BIBLIOGRAPHY OF AMERICAN ETHNOLOGY

Bicentennial First Edition

MARC CASHMAN
Editor

BARRY KLEIN
Research Editor

0094246

TODD Publications

Rye, New York

064441

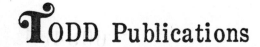 **TODD Publications**   *Rye, New York*

BIBLIOGRAPHY OF AMERICAN ETHNOLOGY

Preface

America is a "nation of nations," a people of many tongues and many traditions. We pride ourselves on being an amalgamation of culturally diversified lifestyles. The editors dedicate this **Bibliography of American Ethnology** to the rising spirit of ethnic self-determination; the realization of an American ideal and an inspiration to the world. However, while certain ethnic groups have been successful in their stride towards recognition and respectability, others have not. It is our hope that this book will remind Americans that our ethnic heritage is our history and our future. It is our way of celebrating America's Bicentennial.

The *Bilbliography of American Ethnology,* a compilation of approximately 4,500 in-print books on ethnology and race relations, is divided into four main categories: General Ethnology, American Indians, Black-Americans, and Other Minority Groups. Each of these major sections is further divided into numerous sub-categories. The listings are arranged alphabetically by title. Annotations have been provided whenever possible. An asterisk (*) has been placed before those books considered appropriate for pre-college level readers, accompanied by an approximate age level. The length of each category reflects the number of in-print books in that area. Further information on listed books can be obtained by writing directly to the addresses given in the Publisher Index.

Every effort has been made to compile a bibliography current through 1975, including a separate section —*Received Too Late For Classification.*

We would appreciate being advised of new and omitted books for inclusion in our second edition.

Marc Cashman, Editor
Barry Klein, Research Editor

Contents

Tribes

Black Americans

Other Minorities

BIBLIOGRAPHY OF AMERICAN ETHNOLOGY

GENERAL ETHNOLOGY

This section includes those subjects and titles that pertain to ethnology in general, or ethnic groups combined for comparative study.

ACCULTURATION AND ASSIMILATION

ACHIEVEMENT AMONG MINORITY AMERICANS
Harry J. Crockett and Jerome L. Schulman 149 pp. Genreal Learning Corp., 1973. $7.95 Pap. $4.25

THE AGE OF CRISIS: DEVIANCE, DISORGANIZATION, AND SOCIETAL PROBLEMS
Alfred M. Mirande
Integrates material on social problems, deviant behavior, and social disorganization. Racial and ethnic problems are discussed. Harper & Row Publishers, 1975.

AMERICAN PLURALISM: A Study of Minority Groups and Social Theory
William M. Newman
Contends that minority groups must be in terms of social stratification and the structure of total societies. 307 pp. Harper & Row Publishers, 1973. Pap. $5.50.

AMERICAN SOCIETY: Problems of Structure
Jonathan H. Turner
Examines how the basic institutions of society exacerbate social problems and outlines strategies for their elimination. Racial and ethnic areas are discussed. 299 pp. Harper & Row Publishers, 1972. Pap. $6.95.

AMERICANIZATION STUDIES: THE ACCULTUATION OF IMMIGRANT GROUPS INTO AMERICAN SOCIETY, 10 Volumes
William S. Bernard, Editor
Volume 1: *Schooling of the Immigrant,* Frank V. Thompson. 147 pp. 1920; Volume 2: *America via the Neighborhood,* John Daniels. 473 pp. 1920; Volume 3: *Old World Traits Transplanted,* William I. Thomas, et al. 315 pp. 1921; Volume 4: *A Stake in the Land,* Peter A. Speek. 226 pp. 1921. Volme 5: *Immigrant Health and the Community,* Michael M. Davis, Jr. 482 pp. Illus. 1921. Volume 6: *New Homes for Old,* Sophonisba P. Breckinridge. 356 pp. 1921; Volume 7: *The Immigrant Press and its Control,* Robert E. Park. 488 pp. 1922; Volume 8: *Americans by Choice,* John Palmer Gavit. 457 pp. 1922;* Volume 9: *The Immigrant's Day in Court,* Kate Holladay Claghorn. 546 pp. 1923; Volume 10: *Adjusting Immigrant and Industry,* William M. Leiserson. 356 pp. 1924. Patterson Smith, 1971. $125.00 the set.

AMERICANS IN THE MAKING: THE NATURAL HISTORY OF THE ASSIMILATION OF IMMIGRANTS
William Carlson Smith
The subjects covered include group reorganization, the marginal man caught between his minority and the majority, the various assimilative processes and the role of the second-generation immigrants. Arno Press, 1970. Reprint of the 1939 edition. $19.00.

ASSIMILATION IN AMERICAN LIFE: THE ROLE OF RACE, RELIGION, AND NATIONAL ORIGINS
Milton M. Gordon
286 pp. Oxford University Press, 1964. Cloth, $8.50; Pap. $3.50

BOSTON'S IMMIGRANTS: A STUDY IN ACCULTURATION
Oscar Handlin
382 pp. Harvard University Press, 1959. $10.00

DEMOCRACY AND ASSIMILATION: THE BLENDING OF IMMIGRANT HERITAGES IN AMERICA
Julius Drachsler
275 pp. Greenwood Press. Reprint of the 1920 edition. Illus. $14.50.

AN ETHNIC SURVEY OF WOONSOCKET, RHODE ISLAND
Bessie Bloom Wessel
This study is a testing of the melting pot theory of assimilation. Arno Press, 1970. Reprint of the 1931 edition. $12.50.

THE LEGISLATIVE HISTORY OF NATURALIZATION IN THE UNITED STATES: FROM THE REVOLUTIONARY WAR TO 1861
Frank George Franklin
Arno Press. Reprint of the 1906 edition. $9.00.

THE NEW IMMIGRATION: A STUDY OF THE INDUSTRIAL AND SOCIAL LIFE OF SOUTHEASTERN EUROPEANS IN AMERICA
Peter Roberts
Jerome S. Ozer Pubs., 1971. Reprint of the 1912 edition. $16.50.

ONE AMERICA: THE HISTORY, CONTRIBUTIONS, AND PRESENT PROBLEMS OF OUR RACIAL AND NATIONAL MINORITIES
Francis J. Brown, and Joseph S. Roucek, Editors
764 pp. Negro Universities Press, 1975. Reprint of the 1952 edition. $24.50.

RED, WHITE AND BLACK: THE PEOPLES OF EARLY AMERICA
Gary B. Nash
History of the social, political, and cultural interaction of Europeans, Africans, and Indians in the 17th and 18th century America. 350 pp. Prentice-Hall, Inc., 1974. Illus. $9.95; Pap. $5.95.

THE SOCIAL REALITY OF ETHNIC AMERICA
Rudolph Gomez, Clement Cottingham, Jr., Russell Endo, and Kathleen Jackson
Identifies and analyzes the social, political, economic, and human condition of four ethnic minorities: blacks, American Indians, Japanese Americans, and Mexican Americans. 320 pp. D.C. Heath and Co., 1974.

THEORIES OF AMERICANIZATION: A CRITICAL STUDY
I. B. Berkson
Arno Press, 1969. Reprint of the 1920 edition. $12.50.

WHITE, RED, BLACK SKETCHES OF SOCIETY IN THE UNITED STATES DURING THE VISIT OF THEIR GUEST, 3 VOLS.
Ferencz and Terizia Pulszky
Negro Universities Press. Reprint of the 1853 edition. $30.00.

ETHNIC LITERATURE

AMERICA'S ETHNIC GROUPS: REVIVAL READER
Jack F. Kinton
American Society Press, 1974. Cloth, $8.95; Pap. $5.95.

THE EMERGENT NATIVE AMERICANS: A READER IN CULTURE CONTACT
Deward E. Walker, Jr.
818 pp. Little, Brown, and Co., 1972. $12.95.

EMERGING HUMANITY: MULTI-ETHNIC LITERATURE FOR CHILDREN AND ADOLESCENTS
Ruth Kearney Carlson
Attempts to aid the student in understanding the various types of ethnic literature, and then focuses on Negro, Indian, and Mexican-American literature. 256 pp. William C. Brown Pubs., 1972. Pap. $5.50.

ETHNOLOGY IN FOLKLORE
G.L. Gomme
Singing Tree Press, 1969. Reprint of the 1892 edition. $7.50.

EUROPEAN FOLKLORE IN AMERICA
R.T.Christiansen
Humanities Press, Inc., 1962. $4.25.

THE FOUNDATIONS OF NATIVISM IN AMERICAN TEXTBOOKS, 1783 TO 1860
Marie L. Fell
Jerome S. Ozer Pubs., 1971. Reprint of the 1941 edition. $10.95.

FROM THE BELLY OF THE SHARK: POEMS BY CHICANOS, ESKIMOS, HAWAIIANS, INDIANS, PUERTO RICANS WITH RELATED POEMS BY OTHERS
Walter Lowenfels, Editor
Vantage Press. $1.95.

FROM NATIVE ROOTS
Felix Sper
A study of the folklore of the United States, including Hill Folks, Creole and Cajun, Negro, Indian, and Spanish among others. 341 pp. Photos. Brown Book Co., 1975. $4.00.

A GATHERING OF GHETTO WRITERS: IRISH, ITALIAN, JEWISH, BLACK, AND PUERTO RICAN
Wayne Charles Miller
New York University Press, 1972. Cloth, $10.50; Pap. $3.95.

A NATION OF NATIONS: ETHNIC LITERATURE IN AMERICA
Theodore L. Gross
Free Press, 1971. Pap. $5.25.

THE OUTNUMBERED: STORIES, ESSAYS AND POEMS ABOUT MINORITY GROUPS BY AMERICA'S LEADING WRITERS
Charlotte Brooks, Editor
Thirteen works by Cather, Malamud, Baldwin, Saroyan, Wright, and others. 160 pp. Dell Publishing Co., 1969. Ages 12 up. $4.95.

SETTLING AMERICA: THE ETHNIC EXPRESSION OF FOURTEEN CONTEMPORARY POETS
David Kheridan, Editor
An Armenian poet is the editor of this anthology of ethnic poetry. 144 pp. MacMillan Publishing Co., 1973. $5.95.

SPEAKING FOR OURSELVES: AMERICAN ETHNIC WRITING
Lillian Faderman and Barbara Bradshaw
Short stories, poems and plays of blacks, Indians, Orientals, Spanish, Jewish, European and near-Eastern peoples of America. 633 pp. Scott, Foresman & Co., 1969. Illus. Pap. $5.95

ETHNICITY AND EDUCATION

ADMISSION OF MINORITY STUDENTS IN MIDWESTERN COLLEGES
Warren W. Willingham
29 pp. College Board Publications, 1970. Free.

AMERICAN EQUATION: LITERATURE IN A MULTI-ETHNIC CULTURE
Katherine D. Newman
Allyn and Bacon, 1971. Pap. $3.95.

AMERICAN MAJORITIES AND MINORITIES: A SYLLABUS OF UNITED STATES FOR SECONDARY SCHOOLS
Warren J. Halliburton and William Loren Katz
An outline of 38 units for a 36-38 week academic year. Selections of readings, audiovisual material, research tools, and classroom activity. Arno Press, 1970. Cloth, $4.95; Pap. $2.95.

ATTITUDE OF CHILDREN AND TEACHERS TOWARD MEXICAN, NEGRO, AND JEWISH MINORITIES: THESIS
Elizabeth K. Cooper
R and E Research Associates, Pubs., 1972. Reprint of the 1945 edition. Pap. $7.00.

CROSS CULTURAL APPROACHES TO LEARNING
Charles Harrington, Editor
MSS Information Corp., 1973. $13.00.

DESEGREGATION INTEGRATION: PLANNING FOR SCHOOL CHANGE
Mark Chesler
Attention given to problem indentification, values clarification, staff development, use of the Force Field analysis, the politics of educational change, resistance to desegregation, community support, and the principles of desegration. 112 pp. National Education Association. Pap. $2.00.

THE EDUCATION OF THE MINORITY CHILD: A COMPREHENSIVE BIBLIOGRAPHY OF 100,000 SELECTED ENTRIES
Covering the education of black, Mexican-American, Indian, and Puerto Rican children. 530 pp. Integrateducation Associates. $12.95; Pap. $5.95.

ELIMINATING ETHNIC BIAS IN INSTRUCTIONAL MATERIALS: COMMENT AND BIBLIOGRAPHY
Maxine Dunfee, Editor
Association for Supervision and Curiculum Development, 1974. Pap. $3.25.

THE EMERGING MINORITIES IN AMERICA: A RESOURCE GUIDE FOR TEACHERS
Santa Barbara County Board of Education
Contains over 500 biographical sketches arranged under four ethnic groups, including a brief historical description of each minority group: Afro-Americans, Asian-Americans, Indian-Americans and Mexican-Americans. 256 pp. Clio Press, 1973. $11.95.

THE FIGHT AGAINST RACISM IN OUR SCHOOLS: *Puerto Rican, Black, and Chinese Community Control in New York City*
Luis Fuentes
16 pp. Pathfinder Press, Inc., 1973. Pap. $.25.

GUIDE TO MEDIA AND MATERIALS ON ETHNIC AMERICAN MINORITIES
Harry A Johnson

Focuses on the selection and utilization of available films, audio and video tapes, slides, transparencies, and recordings for Spanish, Indian, Asian, and Afro-Americans, plus Appalachian, Jewish, Eskimo, and Migrant interests. 375 pp. R.R. Bowker Co., 1975. Price not set.

MAKING IT IN COLLEGE: A GUIDE FOR MINORITY STUDENTS
Marion Walker and Mark Beach
How to select the right college, how to get financial aid, how to improve test-taking skills. 252 pp. Mason-Charter Publishers, 1975. $8.95.

MINORITIES AND THE AMERICAN CITY: A SOCIOLOGICAL PRIMER FOR EDUCATORS
D. N. Alloway and Franesco Cordasco
David McKay Co. Pap. $1.95.

MINORITIES, SCHOOLS, AND POLITICS
Craig Brown, Editor
111 pp. University of Toronto Press, 1969. Pap. $1.95.

THE NEXT GENERATION: AN ETHNO-GRAPHY OF EDUCATION IN AN URBAN NEIGHBORHOOD
John Ogbu
Academic Press, 1973. $11.50.

RACE AND PLACE: A LEGAL HISTORY OF THE NEIGHBORHOOD SCHOOL
An examination of state and federal court decisions since the early 19th century. Integrateducation Associates. $3.00.

RED, BROWN, AND BLACK DEMANDS FOR BETTER EDUCATION
G. Louis Heath
Wanted: A curriculum that is consistent with Indian, Chicano, and black identity and culture and still teaches marketable occupational skills. 224 pp. Westminster Press, 1972. Cloth, $5.95; Pap. $3.50.

THE SCHOOL AND THE IMMIGRANT
Herbert Adolphus Miller
A brief summary of the effectiveness of public

school educational policy in adapting immigrants to American culture. Arno Press. Reprint of the 1916 edition. $4.00.

SELF-CONCEPT: A COMPARISON OF NEGRO, ANGLO AND SPANISH-AMERICAN STUDENTS ACROSS ETHNIC, SEX AND SOCIO-ECONOMIC VARIABLES
Gary W. Healy
Dissertation. R & E Research Associates, 1974. Reprint of the 1969 paper. Pap. $8.00.

SENSITIZING TEACHERS TO ETHNIC GROUPS
Gertrude Noar
Provides the teacher with basic historical and sociological information about black, Jewish, American Indian, Spanish-speaking, and disadvantaged children. 23 pp. Anti-Defamation League of B'nai B'rith. Pap. $.50.

SOCIAL STUDIES FOR LIVING IN A MULTI-ETHNIC SOCIETY: A UNIT APPROACH
Margaret C. Gillespie and A. Gray Thompson
Briefly acquaints the prospective teacher with all the major concepts in social studies teaching and supplies methodology for implementation in the multi-ethnic classroom so that pupils learn how to cope successfully in a multi-ethnic society. 320 pp. Charles E. Merrill Publishing Co., 1973. Pap. $6.95.

TEACHERS, FREE OF PREJUDICE?: TAKE THIS TEST AND SEE
H. Larry Winecoff and Eugene W. Kelly, Jr.
Contains a 30-question racial attitudes test for teachers and one for school administrators. Integraeducation Associates. Pap. $.75.

TEACHERS' SOCIAL KNOWLEDGE AND ITS RELATION TO PUPILS' RESPONS-ES: THE STUDY OF FOUR ST. LOUIS ELEMENTARY SCHOOLS
Ruth Harris
AMS Press, Inc. Reprint of the 1941 edition. $10.00.

TEACHING ETHNIC STUDIES: CON-CEPTS AND STRATEGIES
James A Banks, Ed.
National Council for the Social Studies, 1973. Pap. $6.00; cloth $7.50.

A WEDDING MAN IS NICER THAN CATS, MISS: A TEACHER AT WORK WITH IMMIGRANT CHILDREN
Rachel Scott
St. Martin's Press, 1972. $4.95.

ETHNICITY AND EMPLOYMENT

THE DECISION TO DISCRIMINATE: A STUDY OF EXECUTIVE SELECTION
Robert P. Quinn, Joyce M. Tabor, and Laura K. Gordon
Identifying the forces which perpetuate managerial stratification systems that are based upon factors other than ability or achievement. 162 pp. Institute for Social Research, 1973. Reprint of the 1968 edition. Pap. $6.00.

DIRECTORY OF SPECIAL PROGRAMS FOR MINORITY GROUP MEMBERS: CAREER INFORMATION SERVICES, EMPLOYMENT SKILLS BANKS, FINANCIAL AID
Willis L. Johnson, Editor
Provides special help to black, Spanish speaking, and American Indian candidates, their counselors, and prospective employers. Most of the programs listed are open only to minority group members, however general programs are included for their value to minority candidates. Garrett Park Press, 1974. $7.95.

THE DISADVANTAGED WORKER: READINGS IN DEVELOPING MINORITY MANPOWER
Lloyd Zimpel
Addison-Wesley Publishing Co., 1971. Pap. $6.50.

DISCRIMINATION IN EMPLOYMENT: - AN APPRAISAL OF THE RESEARCH
Dale L. Hiestand
Differential employment patterns, determining factors in discrimination, and dynamics of change in minority group employment patterns and their determinants. 68 pp. Institute of Labor and Industrial Relations, 1970. Pap. $2.50.

DOCUMENT AND REFERENCE TEXT: AN INDEX TO MINORITY GROUP EMPLOYMENT INFORMATION
4850 documents dealing with minority group employment and employment-related problems for blacks, American Indians, Jews, Mexican Americans, Orientals, Puêrto Ricans, and women. 650 pp. Institute of Labor and Industrial Relations, 1967. Pap. $15.00.

ECONOMIC GROWTH AND EMPLOYMENT OPPORTUNITIES FOR MINORITIES
Dale Hiestand
Columbia University Press, 1964. $6.00.

ECONOMIC MINORITIES AND MANPOWER DEVELOPMENT
Eloy Mestre
176 pp. Lexington Books, Inc., 1972. $12.50.

EQUAL EMPLOYMENT OPPORTUNITY FOR MINORITY GROUP COLLEGE GRADUATES: LOCATING, RECRUITING, EMPLOYING
Robert Calvert, Jr.
A listing of sources, techniques and attitudes useful in employing minority group college graduates; lists minority media, black colleges, and bibliography of publications dealing with minority group employment. 248 pp. Garrett Park Press, 1972. Pap. $5.95.

HUMAN FACTORS IN SUPERVISING MINORITY GROUP EMPLOYEES
James H. Morrison
An instructor's manual for training supervisors. Consists of a complete, six-session course covering human relations aspects involved in dealing with minority group members at the work place. 207 pp. International Personnel Management Association, 1970. Pap. $18.00.

MINORITY ENTERPRISE AND THE PRESIDENT'S COUNCIL
Samuel I. Doctors and Anne S. Huff
A review of the objectives of the President's Advisory Council for Minority Business Enterprise (PACMBE). 228 pp. Ballinger Publishing Co. $13.50.

PIECES OF A DREAM: THE ETHNIC WORKER'S CRISIS WITH AMERICA
Michael G. Wenk, et al, Editors
Center for Migration Studies, 1972. Cloth, $8.00; Pap. $4.95.

TRAINING MINORITY JOURNALISTS: A CASE STUDY OF THE SAN FRANCISCO *EXAMINER* INTERN PROGRAM
Judie Telfer
124 pp. Institute of Government Studies at Berkely, 1973. Pap. $4.00.

ETHNICITY AND LANGUAGE

COMPARATIVE STUDIES IN AMERICAN LANGUAGES
Ester Matteson
Humanities Press, 1972. $28.00.

DIRECTIONS IN SOCIOLINGUISTICS: THE ETHNOGRAPHY COMMUNICATION
J. Gumperz and D. Hymes
Holt, Rinehart, and Winston, 1972. $12.50.

FOUNDATIONS IN SOCIOLINGUISTICS: AN ETHNOGRAPHIC APPROACH
Dell Hymes
University of Pennsylvania Press, 1974. Cloth, $12.50; Pap. $5.95.

ETHNICITY AND POLITICS

THE ALIEN AND THE ASIATIC IN AMERICAN LAW
Milton R. Konvitz
299 pp. Johnson Reprint. Reprint of the 1946 edition. $21.00.

AMERICAN MINORITIES: THE JUSTICE ISSUE
Elton Long, et al
A study and report on the minority-group victim of prejudice and discrimination in America. 167 pp. Prentice-Hall, Inc., 1975. $5.95.

AMERICAN PROTEST IN PERSPECTIVE
Robert W. Uphaus, Editor
A survey of important protest writings from 1776 through 1970. Ethnic civil protests are included. 406 pp. Harper & Row Publishers, 1971. Pap. $5.50.

BELEAGURED MINORITIES: CULTURAL POLITICS IN AMERICA
S.J. Makielski, Jr.
W.H. Freeman and Co., 1973. $8.95; Pap. $3.95.

ETHNIC CONFLICT AND POLITICAL DEVELOPMENT: AN ANALYTIC STUDY
Cynthia Enloe
282 pp. Little, Brown, and Co., 1973. Pap. $4.95.

THE ETHNIC FACTOR: HOW AMERICA'S MINORITIES DECIDE ELECTIONS
Mark R. Levy and Michael S. Kramer
Simon and Schuster, 1972. $7.95.

THE ETHNIC FACTOR IN AMERICAN POLITICS
Brett Hawkins and Robert Lorinska
Charles E. Merrill Publishing Co., 1970. Pap. $3.95.

ETHNIC INEQUALITY AND PUBLIC POLICY: A CRITIQUE OF "AFFIRMATIVE ACTION."
Nathan Glazer
A scholarly critique of "Affirmative Action," a governmental policy of requiring educators and employers to actively favor members of discriminated-against groups in decisions on admissions, hiring, and promotions. 300 pp. Harper & Row Pubs., 1975. $10.95.

ETHNIC POLITICS IN AMERICA: BEYOND PLURALISM
Edgar Litt
Analysis of the role of ethnicity in American politics, discussing its origin, persistence manifestations, and variety. 190 pp. Scott, Foresman & Co., 1970. Cloth, $5.95; Pap. $3.25.

ETHNIC VOTERS AND THE ELECTION OF LINCOLN
Frederick C. Luebke,
226 pp. University of Nebraska Press, 1971. Cloth, $11.50; Pap. $3.25.

ETHNO-RELIGIOUS POLITICS
Henry Pratt
Schenkman Publishing Co., 1974. Cloth, $8.95; Pap. $5.95.

IMAGES OF ETHNIC AND RADICAL VIOLENCE IN CALIFORNIA POLITICS, 1917-1930: A SURVEY
Howard A. DeWitt
R & E Research Associates, 1975. Pap. $9.00.

JIM CROW GUIDE TO THE U.S.A.: THE LAWS, CUSTOMS, AND ETIQUETTE GOVERNING THE CONDUCT OF NON-WHITES AND OTHER MINORITIES AS SECOND-CLASS CITIZENS
Stetson Kennedy
230 pp. Greenwood Press, 1959. $9.25.

MINORITIES IN A DEMOCRACY
Humayun Kabir
Lawrence Verry, Inc., 1968. $3.50.

THE WHITE ETHNIC MOVEMENT AND ETHNIC POLITICS
Perry L. Weed
258 pp. Praeger Pubs., 1973. $16.50.

ETHNOGRAPHY

CABOT TO CARTIER: SOURCES FOR A HISTORICAL ETHNOGRAPHY OF NORTH-EASTERN NORTH AMERICA, 1497 TO 1550
Bernard G. Hoffman
288 pp. University of Toronto Press, 1961. $15.00.

COGNITION AND ETHNOGRAPHY
Michael Agar
Burgess Publishing Co., 1973. Pap. $0.95.

THE CULTURAL EXPERIENCE: ETHNOGRAPHY IN COMPLEX SOCIETY
James P. Spradley and David W. McCurdy
Science Research Associates, 1972. Pap. $4.50.

THE CULTURAL GEOGRAPHY OF THE UNITED STATES
Wilbur Zelinsky
Traces the geographic manifestations of culture. 176 pp. Prentice-Hall, Inc., 1973. Pap. $3.85.

DIRECTIONS IN SOCIOLINGUISTICS: THE ETHNOGRAPHY COMMUNICATION
J. Gumperz and D. Hymes
Holt, Rinehart, and Winston, 1972. $12.50.

ETHNOGRAPHIC ATLAS
George Peter Murdock
University of Pittsburgh Press, 1967. $8.95.

ETHNOGRAPHIC BIBLIOGRAPHY OF NORTH AMERICA
George Peter Murdock
395 pp. HRAF Press, 1960. $12.00.

FOUNDATIONS IN SOCIOLINGUISTICS: AN ETHNOGRAPHIC APPROACH
Dell Hymes
University of Pennsylvania Press, 1974. Cloth, $12.50; Pap. $5.95.

ETHNOLOGY—GENERAL

ACHIEVEMENT IN MINORITY AMERICANS: ACONFERENCE REPORT
Harry J. Crockett and Jerome L. Schulman, Editors
Schenkman Publishing Co., 1972. Cloth, $6.96; Pap. $3.95.

THE ALIENS: A HISTORY OF ETHNIC MINORITIES IN AMERICA
Leonard Dinnerstein and Frederic C. Jaher
Explores the history of minority groups from colonial beginnings to the present day. 347 pp. Prentice-Hall, Inc., 1970. Pap. $4.95.

ALL THOSE VOICES: THE MINORITY EXPERIENCE
C.L. Greenspan and L.M. Hirsch
Macmillan Publishing Co., Inc., 1971. Pap. $5.50.

THE AMERICAN COLONIZATION SOCIETY, 1817 TO 1840
Early Lee Fox
AMS Press, Inc. Reprint of the 1919 edition. $8.50.

AMERICAN ETHNIC GROUPS: A SOURCE BOOK
Jack F. Kinton
Social Science and Sociological Resources, 1974. Cloth, $9.95; Pap. $7.25.

THE AMERICAN HERITAGE HISTORY OF THE AMERICAN PEOPLE
Bernard Weisberger, Editor
McGraw Hill Book Co., 1971. $19.95.

AMERICAN MINORITIES IN A CHANGING WORLD
Milton Barron, Editor
Alfred A. Knopf, Inc., 1974. $5.95.

AMERICAN MINORITY RELATIONS
James W. Vander Zanden
Analyzes facts and myths about race, racism, assimilation, and minority relations. 494 pp. Ronald Press Co., 1972. $9.75.

AMERICAN MIX: THE MINORITY EXPERIENCE IN AMERICA
Morris Freedman and Carolyn Banks
Material on Indians, blacks, Chicanos, Japanese-Americans, Polish-Americans, Jews, Catholics, the blind, the old, the poor, the

young, women and homosexuals. 450 pp. J.B. Lippincott Co., 1972. Pap. $5.50.

AMERICAN NATIVISM
    Ira M. Leonard and Robert D. Parmet
Van Nostrand Reinhold Co., 1971. Pap. $3.50.

AMERICAN PLURALISM: A STUDY OF MINORITY GROUPS AND SOCIAL THEORY
    William M. Newman
Harper and Row Pubs., 1973. Pap. $5.95.

AMERICAN SOCIETY FOR ETHNO-HISTORY—MEMBERSHIP LISTING
Lists 620 individual and institutional members, professional anthropologists, and historians, and libraries and museums, as well as all members of the American Society for Ethnohistory. Arizona State Museum, The University of Arizona, Tucson, Ariz. 85721. $.05 per address.

ANNUAL MEETING OF THE AMERICAN ETHNOLOGICAL SOCIETY, 1972; LEARNING AND CULTURE: PRO-CEEDINGS
    Solon T. Kimball and Jacquetta Burnett, Editors
298 pp. University of Washington Press, 1973. Pap. $6.50.

ANTHROPOLOGY AND AMERICAN LIFE
    Marcello Truzzi and Joseph G. Jorgensen
Prentice-Hall, 1974. Pap. $6.95.

ASSESSING MINORITY GROUP CHILDREN
    Beeman N. Phillips
Behavioral Publications, 1974. $9.95.

THE BUREAU OF AMERICAN ETHNOLOGY: A PARTIAL HISTORY
    Neil M. Judd
139 pp. University of Oklahoma Press, 1967. Illus. Cloth, $5.95; Pap. $1.95.

COMPARATIVE ETHNIC RELATIONS: FRAMEWORK FOR THEORY AND RESEARCH
    Richard A. Schermerhorn
Random House, Inc., 1970. $8.95.

CONTRIBUTIONS OF MINORITIES TO THE DEVELOPMENT OF THE WEST
    Larry Stevens

23 pp. Relevant Instructional Materials, 1972. $.75.

CULTURE AND ETHNOLOGY
    Robert H. Lowie
Basic Books, 1966. Cloth, $5.95; Pap. $2.95.

CULTURE AND ETHNOLOGY
    Robert Harry Lowie
R & E Research Associates, 1970. Reprint of the 1929 edition. $9.00.

THE DECLINE OF THE WASP
    Peter Schrag
Simon and Schuster, 1971, $6.95.

DIRECTORY OF PRIVATE PROGRAMS ASSISTING MINORITY BUSINESSES
A geographical list of 350 private and municipal minority business assistance programs in 59 cities. 364 pp. Supt. of Documents, US Government Printing Office, Washington, D.C. 20402. $2.50.

THE DISPOSSESSED MAJORITY
    Wilmot Robertson
The author contends that the traditional Americans of northern European stock have in recent years been reduced to second-class status. 598 pp. Devin-Adair, 1975. Cloth, $12.00; Pap. $3.95.

THE DIVIDED SOCIETY: THE ETHNIC EXPERIENCE IN AMERICA
    Colin Greer
Basic Books, 1974. Cloth, $12.50; Pap. $6.95.

THE EFFECTS OF TWO TYPES OF SOUND MOTION PICTURES ON ATTITUDES OF ADULTS TOWARD MINORITY GROUPS
    Albert L. Goldberg
Dissertation. R & E Research Associates, 1974. Reprint of the 1956 paper. Pap. $8.00.

ENCYCLOPEDIA DIRECTORY OF ETHNIC NEWSPAPERS AND PERIODICALS IN THE UNITED STATES
Lists 900 publications in 43 languages arranged by ethnic groups. Includes an informative essay on the Ethnic Press in the S. S. Libraries Unlimited, Inc., P. O. Box 263, Littleton, Colo. 80120. $12.50.

THE ETHNIC DIMENSION IN AMERICAN SOCIETY
    Salvatore Lagumina and Frank J. Cavaioli
Holbrook Press, 1974. Pap. $5.95.

THE ETHNIC EXPERIENCE IN PENNSYLVANIA
John E. Bodnar
330 pp. Bucknell University Press, 1973. $12.00.

ETHNIC HISTORY IN PENNSYLVANIA: A SELECTED BIBLIOGRAPHY
John E. Bodnar
47 pp. Pennsylvania Historical and Museum - Commission, 1974. Pap. $1.00.

ETHNIC MEDICINE IN THE SOUTHWEST
Edward H. Spicer
A study of different and differing ethnic medicine beliefs in a single community: Indians, Mexican Americans, and blacks in Tucson, Arizona. University of Arizona Press, 1975. Price not set.

THE ETHNIC PRESS IN THE UNITED STATES
Provides information on 646 foreign-language newspapers and periodicals published, arranged by language of publication. American Council for Nationalities Service, 20 W. 40th St., New York, N.Y. 10018. $15.00.

ETHNIC RELATIONS IN THE UNITED STATES
Edward C. McDonagh and Eugene S. Edwards
408 pp. Greenwood Press, 1953. Illus. $23.25.

ETHNIC STRATIFICATION
Tamotsu Shibutani and K.M. Kwan
Macmillan Publishing Co., Inc., 1965. $10.95.

ETHNICITY IN AMERICAN LIFE
John Hope Franklin, Thomas F. Pettigrew, and Raymond W. Mack
Three human-relations specialists discuss ethnicity from distinctive perspectives. 47 pp. Anti-Defamation League of B'nai B'rith. Pap. $.95.

ETHNICITY IN THE UNITED STATES: A PRELIMINARY RECONNAISSANCE
Andrew M. Greeley
Presents extensive empirical evidence about European-American ethnic groups--how they relate to each other and the role they play in American social and political life. 347 pp. John Wiley & Sons, 1974. $14.95.

ETHNOLOGICAL RESULTS OF THE POINT BARROW EXPEDITION
John Murdoch

AMS Press, Inc. Reprint of the 1892 edition. $53.50.

FEDERAL ASSISTANCE PROGRAMS FOR MINORITY BUSINESS ENTERPRISES
Lists assistance programs for minority business enterprises. Includes field offices of the various Government Agencies prepared to aid enterprises, 140 pp. Sales and Distribution Branch, U. S. Department of Commerce, Washington, D. C. 20230. Free.

FOREIGNERS IN THE CALIFORNIA GOLD RUSH
Seville Sylva
Thesis. R & E Research Associates, 1971. Reprint of the 1932 paper. Pap. $7.00.

FOREIGN INFLUENCES IN AMERICAN LIFE
D. F. Bowers
Peter Smith Publishers. $4.50.

GROUP LIFE IN AMERICA: A TASK FORCE REPORT
American Jewish Committee, 1972.

HARVARD UNIVERSITY, PEABODY MUSEUM OF ARCHAEOLOGY AND ETHNOLOGY: AUTHOR AND SUBJECT CATALOGUES OF THE LIBRARY
G.K. Hall and Co., 1970. $840.00, for 12 Vols.

HARVARD UNIVERSITY, PEABODY MUSEUM OF ARCHEAOLOGY AND ETHNOLOGY: AUTHOR AND SUBJECT CATALOGUES OF THE LIBRARY
G.K.Hall and Co., 1963. $3850.00 for 54 Vols.

HARVARD UNIVERSITY, PEABODY MUSEUM OF ARCHAEOLOGY AND ETHNOLOGY: INDEX TO SUBJECT HEADINGS OF THE LIBRARY
G.K.Hall and Co. $28.00.

I, TOO, AM AMERICAN
Romero
United Publishing Corp., 1970. $13.88.

AN INDEX TO BULLETINS 1 TO 100 OF THE BUREAU OF AMERICAN ETHNOLOGY
Biren Bonneruea
Scholarly Press. Reprint of the 1963 edition. $39.50.

KNOWING AND UNDERSTANDING THE SOCIALLY DISADVANTAGED: ETHNIC MINORITY GROUPS
Staten W. Webster
Intext Educational Pubs., 1972. Pap. $8.50.

LAW SCHOOLS AND MINORITY GROUPS
A guide to opportunities in legal education for minorityy group students. 40 pp. Scholarship Information Center, UNC YMCA-YWCA, Chapel Hill, N.C. 27514. $1.00. Free to college students.

THE LEGACY OF THE MELTING POT
Drew L. Smith
Christopher Publishing House, (Mass.), 1971. $6.50.

THE LIFE OF WHITE ETHNICS
Irving M. Levine and Judith Herman
Analysis of the ethnic factor in American history, unions, neighborhoods, politics, economics, social services, young workers, working cless women, and social attitudes. American Jewish Committee. Free.

LIST OF PUBLICATIONS OF THE AMERICAN BUREAU OF ETHNOLOGY, WITH INDEX TO AUTHORS AND TITLES
Scholarly Press. Reprints of the 1906, 1907, 1910, and 1914 editions. $7.50.

A MANUAL ON ORGANIZING A MINORITY TRADE ASSOCIATION
Guidelines. 60 pp. Institute for Minority Business Education, Howard University, P.O. Box 662, Washington, D.C. 20001. $4.00.

THE METHOD AND THEORY OF ETHNOLOGY
Paul Radin
Basic Books, 1966. $7.50.

THE MINGLING OF THE CANADIAN AND AMERICAN PEOPLES, VOLUME I, HISTORICAL
Marcus Lee Hansen
The exchange of peoples between the United States and Canada from about 1600 to 1940 is the subject of this book. Arno Press, 1970. Reprint of the 1940 edition. $12.00.

MINORITIES ALL
Gerald Leinwand
Pocket Books, Inc., Pap. $.95.

MINORITIES AND THE POLICE
D.H.Bayley and H. Mendelsohn

Free Press, 1969. Cloth, $7.95; Pap. $2.45.

*MINORITIES IN AMERICAN HISTORY: EARLY AMERICA, 1492-1812
William Loren Katz
Shows how minority groups were treated from Columbus' treatment of native Americans through the early nineteenth century. 72 pp. Franklin Watts, Inc., 1974. Age 12 up. $4.33.

*MINORITIES IN AMERICAN HISTORY: SLAVERY TO CIVIL WAR 1812-1865
William Loren Katz
72 pp. Franklin Watts, Inc., 1974. Age 12 up. $4.33.

*MINORITIES IN AMERICAN HISTORY: FROM THE PROGRESSIVE ERA TO THE GREAT DEPRESSION, 1900-1929
William Loren Katz
Discusses the immigration of the Japanese and Chinese, and the rise of the Ku Klux Klan. 96 pp. Franklin Watts, Inc., 1974. Age 12 up. $4.33.

*MINORITIES IN AMERICAN HISTORY: YEARS OF STRIFE, 1929-1956
William Loren Katz
Strife, depression, wars, and civil rights. 96 pp. Franklin Watts, Inc., 1975. Age 12 up. $4.33.

MINORITIES IN AMERICAN SOCIETY
Charles F. Marden and Gladys Meyer
D. Van Nostrand Co., 1973. Pap. $7.95.

MINORITIES IN CALIFORNIA HISTORY
George E. Frakes and Curtis B. Solberg, Editors
Random House, Inc., 1971. Pap. $4.95.

MINORITIES IN THE NEW WORLD: SIX CASE STUDIES
Charles Wagley and Marvin Harris
Columbia University Press, 1958. Cloth, $12.00; Pap. $2.45.

MINORITY GROUP ADOLESCENTS IN THE UNITED STATES
Eugene B. Brody
256 pp. Williams and Wilkins, Inc., 1968. $8.25.

A MINORITY GROUP IN AMERICAN SOCIETY
J. Milton Yinger
This text examines the analytic, moral, and strategic questions which relate to the place of

minority groups in a free society. Primary focus is placed on the Negro and the racial situation in contemporary America. 128 pp. McGraw-Hill Book Co., 1965. Cloth, $5.50; Pap. $3.50.

MINORITY GROUP RELATIONS
James Martin and Clyde W. Franklin
Charles E. Merrill Publishing Co., 1973. $9.50.

MINORITY GROUP RELATIONS: AN EXPERIMENTAL HANDBOOK
John J. Sherwood and Howard Fromkin
University Associates, 1974. $6.00.

MINORITY GROUP SERIES
A series of fully annotated bibliographies. Minority Research Center, Inc., 117 R St., N.C., Washington, D.C. 20002. $7.50 each volume.

MINORITY GROUPS AND HOUSING
Bibliography of books, pamphlets, periodicals, government publications published from 1950 to 1970 providing information on the housing problem of minority groups in the United States. Also lists firms and organizations working in the area of minority group housing. 202 pp. Center for Real Estate and Urban Economics Studies, University of Connecticut, School of Business Administration, Storrs, Conn. 06280. $6.50.

MINORITY GROUPS AND HOUSING
Byrl N. Boyce and Sidney Turoff
202 pp. General Learning Press, 1972. $7.50.

MINORITY PEOPLES IN A NATION AT WAR: 1942
The American Academy of Political and Social Science, 1975. Cloth, $5.00; Pap. $4.00.

MINORITY PROBLEMS
Arnold M. Rose and Caroline B. Rose, Editors
Forty-six scholarly contributions to the sociology of minority problems and intergroup relations present a study of the nature of the community, the relation of prejudice to discrimination, community adjustment, and the nature of intergroup conflict. 483 pp. Harper & Row Publishers, 1972. Pap. $8.00.

MINORITY REPORT
Bernard Augustine De Voto
Books for Libraries, Inc. Reprint of the 1940 edition. $13.75.

MINORITY RESPONSES: COMPARITIVE

VIEWS OF REACTIONS TO SUBORDINATION
Minako Kurokawa
Random House, Inc., 1970. Pap. $5.95.

NATION OF NATIONS: THE ETHNIC EXPERIENCE AND THE RACIAL CRISIS
Peter I. Rose, Editor
Random House, 1971. Pap. $5.25.

NATIONAL STATES AND NATIONAL MINORITIES
Charlie Aylmer Macartney
Russell and Russell, 1968. Reprint of the 1934 edition. $18.50.

NEW CONVERTS TO THE AMERICAN DREAM
C.S. Heller
College and University Press. $7.50.

THE OLD AMERICANS:
A PHYSIOLOGICAL PROFILE
Ales Hrdlicka
The term refers to anyone with at least three generations in this country, mostly English, Welsh, Scotch, and German descendants. Arno Press. Reprint of the 1925 edition. $18.00.

ONE AMERICA; THE HISTORY, CONTRIBUTIONS, AND PRESENT PROBLEMS OF OUR RACIAL AND NATIONAL MINORITIES
Francis James Brown and Joseph S. Roucek, Editors
764 pp. Greenwood Press, 1952. Third Edition. $21.50.

THE OTHER AMERICANS: MINORITIES IN AMERICAN HISTORY
Kathleen Wright
Emphasizes the American black, Jew, Indian, Oriental, and Spanish. Fawcett World Library. Pap. $1.25.

OTHER MINORITIES: NON-ETHNIC COLLECTIVITIES CONCEPTUALIZED AS MINORITY GROUPS
Edward Sagarin, Editor
Xerox College Publishing, 1971. Pap. $4.95.

*PEOPLE OF AMERICA: *THEY CAME FROM MANY LANDS*
J. Ralph Randolph and James W. Pohl
An examination of each of the major cultural, ethnic, and racial groups that has contributed to U.S. history. 344 pp. Illus. W.S. Benson & Co., 1974. $6.60. (grade 5)

PLURAL SOCIETY IN THE SOUTHWEST
Edward H. Spicer and Raymond H. Thompson
Essays on the Southwest "melting pot" of the United States' Yankees, Mormons, old Spanish, Chicanos and Indians. 380 pp. Interbook Incorporated, 1972. $5.95.

PROFILES IN ETHNOLOGY
Elman R. Service
A classic description of 21 diverse, nonindustrial societies, arranged according to five basic levels of cultural complexity (bands, tribes, chiefdoms, primitive states, and modern folk societies). 521 pp. Illus. Harper & Row Publishers, 1971. Pap. $7.95.

PROTEST: RED, BLACK, BROWN EXPERIENCE IN AMERICA
James R. Mencarelli and Steven R. Severin
Explains the reasons behind each ethnic power movement, explains its major goals, and includes biographical sketches of its important leaders. Includes American blacks, Mexican Americans and American Indians. 192 pp. William B. Eerdmans Publishing Co., 1975. Pap. $3.45.

RACE AND ETHNICITY IN MODERN AMERICA
Richard J. Meister
An anthology which traces the development of differing attitudes toward race and ethnicity in twentieth-century America. 196 pp. D. C. Heath and Co., 1974. Pap. $2.95.

RACIAL AND ETHNIC RELATIONS
Joseph H. Himes
72 pp. William C. Brown Co., 1974. Pap. $1.50.

THE REALITY OF ETHNOMETHODOLOGY
Hugh Mehan
259 pp. Wiley-Interscience, 1975. $11.50.

REDISCOVERY OF ETHNICITY
Sallie Te Selle, Editor
Harper and Row Pubs., 1974. Pap. $2.25.

RESEARCH MEMORANDUM ON MINORITY PEOPLES IN THE DEPRESSION
Donald Young
Arno Press, 1971. Reprint of the 1937 edition. $10.00.

THE RISE OF THE UNMELTABLE ETHNICS
M. Novak

Macmillan Publishing Co., Inc., 1972. Cloth, $7.95; Pap. $1.95.

SMITHSONIAN INSTITUTION, BUREAU OF AMERICAN ETHNOLOGY BULLETINS, 1 TO 193
Scholarly Press. $3,291.00 for 193 books.

STRANGERS NEXT DOOR ETHNIC RELATIONS IN AMERICAN COMMUNITIES
Robin M. Williams
434 pp. Prentice-Hall, 1964. $12.50.

THEY AND WE: RACIAL AND ETHNIC RELATIONS IN THE UNITED STATES
Peter I. Rose
Random House, Inc., 1964. Pap. $3.95.

THREE AMERICAN EMPIRES
John J. TePaske, Editor
Spanish, English and Indian America during early Colonial America. 168 pp. Harper & Row Publishers, 1967. Pap. $3.95.

TOWARD A THEORY OF MINORITY GROUP RELATIONS
Hubert M. Blalock, Jr.
G.P.Putnam's Sons, 1970. Pap. $2.95.

THE TROUBLE MAKERS: AN ANTI-DEFAMATION LEAGUE REPORT
Arnold Forster
317 pp. Negro Universities Press. Reprint of the 1952 edition. $13.50.

WE, TOO, BELONG
Mary Turner, Editor
An anthology about minority groups in America. 220 pp. Dell Publishing Co., 1969. Pap. $.95.

WHY CAN'T THEY BE LIKE US?: FACTS AND FALLACIES ABOUT ETHNIC DIFFERENCES AND GROUP CONFLICTS IN AMERICA
Andrew M. Greeley
E.P.Dutton and Co., 1971. Cloth, $3.25; Pap. $1.00.

ETHNOPSYCHOLOGY

A COMPARATIVE STUDY OF THE MENTAL CAPACITY OF CHILDREN OF FOREIGN PARENTAGE
May Bere

AMS Press, Inc. Reprint of the 1924 edition. $17.50.

CULTURE AND DEMOCRACY IN THE UNITED STATES: STUDIES IN THE GROUP PSYCHOLOGY OF THE AMERICAN PEOPLES
Horace M. Kallen

This collection of essays by a social psychologist was a rare dissent from the general atmosphere of the Twenties seeking to homogenize American nationalities. The author insists that rather than seeking to anglicize our ethnic subcultures, our policy should be to recognize and encourage cultural pluralism. Arno Press. Reprint of the 1924 edition. $14.00.

ETHNICITY AND MENTAL HEALTH
Joseph Giordano

Reviews literature on the ethnic factor in mental illness and the delivery of mental health services, and makes recommendations concerning training, policy, and community action. American Jewish Committee, 1972. $1.00.

THE FUNCTIONS OF PREJUDICE
Jack Levin

Encompasses sociological and psychological theories involving both functional and conflict points of view. The author argues that majority/minority relations cannot be understood apart from the consequences of prejudice and discrimination. Harper & Row Publishers, 1975. Paper.

OLD WORLD TRAITS TRANSPLANTED
Robert E. Park and Herbert A Miller

A study of the psychology of assimilation. Arno Press, 1969. Reprint of the 1921 edition. $9.50.

PSYCHIATRIC ASPECTS OF SCHOOL DESEGREGATION
GAP Committee on Social Issues

Problems of adjustment for both races. 96 pp. Group for the Advancement of Psychiatry 1957. Pap. $1.00.

A PSYCHOLOGICAL STUDY OF IMMIGRANT CHILDREN AT ELLIS ISLAND
Bertha M. Boody

The results of a psychological survey of immigrant children testing the charge of innate inferiority of recent nationalities. Arno Press. Reprint of the 1926 edition. $7.00.

RACE AND CULTURE: A PSYCHOLOGICAL INSIGHT INTO THE PRESENT AND PAST
Leo Cohen and Ralph J. Erickson

The educational and psychological problems that occur in our multi-racial society. Exposition Press, 1975. $6.00.

RACISM AND PSYCHIATRY
Alexander Thomas and Samuel Sillen

Citadel Press, 1974. Pap. $3.45.

THE SOCIAL PSYCHOLOGY OF PREJUDICE
Howard J. Ehrlich, Editor

A systematic review of published material, in English, by social scientists on the subject of prejudice. 22 principles of prejudice are presented. 208 pp. Wiley-Interscience, 1973. $12.00.

GENEALOGY

AMERICAN ANCESTRY: GIVING THE NAME AND DESCENT, IN THE MALE LINE, OF AMERICANS WHOSE ANCESTORS SETTLED IN THE U.S. PREVIOUS TO THE DECLARATION OF INDEPENDENCE, A.D. 1776
Joel Munsell's Sons

12 volumes. Genealogical Publishing Co., 1968. Reprint of the 1887-1899 editions. $9.00 each.

AMERICAN COLONISTS IN ENGLISH RECORDS: 1ST AND 2ND SERIES, 2 VOLS IN ONE
George Sherwood

Genealogical Publishing Co., 1969. Reprint of the 1932 edition. $10.00.

AMERICAN ORIGINS: SOURCES FOR GENEALOGICAL RESEARCH AND RECORDS ABROAD
Leslie G. Pine

357 pp. Genealogical Publishing Co., 1971. Reprint of the 1960 edition. $10.00.

BRISTOL AND AMERICA: A RECORD OF THE FIRST SETTLERS IN THE COLONIES OF NORTH AMERICA, 1654 TO 1685
R. Hargreaves-Mawdsley

182 pp. Genealogical Publishing Co., 1970. Reprint of the 1929 edition. $10.00.

A COLLECTION OF UPWARDS OF 30,000 NAMES OF GERMAN, SWILL, DUTCH, FRENCH, AND OTHER IMMIGRANTS IN

PENNSYLVANIA, 1727 TO 1776
   Israel Daniel Rupp
Genealogical Publishing Co., 1971. Reprint of
the 1876 edition. $15.00.

**GENEALOGICAL GUIDE TO THE EARLY
SETTLERS OF AMERICA, WITH A BRkIEF
HISTORY OF THOSE OF THE FIRST
GENERATION**
   Henry Whittemore
438 pp. Genealogical Publishing Co., 1967. Re-
print of the 1898-1906 edition. $20.00.

**SURNAMES IN THE UNITED STATES
CENSUS OF 1790**
   American Council of Learned Societies,
Committee on Linguistics, and National Stocks
in the Population of the United States
339 pp. Genealogical Publishing Co., 1971. Reprint of the 1932 edition. $15.00.

IMMIGRATION

**AMERICAN LETTER: IMMIGRANT AND
ETHNIC WRITING**
   Edward Ifkovic
An anthology of essays, poems, plays, and
fiction concerned with immigrant and ethnic
America. 416 pp. Prentice-Hall, Inc., 1975.

***AMERICANS ALL, A NATION OF IM-
MIGRANTS**
   Muriel Stanek and Clinton Hartmann
Emphasizes the role of many diverse cultural
groups. Benefic Press. Age 8-12. $3.85;
Teacher's guide $1.50.

**THE BACKGROUND OF IMMIGRANT
CHILDREN**
   Ivor Morrish
Lawrence Verry, Inc., 1971. $13.50.

**BIBLIOGRAPHY OF IMMIGRATION IN
THE U.S., 1900-1930**
   William R. Janeway
R & E Research Associates, 1972. Reprint of the
1934 edition. Pap. $6.00.

BOSTON'S IMMIGRANTS
   Oscar Handlin
Atheneum Publications, 1968. Illus. Pap. $3.25.

CALL US AMERICANS
   Dorothy A. Chernoff
Seventeen writers dramatize experiences of

emigrants from foreign countries. Doubleday &
Co., 1968. Illus. Cloth, $4.50; Pap. $1.98.

**CITIES AND IMMIGRANTS: A GEOGRA-
PHY OF CHANGE IN 19TH CENTURY
AMERICA**
   David Ward
Oxford University Press, 1971, Cloth, $6.95;
Pap. $3.50.

**EARLY VIRGINIA IMMIGRANTS, 1623 to
1666**
   George Cabell Greer
376 pp. Genealogical Publishing Co., 1973. Reprint of the 1912 edition. $11.50.

EMIGRATION TO THE UNITED STATES
   U.S. Bureau of Statistics
R & E Research Associates, 1970. Reprint of the
1904 edition. $10.00.

**FOREIGN BORN POPULATION OF
CALIFORNIA**
   Allyn C. Loosley
Thesis. R & E Research Associates. Reprint of
the 1928 paper. $7.00.

**FOREIGNERS IN SOUTH CALIFORNIA
DURING THE MEXICAN PERIOD**
   Elizabeth Rhoades
Thesis. R & E Research Associates. Reprint of
the 1925 paper. $7.00.

GREAT IMMIGRANTS
   Cecyle S. Neidle
Twelve outstanding immigrants who had an
impact on our society from 1780 to the present.
Twayne Publishers. $8.95.

**HISTORICAL ASPECTS OF THE IM-
MIGRATION PROBLEM: SELECT
DOCUMENTS**
   Edith Abbott
A collection of letters, diaries and journals that
deals with the historical, legal and social aspects
of European immigration. Arno Press. Reprint
of the 1926 edition. $27.00.

**HISTORY OF IMMIGRATION TO THE
UNITED STATES**
   William J. Bromwell
Exhibiting the number, sex, age, occupation
and country of birth, of passengers arriving in
the United States by sea from foreign countries,
from Sept. 30, 1819 to Dec. 31, 1855, and an
appendix containing the naturalization and
passenger laws of the United States. 225 pp.
August M. Kelley Publishers. Reprint of the
1856 edition. $10.00.

HISTORY OF IMMIGRATION TO THE UNITED STATES, EXHIBITING THE NUMBER, SEX, AGE, OCCUPATION, AND COUNTRY OF BIRTH, OF PASSENGERS ARRIVING IN THE UNITED STATES BY SEA FROM FOREIGN COUNTRIES, FROM SEPTEMBER 30, 1819, TO DECEMBER 31, 1855; COMPILED ENTIRELY FROM OFFICIAL DATA: WITH AN INTRODUCTORY REVIEW OF THE PROGRESS AND EXTENT OF IMMIGRATION TO THE UNITED STATES PRIOR TO 1819 AND AN APPENDIX CONTAINING THE NATURALIZATION AND PASSENGER LAWS OF THE UNITED STATES, AND EXTRACTS FROM THE LAWS OF SEVERAL STATES RELATIVE TO IMMIGRANTS, THE IMPORTATION OF PAUPERS, CONVICTS, LUNATICS, ETC.
William J. Bromwell
A statistical chronicle of immigrants arriving in the United States during a 64 year period. Arno Press. Reprint of the 1856 edition. $6.50.

I AM AN AMERICAN, BY FAMOUS NATURALIZED AMERICANS
Robert Spiers Benjamin, Editor
Books for Libraries, Inc. Reprint of the 1941 edition. $10.50.

ILLUSTRIOUS IMMIGRANTS: THE INTELLECTUAL MIGRATION FROM EUROPE, 1930 TO 1941
Laura Fermi
University of Chicago Press, 1971, 2nd edition. Cloth, $12.50; Pap. $3.95.

THE IMMIGRANT'S DAY IN COURT
Kate Holladay Claghorn
A study on the Americanization of the immigrant, this book is an exposition of how justice and injustice as well was meted out to the foreign-born offender. Arno Press. Reprint of the 1923 edition. $16.50.

THE IMMIGRANT IN AMERICAN HISTORY
M.L.Hansen
Peter Smith Publishers. $4.50

IMMIGRANT ANCESTORS: A LIST OF 2500 IMMIGRANTS TO AMERICA BEFORE 1750
Frederick Adams Virkus
75 pp. Genealogical Publishing Co., 1972. Reprint of the 1942 edition. Pap. $5.00.

THE IMMIGRANT AND THE COMMUNITY
Grace Abbott
Jerome S. Ozer Pubs., 1971. Reprint of the 1917 edition. $12.50.

THE IMMIGRANT EXPERIENCE
Thomas C. Wheeler, Editor
Nine narratives express "the anguish of becoming American." Penguin Books. Pap. $1.25.

IMMIGRANT GIFTS TO AMERICAN LIFE: SOME EXPERIMENTS IN APPRECIATION OF THE CONTRIBUTIONS OF OUR FOREIGN-BORN CITIZENS TO AMERICAN CULTURE
Allen H. Eaton
A record of exhibits of the American Federation of Arts of immigrant art, including metalworking, pottery, dressmaking and carpentry. Arno Press, 1970. Reprint of the 1932 edition. $12.00.

THE IMMIGRANT PRESS AND ITS CONTROL
Robert E. Park
Scholarly Press, 1971. Reprint of the 1922 edition. $11.50.

IMMIGRANT RACES IN NORTH AMERICA
Peter Roberts
R and E Research Associates, Pubs., 1970. Reprint of the 1912 edition. $7.00.

IMMIGRANT SETTLEMENT IN CONNECTICUT: THEIR GROWTH AND CHARACTERISTICS
Samuel Koenig
R & E Research Associates, 1970. Reprint of the 1938 edition. $5.00.

THE IMMIGRANT WOMAN AND HER JOB
Caroline Manning
How the immigrant woman participated in America's industrial order. Arno Press. Reprint of the 1930 edition. $7.50.

IMMIGRANT WORKERS: THEIR IMPACT ON AMERICAN LABOR RADICALISM
Gerald Rosenblum
Basic Books, 1972. $9.95.

*IMMIGRANTS IN AMERICAN LIFE
Arthur Mann

Covers such topics as jobs, religion, housing, ward politics, prejudice, opposition to immigration, pluralism, and assimilation. Houghton-Mifflin, 1974. Illus. Ages 12-18. Pap. $2.96.

IMMIGRANTS AND ASSOCIATIONS
Lloyd A. Fallers, Editor
Humanities Press, Inc., 1967. Pap. $7.50.

IMMIGRANTS AND ETHNICITY: TEN YEARS OF CHANGING THOUGHT
William S. Bernard, Editor
American Jewish Committee, 1972.

THE IMMIGRANTS' INFLUENCE ON WILSON'S PEACE POLICIES
Joseph P. O'Grady, Editor
329 pp. University Press of Kentucky, 1967. $8.50.

IMMIGRANTS TO NEW ENGLAND, 1700-1775
Ethel Stanwood Bolton
235 pp. Genealogical Publishing Co., 1973. Reprint of the 1931 edition. $8.50.

IMMIGRANTS AND THEIR CHILDREN, 1920: A STUDY BASED ON CENSUS STATISTICS RELATIVE TO THE FOREIGN BORN AND THE NATIVE WHITE OF FOREIGN OR MIXED PARENTAGE
Niles Carpenter
This work deals with the distribution, age, sex and occupation of immigrants in America. Arno Press, 1969. Reprint of the 1927 edition. $13.00.

IMMIGRATION: AN AMERICAN DILEMMA
Benjamin Munn Ziegler
118 pp. D.C. Heath & Co., 1953.

IMMIGRATION, THE AMERICAN MOSAIC: FROM PILGRIMS TO MODERN REFUGEES
Michael Kraus
Van Nostrand Reinhold Co., 1966. Pap. $2.95.

IMMIGRATION IN COLONIAL TIMES
Mary Stetson Clarke
Grossman Pubs., 1973. $3.95.

IMMIGRATION, AND THE COMMISSIONERS OF EMIGRATION OF THE STATE OF NEW YORK
Friedrich Kapp
A contemporary account by one of the men who

was responsible for immigration policy, this book provides a glimpse into the administration of immigration in the early 19th century. Arno Press. Reprint of the 1870 edition. $7.50.

IMMIGRATION: CULTURAL CONFLICTS AND SOCIAL ADJUSTMENTS
Lawrence Guy Brown
A sociological analysis of the problem of immigrant assimilation and adjustment to a new environment. Arno Press. Reprint of the 1933 edition. $12.50.

IMMIGRATION: ITS EVILS AND CONSEQUENCES
Samuel C. Busey
A good example of polemical literature, this book espouses the mid-19th century fear of unrestricted immigration, particularly of Catholic immigrants. Arno Press. Reprint of the 1856 edition. $4.50.

IMMIGRATION AND LABOR: THE ECONOMIC ASPECTS OF EUROPEAN IMMIGRATION TO THE UNITED STATES
Isaac A. Hourwich
"The object of this volume is to refute the finding of the Immigration Commission in 1910, that European immigration should be restricted in the interest of the American laboring class...the author deals...with all the important arguments and phrases of the Report of the Commission." Arno Press. Reprint of the 1912 edition. $16.50.

IMMIGRATION AND RACE ATTITUDES
Emory S. Bogardus
Jerome S. Ozer Pubs., 1971. Reprint of the 1928 edition. $10.95.

IMMIGRATION: SELECT DOCUMENTS AND CASE RECORDS
Edith Abbott
A selection of original source material on immigration. Arno Press. Reprint of the 1924 edition. $24.00.

IMMINENT DANGERS TO THE FREE INSTITUTIONS OF THE UNITED STATES THROUGH FOREIGN IMMIGRATION, AND THE PRESENT STATE OF THE NATURALIZATION LAWS
Samuel F.B. Morse
A nativist pamphlet by an inventor and painter which had tremendous impact on anti-Catholic sentiment. Arno Press. Reprint of the 1835 edition. $4.00.

INTELLIGENCE AND IMMIGRATION
Clifford Kirkpatrick

An investigation of the relationship of intelligence to nationality by a psychologist just when the United States was searching for a new immigration policy. Arno Press. Reprint of the 1926 edition. $6.00.

KEEPERS OF THE GATE: *A History of Ellis Island*
Thomas Monroe Pitkin

192 pp. New York University Press, 1975. Illus. $12.50.

MANUAL FOR EMIGRANTS TO AMERICA
Calvin Cotton

An early pocket manual often used by those who were planning to migrate to America. This one in English gives climate, employment opportunities and recommends places for immigrants to settle in the United States. Arno Press. Reprint of the 1832 edition. $4.50.

MENTALITY OF THE ARRIVING IMMIGRANT
E.H. Mullan

The record of the psychological examination of a group of immigrants by the U.S. Public Health Service in order to assess the mentality of the incoming alien. Arno Press. Reprint of the 1917 edition. $5.50.

NATION OF IMMIGRANTS
John F. Kennedy

Harper and Row Pubs., 1970. Cloth, $7.27; Pap. $0.95.

THE NEW IMMIGRATION
John J. Appel and A.S.Eisenstadt

Pitman Publishing Corp., 1971. Cloth, $7.50; Pap. $3.25.

THE NEW IMMIGRATION: A STUDY OF THE INDUSTRIAL AND SOCIAL LIFE OF SOUTHEASTERN EUROPEANS IN AMERICA
Peter Roberts

A portrayal of the Balkan nationalities in the U.S., especially their occupational and housing conditions. Arno Press. Reprint of the 1912 edition. $17.50.

ON THE TRAIL OF THE IMMIGRANT
Edward A. Steiner

Arno Press. Reprint of the 1906 edition. $12.50.

PAPER WALLS: AMERICA AND THE

REFUGEE CRISIS, 1938 To 1941
David S. Wyman

University of Massachusettes Press, 1969. $12.00.

THE PEOPLING OF AMERICA: PERSPECTIVES ON IMMIGRATION
Franklin D. Scott

American Historical Association, 1974. Pap. $1.00.

A PICTORAL HISTORY OF IMMIGRATION
Oscar Handlin

Shows the conditions that led to immigration, rigors of the crossing, and the effect on this country. 352 pp. Crown Publishers, 1972. Over 1,000 illustrations. $12.50.

PORT ARRIVALS AND IMMIGRANTS TO THE CITY OF BOSTON, 1715-1716 AND 1762-1769
William H. Whitmore, Compiler

111 pp. Genealogical Publishing Co., 1973. Reprint of the 1900 edition. $8.50.

PRESENT DAY IMMIGRATION: 1921
The American Academy of Political and Social Science, 1975. $5.00; Pap. $4.00.

RACES AND IMMIGRANTS IN AMERICA
John R. Commons

The attitude of organized labor toward American immigration policy: The author discusses race and democracy; colonial race elements; the Negro; the relationship of urban life to crime and poverty; and amalgamation and assimilation. 242 pp. August M. Kelley Publishers. Reprint of the 1907 edition.

THE RACIAL PROBLEMS INVOLVED IN IMMIGRATION FROM LATIN AMERICA AND THE WEST INDIES
Robert F. Foerster

R and E Research Associates, 1971. Reprint of the 1925 edition. $5.00.

THE RADICAL IMMIGRANT
Sally M. Miller

Covers the period of their greatest activity in the United States, 1820-1920. Twayne Publishers. $8.50.

THE REPORTS OF THE IMMIGRATION COMMISSION
Reprints of 41 volumes put out by the U.S. Immigration Commission. When first issued,

the detailed study of the Commission have what appeared to be official and presumably scientific proof of the innate inferiority of southern and eastern Europeans. The Commission bent whatever evidence it could find to prove their preconceived idea. Arno Press, 1975. $399.00. Individual available.

SOME EMIGRANTS TO VIRGINIA
William G. Stanard
94 pp. Genealogical Publishing Co., 1972. Reprint of the 1915 edition. $5.00.

STRANGERS AT THE DOOR: ELLIS ISLAND, CASTLE GARDEN AND THE GREAT MIGRATION TO AMERICA
Ann Novotny
The story of the port of entry for hundreds of thousands of immigrants. 160 pp. Devin-Adair, 1975. Illus. $12.50

*WE CAME TO AMERICA
Frances Cavanah
Personal accounts by immigrants who help make our nation. 320 pp. Macrae Smith, 1954. $5.79. (Gr. 7 up)

*WE WANTED TO BE FREE: THE STORIES OF REFUGEES AND EXILES IN AMERICA
Frances Cavanah
The accounts of refugees who made their mark in America. 256 pp. Macrae Smith, 1971. $5.95. (Gr. 7 up)

XENOPHOBIA AND IMMIGRATION, 1820-1930
Thomas J. Curran
The hostile reaction of native Americans to the influx of 38 million newcomers to the U.S. Between 1820 and 1930. Twayne Publishers, 1975. $7.95.

MISCEGENATION

INTERMARRIAGE IN NEW YORK CITY: A STATISTICAL STUDY OF THE AMALGAMATION OF EUROPEAN PEOPLES
Julius Drachsler
AMS Press, Inc. Reprint of the 1921 edition. $7.50.

MARRIAGE IN BLACK AND WHITE

Joseph R. Washington, Jr.
The acceptance of intermarriage. Beacon Press. Cloth, $7.50; Pap. $3.95.

MISCEGENATION
David C. Croly
Gregg Press, 1971. $7.00.

RACE MIXTURES: STUDIES IN INTERMARRIAGE AND MISCEGENATION
Edward B. Reuter
224 pp. Negro Universities Press. Reprint of the 1931 edition. $9.50.

RACE RELATIONS IN VIRGINIA AND MISCEGENATION IN THE SOUTH, 1776 TO 1860
James H. Johnston
University of Massachusetts Press, 1970. $15.00.

RACE AND RACISM

ALIEN AMERICANS: A STUDY OF RACE RELATIONS
Bertram Johannes Schrieke
R and E Research Associates, Pubs., 1971. Reprint of the 1936 edition. $10.00.

AM I A RACIST?
Fortune Monte and Robert Heyer
Association Press, 1969. Pap. $1.95.

AMERICA: RED, WHITE, BLACK, YELLOW
Arthur H. Fauset, and Nellie Bright
Franklin Publishing Co., 1969. $4.60.

AMERICAN RACISM: EXPLORATION OF THE NATURE OF PREJUDICE
Roger Daniels and Harry H.L. Kitano
Explores the "culture" of target minorities, and evaluates its role in the development of prejudice. 155 pp. Prentice-Hall, Inc., 1970.

ANTHOLOGIA ANTHROPOLIGICA: THE NATIVE RACES OF AMERICA: A COPIOUS SELECTION OF PASSAGES FOR THE STUDY OF SOCIAL ANTHROPOLOGY
James George Frazer
AMS PRess, Inc. Reprint fo the 1939 edition. $47.50.

BETTER THAN YOU: SOCIAL DISCRIMINATION AGAINST MINORITIES IN AMERICA
Terry Morris
American Jewish Committee, 1971. Pap. $1.00.

BLACK/BROWN/WHITE RELATIONS: RACE RELATIONS IN THE 1970s
Charles V. Willie, Editor
An analysis of the effects of institutional racism on all races in the United States. 300 pp. Transaction Books, 1975, Cloth, $9.95; Pap. $3.95.

THE BLENDING OF RACES
Noel P. Gist and Anthony Gary, Editors
Explores the identity, intergroup harmony,and social structure of racially-mixed minorities in selected societies around the world. 289 pp. Wiley-Interscience, 1972. $11.50.

DESEGREGATION AND THE SUPREME COURT
Benjamin Munn Ziegler
116 pp. D.C. Heath and Co., 1958.

DICTIONARY OF RACES OR PEOPLES
United States Immigration Commission
Gale Research Co., 1969. Reprint of the 1911 edition. $6.50.

DIRTY WORK, RACE, AND SELF-ESTEEM
Edward J. Walsh
A challenge to programs aimed at helping lower-or working-class people based on the assumption that they are "pathological." 95 pp. Institute of Labor and Industrial Relations, 1975. Cloth, $6.50; pap. $2.50.

ETHNIC AND RACIAL SEGREGATION IN THE NEW YORK METROPOLIS: RESIDENTIAL PATTERNS AMONG WHITE ETHNIC GROUPS, BLACKS AND PUERTO RICANS
Nathan Kantrowitz
122 pp. Praeger Pubs., 1973. $12.50

FOUR PERSPECTIVES ON RACE IN AMERICA
Carlos Cortes, et al, Editors
Writings of leading historians and leading historical figures account of the failure of American justice for blacks, Chicanos, native Americans and Puerto Ricans. G.P. Putnam's sons, 1975. $8.95

GROUP IMAGES: RACIAL, ETHNIC AND

RELIGIOUS STEREOTYPING
Frederick Samuels
College and University Press. Pap. $2.45.

MAJORITY AND MINORITY: THE DYNAMICS OF RACIAL AND ETHNIC RELATIONS
Norman R. Yetman and C. Hoy Steele
Emphasizes the institutional and structural aspects of minority group discrimination, including; American and Canadian Indians, Jews, Chicanos, Puerto Ricans, Catholics, Chinese, Jews, Northern Irish, and women. 670 pp. Allyn and Bacon, 1975. Pap. $6.75.

THE MORALITY OF THE COLOR LINE: AN EXAMINATION OF THE RIGHT AND THE WRONG OF THE DISCRIMINATIONS AGAINST THE NEGRO IN THE UNITED STATES
Francis James Gilligan
222 pp. Greenwood Press. Reprint of the 1928 edition. $11.00.

THE NAT TURNER REBELLION: *The Historical Event and the Modern Controversy*
John B. Duff and Peter M. Mitchell, Editors
Tells about the racial polarization in American society. 246 pp. Harper & Row Publishers, 1971. Pap. $3.95.

NATION OF NATIONS: THE ETHNIC EXPERIENCE AND THE RACIAL CRISIS
Peter I. Rose
Random House, Inc., 1971. Pap. $5.95.

NOT BY THE COLOR OF THEIR SKIN: THE IMPACT OF RACIAL DIFFERENCES ON THE CHILD'S DEVELOPMENT
Marjorie McDonald
Observations of the reactions of children in an integrated therapeutic nursery school. 256 pp. International University Press, 1971. $9.00.

PAPERS ON INTER-RACIAL PROBLEMS
G. Spiller, Editor
Communicated to the First Universal Races Congress held at the University of London, 1911. Books for Libraries. Reprint of the 1911 edition. $22.00.

THE PASSING OF THE GREAT RACE: OR THE RACIAL BASIS OF EUROPEAN HISTORY
Madison Grant

This is the essay which constructed a racial theory concerning the ranking of superior and inferior European peoples. The author's emphasis on Nordic superiority was an expression of and influence upon the growing intolerance of Americans for Southern and Eastern Europeans, resulting in the discriminatory national origins principle of immigration restriction in the 1920's. Arno Press. Reprint of the 1918 edition. $13.00.

RACE, CREED, COLOR, OR NATIONAL ORIGIN: A READER ON RACIAL AND ETHNIC IDENTITIES IN AMERICAN SOCIETY
Robert K. Yin
Selections cover historical origins of the concepts, the definition of racial and ethnic groups, institutional discrimination, and emerging issues. 312 pp. F.E. Peacock Publishers, 1973. Pap. $4.95.

RACE DISTINCTIONS IN AMERICAN LAW
Gilbert Thomas Stephenson
Books for Libraries. Reprint of the 1910 edition. $10.50. Johnson Reprint, $16.75.

RACE AND ETHNIC RELATIONS
Brewton Berry
Houghton Mifflin Co., 1965. Cloth, $11.95; Pap. $1.60.

RACE AND ETHNICITY
Pierre Van Den Berghe
Basic Books, 1970. $8.45.

RACE: *The History of an Idea in America*
Thomas F. Gossett
Describes the historical climate in which racial prejudice took root and developed as a part of the American system of beliefs and attitudes. Traces the influence of racial theology on American domestic and foreign policy, on its hemispheric relations, on education, literature, and other channels of public belief and opinion. Schocken Books. Pap. $3.95.

RACE, MARRIAGE, AND THE LAW
Robert J. Sickels
A history of the legal status of interracial marriage in the United States. University of New Mexico Press. $6.95.

RACE AND NATIONALITY IN AMERICAN LIFE
Oscar Handlin
Little, Brown, and Co., 1957. Cloth, $6.95.

Pap. $1.95. Doubleday and Co., Pap. $1.95.

RACE AND RACIALISM
Sami Zubaida, Editor
Barnes and Noble, 1970. Pap. $3.50.

RACE AND RUMOR OF RACE: CHALLENGE TO AMERICAN CRISIS
Howard Washington Odum
245 pp. Greenwood Press. Reprint of the 1943 edition. $10.00.

RACES AND ETHNIC GROUPS IN AMERICAN LIFE
T.J. Woofter
Kraus Reprint Co. Reprint of the 1933 edition. $13.00.

RACES AND IMMIGRANTS IN AMERICA
John R. Commons
The attitude of organized labor toward American immigration policy: The author discusses race and democracy; colonial race elements; the Negro; the relationship of urban life to crime and poverty; and amalgamation and assimilation. 242 pp. August M. Kelley Publishers. Reprint of the 1907 edition. Illus. $10.00.

RACIAL ATTITUDES IN AMERICA:
Analyses and Findings of Social Psychology
John C. Brigham and
Theodore A. Weissbach
Psychological research and theorizing in the area of black-white attitudes. Presents empirical finding within the context of broad social issues. 401 pp. Harper & Row Publishers, 1972. Pap. $7.95

RACIAL CONFLICT AND NEGOTIATIONS: PERSPECTIVES AND FIRST CASE STUDIES
W. Ellison Chalmers and
Gerald W. Cormick, Editors
A series of case studies examining the use of negotiations process in racial conflict. 252 pp. Institute of Labor and Industrial Relations, 1971. Cloth, $12.00; Pap. $5.95.

RACIAL AND CULTURAL MINORITIES: *An Analysis of Prejudice and Discrimination*
George Eaton Simpson and
J. Milton Yinger, Editors
A comprehensive study of minorities and the forces that sustain them. Focus is on the

development of a theory of intergroup conflict, prejudice, and discrimination. 775 pp. Harper & Row Publishers, 1972. $14.50.

RACIAL DISCRIMINATION IN THE UNITED STATES
Thomas F. Pettigrew

A selection of studies on discrimination against blacks in the United States. Harper & Row Publishers, 1975. Pap.

RACIAL AND ETHNIC RELATIONS
Joseph H. Himes

72 pp. william C. Brown Pubs., 1974. Pap. $1.50.

RACIAL AND ETHNIC RELATIONS
Helen M. Hughes, Editor

Holbrook Press, 1972. Pap. $4.50.

RACIAL AND ETHNIC RELATIONS: SELECTED READINGS
Bernard E. Segal, Editor

Thomas Y. Crowell Co., 1972. Pap. $6.50.

RACIAL NEGOTIATIONS: POTENTIALS AND LIMITATIONS
W. Ellison Chalmers

Can the art of negotiation in labor-management relations be used to achieve goals meaningful to both sides in racial conflicts? this question is explored. 281 pp. Institute of Labor and Industrial Relations, 1974. $15.00.

RACIAL OPPRESSION IN AMERICA
Robert Blauner

Eight original essays on Third World movements, the ghetto revolts of the 1960's as a response to internal colonialism, the historical and present-day impulses behind Afro-American culture, and the impact of a white racist society on Chicanos and other colonized groups. 309 pp. Harper & Row Publishers, 1972. Pap. $4.95.

THE RACIAL PROBLEMS INVOLVED IN IMMIGRATION FROM LATIN AMERICA AND THE WEST INDIES
Robert F. Foerster

R E Research Associates, 1971. Reprint of the 1925 edition. $5.00.

*RACISM
Robert Froman

Focuses on the social practices of racism in the United States. 176 pp. Dell Publishing Co., 1972. Ages 12 up. $5.95.

RACISM
Magnus Hirschfeld

The author dissects the whole concept of racism and examines every element from its origin and practice. Kennikat Press, 1973. Reprint of the 1938 edition. $15.00.

RACISM IN CALIFORNIA
R. Daniels and S.C. Olin, Jr.

Macmillan Publishing Co., 1972. Pap. $3.95.

RACISM AND PSYCHIATRY
Alexander Thomas and Samuel Sillen

Citadel Press, 1974. Pap. $3.45.

RED, AND YELLOW, BLACK, AND BROWN
C. Snyder

Holt, Rinehart, and Winston, 1973. $6.95.

RELUCTANT REFORMERS
Robert Allen

A study of the ideological impact of racism on six major social reform movements in the united States. 324 pp. Howard University Press, 1974. $8.95.

THEY AND WE: RACIAL AND ETHNIC RELATIONS IN THE UNITED STATES
Peter I. Rose

Random House, Inc., 1973. Pap. $3.95.

*UNDER THE MASK: AN ANTHOLOGY ABOUT PREJUDICE IN AMERICA
Karel Weiss, Editor

Through songs, poems, documents, periodical and newspaper articles, and excerpts of books, this book traces the decline of racial pride and its subsequent resurgence among Americans of African, Indian, Japanese, Mexican, and Puerto Rican descent. 336 pp. Dell Publishing co., 1972. Age 12 up. $6.95.

THE WHITE MAN'S BURDEN
Matthew Holden, Jr.

Chandler Publishing Co., 1973. Pap. $5.95.

WHITE MAN, LISTEN: THE POSITION OF NON-WHITE PEOPLES
Richard Wright

Doubleday and Co., 1957. $1.45.

WHITE RACISM: ITS HISTORY, PATHOLOGY AND PRACTICE
Barry N. Schwartz and Robert Disch, Editors

A collection of historical and contemporary

writings on white American bigotry. 640 pp. Dell publishing Co. $1.75.

WHITE, RED, BLACK: SKETCHES OF AMERICAN SOCIETY DURING THE VISIT OF THEIR GUESTS

Francis and Theresa Pulszky
673 pp. 2 vols in one. Johnson Reprint Corporation, 1970. Reprint of the 1853 edition. $39.25.

WHITE SETTLERS AND NATIVE PEOPLES: AN HISTORICAL STUDY OF RACIAL CONTACTS BETWEEN ENGLISH SPEAKING WHITES AND ABORIGINAL PEOPLES IN THE UNITED STATES, CANADA, AUSTRALIA, AND NEW ZEALAND

Archibald Grenfell Price
232 pp. Greenwood Press, Inc., 1972. Reprint of the 1950 edition. Illus. $11.50.

RACE AND RELIGION

THE CHURCH IN THE RACIALLY CHANGING COMMUNITY

Robert Wilson and James Davis
Abingdon Press, Pap. $1.25.

THE CHURCH AND RESIDENTIAL DESEGREGATION

henry Clark
College and University Press, 1965. $6.00.

THE PULPIT SPEAKS ON RACE

Alfred T. Davies, Editor
Twenty sermons on race. Abingdon Press. $3.95.

RACE AND THE RENEWAL OF THE CHURCH

Will D. Campbell
The author discusses what he believes to be the church's proper attitudes toward the problems of racial tension. 96 pp. Westminster Press, 1962. Pap. $1.25.

WHITE PROTESTANT AMERICANS: FROM NATIONAL ORIGINS TO RELIGIOUS GROUP

Charles H. Anderson
Information on Scots, Swedes, Norwegians, Finlanders, Dutch and Deutsch. 188 pp. Prentice-Hall, Inc., 1970.

SCHOOL DESEGREGATION

AFFIRMATIVE SCHOOL INTEGRATION: EFFORTS TO OVERCOME DE FACTO SEGREGATION IN URBAN SCHOOLS

Roscoe Hill and Malcolm Feely, Editors
Sage Publications, 1969. $7.50.

BUSING: THE POLITICAL AND JUDICIAL PROCESS

James Bolner and Robert Shanley
175 pp. Praeger Pubs., 1973. $13.50.

THE BUS STOPS HERE: *A Study of School Desegregation in Three Cities*

Anna Holden
Studies the movement toward racial balance in the school districts of Charlottesville, Va., Providence, R.I., and Sacramento, Calif. These cities were chosen for study because they represented — in ethnic composition, geographical location, and patterns of cooperation and resistance — a sampling of problems facing similar-sized cities all over the United States. Schocken Books, 1975. $15.00.

COMBATING DISCRIMINATION IN THE SCHOOLS: LEGAL REMEDIES AND GUIDELINES

Outlines each major antidiscrimination law or regulation covering educational institutions, and specifies what it forbids, who enforces it, and how to file a complaint. 32 pp. National Education Association. Pap. $1.25.

THE DESEGREGATION ERA IN HIGHER EDUCATION

Samuel P. Wiggins
McCutchan Publishing Corp., 1966. Pap. $3.75.

DESEGREGATION WORKS: A PRIMER FOR PARENTS AND TEACHERS

Lillian S. Calhoun
Integrated Education Associates. Pap. $0.75.

THE DYNAMICS OF SCHOOL INTEGRATION: PROBLEMS AND APPROACHES IN A NORTHERN CITY

Donald Bouma and James Hoffman
A critical examination of *de facto* segregation in a typical northern city. William B. Eerdmans Publishing Co., 1968. Pap. $2.25.

EDUCATION AND RACE: AN ANALSIS OF EDUCATIONAL PRODUCTION PROCESS
Eric Hanushek
192 pp. Lexington Books, Inc., 1972. $10.00.

EDUCATION AND RACISM: AN ACTION MANUAL
National Education Association
How teacher organizations have successfully begun to deal with racism in educational settings. 56 pp. National Education Association, 1973. Pap. $2.00.

EMOTIONAL ASPECTS OF SCHOOL DESEGREGATION
GAP Committee on Social Issues
The problems of school desegregation since the Supreme Court decision of 1954. 64 pp. Group for the Advancement of Psychiatry, 1970. Pap. $1.00.

FIFTY-EIGHT LONELY MEN: *Southern Federal Judges and School Desegregation*
J.W. Peltason
The dilemma of Southern Federal judges dedicated to the establishment of justice but under pressure to defeat it in the case of school desegregation. 270 pp. Harcourt Brace Jovanovich, Inc., 1961. $4.95.

IMPACT OF RACIAL ISSUES ON EDUCATIONAL ADMINISTRATION
American Association of School Administrators
26 pp. American Association of School Administrators, 1970. Pap. $2.00.

IMPACT OF SCHOOL DESEGREGATION
Robert R. Mayer, et al
A three-year study of a school desegregation plan in Goldsboro, North Carolina. 143 pp. Lexington Books, 1974. $12.50.

INTEGRATED EDUCATION: A READER
Meyer Weinberg
Glencoe Press, 1968. $5.95.

INTEGRATING THE URBAN SCHOOL
Gordon J. Klopf and Israel A. Laster, eds.
This book presents the important papers read at a conference devoted to promoting integration in urban areas. Topics discussed are cultural factors, school site selection, curriculum planning, grouping of students, guidance services, and teacher training . 136 pp. Teachers College Press, 1963. Pap. $2.25.

JIM CROW IN BOSTON: THE ORIGIN OF THE "SEPARATE BUT EQUAL DOCTRINE"
Leonard Levy and Douglas L. Jones, Editors
Da Capo Press. $12.95.

MODELS FOR INTEGRATED EDUCATION
Daniel U. Levine, Editor
128 pp. C.A. Jones, 1971. Pap. $5.95.

NOW IS THE TIME FOR INTEGRATION IN THE BERKELEY SCHOOLS
Neil V. Sullivan and Evelyn S. Stewart
Indiana University Press, 1970. $6.95.

PAN-AFRICANISM AND EDUCATION: A STUDY OF RACE PHILANTHROPY AND EDUCATION IN THE SOUTHERN STATES OF AMERICAN AND EAST AFRICA
Kenneth King
310 pp. Oxford University Press, 1971. $13.75.

THE POLITICS OF SCHOOL DESEGREGATION: COMPARATIVE CASE STUDIES OF COMMUNITY STRUCTURE AND POLICY-MAKING
Robert L. Crain
Aldine Publishing Co., 1968. $9.95.

THE PRINCIPAL: CHANGE-AGENT IN DESEGREGATION
Martha Turnage
Integrated Education Associates. Pap. $2.25.

PSYCHIATRIC ASPECTS OF SCHOOL DESEGREGATION
GAP Committee on Social Issues
Problems of adjustment for both races. 96 pp. Group for the Advancement of Psychiatry, 1957. Pap. $1.00.

RACE, PREJUDICE, AND EDUCATION
Cyril Bibby
96 pp. Praeger Pubs., 1967. $4.00.

THE RACE WAR IN HIGH SCHOOL: THE TEN YEAR DESTRUCTION OF FRANKLIN K. LANE HIGH SCHOOL IN BROOKLYN
Harold Saltzman
Arlington House Pubs., 1972. $8.95.

RACIAL CRISIS IN PUBLIC EDUCATION
Arthur Davis, Jr.
Vantage Press, Inc., 1974. $7.50.

THE RICHMOND SCHOOL DECISION
Robert P. Merhige
The complete text of ruling by U.S. District Judge Robert P. Merhige, Jr. in the Richmond, Virginia school case. 213 pp. Integrated Education Associates. $5.00.

SCHOOL DESEGREGATION IN THE CAROLINAS: TWO CASE STUDIES
William F. Bagwell
University of South Carolina Press, 1972. $14.95.

SCHOOL DESEGREGATION: OUTCOMES FOR CHILDREN
Nancy H. St. John
This book brings together and classifies over 120 published and unpublished studies of the effects of school desegregation on black and white pupils. The author develops the thesis that school desegregation is a many-sided phenomenon, the effects of which may be simultaneously beneficial to children in some respects and detrimental in others. She points out that the quality of implementation necessary in order to maximize benefits and minimize harm is more important than ratios, quotas, and the fact of racial balance. 236 pp. John Wiley & Sons, 1975. $12.95.

SCHOOL RACIAL POLICY
American Association of School Administrators
Analysis of programs and problems of public school intergration policies. 44 pp. American Association of School Administrators, 1966. Pap. $2.00.

*THE SCHOOL SEGREGATION CASES BROWN VS. THE BOARD OF EDUCATION OF TOPEKA AND OTHERS
Janet Stevenson
Crucial Supreme Court decisions affecting school segregation. 72 pp. FranklinWatts, Inc., 1973. Age 12 up. $3.90.

SCHOOLS IN TRANSITION: COMCUNITY EXPERIENCES INDESEGREGATION
Robin M. Williams, Jr. and Margaret W. Ryan, Editors
279 pp. University of North Carolina Press, 1954. $5.00.

SEPARATE AND UNEQUAL: PUBLIC SCHOOL CAMPAIGNS AND RACISM IN THE SOUTHERN SEABOARD STATES
Louis R. Harlan

Atheneum Publications, 1968. Pap. $2.75.

SOCIAL INTEGRATION IN URBAN COMMUNITIES: *A Program Guide for Educational Leaders*
Robert B. Knapp
The author explores the meaning of social integration in urban-industrial society in a way that may help to define policies and determine the scope of public school programs that will contribute to a higher level of community life. 196 pp. Teachers College Press, 1960. $8.50.

THE TEACHER AND INTEGRATION
National Education Association
Moving from a desegregated to an integrated classroom. 96 pp. National Education Association, 1966. Pap. $2.00.

THEY CLOSED THEIR SCHOOLS: PRINCE EDWARD COUNTY, VIRGINIA, 1951-1964
Bob Smith
The only case where the citizens chose to terminate public education rather than obey a Supreme Court decision. 296 pp. University of North Carolina Press, 1965. Pap. $2.25.

TO KILL A CHILD'S SPIRIT: THE TRAGEDY OF SCHOOL SEGREGATION IN LOS ANGELES
John Caughey
Based on a premise that the segregated school generates a sense of rejection and inferiority that is bitter enough to kill a child's spirit. 255 pp. F.E. Peacock Publishers, 1973. $8.00; Pap. $4.95.

TRIUMPH IN A WHITE SUBURB: THE DRAMATIC STORY OF TEANECK, NEW JERSEY, THE FIRST TOWN TO VOTE FOR INTEGRATED SCHOOLS
Reginald G. Damerell
Apollo Editions, 1969. Pap. $2.50.

WITH ALL DELIBERATE SPEED: SEGREGATION-DESEGREGATION IN SOUTHERN SCHOOLS
Southern Education Reporting Service
239 pp. Neggo Universities Press. Reprint of the 1957 edition. $11.75.

YOUR SCHOOL'S DESEGREGATION: HOW REAL?
Covers teachers, principals, curriculum, extra-curricular activities, and more. Integrateducation Associates. $1.50.

URBAN ETHNICITY

AMERICANS IN PROCESS: A SETTLE-MENT STUDY

Robert A. Woods, Editor
A study of the social conditions of the South, North and West Ends of Boston at the turn of the century. Arno Press. Reprint of the 1903 edition. $17.50.

BEYOND THE MELTING POT: THE NEGROES, PUERTO RICANS, JEWS, ITALIANS, AND IRISH OF NEW YORK CITY

Nathan Glazer and Daniel P. Moynihan
M.I.T. Press, 1970. $15.00; Pap. $2.95.

CITIES AND IMMIGRANTS: GEOGRA-PHY OF CHANGE IN 19TH CENTURY AMERICA

David Ward
Oxfor University Press, 1971. $6.95; Pap. $3.50.

A DIRECTORY OF SPANISH-SPEAKING NEW YORK

Lists businesses, services, manufacturers, distributors, retailers, churches, schools, etc. serving the two million residents of Hispanic background in the New York metropolitan area. 340 bilingual pp. Quadrangle Books, P.O. box 590, Yonkers, N.Y. 10702. $3.95.

THE ETHNIC FACTOR IN THE URBAN POLITY

Richard A. Gabriel
MSS Information Corp., 1973. $10.00.

ETHNIC FACTORS IN THE POPULATION OF BOSTON

Frederick A. Bushee
Studies the social and ethnic diversity in Boston at the turn of the 20th century. Arno Press. Reprint of the 1903 edition. $7.00.

ETHNIC PATTERNS IN AMERICAN CITIES

Stanley Lieberson
Free Press, 1962. $7.95.

A HOUSE FOR ALL PEOPLES: CHICA-GO'S ETHNIC GROUPS AND THEIR POLITICS, 1890 TO 1936

John M. Allswang
253 pp. Universityof Kentucky Press, 1971. $8.95.

IMMIGRANTS AND THE CITY: ETHNI-CITY AND MOBILITY IN A NINETEENTH CENTURY MIDWESTERN CITY

Dean R. Esslinger
Patterns and avenues of mobility, emergence of immigrant neighborhoods, community asimilation, and creation of ethnic leaders in South Bend, Indiana. Kennikat Press, 1975. $9.95.

THE PEOPLES OF PHILADELPHIA

Allen F. Davis and Mark H. Haller, Editors
A history of ethnic groups and lower-class life in Philadelphia, 1790-1940. 311 pp. Temple University Press, 1973. Cloth, $15.00; pap. $3.95.

SOCIAL CHANGE IN URBAN AMERICA

Max Birnbaum and John Mogey, Editors
A collection of readings with commentaries by the editors provides a stimulus to experimental studies of present conditions in urban communities. Social change and race relations are discussed. 249 pp. Harper & Row Publishers, 1972. Pap. $5.95.

URBAN ETHNICITY

Abner Cohen, Editor
Barnes and Noble, 1974. $16.00.

URBAN POLITICAL MOVEMENTS: THE SEARCH FOR POWER BY MINORITY GROUPS IN AMERICAN CITIES

Norman and Susan S. Fainstein
An analysis of fhe mobilizing efforts of minority groups to change the behavior of urban bureaucracies and to create programs that might improve their lives. 271 pp. Prentice-Hall, Inc., 1974.

AMERICAN INDIANS

The first Americans have contributed much to
our ethnic heritage and social development.
Books listed in this section pertain to those areas
the editor believes most relevant to ethnic study.

ARTS AND CRAFTS

ABORIGINAL AMERICAN [INDIAN] BASKETRY
Otis Tufton Mason
A definitive work on basket-making; styles,
design and art. 592 pp. 48 plates. Rio Grande
Press. Reprint of the 1902 edition. Illus. $25.00.

AMERICAN INDIAN ART
Walker Art Center
Twenty color, 150 black-and white-illus.;
Bibliographies, maps. E.P. Dutton & Co., Inc.,
1973, $8.00.

AMERICAN INDIAN ART
Norman Feder
Discusses and illustrates the art forms of the
Amerinds in their various geographic divisions
— the pottery of the Pueblos of the Southwest,
the wooden masks of the Eskimo and the
Tlinget, the beadwork of the Plains and Pacific
Plateau tribes, and the basketry of the
California natives among others. 150 pp. Harry
N. Abrams, Inc., 1971. Illus. $15.00.

*AMERICAN INDIAN ARTS: A WAY OF LIFE
Julia M. Seton
Captures in text and picture the vanishing arts
and handicrafts of the Indians of North
America, from Florida to Alaska. 246 pp.
Ronald Press Co., 1962. $6.00.

AMERICAN INDIAN BOOK OF NEEDLEPOINT DESIGN
M. Boyles, B. Hunt and J.F. Burshears
Macmillan Publishing Co., 1975. Pap. $3.95.

AMERICAN INDIAN CRAFT BOOK
M.N. Minor
Popular Library, 1972. Pap. $1.25.

AMERICAN INDIAN CRAFT INSPIRATIONS
A. D'Amato and J. D'Amato
M. Evans and Co., 1972. $7.95.

AMERICAN INDIAN DESIGN AND DECORATION
L.H. Appleton
Peter Smith Publishers. $6.50.

AMERICAN INDIAN DESIGN AND DECORATION
Leroy H. Appleton
More than 700 drawings catch the spirit of the
art of the Indians of both Americas, from Inca
and Maya to Pueblo and Plains. 279 pp. Dover
Publications, 1971. Illus. Pap. $4.00.

AMERICAN INDIAN PAINTERS: A BIOGRAPHICAL DIRECTORY
Jeanne Owen Snodgrass
269 pp. Museum of the American Indian, 1968.
$7.50.

AMERICAN INDIAN PAINTING OF THE SOUTHWEST AND PLAINS AREA
D. Dunn
University of New Mexico Press, 1968. $30.00.

AN ANNOTATED BIBLIOGRAPHY OF AMERICAN INDIAN PAINTING
Doris Ostrander Dawdy
50 pp. Museum of the American Indian, 1968.
$2.50.

ART AND INDIAN INDIVIDUALISTS
Guy and Doris Monthan
17 contemporary Indian artists work in painting, silversmithing, ceramics, and sculpture 168
pp. 85 plates. Northland Press, 1974. $35.00.
Limited edition of 150 numbered copies signed
by all available artists and the authors, $150.00.

ART OF THE NORTHWEST COAST INDIANS
R.B. Inverarity
University of California Press, 1967. Cloth,
$14.25; Pap. $7.95.

BIBLIOGRAPHY OF ARTICLES AND PAPERS ON NORTH AMERICAN INDIAN ART
A.D. Harding and P. Bolling, Editors
Kraus Reprint Co., 1974. Reprint of the 1938
edition. $15.00.

THE BOOK OF INDIAN-CRAFTS AND COSTUMES
Bernard S. Mason
From the crafts and customs of the Indians of
the Woodlands and Plains — the roamers of the
northern wildwoods, the *wigwam* Indians, the
masters of woodcraft, the *canoe* Indians; and

the riders of the prairies, the *tepee* Indians, the hunters of buffalo, the *horse* Indians — this book has drawn its material. 118 pp. Ronald Press Co., 1974. Reprint of the 1946 edition. $7.95.

*BOOKS OF INDIAN CRAFTS AND IN-DIAN LORE
Julian H. Salomon
Harper and Row Pubs., 1928. Illus. $7.95. Ages 10 and up.

THE CARVER'S ART OF THE INDIANS OF NORTHWESTERN CALIFORNIA
Isabel T. Kelly
Material on the Yurok, Karok, and Hupa Indians living along the lower Klamath and Trinity Rivers, including horn spoons, mush paddles, elk-horn money boxes, relation of carving to basketry design, etc. 33 pp. Ballena Press. Reprint of the 1930 edition. Illus. Pap. $2.50.

DECORATIVE ART OF THE SOUTH-WESTERN INDIANS
S. Sides
Peter Smith Publishers. $4.00.

DECORATIVE ART OF THE SOUTH-WESTERN INDIANS
Dorothy Smith Sides
Contains Pueble pottery designs, Hopi kachina doll decorations, motifs from Zuni masks, Navaho blankets, Apache baskets, and Mohave beadwork among others. 101 pp. Dover Publications. Illus. Pap. $1.50.

INDIAN ART IN AMERICA: THE ARTS AND CRAFTS OF THE NORTH AMERICAN INDIAN
F.J. Dockstader
New York Graphic Society, 1966. $27.50.

INDIAN ART OF THE AMERICAS
Frederick J. Dockstader
Discusses the esthetic accomplishments of the Indians of North, Central and South America from *circa* 3,000 B.C. to 1970 A.D. 304 pp. Museum of the American Indian. $10.00.

INDIAN ART OF THE UNITED STATES
F.H. Douglas and R. D'Harnoncourt
Arno Press, 1970. Reprint of the 1941 edition. $16.00.

*INDIAN ARTS
Robert Hofsinde

Explains the materials and techniques used for decorative, religious, and practical purposes. 96 pp. William Morrow & Co., 1971. Illus. Ages 8-12. $3.95.

INDIAN ARTS AND CRAFTS
M. Miller
Nash Publishing Corp., 1972. Pap. $2.45.

INDIAN BASKET WEAVING: THE MA-TERIALS AND TECHNIQUES OF THE POMO, YUROK, PIMA AND NAVAJO
Sandra Corrie Newman
Describes the weavers, their materials, and shows how the baskets are made. 120 pp. Northland Press, 1973. Illus. Pap. $4.95.

*INDIAN BEADWORK
Robert Hofsinde
Gives the historical background of Indian beadwork, along with instructions for the making and decorating of many items. 128 pp. William Morrow & Co., 1958. Illus. Ages 8-12. $3.78.

INDIAN BLANKETS AND THEIR MAKERS
George Wharton James
An analysis of the technique of primitive hand-weaving. 352 pp. 48 plates. Rio Grande Press, 1971. Reprint of the 1892 edition. Illus. $20.00.

*INDIAN COSTUMES
Robert Hofsinde
Explores beadwork, tattooing, body-painting customs, and hair styles. 96 pp. William Morrow & Co., 1968. Illus. Ages 8-12. $3.78.

INDIAN RAWHIDE: AN AMERICAN FOLK ART
Mable Morrow
Shows patterns and designs representative of tribes from Apache to Yakima. 200 pp. University of Oklahoma Press, 1975. Illus. $20.00

INDIAN SKIN PAINTINGS FROM THE AMERICAN SOUTHWEST: TWO REPRE-SENTATIONS OF BORDER CONFLICTS BETWEEN MEXICO AND THE MISSOURI IN THE EARLY EIGHTEENTH CENTURY
Gottgried Hotz
234 pp. University of Oklahoma Press, 1970. Illus. $9.95.

INTRODUCTION TO AMERICAN INDIAN ART [TWO VOLUMES IN ONE]
Oliver La Farge, et al

Parts I and II of the paperbound books published for the Exposition of the American Indian in 1932-1933. 200 pp. Rio Grande Press. Illus. $10.00.

MASTERWORKS FROM THE MUSEUM OF THE AMERICAN INDIAN

A catalog of the exhibition held in 1973 at the Metropolitan Museum of Art, which featured 200 of the objects in the Museum collection. 64 pp. 200 plates. Museum of the American Indian, 1974. Illus. $2.50.

MY FRIEND THE INDIAN
James McLaughlin

Book is built around 31 color reproductions of Indian paintings by Daniel Shaw Buisson. 142 pp. Superior Publishing Co. Reprint of the 1910 edition. $14.95.

NAKED CLAY: 3000 YEARS OF UNADORNED POTTERY OF THE AMERICAN INDIAN

Introduction to Indian pottery technology and form. 72 pp. 90 plates. Museum of the American Indian, 1974. $3.50.

PICTURE-WRITINGS OF THE AMERICAN INDIAN
G. Mallery

Peter Smith Publishers. $16.00 set.

POTTERY OF THE SOUTHWESTERN INDIANS
Pliny Earle Goddard

Methods of making and ornamenting pottery and how to identify local varities. 30 pp. Ballena Press. Reprint of the 1928 edition. Illus. Pap. $2.00.

*THE RED MAN IN ART
Rena Neumann Coen

Among the artists represented are Benjamin West, Karl Bodmer, George Catlin, Seth Eastman, Frederick Remington, Oscar Howe. 72 pp. Lerner Publications, 1972. Illus. Ages 11-17. $4.95.

ROCK ART OF THE AMERICAN INDIANS
Campbell Grant

192 pp. Apollo Editions, 1972. Pap. $2.95.

SOUTHWEST INDIANS CRAFT ARTS
Clara Lee Tanner

History and descriptions of the various crafts, including baskets, textiles, pottery, silver and jewelry, kachina dolls and other carvings. 206 pp. University of Arizona Press, 1968. Illus. $15.00.

SOUTHWEST INDIAN PAINTING: A CHANGING ART
Clara Lee Tanner

Study of the works and styles of 200 Indian srtists from Arizona and New Mexico. 477 pp. University of Arizona Press, 1973. illus. $35.00.

SOUTHWESTERN INDIAN ARTS AND CRAFTS
Tom Bahti

K C Publications. Illus. Pap. $1.00.

THE TECHNIQUE OF PORCUPINE DECORATION AMONG THE INDIANS OF NORTH AMERICA
William C. Orchard

Detailed commentary on the varieties of technique and styles developed by the several tribes who practiced the art. 53 pp. Museum of the American Indian, 1971. 36 plates. Illus. $3.50.

*TEPEE AND MOCCASIN: INDIAN CRAFT FOR YOUNG PEOPLE
L. Albrectsen

Van Nostrand Reinhold Co., 1972. $4.95. Ages 12 to 16.

THE WOLF AND THE RAVEN: TOTEM POLES OF SOUTHEASTERN ALASKA
Viola E. Garfield and Ernestine Friedl, Editors

161 pp. University of Washington Press, 1961. Illus. Pap. $3.95.

ASSIMILATION

*AMERICAN INDIAN LIFE
Elsie Clews Parsons, Editor

419 pp. University of Nebraska Press, 1967. Illus. Pap. $2.95.

THE AMERICAN INDIAN AND AMERICAN LIFE: 1957
The American Academy of Political and Social Science, 1975. Cloth, $5.00; Pap. $4.00

THE AMERICAN INDIAN IN URBAN SOCIETY
J.O. Waddell and O.M. Watson, Editors

414 pp. Little, Brown, and Co., 1971. Pap. $6.95.

THE AMERICAN INDIAN: OUR RELATIONS AND RESPONSIBILITES
T. Heline
New Age Press. $1.00.

THE AMERICAN INDIAN: PERSPECTIVES FOR THE STUDY OF SOCIAL CHANGE
F. Eggan
Aldine Publishing Co., 1966. $6.00.

THE AMERICAN INDIAN TODAY
Nancy O. Lurie and Stuart Levine, Editors
13 articles by Indian and white anthropologists and educators probe the present condition of the American Indian. Penguin Books. Pap. $1.95.

AMERICAN INDIANS AND AMERICAN LIFE
G. Simpson and M. Yinger, Editors
Russell and Russell, 1974. Reprint of the 1957 edition. $16.00.

AMERICAN INDIANS AND AMERICAN LIFE
American Academy of Political and Social Science of Philadelphia
Kraus Reprint Co. Reprint of the 1957 edition. $13.00.

AMERICAN INDIANS: FACTS — FUTURE TOWARD ECONOMIC DEVELOPMENT FOR NATIVE AMERICAN COMMUNITIES
Subcommittee of Economy in Government
Arno Press, 1970. Reprint of the 1969 edition. $10.00

AMERICAN INDIANS AND OUR WAY OF LIFE
Sylvester M. Morey
32 pp. Waldorf Press, 1961. Pap. $.50.

AMERICAN INDIANS TODAY
O. Hoyt
Abelard, 1972. Illus. $5.95.

AMERICANIZING THE AMERICAN INDIANS: WRITINGS BY THE "FRIENDS OF THE INDIAN," 1880 TO 1900
Francis Paul Prucha, Editors
358 pp. Harvard University Press, 1973. $12.50.

ARISTOTLE AND THE AMERICAN INDIANS: A STUDY IN RACE PREJUDICE IN THE MODERN WORLD
L. Hanke
Indiana University Press, 1970. Pap. $1.95.

CAN THE RED MAN HELP THE WHITE MAN?
Sylvester M. Morey, Editor
Indian elders confer with Franz E. Winkler. Spiritual matters are exchanged. 116 pp. Waldorf Press, 1970. Pap. $1.95.

THE CHARACTER AND INFLUENCE OF THE INDIAN TRADE IN WISCONSIN, A STUDY OF THE TRADING POST AS AN INSTITUTION
Frederick Jackson Turner
94 pp. Johnson Reprint, 1973. Reprint of the 1891 edition. Pap. $7.00.

CONTRIBUTION TO INDIAN SOCIOLOGY: NEW SERIES, NOS. THREE TO SIX
International Pubns. Service, 1972. $5.00.

CONTRIBUTIONS AND ACHIEVEMENTS OF THE AMERICAN INDIAN
R. Costo
Indian Historical Press, 1974. Cloth, $9.00; Pap. $5.00.

*FOODS THE INDIANS GAVE US
W.P. Hays and R.V. Hays
Washburn, Ives, Inc., 1973. Pap. $4.95. Ages 16 and up.

GENOCIDE AGAINST THE INDIANS: ITS ROLE IN THE RISE OF THE UNITED STATES CAPITALISM
G. Novack
32 pp. Pathfinder Press, Inc., 1974. Pap. $.60.

*GETTING TO KNOW AMERICAN INDIANS TODAY
H. Thompson
Coward, McCann and Geohegan, 1965. Illus. $3.68. Below college level.

THE GIFT IS RICH
F. Russell Carter
Contributions Indian Americans have made to American culture: medicine, the arts, music, crafts and spiritual perception. Friendship Press. Pap. $3.50.

*INDIAN HILL
James Spanfeller
The continuing plight of the American Indian in
today's world as he is torn between the old ways
of life on the reservation and the economic ne-
cessity of seeking a new life in the city. 74 pp.
Thomas Y. Crowell., 1963. Illus. Ages 6-10.
$4.95.

THE INDIAN AND HIS PROBLEM
Francis Ellington Leupp
369 pp. Johnson Reprint Corporation. Reprint
of the 1910 edition. $16.75. Arno Press, $17.00.

THE INDIAN IN AMERICA
Wilcomb E. Washburn
Harper and Row Pubs., 1975. $10.00.

THE INDIAN IN AMERICAN LIFE
Gustavus Elmer Lindquist, et al
AMS Press, Inc. Reprint of the 1944 edition.
$11.50.

**INDIAN POPULATION IN THE UNITED
STATES AND ALASKA, 15th CENSUS**
United States Bureau of the Census
Kraus Reprint Co. Reprint of the 1930 edition.
$14.50.

**INDIAN POPULATIONS IN THE UNITED
STATES AND CANADA**
United States Bureau of Census
Kraus Reprint Co. Reprint of the 1930 edition.
Cloth, $35.00; Pap. $14.50.

**INDIAN VOICES: NATIVE AMERICAN
TODAY**
J. Henry, Editor
Discussions on Native American education,
health and medicine, communications, water
and land rights, reservation economy, the
Indian Claims Commission, curriculum
development, and Museums and the Indian.
This was the Second Convocation of American
Indian Scholars. Indian Historian, 1974. Pap.
$6.00.

**INDIANS OF ARIZONA: A CONTEM-
PORARY PERSPECTIVE**
Thomas Weaver, Editor
An anthology of contributing experts discuss
the historical foundations of the Indian affairs
in Arizona; developments in the 20th century;
contemporary Arizona Indians; the legal basis
of tribal government; living conditions, employment, economic development, and assis-

tance programs; and Indian education. 169 pp.
University if Arizona Press, 1974. Pap. $3.95.

THE INDIANS OF TODAY
George Bird Grinnell
AM Press, Inc. Reprint of the 1911 edition.
Illus. $28.50.

**ISHI IN TWO WORLDS: A BIOGRAPHY
OF THE LAST WILD INDIAN IN NORTH
AMERICA**
T. Kroeber
University of California Press, 1961. Cloth,
$7.95; Pap. $2.45.

**MASSACRE: A SURVEY OF TODAY'S
AMERICAN INDIAN**
R. Gessner
Da Capo Press, 1972. Reprint of the 1931
edition. $15.00.

NATIVE AMERICANS TODAY:
Sociological Perspectives
Howard M. Bahr, Bruce A. Chadwick, and
Robert C. Day, Editors
Forty-two studies on the social characteristics
and problems of modern American Indians.
Topics range from Indian education and accul-
turation and identity to suicide, red power and
action programs. 547 pp. Harper and Row
Publishers, 1972. Pap. $7.50.

THE NEW INDIANS
Stan Steiner
Harper and Row Pubs., 1968. Illus. $10.00.

**PERSPECTIVES IN AMERICAN INDIAN
CULTURE CHANGE**
Edward H. Spicer, Editor
University of Chicago Press, 1961. $12.50.

THE RED MAN IN THE UNITED STATES
Gustavus E.E. Lindquist
A study of the social, economic, educational,
and religious life of the American Indian 50
years ago. 461 pp. August M. Kelley Publishers.
Reprint of the 1923 edition. Illus. $16.50.

**SAVAGES OF AMERICA: A STUDY OF
THE INDIAN AND THE IDEA OF CIVIL-
IZATION**
R.H. Pearce and J.H. Millers
Johns Hopkins Press, 1965. $8.50.

*THE SIOUX TODAY
F. LaPointe
Macmillan Publishing Co., Inc., 1972. $5.95.
Below college level.

TRAGEDY STRIKES AT WOUNDED KNEE
Will Spindler
A portrait of Indian life on the reservation in Southwest South Dakota and Northwest Nebraska. 138 pp. Dakota Press, 1972. Pap. $1.95.

THE WORLD OF THE AMERICAN INDIAN
National Geographic Society, 1974. $9.95.

CHILDREN

AMERICAN INDIAN AND WHITE CHILDREN: A SOCIO-PSYCHOLOGICAL INVESTIGATION
Robert J. Havighurst and Bernice L. Neugarten
University of Chicago Press, 1969. $14.50.

FAR FROM THE RESERVATION: THE TRANSRACIAL ADOPTION OF AMERICAN INDIAN CHILDREN
David Fanshel
Extended research on American Indian children adopted by white families. 388 pp. Scarecrow Press, 1972. $10.00.

*INDIAN CHILDREN OF MAERICA: *A Book To Begin On*
M.C. Farquar
Holt, Rinehart, and Winston, 1972. Illus. Pap. $1.25. Below college level.

RESPECT FOR LIFE: THE TRADITIONAL UPBRINGING OF AMERICAN INDIAN CHILDREN
Sylvester M. Morey and Olivia L. Gilliam, Editors
Discussions among members of six Indian tribes focus on the rearing of children from birth to adolescence. 224 pp. Waldorf Press, 1974. Illus. Pap. $3.50.

*SELECTED MEDIA ABOUT THE AMERICAN INDIAN FOR YOUNG CHILDREN
American Library Assn., 1970. Pap. $1.00. - Ages 6 to 10.

CIVIL RIGHTS

THE AMERICAN INDIAN: A RISING ETHNIC FORCE
H.L. Marx, Jr., Editor
H.W. Wilson, 1973. $4.50.

*AMERICAN INDIAN CRISIS
George Pierre, Chief, Coluille Confederated Tribes
224 pp. Naylor Co. $8.95. Below college level.

ANTAP: CALIFORNIA INDIAN POLITICAL AND ECONOMIC ORGANIZATION
Lowell John Bean and Thomas F. King, Editors
Essays argue that Native California was one of the most complex cultural areas known. 177 pp. Ballena Press, 1974. Pap. $5.50.

A CENTURY OF DISHONOR: THE EARLY CRUSADE FOR INDIAN REFORM
Helen Hint Jackson
Harper and Row Pubs. Pap. $3.75. Peter Smith Publishers, $5.75.

CHRONICLES OF AMERICAN INDIAN PROTEST
The Council on Interracial Books for Children, Editors
An anthology of writings that relates the history of the Indian's battle for survival from the 17th century to the Red Power of today. Fawcett World Library, 1971. Pap. $1.25.

A CONSTITUTIONAL ANALYSIS OF THE CRIMINAL JURISDICTION AND PROCEDURAL GUARANTEES OF THE AMERICAN INDIAN
Brent H. Gubler
Dissertation. R & E Research Associates, 1974. Reprint of the 1963 paper. Pap. $10.00.

FROM FEATHER, BLANKET AND TEPEE: THE INDIANS' FIGHT FOR EQUALITY
George A. Trotter
Includes Choctaw, Creek, Pawnee, Sioux, Potawatomi, Kickapoo, Paiute, Zuni and Navajo. Brown Book Co., 1975. $3.50.

THE INDIAN: AMERICA'S UNFINISHED BUSINESS. REPORT OF THE COMMISSION ON THE RIGHTS, LIBERTIES,

AND RESPONSIBILITIES OF THE AMERICAN INDIAN
William A. Brophy, et al
236 pp. University of Oklahoma Press, 1969. Illus. $6.95.

NATIVE AMERICANS: THE NEW INDIAN RESISTANCE
William Meyer
A survey of the present-day struggle for Indian rights and self-determination. 96 pp. International Publishers, 1971. Pap. $1.50.

RECONSTRUCTION IN INDIAN TERRITORY: A STORY OF AVARICE, DISCRIMINATION, AND OPPORTUNISM
M. Thomas Bailey
An account of the political, economic, and educational efforts made by the Five Civilized Tribes. Kennikat Press, 1972. $11.50.

RED POWER: THE AMERICAN INDIANS' FIGHT FOR FREEDOM
Alvin M Josephy, Jr.
Documents and materials illuminating the road along which a new generation of patriot Indians are moving in their fight against the white man's paternalism and for survival as tribal peoples in modern America. McGraw-Hill Book Co., 1972. Pap. $2.95.

THE RIGHT TO BE INDIAN
Ernest Schusky
Considers the difference between the current struggle with civil rights of the minorities in America and the American Indian, whose indigenous status causes complex legal questions and problems. Indian Historian, 1968. Pap. $2.50.

UNCOMMON CONTROVERSY: FISHING RIGHTS OF THE MUCKLESHOOT, PUYALLUP, AND MISQUALLY INDIANS
American Friends Service Committee
Documents the Indians' case in their clash with state agencies and sportsmen's organizations over treaty fishing rights on rivers in western Washington State. 264 pp. University of Washington Press, 1970. Cloth, $5.95; Pap. $2.95.

CULTURE AND CUSTOMS

*THE AMAZING RED MAN: AMERINDIAN CONTRIBUTION TO TODAY'S

CULTURE
Mack Parker
Source book of Indian history, customs and lore with tribal lists. The Naylor Co. Ages 12-18. $3.95.

THE AMERICAN INDIAN AS HUNTER
John Witthoft
Tells the relation of the Indian to wilderness creatures. 23 pp. Pennsylvania Historical and Museum Commission, 1967. Pap. $.50.

AMERICAN INDIAN FOOD AND LORE
C. Neithammer
Macmillan Publishing Co., 1974. Cloth, $6.95; Pap. $3.95.

AMERICAN INDIAN LIFE
E.C. Parsons
Peter Smith Publishers. Cloth, $5.50. Pap. $2.95.

AMERICAN INDIAN MEDICINE
V.J. Vogel
Ballantine Books, 1973. Pap. $1.95.

THE AMERICAN INDIAN READER: ANTHROPOLGY
J. Henry, Editor
An anthology of writings concerned with the anthropology of the American Indian. Indian Historian, 1972. Pap. $4.00.

AMERICAN INDIAN TOMAHAWKS
Harold C. Peterson
Traces the development of Indian cutting tools and reviews the evolution of the trade axe and pipe tomahawk. 142 pp. 113 plates. Museum of the American Indian, 1971. Reprint of the 1965 edition. Illus. $10.00.

ART OF AMERICAN INDIAN COOKING
Jeffe Kimball and Jean Anderson
Doubleday and Co., 1965. $5.95.

CAMP, CLAN, AND KIN, AMONG THE COW, CREEK, SEMINOLE, OF FLORIDA: A STUDY IN THE ACCULTURATION OF THE CREEK, CHEROKEE, AND CHOCTAW
A. Spoehr
Kraus Reprint Co. Reprint of the 1971 edition. Pap. $8.00.

THE CHANGING CULTURE OF AN INDIAN TRIBE
Margaret Mead
AMS Press, Inc., 1932. $14.50.

DANCING GODS: INDIAN CEREMONIALS OF NEW MEXICO AND ARIZONA
    E. Fergusson
University of New Mexico Press, 1957. Cloth, $7.50; Pap. $2.95.

*THE GAMES THE INDIANS PLAYED
    Sigmund A. Lavine
An account of the games of the inventors of lacrosse: the early Indians. 93 pp. Dodd, Mead & Co., 1974. Illus. Age 6-11. $4.25.

GAMES OF THE NORTH AMERICAN INDIANS
    Robert Stewart Culin
AMS Press, Inc. Reprint of the 1907. Illus. $85.00.

HISTORY, MANNERS, AND CUSTOMS OF THE INDIAN NATIONS WHO ONCE INHABITED PENNSYLVANIA AND THE NEIGHBORING STATES.
    J. Heckewelder
Arno Press, 1971. Reprint of the 1819 edition. $19.00.

HOME LIFE AMONG THE INDIANS
    A.C. Fletcher
Shorey Pubs. Reprint of the 1897 edition. Pap. $1.50.

HOUSES AND HOUSE-LIFE OF THE AMERICAN ABORIGINES
    Lewis H. Morgan
University of Chicago Press, 1966. Cloth, $11.00; Pap. $2.95.

*THE INDIAN AND THE BUFFALO
    Robert Hofsinde
Deals with hunting methods, uses of buffalo for food or tools, for robes or rawhide, and a comparison of buffalo dances in different tribes. 96 pp. William Morrow & Co., 1961. Illus. $3.78. Ages 8-12.

*INDIAN CANOE MAKER
    P. Beatty
Caxton Printers, 1960. $4.00. Ages 12 to 16.

*INDIAN CULTURES OF THE SOUTHWEST
    Louis Thomas Jones
Customs, past and present, of the Pueblo, Zuni and Hopi indians in New Mexico, Arizona, and California. The Naylor Co. Age 13 up. $4.95.

INDIAN FAMILIES OF THE NORTH-WEST COAST: THE IMPACT OF CHANGE
    Claudia Lewis
University of Chicago Press, 1970. $9.50.

*INDIAN FESTIVALS
    Lorence Bjorklund
Describes the ways in which modern Indians celebrate traditional rites, and emphasizes the variety of tribes and customs. 33 pp. Thomas Y. Crowell Co., 1969. Illus. $4.95. Ages 4-16.

*INDIAN FISHING AND CAMPING
    Robert Hofsinde
Gives instructions for making Indian fishing gear and cleaning and cooking the catch. 96 pp. William Morrow & Co., 1963. Illus. Ages 8-12. $3.78.

*INDIAN GAMES AND CRAFTS
    Robert Hofsinde
Instructions on how to make twelve different games and play them just as the Indians did. 128 pp. William Morrow & Co., 1965. Illus. Ages 8-12. $3.95.

*THE INDIAN AND HIS HORSE
    Robert (Gray-Wolf) Hofsinde
Details the introduction of the horse to North America by the Spaniards and the cultural changes that resulted. 96 pp. William Morrow & Co., 1960. Illus. Ages 8-12. $3.78.

THE INDIAN AND HIS HORSE
    Frank Gilbert Roe
434 pp. University of Oklahoma Press, 1974. Reprint of the 1955 edition. Illus. $9.95.

*INDIAN HUNTING
    Robert Hofsinde
Methods used by the Indians in hunting small game, large game, and sea life. 96 pp. William Morrow & Co., 1962. Illus. Ages 8-12. $3.78.

THE INDIAN IN AMERICA
    Wilcomb E.Washburn
The story of the Indian in America from pre-Columbian times to the present day. Examines social structure, conduct and beliefs. 352 pp. Harper and Row, 1975. Illus. $10.00.

THE INDIAN IN HIW WIGWAM: OR CHARACTERISTICS OF THE RED RACE OF AMERICA
    Henry Rowe Schoolcraft
AMS Press, Inc. Reprint of the 1848 edition. $29.00.

INDIAN LIFE ON THE UPPER MISSOURI
John C. Ewers
222 pp. University of Oklahoma Press, 1968.
Illus. $7.95.

*THE INDIAN MEDICINE MAN
Robert Hofsinde
Discusses the importance and training of the
Indian medicine man. 96 pp. William Morrow &
Co., 1966. Illus. Ages 8-12. $3.78.

THE INDIAN TIPI: ITS HISTORY, CON-STRUCTION, AND USE, WITH A HISTORY OF THE TIPI BY STANLEY VESTAL
Reginald Laubin and Gladys Laubin
208 pp. University of Oklahoma Press, 1971.
Reprint of the 1957 edition. Illus. Cloth, $6.95.
Ballantine Books, Pap. $1.65.

*INDIANS AT HOME
Robert Hofsinde
Emphasizes the difference in Indian homes and
home life. 96 pp. William Morrow & Co., 1964.
Illus. Ages 8-12. $3.78.

*INDIANS AT WORK AND PLAY
Louis Thomas Jones
The Indians' games of chance and dexterity, his
entertainment in song and dance, his accomplishments in pottery making, weaving and
jewelry design. 172 pp. The Naylor Co., 1971.
Age 12 up. $6.95.

*INDIANS ON HORSEBACK
Alice Marriott
Traces the development of the Plains Indian
culture from the introduction of the horse by
the Spaniards in the 1500's to the annihilation
of tribal ways by white settlers of the mid-nineteenth century. 136 pp. Thomas Y. Crowell Co.,
1968. Reprint of the 1948 edition. Illus. Ages 6-
10. $4.50.

*INDIANS ON THE MOVE
Robert Hofsinde
Introduction to Indian modes of travel. 96 pp.
William Morrow & Co., 1970. Illus. Ages 8-12.
$3.78.

*LOVE—INDIAN STYLE
Louis Thomas Jones
Explores the rituals of several Indian tribes--
Cherokee, Seminole, Pueblo, Navajo, Iroquois,
Apache and Zuni--prior to and during marriage.
168 pp. The Naylor Co. Age 12 up. $5.95.

MANNERS AND CUSTOMS OF SEVERAL

INDIAN TRIBES WEST OF THE MIS-SISSIPPI
John D. Hunter
Personal narrative of a white man captured by
the Indians as an infant and growing to man-
hood among them. 402 pp. Ross & Haines, Inc.
Reprint of the 1832 edition. Illus. $12.50.

MEDICINE POWER: THE AMERICAN INDIAN'S REVIVAL OF HIS SPIRITUAL HERITAGE AND ITS RELEVANCE FOR MODERN MAN
Brad Steiger
Doubleday and Co., 1974. Illus. Cloth, $6.95;
Pap. $2.95.

MONEY OF THE AMERICAN INDIANS AND OTHER PRIMITIVE CURRENCIES OF THE AMERICAS
D. Taxay
Arco Publishing Co., 1972. $5.95.

*NEW WORLD BEGINNINGS: INDIAN CULTURE IN THE AMERICAS
Olivia Vlahos
320 pp. Viking Press, 1970. Illus. Cloth, $6.50;
Pap. $2.75. Ages 12 up.

*NEW WORLD BEGINNINGS: INDIAN CULTURES IN THE AMERICAS
Olivia Vlahos
North and South American Indian cultural
patterns. Fawcett World Library, 1972. Pap.
$1.25. Age 12 up.

PERSPECTIVES IN AMERICAN INDIAN CULTURE CHANGE
Edward H. Spicer, Editor
Cultural change and adaption in six North
American Indian tribes: the Yaquis of Sonora
and Arizona, the Rio Grande Pueblos, the
Mandans of North Dakota, the Navahos of
New Mexico and Arizona, the Wasco-wishrams
of Oregon and the Kwakiutl of British
Columbia. 560 pp. University of Chicago Press,
1961. Pap. $15.00.

SOUTHWESTERN INDIAN CEREMON-IALS
Tom Bahti
K C Publications. Illus. Pap. $1.00.

SPIRITUAL LEGACY OF THE AMERICAN INDIAN
Joseph E. Brown
Understanding and preserving the traditional
values of Indians. Pendle Hill Publications,
1964. Illus. Pap. $.70.

STATUS TERMINOLOGY AND THE SOCIAL STRUCTURE OF THE NORTH AMERICAN INDIANS
   Munro S. Edmondson
92 pp. University of Washington Press, 1958. $7.00.

THE TRAPS OF THE AMERICAN INDIANS
   O.T. Mason
Shorey Publications. Reprint of the 1901 edition. Pap. $1.25.

VOICES OF THE EARTH AND SKY: THE VISIONARY LIFE OF THE NATIVE AMERICANS AND THEIR CULTURE HEROES
   Vinson Brown
224 pp. Stackpole Books, 1974. Illus. $8.95.

THE WORLD OF THE AMERICAN INDIAN
Lifestyles, culture, and the problem of white encroachment provide a narrative in between a wealth of photographs and illustrations. 399 pp. National Geographic Society, 1974. Illus. $10.65.

DANCE

AMERICAN INDIAN CEREMONIAL DANCES
   John Collier
Dances of Indians of the Southwest. 192 pp. Crown Publishers, 1972. Illus. $3.95.

AMERICAN INDIAN DANCE STEPS
   B. Evans and M.G. Evans
Hacker Art Books, 1974. Reprint of the 1931 edition. $20.00

AMERICAN INDIAN DANCES: STEPS, RHYTHMS, COSTUMES, AND INTERPRETATION
   John L Squires and Robert E. McLean
An introductory guide to representative Indian dances, with detailed instructions for executing each dance and making authentic costumes and accessories. 132 pp. Ronald Press Co., 1963. $6.95.

DANCES AND STORIES OF THE AMERICAN INDIAN
   Bernard S. Mason

The story behind 86 Indian dances, the properties and costuming for the conduct of the dances, and the basic steps and body movements essential to recapturing the Indian ritual and routine. 269 pp. Ronald Press Co., 1975. Reprint of the 1944 edition. $7.95.

*HERE IS YOUR HOBBY: INDIAN DANCING AND COSTUMES
   William K. Powers
G.P. Putnam's Sons, 1966. Illus. $4.49. Below college level.

INDIAN GAMES AND DANCES WITH NATIVE SONGS
   Alice Fletcher Cunningham
AMS Press, Inc. Reprint of the 1915 edition. $7.50.

DOCUMENTS AND LAWS

A BIBLIOGRAPHY OF THE CONSTITUTIONS AND LAWS OF THE AMERICAN INDIANS
   L. Hargrett
Kraus Reprint Co. Reprint of the 1947 edition. $9.50.

GREAT DOCUMENTS IN AMERICAN INDIAN HISTORY
   Wayne Moquin and Charles Van Doren, Editors
432 pp. Praeger Publishers, 1973. Illus. $13.50.

EDUCATION

AMERICAN INDIAN EDUCATION: GOVERNMENT SCHOOLS AND ECONOMIC PROGRESS
   E.C. Adams
Arno Press, 1972. Reprint of the 1946 edition. $7.00.

THE AMERICAN INDIAN IN GRADUATE STUDIES: . A BIBLIOGRAPHY OF THESES AND DISSERTATIONS
   Frederick J. Dockstader
3659 completed from 1890-1955. 362 pp. Museum of the American Indian, 1973. Reprint of the 1957 edition. $10.00.

THE AMERICAN INDIAN IN GRADUATE STUDIES: SUPPLEMENT

Frederick J. Dockstader and Alice W. Dockstader

3787 theses completed from 1955-1970. 400 pp. Museum of the American Indian, 1973. $10.00.

THE AMERICAN INDIAN READER: EDUCATION

An anthology of writings concerned with education of the American Indian. Indian Historian, 1972. Pap. $4.00.

*AMERINDIAN EDUCATION: CONTEMPORARY ANALYSIS OF EDUCATIONAL NEEDS

Louis Thomas Jones

This study surveys the first Indian colleges, the educational programs of the Bureau of Indian Affairs, and the growing need for technical training. 212 pp. The Naylor Co., 1972. 12 up. $6.95.

CIVIL SERVICE EXAMINATION PASSBOOK: INDIAN EDUCATION-ELEMENTARY TEACHER

J. Rudman

National Learning. Cloth, $9.00; Pap. $6.00.

CIVIL SERVICE EXAMINATION PASSBOOK: INDIAN EDUCATION-SECONDARY TEACHER

J. Rudman

National Learning. Cloth, $9.00; Pap. $6.00.

CIVIL SERVICE EXAMINATION PASSBOOK: INDIAN EDUCATION-GUIDANCE COUNSELOR

J. Rudman

National Learning. Cloth, $9.00; Pap. $6.00.

EDUCATION AND THE AMERICAN INDIAN 1928 TO 1973: THE ROAD TO SELF DETERMINATION

M. Szaz

University of New Mexico Press, 1974. $10.00.

EFFECTIVE TEACHERS OF INDIAN AND ESKIMO HIGH SCHOOL STUDENTS

J. Kleinfeld

68 pp. University of Washington Press, 1972. Pap. $2.00.

A HISTORY OF INDIAN EDUCATION

P.L. Rawat

International Pubns Service, 1965. $6.00.

IDENTIFICATION OF UNIQUE FEATURES IN EDUCATION AT AMERICAN INDIAN SCHOOLS

Cutis E. Jackson

Dissertation. R & E Research Associates, 1974. Reprint of the 1965 paper. Pap. $8.00.

INDIAN EDUCATION AND CIVILIZATION

United States Bureau of Education

Kraus Reprint Co. $25.00.

INDIAN EDUCATION IN THE CHIAPAS HIGHLANDS

N. Modiano

Holt, Rinehart, and Winston, 1973. Pap. $3.50.

INDIAN STUDENT

John F. Byrde

Seeks to identify the causes of the breakdown of scholastic achievement as well as the social alienation of the American Indian student. 144 pp. Dakota Press, 1970. Pap. $3.00.

INDIAN STUDENTS AND GUIDANCE

J.F. Byrde

Houghton Mifflin Co., 1971. Pap. $1.60.

INDIAN STUDENTS ON AN AMERICAN CAMPUS

Richard D. Lambert and Marvin Bressler

122pp. University of Minnesota Press, 1956. $4.00.

MORAL EDUCATION AMONG THE NORTH AMERICAN INDIANS

Claude Andrew Nichols

AMS Press, Inc. Reprint of the 1930 edition. $10.00.

A STUDY OF THE ROLE OF THE FEDERAL GOVERNMENT IN THE EDUCATION OF THE AMERICAN INDIAN

Theodore Fischbacher

Dissertation. R & E Research Associates, 1974. Reprint of the 1967 paper. Pap. $10.00.

TO LIVE ON THIS EARTH: AMERICAN INDIAN EDUCATION

Estelle Fuchs and Robert J. Havighurst

Doubleday and Co., 1973. Cloth, $8.95; Pap. $3.95.

FEDERAL POLICY

ALTERNATIVE TO EXTINCTION

Robert A. Trennert, Jr.
Federal Indian policy and the beginnings of the reservation system, 1846-51. 272 p.. Temple University Press, 1975. $15.00.

AMERICAN INDIAN UNDER RECONSTRUCTION
Annie Heloise Abel
419 pp. Johnson Reprint, 1971. Reprint of the 1925 edition. $17.50.

AMERICAN INDIANS AND FEDERAL AID
Alan L. Sorkin
231 pp. Brookings Institution, 1971. $8.95.

THE AMERICAN INDIAN POLICY IN THE FORMATIVE YEARS: THE INDIAN TRADE AND INTERCOURSE ACTS, 1790 TO 1834
Francis Paul Prucha
303 pp. Harvard University Press, 1962. $8.50.

AMERICAN INDIAN POLICY IN THE JACKSONIAN ERA
Ronald N. Satz
343 pp. University of Nebraska Press, 1975. $12.95.

APPALACHIAN INDIAN FRONITER: THE EDMOND ATKIN REPORT AND PLAN OF 1755
Edmond Atkin
108 pp. University of Nebraska Press, 1967. Illus. Pap. $1.95.

THE ASSAULT ON INDIAN TRIBAL-ISM: *The General Allotment Law (Dawes Act) of 1887*
Wilcomb E. Washburn
The analysis and documents of the efforts by white Americans to control American Indian lives. 79 pp. J.B. Lippincott Co., 1975. $2.75.

ATTITUDES OF THE COLONIAL POWERS TOWARD THE AMERICAN INDIAN
H. Peckman and C. Gibson
University of Utah Press, 1969. $6.00.

A BIOGRAPHICAL AND HISTORICAL INDEX OF AMERICAN INDIANS AND PERSONS INVOLVED IN INDIAN AFFAIRS
United States Department of the Interior-Bureau of Indian Affairs
G.K. Hall and Co., 1966. $705.00 set.

A CENTURY OF DISHONOR: A SKETCH OF THE UNITED STATES GOVERN-

MENT'S DEALINGS WITH SOME OF THE INDIAN TRIBES
H. Jackson
Scholarly Press, 1972. Reprint of the 1888 edition. $14.50.

DIGEST OF DECISIONS RELATING TO INDIAN AFFAIRS
United States Office of Indian Affairs ·
Kraus Reprint Co. Reprint of the 1901 edition. $20.00.

DISINHERITED: THE LOST BIRTHRIGHT OF THE AMERICAN INDIAN
Dale Van Every
The events preceding the Removal Act, its effect on the eastern Indians. William Morrow & Co., 1971. Illus. Pap. $2.50.

DOCUMENTS OF U.S. INDIAN POLICY
Francis Paul Prucha
303 pp. University of Nebraska Press, 1975. Price not set.

THE ETHICS IN AMERICAN POLITICS: AMERICAN INDIANS
F. Svensson
Burgess Publishing Co., 1973. Pap. $1.25.

FEDERAL CONTROL OF THE WESTERN APACHES, 1848-1886
Ralph H. Ogle
An account of government relations with the western Apaches of Arizona and Southwestern New Mexico. University of New Mexico Press. $6.95.

THE FEDERAL INDIAN POLICY IN CALIFORNIA, 1846-1860
William H. Ellison
Dissertation. R & E Research Associates, 1974. Reprint of the 1959 paper. Pap. $11.00.

FEDERAL INDIAN RELATIONS 1774 TO 1788
Walter Harrison Mohr
AMS Press, Inc. Reprint of the 1933 edition. $10.00.

FEDERAL POLICY AND AMERICAN INDIAN HEALTH NEEDS
E.R. Rhoades
A summary of conference discussions about the effect of Federal health plans on Indians. 38 pp. Interbook Incorporated, 1974. Pap. $1.00.

FRAUD, POLITICS, AND THE DIS-POSSESSION OF THE INDIANS: THE IROQUOIS LAND FRONTIER IN THE COLONIAL PERIOD
Geroge C. Nammack
128 pp. University of Oklahoma Press, 1969. Illus. $4.95.

GENERAL POPE AND UNITED STATES INDIAN POLICY
Richard N. Ellis
University of New Mexico Press, 1970. $4.00.

HANDBOOK OF FEDERAL INDIAN LAW
U.S. Solicitor for the Dept. of the Interior
AMS Press, 1974. Reprint of the 1942 edition. $20.00.

HISTORY OF THE LEGAL STATUS OF THE AMERICAN INDIAN, WITH PARTI-CULAR REFERENCE TO CALIFORNIA
Donald R. Beatty
History 1492-1848. Legal status during American control 1848-1865. Post Civil War 1865-1900. Treaty arrangements, wardship, Reorganization Act of 1934. Thesis. R & E Research Associates, 1974. Reprint of the 1957 edition. Pap. $8.00.

THE INDIAN AFFAIR
Vine Deloria, Jr.
An historical account of legal devices used by the United States to deprive Indians of their lands and rights. Friendship Press. Pap. $2.50.

INDIAN AFFAIRS: LAWS AND TREATIES
Charles J. Kappler, Editor
Indian treaties from 1778-1871; U.S. Presidential Proclamations; statistics of Indian agencies and tribes; letter and documents re-lating to the Executive Orders establishing the reservations; and decisions of the Supreme Court relating to Indian Affairs. AMS Press. Reprint of the 1904-1941 editions. Five volume set. $475.00.

INDIAN AFFAIRS AND THEIR ADMIN-ISTRATION, WITH SPECIAL REFERENCE TO THE FAR WEST
A.W. Hoopes
Kraus Reprint Co. Reprint of the 1930 edition. $13.50.

INDIAN REMOVAL: THE EMIGRATION OF THE FIVE CIVILIZED TRIBES OF INDIANS
Grant Foreman

415 pp. University of Oklahoma Press, 1972. Reprint of the 1932 edition. Illus. Cloth, $8.95; Pap. $3.95.

INDIAN TREATIES, 1778 TO 1883
C.J. KAppler
Interland Publishing, 1972. Reprint of the 1904 edition. $67.50.

INDIANS AND BUREAUCRATS: ADMIN-ISTERING THE RESERVATION POLICY DURING THE CIVIL WAR
Edmund J. Danziger, Jr.
220 pp. University of Illinois Press, 1974. $8.95.

THE INDIANS' LAND TITLE IN CALI-FORNIA: A CASE IN FEDERAL EQUITY, 1851-1942
Ruth C. Dyer
Thesis. R & E Research Associates, 1975. Reprint of the 1945 edition. Pap. $8.00.

THE LEGAL STATUS OF THE INDIAN
Robert Weil
AMS Press, Inc. 1974. Reprint of the 1888 edition. $10.00.

THE NAVAJO INDIANS AND FEDERAL INDIAN POLICY, 1900-1935
Lawrence C. Kelly
The impact on the Navajos of the discovery of oil on their recervations; their efforts to expand the reservation, and the political clashes with whites which ensued. 221 pp. University of Arizona Press, 1968. $7.50.

THE NAVAJO PEACE TREATY
Marie Mitchell
Mason and Lipscomb Publications, 1974. $6.95.

*A NAVAJO SAGA
Kay and Russ Bennett
The history of the broken treaties between the U.S. Government and the Navajos. 252 pp. The Naylor Co. Illus. Age 13 up. $7.95.

THE OFFICE OF INDIAN AFFAIRS: ITS HISTORY, ACTIVITIES, AND ORGAN-IZATION
Laurence Frederick Schmeckebier
AMS PRess, 1972. Reprint of the 1927 edition. $24.50.

OUR RED BROTHERS AND THE PEACE POLICY OF PRESIDENT ULYSSES S. GRANT

Lawrie Tatum
366 pp. University of Nebraska Press, 1970.
Illus. Cloth $12.50; Pap. $3.95.

**THE PROBLEM OF INDIAN ADMIN-
ISTRATION**
Brookings Institute, Washington, D.C.,
Institute for Government Research
Reports of a survey made at the request of
Honorable Hubert Work, Secretary of the In-
terior, and submitted to him, February 21,
1928. 872 pp. Johnson Reprint Corporation,
1971. Reprint of the 1928 edition. $45.50.

**PROCEEDINGS OF THE COMMISSIONERS
OF INDIAN AFFAIRS**
New York State Commissioners of Indian
Affairs
These two volumes contain most of the
documents which record the extinguishment of
the title of the Six Nations to a great portion of
the State of New York in 1784. 501 pp. Burt
Franklin Publishers, 1972. Reprint of the 1861
edition. Illus. $22.50.

**REMOVAL OF THE CHEROKEE NA-
TION: MANIFEST DESTINY OR
NATIONAL DISHONOR**
Louis Filler and Allen Guttmann, Editors
D.C. Heath and Co., 1962. Pap. $2.50.

REMOVAL OF THE CHOCTAW INDIANS
Arthur H. DeRosier, Jr.
224 pp. University of Tennessew Press, 1970.
Illus. $8.75.

**REPORT OF THE COMMISSIONER OF
INDIAN AFFAIRS**
U.S. Office of Indian Affairs
AMS Press, 1974. Reprint of the 1835-1870
edition. 36 volume set. $575.00; per volume,
$16.00.

**REPORT ON INDIANS TAXED AND IN-
DIANS NOT TAXED IN THE UNITED
STATES AT THE ELEVENTH CENSUS,
1890**
Thomas Donaldson
AMS Press, Inc. Reprint of the 1894 edition.
$49.50.

**SEEDS OF EXTINCTION: JEF-
FERSONIAN PHILANTHROPY AND THE
AMERICAN INDIAN**
Bernard W. Sheehan
W.W. Norton and Co., 1974. Pap. $2.95.

**SIXTY YEARS OF INDIAN AFFAIRS,
POLITICAL, ECONOMIC, AND DIP-
LOMATIC**
G.D. Harmon
Kraus Reprint Co. Reprint of the 1941 edition.
$15.50.

***SOLVING "THE INDIAN PROBLEM":
THE WHITE MAN'S BURDENSOME
BUSINESS**
Murray L. Wax and Robert W. Buchanan,
Editors
Four different periods of federal Indian policy
as described by *New York Times* reporters on
the scene. From the 1870's through the 1950's.
272 pp. Franklin Watts, Inc., 1975. Age 16 up.
$12.50; Pap. $4.95.

**SPEECHES ON THE PASSAGE OF THE
BILL FOR THE REMOVAL OF THE IN-
DIANS**
United States 21st Congress, 1st Session,
1829 to 1830
Kraus Reprint Co. Reprint of the 1830 edition.
$15.00.

**THOMAS L. McKENNEY, ARCHITECT OF
AMERICA'S EARLY INDIAN POLICY:
1816-1830**
Herman J. Viola
The prime mover behind the Indian Civilization
Act and the Indian Removal Act. A sympathetic
portrayal. 300 pp. Swallow Press, 1974. Illus.
$12.50.

**THE TRAIL OF TEARS: THE STORY OF
THE AMERICAN INDIAN REMOVALS
1813-1855**
Gloria Jahoda
The government-sponsored forced removal of
thousands of Indians living east of the
Mississippi River and their resettlement in the
west. 320 pp. Holt, Rinehart & Winston, 1975.
Illus. $12.95.

**THE TREATY BETWEEN THE UNITED
STATES AND THE DWAMISH, SUQUAM-
ISH AND OTHER ALLIED AND SUB-
ORDINATE TRIBES OF INDIANS IN
WASHINGTON TERRITORY**
I.I. Stevens
Shorey Publications. Reprint of the 1855
edition. Pap. $2.00.

**THE TREATY BETWEEN THE UNITED
STATES AND THE INDIANS OF THE WIL-
LAMETTE VALLEY**

I.I. Stevens
Shorey Publications. Reprint of the 1855 edition. Pap. $2.00.

THE TREATY BETWEEN THE UNITED STATES AND THE MAKAH TRIBE
   I.I. Stevens
Shorey Publications. Reprint of the 1855 edition. Pap. $2.00.

THE TREATY BETWEEN THE UNITED STATES AND THE NISQUALLY AND OTHER BANDS OF INDIANS
   I.I. Stevens
Shorey Publications. Reprint of the 1855 edition. Pap. $2.00.

TREATY BETWEEN THE UNITED STATES AND THE YAKIMA NATION OF INDIANS
   I.I. Stevens
Shorey Publications. Reprint of the 1855 edition. Pap. $2.00.

UNCLE SAM'S STEPCHILDREN: THE REFORMATION OF THE UNITED STATES INDIAN POLICY, 1865-1887
   L.B. Priest
310 pp. Octagon Books, 1969. Reprint of the 1942 edition. $11.00.

FOLKLORE AND MYTHOLOGY

*AMERICAN INDIAN FAIRY TALES
   Margaret Compton
Collection of Indian legends. 159 pp. Dodd, Mead & Co., 1971. Illus. Age 6-11. $3.95.

AMERICAN INDIAN LEGENDS
   Allan A. MakFarlan
An anthology of 95 legends. Heritage Press, 1974. 432 pp. Illus. $11.95.

*AMERICAN INDIAN MYSTICISM
   Louis Thomas Jones
The traditional sagas and mysterious customs inherent to all Indian Tribes. The Naylor Co. Ages 14 up. $5.95.

AMERICAN INDIAN MYTHOLOGY
   Alice Marriott and Carol K. Rachlin
Thomas Y Crowell Co., 1968. Illus. $10.95.

AMERICAN INDIAN MYTHOLOGY
   A. Marriott and C.K. Rachlin

224 pp. New American Library, 1972. Pap. $1.50.

THE AMERICAN INDIAN AND THE OCCULT
   C. Dane
Popular Library, 1973. Pap. $.95.

A BIBLIOGRAPHY OF NORTH AMERICAN FOLKLORE AND FOLKSONG
   Charles Haywood
A two-volume bibliography of books, articles, periodicals, music, records, etc. First volume covers American social and occupational groups, blues, Negro material; Second volume covers Indian and general material. 1301 pp. Dover Publications. $30.00.

A BOOK OF TALES, BEING MYTHS OF THE NORTH AMERICAN INDIANS
   C.E. Wood
Gordon Press. $25.00.

CREATION MYTHS OF PRIMATIVE AMERICA
   J. Curtain
Benjamin Blom Pubs. Reprint of the 1903 edition. $12.50.

*DOWN FROM THE LONELY MOUNTAIN: *California Indian Tales*
   Jane Louise Curry
A collection of 12 animal tales from the California Indians. 128 pp. Harcourt Brace Jovanovich, Inc. 1965. Ages 8-12. $5.25.

DRAMATIC ELEMENTS IN AMERICAN INDIAN CEREMONIALS
   Virginia S. Heath
Haskell House Pubs., Inc., 1974. Pap. $2.95.

THE ENCHANTED MOCCASINS AND OTHER LEGENDS OF THE AMERICAN INDIANS
   Cornelius Mathews, Editor
AMS Press, Inc. Reprint of the 1877 edition. $9.50.

FIRESIDE BOOK OF AMERICAN INDIAN FOLKTALES
   Allan A. Macfarlan
224 pp. Stackpole Books, 1974. Illus. $8.95.

HEATHER FLOWER AND OTHER INDIAN STORIES OF LONG ISLAND
   V. Dyson
Ira J. Friedman, 1968. $3.50.

INDIAN CAPTIVITIES: OR, LIFE IN THE WIGWAM
Samuel Gardner
AMS Press, Inc. Reprint of the 1872 edition. $23.00.

INDIAN LEGENDS FROM THE NORTHERN ROCKIES
Ella E. Clark
350 pp. University of Oklahoma Press, 1974. Reprint of the 1966 edition. Illus. $7.95.

*INDIAN LEGENDS OF THE PACIFIC NORTHWEST
Ella E. Clark
University of California Press, 1953. Pap. $2.45. Age 16 up.

INDIAN MASKS AND MYTHS OF THE WEST
Joseph H. Wherry
Tales of spirits and heroes of the Indian ancients. 288 pp. Apollo Editions. $3.50.

INDIAN MYTHS, OR LEGENDS, TRADITIONS AND SYMBOLS OF THE ABORIGINES OF AMERICA
Ellen R. Emerson
Various beliefs, superstitions and ceremonies of the American Indian of all tribes. Ross & Haines, Inc., 1965. $10.00.

INDIAN STORIES AND LEGENDS: UPPER PUGET SOUND
N. Bruseth
Ye Galleon Press, 1972. Pap. $2.50.

THE INDIANS' BOOK
Natalie Curtis
Lore, narratives, and dozens of drawings by Indians themselves from a survey of native culture among Plains, Southwestern, Lake and Pueblo Indians. 149 songs. 584 pp. Dover Publications. Illus. Pap. $4.50.

*THE INDIAN'S SECRET WORLD
Robert Hofsinde
An introduction to the rituals and symbolism of Indian religion and philosophy. 96 pp. William Morrow & Co., 1955. Illus. Ages 12-16. $4.81.

METALLIC ORNAMENTS OF THE NEW YORK INDIANS
William Martin Beauchamp
37 plates. AMS Press, Inc. Reprint of the 1903 edition. $12.00.

THE MYTH OF HIAWATHA AND OTHER ORAL LEGENDS, MYTHOLOGIC AND ALLEGORIC, OF THE NORTH AMERICAN INDIANS
H.R. Schoolcraft
Kraus Reprint Co. Reprint of the 1856 edition. $14.50.

MYTHS AND LEGENDS OF THE NORTH AMERICAN INDIANS
L. Spence
Multimedia Publishing Corp., 1974. $5.95.

MYTHS OF THE NEW WORLD INDIANS
Douglas G. Brinton
Multimedia Publishing Corp., 1974. $5.95; Pap. $2.95.

MYTHS OF THE NEW WORLD: A TREATISE ON THE SYMBOLISM AND MYTHOLOGY OF THE RED RACE OF AMERICA
Daniel Garrison Brinton
Haskell House Pubs., Inc., 1974. Reprint of the 1876 edition. $12.95.

THE MYTHS OF THE NEW WORLD: A TREATISE ON THE SYMBOLISM AND MYTHOLOGY OF THE RED RACE IN AMERICA
D.G. Brinton
Gale Research, 1974. Reprint of the 1896 edition. $11.00.

THE MYTHS OF THE NORTH AMERICAN INDIANS
L. Spence
Kraus Reprint Co. Reprint of the 1914 edition. $18.50.

MYTHS AND TALES OF THE SOUTHEASTERN INDIANS
John Reed Swanton
AMS Press, Inc. 1929. $20.00.

ROLLING THUNDER: A PERSONAL EXPLORATION INTO THE SECRET HEALING POWER OF AN AMERICAN INDIAN MEDICINE MAN
Douglas Boyd
Random House, Inc., 1974. $7.95.

*SO SAY THE INDIANS
Louis Thomas Jones
Folklore and verbal history of many tribes native to varied localities incorporate valuable material on Indian customs, language, and

racial differences. 216 pp. The Naylor Co. Age 12 up. $6.95.

*STORIES CALIFORNIA INDIANS TOLD
A.B. Fisher
Parnassus Press, 1957. $3.95. Below college level.

TALES OF THE NORTH AMERICAN INDIANS
S. Thompson
Indiana University Press, 1966. Pap. $2.95.

THE WEEPING SKY: SELECTIONS FROM AMERICAN INDIAN MYSTICISM
C. Hughs, Editor
Sheed and Ward, 1973. Pap. $2.95.

HEALTH CARE

AMERICAN INDIAN MEDICINE
Virgil J. Vogel
The contributions of the Indian toward medical treatment. 581 pp. Integrateducation Associates. $12.50.

EARTH MEDICINE-EARTH FOODS: PLANT REMEDIES, DRUGS AND NATURAL FOODS OF THE NORTH AMERICAN INDIANS
M. Weiner
Macmillan Publishing Co., Inc., 1972. Cloth, $8.95; Pap. $3.95.

THE FIREWATER MYTH: NORTH AMERICAN INDIAN DRINKING AND ALCOHOL ADDICTION
Joy Leland
Rutgers Center of Alcohol Studies, 1974. $7.50.

HEALTH AND DISEASES OF AMERICAN INDIANS NORTH OF MEXICO: A BIBLIOGRAPHY, 1800 TO 1969
Mark V. Barrow, et al, Editors
147 pp. University of Florida Press, 1972. $7.00.

HEALTH PROBLEMS OF UNITED STATES AND NORTH AMERICAN INDIAN POPULATIONS
D. Rabin
MSS Information Corp., 1972. $15.00.

MEDICINE AMONG THE AMERICAN

INDIANS
E. Stone
Hafner Press, 1962. Reprint of the 1932 edition. Pap. $5.95.

HISTORY

ABORIGINAL SOCIETY IN SOUTHERN CALIFORNIA
W.D.Strong
Kraus Reprint Co. Reprint of the 1929 edition. Pap. $25.00.

ADAIR'S HISTORY OF THE AMERICAN INDIANS
S.C.Williams, Editor
Blue and Gray Press. $7.95.

ADAIR'S HISTORY OF THE INDIANS
Samuel Cole Williams, Editor
The customs, beliefs, traditions and history of the Southern Indians, including the Catawbas, Cherokees, Creeks, Choctaws, and Chickasaws. 508 pp. First print, London, 1775. Johnson Publishing Co. $15.00.

AN ALBUM OF THE AMERICAN INDIAN
Rosebud Yellow Robe
Indian culture, history, and problems in America from before the arrival of Columbus to Indian life today, written by the grand-niece of Sitting Bull. 87 pp. Franklin Watts, Inc., 1969. Ages 9-12. $4.90.

ALMOST ANCESTORS: THE FIRST CALIFORNIANS
T.Kroeber and R.F.Heizer
Ballantine Books, 1970. Pap. $3.95.

THE AMERICAN EPIC: THE STORY OF THE AMERICAN INDIAN
Alice Marriott and Carol K. Rachlin
G.P.Putnam's Sons, 1969. Illus. $6.95. New American Library, pap. $.95.

THE AMERICAN HERITAGE BOOK OF INDIANS
William Brandon
The history of all Indians inhabiting North and South America from prehistoric times to the present. 384 pp. Dell Publishing Co. Pap. $1.25.

THE AMERICAN INDIAN
Theodore Heline
A summary of the history and present condition of the American Indian problem. 45 pp. New Age Press, 1975. Reprint of the 1952 edition. Pap. $1.00.

THE AMERICAN INDIAN
Norris Hundley, Editor
An anthology of American Indian history and culture. 150 pp. Clio Press, 1974. Pap. $4.75

*AMERICAN INDIAN
Oliver LaFarge
Western Publishing Co., 1960. $6.96; Pap. $3.95. Below college level.

*THE AMERICAN INDIAN
Anne Terry and William Brandon
Random House, Inc., 1963. $6.95. Ages 10 to 14.

AMERICAN INDIAN, TWO VOLS.
Lee F. Harkins, Editor
Liveright Publishing Corp., 1970. $100.00.

*THE AMERICAN INDIAN
R.F.Locke
Hawthorn Books, 1971. $5.95. Ages 16 and up.

*AMERICAN INDIAN, 1492 TO 1970:
A CHRONOLOGY AND FACT BOOK
Henry C. Dennis
Oceana Pubns., 1971. $5.00. Below college level.

AMERICAN INDIAN ETHNOHISTORY, 118 VOLS
David Agee Horr
40,000 pp. Garland Publishing, 1974. $2,200.00 set; $21.00 each.

*THE AMERICAN INDIAN AS FARMER
L.Morris
Melmont Pubs., 1963. $4.50. Ages 6 to 12.

THE AMERICAN INDIAN: FOCUSING ON FOUR PRINCIPAL TRIBAL GROUPS
Sue Northey
The life of the American Indian from a time "before the Pilgrims came" to the reservations of today. 248 pp. The Naylor Co. Illus. $5.95.

THE AMERICAN INDIAN: FROM COLONIAL TIMES TO THE PRESENT
Michael Gibson
G.P.Putnam's Sons, 1974. Illus. $5.95.

*THE AMERICAN INDIAN IN AMERICA
Jayne Clark Jones
From the Indians' ancestors to the reawakening of Indian pride and heritage. 200 pp. 2 volumes. Lerner Publications, 1973. Illus. Ages 11-17. Each volume $3.95.

THE AMERICAN INDIAN IN NORTH CAROLINA
Douglas L. Rights
A study of the history of the North Carolina Indians, their folklore and mythology, their habits and customs. 298 pp. John F. Blair, Publisher, 1972. Illus. $10.00.

THE AMERICAN INDIAN IN THE UNITED STATES, PERIOD 1850-1914
Warren K. Moorehead
The present condition of the American Indian, his political history and other topics. Books for Libraries. Reprint of the 1914 edition. $33.75.

THE AMERICAN INDIAN: PAST AND PRESENT
R.L.Nichols and G.R.Adams, Editors
Xerox College Publishing, 1971. Pap. $3.95.

THE AMERICAN INDIAN READER: HISTORY
J.Henry, Editor
The culture, tradition and history of the American Indian. Indian Historian, 1974. Pap. $4.00.

*THE AMERICAN INDIAN STORY
M.McNeer
96 pp. Farrar, Strauss, and Giroux, 1963. Illus.- $5.95. Ages 12 and up.

*AMERICAN INDIAN TRIBES
Marion E. Gridley
Dodd, Mead and Co., 1974. Illus. $5.50. Below college level.

THE AMERICAN INDIAN AND THE UNITED STATES, FOUR VOLS.
Wilcomb E. Washburn, Editor
Random House, Inc., 1973. $125.00 set.

AMERICAN INDIANS
Frederick Starr
AMS Press, Inc. Reprint of the 1899 edition. $16.50.

*AMERICAN INDIANS
Florence Randall
Facts about how the early Indians lived, ate, dressed, traveled, and communicated.

Highlights for Children, 1972. Pap. $1.00. Ages 6-12.

AMERICAN INDIANS
William T. Hagan
University of Chicago Press, 1961. Cloth, $6.50; Pap. $1.95.

*AMERICAN INDIANS
S.E.Fletcher
Grosset and Dunlap, Inc., 1954. $1.00. Below college level.

AMERICAN INDIANS: A STUDY GUIDE AND SOURCE BOOK
Lynn P. Dunn
R & E Research Associates, 1975. Pap. $6.00.

*AMERICAN INDIANS: YESTERDAY AND TODAY
Bruce Grant
E.P.Dutton and Co., 1960. Illus. $6.96. Below college level.

ANCIENT INDIAN HISTORY, CIVILIZATION, AND CULTURE
P.S.Joshi, etal
Lawrence Verry, Inc., 1972. $5.00.

ANTIQUITIES OF THE SOUTHERN IN-DIANS PARTICULARLY OF THE GEORGIA TRIBES
Charles Colcock Jones, Jr.
30 plates. AMS press, 1974. Reprint of the 1873 edition. Cloth, $35.00; Pap. $32.50

APPALACHIAN INDIAN FRONTIER: THE EDMOND ATKIN REPORT AND PLAN OF 1775
Edmond Atkin
Peter Smith Publishers. $4.25.

THE BOOK OF AMERICAN INDIANS
R.B. Raphael
Arco Publishing Co., 1973. $3.50.

THE BOOK OF THE INDIANS: OR, BIO-GRAPHY AND HISTORY OF THE INDIANS OF NORTH AMERICA, FROM ITS FIRST DISCOVERY TO THE YEAR 1841
Samuel Gardner
AMS Press, Inc. Reprint of the 1841 edition. $49.00.

A BRIEF HISTORY OF THE INDIAN PEOPLES
William Wilson Hunter

Books for Libraries, Inc., 1973. Reprint of the 1903 edition. $16.75.

THE BROKEN HOOP: THE HISTORY OF NATIVE AMERICANS FROM THE AT-LANTIC COAST TO THE PLAINS, 1600 TO 1890
Dan Georgakas
Doubleday and Co., 1973. Illus. Cloth, $3.75; Pap. $1.45.

BROKEN PEACEPIPES: A FOUR-HUNDRED YEAR OF HISTORY OF THE AMERICAN INDIAN
Irvin M. Peithmann
320 pp. Charles C. Thomas Pubs., 1964. $7.50.

BURY MY HEART AT WOUNDED KNEE: *An Indian History of the American West*
Dee Brown
Bantam Books, 1971. $6.95.

*CALIFORNIA INDIAN DAYS
Helen Bauer
Doubleday and Co., 1968. Illus. $4.50. Up to 12 years old.

CALIFORNIA INDIAN HISTORY: A CLASSIFIED AND ANNOTATED GUIDE TO SOURCE MATERIALS
Robert F. Heizer, et al
Lists of source materials (museum collections, documentary archives, films, pictorial archives, bibliographies) together with a tribal map, index of tribes referred to, and index of authors. 90 pp. Ballena Press. Pap. $4.95.

CALIFORNIA INDIANS: SAGEBRUSH CORNER-OPENING OF CALIFORNIA'S NORTHEAST
W.N.Davis, Jr.
550 pp. Garland Publishing, Inc., 1974. $21.00.

THE CALIFORNIA INDIANS: A SOURCE BOOK
R.F.Heizer and M.A.Whipple, Editors
University of California Press, 1971. Cloth, $14.25; Pap. $5.95.

CALIFORNIA INDIANS: INDIAN LAND USE AND OCCUPANCY IN CALIFORNIA
Harold Driver, et al, Editors
1061 pp. Garland Publishing, Inc., 1974. Three Vols. $21.00.

CALIFORNIA INDIANS VOLUME TWO, INCLUDING:
Indians of California, Robert F. Heizer. *The Luiseno: Analysis of Change in Patterns of Land Tenure and Social Structure,* Herbert R. Harvey. *Division of Labor Among The Indians of California,* Nona C. Willoughby
288 pp. Garland Publishing Co., 1974. $21.00.

CALIFORNIA INDIANS VOLUME THREE, INCLUDING:
Pit River Indians of California, Erminie Wheeler-Voegelin. *Fall River Valley: An Examination of Historical Sources,* Ernest R. Neasham
289 pp. Garland Publishing Co., 1974. $21.00.

CALIFORNIA INDIANS VOLUME FOUR, INCLUDING:
Basic Report on California Indian Holdings, Alfred L. Kroeber
Selected Writings of A.L. Kroeber On Land Use And Political Organization of California Indians, Harold E. Driver
Mexican Land Claims in California, Ralph G. Lounsbury
285 pp. Garland Publishing Co., 1974. $21.00.

CALIFORNIA INDIANS VOLUME SIX, INCLUDING:
Indians Occupancy, Subsistance And Land Use Patterns in California, Ralph L. Beals
Findings of Fact, and Opinion, The Indian Claims Commission
379 pp. Garland Publishing Co., 1974. $21.00.

THE CAROLINA INDIAN FRONTIER
D.H. Corkran
University of South Carolina Press, 1970. Pap. $1.95.

THE CHARACTER AND INFLUENCE OF THE INDIAN TRIBE IN WISCONSIN; A STUDY OF THE TRADING POST AS AN INSTITUTION
Frederick Jackson Turner
Items about the trade organization, goods sold, and the credit system. 75 pp. Burt Franklin Publishers. Reprint of the 1891 edition. $4.50.

CHILDREN OF THE SUN: THE PUEBLOS, NAVAJOS AND APACHES OF NEW MEXICO
Maudie Robinson
Messner, 1973. $5.29.

THE CIVILIZATION OF THE INDIAN NATIVES
H.Jackson
Scholarly Press. Reprint 1830 edition. $9.50.

THE CLASSIC SOUTHWEST: READINGS IN ARCHAEOLOGY ETHNOHISTORY AND ETHNOLOGY
B.C.Hedrick
University of Illinois Press, 1973. $10.00.

THE COAST INDIANS OF SOUTHERN ALASKA AND NORTHERN BRITISH COLUMBIA
Albert Parker Niblack
161 pp. Johnson Reprint, 1971. Reprint of the 1890 edition. Illus. $21.00.

CRY OF THE THUNDERBIRD: THE AMERICAN INDIAN'S OWN STORY
Charles Hamilton, Editor
238 pp. University of Oklahoma Press, 1974. Reprint of the 1972 edition. Illus. $7.95.

A DICTIONARY CATALOG OF THE EDWARD E. AYER COLLECTION OF AMERICANA AND AMERICAN INDIANS, FIRST SUPPLEMENT
Newberry Library-Chicago
G.K.Hall and Co.

DICTIONARY OF PREHISTORIC INDIAN ARTIFACTS OF THE AMERICAN SOUTHWEST
Franklin Barnett
Descriptions and illustrations of prehistoric Indian artifacts, their excavation sites, and uses. 128 pp. Northland Press, 1973. Illus. Pap. $7.95.

THE ENCYCLOPEDIA OF INDIANS OF THE AMERICAS
Scholarly Press. $600.00 set

ETHNOHISTORICAL REPORT ON THE LOCATION OF INDIAN TRIBES IN SOUTHEASTERN MICHIGAN AND NORTHERN OHIO: THE WYANDOT, DELAWARE AND SHAWNEE TRIBES, 1700 TO 1817
Dr. Helen Hornbeck Tanner
55 pp. Clearwater Publishing Co., 1973. $18.15.

ETHNOHISTORY IN SOUTHWESTERN ALASKA AND THE SOUTHERN YUKON: METHOD AND CONTENT

Margaret Lantis
311 pp. University Press of Kentucky, 1970. Illus. $9.75.

ETHNOLOGICAL REPORT ON THE UMATILLA, WALLA WALLA AND CAYUSE INDIANS RELATIVE TO SOCIO-POLITICAL ORGANIZATION AND LAND USE IN OREGON AND WASHINGTON, 1818 TO 1855
Robert J. Suphan
92 pp. Clearwater Publishing Co., 1973. $24.00.

EVERYTHING YOU EVER WANTED TO ASK ABOUT INDIANS BUT WERE AFRAID TO FIND OUT
Don Bibeau, Editor
An Illustrated, cartoon comic look at the American Indian, with Carl Gawboy's ethnic humor. North Star Press. Pap. $1.25.

*FAMOUS INDIAN TRIBES
D.C.Cooke and W. Moyers
Random House, Inc., 1954. Illus. $1.95. Ages 5 to 8.

FINAL REPORT OF INVESTIGATIONS AMONG THE INDIANS OF THE SOUTHWESTERN UNITED STATES, 1880 TO 1885
Adolph Francis Bandelier
AMS Press, Inc. Reprint of the 1890 edition. $58.50.

*THE FIRST AMERICANS
Stanley N. Worton
192 pp. Hayden Book Co., 1974. Illus. Price not set. Below college level.

THE FIRST AMERICANS
Time-Life Editors
Time-Life Books, 1973. Pap. $7.95.

*FIRST COMERS: INDIANS OF AMERICA'S DAWN
Alice Marriott
David McKay Co., 1960. $4.19. Ages 16 and up.

*FIRST ON THE LAND: THE NORTH CAROLINA INDIANS
Ruth Y. Wetmore
The story of North Carolina Indians from the nomadic life of 8000 B.C. to the present-day tourist business of the Cherokee and the militancy of the Lumbee. John F. Blair, Publisher, 1974. $8.95. Jr. High up.

THE FIVE CIVILIZED TRIBES
Grant Foreman
455 pp. University of Oklahoma Press, 1974. Reprint of the 1934 edition. Illus. Cloth, $8.95; Pap. $3.95.

FIVE INDIAN TRIBES OF THE UPPER MISSOURI: SIOUX, ARICKARAS, ASSINIBOINES, CREES, AND CROWS
Edwin Thompson Denig
217 pp. University of Oklahoma Press, 1973. Reprint of the 1961 edition. Illus. $7.95.

FLORIDA INDIANS VOLUME ONE, INCLUDING:
Notes on Colonial Indians and Communities in Florida, 1700-1821, and *Notes on the Treaty of Coweta,* Howard F. Cline
301 pp. Garland Publishing Co., 1974. $21.00.

FLORIDA INDIANS VOLUME TWO, INCLUDING:
Provisional Historical Gazeteer With Locational Notes on Florida Colonial Communities,
Howard F. Cline
251 pp. Garland Publishing Co., 1974. $21.00.

FLORIDA INDIANS VOLUME THREE, INCLUDING:
Ethnological Report on the Florida Indians,
Charles H. Fairbanks
Findings of Fact, and Opinion,
The Indian Claims Commission
363 pp. Garland Publishing Co., 1974. $21.00

FOUR CENTURIES OF SOUTHERN INDIANS
Charles Hudson, Editor
The story of the Indians of the southeastern United States who had the most highly centralized and complex social structure of all the aboriginal peoples in the continental United States. University of Georgia Press, 1974. Cloth, $7.50; Pap. $3.00.

FROM WHOLE LOG TO NO LOG
Edward J. Lettermann
A history of the Indians where the Mississippi and Minnesota Rivers meet. 291 pp. Ross & Haines, Inc. Illus. $8.50.

THE GREAT LAKES INDIANS
W.Kubiac
Baker Book House. $14.95.

A GUIDE TO AMERICA'S INDIANS: CEREMONIES, RESERVATIONS, AND MUSEUMS
Arnold Marquis
400 pp. University of Oklahoma Press, 1974. Illus. Cloth, $9.95; Pap. $4.95.

A GUIDE TO THE INDIAN TRIBES OF OKLAHOMA
Muriel H. Wright
300 pp. University of Oklahoma Press, 1971. Reprint of the 1951 edition. Illus, $6.95.

HALE'S INDIANS OF NORTHWEST AMERICA AND VOCABULARIES OF NORTH AMERICA
Albert Gallitin
AMS Press, Inc. Reprint of the 1848 edition. $22.50.

HANDBOOK OF THE INDIANS OF CALIFORNIA
A.L.Kroeber
Scholarly Press, 1972. Reprint of the 1925 edition. Cloth, $49.50. California Book Co., Pap. $19.50.

HANDBOOK OF MIDDLE AMERICAN INDIANS
R.Wauchope
University of Texas Press, 1974. $20.00.

*A HARDY RACE OF MEN: *America's Early Indians*
Eileen T. Callan
10,000 years of early Indian history on the North American continent. 128 pp. Harcourt Brace Jovanovich, Inc., 1970. Ages 12 and up. $4.95.

HISTORICAL ACCOUNT OF THE EXPEDITION AGAINST THE OHIO INDIANS
W.Smith
University Microfilms, 1966. Reprint of the 1765 edition. $6.75.

HISTORICAL COLLECTIONS OF THE INDIANS IN NEW ENGLAND, OF THEIR SEVERAL NATIONS, NUMBERS, CUSTOMS, MANNERS, RELIGION, AND GOVERNMENT BEFORE THE ENGLISH PLANTED THERE
D.Gookin
Arno Press, 1972. Reprint of the 1792 edition. $10.00.

HISTORICAL AND STATISTICAL IN-

FORMATION RESPECTING THE HISTORY, CONDITION AND PROSPECTS OF THE INDIAN TRIBES OF THE UNITED STATES
Henry Rowe Schoolcraft
Bureau of Indian Affairs. Index compiled 1954. AMS Press. Reprint of the 1851-1857 editions. $1,500.00.

HISTORY OF THE AMERICAN INDIANS
James Adair
464 pp. Johnson Reprint, 1969. Reprint of the 1775 edition. $28.00.

HISTORY OF THE AMERICAN INDIANS
J.Adair
Arno Press. Reprint of the 1930 edition. $22.50.

THE HISTORY OF EVENTS RESULTING IN INDIAN CONSOLIDATION WEST OF THE MISSISSIPPI
Annie Heloise Abel
AMS Press, Inc. Reprint of the 1908 edition. $10.00.

*HISTORY OF THE FIVE INDIAN NATIONS
C.Colden
Peter Smith Publishers, 1958. $4.00. Ages 16 and up.

A HISTORY OF THE INDIANS OF THE UNITED STATES
Angie Debo
386 pp. University of Oklahoma Press, 1974. Reprint of the 1970 edition. Illus. $8.95.

HISTORY OF THE INDIANS OF CONNECTICUT FROM THE EARLIEST KNOWN PERIOD TO 1850
John W. DeForest
509 pp. Shoe String Press, 1964. Reprint of the 1851 edition. Illus. $10.00.

HISTORY OF THE INDIAN TRIBES OF HUDSON'S RIVER
E.M.Ruttenber
Ira J. Friedman, 1971. $14.50.

THE HISTORY OF THE INDIAN WARS IN NEW ENGLAND, TWO VOLS IN ONE
W.Hubbard
Kraus Reprint Co. Reprint of the 1865 edition. $25.00.

HOKAHEY! AMERICAN INDIANS THEN AND NOW

Edith M. Dorian
Groups Indians by culture areas, and outlines their civilizations, the highlights of their history, and their present status. 96 pp. McGraw-Hill Book Co., 1957. Age 8-12. $4.72.

I HAVE SPOKEN: AMERICAN HISTORY THROUGH THE VOICES OF THE INDIANS
Virginia Irving Armstrong, Editor
206 pp. Swallow Press, 1971. Cloth, $6.00; Pap. $2.95.

IN A SACRED MANNER WE LIVE: PHOTOGRAPHS OF THE AMERICAN INDIAN AT THE BEGINNING OF THE TWENTIETH CENTURY
D.D.Fowler
Barre-Westover, 1972. Cloth, $15.00; Pap. $5.95.

AN INDEX TO SCHOOLCRAFT'S "INDIAN TRIBES OF THE UNITED STATES"
F.S.Nichols
Scholarly Press. Reprint of the 1954 edition. $14.50.

INDIAN AFFAIRS IN COLONIAL NEW YORK: THE SEVENTEENTH CENTURY
Allen W. Trelease
Kennikat Press. Reprint of the 1960 edition. $12.00.

INDIAN AFFAIRS IN THE TERRITORIES OF OREGON AND WASHINGTON
J.Ross Brown
48 pp. Ye Galleon Press, 1973. Reprint of the 1858 edition. $3.50.

THE INDIAN TRADERS
393 pp. University of Oklahoma Press, 1972. Reprint of the 1962 edition. Illus. $8.95.

INDIAN TRIBES OF THE LOWER MISSISSIPPI VALLEY AND ADJACENT COAST OF THE GULF OF MEXICO
John R. Swanton
387 pp. Johnson Reprint, 1970. Reprint of the 1911 edition.

INDIAN TRIBES OF TEXAS
186 pp. Texian Press, 1975. Illus. $10.00.

INDIAN TRIBES OF THE UPPER MISSISSIPPI VALLEY AND REGION OF THE GREAT LAKES, 2 VOLS IN ONE
Emma H. Blair, Editor

Kraus Reprint Co. Reprint of the 1911 edition. $25.00.

INDIAN TRIBES OF THE UPPER MISSOURI: EXTRACTS
E. T. Denig
Shorey Publications. Reprint of the 1930 edition. Pap. $7.50.

INDIAN TRIBES OF WASHINGTON TERRITORY
George Gibbs
56 pp. Ye Galleon Press, 1972. Pap. $4.00.

INDIAN VILLAGE SITE AND CEMETERY NEAR MADISONVILLE, OHIO
E. A. Hooton
Kraus Reprint Co., 1974. Reprint of the 1920 edition. Pap. $5.50.

THE INDIAN VILLAGES OF SOUTHEAST ALASKA: *Extracts*
H. W. Krieger
Shorey Publications. Reprint of the 1927 edition. Pap. $2.50.

INDIAN WOMEN OF THE WESTERN MORNING: THEIR LIFE IN EARLY AMERICA
John Upton and Donna Terrell
Reconstructs the state of the American Indian woman at the time of the European exploration of North America. 214 pp. Dial Press, 1974. $8.95.

*THE INDIANS
Benjamin Capps
230 pp. Silver Burdett Co., 1973. Illus. $7.95. Ages 9 up.

THE INDIANS IN AMERICA
Wilcomb E. Washburn
Separates myth from fact in tracing the story of the indian in America from pre-Columbian times to the present. Harper & Row Publishers, 1975.

INDIANS OF THE AMERICAN SOUTH-WEST
Bertha Dutton
An overview of past and present Indian life in the Southwest. Prentice-Hall, 1975. $14.95.

THE INDIANS BOOK
N. Burlin
Gordon Press. $29.95.

INDIANS: THE CAMERA REVEALS THE REALITY OF NORTH AMERICAN INDIAN LIFE: 1847-1928. PHOTOGRAPHS FROM THE SMITHSONIAN INSTITUTION COLLECTION
Joanna Cohan Scherer
The gradual destruction of Indian life and culture as seen through the dispassionate eye of the camera. 192 pp. Crown Publishers, 1974. Illus. $12.95.

*INDIANS: THE FIRST AMERICANS
Patricia Miles Martin
Parents Magazine Press, 1970. Illus. $4.95. Ages 5 to 9.

INDIANS AND PIONEERS: THE STORY OF THE AMERICAN SOUTHWEST BEFORE 1830
Grant Foreman
300 pp. University of Oklahoma Press, 1967. Reprint of the 1936 edition. illus. $7.95.

INDIANS FROM TEXAS: FROM PREHISTORIC TO MODERN TIMES
W. W. N3wcomb Jr.
University of Texas Press. Cloth $7.50; Pap. $2.95.

THE INDIANS IN NORTH CAROLINA
S. A. South
North Carolina Office of Archives and History, 1965. Pap. $.25.

INDIANS IN PESSSYLVANIA
Paul A. W. Wallace
An account of the Indians who met the first settlers. 194 pp. Pennsylvania Historical and Museum Commission, 1975. Cloth, $3.00; Pap. $1.75.

INDIANS IN SEVENTEENTH CENTURY VIRGINIA
Ben C. McCary
93 pp. University Press of Virginia, 1957. Illus. Pap. $1.25.

INDIANS IN NORTH CAROLINA
Stanley A. South
69 pp. Publications of the Division of Archives and History, 1972. Illus. $.25.

INDIANS OF THE AMERICAS
J. Collins
New American Library, 1952. Pap. $1.25.

INDIANS OF THE AMERICAS

E. R. Embree
Macmillan Publishing Co., Inc., 1970. Pap. $1.50.

*INDIANS OF THE EASTERN WOODLANDS
Sally Sheppard
Origins, history, and way of life. 96 pp. Franklin Watts, Inc., 1975. Illus. Age 10 up. $3.90.

*INDIANS OF THE GREAT BASIN AND PLATEAU
Francis Haines
G. P. Putnam's Sons, 1970. Illus. $5.00. Below college level.

THE INDIANS OF GREATER NEW YORK AND THE LOWER HUDSON
Clark Wissler, Editor
Ams Press, Inc., 1974. Reprint of the 1909 edition. $17.50.

INDIANS OF THE HIGH PLAINS: FROM THE PREHISTORIC PERIOD TO THE COMING OF EUROPEANS
George E. Hyde
231 pp. University of Oklahoma press, 1970. Reprint of the 1959 edition. Illus. $6.50.

INDIANS OF ILLINOIS AND IN-DIANA: ILLINOIS, KICKAPOO AND POTOWATOMI INDIANS
Joseph Jablow
320 pp. Garland Publishing, Inc., 1974. $21.00.

INDIANS OF ILLINOIS AND NOR-THWESTERN INDIANA, INCLUDING:
Anthropological Repost on the Chippewa, Ottawa and Pottawatomi Indians in Southwest Michigan, Ermine Wheeler-Voegelin
Report on the Kickapoo, Illinois and Potawa-tomi Indians, David B. Stout
386 pp. Garland Publishing Co., 1974. $21.00.

*INDIANS OF LOUISIANNA
F. B. Kniffen
Pelican Publishing House, 1965. $4.95. Below college level.

INDIANS OF THE LOWER SOUTH
John K. Mahon, Editor
University of West Florida, 1974. Cloth $8.00; Pap. $5.00

INDIANS OF THE NORTH PACIFIC COAST

R. McFeat, Editor
286 pp. University of Washington Press, 1967. Cloth, $5.95; Pap. $2.95.

*THE INDIANS OF NORTHEASTERN AMERICA
Karna L. Bjorklund
The origins, ways of life, dwellings, food, transportation, mythology, religion, arts and crafts, customs and relationship with the white man of the Algonkian and Iroquois tribes. 192 pp. Dodd, Mead & Co., 1969. illus. Age 11-15. $4.95.

INDIANS OF NORTHERN INDIANA AND SOUTHWESTERN MICHIGAN: AN HISTORICAL REPORT ON INDIAN USE AND OCCUPANCY OF NORTHERN INDIANA AND SOUTHWESTERN MICHIGAN
Donald J. Berthrong
325 pp. Garland Publishing, Inc., 1974. $21.00.

INDIANS OF NORTHERN OHIO AND SOUTHEASTERN MICHIGAN, INCLUDING:
An Ethnohistorical Report on the Wyandot, Ottawa, Chippewa, Munsee, Delaware, Shawnee and Potawatomi of Ohio and Southeastern Michigan, Erminie Wheeler-Voegelin
The Location of Indian Tribes in Southeastern Michigan and Northern Ohio, 1700-1817, Helen Nornbeck Tanner
343 pp. Garland publishing Co., 1974. $21.00.

*INDIANS OF THE NORTHERN PLAINS
William K. Powers
G. P. Putnam's Sons, 1969. Illus. $5.00. Below college level.

INDIANS OF THE NORTHWEST COAST
Pliny Earle Goddard
Covers types of housing, tools, clothing, travel, craftsmanship, religion and social organization, along with a pre-history of political and social institutions. Illus. Cooper Square Publishers, 1972. Reprint of 1934 edition. $6.00.

INDIANS OF THE NORTHWEST COAST
Phillip Drucker
An anthropological study. Doubleday & Co. Illus. Pap. $2.50.

INDIANS OF NORTHWEST OHIO: AN ETHNOHISTORICAL REPORT ON THE WYANDOT, POTAWATOMI, OTTAWA,

AND CHIPPEWA OF NORTHWEST OHIO
Erminie Wheeler-Voegelin
300 pp. Garland Publishing, Inc., 1974. $21.00.

INDIANS OF OHIO, INDIANA, ILLINOIS, SOUTHERN MICHIGAN, AND SOUTHERN WISCONSIN: FINDINGS OF FACT AND OPINION, THREE VOLS. INCLUDING: *Wyandots, Delawares, Shawnees, Ottawas, Chippewas, Potawatomi, Miamis, Eel-Rivers, Wea's, Kickapoos, Piankashaws, Kaskaskias, and Peoria*
The Indian Claims Commission
1500 pp. Garland Publishing, 1974. $63.00; $21.00 each.

THE INDIANS OF PUGET SOUND
Hermann Haeberlin and Erna Gunther
84 pp. University of Washington Press, 1930. Illus. Pap. $1.95.

INDIANS OF THE RIO GRANDE VALLEY
Adolph Bandelier and Edgar L. Hewett
AMS Press, Inc. Reprint of the 1937 edition. $33.00.

INDIANS OF THE SOUTHEAST: THEN AND NOW
Jesse Burt and Robert B. Ferguson
The Southeastern tribes, their life-style and beliefs, their triumphs and defeats. 304 pp. Abingdon Books, 1973. Illus. $8.95.

THE INDIANS OF SOUTHEASTERN UNITED STATES
J. R. Swanton
Scholarly Press. Reprint of the 1943 edition. $39.50.

INDIANS OF SOUTHERN ILLINOIS
Irvin M. Peithmann
172 pp. Charles C. Thomas Pubs., 1964. Illus. $6.50.

INDIANS OF SOUTHERN NEW JERSEY
Frank H. Stewart, Editor
Kennikat Press, 1972. Reprint of the 1932 edition. Illus. $7.00.

INDIANS OF THE SOUTHERN PLAINS
William K. Powers
G.P. Putnam's Sons, 1971. Illus. Cloth, $5.00; Pap. $2.75.

*INDIANS OF THE SOUTHWEST
G. C. Baldwin
G. P. Putnam's Sons, 1970. Illus. $5.00. Below college level.

INDIANS OF THE SOUTHWEST
George Amos Dorsey
AMS Press, Inc. Reprint of the 1903 edition.
$13.50.

THE INDIANS OF THE SOUTHWEST: A CENTURY OF DEVELOPMENT UNDER THE UNITED STATES
Edward Everett Dale
288 pp. University of Oklahoma Press, 1971. Reprint of the 1940 edition. Illus. $8.95.

INDIANS OF TEXAS IN 1830
J. L. Berlandier
Smithsonian Institution Press, 1969. $10.00.

INDIANS OF THE UNITED STATES: FOURCENTURIES OF THEIR HISTORY AND CULTURE
Clark Wissler
Doubleday and Co., 1966. Cloth $7.95; Pap. $2.50.

INDIANS OF THE URBAN NORHTWEST
marian Wesley Smith, Editor
AMS Press, Inc., 1969. Reprint of the 1949 edition. $17.50.

THE INDIANS OF WASENTAW COUNTY, MICHIGAN
W. B. Hinsdale
George Wahr Publishing Co. Reprint of the 1927 edition. $1.00.

*MORE INDIAN FRIENDS AND FOES
D. Heiderstadt
David McKay Co., 1963. $3.50. Ages 6 to 12.

NATIVE AMERICANS OF CALIFORNIA AND NEVADA
Jack D. Forbes
From prehistoric times to the present. 210 pp. Naturegraph Publishers, 1969 Illus. 18 Plates. Cloth, $7.95; Pap. $4.95.

NATIVE AMERICANS: 500 YEARS AFTER
Joseph C. Farber and Michael Dorris
A one-time associate of Edward Steichen portrays a story of the number and individuality of the North American Indians. 356 pp. 325 Photos. Thomas Y. Crowell Co., 1975. $14.95.

NATIVE TRIBES MAP
A. L. Kroeber
University of California Press. Pap. $.65.

THE NORTH AMERICAN INDIAN:

BEING A SERIES OF VOLUMES PICTURING AND DESCRIBING THE INDIANS OF THE UNITED STATES AND ALASKA
Edward S. Curtis
20 vols. 5222 pp. 722 plates in 20 portfolios. Johnson Reprint Corporation. Reprint of the 1907-30 edition. $700.00 set. $35.00 ea.; portfolios in 4 vols., ea. $42.00.

THE NORTH AMERICAN INDIANS,
An Account of the American Indians North of Mexico, Compiled From the Original Sources
Rose A. Palmer
The major culture areas are represented by the Eskimo, the Iroquois League of Five Nations, the Cliff Dwellers, several Plains tribes and various West Coast tribes. Illus. Cooper Square Publishers, 1972. Reprint of the 1929 edition. $17.50.

*NORTH AMERICAN INDIANS: LIFE AND LORE
Ernest Berke
Doubleday and Co., 1964. Illus. $5.95. Up to 10 years old.

THE NORTH AMERICAN INDIANS: A SOURCEBOOK
R. C. Owen, et al.
Macmillan Publishing Co., Inc., 1967. $11.95.

NOTES ON THE ETHNOLOGY OF PUGET SOUND INDIANS
T. T. Waterman
96 pp. 36 plates. Museum of the American Indian, 1973. Illus. $3.50.

THE ODYSSEY OF THE AMERICAN INDIAN
Michael Grandees
Vantage Press. $4.95.

THE OLD INDIAN CHRONICLE
Samuel Gardner
AMS Press, Inc. Reprint of the 1867 edition. $21.00.

OREGON INDIANS VOL 1, INCLUDING:
Anthropological Investigation of the Tillamook indians, and, Anthropological Investigation of the Chinook Indians, Herbert C. Taylor, Jr. *Ethnological Report on the Identity and Localization of Certain Native Peoples of Northwestern Oregon,* Robert J. Supan
Findings of Fact, and Opinion, The Indian Claims Commission
280 pp. Garland Publishing, 1974. $21.00.

OREGON INDIANS VOL. 2, INCLUDING:
Ethnological Report on Wasco, Tenind,
Umatilla, Walla Walla, and Cayuse Indians
Relative to Socio-Political Orgaaization and
Land Use, Robert J. Supan
Findings of Fact, and Opinion
   The Indian Claims Commission
251 pp. Garland Publishing, 1974. $21.00.

**THE ORIGIN OF THE AMERICAN IN-
DIANS: EUROPEAN CONCEPTS**
   L. E. Huddleston
University of Texas Press, 1967. $6.00.

**PATTERNS OF INDIAN BURNING IN
CALIFORNIA**
   H. T. Lewis
Ballena Press, 1973. Pap. $6.50.

***THE PEOPLE: THREE INDIAN TRIBES
OF THE SOUTHWEST**
   Gordon Oosterman
A discussion of the history and current life-style
of the Navajo, Cherokee, and Zuni people.
William E. Eerdmans Publishing Co., 1973.
Ages 11-13. Pap. $2.45.

THE PEOPLE WE CALL INDIANS
   Loretto Douglas
The development of the Indians of the United
States from prehistoric times to the present day.
Brown Book Co., 1975. $2.00.

**A PICTORIAL HISTORY OF THE
AMERICAN INDIAN**
   Oliver La Farge
288 pp. Crown Publishers, 1974. 350
illustrations. $9.95.

**PROGRAM OF THE HISTORY OF
AMERICAN INDIANS**
   P. Armillas
Organization of American States, 1962. $1.25;
Spanish, $1.25.

**READINGS IN THE HISTORY OF THE
AMERICAN INDIAN**
   Melvin W. Roe, Editor
MSS Information Corp., 1971. Pap. $5.00.

RED CAROLINIANS
   C. J. Milling
University of South Carolina Press, 1969.
$14.95.

RED MAN'S AMERICA: A HISTORY OF

INDIANS IN THE UNITED STATES
   R. M. Underhill
University of Chicago Press, 1971. Cloth,
$10.00; Pap. $3.95.

**RED SHADOWS: THE HISTORY OF
NATIVE AMERICANS FROM THE DESERT
TO THE PACIFIC COAST, 1600 TO 1900**
   Dan Georgakas
Doubleday and Co., 1973. illus. Cloth, $3.75;
Pap. $1.45.

**RED, WHITE, AND BLACK: SYMPOSIUM
ON INDIANS IN THE OLD SOUTH**
   Charles M. Hudson, Editor
151 pp. University of Georgia Press, 1971. Pap.
$3.75.

**REDSKINS, RUFFLESHIRTS, AND RED-
NECKS: INDIAN ALLOTMENTS IN
ALABAMA AND MISSISSIPPI, 1830-1860**
   Mary Elizabeth Young
217 pp. University of Oklahoma Press, 1961.
Illus. $7.95.

***THE SEA HUNTERS, INDIANS OF THE
NORTHWEST COAST**
   Sonia Bleeker
160 pp. William Morrow and Co., 1951. Illus.
$4.25. Ages 9 to 12.

**SETH EASTMAN: PICTORIAL OF THE
INDIAN**
   John Francis McDermott
270 pp. University of Oklahoma Press, 1961.
Illus. $15.00.

**A SHORT HISTORY OF THE INDIANS OF
THE UNITED STATES**
   E. H. Spicer
Van Nostrand Reinhold Co., 1969. Pap. $3.95.

**SOUTHEASTERN INDIANS: LIFE
PORTRAITS: A CATALOG OF PIC-
TURES, 1564 TO 1860**
   Emma Lila Fundaburk
136 pp. Scarecrow Press, 1969. Reprint of the
1958 edition. Illus. $8.50.

**THE SOUTHERN INDIANS: THE STORY
OF THE CIVILIZED TRIBES BEFORE
REMOVAL**
   R. S. Cotterill
259 pp. University of Oklahoma Press, 1971.
Reprint of the 1954 edition. Illus. Cloth, $6.50;
Pap. $3.25.

SOUTHWESTERN COOKERY: INDIAN AND SPANISH INFLUENCES
Arno Press. Reprint of the 1973 edition. $12.00.

SOUTHWESTERN INDIAN TRIBES
    Tom Bahti
K C Publications, 1968. Illus. Pap. $2.00.

SPEAKING OF INDIANS
    Bernice Johnston
41 articles on Indians of the United States; includes the origin of contemporary tribes in Arizona and New Mexico; cultural aspects; the prehistoric Anasazi, Hohokam, and Mogollon cultures; and modern-day products which originated with the Indians. 112 pp. University of Arizona Press, 1970. Illus. Pap. $2.50.

THE INDIANS OF THE WESTERN GREAT LAKES 1615 TO 1760
    W. V. Kinietz
440 pp. University of MIchigan Press, 1965. $5.95.

INDIANS OF WESTERN ILLINOIS AND SOUTHERN WISCONSIN, INCLUDING:
Anthropological Report on the Chippewa, Ottawas and Potawatomi Residing on the Illinois and Milwaukee Rivers and on the Southwestern Parts of Lake Michigan.
Erminie Wheeler-Voegelin, et al
Anthropological Report on the Chippewa, Ottawa and Potawatomi Indians of Southwest Wisconsin and Northeast Illinois. J. A. Jones
390 pp. Garland Publishing Co., 1974. $21.00

INDIANS OF THE WOODLANDS: FROM PREHISTORIC TIMES TO 1725
    George E. Hyde
295 pp. University of Oklahoma, 1973. Reprint of the 1962 edition. Illus. Cloth, $8.95; Pap. $3.50

J. FODOR'S INDIAN AMERICA
    J. Marks-Highwater
David Mckay Co., 1974. $10.95.

MAN'S RISE TO CIVILIZATION AS SHOWN BY THE INDIANS OF NORTH AMERICA, FROM PRIMEVAL TIMES TO THE COMING OF THE INDUSTRIAL STATE.
    Peter Farb
E. P. Dutton and Co., 1968. Illus. $11.95.

MINES AND QUARRIES OF THE INDIANS OF CALIFORNIA

R. F. Heizer and A. E. Treganza
Ballena Press, 1972. Pap. $3.50.

THE STORY OF THE AMERICAN INDIAN
    Paul Radin
Liveright Publishing Corp., 1944. $7.95.

THE STORY OF THE INDIAN
    George Bird Grinnell
AMS Press, 1974. Reprint of the 1895 edition. $17.50.

THE STORY OF THE RED MAN
    F. W. Seymour
Books for Libraries, Inc., Reprint of the 1929 edition. $18.25.

SYNOPSIS OF THE INDIAN TRIBES WITHIN THE UNITED STATES EAST OF THE ROCKY MOUNTAINS, AND IN BRITISH AND RUSSIAN POSSESSIONS IN NORTH AMERICA
    Albert Gallatin
AMS Press, Inc., Reprint of the 1836 edition. $15.00.

THIS COUNTRY WAS OURS
    Virgil J. Vogel
A documentary survey of American Indian history. 473 pp. Integrateducation Associates; Harper and Row, 1972 Cloth, $12.95; Pap. $3.95.

TOUR OF THE AMERICAN LAKES AND AMONG THE INDIANS OF THE NORTHWEST TERRITORY IN 1830: DISCLOSING THE CHARACTER AND PROSPECTS OF THE INDIAN RACE
    Calvin Colton
Kennikat Press, 1971. Reprint of the 1833 edition. $35.00.

TRADE ROUTES AND ECONOMIC EXCHANGE AMONG THE INDIANS OF CALIFORNIA
    James T. Davis
Ballena Press. Pap. $4.95.

TRAITS OF AMERICAN INDIAN LIFE AND CHARACTER
    Peter Skene Ogden
AMS Press, Inc.Reprint of the 1933 edition. $15.00.

TRIBES OF CALIFORNIA
    Stephen Powers
AMS Press, Inc. Reprint of the 1877 edition. $45.50.

THE TRIBES OF THE EXTREME NORTHWEST, ALASKA, THE ALEUTIANS, AND ADJACENT TERRITORIES

W. H. Dall, et al

Shorey Publications. Reprint of the 1877 edition. Pap. $15.00.

TRIBES OF WESTERN WASHINGTON AND NORTHWESTERN OREGON

G. Gibbs

Shorey Publications. Reprint of the 1877 edition. Pap. $20.00.

TRIBES THAT SLUMBER: INDIANS OF THE TENNESSEE REGION

Thomas M. and Madeline K. Lewis

298 pp. University of Tennessee Press, 1958. Illus. Cloth, $8.50; Pap. $4.95.

URBAN INDIANS IN ARIZONA: PHOENIX, TUCSON AND FLAGSTAFF

Joyatpaul Chaudhuri

A study of Arizona's off-reservation Indians and their unique problems. Examines demography, social and economic environment, and socio-political mobilization. University of Arizona Press, 1975. Price not set.

VILLAGES OF THE ALGONQUIN, SIOUAN, AND CADDOAN TRIBES WEST OF THE MISSISSIPPI RIVER

D. L. Bushnell, Jr.

Scholarly Press. Reprint of the 1922 edition. $14.50.

*WE HAVE NOT VANISHED: EASTERN INDIANS OF THE UNITED STATES

A. A. Tamerin

Follett Publishing Co., 1974. $4.98. Below college level.

THE WESTERN AMERICAN INDIAN: CASE STUDIES IN TRIBAL HISTORY

Richard N. Ellis, Editor

203 pp. University of Nebraska Press, 1972. Cloth, $9.25; Pap. $2.95.

WISCONSIN INDIANS: LIVES AND LANDS

N. O. Lurie

State Historical Society of Wisconsin, 1970. Pap. $.75.

THE WORLD OF THE AMERICAN INDIAN

the story of the American Indian from prehistory to contemporary times. National Geographic Society. Illus. $10.00.

*WOUNDED KNEE: *An Indian History of the American West*

Dee Brown

Adapted for young readers, this book tells of the four Indian nations which held out longest against the white invaders. 224 pp. Holt, Rinehart & Winston, 1975. Illus. Age 11 up. $6.95.

LANGUAGE

THE AMERICAN RACE: A LINGUISTIC CLASSIFICATION AND ETHNOGRAPHIC DESCRIPTION OF THE NATIVE TRIBES OF NORTH AND SOUTH AMERICA

Daniel Garrison Brinton

392 pp. Johnson Reprint, 1970. Reprint of the 1891 edition. $19.50.

BIBLIOGRAPHIES OF THE LANGUAGES OF THE NORTH AMERICAN INDIANS

James Constantine Pilling

In addition to word lists, dictionaries and grammars, the bibliography lists all known biblical and other translations into each Indian language and original writings from those tribes that had been first to adopt a written language. AMS Press, 1976. Reprint of the 1887-1894 editions. 9 parts in 3 volumes. $67.50.

COOS NARRATIVE AND ETHNOLOGIC TEXTS

Melville Jacobs

A collection of phonetic transcriptions and translations of 91 narrative and ethnologic texts in the two Coos dialects, Hanis and Miluk, of western oregon. 125 pp. University of Washington Press, 1939.

HANDBOOK OF AMERICAN INDIAN LANGUAGES, TWO PARTS

Franz Boas, Editor

Humanities Press, Inc., 1969. Reprint of the 1911 edition. Set $82.50. Two Vols.

INDIAN NAMES OF PLACES, ETC. IN AND ON THE BORDERS OF CONNECTICUT: WITH INTERPRETATIONS OF SOME OF THEM

James Hammond Trumbull

93 pp. Shoe String Press, 1971. Reprint of the 1881 edition. $6.00.

*INDIAN PICTURE WRITING
Robert Hofsinde
Includes 248 symbols. Letters are given, and a section on the Cree alphabet with a sentence to translate 96 pp. William Morrow & Co., 1959. Illus. Ages 8-12. $3.78.

INDIAN PLACE NAMES: THEIR ORIGIN, EVOLUTION, AND MEANINGS, COLLECTED IN KANSAS FROM THE SIOUAN, CADDOAN, SHOSHONEAN, ALGONQUIN, IROQUOIAN AND OTHER TONGUES
John Rydjord
380 pp. University of Oklahoma Press, 1968. Illus. $8.95.

*INDIAN SIGN LANGUAGE
Robert Hofsinde
Includes necessary words, descriptions of how to make the signs, and illustrations showing the sign being made. 96 pp. William Morrow & Co., 1956. Illus. Ages 8-12. $3.78.

INDIAN SIGN LANGUAGE
William Tomkins
Over 525 signs developed by the Sioux, Blackfoot, Cheyenne, Arapaho and other tribes. Written instructions and diagrams show the reader how to make the words and construct sentences. 111 pp. Dover Publications, 1969. Pap. $1.25.

INDIAN TALK: HAND SIGNALS OF THE NORTH AMERICAN INDIANS
Iron Eyes Cody
The language used by the Plains Indians for centuries. 80 pp. Naturegraph Publishers. Over 150 illustrations. For all ages.

INTRODUCTION TO THE HANDBOOK OF AMERICAN INDIAN LANGUAGES
Franz Boas
Shorey Publications. Reprint of the 1911 edition. Pap. $5.00.

INTRODUCTION TO HANDBOOK OF AMERICAN INDIAN LANGUAGES AND INDIAN LINGUISTIC FAMILIES OF AMERICA NORTH OF MEXICO
Franz Boas and J. W. Powell
221 pp. University of Nebraska Press, 1966. Pap. $2.45.

*KEE'S HOME: A BEGINNING NAVAJO READER
Geraldine Hall and Irvy Goossen

A dual-language children's story book. 100 pp. Northland Press, 1972. Illus. Ages 6-12. Pap. $4.95.

LIBRARY OF AMERICAN LINGUISTICS
John Gilmary Shea, Editor
Thirteen volumes of vocabularies, grammars, and dictionaries of Indian languages. AMS Press, 1974. Reprint of the 1860-64 edition. 13 Volume Set. $175.00.

NAVAJO MADE EASTER
Irvy W. Goossen
A Navajo language book for English-speaking people. 271 pp. Northland Press, 1968. $6.95.

PICTURE WRITING OF THE AMERICAN INDIANS
Garrick Mallery
An early (1889) report of the Bureau of Ethnology of the Smithsonian Institute, this is a thorough coverage of interpretation and tribal differences in picture writing. Includes: wampum, mnemonic pictures, maps, notices, tribal designations, tatto marks, personal names, and religious symbols among others. 1290 pictures, 822 pp. Dover Publications, 1972. Pap. $10.00.

POPULAR ACCOUNT OF THE KIOWA INDIAN LANGUAGE
Parker MacKenzie with John P. Harrington
A report on the phonetics, morphomatics, and lexics of the Kiowa language, with a text in Kiowa and English. university of New Mexico Press. Pap. $2.50.

STUDIES IN AMERICAN INDIAN LANGUAGES
J. Sawyer
University of California Press, 1974. $13.75.

STUDIES IN CALIFORNIAN LINGUISTICS
W. Bright
University of California Press, 1964. Pap. $5.00.

STUDIES IN SOUTHEASTERN INDIAN LANGUAGES
James M. Crawford, Editor
Essays on Witchita verb structure, Shawnee noun inflection, Yuchi Morphology, Choctaw morphophonemics as well as Chickasaw, Cherokee, Powhatan, Mobilian, and Algonquian. 454 pp. university of Georgia Press, 1974. $13.00.

STUDIES IN SOUTHWESTERN ETHNO-LINGUISTICS: MEANING AND HISTORY IN THE LANGUAGES OF THE AMERICAN SOUTHWEST
    D. Hymes and W. E. Bittle
Humanities Press, Inc., 1967. $29.75.

*TALKING HANDS: INDIAN SIGN LANGUAGE
    Aline Amon
Doubleday and Co., 1968. $3.95. Up to 12 years old.

THE TUSCARORA LANGUAGE
    Elton Greene
Common words prepared for use in Indian schools by Tuscarora Chief Elton Greene. 16 pp. Johnson Publishing Co. $3.75.

LEADERS

AMERICAN INDIAN MOSES
    Timothy Dom Bucci
Vantage Press. $4.95.

*CONTEMPORARY AMERICAN INDIAN LEADERS
    Marion E. Gridley
Biographies of 26 Indian leaders of today. 201 pp. Dodd, Mead & Co., 1972. Illus. Age 11-15. $4.95.

*FAMOUS AMERICAN INDIANS
    William Heuman
The lives of nine of the best-known Indians of the North American continent; King Philip, Pontiac, Joseph Brant, Osceola, Tecumseh, Sequoyah, Chief Joseph, Crazy Horse, and Sitting Bull. 128 pp. Dodd, Mead & Co., 1972. Illus. Age 11-15. $3.95.

*FAMOUS AMERICAN INDIANS OF THE PLAINS
    S. Carl Hirsch
Rand McNally and Co., 1973. Illus. $4.95. Ages 10 up.

THE FIRST LADY OF AMERICA: A ROMANTICIZED BIOGRAPHY OF POCAHONTAS
    L. Phillips
Barre-Westover, 1973. $8.95.

GREAT INDIAN CHIEFS

    Albert Britt
A study of Indian leaders in the 200 year struggle to stop the white advance. Books for Libraries, 1938. $14.25.

*GREAT INDIAN CHIEFS
    A. Roland
Macmillan Publishing Co., Inc., 1966. $4.95. Below College level.

*HEAP MANY TEXAS CHIEF
    Roy D. Holt
The profiles of 50 Indian chiefs in Texas. 400 pp. The Naylor Co. Illus. Age 12 up. $8.95.

*HEROES OF THE AMERICAN INDIAN
    Sol Stember
The many outstanding leaders who were part of the long struggle between the red man and white man are chronicled in this book. Illus. Fleet Press, 1971. $5.00.

INDIAN BIOGRAPHY: NORTH AMERICAN NATIVES DISTINGUISHED AS ORATORS, WARRIORS, STATESMEN
    Benjamin B. Thatcher
Two volumes. 668 pp. Rio Grande Press. Reprint of the 1832 edition. Illus. $20.00.

*INDIAN CHIEFS
    Lynne Deur
14 biographical sketches of American Indian leaders from King Philip to Chief Joseph. 104 pp. Lerner Publications, 1975. illus. Ages 11-16. $3.95.

INDIAN CHIEFS OF PENNSYLVANIA: OR A STORY OF THE PART PLAYED BYTHE AMERICAN INDIAN IN THE HISTORY OF PENNSYLVANIA BASED PRIMARILY ON THE PENNSYLVANIA ARCHIVES AND COLONIAL RECORDS AND BUILT AROUND THE OUT-STANDING CHIEFS
    C. H. Snipe
Arno Press, 1971. Reprint of the 1927 edition. $23.00.

INDIAN CHIEFS OF SOUTHERN MIN-NESOTA
    Thomas Hughes
Ross & Haines, Inc. Reprint of the 1927 edition. 297 pp. $8.75.

INDIAN LEADERS WHO HELPED SHAPE AMERICA
    Ralph W. Andrews

A study of Indians east and west from colonial days to the last treaty. 196 pp. Superior Publishing Co., 1971. Illus. $12.95.

INDIAN ORATORY: A COLLECTION OF FAMOUS SPEECHES BY NOTED INDIAN CHIEFTAINS
W. C. Vanderwerth, Editor
292 pp. University of Oklahoma Press, 1972. Reprint of the 1971. Illus. $8.95.

*INDIAN PATRIOTS OF THE GREAT WEST
Bennett Wayne, Editor
The life stories of Sitting Bull of the Hunkpapa Sioux, Crazy Horse of the Oglala Sioux, Chief Joseph of the Nez Perces, and Quanah Parker of the Comanches. Garrard Books, 1974. Illus. 168 pp. Ages 10 up. $3.98.

*INDIANS
Set of 11 books. 80 pp. Garrard Publishing Co., 1975. Including: *Black Hawk: Indian Patriot,* Lavere Anderson; *Chief Joseph: Guardian of His People,* Elizabeth Rider Montgomery; *Chief Seattle: Great Statesman,* Elizabeth Rider Montgomery; *Crazy Horse: Sioux Warrior,* Enid LaMonte Meadowcroft; *Massasoit: Friend of the Pilgrims,* Virginia Voight; *Osceola: Seminole War Chief,* Wyatt Blassingame; *Pocahontas: Indian Princess,* Katharine E. Wilkie; *Sacagawea: Indian Guide,* Wyatt Blassingame; *Sitting Bull: Great Sioux chief,* LaVere Anderson; *Squanto: Indian Adventurer,* Stewart and Polly Anne Graff; *tecumseh: Shawnee Warrior-Statesman,* James McCague. $34.32. Age 6-10.

*THE INDIANS AND THE STRANGERS
Johanna Johnston
Easy-to-read stories of Squanto, Powhatan, Pontiac, Tecumseh, and Crazy Horse, among others. 109 pp. Dodd, Mead & Co., 1972. Illus. Age 6-11. $4.50.

LIVES OF FAMOUS INDIAN CHIEFS FROM COFACHIQUI, THE INDIAN PRINCESS, AND POWHATAN, DOWN TO AND INCLUDING CHIEF JOSEPH AND GERONIMO
Norman Barton Wood
AMS Press, Inc., 1974. Reprint of the 1906 edition. $48.50.

THE MEMOIRS OF CHIEF RED FOX
Chief William Red Fox Cash Asher
A chief tells of the conquest of the American Indian in the wake of an expanding American frontier. Fawcett World Library. Pap. $.95.

*OUR INDIAN HERITAGE: PROFILES OF 12 GREAT LEADERS
C. Fayne Porter
War leaders, religious mystics and visionaries, a political reformer, a scholar, and a "wild man." 228 pp. Chilton Book Co., 1964. Illus. $4.95.

THE PATRIOT CHIEFS: A CHRONICLE OF AMERICAN INDIAN RESISTENCE
Alvin M. Josephy, Jr.
Viking Press, 1961. Cloth, $7.50; Pap. $1.00.

*RED CHIEFS AND WHITE CHALLENGERS
J. J. Myers
Washington Square Press, 1972. Pap. $1.25. Ages 16 and up.

LITERATURE

AMERICAN ETHNOLOGICAL SOCIETY PUBLICATIONS
Franz Boas, et al, Editors
Amerind texts edited by Franz Boas, Edward Sapir, Ruth Bunzel, and others. Tribes include Fox, Wishram, Haida, Maidu, Ojibway, Kickapoo, Tlingit, and others. AMS Press. Reprint of the 1907-1937 editions. Volumes 1-17, $275.00.

*AMERICAN INDIAN AUTHORS FOR YOUNG READERS
Mary Gloyne Byler, Editor
A bibliography of selected children's books and materials such as records by American Indians and Eskimos, including oral literature for story telling. An introductory essay evaluates the hundreds of children's books written by non-Indians about Indians and explains the misrepresentation of Indian cultures. 26 pp. Interbook Incorporated, 1973. Pap. $1.00.

AMERICAN INDIAN IN ENGLISH LITERATURE OF THE EIGHTEENTH CENTURY
Benjamin Hezekiah Bissell
223 pp. Shoe String Press, 1968. Reprint of the 1925 edition. $8.00.

AMERICAN INDIAN AND ESKIMO AUTHORS

Arlene Hirschfelder, Editor
Bibliography of 389 titles by American Indian and Eskimo authors form 106 tribes. 112 pp. Interbook Incorporated, 1973. Pap. $4.00.

THE AMERICAN INDIAN: THE FIRST VICTIM

Jay David, Editor
A collection of 27 selections, 9 narratives, autobiography, poems, fiction, and essays' written almost entirely by American Indians. William Morrow & Co., 1972. Pap. $2.25.

THE AMERICAN INDIAN READER: CURRENT AFFAIRS

J. Henry, Editor
An anthology of writings concerned with the current situation and relationship between the Indians and the government of the United States. Indian Historian, 1974. Pap. $4.00.

THE AMERICAN INDIAN READER: LITERATURE

An anthology of writings representative of American Indian literature, including poets and story tellers. Indian Historian, 1972. Pap. $4.00.

THE AMERICAN INDIAN SPEAKS

John R. Milton, Editor
Poetry, fiction, art, music, and religion of the American Indian in the 20th century. 194pp. University of South Dakota Press, 1969. Illus. Pap. $5.00.

BIBLIOGRAPHY OF NONPRINT INSTRUCTIONAL MATERIALS ON THE AMERICAN INDIAN

R. Irwin Goodman
A bibliography of every known audiovisual aid available on America's Indians: motion pictures, study prints, maps, charts, filmstrips, and recordings. 221 pp. Brigham Young University Press, 1972. Pap. $2.95.

BOOKS ABOUT INDIANS

Catalog of selected books of all publishers, including most areas, with annotations. 96 pp. Museum of the American Indian, 1974. $.75.

FOUR MASTERWORKS OF AMERICAN INDIAN LITERATURE

John Bierhorst, Editor
The Aztec myth of Quetzalcoatl, the Iroquois Ritual of Condolence, the Mayan epic prophecy Cuceb, and the Night Chant of the Navajo. Farrar, Straus and Giroux, Inc., 1974. Cloth, $10.95; Pap. $4.50.

A GUIDE TO MANUSCRIPTS RELATING TO THE AMERICAN INDIAN IN THE LIBRARY OF THE AMERICAN PHILOSOPHICAL SOCIETY

John F. Freeman and Murphy D. Smith
American Philosophical Society, 1966. $7.50.

HEATHER FLOWER: AND OTHER INDIAN STORIES OF LONG ISLAND

Verne Dyson
Kennikat Press, 1968. Illus. $3.50.

THE INDEX TO LITERATURE ON THE AMERICAN INDIAN: 1970

Jeanette Henry, Editor
A listing of books and articles published during the year, alphabetically indexed by author and subject. Indian Historian, 1972. Pap. $10.00.

THE INDEX TO LITERATURE ON THE AMERICAN INDIAN: 1971

Jeanette Henry, Editor
A listing of books and articles published during the year. Indian Historian, 1972. Pap. $10.00.

THE INDEX TO LITERATURE ON THE AMERICAN INDIAN: 1972

Jeanette Henry, Editor
A listing of books and articles published during the year. Indian Historian, 1974. Pap. $10.00.

INDEX TO LITERATURE ON THE AMERICAN INDIAN: 1973

Jeanette Henry, Editor
A listing of books and articles published during the year. Indian Historian, 1974. Pap. $10.00.

INDIAN HERITAGE, INDIAN PRIDE: STORIES THAT TOUCHED MY LIFE

Jimalee Burton
160 pp. University of Oklahoma Press. Illus. $12.50.

THE INDIAN HISTORIAN

A periodical of history, literature, poetry, book reviews, and Indian culture. Indian Historian. Pap. $1.40.

THE INDIAN IN AMERICAN LITERATURE

Albert Keiser
312 pp. Octagon Books, 1970. Reprint of the 1933 edition. $12.00.

INDIAN JOURNALS
Allen Ginsberg
City Lights Books, 1970. Cloth, $6.50; Pap.
$3.00.

*INDIAN LEGENDS OF THE PACIFIC NORTHWEST
E. E. Clark
University of California Press, 1953. Pap.
$2.45. Ages 16 and up.

INDIAN STORY AND SONG FROM NORTH AMERICA
Alice Cunningham Fletcher
AMS Press, Inc., 1970. Reprint of the 1900
edition. $5.50.

*INDIAN TALES
Jaime de Angulo
Folk tales of the American Indians collected and
retold. Hill & Wang, 1962. Illus. Ages 10-15.
Cloth, $4.50; Pap. $2.65.

INDIAN TALES OF NORTH AMERICA: ANTHOLOGY FOR THE ADULT READER
T. P. Coffin
University of Texas Press, 1961. Pap. $4.00.

THE INDIANS AND ESKIMOS OF NORTH AMERICA: A BIBLIOGRAPHY OF BOOKS IN PRINT
J. W. Marken
University of South Dakota Press, 1973. Pap.
$5.00.

INDIANS OF THE UNITED STATES AND CANADA: A BIBLIOGRAPHY
Dwight L. Smith, Editor
1771 abstracts of articles selected from two
decades of serial publications in the United
States and abroad. 500 pp. Clio Press, 1974.
$40.00.

INLAND WHALE: NINE STORIES TOLD FROM CALIFORNIA INDIAN LEGENDS
T. Kroeber
Peter Smith Publishers. $4.00.

LIBRARY OF ABORIGINAL AMERICAN LITERATURE
Daniel G. Brinton, Editor
Numbers 1-8. AMS Press, 1974. Reprint of the
1882-1890 edition. $60.00; Per No. $8.00.

THE LITERATURE OF AMERICAN ABORIGINAL LANGUAGES

H. E. Ludewig
Kraus Reprint Co. Reprint of the 1858 edition.
$13.00.

LITERATURE OF THE AMERICAN INDIAN
Thomas E. Sanders and Walter W. Peek
An anthology of Indian myths, poems, oratory,
laws, rituals, and autobiography. Macmillan
Publishing Co. $10.95.

THE RED MAN IN THE NEW WORLD DRAMA
J. C. Wise and V. Deloria, Jr.
Macmillan Publishing Co., Inc., 1971. $8.95.

TEXTBOOKS AND THE AMERICAN INDIAN
Jeanette Henry, Editor
An evaluation of 176 books and their in-
terpretation of the American Indian. Indian
Historian, 1969. Pap. $5.00.

THE WAY: AN ANTHOLOGY OF AMERICAN INDIAN LITERATURE
Stan Steiner and Shirley Hill Witt, Editors
Speeches of the great chiefs to the manifestos of
the "New Indians" of modern America.
Vintage Press. $2.45.

MUSIC

*AMERICAN INDIANS SING
C. Hoffmann
John Day Publishing Co., 1967. Illus. $6.27.
Below college level.

AMERICAN RHYTHM: STUDIES AND REEXPRESSIONS OF AMER-INDIAN SONGS
Mary Hunter Austin
A study of the fusion of Amerind poetry and the
natural response to rhythms, which are
manifested in dance. Cooper Square Publishers,
1971. Reprint of the 1930 edition. $6.00.

FRANCES DENSMORE AND AMERICAN INDIAN MUSIC
Charles Hofmann
127 pp. Museum of the American Indian, 1968.
Illus. $5.00.

*INDIAN MUSIC MAKERS
Robert Hofsinde

Material on Indian songs and musical instruments. 96 pp. William Morrow & Co., 1967. Illus. Ages 8-12. $3.95.

INDIAN STORY AND SONG FROM NORTH AMERICA
Alice Cunningham Fletcher
126 pp. JOhnson Reprint, 1970. Reprint of the 1900 edition. $7.75.

THE MAGIC WORLD: AMERICAN INDIAN SONGS AND POEMS
William Brandon, Editor
Representing the literature of the Indian in magic legends, songs, tales, and myth-cycles. William Morrow & Co., 1972. Cloth, $6.00; Pap. $2.50.

MUSIC OF THE AMERICAS: AN ILLUSTRATED MUSIC ETHNOLOGY OF THE ESKIMO AND AMERICAN INDIAN PEOPLES
Paul Collaer
207 pp. Praeger Pubs., 1973. $25.00. 125 photos.

NORTH AMERICAN INDIAN MUSIC STYLES
B. Nettl
university of Texas Press, 1954. Pap. $2.50.

A STUDY OF INDIAN MUSIC
F. Densmore
Shorey Publications. Reprint of the 1941 edition. Pap. $1.50.

NATIONALISM

AWAKENING MINORITIES: AMERICAN INDIANS, MEXICAN AMERICANS, PUERTO RICANS
John R. Howard, Editor
Partial minority groups submerged below the threshhold of national awareness, 191 pp. Transaction Books, 1972. Cloth, $7.95; Pap. $3.45.

AN INDIAN CANNAN: ISAAC McCOY AND THE VISION OF AN INDIAN STATE
George A. Schultz
230 pp. University of Oklahoma Press; 1972. illus. $8.95.

THE INDIAN'S SIDE OF THE INDIAN QUESTION
William Barrows
Books for Libraries, Inc., 1972. Reprint of the 1887 edition. $12.25.

SEARCH FOR AN AMERICAN INDIAN IDENTITY: MODERN PAN-INDIAN MOVEMENTS
Hazel W. Hertzberg
Syracuse University Press, 1971. $12.00.

THE SOUL OF THE INDIAN
Charles Alexander Eastman
170 pp. Johnson Reprint Corporation. Reprint of the 1911 edition. $10.50.

TEACHINGS FROM THE AMERICAN EARTH: PERSPECTIVES ON THE RELIGION, PHILOSOPHY AND SPIRITUALITY OF THE AMERICAN INDIAN
Dennis and Barbara Tedlock
Liveright Publishing Corp., 1975. Cloth, $9.95; Pap. $3.45.

POETRY

AMERICAN INDIAN POETRY: AN ANTHOLOGY OF SONGS AND CHANTS
George W. Cronyn
Liveright Publishing Corp., 1970. Cloth. $7.95; Pap. $2.95.

AMERICAN INDIAN PROSE AND POETRY
Margot Astrov
G. P. Putnam's Sons, 1962. Pap. $2.45.

AMERICAN INDIAN PROSE AND POETRY: WE WAIT IN DARKNESS
Gloria Levitas, et al, Editors
Legends, chants, songs and prose. G. P. Putnam's Sons, 1974. Cloth. $7.95; Pap. $2.95.

ARROWS FOUR: PROSE AND POETRY BY YOUNG AMERICAN INDIANS
T. D. Allen, Editor
Washington Square Press, 1974. Pap. $.95.

COME TO POWER—11 CONTEMPORARY AMERICAN INDIAN POETS
Dick Lourie, ed.
The Crossing Press, 1973. Cloth, $7.95; Pap. $3.95.

FOUR INDIAN POETS
P. G. Allen, et al
University of South Dakota Press, 1974. Pap.
$1.95.

*THE SKY CLEARS: POETRY OF THE AMERICAN INDIANS
A. Grove Day
204 pp. University of Nebraska Press, 1964.
Pap. $2.45. Below college level.

*IN THE TRAIL OF THE WIND: AMERICAN INDIAN POEMS AND RITUAL ORATIONS
John Bierhorst, Editor
Songs, prayers, chants, dreams, and orations
from over forty languages representing tribes of
North and South America. 224 pp. Farrar,
Straus and Giroux, 1971. Illus. Cloth, $4.95;
Pap. $2.45. Age 12 up.

*THE TREES STAND SHINING: POETRY OF THE NORTH AMERICAN INDIANS
Hettie Jones, Editor
32 poems, originally songs which reflect the
Indians' respect for and harmony with nature.
32 pp. Dell Publishing Co., 1971. Illus. Ages
8-12. $4.95.

THE WINGED SERPENT: AN ANTHOLOGY OF AMERICAN INDIAN PROSE AND POETRY
Margot Astrov, Editor
American Indian poetic thought. Fawcett
World Library. Pap. $1.25.

RED-WHITE RELATIONS

AMERICAN INDIAN AND WHITE RELATIONS TO 1830
William Nelson Fenton
Russell and Russell, 1971. Reprint of the 1957
edition. $10.00.

CAN THE RED MAN HELP THE WHITE MAN?
Sylvester M. Morey, Editor
A report of the first conference with American
Indians held by officials of the Myrin Institute,
Denver. Waldorf Press. Pap. $1.95.

A CENTURY OF DISHONOR
Helen Hunt Jackson
A presentation of the white man's violations of

his treaties with the Indians. 528 pp. Ross &
Haines, Inc. $10.00.

INDIAN-AMERICANS: UNITY AND DIVERSITY
Murray L. Wax
Focuses on the interactions between the native
peoples of the Americas and the white invaders
from the time of Cortez to the present. 236 pp.
Prentice-Hall, Inc., 1971. Cloth, $6.40; Pap.
$2.95.

THE INDIAN AND THE WHITE MAN
Wilcomb E. Washburn
Documents relations from Columbus to the
American Indian Conference of 1961.
Doubleday & Co. Pap. $2.95.

INDIAN AND THE WHITE MAN IN CONNECTICUT
C. Whipple
Berkshire Traveller Press, 1972. Pap. $2.95.

THE INDIAN AND THE WHITE MAN IN MASSACHUSETTS AND RHODE ISLAND
C. Whipple
Bershire Traveller Press, 1973. Pap. $3.50.

THE INDIAN IN RELATION TO THE WHITE POPULATION OF THE UNITED STATES
Fayette Avery McKenzie
117 pp. Burt Franklin Publishers. Reprint of the
1908 edition. $11.00.

INDIAN-WHITE RELATIONS: A PERSISTENT PARADOX
Jane F. Smith and Robert M. Kvasnicka,
Editors
Focuses on resources for Indian historica
research in the National Archives and
elsewhere, as well as on facets of Indian-white
relations. Discusses Indian assimilation in the
nineteenth century, the reservation policy, and
some aspects of twentieth century Indian policy.
354 pp. Illus. Howard University Press, 1976
$15.00.

INDIANS AND PIONEERS
Grant Foreman
The forces of the Indians, the pioneers, and the
military in the Mississippi River Valley during
the U.S. westward expansion. 300 pp.
University of Oklahoma Press, 1975. $8.95.

JOHN STUART AND THE SOUTHERN COLONIAL FRONTIER: A STUDY OF INDIAN RELATIONS, WAR, TRADE, AND LAND PROBLEMS IN THE SOUTHERN WILDERNESS
John R. Alden
384 pp. Gordian Press, 1966. Reprint of the 1944 edition. $10.00.

OUR BROTHER'S KEEPER: THE INDIAN IN WHITE AMERICA
E. S. Cahn, Editor
New American Library, 1969. Pap. $3.95.

RED BROTHER
R. Baker
George Wahr Publishing Co., Reprint of the 1927 edition. $1.50.

THE RED MAN AND THE WHITE MAN IN NORTH AMERICA FROM ITS DISCOVERY TO THE PRESENT TIME
George E. Ellis
Reviews Indian origins, population, environment, colonial relations, missionary efforts, and peace treaties with the United States government. 642 pp. August M. Kelley Publishers. Reprint of the 1882 edition. $17.50.

RED MEN CALLING ON THE GREAT WHITE FATHER
Katharine C. Turner
236 pp. University of Oklahoma Press. Reprint of the 1951 edition. Illus. $7.95.

*WHITE CAPTIVE OF THE SIOUX
M. Miller
Holt, Rinehart, and Winston, 1952. Illus. $2.50. Ages 10 to 14.

WHITE INTO RED: A STUDY OF THE ASSIMILATION OF WHITE PERSONS CAPTURED BY INDIANS
J. Norman Heard
189 pp. Scarecrow Press, 1973. Illus. $7.00.

REFERENCE

REFERENCE ENCYCLOPEDIA OF THE AMERICAN INDIAN
Barry Klein and Dan Icolari, Editors
Volume I — Lists Government Agencies, associations and organizations, museums displaying Indian artifacts, reservations and tribal councils, special library collections, craft shops, audio-visual aids, and a complete bibliography of in-print books. Each listing is fully annotated and listed alphabetically and alpha-geographically. 550 pp. 1974. $15.00 Volume II — Contains a biography of over 2,000 prominent Indians and non-Indians who are active in Indian Affairs. 300 pp. 1974. $15.00. Volumes published by Todd Publications, 11 Third St., Rye, N. Y. 10580.

RELIGION

AMERICAN INDIAN RELIGIONS
J. M. Hurdy
Sherbourne Press, 1971. Pap. $2.50.

THE CATHOLIC INDIAN MISSIONS IN MAINE
Sister Mary Celeste Leger
AMS Press, Inc. Reprint of the 1929 edition. $8.00.

CHURCH, STATE, AND THE AMERICAN INDIANS
R. P. Beaver
Concordia Publishing House, 1966. $6.75.

GOVERNMENT AND RELIGION OF THE VIRGINIA INDIANS
Samuel Rivers Hendren
58 pp. Johnson Reprint, 1973. Reprint of the 1895 edition. Pap. $6.25.

HISTORICAL ACCOUNT OF THE DOINGS AND SUFFERINGS OF THE CHRISTIAN INDIANS IN NEW ENGLAND IN THE YEARS 1675, 1676, AND 1677
D. Gookin
Arno Press, 1972. Reprint of the 1836 edition. $10.00.

HISTORY OF THE CATHOLIC MISSIONS AMONG THE INDIAN TRIBES OF THE UNITED STATES, 1529 TO 1854
John Dawson Shea
AMS Press, Inc., Reprint of the 1855 edition. $17.50.

HISTORY OF THE CATHOLIC MISSIONS AMONG THE INDIAN TRIBES OF THE· UNITED STATES
J. G. Shea
Arno Press. Reprint of the 1857 edition. $17.50.

AN INDIAN CANAAN: ISSAC McCOY AND THE VISION OF AN INDIAN STATE
George A. Schultz
A Baptist missionary in the Old Northwest who

wanted to establish an organized political Indian state offering self-government, educational opportunities, and economic assistance for all. 230 pp. University of Oklahoma Press, 1975. Illus. Pap. $3.95.

ON THE GLEAMING WAY: NAVAJOS, EASTERN PUEBLOS, ZUNIS, HOPIS, APACHES AND THEIR LAND: AND THEIR MEANING TO THE WORLD
John Collier
Spiritual survival of the Indian. 163 pp. Swallow Press, 1962. Illus. Pap. $2.25.

RED MAN'S RELIGION: BELIEFS AND PRACTICES OF THE INDIANS NORTH OF MEXICO
R. M. Underhill
University of Chicago Press, 1965. Cloth, $10.00; Pap. $2.95.

SLAVERY

INDIAN SLAVE A TRADE IN THE SOUTHWEST: A STUDY OF SLAVE-TAKING AND THE TRAFFIC IN INDIAN CAPTIVES FROM 1700-1935
L. R. Bailey
The story of the buying and selling of Apache, Ute, Comanche, Paiute, and Navajo Indians. Westernlore Press, 1966. Illus. $7.95.

INDIAN SLAVERY IN COLONIAL TIMES WITHIN THE PRESENT LIMITS OF THE UNITED STATES
Almon Wheeler Lauber
Discusses in detail the enslavement of Indians by Indians, by the Spaniards, the French and the English during the colonial period. Describes methods of enslavement, the slave trade, treatment of slaves and the eventual decline of the practice. 352 pp. Corner House Publishers, 1974. Reprint of the 1913 edition of Columbia University. $12.50.

SLAVEHOLDING INDIANS, 3 VOLS.
A. H. Abel
Scholarly Press, 1925. Reprint of the 1919 edition. $39.00 set.

WARS

THE AMERICAN INDIAN AS PAR-

TICIPANT IN THE CIVIL WAR
Annie Heloise Abel
403 pp. Johnson Reprint, 1970. Reprint of the 1919 edition. $14.75.

CRIMSON DESERT: INDIAN WARS OF THE AMERICAN SOUTHWEST
O. B. Faulk
250 pp. Oxford UNiversity Press, 1974. $8.95.

FIGHTING INDIANS OF THE WEST
D. Brown
Ballantine Books, 1974. Pap. $2.00.

*THE FIRST BOOK OF THE INDIAN WARS
Richard B. Morris
History of the strife between the Indians and the early American settlers in the area east of the Mississippi River through the 1780's. 86 pp. Franklin Watts, Inc., 1959. Illus. Ages 9-12. $3.90.

FOLLOWING THE INDIAN WARS: THE STORY OF THE NEWSPAPER CORRESPONDENTS AMONG THE INDIAN CAMPAIGNERS
Oliver Knight
348 pp. University of Oklahoma Press, 1960. Illus. $8.95.

FRONTIER REGULARS: THE UNITED STATES ARMY AND THE INDIAN, EIGHTEEN SIXTY-SIX TO EIGHTEEN NINETY
R. M. Utley
Macmillan Publishing Co., Inc., 1974. $12.95.

HISTORY OF THE EARLY SETTLEMENT AND INDIAN WARS OF WESTERN VIRGINIA
Wills DeHass
An early history of what is now West Virginia. McClain Printing Co.; 1960. Reprint of the 1851 edition. $10.00.

HISTORY OF THE INDIAN WARS
Samuel Penhallow
The indian Wars of New England from 1703-1726. This edition is an exact copy of the 1924 facsimile reprint of the first edition of 1726. 208 pp. Corner House Publishers, 1974. $8.50.

THE HISTORY OF THE INDIAN WARS IN NEW ENGLAND FROM THE FIRST SETTLEMENT TO THE TERMINATION OF THE WAR WITH KING PHILLIP IN 1677
William Hubbard, 1621-1704

The first history of the intense conflicts between New England tribes and the colonists. 628 pp. 2 volumes in 1. Burt Franklin Publishers, 1971. Reprint of the 1865 edition. $23.50.

THE HISTORY OF THE WARS OF NEW ENGLAND WITH THE EASTERN INDIANS
S. Penhallow
Kraus Reprint Co. Reprint of the 1859 edition. $10.00.

INDIAN BATTLES AND SKIRMISHES ON THE AMERICAN FRONTIER
J. P. Peters
Arno Press, 1966. $27.50.

INDIAN FIGHTS: NEW FACTS ON SEVEN ENCOUNTERS
J. W. Vaughn
250 pp. University of Oklahoma Press, 1966. Illus. $6.95.

THE INDIAN UPRISING IN LOWER CALIFORNIA, 1734-1737
Sigismundo Taraval
AMS Press, 1974. Reprint of the 1931 edition. $12.00.

INDIAN WAR OF EIGHTEEN SIXTY-FOUR
Captain Eugene F. Ware
483 pp. University of Nebraska Press, 1963. Pap. $3.75.

*INDIAN WARRIORS AND THEIR WEAPONS
Robert Hofsinde
Describes the war dress, weapons, and fighting methods of seven tribes. 96 pp. William Morrow & Co., 1965. Illus. Ages 8-12. $3.78.

THE INDIAN WARS IN NORTH CAROLINA, 1663 TO 1763.
E. L. Lee
North Carolina Office of Archives and History, 1968. Pap. $.50.

INDIAN WARS OF THE PACIFIC NORTHWEST
Ray Glassley
Cayuse, Rogue River, Yakima, Coeur d'Alene, Modoc, Nez Perce, Bannock, Sheepeater. 286 pp. Binford & Mort, 1972. Illus. $6.95.

INDIAN WARS OF TEXAS
Mildred P. Mayhall
308 pp. Texian Press, 1975. Illus. $7.50.

INDIAN WARS OF THE WEST, CONTAINING BIOGRAPHICAL SKETCHES OF THOSE PIONEERS WHO HEADED THE WESTERN SETTLERS IN REPELLING THE ATTACKS OF THE SAVAGES
T. Flint
Arno Press, 1971. Reprint of the 1833 edition. $11.00.

MASSACRES OF THE MOUNTAINS: A HISTORY OF INDIAN WARS OF THE FAR WEST
J. P. Dunn
Peter Smith Publishers. $5.50.

MEMOIR OF INDIAN WARS AND OTHER OCCURRENCES
J. Stuart
Arno Press, 1970. Reprint of the 1833 edition. $6.00.

NOTES ON THE SETTLEMENT AND INDIAN WARS
Joseph Doddridge
Describes the settlement and Indian wars of the western parts of Virginia and Pennsylvania from 1763 to 1783. McClain Printing Co., 1960. Reprint of the 1824 edition. $9.00.

NOTES ON THE SETTLEMENT AND INDIAN WARS OF THE WESTERN PARTS OF VIRGINIA AND PENNSYLVANIA FROM 1763-1783
Joseph Doddridge, 1769-1826
Contains chapters on Indian remains, origin of the Indians, dress of the Indians, and Indian modes of warfare. 331 pp. Burt Franklin Publishers, 1973. Reprint of the 1876 edition. $16.50.

A REPORT TO THE SECRETARY OF WAR OF THE UNITED STATES ON INDIAN AFFAIRS
J. A. Morse
Scholarly Press, 1972. Reprint of the 1822 edition. $19.50.

THE SAND CREEK MASSACRE
Stan Hoig
217 pp. University of Oklahoma Press, 1974. Reprint of the 1961 edition. Illus. Cloth, $5.25; Pap. $2.95.

SELECTION OF SOME OF THE MOST INTERESTING NARRATIVES OF OUTRAGES COMMITTED BY THE INDIANS IN THEIR WARS WITH THE

WHITE PEOPLE
A. Loudon
Arno Press, 1971. Reprint of the 1808 edition. $30.00.

SOUTHERN INDIANS IN THE AMERICAN REVOLUTION
James H. O'Donnell
188 pp. University of Tennessee Press, 1973. $8.50.

*THE UNITED STATES IN THE INDIAN WARS
Don Lawson
The 300 year history of the "Indian Problem." 160 pp. Thomas Y. Crowell, Co., 1975. Illus. Age 12 up. $6.95.

WILD LIFE ON THE PLAINS AND HORRORS OF INDIAN WARFARE
G. A. Custer
Arno Press. Reprint of the 1891 edition. $20.50.

TRIBES

ACOMA

THE ACOMA INDIANS
Leslie A. White
A paper from the Bureau of American ethnology, including Acoma ceremonial masks for the first time in full color. 238 pp. 32 plates. Rio Grande Press, 1975. Reprint of the 1932 edition. Illus. $15.00.

MUSIC OF ACOMA, ISLETA, COCHITI AND ZUNI PUEBLOS
F. Densmore
Da Capo Press, 1972. Reprint of the 1957 edition. $8.95.

ALGONQUIAN

ALGONQUIAN LEGENDS OF NEW ENGLAND
C. G. Leland
Singing Tree Press, 1968. Reprint of the 1884 edition. $12.50.

THE ALGONQUIANS, VOL I

F. Roy Johnson
A pre-history of the Algonquian Indians of Coastal Virginia and North Carolina. 112 pp. Johnson Pub. Co., 1972. $6.50.

THE ALGONQUIANS, VOL. II
F. Roy Johnson
This book relates the history and traditions of the Algonquians, plus the adventures of the Spanish and French explorers, Raleigh's explorers and colonists, the Lost Colonists and decaying Indian tribes. 240 pp. Johnson Publishing Co., 1972. $8.50.

POWHATAN
Kay Bonner Nee
The seventeenth-century Algonquian leader, father of Pocahontas, who befriended and fought the settlers of Jamestown Colony, Virginia. 41 pp. Dillon Press. $4.95.

APACHE

ATHROPOLOGICAL REPORT ON THE JICARILLA APACHE IN NEW MEXICO AND OKLAHOMA, 1540 TO 1898
Charles C. DiPeso
430 pp. Clearwater Publishing Co., 1974. $78.15.

APACHE INDIANS: A STUDY OF THE APACHE INDIANS: "TONTO" AND WESTERN APACHE INDIANS, 2 VOLS.
Albert H. Schroeder
325 pp. Garland Publishing, Inc., 1974. $21.00 each.

APACHE INDIANS: JICARILLA APACHE TRIBE: HISTORICAL MATERIALS, 1540 TO 1887
251 pp. Garland Publishing, Inc., 1974. $21.00.

APACHE INDIANS VOLUME 2: *The Ascarate Grant,* Jocelyn J. Bowden;
An Ethnological Study of Torugas, New Mexico, Alan J. Oppenheimer.
361 pp. Garland Publishing, 1974. $21.00.

APACHE INDIANS VOLUME 3 INCLUDING: *Aboriginal Use and Occupation of Certain Lands by Tigua, Manso, and Suma Indians,* Rex E. Gerald;
History and Administration of the Tigua Indians of Ysleta Del Sur During the Spanish

Colonial Period, Myra Ellen Jenkins,
*Apache Ethnohistory: Government Land, and
Indian Policy Relative to Lipan, Mescalero and
Tigua Indians.*
358 pp. Garland Publishing, 1974. $21.00.

**APACHE INDIANS VOLUME 5, IN-
CLUDING:** *A Study of Western Apache
Indians, 1846-86,* Averan B Bender;
*Environment and Ecology in the "Northern
Tonto" Claim Area,* Homer Aschmann
260 pp. Garland Publishing Co., 1974. $21.00.

**APACHE INDIANS VOLUME 6, IN-
CLUDING:** *Environment, Settlement and
Land Use in the Jicarilla Apache Claim Area,* B.
L. Gordon, et al; *Indian Land Rights in the
American Southwest in the Jicarilla Apache
Area,* Donald C. Cutter. 286 pp. Garland
Publishing Co., 1974. $21.00.

**THE APACHE INDIANS VOLUME 8 IN-
CLUDING:** *The Jicarilla Apache Indians: A
History 1598 to 1888,* Alfred B. Thomas;
*Mode of Life and Tribal Lands of the Jicarilla
Apache During the Spanish-American Period
1601 to 1849,* Elizabeth V. Atwater;
*Mode of Life and Aboriginal Tribal Lands of
the Jicarilla Apache,* Jean W. Nelson. 4 Vols.
262 pp. Garland Publishing Co., 1974. $21.00.

**APACHE INDIANS VOLUME 9, IN-
CLUDING:**
*A Study of the Jicarilla Apache Indians 1846-
1887,* Averan B. Bender. 210 pp. Garland
Publishing Co., 1974. $21.00.

**APACHE INDIANS VOLUME 10, IN-
CLUDING:** *Ethnohistorica Analysis of
Documents Relating to the Apache Indians of
Texas,* Verne F.Ray;
Lipan and Mescalero Apache in Texas,
Morris E. Opler
441 pp. Garland Publishing Co., 1974. $21.00.

**APACHE INDIANS VOLUME 11, IN-
CLUDING:** *The Mescalero Apache 1653 to
1874,* Alfred B. Thomas;
*A Study of Mescalero Apache Indians 1846 to
1880,* Averam B. Bender.
310 pp. Garland Publishing, 1974. $21.00.

**APACHE INDIANS VOLUME 12, IN-
CLUDING:** *Mescalero Apache Subsistence
Patterns and Socio-Political Organization,*
Harry W. Basehaat; *Findings of Fact, and
Opinion,* The Indian Claims Commission.

323 pp. Garland Publishing Co., 1974. $21.00.

***THE APACHE INDIANS, RAIDERS OF
THE SOUTHWEST**
Sonia Bleeker
160 pp. William Morrow and Co., 1951. Illus.
$3.94. Ages 9 to 12.

APACHE INDIANS OF NEW MEXICO
*12 photos with explanatory text, background
information and bibliography.* Museum of New
Mexico Press, 1974. $1.00.

APACHE, NAVAJO, AND SPANIARD
Jack D. Forbes
340 pp. University of Oklahoma Press, 1971.
Reprint of the 1960 edition. Illus. Cloth, $7.95;
Pap. $2.95.

**APACHEAN CULTURE, HISTORY AND
ETHNOLOGY**
Keith H. Basso and Morris Opler, Editors
Fourteen contributors highlighting the treatment of material on southern Athapaskan
cultures. 168 pp. University of Arizona Press,
1971. Pap. $6.95.

*THE APACHES
M. L. Israel
Melmont Pubs., 1959. $4.50. Ages 6 to 10.

**ETHNOHISTORICAL ANALYSIS OF
DOCUMENTS RELATING TO THE
APACHE INDIANS OF TEXAS, 1772 TO
1860**
Verne F. Ray
270 pp. Clearwater Publishing co., 1973.
$52.55.

**ETHNOHISTORICAL REPORT, WITH
SUPPORTING EXHIBITS, RELATING TO
THE LIPAN APACHE TRIBE AND
MESCALERO APACHE TRIBE IN TEXAS
AND NEW MEXICO**
Kenneth F. Neighbours
83 pp. Clearwater Publishing Co., 1973. $22.60.

**AN ETHNOHISTORICAL STUDY OF
JICARILLA APACHE INDIANS IN NEW
MEXICO AND ARIZONA, 1846 TO 1887**
Averam B. Bender
199 pp. Clearwater Publishing Co., 1973.
$41.20.

**FORMAL EDUCATION AND CULTURE
CHANGE: A MODERN APACHE INDIAN
COMMUNITY AND GOVERNMENT**

EDUCATION PROGRAMS
Edward A. Parmee
Points up the problem arising when changes are imposed upon people who are unprepared to meet the consequences. 132 pp. University of Arizona Press, 1968. $5.00.

GERONIMO
Charles Morrow Wilson
The story of the famed Apache warrior who died in 1909 on a reservation. 74 pp. Dillon Press. $4.95.

GERONIMO: A BIOGRAPHY
Alexander B. Adams
G. P. Putnam's Sons, 1971. Illus. $8.95.

*GERONIMO: THE FIGHTING APACHE
Ronald Syme
The biography of one of the great American Indian chieftains. 96 pp. William Morrow & Co., 1975. Illus. $4.95. Ages 8-12.

GERONIMO'S STORY OF HIS LIFE
S. M. Barret, editor
The autobiography of the famed Apache warrior as dictated in his later years to S. M. Barret. Discusses his reasons for the uprisings he led, Apache folklore, religious ceremonies and festivals. 216 pp. Corner House Publisher, 1974. Illus. Reprint of the 1906 edition. $9.00.

HISTORICAL AND DOCUMENTARY EVIDENCE CONCERNING THE JICARILLA APACHE TRIBE OF THE JICARILLA INDIAN RESERVATION IN NEW MEXICO, 1849-1870
Stanfor Research Institute
108 pp. Clearwater Publishing Co., 1973. $26.60.

A HISTORY OF THE APACHE INDIANS IN NEW MEXICO, TEXAS, AND MEXICO, 1540 TO 1800
Albert H. Schroeder
973 pp. Clearwater Publishing Co., 1973. $227.70 Six Vols.

INDEH [THE DEAD]: REMINISCENCES OF A NEDNHI APACHE
Eve Ball and Ace Daklugie
Apache religion, witchcraft, pride, peyote, humor, battles, family life, and death. 400 pp. Swallow Press, 1975. Photos. $15.00.

THE JICARILLA APACHE INDIANS IN NEW MEXICO AND COLORADO, A

HISTORY
Alfred B. Thomas
156 pp. Clearwater Publishing Co., 1973. $34.30.

*JICARILLA APACHES
Gertrude Van Roekel
Education that has changed the Apache way of life. The Naylor Co. Photos. Age 13 up. $6.95.

THE LIPAN AND MESCALERO APACHE IN TEXAS, 1650 TO 1800'S
Morris E. Opler
170 pp. Clearwater Publishing Co., 1973. $36.55.

THE MARVELOUS COUNTRY
Samuel W. Cozzens
An account of Cochise and the Apaches. 532 pp. Ross & Haines, Inc. Reprint of the 1874 edition. Illus. $10.00.

THE MEDICINE MEN OF THE APACHES
John Gregory Bourke
A study of America's "wildest" Indians. 196 pp. Rio Grande Press. Reprint of the 1892 edition. Illus. $15.00.

THE MESCALERO APACHE IN NEW MEXICO AND TEXAS, 1650 TO 1874
Alfred B. Thomas
50 pp. Clearwater Publishing Co., 1973. $17.35.

THE MESCALERO APACHES
C. L. Sonnichsen
303 pp. University of Oklahoma Press, 1973. Reprint of the 1958 edition. Illus. $8.95.

MYTHS AND TALES OF THE CHIRACAHUA APACHE INDIANS
M. E. Opler
Kraus Reprint Co., 1974. Reprint of the 1942 edition. $7.50.

MYTHS AND TALES OF THE JICARILLA APACHE INDIANS
E. M. Opler
Kraus Reprint Co. Reprint of the 1938 edition. $18.00

MYTHS AND TALES OF THE WHITE MOUNTAIN APACHE
G. Goodwin
Kraus Reprint Co. Reprint of the 1939 edition. $10.00.

ON THE BLOODY TRAIL OF GERONIMO

John Bigelow, Jr.
The campaign against the Apache Chief
Geronimo, written by the Lieutenant who led
the Tenth Cavalry. Westernlore Press. illus.
$7.50.

A STUDY OF MESCALERO AND APACHE INDIANS IN NEW MEXICO AND ARIZONA, 1846 TO 1880
Averam B. Bender
Clearwater Publishing Co., 1974. $47.40.

WESTERN APACHE WITCHCRAFT
Keith H. Basso
An ethnographic study describing the beliefs
and ideas associated with witchcraft as shared
"knowledge" that the Apaches have about their
universe. 75 pp. University of Arizona Press.
Pap. $5.95.

YESTERDAY AND TODAY IN THE LIFE OF THE APACHES
Irene Burlison
Dorrance and Co., 1973. $4.95.

ARAPAHO

ARAPAHO-CHEYENNE INDIANS, IN-CLUDING: *Ethnological Report on Cheyenne and Arapaho; Aboriginal Occupation,* Zachary Gussow;*Historical Development of the Arapaho-cheyenne Land Area,* Leroy R. Hafen; *Cheyenne and Arapaho Indians? Historical Background, Social and Economic Conditions,*Arthur A. Ekirch, Jr.; *Findings of Fact, and Opinion;* The Indian Claims. Commission;
199 pp. Garland Publishing Co., 1974. $21.00.

THE ARAPAHOES, OUR PEOPLE
Virginia Cole Trenholm
372 pp. University of Oklahoma Press, 1973.
Reprint of the 1970 edition. Illus. $8.95.

HISTORICAL BACKGROUND OF THE CHEYENNE AND ARAPAHO
Arthur A. Ekirch
45 pp. Clearwater Publishing Co., 1973. $16.55.

ETHNOLOGICAL REPORT ON CHEYENNE AND ARAPAHOE: ABORIGINAL OCCUPATION IN COLORADO, KANSAS, AND WYOMING, 1865

Zachary Gussow
68 pp. Clearwater Publishing Co., 1973. $20.20.

TRADITIONS OF THE ARAPAHO
G. A. Dorsey and A. L. Kroeber
Kraus Reprint Co., 1974. Reprint of the 1903
edition. Pap. $6.25.

BLACKFEET-BLACKFOOT

BLACKFEET AND BUFFALO: MEMORIES OF LIFE AMONG THE INDIAN
J. Willard (Apikuni) Schultz
384 pp. University of Oklahoma Press, 1968.
Reprint of the 1962 edition. Illus. $8.95.

BLACKFEET INDIANS: ETHNOLOGICAL REPORT ON THE BLACKFEET AND GROS VENTRE TRIBES
John C. Ewers
312 pp. Garland Publishing, inc., 1974. $21.00.

THE BLACKFEET: RAIDERS ON THE NORTHWESTERN PLAINS
John C. Ewers
348 pp. University of Oklahoma Press, 1971.
Reprint of the 1958 edition. Illus. $7.95.

BLACKFOOT LODGE TALES
George Bird Grinnell
A collection of Indian myths, legends and
customs in the late 19th century. 310 pp. Corner
House Publishers, 1974. Reprint of the 1892
edition. $9.00.

THE EFFECTS OF WHITE CONTACT UPON BLACKFOOT CULTURE, WITH SPECIAL REFERENCE TO THE ROLE OF THE FUR TRADE
Oscar Lewis
79 pp. University of Washington Press, 1942.
$7.00.

ETHNOLOGICAL REPORT ON THE BLACKFEET AND GROS VENTRE LANDS IN NORTHERN MONTANA, 1888
John C. Ewers
182 pp. Clearwater Publishing Co., 1973.
$38.45.

MATERIAL CULTURE OF THE BLACKFOOT INDIANS
Clark Wissler
AMS Press, Inc., 1974. Reprint of the 1910

edition. $12.50.

MISSION AMONG THE BLACKFEET
Howard L. Harrod
Christian missions, Protestant and Catholic, among the Indians from the 1840's to the present day. 256 pp. University of Oklahoma Press, 1975. illus. Pap. $3.95.

MYTHOLOGY OF THE BLACKFOOT INDIANS
Clark Wissler
AMS Press, 1974. Reprint of the 1908 edition. $11.50.

THE OLD NORTH TRAIL: OR LIFE, LEGENDS, AND RELIGION OF THE BLACKFEET INDIANS
W. McClintock
Peter Smith Publishers. $6.00.

SOCIAL ORGANIZATION AND RITUALISTIC CEREMONIES OF THE BLACKFOOT INDIANS
Clark Wissler
Two parts in one volume. AMS Press, 1974. Reprint of the 1912 edition. $20.00.

CADDOAN

THE CADDO INDIANS IN LOUISIANA AND TEXAS: THEIR HISTORY AND CULTURE
Stuart Omer Landry
60 pp. Clearwater Publishing Co., 1974. Illus. $18.95.

CADDOAN INDIANS VOLUME 1, IN-CLUDING: *The Caddoan Cultural Area: An Archaeological Perspective,* Donald G. Wyckoff; *The Aboriginal Location of the Kadohadacho and Related Indian Tribes,* Stephen Williams;
33 pp. Garland Publishing Co., 1974. $21.00.

CADDOAN INDIANS VOLUME 2, IN-CLUDING: *Historical Locations of Certain Caddoan Tribes;* Robert W. Neuman; *Caddo Treaty of July 1, 1835: The Historical and Anthropological Background and Aftermath,* Charles H. Lange;
316 pp. Garland Publishing Co., 1974. $21.00.

CADDOAN INDIANS VOLUME 3, IN-

CLUDING: *Prehistory of the Caddoan-Speaking Tribes,*
Jack Thomas Hughes.
435 pp. Garland Publishing Co., 1974. $21.00.

CADDOAN INDIANS VOLUME 4, IN-CLUDING: *The Territory of the Caddo Tribe of Oklahoma,* Helen Hornbeck Tanner; *Rebuttal Statement of Helen Hornbeck Tanner to Evidence of Alabama Coushatta Indians and Wichita Tribe of Oklahoma Findings of Fact, and Opinion,* The Indian Claims Commission.
177 Garland Publishing Co., 1974. $21.00.

SOURCE MATERIAL ON THE HISTORY AND ETHNOLOGY OF THE CADDO INDIANS
J. R. Swanton
Scholarly Press. Reprint of the 1911 edition. $19.50.

TRADITIONS OF THE CADDO
George Amos Dorsey
AMS Press, 1974. Reprint of the 1905 edition. $16.50.

CAHUILLA

THE CAHUILLA INDIANS OF THE COLORADO DESERT: ETHNOHISTORY AND PREHISTORY
Lowell John Bean, Editor
The California Indians, the native occupants of Coachella Valley, the historical value of oral tradition, and the early history of the Colorado desert. 73 pp. Ballena Press. Pap. $4.95.

THE CAHUILLA INDIANS: A HISTORY IN SOUTHERN CALIFORNIA
Lucile Hooper
Information on Shamanism, burial customs, naming of children, food, clothing, bows and arrows, pottery, religion, their calendar, and more. 65 pp. Ballena Press. Reprint of the 1920 edition. Pap. $2.95.

CHEROKEE

CHEROKEE CAVALIERS: FORTY YEARS OF CHEROKEE HISTORY AS TOLD IN

THE CORRESPONDENCE OF THE RIDGE-WATIE-BOUDINOT FAMILY
Edward Everett Dale
319 pp. University of Oklahoma Press, 1969. Reprint of the 1939 edition. Illus. $8.95.

CHEROKEE AND CREEK INDIANS, INCLUDING: *Ethnographic Report on Royce Area 79, Docket 275, Chickasaw, Cherokee, Creek,* Charles H. Fairbanks; *Cherokee Treaties,* John G. Goff; *Findings of Fact, and Opinion,* The Indian Claims Commission.
451 pp. Garland Publishing Co., 1974. $21.00.

THE CHEROKEE FRONTIER: CONFLICT AND SURVIVAL, 1740 TO 1762
David H. Corkran
302 pp. university of Oklahoma Press, 1966. Reprint of the 1962 edition. Illus. $8.95.

*THE CHEROKEE, INDIANS OF THE MOUNTAINS
Sonia Bleeker
160 pp. William Morrow and Co., 1952. Illus. $4.25. Ages 9 to 12.

THE CHEROKEE REMOVAL, 1838: AN ENTIRE INDIAN NATION IS FORCED OUT OF ITS HOMELAND
Glen H. Fleischmann
88 pp. Franklin Watts, Inc., 1971. Cloth $3.90; Pap. $1.25.

CHEROKEE TRAGEDY: THE STORY OF THE RIDGE FANILY AND OF THE DECIMATION OF A PEOPLE
Thurman Wilkins
A narrative of the expulsion of the Cherokees from their native Appalachia to Oklahoma in 1835. Macmillan Publishing Co. $10.00.

CHEROKEE WOMAN
Francis M. Daves
Branden Press, 1973. $8.95.

*THE CHEROKEES
M. L. Israel
Melmont Pubs., 1961. $4.50. Ages 6 to 12.

THE CHEROKEES
Grace Steele Woodward
359 pp. University of Oklahoma Press, 1972. Reprint of the 1963 edition. Illus. $7.50.

CHEROKEES OF THE OLD SOUTH: A PEOPLE IN TRANSITION

Henry T. Malone
238 pp. University of Georgia Press, 1956. $5.50.

CHIEF BOWLES AND THE TEXAS CHEROKEES
Mary Whatley Clark
154 pp. University of Oklahoma Press, 1971. Illus. $6.95.

THE CONSTITUTION AND LAWS OF THE CHEROKEE NATION
Scholarly Resource, Inc., 1973. Reprint of the 1893 edition. $40.00.

FIRE AND THE SPIRITS: CHEROKEE LAW FROM CLAN TO COURT
Rennard Strickland
Traces the emergence of the Cherokee legal system from the ancient "spirit" decrees to the fusion of tribal law ways with Anglo-American Law. 350 pp. University of Oklahoma Press, 1975. Illus. $9.95.

GIVE ME THE WIND: A BIOGRAPHICAL NOVEL OF JOHN ROSS, CHIEF OF THE CHEROKEE
J. Jordan
Prentice-Hall, 1973. $6.95.

HISTORY OF THE CHEROKEE INDIANS AND THEIR LEGENDS AND FOLKLORE
E. Starr
Kraus Reprint Co. Reprint of the 1921 edition. $25.00.

THE LAST CHEROKEE WARRIORS
Phillip Steele
The documentation of the lives of Ezekiel Proctor and Ned Christie, who struggled against the power of the government of the United States in an effort to stop the encroaching whites and preserve the Cherokee heritage. 111 pp. Pelican Publishing Co., 1974. Illus. $5.95.

MYTHS OF THE CHEROKEE
James Mooney
Contains Sacred Formulas of the Cherokees. 673 pp. Johnson Publishing Co. $15.00.

RED MEN OF FIRE: A HISTORY OF THE CHEROKEE INDIANS
Irvin M. Peithmann
184 pp. Charles C. Thomas Pubs., 1964. Illus. $6.50.

THE REMOVAL OF THE CHEROKEE NATION: MANIFEST DESTINY OR NATIONAL DISHONOR?

Louis Filler and Allen Guttmann
113 pp. D. C. Heath and Co., 1962. Pap. $2.50.

SEQUOYAH

C. W. Campbell
Born in Tennessee around 1770, created a writing system for the Cherokee language. 74 pp. dillon Press. $4.95.

SE-QUO-YAH [1770-1843], THE AMERICAN CADMUS AND MODERN MOSES. A COMPLETE BIOGRAPHY OF THE GREATEST OF REDMEN, AROUND WHOSE WONDERFUL LIFE HAS BEEN WOVEN THE MANNERS, CUSTOMS AND BELIEFS OF THE EARLY CHEROKEES

George Everett Foster
The story of the inventor of the Cherokee Language. 244 pp. Burt Franklin Publishers, 1972. Reprint of the 1885 edition. $12.50.

SHADOW OF SEQUOYAH: SOCIAL DOCUMENTS OF THE CHEROKEES, 1862-1964

Jack Frederick Kilpatrick and Anna Gritts, Editors
129 pp. University of Oklahoma Press, 1965. $5.95.

A SYMPOSIUM ON CHEROKEE AND IROQUOIS CULTURE

W. Fenton and J. Gulick
Scholarly Press. Reprint of the 1961 edition. $14.50.

TSALI

Denton R. Bedford
The unsung hero of the Cherokee people. Indian Historian, 1972. Pap. $6.00.

*WHEN SHALL THEY REST? THE CHEROKEES' LONG STRUGGLE WITH AMERICA

P. Collier
Holt, Rinehart, and Winston, 1973. $6.95. Below college level.

CHEYENNE

ARAPAHO-CHEYENNE INDIANS, INCLUDING: *Ethnological Report on Cheyenne and Arapaho: Aboriginal Oc-*

cupation, Zachary Gussow; *Historical Development of the Arapaho-Cheyenne Land Area,* Leroy R. Fafen; *Cheyenne and Arapaho Indians: Historical Background, Social and Economic Conditions,* Arthur A. Ekirch, Jr.; *Findings of Fact, and Opinion,* The Indian Claims Commission.
199 pp. Garland Publishing Co., 1974. $21.00.

THE CHEYENNE

G. A. Dorsey
Kraus Reprint Co. 1974. Reprint of the 1905 edition. Pap. $15.00.

CHEYENNE AND SIOUX: THE REMINISCENCES OF FOUR INDIANS AND A WHITE SOLDIER

R. H. Limbaugh and T. B. Marquis
University of the Pacific, 1973. $5.50.

THE CHEYENNE IN PLAINS INDIAN TRADE RELATIONS 1795 TO 1840

Joseph Jablow
110 pp. University of Washington Press, 1951. $5.00.

THE CHEYENNE INDIANS

J. Mooney
Kraus Reprint Co., 1974. Reprint of the 1907 edition. Pap. $3.50.

THE CHEYENNE INDIANS: THE SUN DANCE

George A. Dorsey
A study of an American Indian ceremonial. 286 pp. 24 plates. Rio Grande Press, 1972. Illus. $20.00.

THE CHEYENNE INDIANS, THEIR HISTORY AND WAYS OF LIFE

George B. Grinnell
New Introduction by Mari Sandoz. Photos. Cooper Square Publishers, 1972. Reprint of the 1923 edition. Two Volumes, Cloth, $20.00. University of Nebraska Press, Pap., each volume, $3.00.

THE CHEYENNE WAY: CONFLICT AND CASE LAW IN PRIMITIVE JURISPRUDENCE

Karl N. Llewellyn and E. Adamson Hoebel
360 pp. University of Oklahoma Press, 1967. Reprint of the 1941 edition. Illus. $8.95.

ETHNOLOGICAL REPORT ON CHEYENNE AND ARAPAHOE: ABORIGINAL OCCUPATION IN COLORADO,

KANSAS AND WYOMING, 1865
Zachary Gussow
68 pp. Clearwater Publishing co., 1973. $20.20.

THE FIGHTING CHEYENNES
George Bird Grinnell
453 pp. University of Oklahoma Press, 1971.
Reprint of the 1956 edition. Illus. $8.95.

HISTORICAL BACKGROUND OF THE CHEYENNE AND ARAPAHO
Arthur A. Ekirch
45 pp. Clearwater Publishing Co., 1973. $16.55.

THE SOUTHERN CHEYENNES
Donald J. Berthrong
446 pp. University of Oklahoma Press, 1972.
Reprint of the 1963 edition. Illus. $8.95.

THE SOUTHERN CHEYENNES
Donald J. Berthrong
An account of one of the tribes of the Great Plains, noted for their advanced religious beliefs, tribal government, and fierce defense of lands they considered their own. 456 pp. University of Oklahoma Press, 1975. Illus. Pap. $3.95.

SWEET MEDICINE: THE CONTINUING ROLE OF THE SACRED ARROWS, THE SUN DANCE, AND THE SACRED BUF-FALO HAT IN NORTHERN CHEYENNE HISTORY
Peter J. Powell
935 pp. University of Oklahoma Press, 1969.
Illus. Two volumes. $25.00.

CHICKASAW

THE CHICKASAWS
Arrell M. Gibson
320 pp. University of Oklahoma Press, 1972.
Illus. Cloth $8.95; Pap. $3.95.

THE CONSTITUTION, LAWS, AND TREATIES OF THE CHICKASAWS
Scholarly Resource, Inc., 1973. Reprint of the 1878 edition. $25.00.

HISTORY OF THE CHOCTAW, CHICKASAW, AND NATCHEZ INDIANS
Horatio Bardwell Cushman
Russell and Russell. Reprint of the 1899 edition. Illus. $20.00.

CHIPPEWA

CHIPPEWA INDIANS: ETHNOHISTORY OF CHIPPEWA IN CENTRAL MINNESOTA
Harold Hickerson
321 pp. Garland Publishing, Inc., 1974. $21.00.

CHIPPEWA INDIANS VOLUME 2, IN-CLUDING: *Ethnohistory of Mississippi Bands, and Pillager and Winnibigoshish Bands of Chippewa,* Harold Hickerson.
338 pp. Garland Publishing Co., 1974. $21.00.

CHIPPEWA INDIANS VOLUME 3, IN-CLUDING: *Ethnohistory of Chippewa of Lake Superior,* Harold Hickerson;
Economic and Historical Background of Northeastern Minnesota Lands: Chippewa Indians of Lake Superior, Helen E. Knuth.
294 pp. Garland Publishing Co., 1974. $21.00.

CHIPPEWA INDIANS VOLUME 5, IN-CLUDING: *An Anthropological Report on Indian Use and Occupancy of Northern Michigan,* Erminie Wheeler-Voegelin;
Ethnohistorical Report on the Saginaw Chippewa, David B. Stout; *Economic and Historical Report on Northern Michigan: From Early Times to 1850,* Robert Warner; *Historical Report on the Sault Ste. Marie Area,* Robert Warner/Lois J. Groesbeck;
The Chippewa of Eastern Lower Michigan, Helen Hornbeck Tanner
327 pp. Garland Publishing Co., 1974. $21.00.

CHIPPEWA INDIANS VOLUME 6, IN-CLUDING: *Ethnological Report on the Chippewa Cree Tribe of the Rocky Boy Reservation, Montana, and the Little Shell Bank of Indians,* John C. Ewers;
History of the Cree Indian Territorial Expansion from the Hudson Bay Area to the Interior Saskatchewan and Missouri Plains, Floyd and Susan Sharrock.
379 pp. Garland Publishing Co., 1974. $21.00.

CHIPPEWA INDIANS VOLUME 7, IN-CLUDING: *Findings of Fact, and Opinion*
The Indian Claims Commission
516 pp. Garland Publishing Co., 1974. $21.00.

CHIPPEWA AND DAKOTA INDIANS: A SUBJECT CATALOG OF BOOKS, PAM-PHLETS, PERIODICAL ARTICLES, AND MANUSCRIPTS IN THE MINNESOTA

HISTORICAL SOCIETY
Minnesota Historical Society
Minnesota Historical Society, 1970. Pap. $7.50.

THE CHIPPEWA AND THEIR NEIGH-BORS: A STUDY IN ETHNOHISTORY
H. Hickerson
Holt, Rinehart, and Winston, 1970. Pap. $3.25.

CHIPPEWA CUSTOMS
Frances Densmore
Cultural aspects of the Chippewa (Ojibway) Nation. 204 pp. Ross & Haines, Inc. Illus. 80 plates. Reprint of the 1929 edition. $10.00.

CHIPPEWA INDIANS: RED LAKE AND PEMBINA CHIPPEWA
Erminie Wheeler-Voegelin
255 pp. Garland Publishing, Inc., 1974. $21.00.

*THE CHIPPEWA INDIANS, RICE GATHERERS OF THE GREAT LAKES
Sonia Bleeker
160 pp. William Morrow and Co., 1955. Illus. $3.94. Ages 9 to 12.

CHIPPEWA MUSIC
Frances Densmore
An inquiry into the music, mythology and customs of Chippewa (Ojibway) Indians. Two volumes in one. 605 pp. Ross & Haines, Inc. Illus. 57 plates. Reprint of the 1910 and 1913 editions. $15.00.

ETHNOLOGICAL REPORT ON THE CHIPPEWA CREE TRIBE OF THE ROCKY BOY RESERVATION, AND THE LITTLE SHELL BAND, MONTANA, 1888
John C. Ewers
173 pp. Clearwater Publishing Co., 1973. $37.00.

*THE FIRE PLUME: LEGENDS OF THE AMERICAN INDIANS
John Bierhorst, Editor
A selection of seven Chippewa legends, originally collected by Henry Rowe Schoolcraft 96 pp. Dell Publishing Co., 1969. Illus. Ages 7-11. $4.50.

HISTORICAL REPORT ON THE CHIP-PEWA OF EASTERN LOWER MICHIGAN, 1785 TO 1837
Dr. Helen Hornbeck Tanner
25 pp. Clearwater Publishing Co., 1973. $13.35.

INDIAN AND FREE: A CONTEMPORARY

PORTRAIT OF LIFE ON A CHIPPEWA RESERVATION
Charles Brill
A collection of 160 photographs and accompanying text. University of Minnesota Press, 1975. $9.75.

INDIANS OF NORTHEASTERN ILLINOIS: THE CHIPPEWA, OTTAWA, AND POTAWATOMI INDIANS
David A. Baerreis, et. al, Editors
Garland Publishing, Inc., 1974. $21.00.

RED WORLD AND WHITE: MEMORIES OF A CHIPPEWA BOYHOOD
J. Rogers, (Chief Snow Clouds)
158 pp. University of Oklahoma Press, 1974. $4.95.

SIX STUDIES OF THE CHIPPEWA INDIANS
Anthony Paredes, Editor
University of Florida Press.

*SONGS OF THE CHIPPEWA
John Bierhorst
Ritual chants, dream songs, medicine charms and lullabies arranges for piano and guitar. 48 pp. Farrar, Straus and Giroux, 1975. Illus. Ages 8-12. $6.95.

*WORLD OF MANABOZHO: TALES OF THE CHIPPEWA INDIANS
T. B. Leekley
Vanguard Press. Illus. $3.50. Below college level.

CHOCTAW

THE ACTS AND RESOLUTIONS OF THE GENERAL COUNCIL OF THE CHOCTAW NATION PASSED AT ITS REGULAR SESSION, 1903
Scholarly Resource, Inc., 1973. Reprint of the 1904 edition. $7.50.

*CHOCTAW LITTLE FOLK
Novella Goodman Martin
Legends about animals and birds beloved by Choctaw children. The Naylor Co. 8 up. $4.95.

CHOCTAW MUSIC
F. Densmore
Da Capo Press, 1972. Reprint of the 1943 edition. $7.95.

THE CONSTITUTION AND LAWS OF THE CHOCTAW NATION: TOGETHER WITH THE TREATIES OF 1837, 1855, 1865, AND 1866

A. R. Durant and A. D. Homer, Editors
Scholarly Resources, Inc., 1973. Reprint of the 1894 edition. $30.00.

AN EARLY ACCOUNT OF THE CHOCTAW INDIANS

John R. Swanton
Kraus Reprint Co. Reprint of the 1918 edition. Pap. $3.50.

HISTORY OF THE CHOCTAW, CHICKASAW, AND NATCHEZ INDIANS

Horatio Bardwell Cushman
Russell and Russell. Reprint of the 1899 edition. Illus. $20.00.

LIFE AMONG THE CHOCTAW INDIANS AND SKETCHES OF THE SOUTHWEST

Henry Clark Benson
314 pp. Johnson Reprint, 1970. Reprint of the 1860 edition. $14.00.

THE REMOVAL OF THE CHOCTAW INDIANS

Arthur H. DeRosier, Jr.
Harper and Row Pubs., 1972. Pap. $2.95.

THE RISE AND FALL OF THE CHOCTAW REPUBLIC

Angie Debo
The record of a people whose forced migration and from their ancestral homes and whose subsequent efforts to maintain an autonomous government and institutions form a chapter in the history of the West. 314 pp. University of Oklahoma Press. Reprint of the 1934 edition. Illus. Pap. $3.50.

COMANCHE

*COMANCHE LAND

J. Emmor Harston
Comanche living, social life, ethnology and artwork. 240 pp. Photos. The Naylor Co. Age 12-18. $6.95.

COMANCHES

T. R. Fehrenbach
Alfred A. Knopf, Inc., 1974. $12.50.

*COMANCHES AND OTHER INDIANS OF TEXAS

Marian T. Place
A detailed description of the early peoples who made their home in Texas, with an emphasis on the tribal culture of the Comanches. 144 pp. Harcourt Brace Jovanovich, Inc., 1970. $4.95. Ages 12 up.

THE COMANCES: LORDS OF THE SOUTH PLAINS

Ernest Wallace and E. Adamson Hoebel
382 pp. University of Oklahoma Press, 1972. Reprint of the 1952 edition. Illus. $7.95.

KIOWA-COMMANCHE INDIANS 2 VOLS.

David Agee Horr, Editor
500 pp. Garland Publishing, Inc., 1974. $21.00 each; $42.00 per set.

THE POLITICAL ORGANIZATION AND LAW-WAYS OF THE COMANCHE INDIANS

A. Hoebel
Kraus Reprint Co., 1974. Reprint of the 1940 edition. $13.50.

CREEK

ALABAMA-COUSHATTA [CREEK] INDIANS, INCLUDING: *Alabama-Coushatta Indians: Ethnological Report and Statement of Testimony,* Daniel Jacobson; *Ethnological Analysis of Documents Relating to the Alabama and Coushatta Tribes of the State of Texas,* Howard Martin; *A History of Polk County, Texas, Indians,* Ralph H. Marsh.
249 pp. Garland Publishing Co., 1974. $21.00.

CHEROKEE AND CREEK INDIANS, INCLUDING: *Ethnographic Report on Royce Area 79, Docket 275, Chickasaw, Cherokee, Creek,* Charles H. Fairbanks; *Cherokee Treaties,* John G. Goff; *Findings of Fact, and Opinion,* The Indian Claims Commission.
451 pp. Garland Publishing Co., 1974. $21.00.

THE CREEK FRONTIER, 1540 TO 1783

David H. Corkran
343 pp. University of Oklahoma Press, 1967. Illus. $8.95.

THE CREEK INDIANS AND THEIR
FLORIDA LANDS 1740 TO 1805
James F. Doster
268 pp. Clearwater Publishing Co., 1974.
$52.50.

CREEK INDIANS, INCLUSING: *The Creek
Indians and Their Florida Lands, 1740-1823,*
James F. Dorster; *Findings of Fact, and
Opinion,* The Indian Claims Commission.
652 pp. Garland Publishing Co., 1974. Two
volumes, $42.00.

CREEK WAR OF 1813 AND 1814
H. S. Halbert and T. H. Ball
331 pp. University of Alabama Press. Reprint
of the 1895 edition. $8.00.

AN EARLY HISTORY OF THE CREEK
INDIANS AND THEIR NEIGHBORS
J. R. Swanton
Scholarly Press. Reprint of the 1922 edition.
$29.00.

EARLY HISTORY OF THE CREEK IN-
DIANS AND THEIR NEIGHBORS
John R. Swanton
492 pp. Johnson Reprint Corp. Reprint of the
1922 edition. $35.00.

ETHNOLOGICAL REPORT ON THE
ALABAMA-COUSHATTA INDIANS OF
TEXAS AND THE COUSHATTA INDIANS
OF LOUISIANA 1540 TO 1855
Daniel Jacobson
150 pp. Clearwater Publishing Co., 1974.
$33.35.

A MIGRATION LEGEND OF THE CREEK
INDIANS WITH A LINGUISTIC,
HISTORICAL, AND ETHNOGRAPHIC
INCTRODUCTION, TWO VOLS. IN ONE
A. S. Gatschet
Kraus Reprint Co. Reprint of the 1888 edition.
$17.50.

A MIGRATION LEGEND OF THE CREEK
INDIANS
Albert Samuel Gatschet
With a linguistic, historic and ethnographic
introduction. AMS Press, 1972. Reprint of the
1884 edtion. $8.00.

THE ROAD TO DISAPPEARANCE: A
HISTORY OF THE CREEK INDIANS
Angie Debo
339 pp. University of Oklahoma Press. Reprint

of the 1941 edition. Illus. $8.95.

*SAM HOUSTON'S INDIANS, THE
ALABAMA-COUSHATTI
P. V. Malone
An ethnological study. The Naylor Co., 1960.
Age 12-18. $4.95.

SOCIAL ORGANIZATION AND SOCIAL
USAGES OF THE INDIANS OF THE CREEK
CONFEDERACY
John R. Swanton
472 pp. Johnson Reprint. Reprint of the 1928
edition. $28.00.

CROW

CROW INDIAN BEADWORK: A DES-
CRIPTIVE AND HISTORICAL STUDY
William Wildshut and John C. Ewers
55 pp. 47 plates Museum of the American
Indian. Reprint of the 1959 edition. Cloth
$5.00; Pap. $3.50.

*THE CROW INDIANS, HUNTERS OF THE
NORTHERN PLAINS
Sonia Bleeder
160 pp. William Morrow and Co., 1953. Illus.
$4.25. Ages 9 to 12.

CROW INDIANS, INCLUDING: *The Crow
Tribe of Indians,* Norman B. Plummer;
Findings of Fact, and Opinion, The Indian
Claims Commission.
243 pp. Garland Publishing, 1974. $21.00.

LIFE AND ADVENTURES OF JAMES P.
BECKWOURTH, MOUNTAINEER, SCOUT
PIONEER, AND CHIEF OF THE CROW
NATION OF INDIANS
T. D. Bonner, Editor
Arno Press. Reprint of the 1856 edition. $16.00.

THE MATERIAL CULTURE OF THE
CROW INDIANS
Robert Harry Lowe
AMS Press. Reprint of the 1922 edition. $10.00.

MEMOIRS OF A WHITE CROW INDIAN
Thomas H. LeForge
356 pp. University of Nebraska Press, 1974.
Pap. $3.95.

MYTHS AND TRADITIONS OF THE CROW INDIANS
Roberr Harry Lowie
AMS Press, Inc. Reprint of the 1918 edition. $22.00.

PLENTY-COUPS, CHIEF OF THE CROWS
F. B. Linderman
John Day Co., 1972. $8.95.

PRETTY-SHIELD, MEDICINE WOMAN OF THE CROWS
F. B. Linderman
John Day Publishing Co. Reprint of the 1932 edition. $7.95.

THE RELIGION OF THE CROW INDIANS
Robert Harry Lowie
AMS Press. Reprint of the 1922 edition. $10.00.

SOCIAL LIFE OF THE CROW INDIANS
Robert Harry Lowie
AMS Press, Inc. Reprint of the 1912 edition. $10.00.

THE TOBACCO SOCIETY OF THE CROW INDIANS
Robert Harry Lowie
AMS Press, Inc. Reprint of the 1919 edition. $10.00.

DAKOTA

CHIPPEWA AND DAKOTA INDIANS: A SUBJECT CATALOG OF BOOKS, PAMPHLETS, PERIODICAL ARTICLES, AND MANUSCRIPTS IN THE MINNESOTA HISTORICAL SOCIETY
Minnesota Historical Society
Minnesota Historical Society, 1970. Pap. $7.50.

*DAKOTA INDIAN LORE
Darrel Woodyard
Chantlike legends portraying the history and customs of Kakota Indians. 180 pp. The Naylor Co. Age 11-14. $4.95.

*THE DAKOTAS
M. L. Israel
Melmont Pubs., 1959. Ages 6 to 10.

A HISTORY OF THE DAKOTA OR SIOUX INDIANS
Doane Robinson
523 pp. Ross & Haines, Inc. Reprint of the 1904 edition. Illus. $12.50.

DELAWARE

A DELAWARE INDIAN SYMPOSIUM
Herbert C. Kraft, ed.
Includes a prehistory of New Jersey. 160 pp. Pennsylvanis Historical Museum Commission, 1974. Cloth, $4.50; Pap. $3.00.

*THE DELAWARE INDIANS: EASTERN FISHERMEN AND FARMERS
Sonia Bleeker
160 pp. William Morrow and Co., 1953. Illus. $3.94. Ages 9 to 12.

THE DELAWARE INDIANS: A HISTORY
C. A. Weslager
Rutgers University Press, 1972. $17.50.

NARRATIVE OF THE MISSION OF THE UNITED BRETHEREN AMONG THE DELAWARE AND MOHEGAN INDIANS
J. Heckwelder
Arno Press, 1971. Reprint of the 1820 edition. $17.00.

FLATHEAD

THE ETHNOMUSICOLOGY OF THE FLATHEAD INDIANS
A. P. Merriam
Aldine Publishing Co., 1967. $12.95.

THE FLATHEAD INDIANS OF MONTANA
H. H. Turney-High
Kraus Reprint Co. Reprint of the 1937 edition. Pap. $6.00.

HISTORICAL SKETCH OF THE FLATHEAD INDIAN NATION
Peter Ronan
Ross & Haines, Inc. Reprint of the 1890 edition. 108 pp. $4.95.

HAIDA

CONTRIBUTIONS TO THE ETHNOLOGY OF THE HAIDA
John Reed Swanton
AMS Press, Inc. Reprint of the 1905 edition. $72.50.

HAIDA TEXTS AND MYTHS
John R. Swanton
448 pp. Johnson Reprint Corp. Reprint of the 1905 edition. $25.25.

THE STORY OF THE HAIDA
Marion E. Gridley
G. P. Putnam's Sons, 1972. Illus. $4.97.

HAVASUPAI

HAVASUPAI INDIANS: AN ETHNO-HISTORICAL REPORT, ARIZONA
Robert A. Manners
154 pp. Clearwater Publishing Co., 1973. $34.00.

HAVASUPAI INDIANS, INCLUDING:
Havasupai Indians, An Ethnohistorical Report, Robert A. Manners; *Socio-Political Structure and Ethnic Group Concept of the PAI,* Henry F. Dobyns, et al; *Finding of Fact, and Opinion,* The Indian Claims Commission.
285 pp. Garland Publishing, 1974. $21.00.

THE HAVASUPAI-PRISONERS OF THE GRAND CANYON
An explanation of the effort to give the Havasupai Indians enough of their ancient homeland to support them. 16 pp. Interbook Incorporated, 1974. Illus. Pap. $1.00.

HAVASUPAI RELIGION AND MYTHOL-OGY
Carma Lee Smithson and Robert C. Euler
112 pp. Johnson Reprint. Reprint of the 1964 edition. $14.00.

THE HAVASUPAI WOMEN
Carna Lee Smithson
170 pp. Johnson Reprint . Reprint of the 1959 edition. Illus. $16.75.

HISTORICAL REPORT ON THE HAVASUPAI INDIANS 1150 TO 1890
Robert C. Euler
50 pp. Clearwater Publishing Co., 1974. $17.35.

LIFE IN A NARROW PLACE: THE HAVASUPAI OF THE GRAND CANYON
S. Hirst
David McKay Co., 1974. $7.95.

HOPI

THE CHANGING PHYSICAL EN-VIRONMENT OF THE HOPI INDIANS OF ARIZONA
John T. Hack
Kraus Reprint Co. Reprint of the 1942 edition. Pap. $2.00.

CULTURE IN CRISIS: A STUDY OF THE HOPI INDIANS
Laura Thompson
Russell and Russell. Reprint of the 1950 edition. Illus. $22.00.

*A DAY WITH HONAU: A HOPI INDIAN BOY
H. C. James
Melmont Pubs., 1957. $4.50. Ages 6 to 10.

THE FOURTH WORLD OF THE HOPIS
Harold Courlander
Accounts of events and adventures in the life of Hopi clans and villages from legendary to historical times. Fawcett World Library. Pap. $.95.

HOPI INDIANS, INCLUDING:
The Hopi: Their History and Use of Lands, Florence H. Ellis; *Hopi History and Ethnobotany,* Harold S. Colton; *Findings of Fact, and Opinion,* The Indian Claims Commission.
403 pp. Garland Publishing, 1974. $21.00.

HOPI JOURNAL
Alexander M. Stephen
AMS Press. Reprint of the 1936 edition. Two volume set, $84. 50. $45.00 per volume.

HOPI KATCHINAS DRAWN BY NATIVE ARTISTS
Jesse Walter Fewkes
A collection of aboriginal Indian art. 190 pp. 65 plates. Rio Grande Press. Reprint of the 1903 edition. Illus. $15.00.

THE HOPI: THEIR HISTORY AND USE OF LANDS IN NEW MEXICO AND ARIZONA, 1200s to 1900s
Florence Hawley Ellis
248 pp. Clearwater Publishing Co., 1973. $49.00.

THE HOPIS: PORTRAIT OF A DESERT PEOPLE

W. C. O'Kane
267 pp. University of Oklahoma Press. Reprint of the 1953 edition. Illus. $8.95.

KACHINAS: A HOPI ARTISTS DOCUMENTARY
Barton Wright
Explains the Kachina cult, its origins and fuctions. 272 pp. 237 plates. Northland Press, 1973. Illus. $40.00.

NAVAJO AND HOPI WEAVING TECHNIQUES
Mary Pendleton
Describes how to make your own loom and tools; the various yarns and their uses; the different weaves; how to set up your own loom; and how to analyze your finished piece. Macmillan Publishing Co. Cloth, $9.95; Pap. $4.95.

NOTES ON HOPI CLANS AND HOPI KINSHIP
Robert Harry Lowie
AMS Press. Reprint of the 1929 edition. $10.00.

RITUAL IN PUEBLO ART: HOPI LIFE IN HOPI PAINTINGS
Byron Harvey III
185 watercolor paintings portray various aspects of Pueblo life along with a text. 80 pp. 185 plates. Museum of the American Indian, 1970. Cloth, $15.00; Pap. $10.00.

THE SNAKE DANCE OF THE HOPI INDIANS
Earle R. Forrest
Includes photographs taken before the tribal ban on photography, with an explanation of the ritual; its background, meaning, and religious significance. Westernlore Press, 1961. Illus. $7.50.

SUN IN THE SKY: THE HOPI INDIANS OF THE ARIZONA MESA LANDS
Walter Collins O'Kane
Describes ingenious agriculture on arid sands, houses and furnishings, dress and personal traits, and child-rearing. 280 pp. Universtiy of Oklahoma Press, 1975. Illus. Pap. $3.95.

TRADITIONS OF THE HOPI
H. R. Voth
Kraus Reprint Co. Reprint of the 1903 edition. Pap. $4.50.

TRUTH OF A HOPI
Edmund Nequatewa
A collection of stories relating to the origin, myths and history of the Hopi clans. 137 pp. Northland Press, 1973. Pap. $4.95.

THE UNCHANGING HOPI
Barton Wright
Scratchboard portrayal of the Indians in northeastern Arizona. 128 pp. Northland Press, 1974. Illus. $12.50. Limited edition of 100 with original art by the author, $100.00.

HUALAPAI

ETHNOLOGICAL REPORT ON THE HUALAPAI INDIANS OF ARIZONA
Robert A. Manners
189 pp. Clearwater Publishing Co., 1973. $39.60.

HUALAPAI INDIANS: AN ETHNOLOGICAL REPORT ON THE HUALAPAI INDIANS OF ARIZONA
Robert A. Manners
194 pp. Garland Publishing, Inc., 1974. $21.00.

HUALAPAI INDIANS: PREHISTORIC INDIAN OCCUPATION WITHIN THE EASTERN AREA OF THE YUMAN COMPLEX: A STUDY IN APPLIED ARCHAEOLOGY
Henry F. Dobyns
713 pp. Garland Publishing, Inc., 1974. $21.00.

IROQUOIS

A HISTORY OF THE NEW YORK IROQUOIS, NOW COMMONLY CALLED THE SIX NATIONS
William Martin Beauchamp
AMS Press, Inc. Reprint of the 1905 edition. $21.50.

*INDIANS OF THE LONGHOUSE, THE STORY OF THE IROQUOIS
Sonia Bleeker
160 pp. William Morrow and Co., 1950. Illus. $3.94. Ages 9 to 12.

THE IROQUOIS BOOK OF RITES
Horation Emmons Hale
AMS press. Reprint of the 1883 edition. $8.00.

THE IROQUOIS IN THE AMERICAN REVOLUTION
Barbara Graymont
359 pp. Syracuse University Press, 1972. Illus. Cloth, $11.50; Pap. $5.75.

IROQUOIS INDIANS: HISTORY OF PENNSYLVANIA PURCHASES FROM THE INDIANS
Donald H. Kent
Garland Publishing, Inc., 1974. $21.00.

IROQUOIS INDIANS VOLUME 2, INCLUDING:
Historical Report on the Niagra River to 1759, Donald H. Kent; *Findings of Fact, and Opinion,* The Indian Claims Commission.
346 pp. Garland Publishing Co., 1974. $21.00.

IROQUOIS MUSIC AND DANCE: CEREMONIAL ARTS OF TWO SENECA LONGHOUSES
G. P. Kurath
Scholoarly Press. Reprint of the 1964 edition. $14.50.

IROQUOIS PAST AND PRESENT
Edward Hale Brush
AMS Press, Inc. Reprint of the 1901 edition. $10.00.

MYTHS AND LEGENDS OF THE NEW YORK STATE IROQUOIS
H. M. Converse
Gordon Press. Reprint of the 1908 edition. $14.00.

NOTES ON THE IROQUOIS: OR, CONTRIBUTIONS TO AMERICAN HISTORY, ANTIQUITIES, AND GENERAL ETHNOLOGY
Henry Rowe Schoolcraft
AMS Press, Inc. Reprint of the 1847 edition. $31.00.

PARKER ON THE IROQUOIS: IROQUOIS USES OF MAIZE AND OTHER FOOD PLANTS; THE CODE OF HANDSOME LAKE, THE SENECA PROPHET; THE CONSTITUTION OF THE FIVE NATIONS
Arthur C. Parker
480 pp. Sygacuse University Press, 1968. Illus. Pap. $4.95.

*THE STORY OF THE IROQUOIS
Marion E. Gridley
G. P. Putnam's Sons, 1969. Illus. $4.97. Below college level.

A SYMPOSIUM ON CHEROKEE AND IROQUOIS CULTURE
W. Fenton and J. Gulick
Scholarly Press. Reprint of the 1961 edition. $14.50.

THE TUSCARORAS, VOL. I
F. Roy Johnson
The mythology, medicine and culture of the once powerful Iroquoian group of Eastern North Carolina which joined their Five Nations kinsmen after colonial warfare with the English. 264 pp. Johnson Publishing Co., 1968. $6.50.

THE TUSCARORAS, VOL. II
F. Roy Johnson
The history, traditions and cultural modifications of one of the important Indian groups of the Southeast, from the Carolina wars through migration and reservation building. 285 pp. Johnson Publishing Co., 1968. $8.50.

THE WARS OF THE IROQUOIS: A STUDY IN INTERTRIAL TRADE RELATIONS
G. T. Hunt
University of Wisconsin Press, 1960. Pap. $3.50.

KICKAPOO

KICKAPOO, ILLINOIS AND POTAWATOMIE INDIANS IN ILLINOIS AND INDIANA, 1819 TO 1832
David B. Stout
124 pp. Clearwater Publishing Co., 1973. $29.20.

KICKAPOO TALES
William Jones, Compiler
Translated by Truman Michelson. AMS Press. Reprint of the 1915 edition. $7.50.

THE KICKAPOOS: LORDS OF THE MIDDLE BORDER
Arrell M. Gibson
The tribe who fought with encroaching settlers for over 300 years. University of Oklahoma Press, 1974. 408 pp. Illus. $8.95.

KIOWA

*INDIAN ANNIE: KIOWA CAPTIVE
Alice Marriott
David McKay Co., 1965. $3.75. Ages 16 and up.

LAW AND STATUS AMONG THE KIOWA INDIANS
Jane Richardson
The kiowa are shown to have had an articulate legal procedure with a wide range of choices in criminal and dispute situations. 144 pp. University of Washington Press, 1940. $5.00.

KLAMATH

ETHNOGRAPHIC SKETCH OF THE KLAMATH INDIANS OF SOUTH-WESTERN OREGON
Albert Samuel Gatschet
AMS Press, Inc. Reprint of the 1890 edition. $106.50.

KLAMATH ETHNOGRAPHY
L. Spier
Kraus Reprint Co. Reprint of the 1930 edition. Pap. $25.00.

THE KLAMATH TRIBE: A PEOPLE AND THEIR RESERVATION
Theodore Stern
372 pp. University of Washington Press, 1965. Illus. $7.50.

KWAKIUTL

KWAKIUTL CULTURE AS REFLECTED IN MYTHOLOGY
Franz Boas, Editor
Kraus Reprint Co. Reprint of the 1935 edition. $9.00.

KWAKIUTL ETHNOGRAPHY
Franz Boas
University of Chicago Press, 1966. $13.75.

THE MOUTH OF HEAVEN, *An Introduction to Kwakiutl Religious Thought*
Irving Goldman
The synthesis of the encyclopedic Kwakiutl and English language texts of Franz Boas and George Hunt. a reinterpretation of the ethnographic and cultural record. 265 pp. Wiley-Interscience, 1975., $13.50.

MACKINAC

LORE OF THE GREAT TURTLE: INDIAN LEGENDS OF THE MACKINAC RETOLD
D. Gringhuis
96 pp. Mackinac Island State Park Commission, 1970. Pap. $2.00.

MYTHS AND LEGENDS OF THE MACKINACS AND THE LAKE REGION
Grace Franks Kane
This is a reprint of the 1897 first edition with the original photographs and drawings of Indian Mythology of the Great Lakes Region. 160 pp. Black Letter Press. $2.95.

MANDAN-HIDATSA

ETHNOGRAPHY AND PHILOLOGY OF THE HIDATSA INDIANS: UNITED STATES GEOLOGICAL AND GEOGRAPHICAL SURVEY OF THE TERRITORIES
Wahington Matthews
239 pp. Johnson Reprint, 1971. Reprint of the 1877 edition. $17.50.

MANDAN AND HIDATSA MUSIC
F. Densmore
Scholarly Press. $9.50.

MANDAN-HIDATSA MYTHS AND CEREMONIES
M. W. Beckwith
Kraus Reprint Co. Reprint of the 1938 edition. $14.00.

NOTES ON THE SOCIAL ORGANIZATION AND CUSTOMS OF THE MANDAN-HIDATSA, AND CROW INDIANS
Robert Harry Lowie
AMS Press, Inc. Reprint of the 1917 edition. $9.00.

MENOMINI

DREAMERS WITHOUT POWER: THE MENOMINI INDIANS
G. Spindler and L. Spindler
Holt, Rinehart, and Winston, 1971. $3.75.

MENOMINEE MUSIC
F. Densmore
Da Capo Press. Reprint of the 1932 edition.
$12.95.

MENOMINEE MUSIC
F. Densmore
Scholarly Press. Reprint of the 1932 edition.
$14.50.

THE MENOMINI INDIANS
Walter James Hoffman
328 pp. Johnson Reprint. Reprint of the 1896 edition. Illus. $35.00.

THE MENOMINI INDIANS OF WISCONSON: A STUDY OF THREE CENTURIES OF CULTURAL CONTACT AND CHANGES
Felix Maxwell Keesing
261 pp. Johnson Reprint. Reprint of the 1939 edition. $18.25.

MIAMI

THE MIAMI INDIANS
B. Anson
329 pp. University of Oklahoma Press, 1970.
Illus. $8.95.

MIAMI, WEA, AND EEL-RIVER INDIANS OF SOUTHERN INDIANA
Erminie Wh3eler-Voegelin, et al
442 pp. Garland Publishing, 1974. $21.00.

MISSION

BASKET DESIGNS OF THE MISSION INDIANS OF CALIFORNIA
A. L. Kroeber
Ballena Press, 1973. Pap. $3.50.

*THE MISSION INDIANS OF CALIFORNIA
Sonia Bleeker

160 pp. William Morrow and Co., 1956. Illus.
$3.94. Ages 9 to 12

MODOC

THE MYTHS OF THE MODOCS: INDIAN LEGENDS FROM THE NORTHWEST
J. Curtain
Benjamin Blom Pubs. Reprint of the 1912 edition. $12.50.

PRIMITIVE PRAGMATISTS: THE MODOC INDIANS OF NORTHERN CALIFORNIA
V. F. Ray
256 pp. University of Washington Press, 1963.
Illus. $8.50.

MOHAVE

MOHAVE ETHNOPSYCHIATRY AND SUICIDE: THE PSYCHIATRIC KNOWLEDGE AND THE PSYCHIC DISTURBANCES OF AN INDIAN TRIBE
G. Devereux
Scholarly Press. Reprint of the 1961 edition.
$34.50.

MOHAVE INDIANS, INCLUDING:
Report on Aboriginal Territory and Occupancy of the Mohave Tribe, Alfred Kroeber;
Findings of Fact, and Opinion, The Indian Claims Commission.
158 pp. Garland Publishing Co., 1974. $21.00.

*MOHAVE PEOPLE
Fulsom Charles Scrivner
The account of desert confrontations between the Mohave Indians and successive waves of Spaniards, American surveyors, settlers, Mormons and the U. S. Army. the Naylor co.
Age 13 up. $6.95.

TALES FROM THE MOHAVES
Herman Grey
96 pp. University of Oklahoma Press, 1971.
$4.95.

NAVAJO

APACHE, NAVAJO, AND SPANIARD

Jack D. Forbes
340 pp. University of Oklahoma Press. Reprint of the 1960 edition. Illus. $7.95; Pap. $2.95.

A BIBLIOGRAPHY OF THE NAVAJO INDIANS

Clyde Kluckhohn and Katherine Spencer
AMS Press, Inc., Reprint of the 1940 edition. $7.50.

*CHILD OF THE NAVAJOS

Seymour Reit
The true story of a nine-year-old Navajo boy living on his reservation in Arizona, and how he preserves his centuries-old identity. 64 pp. Dodd, Mead & Co., 1971. Age 6-11. $4.50.

DEZBA, NAVAJO WOMAN OF THE DESERT

Gladys A. Reichard
An account of the day to day life of a Navajo family. 236 pp. Rio Grande Press. Reprint of the 1939 edition. Illus. $8.00.

HISTORICAL REPORT ON THE NAVAJO INDIANS IN NEW MEXICO TO 1870

Frank D. Reeve
100 pp. Clearwater Publishing Co., 1973. $25.35.

HOSTEEN KLAH: NAVAJO MEDICINE MAN AND SAND PAINTER

Franc Johnson Newcomb
227 pp. University of Oklahoma Press. Reprint of the 1964 edition. Illus. $6.95; Pap. $2.50.

INDIAN DRINKING: NAVAJO PRACTICES AND ANGLO-AMERICAN THEORIES

Jerrold E. Levy
This book investigates several small groups of Navajos in the Southwest. Intertribal comparisons of epidemiological date are used to provide a framework for the study. The author examines the interworkings of social theory and myths of deviance and drinking, reviews the history of alcohol in the southwest, and discusses the disparity between Indians' drinking patterns and white misconceptions. 272 pp. John Wiley & Sons, 1974. $12.95.

*LORDS OF THE EARTH: THE HISTORY OF THE NAVAJO INDIANS

J. Loh
Macmillan Publishing Co., Inc., 1971. $4.95. Below college level.

MASKED GODS: NAVAJO AND PUEBLO CEREMONIALISM

Frank Waters
Swallow Press, 1973. Cloth, $10.00; Pap. $4.95.

THE MOUNTAIN CHANT OF THE NAVAJO: A MYSTIC CEREMONY

Washington Matthews
A report of the mystic ceremony with analysis. 304 pp. Rio Grande Press. Reprint of the 1887 edition. Illus. $10.00.

*THE NAVAJO: HERDERS, WEAVERS AND SILVERSMITHS

Sonia Bleeker
160 pp. William Morrow and Co., 1958. Illus. $3.94. Ages 9 to 12.

THE NAVAJO AND HIS BLANKET

U. S. Hollister
A rare book on Navajo weaving and primitive textiles. 176 pp. Rio Grande Press. Reprint of the 1903 edition. Illus. $12.00.

NAVAJO AND HOPI WEAVING TECHNIQUES

Mary Pendleton
Describes how to make your own loom and tools; the various yarns and their uses; the different weaves; how to set up your own loom; and how to analyze your finished piece. Macmillan Publishing Co. Cloth, $9.95; Pap.

THE NAVAJO HUNTER TRADITION

Karl W. Luckert
A study of myths relating to the origin of the Navajo Indian. University of Arizona Press, 1975. Price not set.

NAVAJO INDIAN ETHNOENTOMOLOGY

Leland C. wyman and Flora L. Baily
University of New Mexico Press, 1964. Pap. $1.50.

NAVAJO INDIANS: ANTHROPOLOGICAL STUDY OF THE NAVAJO INDIANS

Florence H. Ellis
580 pp. Garland Publishing, Inc., 1974. $21.00.

THE NAVAHO INDIANS OF NEW MEXICO

In 12 photos with explanatory text, the story of six centuries of Navaho residence in New Mexico. Museum of New Mexico Press, 1974. $1.00.

*NAVAJO INDIANS TODAY

Dorothy F. Robinson

Condensed account of Navajo history up to their resettlement on their reservation in Arizona, with a report of what is being done today in education, sanitation and modern farm and ranch management. The Naylor Co. Photos. Ages 12-18. $4.95.

NAVAJO INDIANS VOLUME 2, INCLUDING: *Navajo Activities Affecting the Acoma-Laguna Area, 1746-1910,* Myra Jenkins and Ward Alan Minge; *Navajo Indians,* Frank D. Reeve.
317 pp. Garland Publishing Co., 1974. $21.00.

NAVAJO INDIANS VOLUME 3, INCLUDING: *Navajo Sacred Places [83 Photographs Plus Notes],* Richard Van Valkenburgh; *Findings of Fact, and Opinion,* The Indians Claims Commission.
226 pp. Garland Publishing Co., 1974. $21.00.

THE NAVAJO IN NEW MEXICO, 1800-1870
Frank D. Reeve
100 pp. Clearwater Publishing Co., 1973. $25.35.

NAVAHO LEGENDS
W. Matthews
Kraus Reprint Co. Reprint of the 1897 edition. Illus. 12.00.

NAVAJOLAND MAP
A cartoon map of the Navajo Reservation, endorsed by the Bribal Council. K C Publications. Illus. Pap. $.50.

NAVAJO NEIGHBORS
F. J. Newcomb
236 pp. University of Oklahoma Press, 1966. Illus. Cloth, $6.95; Pap. $2.95.

NAVAJO POTTERY-MAKING
H. Tschopik
Kraus Reprint Co. Reprint of the 1941 edition. Pap. $6.00.

NAVAJO SHEPHERD AND WEAVER
Gladys A. Reichard
A study of the art and technique of primitive weaving, as practiced by the Navajo women. 280 pp. Rio Grande Press. Reprint of the 1936 edition. Illus. $8.00.

A NAVAJO SKETCH BOOK
Don Perceval and Clay Lockett
98 pp. 187 illus. Northalnd Press, 1968. $14.50.

NAVAJO WEAVING, ITS TECHNIQUE AND HISTORY
Charles Avery Amsden
A complete study of primitive textile weaving. 460 pp. Rio Grande Press. Reprint of the 1934 edition. Illus. $12.00.

NAVAHO WITCHCRAFT
Clyde Kluckholm
Traces the impact of supernatural beliefs on a society emerging from primitivism. Beacon Press. Pap. $2.95.

THE NAVAJOS
Ruth M. Undershill
299 pp. University of Oklahoma Press, 1971. Reprint of the 1956 edition. Illus. $6.95.

NAVAJOS HAVE FIVE FINGERS
T. D. Allen
249 pp. University of Oklahoma Press, 1970. Reprint of the 1963 edition. Illus. $6.95.

PEOPLES HEALTH: MEDICINE AND ANTHROPOLOGY IN A NAVAJO COMMUNITY
J. Adair and K. Deuschle
Prentice-Hall, 1970. $7.30.

RED CAPITALISM: AN ANALYSIS OF THE NAVAJO ECONOMY
Kent Gilbreath
168 pp. University of Oklahoma Press, 1973. Pap. $2.95.

SOCIAL LIFE OF THE NAVAJO INDIANS
Gladys Amanda Reichard
With some attention to minor ceremonies. AMS Press. Reprint of the 1928 edition. $27.50.

SOME SEX BELIEFS AND PRACTICES IN A NAVAJO COMMUNITY
F. L. Baily
Kraus Reprint Co. Reprint of the 1950 edition. Pap. $5.00.

THE STORY OF THE NAVAJO
Marion E. Gridley
G. P. Putnams's Sons, 1969. Illus. $4.97.

A STUDY OF NAVAJO SYMBOLISM
F. J. Newcomb
Kraus Reprint Co., 1974. Reprint of the 1956 edition. Pap. $9.50.

WHEN NAVAJOS HAD TOO MANY SHEEP: THE 1940'S

George A. Boyce
Navajo education, housing, health, and
economy during the 1940's. Indian Historian.
Pap. $5.00.

NEZ PERCE

CHIEF JOSEPH
R. P. Johnson
The leader who helped guide the Nez Perce
Indians on a swventeen-hundred-mile retreat
from United States Military Forces. 74 pp.
Dillon Press. $4.95.

*CHIEF JOSEPH: WAR CHIEF OF THE NEZ PERCE
Russell Davis and Brent Ashabranner
The story of the greatest fighting chief of the
Western Indian wars. 192 pp. McGraw-Hill
Book Co., 1962. Age 8-12. $4.72.

ETHNOHISTORICAL STUDY OF ABORIGINAL TERRITORY OF THE NEZ PERCE INDIANS IN IDAHO, OREGON, AND WASHINGTON, 1805 TO 1855
Stuart S. Chalfant
135 pp. Clearwater Publishing Co., 1973.
$30.95.

ETHNOHISTORY OF THE JOSEPH BAND OF NEZ PERCE INDIANS, 1805 TO 1905
Verne F. Ray.
111 pp. Clearwater Publishing Co., 1973.
$27.00.

*HORSEMEN OF THE WESTERN PLATEAUS, THE NEZ PERCE INDIANS
Sonia Bleeker
160 pp. William Morrow and Co., 1957. Illus.
$4.32. Ages 9 to 12.

"I WILL FIGHT NO MORE FOR-EVER": CHIEF JOSEPH AND THE NEZ PERCE WAR
Merrill D. Beal
384 pp. University of Washington Press, 1966.
Illus. Cloth, $8.95; Pap. $3.95.

THE NEZ PERCE INDIANS
H. J. Spinden
Kraus Reprint Co. Reprint of the 1908 edition.
Pap. $6.00.

NEZ PERCE INDIANS, INCLUDING:
Aboriginal Territory of the Nez Perce Indians,

Stuart A. Chalfant; Ethnology of the Joseph
Band of the Nez Perce Indians, 1805 to 1905,
verne F. Ray; *Findings of Fact, and Opinion,*
The Indian Claims Commission.
301 pp. Garland Publishing, 1974. $21.00.

THE NEZ PERCE: TRIBESMEN OF THE COLUMBIA PLATEAU
Francis Haines
329 pp. University of Oklahoma Press. Reprint
of the 1955 edition. Illus. Cloth, $8.95; Pap.
$.95.

OJIBWA

HISTORY OF THE OJIBWAY NATION
William W. Warren
A history of the people, their migrations,
conflicts with the Sioux, and eventual settlement. 527 pp. Ross & Hain3s, Inc. Reprint of
the 1885 edition. $12.50.

OJIBWA SOCIOLOGY
Ruth Landes
AMS Press. Reprint of the 1937 edition. $7.50.

THE OJIBWA WOMAN
Ruth Landes
AMS Press, Inc. Reprint of the 1938 edition.
$12.50.

*THE OJIBWAY
M. L. Israel
Melmont Pubs., 1962. $4.50. Ages 6 to 10.

OMAHA

BRIGHT EYES: THE STORY OF SUETTE LA FLESCHE, AN OMAHA INDIAN
D. C. Wilson
The traditional clash between indian and white
man's ways. 324 pp. McGraw-Hill Book Co.,
1974. $8.95.

ETHNOGRAPHIC REPORT ON THE OMAHA INDIANS
G. Hubert Smith
216 pp. Clearwater Publishing Co., 1974.
$43.50.

MIDDLE FIVE: INDIAN SCHOOL-BOYS
OF THE OMAHA TRIBE
F. LaFlesche
University of Wisconsin Press, 1963. Pap.
$2.50.

OMAHA INDIAN MYTHS AND
TRICKSTER TALES
Roger Welsch
Over 70 tribal tales. 350 pp. Swallow Press,
1975. $10.00.

OMAHA INDIANS: AN ETHNOHISTORY
G. Hubert Smith
286 pp. Garland Publishing, Inc., 1974. $21.00.

THE OMAHA TRIBE
Alice Cunningham Fletcher and Francis La
Flesche
653 pp. Johnson Reprint Corporation. Reprint
of the 1911 edition. $38.50.

THE OMAHA TRIBE
Alice C. Fletcher and Francis La Flesche
Vol. I: 312 pp., Illus. Vol. II: 347 pp., Illus.
University of Nebraska Press, 1972. Each
volume, $3.50.

A STUDY OF OMAHA INDIAN
MUSIC: INCLUDING TRANSCRIPTIONS
OF 92 SONGS, WORDS AND MUSIC
A. C. Fletcher and F. LaFlesche
Kraus Reprint Co., 1974. Reprint of the 1893
edition. Pap. $6.00.

OSAGE

ANTHROPOLOGICAL STUDY OF THE
OSAGE INDIANS IN KANSAS, MISSOURI,
ARKANSAS, AND OKLAHOMA, 1700 TO
1825
Alice Marriott
319 pp. Clearwater Publishing co., 1973.
$60.40.

LAWS RELATING TO THE OSAGE TRIBE
OF INDIANS FROM MAY 18, 1824 TO
MARCH 2, 1929
R. A. Barney
Scholarly Resources, Inc. Reprint of the 1929
edition. $12.00.

MARIA TALLCHIEF
Marion Gridley
Osage Indian Maria Tallchief achieved world

reknown as a ballerina. 74 pp. Dillon Press.
$4.95.

THE ORIGIN OF THE OSAGE INDIAN
TRIBE: AN ETHNOGRAPHICAL,
HISTORICAL AND ARCHAEOLOGICAL
STUDY, MISSOURI, 1673 TO 1872
Carl H. Chapman
324 pp. Clearwater Publishing Co., 1973. Illus.
$61.20.

OSAGE INDIANS: THE ORIGIN OF THE
OSAGE INDIAN TRIBE: AN ETHNO-
GRAPHICAL, HISTORICAL, AND AR-
CHAEOLOGICAL STUDY
Carl H. Chapman
326 pp. Garland Publishing, Inc., 1974. $21.00.

OSAGE INDIANS VOLUME 1, IN-
CLUDING: *Osage Research Project,*
Fred W. Voget
444 pp. Garland Publishing Co., 1974. $21.00.

OSAGE INDIANS VOL. 4, INCLUDING: *A
Preliminary Survey of Missouri Archaeology,
and Osage Village Locations and Hunting
Territories to 1808,* and *Osage Village Sites and
HuntingTerritory 1808 to 1825,*Carl H. Chap-
man; *The Osage Nation 1775 to 1818,* Dale
R. Henning.
313 pp. Garland Publishing, 1974. $21.00.

OSAGE INDIANS VOLUME 5, INCLUD-
ING: *Findings of Fact, and Opinion,*
The Indian Claims Commission
223 pp. Garland Publishing Co., 1974. $21.00.

TRADITIONS OF THE OSAGE
George Amos Dorsey
AMS Press, 1974. Reprint of the 1904 edition.
$7.50.

PAIUTE

ANTHROPOLOGICAL REPORT ON THE
NORTHERN PAIUTE INDIANS IN
NEVADA, OREGON, AND CALIFORNIA,
1826 TO 1880
Julian H. Steward and Erminie Wheeler-
Voegenlin
313 pp. Clearwater Publishing Co., 1973.
$59.40.

PAIUTE INDIANS: FINDINGS OF FACT, AND OPINION
The Indian Claims Commission
164 pp. Garland Publishing, Inc., 1974. $21.00.

PAIUTE INDIANS: THE NORTHERN PAIUTE INDIANS
Junian H. Steward and Erminie Wheeler-Voegelin
318 pp. Garland Publishing, Inc., 1974. $21.00.

PAIUTE INDIANS VOL. 2, INCLUDING:
Southern Paiute Ethnography, Isabel T. Kelly; *Chemehuevi Notes,* Richard F. Van Valkenburgh.
192 pp. Garland Publishing, 1974. $21.00.

PAIUTE INDIANS VOL. 4, INCLUDING:
Northern Paiute Archaelogy, Gordon L. Grosscup; *Medicinal Uses of Plants by Indian tribes of Nevada,* Percy Train, et al; *Notes on Snakes, Paiutes, Nez Perces at Malheur Reservation,* A.B. Meacham, et al.
349 pp. Garland Publishing, 1974. $21.00.

PAIUTE INDIANS: SOUTHERN PAIUTE AND CHEMEHEUVI: AN ETHNOHISTORICAL REPORT
Robert A. Manners
278 pp. Garland Publishing, Inc., 1974. $21.00.

SAND IN A WHIRLWIND: THE PAIUTE INDIAN WAR OF 1860
Ferol Egan
Doubleday and Co., 1972. Illus. $8.95.

SOUTHERN PAIUTE AND CHEMEHEUVI: AN ETHNOHISTORICAL REPORT, ARIZONA
Robert A. Manners
272 pp. Clearwater Publishing Co., 1973. $52.85.

SOUTHERN PAIUTE ETHNOGRAPHY: THE EASTERN BANDS IN ARIZONA, UTAH, AND NEVADA
Isabel T. Kelly
192 pp. Clearwater Publishing Co., 1973. $40.00.

SOUTHERN PAIUTE ETHNOHISTORY
Robert C. Euler
Dr. Euler reconstructs Southern Paiute culture-history using techniques and data from ethnology and history. 176 pp. University of Utah Press. Reprint of 1966 edition. Pap. $6.00.

PAPAGO

BASKETRY OF THE PAPAGO AND PIMA INDIANS
Mary Lois Kissell
Study of the art and handicraft of aboriginal basket weaving. 158 pp. Rio Grande Press. Reprint of the 1916 edition. Illus. $8.00.

LEGENDS AND LORE OF THE PAPAGO AND PIMA INDIANS
Dean and Lucille Saxton
Oral literature, as told by the Indians themselves. 441 pp. University of Arizona Press, 1973. Pap. $5.95.

PAPAGO INDIAN POTTERY
Bernard L. Fontana, et al
185 pp. University of Washington Press, 1962. Illus. $6.50.

PAPAGO INDIANS: PAPAGO POPULATION STUDIES
William S. King and Delmos J. Jones
361 pp. Garland Publishing, Inc., 1974. $21.00.

PAPAGO INDIANS VOL. 1, INCLUDING:
Papago Indians: Aboriginal Land Use and Occupancy, Robert A. Hackenbert; *Acculturation at the Papago village of Santa Rosa,* Ruth M. Underhill; *the Cattle Industry of the Southern Papago districts with Some Information on the Reservation Cattle Industry as a Whole,* Gwyneth H. Xavier.
303 pp. Garland Publishing, 1974. $21.00.

PAPAGO INDIANS VOL. 3, INCLUDING:
The Papago Indians of Arizona, William H. Kelley; *The Papago Tribe of Arizona,* Bernard I. Fontana; *Findings of Fact, and opinion,* The Indian Claims commission.
252 pp. Garland Publishing, 1974. $21.00.

PAPAGO MUSIC
F. Densmore
Da Capo Press. Reprint of the 1929 edition. $12.50.

THE PAPAGO TRIBE OF ARIZONA: ANTHROPOLOGICAL REPORT, 1539 TO 1937
Bernard L. Fontana
70 pp. Clearwater Publishing Co., 1973. $20.55.

SINGING FOR POWER: THE SONG MAGIC OF THE PAPAGO INDIANS OF SOUTHERN ARIZONA
R. M. Underhill
University of California Press, 1975. Reprint of the 1938 edition. $6.75.

PAWNEE

THE PAWNEE GHOST DANCE HAND GAME
Alexander Lesser
AMS Press, Inc. Reprint of the 1933 edition. $17.00.

THE PAWNEE INDIANS
George E. Hyde
372 pp. University of Oklahoma Press, 1974. Illus. $8.95.

PAWNEE AND KANSA [KAW] INDIANS, INCLUDING:
Notes on the Pawnee, John L. Champe and Franklin Fenenga; *Historical and Economic Geography of the Pawnee Lands,* Thomas M. Griffiths; *The prehistoric and Historic Habitat of the Kansa Indians,* Waldo R. Wedel; *Findings of Fact, and Opinion,* The Indian Claims Commission.
492 pp. Garland Publishing Co., 1974. $21.00.

PAWNEE MUSIC
F. Densmore
Scholarly Press. Reprint of the 1929 edition. $9.50.

THE PAWNEE: MYTHOLOGY
George Amos Dorsey
AMS Press, Inc. Reprint of the 1906 edition. $65.50.

PIANKASHAW

ANTHROPOLOGICAL REPORT ON THE PIANKASHAW INDIANS IN ILLINOIS, 1682 TO 1832.
Dorothy Libby
313 pp. Clearwater Publishing Co., 1973. $59.40.

PIANKASHAW AND KASKASKIA INDIANS, INCLUDING:

An Anthropological Report on the Piankashaw Indians, Dorothy Libby; *Report on the Piankashaw and Kaskaskia and the Treaty of Greene Vile,* David B. Stout.
332 pp. Garland Publishing Co., 1974. $21.00.

PIMA

BASKETRY OF THE PAPAGO AND PIMA INDIANS
Mary Lois Kissell
Study of the art and handicraft of aboriginal basket weaving. 158 pp. Rio Grande Press. Reprint of the 1916 edition. Illus. $8.00.

LEGENDS AND LORE OF THE PAPAGO AND PIMA INDIANS
Dean and Lucille Saxton
Oral literature, as told by the Indians themselves. 441 pp. University of Arizona Press, 1973. Pap. $5.95.

PIMA INDIAN LEGENDS
Anna Moore Shaw
The author, a Pima herself, unfolds 24 Indian tales. 111 pp. University of Arizona Press, 1968. Pap. $2.50.

THE PIMA INDIANS
Frank Russell
A study of Pima history and culture, and includes texts of speeches in the Piman language. University of Arizona Press, 1975. Illus. Pap. $5.95.

PIMA-MARICOPA INDIANS, INCLUDING:
Aboriginal Land Use and Occupancy of the Pima-Maricipa Indians, Robert Hackenberg; *Findings of Fact, and Opinion,* The Indian Claims Commission.
698 pp. Garland Publishing, 1974. $42.00. Two volume set.

A PIMA PAST
Anna Moore Shaw
Recollections of a Pima Indian woman. 263 pp. University of Arizona Press, 1974. Pap. $3.95.

PLAINS

*AMONG THE PLAINS INDIANS

Lorenz Engel
Visiting the villages of the Mandan, Assiniboin,
Blackfoot and Sioux. 112 pp. Lerner
Publications, 1970. Illus. Ages 11-17. $6.95.

COSTUMES OF THE PLAINS INDIANS
Clark Wissler
AMS Press, Inc. Reprint of the 1915 to 1916
edition. $9.00.

DOG SOLDIERS, BEAR MEN, AND BUF-FALO WOMEN: THE SOCIETIES AND CULTS OF THE PLAINS INDIAN
T. E. Mails
Prentice-Hall, 1973. $20.00.

HAPPY HUNTING GROUNDS
Stanley Vestal
A comprehensive picture of Plains Indian life.
228 pp. universtiy of Oklahoma Press, 1975.
Illus. $5.95.

NORTH AMERICAN INDIANS OF THE PLAINS
Clark Wissler
Not only a guide to museum collections from
the Plains Indians but a summary of the facts
and interpretations making up the anthropology
of these tribes. 172 pp. Burt Franklin
Publishers. Reprint of the 1934 edition. Illus.
$12.50.

THE PLAINS APACHE
John Upton Terrell
The history of the Plains Apache from the
arrival of the first Spanish Missionaries to their
near destruction by the United States Army in
the nineteenth century. 224 pp. Thomas Y.
Crowell Co., 1975. $7.95.

PLAINS INDIAN MYTHOLOGY
Alice Marriott and Carol Rachlin
Tales that reflect the history of the Plains Indians: the coming of the horse, the appearance
of the white man on the Plains, the Plains wars,
the Ghost Dance Revolt, stories of missionaries,
and life on reservations today. 224 pp. Thomas
Y. Crowell Co. $7.95. 1974.

PLAINS INDIAN RAIDERS: THE FINAL PHASES OF WARFARE FROM THE ARKANSAS TO THE RED RIVER
Wilbur Sturtevant Nye
418 pp. University of Oklahoma Press. Reprint
of the 1968 edition. illus. Cloth, $10.50; Pap.
$4.95.

RANK AND WARFARE AMONG THE PLAINS INDIANS
Bernard Mishkin
Examines the economic implications and the
historical interrelationships of horse culture,
rank, warfare, and their roles in the framework
of Plains society. 73 pp. University of
Washington Press, 1940. $7.00.

REALITY AND DREAM: PSYCHOTHER-APY OF A PLAINS INDIAN
G. Devereaux
New York University Press. Reprint of the 1951
edition. $12.00.

SITTING BULL: AN EPIC OF THE PLAINS
Alexander B. Adams
G. P. Putnam's Sons, 1973. Illus. Cloth, $9.95;
Pap. $3.50.

SOCIETIES OF THE PLAINS INDIANS
Clark Wissler
13 parts in one volume. AMS Press. Reprint of
the 1912-1916 editions. $70.00.

THE SUNDANCE PEOPLE: THE PLAINS INDIANS, THEIR PAST AND PRESENT
Richard Erdoes
Portrait of the Plains Indians. Vintage Press.
$1.50. Teacher's guide, $1.00.

WARRIORS OF THE PLAINS
C. Taylor
Arco Publishing Co., 1975. $15.00.

POMO

POMO INDIAN MYTHS AND SOME OF THEIR SACRED MEANINGS
Cora Clark and Texa Bowen Williams
Pomo Indian priests, in violation of strictest
rules, have for the first time revealed their
folklore and legends in an attempt to per-
manently record their culture. Brown Book Co.,
1975. $3.00.

THE POMO INDIANS OF CALIFORNIA AND THEIR NEIGHBORS
Vinson Brown
64 pp. Naturegraph, 1969. Illus. Cloth,
$5.95; Pap. $2.95.

PONCA

ETHNOHISTORY OF THE PONCA IN-DIANS WITH REFERENCE TO THEIR CLAIM TO CERTAIN LANDS IN NEBRASKA AND SOUTH DAKOTA, 1858
Joseph Jablow
356 pp. Clearwater Publishing Co., 1973. $66.30.

PONCA INDIANS, INCLUDING:
Ethnology of the Ponca,
Joseph Jablow; *Findings of Fact, and Opinion,* The Indian Claims Commission. 403 pp. Garland Publishing, 1974. $21.00.

POTAWATOMI

ANTHROPOLOGICAL REPORTS ON THE KICKAPOO, ILLINOIS AND POTAWA-TOMIE INDIANS IN ILLINOIS AND INDI-ANA, 1819 TO 1832
David B. Stout
124 pp. Clearwater Publishing Co., 1973. $29.20.

INDIANS OF NORTHEASTERN ILLI-NOIS: THE CHIPPEWA, OTTAWA, AND POTAWATOMI INDIANS
David A. Baerreis, et al, Editors
Garland Publishing, Inc., 1974. $21.00.

THE MASCOUTENS OF PRAIRIE POTAWATOMI INDIANS: SOCIAL LIFE AND CEREMONIES
Alanson Buck Skinner
262 pp. Greenwood Press. Reprint of the 1924 edition. Illus. $15.00.

PRAIRIE POTAWATOMI: TRADITION AND RITUAL IN THE TWENTIETH CENTURY
R. Landes
University of Wisconsin Press, 1969. $15.00.

PUEBLO

THE AMERICAN INDIAN AS A PRODUCT OF ENVIRONMENT
A. J. Fynn

An examination of Pueblo ethnology; land homes: food and clothing; government and social life; education; industries, arts and sciences; religion; and dances and festivals. 275 pp. August M. Kelley Publishers. Reprint of the 1907 edition. Illus. $12.50.

AMONG THE PUEBLO INDIANS
Carl and Lilian Westcott Eickemeyer
AMS Press, Inc., 1900. Illus. $12.50.

GLEN CANYON: *A Summary*
Jesse D. Jennings
Summary of the Glen Canyon research achievements from 1956 through 1963. This Canyon located in northern Arizona, was once inhabited by the Pueblo Indians. Their culture is put into perspective. 86 pp. The University of Utah Press. Reprint of 1966 edition. Pap. $6.00.

THE INDIANS OF POINT PINES, ARIZONA: A COMPARATIVE STUDY OF THEIR PHYSICAL CHARACTERISTICS
Kenneth A. Bennett
Based on skeletal remains of more than 500 individuals from one of the largest population centers in the prehistoric Western Pueblo culture. 75 pp. University of Arizona Press. Pap. $3.95.

INDIANS OF THE RIO GRANDE
Adolph F. Bandelier and Edgar L. Hewett
This book explores, in two parts, the cultural life of the Pueblos as well as a documentary history. Cooper Square Publishers, 1973. $12.50.

INDIANS OF THE SOUTHWEST
Pliny Earle Goddard
Following the earliest archeological evidence of the Basket-maker culture and the outgrowth of the modern Pueblo. Illus. Cooper Square Publishers. Reprint of the 1931 edition. 6.50.

INDIANS OF THE TERRACED HOUSES: THE PUEBLO INDIANS OF NEW MEXICO AND ARIZONA, 1902-1910
Charles Francis Saunders
An account of the Pueblo Indians in Territorial times. 430 pp. 51 plates. Rio Grande Press. Reprint of the 1912 edition. Illus. $10.00.

KERESAN BRIDGE: A PROBLEM IN PUEBLO ETHNOLOGY
R. Fox
Humanities Press, Inc., 1967. $8.00.

MANY WINTERS: PROSE AND POETRY OF THE PUEBLOS
  Nancy C. Wood
80 pp. Doubleday, 1974. Illus. $6.95.

MASKED GODS: NAVAJO AND PUEBLO CEREMONIALISM
  Frank Waters
Swallow Press, 1973. Cloth, $10.00; Pap. $4.95.

POTTERY OF THE ANCIENT PUEBLOS
  W. H. Holmes
Shorey Pubns. Reprint of the 1886 edition. Pap. $6.00.

PUEBLO ANIMALS AND MYTHS
  Hamilton A. Tyler
Explains the Indians' naturalistic view of animals, and how they came to be elevated to the status of spirits and gods. 300 pp. University of Oklahoma Press, 1975. Illus. $8.95.

PUEBLO GODS AND MYTHS
  Hamilton A. Tyler
313 pp. University of Oklahoma Press. Reprint of the 1964 edition. Cloth, $7.95; Pap. $3.50.

PUEBLO INDIANS: ARCHAEOLOGIC AND ETHNOLOGIC DATA: ACOMA-LAGUNA LAND CLAIMS
  Florence H. Ellis
326 pp. Garland Publishing, Inc., 1974. $21.00.

*THE PUEBLO INDIANS, FARMERS OF THE RIO GRANDE
  Sonia Bleeker
160 pp. William Morrow and Co., 1954. Illus. $3.94. Ages 9 to 12.

THE PUEBLO INDIANS OF NEW MEXICO: THEIR LAND, ECONOMY, AND CIVIL ORGANIZATION
  S. B. DeAberle
Kraus Reprint Co. Reprint of the 1948 edition. Pap. $5.00.

PUEBLO INDIANS VOL. 1, INCLUDING:
Anthropological Data Pertaining to the Taos Land Claim, Florence H. Ellis; *Spanish and Mexican Land Policies and Grants in the Taos Pueblo Region, New Mexico,* Harold Dunham; *Findings of Fact and Opinion,* The Indian Claims Commission; *A Historical Study of Land Use Eastward of the Taos Indians' Pueblo Land Grant Prior to 1848,* Harold Dunham. 386 pp. Garland Publishing, 1974. $21.00.

PUEBLO INDIANS VOL. 3, INCLUDING:
Anthropology of Languna Pueblo Land Claims, Florence H. Ellis; *Historical Treatise in Defense of the Pueblo of Acoma Land Claims,* Ward A. Minge; *Acoma Land Utilization,* Robert L. Rands. 391 pp. Garland Publishing, 1974. $21.00.

PUEBLO INDIANS VOL. 4, INCLUDING:
History of the Laguna Pueblo Land Claims, Myra Ellen Jenkins; *Laguna Land Utilization; An Ethnohistorical Report,* Robert L. Rands. 386 pp. Garland Publishing, 1974. $21.00.

PUEBLO INDIANS VOLUME 5, INCLUDING: *Findings of Fact, and Opinion,*
  The Indian Claims Commission
249 pp. Garland Publishing Co., 1974. $21.00.

THE RE-ESTABLISHMENT OF THE INDIANS IN THEIR PUEBLO LIFE THROUGH THE REVIVAL OF THEIR TRADITIONAL CRAFTS: A STUDY IN HOME EXTENDION EDUCATION
  Mrs. Henrietta Kolshorn Burton
AMS Press, Inc., Reprint of the 1936 edition. $10.00.

QUILEUTE

ETHNOLOGICAL AND HISTORICAL EVIDENCE: THE QUILEUTE TRIBE AND THE QUINAIELT TRIBE IN OREGON, 1808 TO 1956
  Anonymous
192 pp. Clearwater Publishing Co., 1973. $40.00.

NOOTKA AND QUILEUTE MUSIC
  F. Densmore
Scholarly Press. Reprint of the 1939 edition. $24.50.

SAC AND FOX

CONTRIBUTIONS TO FOX ETHNOLOGY
  T. Michelson
Scholarly Press. Reprint of the 1927 edition. $9.50.

ETHNOLOGICAL REPORT ON THE HISTORIC HABITAT OF THE SAUK, FOX AND IOWA TRIBES IN IOWA, 1665 TO 1820
Zachary Gussow
62 pp. Clearwater Publishing Co., 1973. $19.25.

THE ETHNOGRAPHY OF THE FOX INDIANS
W. Jones
Scholarly Press. Reprint of the 1939 edition. $9.50.

FOX TEXTS
William Jones
AMS Press. Reprint of the 1907 edition. $17.50.

JIM THORPE
Robert Reising
Jim Thorpe won the Olympic Pentathlon and Decathlon events and played professional baseball and football leagues. This book opens with a brief history of the Sac and Fox Indians. 58 pp. Dillon Press. $4.95.

NOTES ON THE BUFFALO-HEAD DANCE OF THE BEAR GENS OF THE FOX INDIANS
T. Michelson
Scholarly Press. Reprint of the 1928 edition. $9.50.

OBSERVATIONS ON THE ETHNOLOGY OF THE SAUK INDIANS
Alanson buck skinner
180 pp. Greenwood Press. Reprint of the 1923 edition. Illus. $12.50.

SAC, FOX AND IOWA INDIANS VOLUME 1, INCLUDING:
An Anthropological Report on the Sac, Fox and Iowa Indians, and *An Ethnohistorical Report on the Historic Habitat of the Sauk, Fox and Iowa Indians,* Zachary Gussow; *Spanish Land Grants in Missouri,* Raleigh Barlowe; *Manners and customs of the Suuk Nation of Indians,* The Indian Claims Commission.
Garland Publishing, Inc., 1974. $21.00.

SAC, FOX, AND IOWA INDIANS: INDIANS OF EAST MISSOURI, WEST ILLINOIS, AND SOUTH WISCONSIN FROM THE PROTO-HISTORIC PERIOD TO 1804
David B. Stout and Erminie Wheeler-Voegelin
321 pp. Garland Publishing, Inc., 1974. $21.00.

SAC, FOX AND IOWA INDIANS VOLUME 3, INCLUDING: *Findings of Fact, and Opinion,*
The Indian Claims Commission
299 pp. Garland Publishing Co., 1974. $21.00.

THE SAC AND FOX INDIANS
William T. Hagen
287 pp. University of Oklahoma Press, 1958. Illus. $7.95.

SALISH

ANTHROPOLOGICAL AND ETHNOHISTORICAL REPORT ON COLUMBIA SALISH OF CENTRAL WASHINGTON: ABORIGINAL LAND USE AND OCCUPANCY
Stuart A. Chalfant
78 pp. Clearwater Publishing Co., 1973. $21.80.

COAST SALISH AND WESTERN WASHINGTON INDIANS: THE ECONOMIC LIFE OF THE COAST SALISH OF HARO AND ROSARIO STRAITS, VOL 1
Wayne P. Suttles
516 pp. Garland Publishing, Inc., 1974. $21.00.

COAST SALISH AND WESTERN WASHINGTON INDIANS VOLUME 2, INCLUDING:
Ethnological Filed Investigation and Analysis of the Puget Sound Indians, Carroll L. Riley; *Influence of White Contact on Class Distinctions and Political Authority Among the Indians of Northern Puget Sound,* June McCollins; *The Quileute Indians of Puget Sound,* The Indian Claims Commission, et al; *Anthropological Investigation of the Medicine Creek Tribes,* Herbert Taylor; *Historical and Ethnological Study of the Snohomish Indian People,* Colin Tweddell.
538 pp. Garland Publishing Co., 1974. $21.00.

COAST SALISH AND WESTERN WASHINGTON INDIANS VOLUME 3, INCLUDING:
Anthropological Investigation of Makah Indians, Anthropological Investigation of the Chehalis Indians, John Work on the Chehalis Indians, All by Herbert C. Taylor, Jr.; *Territorial Distribution of the Aboriginal Population of Western Washington State and the Economic and Political Characteristics of their Culture,* Jacob Fried; *Handbook of*

Cowlitz Indians, Verne F. Ray
299 pp. Garland Publishing Co., 1974. $21.00.

COAST SALISH AND WESTERN WASHINGTON INDIANS VOL. 4, INCLUDING: *Structure of Twana Culture,* William W. Elmendorf; *A Study of Religious Change Among the Skagit Indians,* June M. Collins.
367 pp. Garland Publishing, 1974. $21.00.

COAST SALISH AND WESTERN WASHINGTON INDIANS: FINDINGS OF FACT AND OPINION
The Indian Claims Commission
412 pp. Garland Publishing, Inc., 1974. $21.00.

ETHNOGRAPHIC REPORT ON THE SALISH AND CHIMAKUA-SPEAKING INDIANS OF THE PUGET SOUND BASIN WASHINGTON, 1853
Carroll l. Riley
68 pp. Clearwater Publishing Co., 1973. $20.20.

FOLK-TALES OF THE COAST SALISH
Thelma Adamson, Editor
Kraus Reprint co., 1974. Reprint of the 1934 edition. $18.00.

INTERIOR SALISH AND EASTERN WASHINGTON INDIANS VOL. 1, INCLUDING:
Ethnological Field Investigation and Analysis of Historical Material Relative to Coeur D'Alene Indian Aboriginal Distribution, Stuart A. Chalfnat; *The Coeur D'Alene Country 1805 to 1892-An Historical Sketch,* William N. Bischoff; *Findings of Fact, and Opinion,* The Indian Claims Commission.
280 pp. Garland Publishing, 1974. $21.00.

INTERIOR SALISH AND EASTERN WASHINGTON INDIANS VOL. 2, INCLUSIVE
Garland Publishing, Inc. $21.00.

INTERIOR SALISH AND EASTERN WASHINGTON INDIANS VOLUME 3, INCLUDING:
The Confederated Salish and Kutenal Tribes of the Flathead Reservation, Montana, E.O. Fuller; *Aboriginal Territory of the Kalispel Indians,* Stuart A. Chalfnat; *History of the Confederated Salish and Kutenal Tribes of the Flathead Reservation, Montana,* Paul C. Phillips; *Flathead, Kutenai and Upper Pend D'Oreille Genealogies,* Carling Maluof and Paul C.

Phillips; *Findings of Fact, and Opinion,* The Indian Claims Commission.
371 pp. Garland Publishing Co., 1974. $21.00.

INTERIOR SALISH AND EASTERN WASHINGTON INDIANS VOLUME 4, INCLUDING:
Ethnohistorical Report on Aboriginal Land Use and Occupancy by Spokane Indians, Ethnohistorical Report on Aboriginal Land Occupancy and Utilization by Palus Indians, Anthropological and Ethnohistorical Material Relative to Aboriginal Land Use and Occupancy by the Columbia Salish of Central Washington, Anthropological and Ethnohistorical Material Relative to Aboriginal Land Use and Occupancy by the Wentachi Salish of Central Washington, All by Stuart A. Chalfant. *Ethnohistory of the Spokane Indians,* Angelo Anastasio; *Ethnological Notes on the Columbia, Chelan, Entiat and Wenatchi Tribes,* Verne F. Ray; *Findings of Fact, and Opinion,* The Indian Claims Commission.
541 pp. Garland Publishing Co., 1974. $21.00.

SALISH LANGUAGE AND CULTURE: A STATISTICAL ANALYSIS OF INTERNAL RELATIONSHIPS, HISTORY AND EDUCATION
J. C. Jorgensen
Indiana University Research Center for the Language Sciences, 1969, Pap. $9.00.

SEMINOLE

ETHNOHISTORICAL REPORT OF THE FLORIDA SEMINOLE TO 1823
Charles H. Fairbanks

FLORIDA'S SEMINOLE INDIANS
W. T. Neill and E. R. Allen
Great Outdoors Publishing Co., Pap. $1.50.

NOTES ON COLONIAL INDIANS [SEMINOLE] AND COMMUNITIES IN FLORIDA, 1700 TO 1821
Howard F. Cline
220 pp. Clearwater Publishing co., 1974. $49.20.

OSCEOLA
R. P. Johnson
The military genius of Osceola, who led the

Seminoles in the defense of their Florida homeland. 90 pp. Dillon Press. $4.95.

RED PATRIOTS: THE STORY OF THE SEMINOLES
Charles H. Coe
347 pp. University of Florida Press, 1974. Reprint of the 1898 edition. Illus. $12.00.

REMINISCENCES OF THE SECOND SEMINOLE WAR
John Bemrose
115 pp. University of Florida Press, 1966. $5.00.

*THE SEMINOLE INDIANS
Sonia Bleeker
160 pp. William Morrow and Co., 1954. Illus. $4.25. Ages 9 to 12.

SEMINOLE MUSIC
F. Densmore
Da Capo Press. Reprint of the 1956 edition. $12.50.

THE SEMINOLES
Edwin C. McReynolds
430 pp. University of Oklahoma Press, 1972. Reprint of the 1957 edition. Illus. $8.95.

THE SEMINOLES
Edwin C. McReynolds
The story of the only Indian tribe never to make official peace with the government of the United States. 414 pp. University of Oklahoma Press, 1975. Illus. Pap. $3.95.

THE STORY OF THE SEMINOLE
Marion E. Gridley
G. P. Putnam's Sons, 1973. Illus. $4.97.

*WAR WITH THE SEMINOLES, 1835-1842: THE FLORIDA INDIANS FIGHT FOR THEIR FREEDOM AND HOMELAND
Kenneth M. Jones
The fight against the American government, led by Osceola. 96 pp. Franklin Watts, Inc., 1975. Age 12 up. $3.90.

SENECA

THE DEATH AND REBIRTH OF THE SENECA
A. F. Wallace

Random House, Inc., 1972. Pap. $2.45.

THE HISTORY OF THE SENECA INDIANS
Arthur Caswell Parker
Kennikat press. Reprint of the 1926 edition. Illus. $6.00.

SENECA INDIAN MYTHS
J. Curtain
Gordon Press. $27.00.

SENECA THANKSGIVING RITUALS
W. L. Chafe
Scholarly Press. Reprint of the 1961 edition. $19.50.

SHAWNEE

HISTORY OF THE SHAWNEE INDIANS FROM THE YEAR 1681 TO 1854
H. Harvey
Kraus Reprint Co. Reprint of the 1855 edition. $13.50.

LIFE OF TECUMSEH AND HIS BROTHER THE PROPHET; WITH AN HISTORICAL SKETCH OF THE SHAWANOE INDIANS
B. Drake
Kraus Reprint Co., 1974. Reprint of the 1852 edition. $10.00.

TECUMSEH
C. Klinck
The biography of the Indian chief who organized an Indian confederacy from the Canadian to the Mexican border to fight U. S. troops. Brown Book Co., 1961. Pap. $2.50.

TECUMSEH
Kent Pellett
Tecumseh, son of a Shawnee chief, traveled from his home in Ohio to almost every tribe east of the Rockies trying to form an Indian confederacy to halt the flow of whites into the west. He later commanded the Indian allies of the British armies in the War of 1812 in the hope that the Americans could be defeated. 70 pp. Dillon Press. $4.95.

*TECUMSEH AND THE INDIAN CONFEDERATION, 1811-1813: THE INDIAN NATIONS EAST OF THE MISSISSIPPI ARE DEFEATED
Joseph B. Icenhower

The great Shawnee leader of the Indian Confederation. 96 pp. Franklin Watts, Inc., 1975. Age 12 up. $3.90.

SHOSHONI

BASIN-PLATEAU ABORIGINAL SOCIO-POLITICAL GROUPS
Julian H. Steward
An ethnographic reconnaissance of the Western Shoshoni and some of their Northern Paiute, Ute, and Southern Paiute neighbors of the Great Basin. Attempts to ascertain the types of Shoshonean socio-political groups and to discover their ecological and social determinats. 346 pp. The University of Utah Press. Reprint of 1938 edition. Pap. $5.00.

NEWE NATEKWINAPPEH: *Shoshoni Stories and Dictionary*
Wick R. Miller, Compiler
A collection of tales depicting a spectrum of Shoshoni verbal literature. Imbedded in the stories are ethnographic data, information on hunting practices, and descriptions of the native view of natural history. A dictionary of Shoshoni words are found in the back of the text. 172 pp. The University of Utah Press. Pap. $6.00. Distributed free to Shoshoni Indians by writing the Dept. of Anthropology, University of Utah, Salt Lake City, Utah 84112, Attention Wick R. Miller.

THE NORTHERN SHOSHONE
Robert Harry Lowie
AMS Press, 1974. Reprint of the 1909 edition. $10.00

SHOSHONE INDIANS, INCLUDING:
The Gosiute Indians, Carling Malouf; *The Shoshones in the Rocky Mountain Area, and the Indians in Yellowstone Park,* Ake Hultkrantz; *Findings of Fact, and Opinion,* The Indian Claims Commission.
323 pp. Garland Publishing, 1974. $21.00.

THE SHOSHONIS: SENTINELS OF THE ROCKIES
Virginia Cole Trenholm and Maurine Carley
367 pp. University of Oklahoma Press. Reprint of the 1964 edition. Illus. $8.95; Pap. $3.95.

SIOUX

AIRLIFT TO WOUNDED KNEE
Bill Zimmerman
The story of the airlift to the Sioux Indians who seized the village in 1973. 400 pp. Swallow Press, 1975. Photos. $10.00.

CHEYENNE AND SIOUX: THE REMINISCENCES OF FOUR INDIANS AND A WHITE SOLDIER
R. H. Limbaugh and T. B. Marquis
University of the Pacific, 1973. $5.50.

CRAZY HORSE
John Milton
This Indian warrior's biography is of the Sioux way of life, of the Sioux wars, and of the tragic conflict between the namad Sioux and white settlers. 58 pp. Dillon Press. $4.95.

CRAZY HORSE, THE STRANGE MAN OF THE OGLALAS: A BIOGRAPHY
Mari Sandoz
429 pp. University of Nebraska Press, 1961. Pap. $2.95.

CUSTER DIED FOR YOUR SINS: AN INDIAN MANIFESTO
Vine Deloria, Jr.
An American Indian of the Standing Rock Sioux expounds his people's problems. Macmillan Publishing Co. $5.95.

THE FORGOTTEN SIOUX
Ernest L. Schusky
The story of the Sioux who remained peaceful with the white man. 272 pp. Nelson-Hall Publishers, 1975. Illus. $12.95.

THE GREAT SIOUX NATION
Frederick Hans
A history of the war-like Sioux and a study of their manners and customs A fifty-page dictionary of the language is included. 586 pp. Ross & Haines, Inc. Illus. $15.00.

HISTORY OF THE SANTEE SIOUX: UNITED STATES INDIAN POLICY ON TRIAL
Roy W. Meyer
434 pp. University of Nebraska Press, 1968. $11.95.

INDIAN OUTBREAKS
Daniel Buck

History of the Sioux uprising of 1862 by a witness of many of the incidents. 299 pp. Ross & Haines, Inc. Reprint of the 1904 edition. Illus. $8.75.

LAST DAYS OF THE SIOUX NATION
R. M. Utley
Yale University Press, 1963. Cloth, $12.50; Pap. $2.75.

LEGENDS OF THE MIGHTY SIOUX
Writers Program, South Dakota
AMS Press, Inc. Reprint of the 1941 edition. $10.00.

THE MODERN SIOUX: SOCIAL SYSTEMS AND RESERVATION CULTURE
Ethel Nurge, Editor
352 pp. University of Nebraska Press, 1970. Cloth, $15.00; Pap. $3.95.

NEW SOURCES OF INDIAN HISTORY, 1850-1891; THE GHOST DANCE — THE PRAIRIE SIOUX
Stanley Vestal, Compiler
A study of the ceremonial dance which originated among the Paiutes of Nevada during the 19th century. The ritual was performed in the belief that it would restore to the Indians their hunting grounds and reunite them with departed friends. 351 pp. Burt Franklin Publishers. Reprint of the 1934 edition. Illus. $14.50.

A PICTOGRAPHIC HISTORY OF THE OGLALA SIOUX
Amos Bad Heart Bull
530 pp. University of Nebraska Press, 1968. Illus. $17.95.

RED CLOUD
Ed McGaa
A Sioux chief who fought white settlers and won, Red Cloud signed the 1868 Peace Treaty and became an eloquent spokesman for his people. 54 pp. Dillon Press. $4.95.

RED CLOUD'S FOLK: A HISTORY OF THE OGLALA SIOUX
George E. Hyde
The epic migration of the westward drive of the Sioux Indians from the Plains to the mountains. 331 pp. University of Oklahoma Press, 1975. Illus. $8.95.

SIOUX INDIAN LEADERS
Mildred Fielder

Featured are Crazy Horse, Spotted Tail, Sitting Bull, Gall, Martin Charger, Red Cloud, Chauncey Yellow Robe, and Ben Reifel. 160 pp. Superior Publishing Co., 1975. Illus. $13.95.

SIOUX INDIANS: DAKOTA SIOUX INDIANS
Wesley R. Hurt
266 pp. Garland Publishing, Inc. $21.00.

*THE SIOUX INDIANS, HUNTERS AND WARRIORS OF THE PLAINS
Sonia Bleeker
160 pp. William Morrow and Co., 1962. Illus. $4.32. Ages 9 to 12.

SIOUX INDIANS VOLUME 1, INCLUDING:
Mdewakanton Band of Sioux Indians,
Harlod Hickerson
303 pp. Garland Publsihing Co., 1974. $21.00.

SIOUX INDIANS VOL. 3, INCLUDING:
Ehtnohistorical Report on the Yankton Sioux,
Alan R. Woolworth; *Yankton Chronology,*
John L. Champe.
274 pp. Garland Publishing, 1974. $21.00.

THE SIOUX: LIFE AND CUSTOMS OF A WARRRIOR SOCIETY
Royal B. Hassrick, et al
400 pp. University of Oklahoma Press. Reprint of the 1964 edition. Illus. $8.95.

THE SIOUAN TRIBES OF THE EAST
James Mooney
101 pp. Johnson Reprint. Reprint of the 1895 edition. $7.00.

SIOUX UPRISING OF 1862
K. Carley
Minnesota Historical Society, 1961. Cloth, $3.75; Pap. $2.50.

SITTING BULL
Faith Yinling Knoop
Medicine man, artist, singer, storyteller, and warrior — Sitting Bull was the only man ever to be chief of all the Plains Sioux. 74 pp. Dillon Press. $4.95.

SITTING BULL: CHAMPION OF THE SIOUX: A BIOGRAPHY
Stanley Vestal
349 pp. University of Oklahoma Press. Reprint of the 1957 edition. Illus. $7.95.

SONGS OF THE TETON SIOUX
Harry W. Paige
A study of the oral expression of the Sioux and the Plains Indians. Westernlore Press. Illus. $7.50.

SPOTTED TAIL'S FOLK: A HISTORY OF THE BRULE SIOUX
George E. Hyde
362 pp. University of Oklahoma Press, 1974. Reprint of the 1962 edition. Illus. $8.95.

*THE STORY OF THE SIOUX
Marion E. Gridley
G. P. Putnam's Sons, 1972. Illus. $4.97. Below college level.

TETON SIOUX MUSIC
F. Densmore
Da Capo Press. Reprint of the 1918 edition. $24.50.

WAR-PATH AND BIVOUAC: OR, THE CONQUEST OF THE SIOUX
John F. Finerty
357 pp. University of Oklahoma Press. Reprint of the 1961 edition. Illus. $3.95.

SKAGIT

THE SKAGIT TRIBE AND THE SNOQUALMIE TRIBE IN WASHINGTON: ETHNOLOGICAL AND HISTORICAL EVIDENCE FROM 1792
Anonymous
265 pp. Clearwater Publishing Co., 1973. $51.75.

VALLEY OF THE SPIRITS: THE UPPER SKAGIT INDIANS OF WESTERN WASHINGTON
June Collins
282 pp. University of Washington Press, 1974. Illus. $9.50.

TEWA

THE ETHNOBOTANY OF THE TEWA INDIANS
Wilfred Robbins, et al
Scholarly Press. $9.50.

ETHNOZOOLOGY OF THE TEWA INDIANS
Henderson and Harrison
Scholarly Press. Reprint of the 1914 edition. $7.50.

THE SOCIAL ORGANIZATION OF THE TEWA OF NEW MEXICO
E. C. Parsons
Kraus Reprint Co. Reprint of the 1929 edition. Pap. $15.00.

TILLAMOOK

ETHNOGRAPHIC REPORT ON THE IDENTITY AND LOCALIZATION OF THE TILLAMOOK BAND OF NORTHWESTERN OREGON
Robert J. Suphan
86 pp. Clearwater Publishing Co., 1974. $23.10.

TILLAMOOK INDIANS OF THE OREGON COAST
Sauter B. Johnson
The Tillamook (Salish) methods of fishing, hunting, and food-gathering; their traditions, spirit stories, and general way of life. 208 pp. Binford & Mort Publishers, 1972. $6.95.

UTE

ABORIGINAL AND HISTORIC GROUPS OF THE UTE INDIANS OF UTAH: AN ANALYSIS
Julian H. Steward
121 pp. Clearwater Publishing Co., 1973. $28.70.

ETHNOGRAPHY OF THE NORTHERN UTES
Anne Smith
Material on the lifestyles which differentiate the various groups of Northern Ute Indians in Colorado and Utah. Museum of New Mexico Press, 1974. $9.95.

HISTORICAL SUMMARY OF THE UTE INDIANS AND THE SAN JUAN MINING REGION
Leroy R. Hafen
54 pp. Clearwater Publishing Co., 1973. $18.00.

INDIANS OF THE PIKE'S PEAK REGION
    Irving Howbert
An account of the Sand Creek massacre in December, 1864; the story of the Ute Indians of the area east of the Rockies. 262 pp. Rio Grande Press. Reprint of the 1914 edition. Illus. $7.50.

THE LAST WAR TRAIL: THE UTES AND THE SETTLEMENT OF COLORADO
    Robert Emmitt
333 pp. University of Oklahoma Press. Reprint of the 1954 edition. Cloth, $8.95; Pap. $3.50.

NORTHERN UTE MUSIC
    F. Densmore
Scholarly Press. Reprint of the 1922 edition. 14.50.

UTE INDIANS VOL. 1, INCLUDING:
Analysis: Aboriginal and Historical Groups of the Ute Indians of Utah. and *Supplement: Native Components of the White River Ute Indians,*
    Julian H. Steward
159 pp. Garland Publishing, 1974. $21.00.

UTE INDIANS VOL. 2, INCLUDING:
Map and Confederated Ute Indian Lands, The Indian Claims Commission; *Historical Summary of the Ute and the San Juan Mining Region,* Leroy R. Hafen; *Cultural Differences and Similarities Between Unitah and White River Indians,* Anne M. Smith; *Finding of Fact and Opinion,* The Indian Clamis Commission. 341 pp. Garland Publishing, 1974. $21.00.

WASHO

THE TWO WORLDS OF THE WASHO: AN INDIAN TRIBE OF CALIFORNIA AND NEVADA
    J. F. Downs
Holt, Rinehart, and Winston, 1966. Pap. $3.00.

THE WASHO INDIANS OF CALIFORNIA AND NEVADA
    Warren L. d'Azevedo, Compiler and Editor
A collection of papers of those engaged in ethnological investigation among the Washo from 1952 to 1963. Includes a bibliography of Washo sources. 201 pp. The University of Utah Press. Reprint of 1963 edition. Pap. $6.00.

THE WASHOE TRIBE OF NEVADA AND CALIFORNIA, 1853
    Noble T. Murray
282 pp. Clearwater Publishing Co., 1973. $54.45.

WINNEBAGO

THE AUTOBIOGRAPHY OF A WINNEBAGO INDIAN
    Paul Radin
This autobiography relates first-hand experiences at the end of the 19th and the beginning of the 20th centuries of tribal life, acculturation, relations with the white society, and entry into the peyote cult. 91 pp. Dover Publications, 1920. Pap. $1.25.

WINNEBAGO, INCLUDING:
Winnebago Ethnology,
    J. A. Jones; *Economic and Historical Background for the Winnebago Indian Claims,* Alice E. Smithe and Vernon Carstensen. 459 pp. Garland Publishing, 1974. $21.00.

THE WINNEBAGO TRIBE
    Paul Radin
526 pp. Johnson Reprint Corporation, 1971. Reprint of the 1923 edition. Illus. $38.50.

WICHITA

THE MYTHOLOGY OF THE WICHITA
    George Amos Dorsey
AMS Press, Inc. Reprint of the 1904 edition. $42.00.

A PILOT STUDY OF WICHITA INDIAN ARCHAEOLOGY AND ETHNOHISTORY
    Robert E. Bell, et al, Editors
340 pp. Clearwater Publishing Co., 1973. $63.75.

WICHITA INDIANS, INCLUDING:
Wichita Indian Archaelogy and Ethnolgy; A Pilot Study, Robert E. Bell, et al
169 pp. Garland Publishing Co., 1974. $21.00.

YAVAPAI

A STUDY OF YAVAPAI HISTORY IN ARIZONA, 1540 TO 1942
Albert H. Schroeder
330 pp. Clearwater Publishing Co., 1973. $62.15.

YAVAPAI INDIANS, INCLUDING:
A Study of Yavapai History, Albert H. Schroeder; *Findings of Fact, and Opinion,* The Indian Claims Commission.
386 pp. Garland Publishing, 1974. $21.00.

YUMAN

YUMAN POTTERY MAKING
Malcolm J. Rogers
Step by step from the gathering of raw clay through the various stages of building, finishing, decorating and firing of paddle-and-anvil vessels. 53 pp. Ballena Press. Reprint of the 1936 edition. Illus. Pap. $2.95.

YUMAN AND YAQUI MUSIC
F. Densmore
Da Capo Press. Reprint of the 1932 edition. $12.50.

ZUNI

THE ZUNI INDIANS: THEIR MYTHOLOGY, ESOTERIC FRATERNITIES, AND CEREMONIES
Mrs. Matilda Coxe (Evans) Stevenson
634 pp. Johnson Reprint. Reprint of the 1905 edition. $63.00.

THE ZUNI INDIANS: THEIR MYTHOLOGY, ESOTERIC FRATERNITIES AND CEREMONIES
Matilda Coxe Stevenson
A study of the Zuni Indians of New Mexico. 760 pp. 48 plates. Rio Grande Press. Reprint of the 1904 edition. Illus. $25.00.

ZUNI KATCHINAS
Ruth L. Bunzel
A Paper from the Bureau of American Ethnology including rare Zuni Katchina plates printed for the first time in full color. 360 pp. Rio Grande Press. Reprint of the 1932 edition. Illus. $20.00.

THE ZUNIS: SELF-PORTRAYALS
Zuni People
University of New Mexico Press, 1972. Cloth, $7.95; Pap. $3.95.

MISCELLANEOUS

ABORIGINAL LOCATION OF THE KADOHADACHO AND RELATED INDIAN TRIBES IN ARKANSAS AND LOUISIANA, 1542 TO 1954
Stephen Williams
60 pp. Clearwater Publishing Co., 1974. $18.95.

BIBLIOGRAPHY OF THE DIEGUENO INDIANS
R. F. Almstedt
Ballena Press, 1974. Pap. $2.95.

CATAWBA INDIANS: THE PEOPLE OF THE RIVER
D. S. Brown
University South Carolina Press. Reprint of the 1966 edition. $14.95.

THE CAYUSE INDIANS: IMPERIAL TRIBESMEN OF OLD OREGON
Robert H. Ruby and John A. Brown
345 pp. University of Oklahoma Press, 1972. Illus. $8.95.

COCOPA ETHNOGRAPHY
William H. Kelly
Describes the customs, beliefs, traditions, and values during the late 1800's of the Cocopa Indians of the Colorado River Delta. University of Arizona Press, 1975. Price not set.

COCHITI: NEW MEXICO PUEBLO PAST AND PRESENT
C. H. Lange
University of Illinois Press, 1968. Cloth, $10.00;Pap. $4.95.

THE CONSTITUTION AND LAWS OF THE MUSKOGEE NATION, AS COMPILED AND CODIFIED BY A. P. McKELLOP, UNDER ACT OF OCTOBER 15, 1892
A. P. McKellop
Scholarly Resource, Inc. Reprint of the 1893 edition. $25.00.

THE CULTURE OF THE LUISENO INDIANS
Philip H. Sparkman
Indians of Southern California. 47 pp. Ballena Press. Reprint of the 1908 edition. Illus. Pap. $2.50.

THE ETHNO-BOTANY OF THE GOSIUTE INDIANS OF UTAH
Ralph V. Chamberlin
Kraus Reprint Co. Reprint of the 1911 edition. Pap. $5.00.

THE ETHNOGRAPHY OF THE KUTENAI
H. H. Turney-High
Kraus Reprint Co. Reprint of the 1941 edition. Pap. $10.00.

ETHNOHISTORICAL REPORT ON THE SISSETON AND WAHPETON TRIBES IN NORTH DAKOTA AND THE TREATY OF 1867 AND THE AGREEMENT OF 1872
Dr. Helen Hornbeck Tanner
134 pp. Clearwater Publishing Co., 1974. Maps. $30.80.

ETHNOLOGICAL REPORT ON THE WASCO AND TENINO INDIANS: POLITICAL ORGANIZATION AND LAND USE IN OREGON, 1855
Robert J. Suphan
74 pp. Clearwater Publishing Co., 1973. $21.20.

AN ETHNOLOGY OF THE HURON INDIANS, 1615 TO 1649
E. Tooker
Scholarly Press. Reprint of the 1964 edition. $9.50.

THE EYAK INDIANS OF THE COPPER RIVER DELTA, ALASKA
K. Birlet-Smith and F. DaLaguna
AMS Press, Inc. Reprint of the 1938 edition. $42.50.

GLOOSKAP'S CHILDREN
Peter Anastas
Narratives of the world of the Penobscot Indians of Maine, living on a reservation in the 1970's. Beacon Press, 1973. $6.95.

HISTORIC AND ETHNOGRAPHIC STUDY OF THE SNOHOMISH, SPECIFICALLY CONCERNING THEIR ABORIGINAL AND CONTINUED EXISTENCE
Colin E. Tweddell
237 pp. Clearwater Publishing co., 1973. $47.25.

HISTORICAL, ETHNOGRAPHICAL AND ARCHAEOLOGICAL REPORT ON THE CHEHALIS
Herbert C. TAylor
35 pp. Clearwater Publishing Co., 1974. $14.95.

HISTORICAL AND ETHNOLOGICAL MATERIAL ON THE JUVARE INDIANS
M. W. Stirling
Scholarly Press. Reprint of the 1938 edition. $9.50.

A HISTORY OF THE CREE INDIAN TERRITORIAL EXPANSION: THE HUDSON BAY AREA TO INTERIOR SASKATCHEWAN AND MISSOURI PLAINS, 1640 TO 1916
Floyd W. Sharrock and Susan R. Sharrock
230 pp. Clearwater Publishing Co., 1973. $46.15.

HISTORY OF THE MINGO INDIANS
Articles by William H. Cobb, Andrew Price, and Hu Maxwell
West Virginia history of the Mingo Indians. McClain Printing Co. Reprint of 1921 edition. $2.50.

ISHI, LAST OF THE YANA INDIANS
Curtis Campbell
In 1911, a small, copper-skinned man stumbled into 20th century civilization in Northern California. For more than forty years he had watched his people die, one by one, until he alone remained — Ishi, the last of an unknown tribe, the last of the Yana Indians. This book is based on his true life story. 120 pp. Dillon Press. $5.95.

THE KANSA INDIANS: A HISTORY OF THE WIND PEOPLE, 1673 TO 1873
William E. Unrau
244 pp. University of Oklahoma Press, 1971. Illus. $8.95.

THE KARANKAWA INDIANS, THE COAST PEOPLE OF TEXAS
A. S. Gatschet
Kraus Reprint Co. Reprint of the 1891 edition. Pap. $5.50.

KARUK INDIAN MYTHS
John P. Harrington

The upriver Indians of northwestern California. 34 pp. Ballena Press. Reprint of the 1932 edition. Pap. $2.00.

THE LUMMI INDIANS OF NORTHWEST WASHINGTON
Bernhard Joseph Stern
AMS Press, Inc. Reprint of the 1934 edition. $8.50.

MARTYRS OF THE OBLONG AND LITTLE NINE
DeCost Smith
The story of the once warlike Mohican tribe who tried to live in peace with the early white settlers. Brown Book Co., 1975. $6.00.

THE MOHAWK INDIANS AND THEIR VALLEY
T. Grassmann
Magi Books, 1969. $25.00.

THE OKANAGAN INDIANS
J. A. Teit and Franz Boas
Shorey Pubns. Reprint of the 1930 edition. Pap. $7.50.

OTO AND MISSOURI INDIANS, INCLUDING:
Prehistoric and Historic Habitats of the Missouri and Oto Indians, The Indian Claims Commission; *History of the Oto and Missouri Lands,* Berlin B. Chapman; *Findings of Fact, and Opinion,* The Indian Claims Commission. 328 pp. Garland Publishing Co., 1974. $21.00.

PEOPLE OF THE NOATAK
Claire Fejes
Alfred A. Knopf, Inc., 1966. $7.95.

REQUIEM FOR A PEOPLE: THE ROUGE INDIANS AND THE FRONTIERSMEN
Stephen Dow Beckham
214 pp. Universtiy of Oklahoma Press, 1972. Ellus. Cloth, $7.95; Pap. $2.95.

SALINAN INDIANS OF CALIFORNIA AND THEIR NEIGHBORS
Betty War Brusa
Includes the area from San Francisco to Santa Barbara on the coast, east to Bakersfield and Fresno. 84 pp. Naturegraph Publishers. Illus.

THE SPOKANE INDIANS: CHILDREN OF THE SUN
Robert H. Ruby and John A. Brown
346 pp. University of Oklahoma Press, 1970. Illus. $8.95.

THE SUBARCTIC ATHABASCANS: A SELECTED ANNOTATED BIBLIOGRAPHY
Arthur E. Hippler and John R. Wood
University of Alaska Institure of Research, 1974. $15.00.

SYNOPSIS OF THE INDIAN TRIBES WITHIN THE UNITED STATES EAST OF THE ROCKY MOUNTAINS, AND IN THE BRITISH AND RUSSIAN POSSESSIONS IN NORTH AMERICA
Albert Galiatin
AMS Press. Reprint of the 1836 edition. $15.00.

THE TIGUA, SUMA AND MANSO INDIANS OF WESTERN TEXAS AND NEW MEXICO: FROM ABORIGINAL TIMES TO THE 1880'S
Rex E. Gerald
116 pp. Clearwater Publishing Co., 1974. $27.00.

TLINGIT MYTHS AND TEXTS
John R. Swanton
451 pp. Johnson Reprint Corp. Reprint of the 1909 edition. $25.25.

TSIMSHIAN INDIANS AND THEIR ARTS
Viola E. Garlfield and Paul S. Wingert
108 pp. University of Washington Press, 1966. Illus. Cloth, $6.50; Pap. $2.95.

TWANA, CHEMAKU, AND KLALLAM INDIANS OF WASHINGTON TERRITORY: EXTRACTS
M. Eells
Shorey Pubns. Reprint of the 1887 edition. Pap. $4.00.

WALAPAI ETHNOGRAPHY
A. L. Kroeber
Kraus Reprint Co. Reprint of the 1935 edition. Pap. $15.00.

THE WAMPANOAG INDIAN FEDERATION
Milton A. Travers
The Wampanoag Indians, their surroundings and their relations with the Pilgrim settlement. 247 pp. Christopher Publishing House. Illus. $4.50.

WAUBA YUMA'S PEOPLE: THE COMPARATIVE SOCIO-POLITICAL STRUCTURE OF THE PAI INDIANS OF ARIZONA
H. F. Dobyns and R. C. Euler
Prescott College Press, 1970. Pap. $6.50.

BLACK-AMERICANS

Black-Americans, the largest of America's minority groups, have a long and diverse history of participation in the institutions of the United States. Included in this section are those books which the editor feels are most important in distinguishing their ethnicity and contribution toward the development of the nation.

ACTIVISM

AGONY IN NEW HAVEN: THE TRIAL OF BOBBY SEAL, ERICA HUGGINS, AND THE BLACK PANTHER PARTY
Donald Freed
Simon and Schuster, 1973. $8.95.

BLACK ACTIVISM: RACIAL REVOLUTION IN THE UNITED STATES 1954-1970
Robert H. Brisbane
A detailed history of the black social and political revolution. 336 pp. Judson Press, 1974. $10.00.

THE BLACK CRUSADERS: *A Case Study of a Black Militant Organization*
William B. Helmreich
Traces the activities of a black militant group from its formation to its collapse, describing and analyzing the members' backgrounds, motives, political beliefs and racial attitudes. 186 pp. Harper & Row Publishers, 1973. Pap. $3.25.

BLACK DEFIANCE
Jay David, Editor
A personal history of black defiance in America from the 18th century to the present. in autobiography, dramatic account, and poetry, 23 blacks tell of their struggles to combat racism. William Morrow & co., 1972. cloth, $6.95; Pap. $2.45.

BLACK EXPERIENCE: THE TRANS-FORMATION OF ACTIVISM
August Meier, Editor
A collection of essays traces the transformation of black activism in the past two decades. 203 pp. Transaction Books, 1973. Cloth, $7.95; Pap. $2.95.

BLACK MANIFESTO: RELIGION, RACISM, AND REPARATION
Robert Lecky and H. Elliot Wright
Sheed and Ward, 1969. Cloth, $5.00; Pap. $2.45.

BLACK PANTHER MENACE: AMERICA'S NEO-NAZIS
N. Hill, Editor
Popular Library, 1971. Pap. $.95.

THE BLACK PANTHERS
G. Marine
New American Library, 1969. Pap. $.95.

THE BLACK POWER REVOLT
Floyd B. Barbour, Editor
Black authors from Nat Turner to Stokely Carmichael trace the concept of Black Power from past to present. 288 pp. Porter Sargent Publisher, Inc., $5.95.

BLACK PROTEST: HISTORY, DOCUMENTS, AND ANALYSES FROM 1619 TO THE PRESENT
Joanne Grant, Editor
Fawcett World Library, 1972. Pap. $1.50.

BLACK RAGE
William H. Grier and Price M. Cobbs
Basic Books, 1968. $7.95.

BLACK REVOLUTION: AN EBONY SPECIAL ISSUE
Ebony Editors
Johnson Publishing Co., Chicago, 1970. $5.95.

CONFRONTATION: BLACK AND WHITE
Lerone Bennett, Jr.
An analysis of the Negro revolt in American, its origins, history, and implications for the future. Penguin Books. $2.45.

FREE HUEY! THE STORY OF THE TRIAL OF HUEY P. NEWTON FOR MURDER
Edward M. Keating
The story of the politically overtoned trial of Huey Newton, and of his defense of the Black Panther Party's policies and goals. 280 pp. Ramparts Press. $6.95.

I WAS A BLACK PANTHER
Chuck Moore
Doubleday and Co., 1970. Cloth, $3.95; Pap. $1.45.

**THE MAKING OF BLACK REVOLUTION-
ARIES: A MEMOIR**
 J. Forman
Macmillan Publishing Co., Inc., 1972. $12.50.

NEGROES WITH GUNS
 Robert F. Williams
Third World Press. $1.95.

**THE RIVER OF NO RETURN: THE
AUTOBIOGRAPHY OF A BLACK
MILITANT AND THE LIFE AND DEATH
OF SNCC**
 Cleveland Sellers and Robert Terrell
William Morrow and Co., 1973. Cloth,
$7.95; Pap. $3.50.

**SEIZE THE TIME: THE STORY OF THE
BLACK PANTHER PARTY AND HUEY P.
NEWTON**
 Bobby Seale
Random House, Inc., 1970. Cloth, $6.95; Pap.
$1.95.

**A SPECIAL RAGE: A BLACK REPORTER
WITH HUEY P. NEWTON'S MURDER
TRIAL, THE BLACK PANTHERS AND HIS
OWN DESTINY**
 Gilbert Moore
Harper and Row Pubs., 1972. Pap. $2.95.

**THE WAR WITHIN: VIOLENCE OR
NONVIOLENCE IN THE BLACK REVOLU-
TION**
 Eldridge Cleaver, et al
Sheed and Ward, 1971. Cloth, $6.50; Pap.
$3.95.

AFRICAN HERITAGE

**AFRICA AND THE AFRO-AMERICAN
EXPERIENCE**
 Lorraine A. Williams, Editor
A collection of analytical and evaluative essays
dispelling longstanding myths about the role
black people have played in the historical
process, nationally and internationally. 128 pp.
Howard University press, 1976. $8.95.

**AFRICA AND AMERICA: ADDRESSES
AND DISCOURSES**
 Alexander Crummell
466 pp. Negro Universities Press. Reprint of the
1891 edition. $17.00.

AFRICA AND THE AMERICAN NEGRO
 Congress on Africa
Addresses and proceeding of the Congress on
Africa held under the auspices of the Stewart
Missionary Foundation for Africa. Books for
Libraries. Reprint of the 1896 edition. $11.25.

AFRICA'S GIFT TO AMERICA
 J. A. Rogers
Americans of African ancestry in the making of
the United States. 256 pp. Illus. Helga M.
Rogers Publishing co., 1961. $7.95.

**AFRICA'S REDEMPTION, THE SALVA-
TION OF OUR COUNTRY**
 Frederick Freeman
383 pp. Negro Universities Press. Reprint of the
1852 edition. $16.00. Scholarly Press, $19.50.

**THE AFRICAN BACKGROUND OUTLIN-
ED: OR HANDBOOK FOR THE STUDY
OF THE NEGRO**
 Carter Godwin Woodson
478 pp. Negro Universities Press. Reprint of the
1936 edition. $15.00.

THE AFRICAN'S ODYSSEY IN AMERICA
 Livnus A. Ukachi
Carlton Press. $3.50.

AFRICANISMS IN THE GULLAH DIALECT
 Lorenzo D. Turner
A linguistic study of an American creole,
relevant ot contemporary students of "black
English," language admixture, and American
speech. University of Michigan Press. 336 pp.
Pap. $4.95.

**APROPOS OF AFRICA: SENTIMENTS OF
AMERICAN NEGRO LEADERS ON
AFRICA FROM THE 1800'S TO THE 1950'S**
 Adelaide Cromwell Hill and Martin Kilson
Doubleday and Co., 1971. $2.50.

**A BIBLIOGRAPHY OF THE NEGRO IN
AFRICA AND AMERICA**
 Monroe Work
Argosy-Antiquarian. Reprint of the 1928
edition. $22.50.

**BLACK BROTHERHOOD: AFRO-
AMERICANS AND AFRICA**
 Okon E. Uya, Editor
Explores the attitude of Afro-Americans toward
Africa. 282 pp. D. C. Heath & Co., 1971. Pap.
$4.95.

**BLACK EXODUS: BLACK NATIONALIST
AND BACK-TO-AFRICA MOVEMENTS,
1890 TO 1910**
Edwin S. Redkey
Yale University Press, 1969. Cloth, $13.50;
Pap. $2.95.

BLACK FAITH AND BLACK SOLIDARITY
Priscilla Massie, Compiler and Editor
A series of addresses by Africans and black
Americans presented originally at the East
African consultation, Dar es Salaam, Tanzania,
1971. Friendship Press, 1974. Pap. $2.50.

**BLACK HOMELAND/BLACK
DIASPORA:** *Cross-Currents of the African
Relationship*
Jacob Drachler, Editor
An anthology of Afro-American and African
writings explores Zionism. Kennikat Press,
1975. $12.00.

**EBONY KINSHIP: AFRICA, AFRICANS
AND THE AFRO-AMERICAN**
Robert G. Weisbord
256 pp. Greenwood Press, Inc., 1973. $11.95.

**THE DESTRUCTION OF BLACK CIVILIZA-
TION**
Chancellor Williams
Third World Press, 1974. Cloth, $10.00; Pap.
$4.95.

**THE GREAT FUTURE OF AMERICA AND
AFRICA**
Jacob Dewees
Scholarly Press. Reprint of the 1854 edition.
$9.00.

**A HISTORY OF COLONIZATION OF THE
WESTERN COAST OF AFRICA**
Archibald Alexander
Negro Universities Press. Reprint of the 1846
edition. $17.75.

**LIFE OF YEHUDI ASHMUN: LATE
COLONIAL AGENT IN LIBERIA**
Ralph Randolph Gurley
160 pp. Negro Universities Press. Reprint of the
1835 edition. $16.50.

**MARYLAND IN AFRICA: THE MARY-
LAND STATE COLONIZATION SOCIETY,
1831 TO 1857**
Penelope Campbell
272 pp. University of Illinois Press, 1971. $7.95.

THE NEGRO FROM AFRICA TO AMERICA
Willis Duke Weathford
487 pp. Negro Universities Press. Reprint of the
1924 edition. $15.00.

THE NEGRO IN AFRICA AND AMERICA
Joseph Alexander Tillinghast
Books for libraries, Inc. Reprint of the 1902
edition. $10.00.

**THE NEGRO PROBLEM SOLVED: OR,
AFRICA AS SHE WAS, AS SHE IS, AND AS
SHE SHALL BE: HER CURSE AND HER
CURE**
Hollis Read
Books for Libraries. Reprint of the 1864
edition. $13.75.

**PHILOSOPHY AND OPINIONS OF
MARCUS GARVEY: OR, AFRICA FOR
THE AFRICANS**
Amy J. Garvey
Humanities Press, 1967. $14.75.

**RESPECT BLACK: THE WRITINGS AND
SPEECHES OF HENRY McNEAL TURNER**
Edwin S. Redkey, Editor
An advocate of militant black nationalism who
urged Afro-Americans to emigrate to Africa.
Arno Press, 1971. $9.00.

**THE SEARCH FOR A BLACK NATIONA-
LITY: BLACK COLONAZATION AND
EMIGRATION, 1787-1863**
Floyd J. Miller
The persistent and central concern of Afro-
Americans between the Revolution and the Civil
War. 320 pp. University of Illinois Press.
$10.95.

**SEARCH FOR A PLACE: BLACK
SEPARATISM AND AFRICA, 1860**
M. R. Delaney and Robert Campbell
256 pp. University of Michigan Press, 1969.
Cloth, $5.95; Pap. $2.25.

**THOUGHTS ON AFRICAN
COLONIZATION**
William Lloyd Garrison
A leading white abolitionist's answer to those
who advocated coupling abolition of slavery
with the removal of American Negroes to
Africa. Arno Press, 1968. Reprint of the 1832
edition. Cloth, $9.00; Pap. $3.25.

ANTEBELLUM

FREE BLACKS IN AMERICA, 1800-1860
    John H. Bracey, Jr. Editor
A collection of essays and articles about free
Negroes in the United States between 1800 and
1860. 160 pp. Wadsworth Publishing Co., 1971.
Pap. $4.50.

THE FREE NEGRO IN MARYLAND, 1634-1860
    James M. Wright
Octagon Books, 1975. 362 pp. Reprint of the
1921 edition. $13.00.

THE FREE NEGRO IN NORTH CAROLINA, 1790 TO 1860
    John Franklin
W. W. Norton and Co., 1971. Pap. $2.25.

FREE NEGRO OWNERS OF SLAVES IN THE UNITED STATES IN 1830
    Carter Godwin Woodson, Editor
78 pp. Negro Universities Press. Reprint of the
1924 edition. $7.00.

THE FREE NEGRO IN VIRGINIA 1619 TO 1865
    John H. Russell
Peter Smith Publishers. $4.75.

THE FREE NEGRO IN VIRGINIA, 1619-1865
    John Henderson Russell
194 pp. Greenwood Press. Reprint of the 1913
edition. $9.00.

FREE NEGROES IN THE DISTRICT OF COLUMBIA, 1790 TO 1846
    Lettia Woods Brown
236 pp. Oxford University Press, 1972. $7.95.

THE FREE PEOPLE OF COLOR: ON THE CONDITION OF THE FREE PEOPLE OF COLOR IN THE UNITED STATES AND PRESENT CONDITION OF THE FREE COLORED PEOPLE OF THE UNITED STATES
    William Jay and James Freeman Clarke
Two abolitionist studies on the plight of the free
Negro class in the mid-nineteenth century.
Although legally free from bondage, free
Negroes were nonetheless barred from political,
economic, educational, and social intercourse
by Jim Crow codes. Arno Press, 1975. Reprint
of the 1853 edition. $4.50.

NEITHER SLAVE NOR FREE: THE FREED-MAN OF AFRICAN DESCENT IN THE SLAVE SOCIETIES OF THE NEW WORLD
    David W. Cohen and Jack P. Greene,
    Editors
Story of the freedman in North and South
American slave societies. 352 pp. Johns
Hopkins University Press, 1974. Cloth, $13.50;
Pap. $3.45.

NORTH OF SLAVERY: THE NEGRO IN THE FREE STATES, 1790 TO 1860
    Leon F. Litwack
University of Chicago Press, 1961. Cloth,
$9.50; Pap. $2.45.

SLAVES WITHOUT MASTERS: THE UNITED STATES FREE NEGRO IN THE ANTEBELLUM SOUTH
    Ira Berlin
Pantheon Books, 1974. $15.00.

SOME ASPECTS OF THE FREE NEGRO QUESTION IN SAN FRANCISCO
    Phillip Montesano
Historical and sociological study of the Negro in
early San Francisco. Thesis. R & E Research
Associates. Reprint of the 1967 edition. Pap.
$8.00.

A WORLD IN SHADOW: THE FREE BLACK IN ANTEBELLUM SOUTH CAROLINA
    Marina Wikramanayake
University of South Carolina Press, 1973.
$14.95.

ART

AFRO-AMERICAN ART AND CRAFT
    Judith W. Chase
Van Nostrand Reinhold Co., 1971. $12.95.

THE AFRO-AMERICAN ARTIST
    Elsa H. Fine
Holt, Rinehart, and Winston, 1973. Cloth,
$12.95; Pap. $10.95.

AMERICAN NEGRO ART
    Cedric Dover
New York Graphic Society, 1965. Cloth,
$12.50; Pap. $6.95.

BLACK ART

Ralph Hudson, Editor
A bibliography of Afro-American art; books, monographs, exhibition catalogues, periodicals, and related material. 16 pp. National Art Education Association, 1970. Pap. $.25.

BLACK ARTS: AN ANTHOLOGY OF BLACK CREATIONS

Almed Alhamisi and Kofe Wangara
Broadside Press, Pubns., 1969. Pap. $3.50.

*THE BLACK MAN IN ART

Rena Neumann Coen
The author focuses on the artistic and social significance of each work of art depicting the Negro, beginning with a survey of African sculpture and the art of ancient Egypt, Greece, and Rome. 72 pp. Lerner Publications, 1970. Illus. Ages 11-17. $4.95.

BUSH NEGRO ART: AFRICAN ART IN THE AMERICAS

Philip J. Dark
St. Martin's Press, 1974. $10.00

THE IMAGE OF THE INDIAN AND THE BLACK MAN IN AMERICAN ART, 1590 TO 1900

Ellwood Parry
George Braziller, Inc., 1974. $12.50.

MODERN NEGRO ART

James A. Porter
An evaluation of pre-World War II black contributions to American art. Arno Press. Reprint of the 1943 edition. $10.00.

THE NEGRO-AMERICAN ARTISAN

W. E. B. DuBois
Kraus Reprint Co. Reprint of the 1912 edition. Pap. $3.00.

THE NEGRO IN ART: A PICTORIAL RECORD OF THE NEGRO ARTIST AND THE NEGRO THEME IN ART

Alain Locke, Editor
Hacker Art Books, Reprint of the 1940 edition. Illus. $15.00. Metro Books, Inc., $22.50.

THE NEGRO ARTISAN

W. E. B. DuBois
Kraus Reprint Co. Reprint of the 1902 edition. Pap. $4.00.

NEGRO ARTISTS

Harmon Foundation, Inc.

An illustrated view of their achievements. Books for Libraries. Reprint of the 1935 edition. $11.00.

NEGRO IN MUSIC AND ART

Patterson
United Publishing Corp., 1970. $13.88.

NEW BLACK ARTISTS

American Federation of Arts, Editors
American Federation of Arts, 1970. Pap. $2.00.

SIX BLACK MASTERS OF AMERICAN ART

Romare Bearden and Harry Henderson
Doubleday and Co., 1972. Illus. Cloth, $3.95; Pap. $1.95.

ASSIMILATION

AFRICAN CIVILIZATIONS IN THE NEW WORLD

Roger Bastide
Harper and Row Pubs., 1972. Cloth, $12.50 Pap. $2.75.

ALL OUR KIN: STRATEGIES FOR SURVIVAL IN A BLACK COMMUNITY

Carol B. Stack
Harper and Row Pubs., 1974. Illus. $7.95.

AMERICAN CIVILIZATION AND THE NEGRO: THE AFRO-AMERICAN IN RELATION TO NATIONAL PROGRESS

Charles Victor Roman
434 pp. Metro Books, Inc. Reprint of the 1916 edition. Illus. $17.50. Books for Libraries, Inc., $25.75.

AN AMERICAN DILEMMA: THE NEGRO PROBLEM AND MODERN DEMOCRACY, VOL. VI

Gunnar Myrdal
Harper and Row Pubs., 1962. Cloth, $20.00; Pap. $3.95.

AMERICAN NEGRO

Lulamae Clemons
McGraw Hill Book Co., 1965. $2.00.

THE AMERICAN NEGRO

American Academy of Political and Social Science
Kraus Reprint Co. Reprint of the 1928 edition. $16.00.

AMERICAN NEGRO
    William Thomas
Haskell House Publishing, Inc. Reprint of the
1901 edition. $13.95

THE AMERICAN NEGRO
    Melville J. Herskovitz
Indiana University Press, 1964. Pap. $1.65.

**AMERICAN SOCIETY AND BLACK
REVOLUTION**
    Frank Hercules
An analysis of the black experience throughout
American history and an assessment of black
leaders from Frederick Douglass to Angela
Davis. 437 pp. Harcourt Brace Jovanovich,
Inc., $12.95. Peter Smith Publishers; Pap.
$5.00.

BLACK AMERICA
    John Szwed, Editor
Basic Books, 1970. $10.00.

BLACK AMERICA
    Scott Nearing
275 pp. Johnson Reprint. Reprint of the 1929
edition. Illus. $11.25.

**BLACK   AMERICA: ACCOMODATION
AND   CONFRONTATION   IN   THE
TWENTIETH CENTURY**
    Richard Resh
A chronological series of readings on social,
political, and economic events as witnessed by
black-Americans from 1900-1968. 261 pp. D.C.
Heath & Co., 1969. Pap. $3.95.

**THE BLACK AMERICAN IN SOCIOLOLO-
GICAL   THOUGHT: A   FAILURE   IN
PERSPECTIVE**
    Stanford M. Lyman
G. P. Putnam's Sons, 1972. Cloth, $6.95; Pap.
$2.95.

THE BLACK AMERICAN EXPERIENCE
    Frances Freedman, Editor
Bantam Books, 1970. Pap. $.95.

BLACK AMERICANS
    Alphonso Pinkney
A sociological study of black people in the
United States from their first importation in
1619 to the current Black Power movement. 242
pp. Prentice-Hall, Inc., 1973. Cloth, $8.95;
Pap. $3.75.

BLACK   AMERICANS: IMAGES   IN

CONFLICT
    Phyllis Banks and Virginia Burke, Editors
64 pp. Bobbs-Merrill Co., 1970. Pap. $1.00.

**BLACK   AWAKENING   IN   CAPITALIST
AMERICA: AN ANALYTIC HISTORY**
    Robert L. Allen
Doubleday & Co., 1969. Pap. $2.50.

**BLACK BOURGEOSIE: THE RISE OF A
NEW MIDDLE CLASS IN AMERICA**
    E. Franklin Frazier
Macmillan Publishing Co., Inc., 1962. Pap.
$.95.

**BLACK AMERICANS: IMAGES IN CON-
FLICT**
    J. Edward Atkinson, Editor
New American Library. $3.95.

THE BLACK EXPERIENCE
A special issue of *Social Casework* containing
seven articles, written by black authors, in-
tended to increase knowledge of and insight into
the meaning of the black experience. Family
Service Association of America, 1970. $2.25.

**THE BLACK EXPERIENCE: A BIBLIO-
GRAPHY**
    Tad Kumatz and Janyce Wolf, Editors
268 pp. Long Island University Press. Pap.
$5.00.

**THE BLACK EXPERIENCE IN AMERICAN
SOCIALISM, 2 VOLS.**
    Philip S. Foner, Editor
G. P. Putnam's Sons, 1974. .$7.95 each.

BLACK IN WHITE AMERICA
    Leonard Freed
Grossman Publishers, 1968. Cloth, $10.00;
Pap. $3.95.

THE BLACK MAFIA
    Francis J. Ianni
Simon and Schuster, 1974. $7.95.

**THE BLACK MAN: HIS ANTECEDENTS,
HIS GENIUS AND HIS ACHIEVEMENTS**
    William W. Brown
312 pp. Johnson Reprint, 1969, 2nd edition.
Reprint of the 1863 edition. $12.00.

BLACK MIDDLE CLASS
    Sidney Kronus
Charles E. Merrill Publishing Co., 1971. Pap.
$2.95.

BLACK NEIGHBORS: NEGROES IN A NORTHERN RURAL COMMUNITY
George K. Hesslink
345 pp. Bobbs-Merrill Co., 1974. Cloth, $6.95; Pap. $3.95.

BLACK RAGE
William H. Grier and Price Cobbs
Bantam Books, 1969. Pap. $.95.

THE BLACK SEVENTIES
Floyd B. Barbour, Editor
Peter Sargent Pubs., 1970. Cloth, $5.95; Pap. $2.95.

THE BLACK SITUATION
Addison Gayle, Jr.
The American black experience and its consequences. 224 pp. Dell Publishing Co. $2.25.

BLACK SOCIETY IN THE NEW WORLD
Richard Frucht, Editor
Random House, Inc., 1971. Pap. $5.95.

THE BLACK SOCIOLOGISTS: THE FIRST HALF CENTURY
John H. Bracey, Editor
A collection of essays of prominent black sociologists during the first half of the 20th century. Twelve readings by Dubois, Frazier, Johnson, and Doyle, among others. 180 pp. Wadsworth Publishing Co., 1974. Pap. $4.50

BLACK SOCIOLOGISTS: HISTORICAL AND CONTEMPORARY PERSPECTIVES
James Blackwell and Morris Janowitz, Editors
University of Chicago Press, 1974. 15.00.

BLACK UTOPIA: NEGRO COMMUNAL EXPERIMENTS IN AMERICA
William H. Pease and Jane H. Pease
State Historical Society of Wisconsin, 1972. Pap. $2.00.

BLACKLASH
Stewart Benedict, Editor
Popular Library, 1970. Pap. $.95.

BLACKS AND AMERICAN MEDICAL CARE
Max Seham
The author describes and documents the black health crisis and makes recommendations for changes which will alleviate existing conditions. University of Minnesota Press, 1975. $7.95.

BLACKS IN THE DEEP SOUTH
Emily Parker Robinson
A narrative of a black girl's social and intellectual development in the Seep South. Vantage Press, $4.50.

BLACKS IN THE UNITED STATES NOW AND FUTURE: A CROSS-DISCIPLINARY EXAMINATION
Norval D. Glenn and Charles Bonjean
Chandler Publishing Co., 1969. $8.95.

BLACKS IN WHITE AMERICA BEFORE 1865 ISSUES AND INTERPRETATIONS
Robert Haynes, Editor
David McKay Co., 1972. Cloth, $7.95; Pap. $4.95.

BLACKS IN WHITE AMERICA SINCE 1865; ISSUES AND INTERPRETATIONS
Robert Twombly
David McKay Co., 1972. Cloth, $7.95; Pap. $4.95.

BLACKWAYS OF KENT
Hylan Lewis
Social change in the American South. 362 pp. University of North Carolina press, 1955. $6.00.

THE CHALLENGE OF BLACKNESS
Lerone Bennett, Jr.
Johnson Publishing Co., 1972. $6.95.

COLOR, CLASS, AND PERSONALITY
Robert Lee Sutherland
135 pp. Greenwood press, Inc. Reprint of the 1942 edition. Illus. $9.00.

THE COLORED GENTLEMAN, A BY PRODUCT OF MODERN CIVILIZATION
Dennis I. Imbert
AMS Press, Inc. Reprint of the 1931 edition. $6.00.

CONTENDING FORCES: ROMANCES ILLUSTRATIVE OF NEGRO LIFE, NORTH AND SOUTH
Pauline E. Hopkina
Books for Libraries, Inc., Reprint of the 1900 edition. Illus. 13.75.

DRUMS OF LIFE: A PHOTOGRAPHIC ESSAY ON THE BLACK MAN IN AMERICA
Orde Coombs and Chester Higgins, Jr.
Doubleday & Co., 1973. illus. $5.95.

*THE EBONY BOOK OF BLACK ACHIEVEMENT
Margaret W. Peters
Johnson Publishing, Co., 1974. $5.50. Below college level.

THE EBONY HANDBOOK
Doris E. Saunders, Editor
Covers topics from books to business, politics to population statistics, music to medicine, and many other facts about blacks in America today. 576 pp. Johnson Publishing Co., 1974. $20.00.

EBONY SUCCESS LIBRARY, VOLS. 1 TO 3
Ebony Editors
Johnson Publishing Co., 1973. $27.95. per set.

EFFORTS FOR SOCIAL BETTERMENT AMONG NEGRO AMERICANS
W. E. B. DuBois
Kraus Reprint Co., 1969. Pap. $3.00.

EVIDENCES OF PROGRESS AMONG COLORED PEOPLE
C. R. Richings
Johnson Reprint. Reprint of the 1900 edition. $25.25.

FROM PLANTATION TO GHETTO
August Meier and Elliott Rudwick
An updated view of the Negro experience. Hill & Wang, 1970. Cloth, $6.95; Pap. $2.45.

GROWING UP BLACK
Jay David, Editor
Simon and Schuster, 1970. Pap. $2.45. Pocket Books, Inc., Pap. $.95.

HOW A MINORITY CAN CHANGE SOCIETY: THE REAL POTENTIAL OF THE AFRO-AMERICAN STRUGGLE
George Breitman
32 pp. Pathfinder Press, Inc., Pap. $.50.

I AM THE AMERICAN NEGRO
Frank Marshall Davis
Books for Libraries, Inc., Reprint of the 1937 edition. $8.75.

IN WHITE AMERICA
Martin N. Duberman
New American Library, 1974. Pap. $.95.

THE MIDDLE-CLASS NEGRO IN THE WHITE MAN'S WORLD

Eli Ginzberg
Columbia University Press, 1969. Cloth, $10.00 Pap. $2.25.

MORALS AND MANNERS AMONG NEGRO AMERICANS
W. E. B. DuBois
Kraus Reprint Co. Reprint of the 1914 edition. Pap. $3.00.

MY FACE IS BLACK
C. Eric Lincoln
What it feels like to be a black man in America, by a black sociologist. Beacon Press, 1964. $3.50.

MUTH TO MAN: BLACK AMERICANS
Florette Henri
Doubleday and Co., 1975. $8.95.

THE NEGRO AMERICAN
Talcott Parsons and Kenneth B. Clark, Editors
A symposium on the status and problems of black-Americans. Beacon Press. Pap. $3.95.

NEGRO AMERICANS, WHAT NOW?
James Johnson
AMS Press, Inc. Reprint of the 1938 edition. $6.00

THE NEGRO AND HIS NEEDS
Raymond Patterson
Books for Libraries, Inc., Reprint of the 1911 edition. $12.25.

NEGRO HOUSING
President's Conference on Home Building, and Home Ownership.
282 pp. Negro Universities Press. Reprint of the 1932 edition. Illus. $13.75.

NEGRO IMMIGRANT: HIS BACKGROUND, CHARACTERISTICS, AND SOCIAL ADJUSTMENT, 1899 TO 1937
Ira deAugustine Reid
AMS Press, Inc. Reprint of the 1939 edition. $10.00.

THE NEGRO IN AMERICA: A BIBLIOGRAPHY
Elizabeth Miller and Mary Fisher
351 pp. Harvard university Press, 1970. Cloth, $10.00; Pap. $4.95.

THE NEGRO IN AMERICA: A CONDENSED VERSION OF GUNNAR MYR-

DAL'S *An American Dilemma*
  Arnold Rose
Harper and Row Pubs. Pap. $2.25.

THE NEGRO IN AMERICAN LIFE
  Jerome Dowd
600 pp. Greenwood Press, 1974. Reprint of the 1926 edition. $20.25. Negro Universities Press, $23.35.

*NEGRO IN THE MAKING OF AMERICA
  Benjamin Quarles
Macmillan Publishing Co., Inc., 1964. Pap. $1.25. Below college level.

THE NEGRO MOOD
  Lerone Bennette, Jr.
Johnson Publishing Co., 1964. $3.95.

THE NEGRO AND THE NATION
  George S. Merriam
Haskell House Pubs., Inc. Reprint of the 1906. $13.95.

THE NEGRO IN THE NEW WORLD
  Harry Johnston
Beekman Publishers. Reprint of the 1868 edition. $24.00.

THE NEGRO IN NEW YORK: AN IN-FORMAL SOCIAL HISTORY
  R. Ottley and W. Weatherby
Oceana Publications, 1967. $10.00.

THE NEGRO PROBLEM: ABRAHAM LINCOLN'S SOLUTION
  William Passmore Pickett
580 pp. Negro Universities Press. Reprint of the 1909 edition. $20.00.

THE NEGRO PROBLEM A SERIES OF ARTICLES BY REPRESENTATIVE AMERICAN NEGROES OF TODAY
  Booker T. Washington, et al
Books for Libraries. Reprint of the 1903 edition. $8.25.

THE NEGRO PROBLEM IN THE UNITED STATES, ITS RISE, DEVELOPMENT AND SOLUTION
  Frank Wellington Gage
116 pp. Greenwood Press. Reprint of the 1892 edition. $7.25.

THE NEGRO'S IMAGE IN THE SOUTH: THE ANATOMY OF WHITE SUPREMACY

  Claude H. Nolen
232 pp. The University Press of Kentucky. Pap. $2.50.

THE NEGRO'S PROGRESS IN 50 YEARS
  American Academy of Political and Social Science
266 pp. Greenwood Press. Reprint of the 1913 edition. $10.50.

THE NEGRO'S SHARE: A STUDY OF INCOME, CONSUMPTION, HOUSING, AND PUBLIC ASSISTANCE
  Richard Edward Sterner
433 pp. Negro Universities Press, 1971. Reprint of the 1943 edition. $17.50.

A NEW NEGRO FOR A NEW CEN-TURY: AN ACCURATE AND UP-TO-DATE RECORD OF THE UPWARD STRUGGLES OF THE NEGRO RACE
  Booker T. Washington
Books for Libraries, Inc. Reprint of the 1900 edition. $14.25. AMS Press, $17.00.

NIGGER
  Dick Gregory and Robert Lipsyte
Pocket Books, Inc. Pap. $.95.

ODYSSEY: JOURNEY THROUGH BLACK AMERICA
  Earl and Miriam Selby
G. P. Putnam's Sons, 1971. $7.95.

PERSPECTIVES ON BLACK AMERICA
  Russell Endo and William Strawbridge
Irvington Books Press, 1970. Pap. $4.95. Prentice-Hall, $8.95.

POLICE AND THE BLACK COMMUNITY
  Robert Wintersmith
A historical and contemporary account of the relationship between the police force and the black community. 176 pp. Lexington Books, 1974. $12.50.

THE POSSIBEL DREAM: TOWARD UNDERSTANDING THE BLACK EX-PERIENCE
  Peter A. Angeles
Case studies, facts and statistics try to answer the question: Can white America come to appreciate the black experience. Friendship Press, 1971. Pap. $1.95.

A PROFILE OF THE NEGRO AMERICAN
  Thomas Pettigrew

Van Nostrand Reinhold Co., 1964. $5.95.

PROGRESS OF A RACE: OR THE REMAKABLE ADVANCEMENT OF THE AMERICAN NEGRO
   J. W. Gibson and W. H. Crogman
Books for Libraries, Inc. Reprint of the 1902 edition. $24.75.

PROTEST AND PREJUDICE: A STUDY OF BELIEF IN THE BLACK COMMUNITY
   Gary T. Marx
Harper and Row Pubs., 1969. Pap. $1.95.

REPORT FROM BLACK AMERICA
   Peter Goldman
Simon and Schuster, 1970. $6.95.

THE RISING SUN: OR, THE ANTECEDENTS AND ADVANCEMENT OF THE COLORED RACE
   William W. Brown
552 pp. Johnson Reprint. Reprint of the 1874 edition. $23.00.

SELECT DISCUSSIONS OF RACE PROBLEMS: A COLLECTION OF PAPERS OF SPECIAL USE IN THE STUDY OF NEGRO AMERICAN PROBLEMS
   John Alvin Bigham, Editor
108 pp. Greenwood Press. Reprint of the 1919 edition. $8.00.

THE SHAPING OF BLACK AMERICA
   Lerone Bennett, Jr.
Johnson Publishing Co., 1975. $15.95.

SOCIAL AND MENTAL TRAITS OF THE NEGRO: RESEARCH INTO THE CONDITIONS OF THE NEGRO RACE IN SOUTHERN TOWNS; A STUDY IN RACE TRAITS, TENDENCIES, AND PROSPECTS
   Howard Washington Odum
AMS Press. Reprint of the 1910 edition. $12.50.

SOCIOLOGY OF THE BLACK EXPERIENCE
   Daniel C. Thompson
Writings on key experiences of the past two decades. 261 pp. Greenwood Press, 1974. $12.50.

SOME NOTES ON NEGRO CRIME PARTICULARLY IN GEORGIA
   W. E. B. DuBois
Kraus Reprint Co. Reprint of the 1904 edition. Pap. $2.00.

A STUDY OF SOME NEGRO-WHITE FAMILIES IN THE U. S.
   Caroline (Bond) Day
126 pp. Greenwood Press. Illus. Reprint of the 1932 edition. $20.75.

TRANSFORMATION OF THE NEGRO AMERICAN
   Leonard Broom and Norval Glenn
Basic Books, 1969. Cloth, $5.50; Pap. $1.75.

WATCH WHAT IS LACKING IN NEGRO PROGRESS
   Eva A. Warren
Carlton Press. $3.00.

WHITE-COLLAR BLACKS: A BREAKTHROUGH?
   John S. Morgan, and Richard L. Van Dyke
AM Management Assn., 1970. $10.00.

WHITE PROBLEM IN AMERICA
   Ebony Editors
Johnson Publishing Co. 1966. $3.50.

WHO NEEDS THE NEGRO?
   Sidney M. Willhelm
An analysis of the American social and economic situation; the thesis develops that the black American is no longer needed in post-industrial society. Doubleday & Co., Cloth, $9.50. Pap. $1.95. General Learning Corp., Cloth, $6.50; Schenkman Publishing Co. Cloth, $9.50.

WHO SPEAKS FOR THE NEGRO?
   Robert Penn Warren
Random House, Inc., 1965. Cloth, $7.95; Pap. $1.95.

ATHLETES

BAD NIGGER! THE NATIONAL IMPACT OF JACK JOHNSON
   Al-Tony Gilmore
This study explores Johnson's role as a major force in American intellectual, social, and folk history from 1908-1915 and beyond because of his achievement of the first black heavyweight championship of the world.

*THE BERLIN OLYMPICS, 1936: BLACK AMERICAN ATHLETES COUNTER NAZI PROPAGANDA

James P. Barry
Black athletes upstage Hitler's racist ideology.
88 pp. Franklin Watts, Inc., 1975. Age 12 up.
$3.90.

BLACK ATHLETE
Henderson and *Sport Magazine*
United Publishing Corp., 1970. $13.88.

BLACK CHAMPIONS CHALLENGE AMERICAN SPORTS
Wally Jones and Jim Washington
David McKay Co., 1972. $5.95.

*BLACK CHAMPIONS OF THE GRID-IRON: O.J. SIMPSON AND LEROY KEYES
A. S. "Doc" Young
The backgrounds, personalities and football
careers of two famous black athletes. 120 pp.
Harcourt Brace Jovanovich, Inc. $4.95. Ages 10
up.

BLACKTHINK: MY LIFE AS BLACK MAN AND WHITE MAN
Jesse Owens and Paul G. Neimark
Athlete Jesse Owens gives his views on
America's racial crisis. William Morrow & Co.,
1970. $5.95.

DISCRIMINATION AGAINST THE NEGRO IN AMERICAN ATHLETICS
Thomas E. Foreman
Thesis. R & E Research Associates. Reprint of
the 1957 edition. Pap. $8.00.

*FAMOUS NEGRO ATHLETES
Arna Bontemps
Biographies of Negro athletic greats Sugar Ray
Robinson, Willie May, Jim Brown and Jackie
Robinson, among others. 155 pp. Dodd, Mead
& Co., 1964. Illus. Age 11-15. $3.95. Apollo
Editions, Pap. $1.95.

GREAT BLACK ATHLETES
Bert Schwartz
Pendulum Press, Inc., 1971. Pap. $.60.

NEGRO FIRST IN SPORTS
A. S. Young
Johnson Publishing Co. 1963. $4.95.

*PIONEERS OF BLACK SPORT
Ocania Chalk
The pioneers who first played on all-black
teams, in all-black championships, and the
occasional exhibition game against white ad-
versaries. 300 pp. Dodd, Mead & Co., 1974.

Illus. Age 16 up. $7.95.

THE REVOLT OF THE BLACK ATHLETE
Harry Edwards
Free Press, 1969. Cloth, $5.95; Pap. $2.95.

AUTHORS

*AFRO-AMERICAN AUTHORS
William Adams, Editor
Houghton Mifflin Co., 1971. Pap. $2.64. Below
college level.

AFRO-AMERICAN WRITERS
Compiled by DArwin T. Turner
AHM Publishing Corp., 1970. Pap. $2.95.

ANGER AND BEYOND: THE NEGRO WRITER IN THE UNITED STATES
Herbert Hill, Editor
Harper and Row Pubs., 1966. $7.95.

THE BLACK AMERICAN WRITER, VOLUMES I AND II
C. W. E. Bigsby, Editor
A two-volume collection of essays on the Negro
literary achievement. Penguin Books. $1.45
each.

BLACK AMERICAN WRITERS 1773-1949: *A Bibliography and Union List*
Geraldine O. Matthews, Editor
Identifies and lists monographic works by more
than 1,500 black aathors who wrote prior to
1950 about black experience. 221 pp. Hall,
1975. $16.95.

BLACK AMERICAN WRITERS PAST AND PRESENT: A BIOGRAPHICAL AND BIB-LIOGRAPHICAL DICTIONARY
Theressa Gunnels Rush, Carol Fairbanks
Myers, and Esther Spring Arata
Furnishes information about the lives and
works of more than 2,000 black American
writers from the early 18th century to the
present. 2 vols. 865 pp. Scarecrow Press, 1975.
Illus. $30.00.

THE BLACK NOVELIST
Robert Hemenway
Charles E. Merrill Publishing Co. Cloth, $8.95;
Pap. $3.95.

THE BLACK NOVELIST
Hemenway, Editor

Nineteen essays by and about the black American novelist. Stories by W. E. B. DuBois, Arna Bontemps, Richard Wright, Ralph Ellison, James Baldwin, J. Saunders Redding, and William Gardner Smith among others. Brown Book Co., 1975. Cloth, $7.95; Pap. $2.95.

BLACK WRITER IN AFRICA AND THE AMERICAS
Lloyd W. Brown, Editor

Hennessey and Ingalls, 1973. Pap. $5.95.

BLACK WRITERS OF AMERICA: A COMPREHENSIVE ANTHOLOGY
R. Barksdale and K. Kinnamon

Macmillan Publishing Co., Inc., 1972. $12.50.

BLACK WRITERS OF THE THIRTIES
James O. Young

Intellectual currents within the American black community shift during the 1930s. Louisiana State University Press, 1975. $10.00.

EARLY AMERICAN NEGRO WRITERS
Benjamin Brawley, Editor

An anthology of the earliest Black writers in America, 1761 through the Civil War. 305 pp. Reprint of the 1935 edition. Dover Publications, 1970. Pap. $2.50. Books for Libraries, Inc.; Cloth, $13.75.

EARLY NEGRO AMERICAN WRITERS: SELECTIONS WITH BIOGRAPHICAL AND CRITICAL INTRODUCTIONS
Benjamin Brawley

Peter Smith Publishers. $4.75.

FIVE BLACK WRITERS
Donald B. Gibson

New York University Press. Cloth, $10.00; Pap. $3.50.

FROM THE DARK TOWER: AFRO-AMERICAN WRITERS FROM 1900 TO 1960
Arthur P. Davis

Howard University Press, 1974. $10.95.

IN A MINOR CHORD: THREE AFRO-AMERICAN WRITERS AND THEIR SEARCH FOR IDENTITY
Darwin T. Turner

Southern Illinois University Press, 1971. $5.95.

JOHN A. WILLIAMS: THE EVOLUTION OF A BLACK WRITER
Earl A. Cash

Traces Williams' literary development and examines his thinking with regard to the future of black-American literature. 200 pp. Third Press, 1974. $7.95.

LIVING BLACK AMERICAN AUTHORS: A BIOGRAPHICAL DIRECTORY
Ann Allen Shockley and Sue P. Chandler, Editors

425 Black authors are profiled, covering novelist, poets, film critics, educators, librarians, publishers, and media specialists. 220 pp. R. R. Bowker Co., 1973. $12.95.

THE MILITANT BLACK WRITER IN AFRICA AND THE UNITED STATES
M. Cook and S. E. Henderson

University of Wisconsin Press, 1969. Pap. $1.95.

MODERN BLACK NOVELISTS: A COLLECTION OF CRITICAL ESSAYS
Michael Cooke, Editor

Prentice-Hall, 1972. Pap. $1.95.

NATIVE SONS: A CRITICAL STUDY OF TWENTIETH-CENTURY NEGRO-AMERICAN AUTHORS
E. Margolies

J. B. Lippincott Co., 1969. Cloth, $5.95; Pap. $1.95.

THE NEGRO NOVELIST, 1940 TO 1950
Carl M. Hughs

Citadel press, 1970. Pap. $2.25.

AUTOBIOGRAPHIES

AUTOBIOGRAPHY OF AN EX-COLORED MAN
James W. Johnson

Alfred A. Knopf, Inc., 1927. $5.95.

BLACK AMERICANS IN AUTOBIOGRAPHY: AN ANNOTATED BIBLIOGRAPHY OF AUTOBIOGRAPHIES AND AUTOBIOBRAPHICAL BOOKS WRITTEN SINCE THE CIVIL WAR
Russell C. Brigano

Duke University Press, 1974. $5.75.

BLACK AUTOBIOGRAPHY IN AMERICA
Stephen Butterfield

Traces the growth and progress of black autobiography in America from the slave narratives of the abolitionist era to the revolutionary works of the 1960s and 1970s. 320 pp. University of Massachusetts Press, 1974. Cloth, $15.00; Pap. $6.00.

BOOKER T. WASHINGTON'S OWN STORY OF HIS LIFE AND WORK: *The Original Autobiography Brought Up to Date With a Complete Account of Dr. Washington's Sickness and Death*
Albon L. Holsey
Containing the only photos of the funeral and burial. The authentic edition. 462 pp. Greenwood Press. Reprint of the 1915 edition. Illus. $19.00.

GROWING UP BLACK
Jay David, Editor
Nineteen autobiographical selections tell the stories of Negro children raised white America during the past two centuries. William Morrow & Co., 1968. $7.95.

I NEVER HAD IT MADE
Jackie Robinson
G. P. Putnam's Sons, 1972. Illus. $7.95.

LIVING BLACK IN WHITE AMERICA
Jay David and Elaine Crane
200 years of adult experience told through 22 autobiographical sections. William Morrow & Co., 1971. Cloth, $6.95; Pap. $2.95.

A MAN CALLED WHITE: THE AUTOBIOGRAPHY OF WALTER WHITE
Walter White
Indiana University Press, 1970. Pap. $3.25.

MANY SHADES OF BLACK
Stanton L. Wormley and Lewis H. Federson
Lena Horne, Louis Armstrong, and many other prominent Negroes tell about America and themselves, their struggles, their hopes. William Morrow & Co., 1969. $7.95.

MY LARGER EDUCATION
Booker T. WAShington
An autobiography of Washinngton's later life. Mnemosyne Publishing Co. Reprint of the 1911 edition. $3.50.

NIGGER: AN AUTOBIOGRAPHY
Dick Gregory and Robert Lipsyte
E. P. Dutton and Co., 1964. $4.95.

OSSIE: THE AUTOBIOGRAPHY OF A BLACK WOMAN
Ossie Guffy
Bantam Books, 1972. Pap. $1.25.

THE STORY OF MY LIFE AND WORK
Booker T. Washington
423 pp. Greenwood Press, 1970. Reprint of the 1900 edition. Illus. $16.75.

UP FROM SLAVERY
Booker T. Washington
The story of a man's rise from slavery to the national leadership of his people in their struggle for political and economic freedom. 330 pp. Corner House Publishers. Reprint of the 1900 edition. $5.98.

*UP FROM SLAVERY
Booker T. Washington
The autobiography of the founder of the Tuskegee Institute in Alabama. 212 pp. Dodd, Mead & Co., 1965. Illus. Age 16 up. $5.50.

BIBLIOGRAPHIES AND REFERENCES

AFRO-AMERICAN HISTORY: A BIBLIOGRAPHY
Dwight L. Smith, Editor
2285 abstracts of articles selected from two decades of serial publications in the United States and abroad. Clio Press, 1974. $45.00.

AMERICAN NEGRO REFERENCE BOOK
J. Davis, Editor
Prentice-Hall, 1966. $24.95.

ANALYTICAL GUIDE AND INDEXES TO *The Colored American Magazine, 1900-1909*
"Devoted to the interest of American citizens of color and to the development of Afro-American art and literature." Two volumes. Greenwood Press, 1974. $75.00.

AN ANNOTATED GUIDE TO BASIC REFERENCE BOOKS ON THE BLACK AMERICAN EXPERIENCE
Guy Westmoreland
Scholarly Resources, Inc. $12.50.

BIBLIOGRAPHY OF AFRO-AMERICAN AND OTHER MINORITIES REPRESENTED IN LIBRARY LISTINGS
Clara O. Jackson

American Institute for Marxist Studies, 1970.
$1.00.

**A BIBLIOGRAPHY OF NEGRO HISTORY
AND CULTURE FOR YOUNG READERS**
Miles Jackson, Jr., Editor
University of Pittsburgh Press, 1969. Pap.
$2.95.

**THE BLACK AMERICAN REFERENCE
BOOK**
Mabel M. Smythe, Editor
The revised and updated successor to *The
American Negro Reference Book*. 1240 pp.
Prentice-Hall, Inc., 1975. Illus. $35.00.

**BLACK IMAGE ON THE AMERICAN
STAGE: A BIBLIOGRAPHY OF PLAYS
AND MUSICALS 1770 TO 1970**
James V. Hatch
Drama Book Specialists, Pubs., 1970. $8.00.

**BLACK NAMES IN AMERICA: A GUIDE
TO THEIR HISTORY AND MEANING**
Murray Heller and Puckett Newbell
G. K. Hall and Co., 1974. Price not set

**THE CHICAGO AFRO-AMERICAN UNION
ANALYTIC CATALOG: AN INDEX TO
MATERIALS ON THE AFRO-AMERICAN
IN THE PRINCIPAL LIBRARIES IN
CHICAGO, 5 VOLS.**
G. K. Hall and Co., 1972. $345.00.

**A CLASSIFIED CATALOG OF THE NEGRO
COLLECTION IN THE COLLINS P.
HUNTINGTON LIBRARY-WRITERS' PRO-
GRAM**
W. P. A. Hampton Institute, Virginia
Scholarly Press, 1971. $19.50.

**A DICTIONARY CATALOG OF THE JESSE
E. MOORLAND COLLECTION OF NEGRO
LIFE AND HISTORY, 9 VOLS.**
Howard University Libraries
G. K. Hall and Co., 1970. $665.00.

**A DICTIONARY CATALOG OF THE
NEGRO COLLECTION OF THE FISK
UNIVERSITY LIBRARY, 6 VOLS.**
Fisk University Library
G. K. Hall and Co., 1974. $375.00.

**A DICTIONARY CATALOG OF THE
SCHOMBURG COLLECTION OF NEGRO
LITERATURE AND HISTORY**
New York Library, Research Libraries

G. K. Hall and Co., 1962. $730.00 set.

**A DIRECTORY CATALOG OF THE AR-
THUR B. SPINGARN COLLECTION OF
NEGRO AUTHORS, 2 VOLS.**
Howard University Libraries
G K. Hall and Co., 1970. $150.00

EIGHT NEGRO BIBLIOGRAPHIES
D. T. Williams
Kraus Reprint Co., 1969. $25.00.

***EXPLORING BLACK AMERICA: A HIS-
TORY AND GUIDE**
Marcella Thum
A history and guidebook to museums,
monuments and historical sites that com-
memorate achievements of black Americans.
Atheneum Pubs., 1974. Age 10 up. $10.95.

**FIFTEEN TOPICS ON AFRO-AMERICA:
AN ANNOTATED BIBLIOGRAPHY**
Charles Irby
A collection of periodical articles focusing on all
aspects of the black experience in America. 86
pp. Relevant Instructional Materials, 1973.

**A GUIDE TO BLACK MEDIA: MAGA-
ZINES, NEWSPAPERS, RADIO AND
COLLEGE**
Lists 500 magazines, newspaper titles, radio call
signals; college names, publication titles. 25 pp.
Deutsch, Shea & Evans, Inc., 49 E. 53rd St.,
New YOrk, N. Y. 10022. $10.00.

GUIDE TO FILMS ABOUT NEGROES
Contains information on over 750 motion
pictures covering the lives, culture, history and
problems of Negroes in the United States and
Africa. 86 pp. Serina Press, $3.95.

**AN INDEX TO PERIODICAL ARTICLES BY
AND ABOUT NEGROES, DECENNIAL
CUMULATION 1950 TO 1959**
Hallie Q. Brown Memorial Library
G. K. Hall and co., 1962. $40.00.

**AN INDEX TO PERIODICAL ARTICLES BY
AND ABOUT NEGROES, ANNUALS, 1960
TO 1969**
Hallie Q. Brown Memorial Library
G. K. Hall and Co., 1971. $13.00 each.

**AN INDEX TO PERIODICAL ARTICLES BY
AND ABOUT NEGROES, 1906 TO 1970**
Hallie Q.Brown Memorial Library
G. K. Hall and Co., 1971. $50.00.

AN INDEX TO PERIODICAL ARTICLES BY AND ABOUT NEGROES
Hallie Q. Brown Memorial Library
G. K. Hall and Co., 1972 to 1974. $49.00.

AN INDEX TO PERIODICALS BY AND ABOUT NEGROES, ANNUAL
Hallie Q. Brown Memorial Library
G. K. Hall and Co., 1971. $39.00.

THE NEGRO IN AMERICA: A BIBLIOGRAPHY
Lists 6,500 materials on the American Negro published from 1954 through 1970. 351 pp. Harvard University Press. Cloth, $10.00; Pap. $4.95.

*THE NEGRO AMERICAN IN PAPERBACK
An annotated list for secondary school students. 45 pp. National Education Association, 1968. Pap. $.50.

THE NEGRO IN THE UNITED STATES
A selected bibliography of books and other material on the Negro in the U. S. 313 pp. Supt. of Documents, U. S. Government Printing Office, $3.25.

THE NEGRO IN THE UNITED STATES: A RESEARCH GUIDE
Erwin K. Welsch
Indiana UniversityPress, 1965. Pap. $2.25.

NO CRYSTAL STAIR: A BIBLIOGRAPHY OF BLACK LITERATURE
Office of Adult Services
New York Public Library, 1971. Pap. $2.00.

A SELECT BIBLIOGRAPHY OF THE NEGRO AMERICAN
W. E. B. DuBois
Kraus Reprint Co. Reprint of the 1905 edition. Pap. $2.00.

A WORKING BIBLIOGRAPHY OF THE NEGRO IN THE UNITED STATES
Dorothy B. Porter
University Microfilms, 1969. $7.50.

BIOGRAPHIES

*AFRO-AMERICAN CONTRIBUTORS TO AMERICAN LIFE
John M. Franco
A collection of twenty biographies of Afro-Americans of high achievement, from 1731 to the present. Benefic Press. Age 8-14. Illus. $3.70.

*AFRO-AMERICANS THEN AND NOW
Doris Haynes and Jane Hurley
Biographies of prominent blacks organized into historical groupings. Benefic Press. Age 7-10. $4.00.

A BIOGRAPHICAL HISTORY OF BLACKS IN AMERICA SINCE 1528.
Edgar Toppin
David McKay Co., 1971. Cloth, $7.95; Pap. $4.95.

BIOGRAPHICAL SKETCHES OF PROMINENT MEN AND WOMEN OF KENTUCKY
William D. Johnson
Books for Libraries, Inc. Reprint of the 1897 edition. $12.75.

*BIOGRAPHIES OF BLACK AMERICANS FOR ALL AMERICANS
Mabelle E. martin, et al
18 historic black Americans; scientists, singers, writers, and others. Highlights for Children, 1971. Ages 6-12. Pap. $1.00.

*BALCK AMERICAN LEADERS
Margaret B. Young
Harriet Tubman, Frederick Douglass, Senator Edward Brooke, Carl Stokes and others. 120 pp. Franklin Watts, Inc., 1969. Illus. Age 12 up. $3.95.

*BLACK COP
Ina R. Friedman
A biography of Tilmon B. O'Bryant, An assistant Chief of Police in Washington, D. C. Westminster Press, 1974. Illus. Age 12-16. $5.95.

BLACK COURAGE
A. E. Schraff
True stories of Afro-American heroes of the American West. 160 pp. Illus. Macrae Smith, 1969. $5.47. (Grade three up)

BLACK CRUSADER: ABIOGRAPHY OF ROBERT FRANKLIN WILLIAMS
Robert Carl Cohen
Lyle Stuart, Inc., 1972. $10.00.

*BLACK CRUSADERS FOR FREEDOM
Bennett Wayne, Editor

The life stories of four Civil War heroes: Sojourner Truth, Frederick Douglass, Harriet Tubman, and Booker T. Washington. 168 pp. Garrard books, 1974. Illus. Age 10 up. $3.98.

BLACK ENGINEERS IN THE UNITED STATES
James K. K. Ho, Editor

A reference book giving the educational backgrounds and professional experiences of blacks in virtually every field of engineering. 308 pp. Howard University Press, 1974. $18.00.

THE BLACK MAN, HIS ANTECENDENTS, HIS GENIUS, AND HIS ACHIEVEMENTS
William Wells Brown

Biographical sketches of individuals who have surmounted the obstacles of slavery and reised their status in society. Mnemosyne Publishing Co., 1975. Reprint of the 1865 edition. $2.95.

BLACK PROFILES
George R. Metcalf

Biographies of seven key figures in the black struggle for freedon in America; DuBois, Tubman, Malcolm X, Medgar Evers, King, Young, and Cleaver. 240 pp. McGraw-Hill book Co., 1972. Pap. $2.95.

CHARLES WADDELL CHESNUTT
Helen M. Chesnutt

The biography of a great black man of letters. 352 pp. University of North Carolina Press, 1952. $5.95.

*CHEER THE LONESOME TRAVELER: THE LIFE OF W. E. B. DuBOIS
Leslie Alexander Lacy

A biography of the black leader and philosopher by a writer who knew him. 160 pp. Dell Publishing Co., 1970. Photos. Age 12 up. $5.95.

*CONTEMPORARY BLACK LEADERS
Elton C. Fax

Stories of 14 famous black men and women, including Martin Luther King, Malcolm X, Carl Stokes, and Whitney Young, among others. 243 pp. Dodd, Mead & Co., 1970. illus. Age 11-15. $4.95.

*COUNTEE CULLEN AND THE NEGRO RENAISSANCE
Blanche E. Ferguson

Story of the young poet who was active during the 1920's in the Harlem-centered Negro

Renaissance. 213 pp. Dodd, Mead & Co., 1966. Illus. Age 16 up. $5.00.

*DANIEL HALE WILLIAMS, OPEN HEART DOCTOR
Lewis H. Fenderson

The story of a famous black physician and surgeon. 128 pp. McGraw-Hill Book Co., 1972. Illus. Age 8-12. $4.72.

DARK VALOR: THE MAN HISTORY FORGOT
Don Benn Owens, Jr.

The story of Columbus' first mate, Ricardo, who supposedly stopped Columbus from turning back on his quest for the New World. Commonsense Publications, 1975. $5.95.

THE EARLY RECOLLECTIONS AND LIFE OF DR. JAMES STILL
James Still

Rutgers University Press, 1973. $7.50.

*EDWARD ROSE, NEGRO TRAIL BLAZER
Harold Felton

The black pioneer who was a mountain man, trapper, interpreter, guide, and Chief of the Crow Indians. 111 pp. Dodd, Mead & Co., 1967. Illus. Age 11-15. $4.50.

*FAMOUS AMERICAN NEGROES
Langston Hughes

Biographical sketches of 17 outstanding Negro Americans include Phillis Wheatley, Paul Laurence Dunbar, Ralph Bunche, and Marion Aneerson, among others. 148 pp. Dodd, Mead & Co., 1954. Illus. Age 11-15. $3.95.

*FAMOUS BLACK AMERICANS
Morrie and Letha Turner

Facts about the important contributions black Americans have made to the history of the U. S. from colonial times to the 20th century. Judson Press. Age 6-12. Pap. $.95. Cartoons.

FAMOUS FIRST BLACKS
Sterling G. Afford

A record of Negro pioneers in every major field of endeavor, from art to stage and screen. Vantage Press. $3.95.

FAMOUS FIRST FACTS ABOUT NEGROES
Romeo B. Garrett

The roles, achievements and contributions of black men and women in American history. Arno Press, 1972. $7.95.

*FAMOUS NEGRO HEROES OF AMERICA
Harriet Tubman, Crispus Attucks, Matthew A. Henson, and Frederick Douglass, among others.
202 pp. Dodd, Mead & Co., 1958. Illus. Age 11-15. $3.95.

FIVE NEGRO PRESIDENTS
J. A. Rogers
H. M. Rogers Publishing Co., 1965. Pap. $1.25.

FOR FREEDOM: A BIOGRAPHICAL STORY OF THE AMERICAN NEGRO
Arthur Huff Fauset
200 pp. Negro Universities Press. Reprint of the 1927 edition. Illus. $9.75.

FOUR TOOK FREEDOM
Philip Sterling and Rayford Logan
The lives of Harriet Tubman, Frederick Douglass, Robert Smalls and Blanche K. Bruce. Doubleday & Co., 1965. Illus. Cloth, $3.75;

FREDERICK DOUGLASS
Charles P. Graves
G. P. Putnam's Sons, 1970. Illus. $3.59.

FREDERICK DOUGLASS THE ORATOR
James Monroe Gregory
Containing an account of his life, public services, and selections from his speeches and writings. 309 pp. Metro Books, Inc. Reprint of the 1893 edition. $12.00.

*FREE AT LAST, THE LIFE OF FREDERICK DOUGLASS
Arna Bontemps
The story of one of the original leaders of the abolitionist movement in America. 308 pp. Dodd, Mead & Co., 1971. Illus. Age 16 up. $7.95.

*FREEDOM TRAIN: THE STORY OF HARRIET TUBMAN
Dorothy Sterling
A biography of a slave who helped form the underground railroad. Doubleday & Co., 1954. Illus. Age 16 up. $3.95.

*FROM LEW ALCINDOR TO KAREEM ABDUL JABBAR
Jim Haskins
This biography discusses his career, conversion to the Muslim religion, reactions as a black man, and his personal life. 96 pp. William Morrow & Co., 1972. Illus. Ages 12-16. $3.95.

A GALLERY OF GREAT AFRO-AMERICANS
John Peterson
Initial Teaching Alphabet Publications, 1968. $20.00.

*GARVEY: THE STORY OF A PIONEER BLACK NATIONALIST
Elton C. Fax
The first black nationalist to coin "Black is Beautiful." 305 pp. Dodd, Mead & co., 1972. Illus. Age 16 up. $7.95.

GREAT BLACK AMERICANS
Harold C. Allen
Pendulum Press, Inc., 1971. Pap. $.60.

*GREAT NEGROES: PAST AND PRESENT
Russell L. Adams
175 biographies, 180 illustrations, historical summaries and bibliography. 212 pp. Afro-Am Publishing Company. Age 13 up. Cloth, $8.95; Pap. $4.95.

HARRIET BEECHER STOWE
Catherine Gilbertson
A biography of the author of *Uncle Tom's Cabin*. Kennikat Press. Reprint of the 1937 edition. $11.00.

HISTORICAL NEGRO BIOGRAPHIES
Robinson
United Publishing Corp., 1970. $13.88.

JESSE JACKSON: THE MAN, THE MOVEMENT, THE MYTH
Barbara Reynolds
A biography of Jesse Jackson and the story of the black man in America during the last decade. 416 pp. Nelson-Hall Publishers, 1974. $9.95.

*JIM BECKWOURTH, NEGRO MOUNTAIN MAN
Harold Felton
A famous mountain man who became a chief of the Crow Indians. 173 pp. Dodd, Mead & Co., 1966. Illus. Age 11-15. $4.50.

KING: A CRITICAL BIOGRAPHY
David L. Lewis
An in-depth biography of Martin Luther King, Jr. Penguin Books. $1.45.

LIFT EVERY VOICE
Dorothy Sterling and Benjamin Quarles
The lives of Booker T. Washington, W. E. B.

DuBois, Mary Church Terrell and James Weldon Johnson. Doubleday & Co., 1965. Cloth, $3.75; Pap. $1.45.

THE LONESOME ROAD: BIOGRAPHICAL HISTORY OF BLACK AMERICA
    Saunders Redding
Doubleday and Co., 1972. Pap. $2.95.

THE MAKING OF AN AFRO-AMERICAN: MARTIN ROBINSON DELANY, 1812-1885
    Dorothy Sterling
Doubleday & Co., Cloth, $4.95; Pap. $1.95.

MARCHING TO FREEDOM THE LIFE OF MARTIN LUTHER KING, JR.
    R. Bleiweiss
New American Library, 1975.

*MARCUS GARVEY
    Daniel S. Davis
Story of the man who advocated racial pride, separatism and black nationalism. 192 pp. Franklin Watts, Inc., 1972. Illus. Age 12 up. $4.90.

MARTIN R. DELANY: THE BEGINNINGS OF BLACK NATIONALISM
    Victor Ullman
The biography of a black abolitionist. Beacon Press, 1974. Cloth, $9.95; Pap. $3.95.

*MONUMENT TO A BLACK MAN
    Daniel James Kubiak
The brief biography of William Goyens. The Naylor Co. Illus. Age 11 up. $6.95.

THE MOST NATIVE OF SONS: A BIOGRAPHY OF RICHARD WRIGHT
    John A. Williams
Doubleday & Co. Cloth, $3.95; Pap. $1.45.

MR. BLACK LABOR: THE STORY OF A. PHILIP RANDOLPH, FATHER OF THE CIVIL RIGHTS MOVEMENT
    Daniel S. Davis
E. P. Dutton and Co. $6.50.

*THE NEGRO IN AMERICAN LIFE
    Mabel Morsbach
An up-to-date history of the American Negro, featuring capsule biographies of Dr. Martin Luther King, Jr., Ralph Ellison, Senator Edward Brooke, and Jackie Robinson among others. 273 pp. Illus. Harcourt Brace Jovanovich, Inc., 1968. $7.50. Ages 12 up.

12 NEGRO AMERICANS
    Mary Jenness
Books for libraries, Inc. Reprint of the 1936 edition. $10.50.

A NEGRO EXPLORER AT THE NORTH POLE
    Matthew A. henson
Peary's assistant on the Peary Polar Expedition at the top of the world in 1909. Arno Press. Reprint of the 1912 edition. $6.00.

NEGRO LEADERSHIP IN A SOUTHERN CITY
    M. Elaine Burgess
College and University Press, 1962. Pap. $2.25.

NEW DIRECTIONS FROM DON L. LEE
    Marlene Mosher
Full-length study of an acclaimed black poet, essayist, and teacher. Exposition Press. $6.50.

*PIONEERS AND PATRIOTS: THE LIVES OF SIX NEGROES OF THE REVOLTIONARY ERA
    Lawinia Dobler and Edgar Toppin
Doubleday and Co., 1965. Cloth, $3.75; Pap. $1.45. Below college level.

PRIVATE   PRESSURE   ON   PUBLIC LAW: THE LEGAL CAREER OF JUSTICE THURGOOD MARSHALL
    Randall W. Blank
The story of the first Negro appointed to the Supreme Court. Kennikat Press, 1973. Cloth, $9.95; Pap. $3.95.

*PROFILES OF BLACK AMERICANS, TWO VOLUMES
    Richard A. Boning
A treasury of art and information about famous black Americans. Dexter & Westbrook, Ltd., 1969. $88.70. Jr. High up.

*SEVENTEEN BLACK ARTISTS
    Elton c. Fax
Biographies of leading black American artists. 288 pp. Dodd, Mead & Co., 1971. Illus. Age 16 up. $7.95.

*THADDEUS STEVENS AND THE FIGHT FOR NEGRO RIGHTS
    Milton Meltzer
Thomas Y. Crowell Co., 1967. $4.50. Below college level.

*THEY SHOWED THE WAY: FORTY AMERICAN NEGRO LEADERS
Charlemae Rollins
Thomas Y. Crowell Co., 1964. $3.95. Below college level.

*THURGOOD MARSHALL, FIGHTER FOR JUSTICE
Lewis H. Fenderson
The important events in Marshall's private life and public career from boyhood to his appointment as Supreme Court justice are highlighted. 128 pp. McGraw-Hill Book Co. Age 8-12. $4.72.

*TOGETHER IN AMERICA
Johanna Johnston
Contributions of individual Negroes throughout American history. 158 pp. Dodd, Mead & Co., 1965. Illus. Age 11-15. $3.95.

*UNSUNG BLACK AMERICAN HEROES AND HEROINES
Edith Stull
Grosset and Dunlap, Inc., 1970. $2.95. Ages 6 to 12.

UP FROM WITHIN: TODAY'S NEW BLACK LEADERS
George R. Metcalf
304 pp. McGraw-Hill Book Co., 1971. $7.95.

W. E. B. DuBOIS: NEGRO LEADER IN A TIME OF CRISIS
Francis L. Broderick
259 pp. Stanford University Press, 1959. Cloth, $8.50; Pap. $2.95.

W. E. DuBOIS: PROPAGANDIST OF THE NEGRO PROTEST
Elliot Rudwick
Atheneum Publications, 1968. Pap. $3.25.

WHO'S WHO OF THE COLORED RACE
Frank L. Mather
Gale Research. Reprint of the 1915 edition. $18.00.

*YOUNG BOOKER: BOOKER T. WASHINGTON'S EARLY DAYS
Arna Bontemps
The story of the founder of the Tuskegee Institute. 196 pp. Dodd, Mead & Co., 1972. Illus. Age 16 up. $6.95.

*YOUNG JIM: THE EARLY YEARS OF JAMES WELDON JOHNSON
Ellen Tarry

The story of the boyhood and youth of a great Negro poet. 230 pp. Dodd, Mead & Co., 1967. Illus. Age 11-15. $4.50.

BLACK POWER

BLACK POWER U.S.A.: THE HUMAN SIDE OF RECONSTRUCTION 1867-1877
Lerone Bennett, Jr.
A detailed account of the Reconstruction era. Penguin Books. Pap. $1.95.

*BLACK PRIDE: A PEOPLE'S STRUGGLE
Janet Harris and Julius Hobson
How black power grew and what both SNCC workers and Black Panthers feel that it means today. 128 pp. McGraw-Hill Book Co., 1969. Age 16 up. $4.95.

BLACK POWER AND THE GARVEY MOVEMENT
Theodore G. Vincent
Monthly Review Press, 1975. Cloth, $7.95; Pap. $2.95.

BLACK POWER AND THE GARVEY MOVEMENT
Theodore G. Vincent
299 pp. Ramparts Press, 1975. $5.95; Pap. $2.95.

BLACK POWER GARY STYLE: THE MAKING OF MAYOR RICHARD GORDON HATCHER
Alex Poinsett
Johnson Publishing Co., Chicago, 1970. $6.95.

BLACK POWER: THE POLITICS OF LIBERATION IN AMERICA
Stokely Carmichael and Charles V. Hamilton
Random House, Inc., 1968. Cloth, $5.95; Pap. $1.95.

BLACK POWER: THE RADICAL RESPONSE TO WHITE AMERICA
Thomas Wagstaff
Glencoe Press; Macmillan Publishing Co.; 1969. Pap. $2.95.

BLACK POWER REVOLT
Floyd B. Barbour
Peter Sargent Pubs., 1969. $5.95.

BLACK POWER, UNITED STATES OF AMERICA: THE HUMAN SIDE OF RECONSTRUCTION, 1867 TO 1877
Lerone Bennett, Jr.
Johnson Publishing Co. 1967. $6.95.

BLACK POWER AND URBAN UNREST
N. Wright, Jr.
Hawthorn Books, 1967. Pap. $1.95.

BLACK POWER/WHITE RESISTANCE
Fred Powledge
Simon and Schuster, Inc., 1971. $2.95.

*CHRONICLES OF NEGRO PROTEST, DOCUMENTING THE HISTORY OF BLACK POWER
Bradford Chambers
320 pp. Parents Magazine Press, 1968. $4.95. Ages 12 up.

*IF NOT NOW, WHEN?: THE MANY MEANINGS OF BLACK POWER
Dora Pantell and Edwin Greenidge
A study of the Black Power movement and of the major civil rights groups. 216 pp. Dell Publishing Co., 1970. Age 12 up. $5.95.

THE IMPOSSIBLE REVOLUTION: - BLACK POWER AND THE AMERICAN DREAM
Lewis M. Killian
Random House, Inc., 1968. Cloth, $7.95; Pap. $3.95.

THE LONG STRUGGLE FOR BLACK POWER
Edward Peeks
From the days of slavery to the Black Panthers. Charles Scribner's Sons, 1972. Cloth, $7.95; Pap. $4.95.

*PROFILES IN BLACK POWER: HISTORY OF THE BLACK POWER MOVEMENT IN AMERICA
James Haskins
Doubleday and Co., 1972. $3.95. Up to 14 years old.

REALITY IN BLACK AND WHITE: A PRIMER FOR WHITE AMERICANS
William L. Eichelberger
A strong statement for Black Power. 160 pp. Westminster Prees, 1969. Pap. $2.65.

THE RHETORIC OF BLACK POWER
Robert L. Scott and Wayne E. Brockriede, Editors

Harper and Row Pubs., 1969. Pap. $5.95.

STOKELY SPEAKS: BLACK POWER TO PAN-AMERICANISM
Stokely Carmichael
Random House, Inc., 1971. Cloth, $6.95; Pap. $1.95.

WADE HAMPTON AND THE NEGRO: THE ROAD NOT TAKEN
Hamton M. Jarrel
University of South Carolina Press. Reprint of the 1949 edition. $9.95.

WHITE ETHICS AND BLACK POWER: THE EMERGENCE OF THE WEST SIDE ORGANIZATION
William W. Ellis
Aldine Publishing Co., 1969. $7.95.

WHITE REFLECTIONS ON BLACK POWER
Charles E. Fager
The author sees political organization as the power by which minority groups develop social self-reliance and responsibility. William B. Eerdmans Publishing Co., 1967. Pap. $1.65.

WHY BLACK POWER?
Joseph R. Barndt
Explains the Black Power ideology and how it grew. Friendship Press. Pap. $.95.

BLACK STUDIES

AFRICAN AND BLACK AMERICAN STUDIES
Alexander S. Birkos and Lewis A. Tambs
Serial pubications in Africa, Canada, Latin American, and the United States. Data includes title, editor, address, sponsor, frequency, subscription rate, circulation, editorial interests and policies, notes, and special features. 295 pp. Libraries Unlimited, 1975. $11.50.

AFRO-AMERICAN STUDIES: A RESOURCE GUIDE FOR STUDENTS, TEACHERS, AND LIBRARIANS
Ann Knight Randall
Provides an annotated bibliography of directories, biographical sources, organizations, library collections, and key figures in black studies programs. 300 pp. R. R. Bowker Co., 1975.

THE BLACK AESTHETIC
Addison Gayle, Jr., Editor
Essays on black studies, literature and criticsm.
Doubleday & Co., 1971. Illus. $2.95.

BLACK STUDIES
R. L. Cortada
Xerox College Publishing, 1974. Pap. $6.95.

BLACK STUDIES: A BIBLIOGRAPHY
Leonard B. Irwin
Included are works of history, biography, autobiography and memoirs, exposition and argument of all views. McKinley Publishing Co., 1973. $8.50.

BLACK STUDIES IN PUBLIC SCHOOLS
Raymond H. Giles, Jr.
250 pp. Praeger Pubs., 1974. $15.00.

BLACK STUDIES IN THE UNIVERSITY: A SYMPOSIUM
A. L. Robinson
Yale University Press, 1969. Cloth, $10.00; Pap. $2.45.

BLACK STUDIES: THREAT OR CHALLENGE?
Nick Aaron Ford
A documented report on the history, scope, effects, and future development of Black Studies programs in American schools and colleges. Kennikat Press, 1973. Cloth, $8.95; Pap. $3.95.

DIRECTORY OF AFRO-AMERICAN RESOURCES
Walter Schatz
Lists organizations and institutions holding research materials in Afro-American studies. Lists 2100 resource centers, with 4500 listings of holdings. 512 pp. R. R. Bowker Co., $21.00.

LECTURES IN BLACK STUDIES
Ira Lunan Ferguson
The Lunan-Ferguson Library, 1972. 352 pp. $8.95.

MULTIMEDIA MATERIALS FOR AFRO-AMERICAN STUDIES
Harry A. Johnson
An annotated bibliography of films, filmstrips, audio and video tapes, and other educational media available for rental or purchase in the United States. 353 pp. R. R. Bowker Co., 1971. $21.50.

NEW PERSPECTIVES ON BLACK STUDIES
John W. Blassingame, Editor
236 pp. University of Illinois Press. Reprint of the 1971 edition. Pap. $2.95.

THE NEW WORLD NEGRO: SELECTED PAPERS IN AFRO-AMERICAN STUDIES
Melville J. Herskovitz
Funk and Wagnall Publishers. Illus. Pap. $2.95.

OPINIONS FIFFER ON BLACK STUDIES
Thomas Sowell and Ronald Beresford Bailey
National Education Association, 1975. Pap. $.50.

PRIDE: A HANDBOOK OF CLASSROOM IDEAS TO MOTIVATE THE TEACHING OF ELEMENTARY BLACK STUDIES
Educational Services. $5.25.

SOURCE BOOK IN BLACK STUDIES
Walter D. Abilla
MSS Information Corp., 1972. $10.00.

SURVEY OF BIBLIOGRAPHIC ACTIVITIES OF U. S. COLLEGES AND UNIVERSITIES ON BLACK STUDIES
Information on 200 colleges and universities doing bibliographic work in regard to Black Studies with programs and key personnel. 60 pp. St. Louis University, Pius XII Library, 3655 W. Pine St., St. Louis, Mo. 63108. $3.00.

TEACHING THE BLACK EXPERIENCE: METHODS AND MATERIALS
James A. Banks
Fearon Pubs., 1970. Pap. $2.75.

CHILD WELFARE

BLACK CHILDREN—WHITE PARENTS: A STUDY OF TRANSRACIAL ADOPTION
Grow and Shapiro
A research examination of black children over six growing up with white parents. 239 pp. Child Welfare League of America, Inc., 1974. $6.95.

CHILD WELFARE, WITH SUPPLEMENT ON THE STANDARD OF LIVING AMONG 100 NEGRO MIGRANT FAMILIES IN PHILADELPHIA: 1921
The American Academy of Political and Social Science, 1975. Cloth, $5.00; Pap. $4.00.

CHILDREN OF THE STORM: *Black Children and American Child Welfare*
 Andrew Billingsley and Jeanne M. Giovannoni
An analysis of the general inadequacies and racial inequities in the American child welfare system. 288 pp. Harcourt Brace Jovanovich, Inc., 1974. Cloth, $8.50; Pap. $3.95.

NEGRO CHILD WELFARE IN NORTH CAROLINA
 Wiley B. Sanders
326 pp. Patterson Smith Publishing Corp. Reprint of the 1933 edition. Illus. $12.00.

CIVIL RIGHTS

THE AMERICAN NEGRO: 1928
The American Academy of Political and Social Science, 1975. Cloth, $5.00; Pap. $4.00.

THE AMERICAN NEGRO REVOLUTION
 Benjamin Muse
Citadel Press, 1970. Pap. $2.95.

AMERICAN NEGRO REVOLUTION: FROM NONVIOLENCE TO BLACK POWER, 1963 TO 1967
 Benjamin Muse
Indiana University Press, 1968. $8.50.

AN APPEAL IN FAVOR OF THAT CLASS OF AMERICANS CALLED AFRICANS
 Lydia maria Child
An early defense of Negro rights by a leading abolitionist. Arno Press. Reprint of the 1836 edition. $7.00.

BALANCE OF POWER: THE NEGRO VOTE
 H. L. Moon
Kraus Reprint Co. Reprint of the 1948 edition. $10.50.

BLACK FREEDOM
 C. Mabee
Macmillan Publishing Co., 1969. $9.95.

BLACK CIVIL RIGHTS DURING THE JOHNSON ADMINISTRATION
 James C. Harvey
University Press of Mississippi, 1973. Pap. $4.95.

BLACK LAWS OF VIRGINIA: A SUMMARY OF THE LEGISLATIVE ACTS OF VIRGINIA CONCERNING NEGROES FROM EARLIEST TIME TO THE PRESENT
 June Purcell Guild
249 pp. Greenwood Press. Reprint of the 1936 edition. $11.00.

THE BLACK MAN IN THE LAND OF EQUALITY
 Thomas J. Ladenburg and William S. McFeely
184 pp. Hayden Book Co., 1969. Illus. Pap. $4.30.

THE BLACK RESPONSE TO AMERICA: MEN, IDEALS, AND ORGANIZATION FROM FREDERICK DOUGLASS TO THE NAACP
 Robert Factor
Addison-Wesley Publishing Co., 1970. Pap. $3.95.

THE BLACK REVOLT: THE CIVIL RIGHTS MOVEMENT, GHETTO UPRISINGS, AND SEPARATISM
 James A. Geschwender, Editor
A selection of social science writing on black protest in America. 483 pp. Prentice-Hall, Inc., Pap. $6.95.

*BLACK STRUGGLE: A HISTORY OF THE NEGRO IN AMERICA
 Bryan Fulks
From origins in Africa through the Revolution, Civil War, and up to the present. 368 pp. Dell Publishing Co., 1970. Ages 12 up. $5.95.

THE BLACK VANGUARD
 Robert H. Brisbane
Probes the origins of the Negro social revolution from 1900. Judson Press, 1970. Cloth, $6.95; Pap. 3.95.

BLACKS AND THE LAW
American Academy of Political and Social Science, 1975. Cloth, $5.00; Pap. $4.00.

CAUCASIANS ONLY: THE SUPREME COURT, THE NAACP AND THE RESTRICTIVE COVENANT CASES
 Clement Vose
University of California Press, 1959. Cloth, $10.95; Pap. $3.45.

A CENTURY OF CIVIL RIGHTS
 Milton Konivitz and Theodore Leskes

Columbia University Press. Cloth, $12.00; Pap. $2.25.

CHRONICLES OF BLACK PROTEST
Bradford Chambers
New American Library, 1969. Pap. $.95.

CIVIL RIGHTS/1960-68
The history of the civil rights movement from the sit-ins of 1960 to the "long hot summers" toward the end of the decade. Volume 1 chronicles the nonviolent period of the movement, the freedom rides, the passage of the Voting Rights Act of 1965, the search for equality in education and the beginning of the major race riots. Volume 2 covers the riots in Newark and Detroit and the assassination of Martin Luther King, Jr. Volume 1, 1960-66, 504 pp. Volume 2, 1967-68, 437 pp. Facts on File Reference Books, 1974. Volume 1, Pap. $4.45; Volume 2, Pap. $5.95.

CIVIL RIGHTS AND THE AMERICAN NEGRO
Albert Blaustein and Robert L. Zangrando, Editors
Trident Press, 1968. Cloth, $7.95; Pap. $4.95.

CIVIL RIGHTS, THE CONSTITUTION AND THE COURTS
Archibald Cox, et al,
76 pp. Harvard University Press, 1967. $2.95.

CIVIL RIGHTS DURING THE KENNEDY ADMINISTRATION
James C. Harvey
University Press of Mississippi. $2.95.

CIVIL RIGHTS IN AMERICA: 1951
The American Academy of Political and Social Science, 1975. Cloth, $5.00; Pap. $4.00.

CONFLICT AND COMPETITION: STUDIES IN THE RECENT BLACK PROTEST MOVEMENT
John H. Bracey, et al, Editors
Fourteen essays on black civil rights in the 20th century. 226 pp. Wadsworth Publishing Co., 1971. Pap. $4.50.

CORE: A STUDY IN THE CIVIL RIGHTS MOVEMENT, 1942 TO 1968
August Meier and Elliot Rudick
576 pp. Oxford University Press, 1973. $15.00.

DEVELOPMENT OF SENTIMENT ON

NEGRO SUFFRAGE TO 1860
Emil Olbrich
Books for Libraries, Inc. Reprint of the 1912 edition. $11.00.

DIARY OF A SIT-IN
Merrill Proudfoot
Insight into the passive resistance phase of the Negro's struggle for equality. 22 pp. University of North Carolina Press, 1962. $5.95.

DOWN TO NOW: *Recollections of the Civil Rights Movement*
Pat Watters
Pantheon Books, 1972. $8.95.

EQUALITY
Robert Carter, et al, Editors
Pantheon Books, 1965. $6.95.

FETTERED FREEDOM: CIVIL LIBERTIES AND THE SLAVERY CONTROVERSY, 1830--1860
Russel B. Nye
353 pp. University of Illinois Press. Reprint of the 1963 edition. Pap. $3.45.

FIRE-BELL IN THE NIGHT: THE CRISIS IN CIVIL RIGHTS
Oscar Handlin
Little, Brown, and Co., 1964. $3.95.

FIRST FREEDOM: THE RESPONSES OF ALABAMA'S BLACKS TO EMANCIPATION UNDER RECONSTRUCTION
Peter Kolchin
215 pp. Greenwood Press, Inc., 1972. $11.00.

FOLLOWING THE COLOR LINE: AMERICAN NEGRO CITIZENSHIP IN THE PROGRESSIVE ERA
Ray S. Baker
Peter Smith Publishers. $5.25.

FREE BUT NOT EQUAL: THE MIDWEST AND THE NEGRO DURING THE CIVIL WAR
V. Jacque Voegeli
University of Chicago Press, 1967. Cloth, $7.50; pap. $2.95.

*FROM RECONSTRUCTION TO REVOLUTION
Joseph A. Alvarez
The record of the black struggle for civil rights, from Reconstruction to today. Atheneum Publishers, 1971. Age 12 up. $6.50.

HISTORY OF THE NEGRO REVOLT
C. L. R. James
Haskell House Pubs., Inc. Reprint of the 1938 edition. $8.95.

HISTORY OF SUFFRAGE IN THE UNITED STATES
Kirk Harold Porter
AMS Press, Inc. Reprint of the 1918 edition. $6.75.

IN BLACK AMERICA, 1968: THE YEAR OF AWAKENING
Patricia W. Romero
United Publishing Corp., 1969. $11.25.

LAW AND EQUAL OPPORTUNITY: A STUDY OF THE MASSACHUSETTS COMMISSION AGAINST DISCRIMINATION
Leon Mayhew
313 pp. Harvard University Press, 1968. $9.00.

THE LEGAL STATUS OF THE NEGRO
C. S. Mangum
436 pp. Johnson Reprint. Reprint of the 1940 edition. $19.00.

THE LONG SHADOW OF LITTLE ROCK
Daisy Bates
David McKay Co., 1962. $5.50.

*THE MONTGOMERY BUS BOYCOTT, DECEMBER, 1955: AMERICAN BLACKS DEMAND AN END TO SEGREGATION
Janet Stevenson
The fight against "Jim Crow," led by Martin Luther King, Jr. 72 pp. Franklin Watts, Inc., 1971. $3.90. Age 12 up.

THE MOVEMENT: DOCUMENTARY OF A STRUGGLE FOR EQUALITY
Lorraine Hansberry
Simon and Schuster, 1964. Illus. $5.95.

MR. LINCOLN AND THE NEGROES: THE LONG ROAD TO EQUALITY
William O. Douglas
The position of the Negro today in light of Lincoln's actions and principles. Atheneum Publishers, 1963. $4.95.

NAACP: A HISTORY OF THE NATIONAL ASSOCIATION FOR THE ADVANCEMENT OF COLORED PEOPLE, VOLUME 1, 1909-1920
Charles Flint Kellog

The structure, compostion, and objectives of the NAACP. 360 pp. Johns Hopkins University press, 1975. Cloth, $11.00; Pap. $2.95.

NEGRO IN 20th CENTURY AMERICA: A READER ON THE STRUGGLE FOR CIVIL RIGHTS
J. Franklin and I. Starr
Peter Smith Publishers. $5.00.

THE NEGRO AND THE FIRST AMENDMENT
Harry Kalven, Jr.
University of Chicago Press, 1966. Pap. $2.45.

THE NEGRO AT HOME: AN INQUIRY AFTER HIS CAPACITY FOR SELF GOVERNMENT AND THE GOVERNMENT OF WHITES
Lindley Spring
Books for Libraries, Inc. Reprint of the 1868 edition. $12.25.

NEGRO PROTEST PAMPHLETS: A COMPENDIUM
Dorothy Porter, Editor
A collection of rare pamphlets which document Negro civil rights activities prior to the Civil War. Arno Press, 1969. $7.00.

NEGRO PROTEST THOUGHT IN THE TWENTIETH CENTURY
Francis L. Broderick and August Meier, Editors
54 selections by famous figures in the negro revolt, as well as little-known material from convention speeches, the declarations of conferences, pamphlets, and articles in magazines of small circulation. 486 pp. Bobbs-Merrill Co., 1965. Cloth, $7.50; Pap. $3.45.

NEGRO QUESTION: A SELECTION OF WRITINGS ON CIVIL RIGHTS IN THE SOUTH
George W. Cable
W. W. Norton and Co., 1968. Pap. $1.95.

THE NEGRO REVOLT
Louise Lomax
Harper and Row Pubs., 1962. Cloth, $7.95; Pap. $1.25.

*THE NEGRO REVOLUTION: FROM ITS AFRICAN GENESIS TO THE DEATH OF MARTIN LUTHER KING
Robert Goldston
Macmillan Publishing Co., Inc., 1968. Cloth, $5.95; Pap. $2.96. Below college

NEGROES, BALLOTS, AND JUDGES
Donald S. Strong
100 pp. University of Alabama Press, 1968.
$5.00.

THE NEW NEGRO OF THE SOUTH
Wilmoth A. Carter
Analysis of Southern black leadership and the
Civil Rights movement. Exposition Press, 1967.
$4.00.

**NORTHERN SCHOOLS AND CIVIL
RIGHTS: THE RACIAL IMBALANCE
ACT OF MASSACHUSETTS**
Frank Levy
Markham Publishing Co., 1971. $7.95.

***OUR BLOOD AND TEARS: BLACK
FREEDOM FIGHTERS**
Ruth Wilson
G. P. Putnam's Sons, 1972. $4.69. Below
college level.

**THE PETITIONERS: THE STORY OF THE
NEGRO AND THE UNITED STATES
SUPREME COURT**
Loren Miller
Pantheon Books, 1966. $10.95.

POLICE AND THE BLACKS
U.S. Commission on Civil Rights
Excerpts from several volumes of testimony
heard by the U. S. Commission on Civil Rights
discusses the issues of police mistreatment of
blacks, including techniques of arrest and in-
stances of police harrassment and brutality.
Arno Press. Reprint of the 1960 edition. $14.00.

**THE PRESIDENCY AND BLACK CIVIL
RIGHTS: EISENHOWER TO NIXON**
Allan Wolk
Fairleigh Dickinson University Press. $12.00.

**QUEST AND RESPONSE: MINORITY
RIGHTS AND THE TRUMAN AD-
MINISTRATION**
Donald R. McCoy and Richard T. Ruetten
University Press of Kansas. $12.00.

**RACE, CLASS, AND PARTY: A HISTORY
OF NEGRO SUFFRAGE AND WHITE
POLITICS IN THE SOUTH**
Paul Lewinson
Russell and Russell. Reprint of the 1932 edition.
Illus. $16.00.

REMUS, RASTUS, REVOLUTION
Marshall Fishwick

Bowling Green University Press, 1975. Cloth,
$5.00; Pap. $2.50.

A REPUBLIC OF EQUALS
Leslie W. Dunbar
144 pp. University of Michigan Press, 1966.
$4.00.

**RHETORIC OF THE CIVIL RIGHTS
MOVEMENT**
Haig Bosmajian and Hamida Bos
Philadelphia Book Co., 1969. Pap. $2.95.

**RIGHTS OF COLORED MEN TO SUF-
FRAGE, CITIZENSHIP, AND TRIAL BY
JURY**
William Yates
Books for Libraries, Inc. Reprint of the 1838
edition. $8.00.

***THE RISE AND FALL OF "JIM CROW":
THE LONG STRUGGLE AGAINST THE
SUPREME COURT'S "SEPARATE-BUT-
EQUAL" RULING**
Frank B. Latham
An examination of the "Jim Crow" laws in the
United States. 72 pp. Franklin Watts, Inc.,
1969. Cloth, $3.90; Pap. $1.25. Age 12 up.

**SOUNDS OF THE STRUGGLE: PERSONS
AND PERSPECTIVES IN CIVIL RIGHTS**
C. Eric Lincoln
Essays treating many aspects of the struggle for
racial justice. Friendship Press. $1.95.

**STRIDE TOWARD FREEDOM: THE
MONTGOMERY STORY**
Martin L. King, Jr.
Harper and Row Pubs., 1958. $5.95.

**STRUGGLE FOR EQUALITY: ABOLI-
TIONISTS AND THE NEGRO IN THE CIVIL
WAR**
James McPherson
Princeton University Press, 1964. Cloth,
$15.00; Pap. $3.95.

***TEAR DOWN THE WALLS!: A HISTORY
OF THE AMERICAN CIVIL RIGHTS
MOVEMENT**
Dorothy Sterling
Doubleday & Co., 1968. Age 12 up. $6.95.

**THIN DISGUISE: TURNING POINT IN
NEGRO HISTORY-PLESSY VS. FERGU-
SON-A DOCUMENTARY PRESENTATION**
Otto Olsen, Editor
Humanities Press, 1967. $4.50.

TO BE EQUAL
Whitney M. Young
256 pp. McGraw-Hill Book Co., 1966. Pap. $1.95.

THE TROUBLE I'VE SEEN, *White Journalist/Black Movement*
Paul Good
A first hand account by a white journalist of the Civil Rights Movement. The author constructs a personal portrait of himself in relation to the realities of being black or white in America. 354 pp. Howard University Press, 1975. $9.95.

THE TROUBLESOME PRESENCE: AMERICAN DEMOCRACY AND THE NEGRO
Eli Ginzberg, and Alfred S. Eichner
Free Press, 1964. $6.95.

VOICES OF NEGRO PROTEST IN AMERICA
W. Haywood Burns
102 pp. Oxford University Press, 1963. $2.50.

VOLUNTARY SERVITUDE: WHITES IN THE NEGRO MOVEMENT
Charles J. Levy
Irvington Books Press, 1968. Pap. $4.95.

WALLS COME TUMBLING DOWN: A HISTORY OF THE CIVIL RIGHTS MOVEMENT, 1940 TO 1970
Thomas R. Brooks
Prentice-Hall, 1974. $10.00.

WE CHARGE GENOCIDE: THE CRIME OF GOVERNMENT AGAINST THE NEGRO PEOPLE
William L. Patterson
The full text of the historic petition placed before the U. N. in 1951. 256 pp. International Publishers. Reprint of the 1951 edition. Cloth, $5.95; Pap. $1.95.

WHEN NEGROES MARCH
Herbert Garfinkel
Study of the mass-demonstration March on Washington Movement. Atheneum Publishers, 1969. Pap. $3.25. Free Press, $4.95.

WHITE RESPONSE TO BLACK EMANCIPATION: SECOND-CLASS CITIZENSHIP IN THE UNITED STATES SINCE RECONSTRUCTION
Sig Synnestvedt
Macmillan Publishing Co., Inc., 1972. Pap. $3.95.

CONVENTIONS

CALIFORNIA STATE CONVENTION OF COLORED CITIZENS FOR 1855, 1856, 1865
R and E Research Associates, Pubs. Reprint of the 1855, 1856, and 1865 editions. $8.00.

MINUTES OF THE PROCEEDINGS OF THE NATIONAL NEGRO CONVENTIONS, 1830-1864
Howard H. Bell, Editor
Arno Press. Reprint of the 1969 edition. $17.00.

PROCEEDINGS
National Conference of Colored Men of the United States-Nashville, Tennessee-1879
107 pp. Negro Universities Press. Reprint of the 1879 edition. $8.50.

A SURVEY OF THE NEGRO CONVENTION MOVEMENT, 1830-1861
Howard H. Bell
A survey of black conventions prior to the Civil War; studies the entire convention movement, emphasizing education, temperance, moral reform, frugality, and self-help. Arno Press. Reprint of the 1953 edition. $12.00.

CULTURE

AFRO-AMERICAN ANTHROPOLOGY: CONTEMPORARY PERSPECTIVES ON THEORY AND RESEARCH
Norman Whitten and John Szwed
Free Press, 1970. Cloth, $12.00; Pap. $5.95.

THE AFRO-AMERICAN EXPERIENCE: A CULTURAL HISTORY THROUGH EMANCIPATION
James H. Dormon and Robert R. Jones
Presents the Afro-American experience as a process of culture dynamics, from the African beginnings through Emancipation. 279 pp. John Wiley & Sons, 1974. Cloth, $8.95; Pap. $4.50.

AFTER FREEDOM: A CULTURAL STUDY IN THE DEEP SOUTH
Hortense Powdermaker
Local Negro culture in relation to the white community in a cotton-growing town in Mississippi 75 years after Emancipation. Atheneum Publishers, 1968. Pap. $3.45.

100 AMAZING FACTS ABOUT THE NEGRO
J. A. Rogers
H. M. Rogers Publishing Co., 1952. Pap. $1.25.

ANTHROPOMETRY OF THE AMEEICAN NEGRO
Melville J. Herskovitz
Haskell House Pubs., Inc. Reprint of the 1930 edition. 12.95. AMS Press, Inc., 15.00.

BEYOND THE ANGRY BLACK
John A. Williams
Deals with sociological and cultural aspects of the black American, by both black and white authors. Cooper Square Publishers, 1966. $6.00

BLACK CULTURE
G. Simons, and H. Huthinson
Holt, Rinehart, and Winston, 1972. Pap. $5.25.

BLACK EXPERIENCE: SOUL
Lee Rainwater, Editor
The expression of black culture in soul food, music, and language. 266 pp. Transaction Books, 1973. cloth, $7.95; Pap. $3.45.

BLACK FOLK: THEN AND NOW
W. E. Burghardt Du Bois
401 pp. Octagon Books. Reprint of the 1939 edition. $14.00.

*BLACK LIFE AND CULTURE IN THE UNITED STATES
Rhoda L. Goldstein, Editor
Topics include slavery, liberation, survival techniques, black nationalism, black heritages and influences on the New World, black music, dance, and race and class in the urban ghetto, among others. 352 pp. Thomas Y. Crowell Co., 1971. $7.95. Age 16 up.

BLACK RITUALS
Sterling Plumpp
Third World Press, 1972. Pap. $1.95.

BLACK TOMORROW: A PORTRAIT OF NEGRO CULTURE
Frank Milton McCoy
Vantage Press. $3.95.

BLACKWAYS OF KENT
Hylan Lewis
337 pp. University of North Carolina Press, 1955. Cloth, $6.00; Pap. $3.45.

CONGAREE SKETCHES
E. C. L. Adams

Scenes from Negro life in the swamps of the Congaree. Kraus Reprint Co. Reprint of the 1927 edition. $10.00.

DARKWATER: *Voices from Within the Veil*
W. E. B. DuBois
A companion volume to *The Souls of Black Folk,* a collection of essays on black pride. Schocken Books. Pap. $2.75.

DICTIONARY OF BLACK CULTURE
Wade Baskin and Richard N. Runes
An encyclopedic survey of the cultural background and development of American blacks, with issues, events, contributions and biographies. 460 pp. Philosophical Library, 1973. $15.00.

DO NEGROES REALLY BELIEVE BLACK IS BEAUTIFUL?
George W. Williams
Vantage Press. $4.50.

DRUMS AND SHADOWS: SURVIVAL STUDIES AMONG THE GEORGIA COASTAL NEGROES
Georgia Writers' Project, Work Projects Administration, Savannah Unit
274 pp. Greenwood Press. Reprint of the 1940 edition. Illus. Cloth, $12.50. Doubleday and Co., Pap. 1.95.

HARLEM ON MY MIND: CULTURAL CAPITAL OF BLACK AMERICA, 1900-1968
Allon Schoerner, Editor
Hundreds of photographs of Harlem, plus an accompanying text. 255 pp. Morgan & Morgan, 1975. Pap. $3.50.

MARGINALITY AND IDENTITY: A COLORED CREOLE FAMILY THROUGH TEN GENERATIONS
Sister Frances Jerome Woods
396 pp. Louisiana State University Press, 1972. $15.00.

"THE MISSING LINK," OR THE NEGRO'S ETHNOLOGICAL STATUS
Gottlieb Christopher Hasskarl
AMS Press, Inc. Reprint of the 1898 edition. $10.00.

THE NEGRO IN AMERICAN CULTURE
Margaret J. Butcher
Alfred A. Knopf, Inc., 1972. Cloth, $7.95. New American Library, 1971. Pap. $1.50.

SEEDS BENEATH THE SNOW
    Arthenia J. Bates
A collection of twelve vignettes of black life in the rural South. 146 pp. Illus. Howard University Press, 1975. $6.95.

TWENTY-FIVE YEARS IN THE BLACK BELT
    William James Edwards
143 pp. Greenwood Press. Reprint of the 1918 edition. Illus. $9.00.

*WITCHCRAFT, MYSTICISM AND MAGIC IN THE BLACK WORLD
    James Haskins
Doubleday & co., 1973. Age 12 up. $4.50.

ECONOMICS

BLACK AMERICANS AND WHITE BUSINESS
    David Hampton and Edwin Epstein
Dickenson Publishing Co., 1971. $10.95.

BLACK BUSINESS ENTERPRISE: HISTORICAL AND CONTEMPORARY PERSPECTIVES
    Ronald W. Barley
Basic Books, 1971. $13.00.

BLACK BUSINESS IN THE NEW SOUTH: A SOCIAL HISTORY OF THE NORTH CAROLINA MUTUAL LIFE INSURANCE COMPANY
    Walter B. Weare
322 pp. University of Illinois Press, 1973. Photos. $10.95.

BLACK CAPITALISM
    Laird Durham
Communication Service Corp., 1970. Pap. $3.00.

BLACK CAPITALISM: PROBLEMS IN DEVELOPMENT: A CASE STUDY OF LOS ANGELES
    Frederick E. Case
102 pp. Praeger Pubs., 1972. $11.00.

BLACK CAPITALISM: A QUANTITATIVE ANALYSIS
    Timothy Bates
150 pp. Praeger Pubs., 1973. $13.50.

BLACK CAPITALISM: STRATEGY FOR BUSINESS IN THE GHETTO
    Theodore L. Cross
Atheneum Publications, 1969. Pap. $3.95.

BLACK CONSUMER: DIMENSIONS OF BEHAVIOR AND STRATEGY
    George Joyce and Norman A. Govoni, Editors
Random House, Inc., 1971. Pap. $4.95.

BLACK ECONOMIC DEVELOPMENT
    Flournoy A. Coles, Jr.
Discusses the nature of, obstacles to, psychological factors involved with, planning and strategies for, and management of black economic development. 232 pp. Nelson-Hall Publishers, 1975. $9.95.

BLACK ECONOMIC DEVELOPMENT
    William Haddad and G. Douglas Pugh, Editors
Prentice-Hall, 1969. Pap. $1.95.

BLACK ENTERPRISE, INC.: CASE STUDIES OF A NEW EXPERIMENT IN BLACK BUSINESS DEVELOPMENT
    Alvin N. Puryear and Charles A. West
Doubleday and Co., 1973. Cloth, $9.95; Pap. $4.95.

BLACK ENTREPRENEURSHIP
    James Hund
Wadsworth Publishing Co., 1970. Pap. $4.95.

BLACK EXECUTIVE
    W. T. Whitsitt
Broadside Press, Pubns., 1974.

BLACK MEN AND BUSINESSMEN: THE GROWING AWARENESS OF A SOCIAL RESPONSIBILITY
    Steven M. Gelber
This historical analysis explores black inroads in business as part of the larger question of business social responsibility. It relates black employment problems to the businessman's concept of his role in society, examining underlying legal, moral, and economic issues and the profound influence of two traditional business values; the capitalist ethic and the America creed of equal opportunity. Kennikat Press, 1974. $15.00.

BLACK SELF-DETERMINATION: THE STORY OF THE WOODLAWN ORGANIZATION

Arthur Brazier, Robert and Roberta DeHann, Editors

T. W. O., the model black self-help organization, is analyzed from its inception, through its years of struggle, to its confrontation with Senator McClellan's Sub-Committee. William B. Eerdmans Publishing Co., 1969. $4.95.

BLACK IN BUSINESS
Edward H. Jones
Grosset and Dunlap, Inc., 1971. $5.95.

BUILDING BLACK BUSINESS: AN ANALYSIS AND A PLAN
Abraham Venable
Thomas Y. Crowell Co., 1972. $5.95.

BUSINESS CORPORATIONS AND THE BLACK MAN-AN ANALYSIS OF SOCIAL CONFLICT: THE KODAK-FIGHT CONTROVERSY
S. P. Sethi
Chandler Publishing Co., 1970. Cloth, $7.00; Pap. $4.00.

BUSINESS LEADERSHIP AND THE NEGRO CRISIS
Eli Ginzberg
McGraw-Hill Book Co., 1968. $6.95.

CAPITAL FLOWS IN MINORITY AREAS
John R. Dominguez
A three-year study of banking and capital flows focuses on the inner city of the ghetto. Lexington Books, 1975.

CITY DIRECTORIES OF BLACK BUSINESSES
Lists city directories of black businesses. 5 pp. Minority Business Education, Howard University, 2345 Sherman Ave., N.W., Washingtin, D.C. 20001. Free

ECONOMIC CO-OPERATION AMONG NEGRO AMERICANS
W. E. B. DuBois
Kraus Reprint Co. Reprint of the 1907 edition. Pap. $4.00.

ECONOMIC CO-OPERATION AMONG THE NEGROES OF GEORGIA
T. I. Brown, Editor
Kraus Reprint Co. Reprint of the 1917 edition. Pap. $4.00.

AN ECONOMIC DETOUR: A HISTORY

OF INSURANCE IN THE LIVES OF AMERICAN NEGROES
M. S. Stuart
351 pp. Johnson Reprint. Reprint of the 1940 edition. $17.50. McGrath Publishing Co., $18.00.

THE ECONOMICS OF BLACK AMERICA
Harold G. Vatter and Thomas Palm
A brief, nontechnical survey of the socioeconomic problems of black Americans through secondary readings and editorial materials. 296 pp. Harcourt Brace Jovanovich, Inc., 1972. Pap. $3.95.

THE ECONOMICS OF DISCRIMINATION
Gary S. Becker
University of Chicago Press, 1971, 2nd edition. Cloth, $7.50; Pap. $2.95.

EMPLOYING THE NEGRO IN AMERICAN INDUSTRY
Paul H. Norgren, et al
A study of management practices. Brown Book Co., 1975. $6.00.

ETHNIC ENTERPRISE IN AMERICA: BUSINESS AND WELFARE AMONG CHINESE, JAPANES, AND BLACKS
Ivan H. Light
University of California Press, 1973. Pap. $2.85.

FEDERAL GOVERNMENT POLICY AND BLACK BUSINESS ENTERPRISE
Robert J. Yancy
An evaluation of the long and short-term value of the federal efforts to help minority business. 196 pp. Ballinger Publishing Co., 1974. $13.50.

A FRANCHISING GUIDE FOR BLACKS
Thomas B. Jones
A guide to owning a franchised business, including suggested businesses and required investment. Also explains how the black community can profit from black ownership. Pilot Books, 1973. Pap. $2.00.

THE FRAUD OF BLACK CAPITALISM
Dick Roberts
16 pp. Pathfinder Press. $.25.

GETTING IT TOGETHER: *Black Businessmen in America*
Accounts, distilled from taped interviews, of black men who have made it as professionals or as business proprietors. 233 pp. Harcourt Brace Jovanovich, Inc., 1971. $6.95.

JOBS AND INCOME FOR NEGROES
Charles C. Killingsworth
Examines the forces in the labor market which retard the economic growth of black Americans. Also touches upon black out-migration from the South in the last 50 years. 92 pp. Institute of Labor and Industrial Relations, 1968. Pap. $2.50.

THE MERCHANTS OF HARLEM: A STUDY OF SMALL BUSINESS IN A BLACK COMMUNITY
David Caplovitz
Sage Publications, 1972. Pap. $6.50.

THE MYTH OF BLACK CAPITALISM
Earl Ofari
Monthly Review Press, 1970. Cloth, $4.95; Pap. $2.65.

THE NEGRO AS A BUSINESSMAN
John H. Harmon, et al
McGrath Publishing Co. Reprint of the 1928 edition. $12.00.

NEGRO AS A CAPITALIST
Abram L. Harris
Haskell House Pubs., Inc. Reprint of the 1936 edition. $6.95.

THE NEGRO AS CAPITALIST: 1936
Abram L. Harris
The American Academy of Political and Social Science, 1975. Cloth, $5.00;Pap. $4.00.

THE NEGRO AS CAPITALIST: A STUDY OF BANKING AND BUSINESS AMONG AMERICAN NEGROES
Abram Lincoln Harris
205 pp. Negro Universities Press; Greenwood Press. Reprint of the 1936 edition. Illus. $9.00.

THE NEGRO AS CAPITALIST: A STUDY OF BANKING AND BUSINESS AMONG AMERICAN NEGROES
Abram L. Harris
Peter Smith Publishers. Reprint of the 1936 edition. Pap. $4.50.

THE NEGRO AS AN ECONOMIC FACTOR IN ALABAMA
Waight Gibbs Henry
111 pp. Greenwood Press. Reprint of the 1919 edition. $7.50.

NEGRO BUSINESS AND BUSINESS EDUCATION: THEIR PRESENT AND

PROSPECTIVE DEVELOPMENT
Joseph Alphonse Pierce
338 pp. Greenwood Press. Reprint of the 1947 edition. $13.00.

THE NEGRO IN BUSINESS
William E. DuBois
AMS Press, Inc. Reprint of the 1899 edition. $8.00.

THE NEGRO IN BUSINESS
Booker T. Washington and W. E. DuBois
AMS Press, Inc., 1971. Reprint of the 1907 edition. $12.50.

THE NEGRO IN BUSINESS
Booker T. Washington
379 pp. Metro Books, Inc. Reprint of the 1907 edition. $16.00.

THE NEGRO CHALLENGE TO THE BUSINESS COMMUNITY
Eli Ginzberg, Editor
An analysis of what the Negro's search for equality means to the business community. 111 pp. McGraw-Hill Book Co., 1964. Cloth, $5.50; Pap. $1.65.

THE NEGRO IN THE FIELD OF BUSINESS
A bibliography of black involvement in business. Lists more than 200 books, government reports, etc. Minority Business Education, P. O. Box 662, Howard University, Washington, D. C. 20001. $2.00.

THE NEGRO IN PENNSYLVANIA: A STUDY IN ECONOMIC HISTORY
Richard R. Wright, Jr.
Negro life in Pennsylvania From the days of William Penn to the first decade of the 20th century. Arno Press. Reprint of the 1912 edition. $7.00.

THE NEGRO IN THE SOUTH: HIS ECONOMIC PROGRESS IN RELATION TO HIS MORAL AND RELIGIOUS DEVELOPMENT
Booker T. Washington and W. E. Burghardt DuBois
222 pp. Metro books, Inc. Reprint of the 1907 edition. $11.50.

THE NEGRO'S ADVENTURE IN GENERAL BUSINESS
Vishnu Vitthal Oak
223 pp. Greenwood Press. Reprint of the 1949 edition. $9.50.

NEGROES AND THE GREAT DEPRESSION: THE PROBLEM OF ECONOMIC RECOVERY
Raymond Wolters
398 pp. Greenwood Press, Inc., 1970. Cloth, $15.00; Pap. $3.95.

ON BLACK ECONOMIC DEVELOPMENT: MYTHS AND FACTS
Edward D. Irons
University of Texas, Bureau of Business Research, 1971. Pap. $1.00.

THE SETTING FOR BLACK BUSINESS DEVELOPMENT: A STUDY IN SOCIOLOGY AND POLITICAL ECONOMY
Roy F. Lee
Investigates black bankers and insurance executives to determine what standards are required for success. 272 pp. New York State School of Industrial and Labor Relations, 1973. Pap. $7.00.

THE SOUTHERN URBAN NEGRO AS A CONSUMER
Paul K. Edwards
323 pp. Negro Universities Press. Reprint of the 1932 edition. illus. $13.00.

STATE OF THE BLACK ECONOMY: PROCEEDINGS
Symposium on Minority Economy, Chicago, April, 1972
University of Michigan Institute of Labor and Industrial Relations, 1973. Pap. $3.00.

THIRTY BILLION DOLLAR NEGRO
D. P. Gibson
Macmillan Publishing Co., Inc., 1969. $6.95.

EDUCATION

AN ANALYSIS OF THE SPECIFIC REFERENCES TO NEGROES IN SELECTED CURRICULA FOR THE EDUCATION OF TEACHERS
Edna Meade Colson
AMS Press, Inc. Reprint of the 1940 edition. $10.00.

BIBLIOGRAPHY OF DOCTORAL RESEARCH ON THE NEGRO, 1933 TO 1966
Earl H. West, Editor
University Microfilms, 1969. $5.00.

BLACK EDUCATION: MYTHS AND TRAGEDIES
Thomas Sowell
David McKay Co., 1972. Cloth, $6.95; Pap. $3.95.

THE BLACK EXPERIENCE IN CHILDREN'S AUDIOVISUAL MATERIALS
32 pp. New York Public Library, 1973. $1.00.

THE BLACK HIGH SCHOOL AND ITS COMMUNITY
Frederick A. Rodgers
The analysis of the black high school in the North Carolina dual educational system. Lexington Books, 1975.

BLACK IMAGE: EDUCATION COPES WITH COLOR
Jean D. Grambs, et al
A collection of original research and published material that analyzes the social values implicit in instructional media for elementary and secondary pupils, as well as textbook material and general literature. 196 pp. William C. Brown Pubs., 1972. Pap. $3.95.

BLACK MANIFESTO FOR EDUCATION
James Haskins, Editor
America's leading black educators speak out and offer plans for the future on education from the black point of view. William Morrow & Co., 1973. Cloth, $7.95; Pap. $2.95.

BLACK POWER AND STUDENT REBELLION:CONFLICT ON THE AMERICAN CAMPUS
James McEvoy and Abraham Miller, Editors
A selection of analytical essays covering the current phase of student unrest on the American college campus. 440 pp. Wadsworth Publishing Co., 1969. Pap. $5.95.

BLACK STUDENTS
Harry Edwards
Free Press, 1970. Cloth, $6.00; Pap. $2.45.

BLACK STUDENTS IN WHITE SCHOOLS
Edgar A. Epps, Editor
128 pp. C A Jones, 1972. Pap. $5.95.

BLACK STUDIES IN PUBLIC SCHOOLS
Raymond H. Giles, Jr.
250 pp. Praeger Pubs., 1973. $15.00.

THE BLACK TEACHER AND THE

DRAMATIC ARTS: A DIALOGUE, BIBLI-OGRAPHY AND ANTHOLOGY
William R. Reardon and Thomas D. Pawley, Editors
487 pp. Greenwood Press, 1970. Illus. $14.00.

BLACK TEACHERS IN GHETTO SCHOOLS: THE CASE OF WASHINGTON, D.C.
Catherine B. Silver
275 pp. Praeger Pubs., 1973. $16.50.

COLORED SCHOOL CHILDREN IN NEW YORK
Frances Blascoer
Traces 531 children through a year of school in an attempt to relate academic and social success with general school conditions, home-life, and after-school activities. A sociological study of the Afro-American community prior to World War. I. 176 pp. August M. Kelley Publishers. Reprint of the 1915 edition. $8.50. Negro Universities Press, $8.00.

THE COMMON SCHOOL AND THE NEGRO AMERICAN
W. E. B. DuBois
Kraus Reprint Co. Reprint of the 1911 edition. Pap. $3.00.

THE CONTROL OF STATE-SUPPORTED TEACHER TRAINING PROGRAMS FOR NEGROES
Felton Grandison Clark
AMS Press, Inc. Reprint of the 1934 edition. $17.50.

COUNTY TRAINING SCHOOLS AND PUBLIC SECONDARY EDUCATION FOR NEGROES IN THE SOUTH
Edward Redcay
168 pp. Negro Universities Press. Reprint of the 1935 edition. Illus. $11.25.

DEATH AT AN EARLY AGE: THE DESTRUCTION OF THE HEARTS AND MINDS OF NEGRO CHILDREN IN THE BOSTON PUBLIC SCHOOLS
Jonathan Kozol
Houghton Mifflin Co., 1967. $5.95.

THE DEVELOPMENT AND PRESENT STATUS OF NEGRO EDUCATION IN EAST TEXAS
William Davis
AMS Press, Inc., Reprint of the 1934 edition. $10.00.

THE EDUCATION OF BLACK AMERI-CANS
Statton Webster
John Day Publishing Co., 1974. Cloth, $6.50. Intext Educational Pubs. Pap. $3.95.

THE EDUCATION OF BLACK FOLK: THE AFRO-AMERICAN STRUGGLE FOR KNOWLEDGE IN WHITE AMERICA
Allen B. Ballard
Harper and Row Pubs., 1974. Cloth, $6.95; Pap. $2.95.

THE EDUCATION OF BLACK PEOPLE IN FLORIDA
J. Irving Scott
The professional and personal struggles involved in the desegregation, both legal and attitudinal, of the Florida public and private schools. 145 pp. Dorrance & Co., 1974. $5.95.

THE EDUCATION OF BLACK PEOPLE: TEN CRITIQUES, 1906-1960
W. E. B. DuBois
Seven critiques and three essays on black education. 192 pp. Monthly Review Press, 1975. Pap. $3.75.

EDUCATION FOR NEGROES IN MISSIS-SIPPI SINCE 1910
Charles H. Wilson, Sr.
Crofton Publishing Corp., 1947. 641 pp. Photos. $20.00

THE EDUCATION OF NEGROES IN NEW JERSEY
Marion M. Thompson Wright
Negro schooling in New Jersey, from the missionary efforts of the 18th century through the enactment of an 1881 law prohibiting racial discrimination in the public schools and the subsequent failure to honor the law. Arno Press. Reprint of the 1941 edition. $11.00. AMS Press, $10.00.

THE EDUCATION OF THE NEGRO PRIOR TO 1861: A HISTORY OF THE EDUCATION OF THE COLORED PEOPLE OF THE UNITED STATES FROM THE BEGINNINGS OF SLAVERY TO THE CIVIL WAR
Carter G. Woodson
Arno Press. Reprint of the 1919 edition. $14.00.

EDUCATION OF NEGRO TEACHERS
Ambrose Caliver

123 pp. Negro Universities Press. Reprint of the 1933 edition. Illus. $12.75.

FORTY YEARS OF PUBLIC SCHOOLS IN MISSISSIPPI: WITH SPECIAL REFERENCE TO THE EDUCATION OF THE NEGRO
Stuart Noble
AMS Press, Inc. Reprint of the 1918 edition. $8.50.

HISTORICAL HIGHLIGHTS IN THE EDUCATION OF BLACK AMERICANS
Presents the continuity of the educational development of black people in the United States from 1619 to the present. 36 pp. National Education Association, 1969. Pap. $.50.

A HISTORY OF NEGRO EDUCATION IN THE SOUTH: FROM 1619 TO THE PRESENT
Henry A. Bullock
339 pp. Harvard University Press, 1967. Cloth, $9.95; Pap. $3.45.

HISTORY OF THE NEW YORK AFRICAN FREE-SCHOOLS, FROM THEIR ESTABLISHMENT IN 1787 TO THE PRESENT TIME
Charles C. Andrews
148 pp. Negro Universities Press. Reprint of the 1830 edition. illus. $9.00.

HISTORY OF SCHOOLS FOR THE COLORED POPULATION
Commissioner of Education in the District of Columbia
An evaluation of black education in the nation and the nation's capitol. Arno Press. Reprint of the 1871, edition. $7.50.

THE JEANS TEACHER IN THE UNITED STATES, 1908 TO 1933: AN ACCOUNT OF 25 YEARS EXPERIENCE IN THE SUPERVISION OF NEGRO RURAL SCHOOLS
Lance Jones
Russell and Russell, 1974. Reprint of the 1937 edition. Illus. $9.00.

A LAYMAN'S GUIDE TO NEGRO HISTORY
Erwin Salk
A bibliography of books and teaching aids concerned with the history of the Negro in the United States. 196 pp. McGraw-Hill Book Co., 1967. $6.95.

MESSIAH OR SACRIFICIAL LAMB?
Hugh J. Scott
Explores the specifics of the challenges of urban education and the emerging black school superintendent. 300 pp. Howard University Press, 1976. $8.95.

THE MIS-EDUCATION OF THE NEGRO
Carter Godwin Woodson
AMS Press, Inc. Reprint of the 1933 edition. $10.00.

THE MOVABLE SCHOOL GOES TO THE NEGRO FARMER
thomas Monroe Campbell
A semi-autobiographical account of an early 20th century educator who went to be the first Negro agricultural extension worker. Arno Press. Reprint of the 1936 edition. $6.50.

THE NATIONAL EDUCATION ASSOCIATION AND THE BLACK TEACHER: THE INTERGRATION OF PROFESSIONAL ORGANIZATION
Michael J. Schultz, Jr.
224 pp. University of Miami Press, 1970. $7.95.

THE NEGRO AND THE SCHOOLS
Harry Ashmore
228 pp. University of North Carolina Press, 1970. Pap. $2.50.

NEGRO EDUCATION: A STUDY OF THE PRIVATE AND HIGHER SCHOOLS FOR COLORED PEOPLE IN THE UNITED STATES
Thomas Jesse Jones, Editor
A study of Negro higher education. Arno Press. Reprint of the 1917 edition. $35.00. Negro Universities Press, $58.00. Illus.

NEGRO EDUCATION IN ALABAMA: A STUDY IN COTTON AND STEEL
Horace Mann Bond
Public education studied against the background of the cast-based social and economic order. Atheneum Publishers, 1969. Pap. $3.45.

NEGRO EDUCATION IN KENTUCKY: A COMPARITIVE STUDY OF WHITE AND NEGRO EDUCATION ON THE ELEMENTARY AND SECONDARY SCHOOL LEVELS
Leonard Meece
180 pp. Negro Universities Press. Reprint of the 1938 edition. Illus. $9.50.

THE NEGRO RURAL SCHOOL AND ITS RELATION TO THE COMMUNITY
Tuskegee Normal and Industrial Institute-Extension Department
133 pp. Negro Universities Press. Reprint of the 1915 edition. Illus. $9.50.

NEGRO SELF-CONCEPT IMPLICATIONS FOR SCHOOL AND CITIZENSHIP
W. C. Kvaraceus, Editor
192 pp. McGraw-Hill Book Co., 1964. Pap. $2.45.

ORIGIN AND DEVELOPMENT OF THE NEGRO VISITING TEACHER IN ALABAMA
Ruth F. Boatwright
Vantage Press. $4.50.

PHILANTHROPY IN NEGRO EDUCATION
Ullin Leavell
188 pp. Negro Universities Press. Reprint of the 1930 edition. $11.00.

PORTRAIT OF A GHETTO SCHOOL
Addie D. Jones
The author shows how segregated black Southern schools have been able to achieve despite overwhelming odds. Vantage Press. Illus. $6.95.

PUBLIC SECONDARY EDUCATION FOR NEGROES IN NORTH CAROLINA
Hollia Long
AMS Press, Inc. Reprint of the 1932 edition. $10.00.

QUALITY EDUCATION FOR ALL AMERICANS: AN ASSESSMENT OF GAINS OF BLACK AMERICANS WITH PROPOSALS FOR PROGRAM DEVELOPMENT IN AMERICAN SCHOOLS AND COLLEGES FOR THE NEXT QUARTER CENTURY
William F. Brazziel
Howard University Press, 1974. $8.95.

RACIAL INTERACTION IN SCHOOL AND SOCIETY
Samuel S. Rubin and Alice Pisciotto
An analysis of the black student in a predominantly white school system. Vantage Press. $5.00.

SECONDARY EDUCATION FOR NEGROES
Ambrose Caliver
121 pp. Negro Universities Press, 1975. Reprint

of the 1933 edition. Illus. $8.50.

A SCHOOL HISTORY OF THE NEGRO RACE IN AMERICA, FROM 1619 TO 1890; ALSO A SHORT SKETCH OF LIBERIA. COMBINED WITH THE HISTORY OF THE NEGRO SOLDIERS IN THE SPANISH-AMERICAN WAR
Edward Augustus Johnson
Two Parts in One Volume. AMS Press. Reprint of the 1911 edition. $9.50.

SELF-CONCEPT: A COMPARISON OF NEGRO, ANGLO AND SPANISH-AMERICAN STUDENTS ACROSS ETHNIC, SEX AND SOCIO-ECONOMIC VARIABLES
Gary W. Healy
Dissertation. R & E Research Associates. Reprint of the 1969 paper. Pap. $8.00.

SHUT THOSE THICK LIPS: A CULTURAL STUDY ON A SLUM SCHOOL
G. Rosenfeld
Holt, Rinehart, and Winston, 1972. Pap. $3.25.

SPECIAL PROBLEMS OF NEGRO EDUCATION
Doxey Wilkerson
171 pp. Negro Universities Press. Reprint of the 1939 edition. $9.75.

STRUGGLE FOR BLACK EDUCATION
Center for Black Education
Drum and Spear Press, 1972. Pap. $1.50.

TEACH THE FREEMAN: THE CORRESPONDENCE OF RUTHERFORD B. HAYS AND THE SLATER FUND FOR NEGRO EDUCATION, 1881 TO 1887, 2 VOLS. IN 1
R. B. Hayes
Kraus Reprint Co. Reprint of the 1959 edition. $22.00 per set.

TEACHER'S GUIDE TO AMERICAN NEGRO HISTORY
William Loren Katz
Provides bibliographic, text and audio-visual information, a core reference library, and guidelines and objectives for class exercises. 192 pp. Afro-Am Publishing Company. Pap. $3.50.

THE TESTING OF BLACK STUDENTS: A SYMPOSIUM
LaMar P. Miller, Editor
Prentice-Hall, 1974. $6.95.

THE TRAINING OF NEGRO TEACHERS IN LOUISIANA

Jane Ellen McAllister
AMS Press. Reprint of the 1929 edition. $17.50.

TWO BLACK TEACHERS DURING THE CIVIL WAR

Lewis C. J. Lockwood and Charlotte Forten
Two teachers who educated ex-slaves under Yankee missionary auspices. Arno Press. Reprint of the 1864 edition. $5.00.

VOCATIONAL EDUCATION AND GUIDANCE OF NEGROES

Ambrose Caliver
137 pp. Negro Universities Press. Reprint of the 1937 edition. Illus. $9.50.

WHAT BLACK EDUCATORS ARE SAYING

Nathan Wright, Editor
Hawthorn Books, 1970. Cloth, $7.95; Pap. $3.95.

THE WHITE SUPERINTENDENT AND THE NEGRO SCHOOLS IN NORTH CAROLINA

Dennis Cooke
176 pp. Negro Universities Press. Reprint of the 1930 edition. $9.75.

WHITE TEACHER IN A BLACK SCHOOL

Robert Kendall
Two years of teaching in Los Angeles black schools. 224 pp. Devin-Adair, 1975. $5.95.

FAMILY

BEHIND GHETTO WALLS: BLACK FAMILY LIFE IN A FEDERAL SLUM

Lee Rainwater
Aldine Publishing Co., 1970. Cloth, $12.50; Pap. $4.95.

BLACK FAMILIES AND THE STRUGGLE FOR SURVIVAL: TEACHING OUR CHILDREN TO WALK TALL

Andrew Billingsley
Presents the black family as essential to the understanding of the culture, consciousness, community and competence in the black world. Friendship Press, 1974. Pap. $1.95.

BLACK FAMILIES IN WHITE AMERICA

Andrew Billingsley

Prentice-Hall, 1968. Cloth, $5.45; Pap. $2.45.

THE BLACK FAMILY: ESSAYS AND STUDIES

Robert Staples, Editor
A collection of essays and research studies on major aspects of the black family. Readings delve into the behavior of the black family and examine cross-cultural variations, interracial patterns, socio-sexual activities, socialization, and marital practices. 524 pp. Wadsworth Publishing Co., 1970. Pap. $5.95.

THE BLACK FAMILY IN MODERN SOCIETY

John H. Scanzoni
Focuses on the "middle-class" black family in urban America. 353 pp. Allyn and Bacon, 1971. Pap. $4.95.

THE BLACK GHETTO FAMILY IN THERAPY

Clifford J. Sager
Grove Press, Inc., 1970. $6.50.

BLACK MATRIARCHY: SOCIOLOGICAL INTERPRETATIONS

John H. Bracey, Jr., Editor
A collection of 10 essays on the black family and the role of the matriarchy. 217 pp. Wadsworth Publishing Co., 1974. Pap. $4.50.

THE CASE OF THE BLACK FAMILY: A SOCIOLOGICAL INQUIRY

Jerold Heiss
The structure of the black family and its place within the U. S. Columbia University Press, 1975. $12.50.

FAMILY EXPERIENCES IN OPERATION EXODUS: THE BUSING OF NEGRO CHILDREN

James Teele
Behavioral Pubns., 1967. Pap. $3.25.

THE FAMILY LIFE OF BLACK PEOPLE

Charles V. Willie
Charles E. Merrill Publishing Co., 1970. Pap. $5.95.

THE FREE NEGRO FAMILY: A STUDY OF FAMILY ORIGINS BEFORE THE CIVIL WAR

E. Franklin Frazier
A study of family origins of antebellum free Negroes by the President of the American Sociological Association. Arno Press. Reprint of the 1932 edition. $2.50.

MARRIAGE AND FAMILY AMONG NEGROES
Jessie Bernard
Prentice-Hall, 1965. pap. $1.95.

THE NEGRO AMERICAN FAMILY: A REPORT OF A SOCIAL STUDY MADE PRINCIPALLY BY THE COLLEGE CLASSES OF 1909 AND 1910 OF ATLANTA UNIVERSITY, UNDER THE PATRONAGE OF THE TRUSTEES OF THE JOHN F. SLATER FUND; TOGETHER WITH THE PROCEEDINGS OF THE 13TH ANNUAL CONFERENCE FOR THE STUDY OF NEGRO PROBLEMS, HELD AT ATLANTA UNIVERSITY ON TUESDAY, MAY THE 26TH, 1908
William Edward Burghardt DuBois, Editor
156 pp. Greenwood Press. Reprint of the 1908 edition. Illus. Kraus Reprint Co., Pap. $3.00; M. I. T. Press, Pap. $3.45; Cloth, $9.75.

THE NEGRO FAMILY IN THE UNITED STATES
E. Franklin Frazier
University of Chicago Press, 1966. Cloth, $7.50; Pap. $2.95.

THE STRENGTHS OF BLACK FAMILIES
Robert B. Hill
Upsets negative stereotypes about black families. 76 pp. Emerson Hall Publishers, 1972. A National Urban League Research Study. $1.95.

A STUDY OF BLACK ADOPTION FAMILIES: A COMPARISON OF A TRADITIONAL AND A QUASI-ADOPTION PROGRAM
Elizabeth A. Lawder, et al
Doubling the number of inracial placements. 77 pp. Child Welfare League of America, 1971. Pap. $3.95.

FILM AND THEATRE

ANTHOLOGY OF THE AMERICAN NEGRO IN THE THEATRE
Pattersno
United Publishing Corp., 1970. $13.88.

BLACK DRAMA IN AMERICA: AN ANTHOLOGY
Darwin T. Turner, Editor

A collection of plays by America's leading black playwrights: Hughes, Davis, Jones, Ward, and Richardson, among others. Fawcett World Library. $1.95.

*BLACK DRAMA: THE STORY OF THE AMERICAN NEGRO IN THE THEATRE
Liften Mitchell
Hawthorn Books, 1970. Cloth, $7.95; Pap. $2.45. Below college level.

*BLACK FILMS AND FILM-MAKERS
Lindsay Patterson, Editor
A collection of 30 articles by James Baldwin, Melvin Van Peebles, Lena Horne, Pauline Kael, Bosley Crowther, and the author himself. 400 pp. Dodd, Mead & Co., 1974. Illus. Age 16 up. $12.50.

BLACK LIST: THE CONCISE REFERENCE GUIDE TO PUBLICATIONS, FILMS, AND BROADCASTING MEDIA OF BLACK AMERICA, AFRICA, AND THE CARRIBEAN
Panther House, 1974. Pap. $17.00.

BLACK MAGIC: A PICTORIAL HISTORY OF THE NEGRO IN AMERICAN ENTERTAINMENT
Langston Hughes and Milton Meltzer
Prentice-Hall, 1967. $14.95.

*THE BLACK MAN ON FILM: RACIAL STEREOTYPING
Richard A. Maynard
144 pp. Hayden Book Co., 1974. Illus. Price not set. Below college level.

BLACK SCENES: COLLECTION OF SCENES FROM PLAYS WRITTEN BY BLACK PEOPLE ABOUT BLACK EXPERIENCE
Alice Childress, Editor
Doubleday and Co., 1970. Cloth, $3.95; Pap. $1.75.

*BLACK THEATER: A 20TH CENTURY COLLECTION OF ITS BEST PLAYWRIGHTS
Lindsay Patterson, Editor
12 full-length plays representing the best of the work of black playwrights. 493 pp. Dodd, Mead & Co., 1971. Age 16 up. $12.95.

BLACK THEATER, U. S. A.: FORTY-FIVE PLAYS BY BLACK AMERICANS, 1847-1972
James Hatch, Editor-Author

45 works ranging from 1847 to the present. Macmillan Publishing Co. $19.95.

*BLACK AND WHITE BABY
Bobby Short
The show business story of Bobby Short. 304 pp. Dodd, Mead & Co., 1971. Illus. Age 16 up. $7.95.

BLACKS IN AMERICAN FILMS: TODAY AND YESTERDAY
Edward Mapp
278 pp. Scarecrow Press, 1972. Illus. $8.50.

BLACKS IN AMERICAN MOVIES: A SELECTED BIBLIOGRAPHY
Anne Powers, Editor
A selective listing of books, articles and other materials on blacks in American films. 167 pp. Scarecrow Press, 1974. $6.00.

*FAMOUS BLACK ENTERTAINERS OF TODAY
Raoul Abdul
Personal portraits of Melvin Van Peebles, Aretha Franklin, Cecily Tyson, Andre Watts, among others. 192 pp. Dodd, Mead & Co., 1974 Illus. Age 11-15. $3.95.

*FAMOUS NEGRO ENTERTAINERS OF STAGE, SCREEN AND TV
Charlemae Rollins
Profiles on Sidney Poitier, Lena Horne, Duke Ellington, and Sammy Davis, Jr., among fifteen. 122 pp. Dodd, Mead & Co., 1967. Illus. Age 11-15. $3.95.

GUIDE TO FILMS ABOUT NEGROES, 16 MM
Daniel Sprecher, Editor
Serina Press, 1970. Pap. $4.95.

THE NEGRO AND THE DRAMA
Frederick W. Bond
McGrath Publishing Co. Reprint of the 1940 edition. $12.00.

THE NEGRO IN THE AMERICAN THEATER
Edith J. Issacs
McGrath Publishing Co. Reprint of the 1947 edition. $18.00.

THE NEGRO IN FILMS
Peter Noble
An extended study of the role of the Negro in American theatre and in both silent and sound films. Arno Press. Reprint of the 1949 edition. $9.00.

PLAYS OF NEGRO LIFE: A SOURCE BOOK OF NATIVE AMERICAN DRAMA
Alain Roy Locke and Montgomery Gregory, Editors
430 pp. Negro universities Press. Reprint of the 1927 edition. Illus. $16.50.

TOMS, COONS, MULATTOES, MAMMIES, AND BUCKS: AN INTERPRETIVE HISTORY OF BLACKS IN AMERICAN FILMS
Donald Bogle
How the movie roles of black performers have reflected the changing status of their race. 280 pp. Viking Press, 1973. $12.50.

VOICES OF THE BLACK THEATER
Loften Mitchell
James T. White, 1974. $12.50.

FOLKLORE

AFRO-AMRICAN FOLK LORE
Abigail M. Holmes Christensen
Told around cabin fires on the Sea Islands of South Carolina. Books for Libraries. Reprint of the 1892 edition. $7.00.

AMERICAN AESOP: NEGRO AND OTHER HUMOR
William Pickens
AMS Press, Inc. Reprint of the 1926 edition. $10.00.

AMERICAN NEGRO FOLKTALES
Richard M. Dorson, Editor
Ranges from supernatural accounts of spectres and bogies, through comical and satirical anecdotes, to the more realistic reports of racial injustice. Fawcett World Library, 1972. Pap. $1.50. Peter Smith Pubs. Cloth, $3.25.

A BIBLIOGRAPHY OF NORTH AMERICAN FOLKLORE AND FOLKSONG
Charles Haywood
A two-volume bibliography of books, articles, periodicals, music, records, etc. First volume covers American social and occupational groups. blues, Negro material; Second volume covers Indian and general material. 1301 pp. Dover Publications. $30.00.

THE BLACK CAT CLUB: NEGRO HUMOR AND FOLKLORE
James David Corrothers
AMS Press, Inc. Reprint of the 1902 edition. $10.50.

BLACK FOLKTALES
Julius Lester
Richard W. Baron Publishing Co., 1969. $4.50.

BLACK HUMOR
Charles Johnson
Johnson Publishing Co. 1970. Pap. $3.95.

*THE BOOK OF NEGRO FOLKLORE
Langston Hughes and Arna Bontemps, Editors
Representative selections from the folklore of the Negro in the United States, from its beginning to the present day. 624 pp. Dodd, Mead & Co., 1958. Age 16 up. $8.00.

*THE BOOK OF NEGRO HUMOR
Langston Hughes, Editor
Prose and verse, songs and the spoken word representing, in the editor's opinion, the best of Negro humor. 265 pp. Dodd, Mead & Co., 1966. Age 16 up. $5.00.

*COAL BLACK AND THE SEVEN DUDES
Kermit T. Mehlinger, M.D.
A christmas fable for children that features a black hero by reworking the Snow White story. Vaatage Press. 1974. $3.95.

DEEP DOWN IN THE JUNGLE: NEGRO NARRATIVE FOLKLORE FROM THE STREETS OF PHILADELPHIA
R. D. Abrahams
Aldine Publishing Co., 1970. Cloth, $10.95; Pap. $3.95.

ENCYCLOPEDIA OF BLACK FOLKLORE AND HUMOR
Henry D. Spalding, Editor
Tales, stories, legends and music of black folklore. 600 pp. Jonathan David Pub., 1972. Illus. $12.95.

FOLK BELIEFS OF THE SOUTHERN NEGRO
Newbell N. Puckett
Peter Smith Publishers. $7.50.

*HISTORY OF NEGRO HUMOR IN AMERICA
William Schechter

The history of the development of Negro humor in America. Illus. Fleet Press, 1971. $8.95.

JOHN HENRY: A FOLK-LORE STUDY
Louis W. Chappell
As a folk-lore figure, especially in the American Black Belt and border regions, John Henry belongs to the rock-tunnel gangs, the hand-drillers of the frontier. Kennikat Press. Reprint of the 1933 edition. $6.00.

JOHN HENRY: TRACKING DOWN A NEGRO LEGEND
Guy Benton Johnson
AMS Press, Inc. Reprint of the 1929 edition. $5.00.

*JOKES FROM BLACK FOLKS
James Haskins
Jokes, riddles, anecdotes. Doubleday & Co., 1972. Ages 6-14. $3.95.

MAGIC AND FOLK BELIEFS OF THE SOUTHERN NEGRO
N. N. Puckett
Some of the thousands of beliefs collected over a 20-year period, mostly in Mississippi. Animal tales, nature lore, games, funeral customs, ghosts and witches, charms and fetishes, hoodoo medicine and conjuring. 644 pp. Dover Publications, 1969. $4.50.

NEGRO FOLK SINGING GAMES AND FOLK GAMES OF THE HABITANTS
Grace C. Porter
Norwood Editions. Reprint of the 1914 edition. $6.50.

NEGRO MYTHS FROM THE GEORGIA COAST
C. C. Jones, Jr.
Singing Tree Press. Reprint of the 1888 edition. $8.50.

NEGRO TALES
Joseph Seamon Cotter
Books for Libraries, Inc. Reprint of the 1912 edition. $8.75.

NEGRO TALES FROM PINE BLUFF, ARKANSAS, AND CALVIN, MICHIGAN
Richard M. Dorson
Kraus Reprint Co. Reprint of the 1958 edition. $13.00.

TIS SO: NEGRO FOLK TALES
Sam Short

Claitors Publishing Division, 1972. Cloth, $3.50; Pap. $1.95.

THE TRUE AMERICAN
Melvin Van Peebles
A modern folk fable about two American men that become an allegory for racial relations from the 1920's to the 1960's. Illus. Doubleday, 1976. $6.95.

TWELVE MILLION BLACK VOICES: A FOLK HISTORY OF THE NEGRO IN THE UNITED STATES
Richard Wright
A photographic essay on black America during the Great Depression. Arno Press. Reprint of the 1941 edition. $10.00.

VOODOO TALES AS TOLD AMONG THE NEGROES OF THE SOUTHWEST
Mary Alicia Owen
Books for Libraries, Inc. Reprint of the 1893 edition. $12.75.

GHETTOS

BLACK AND FREE
Tom Skinner
The account of a black gang leader's search for identity in the "concrete jungles" of Harlem. Zondervan Books, 1970. Cloth, $3.95; Pap. $.95.

BLACK CHICAGO: THE MAKING OF A NEGRO GHETTO, 1890 TO 1920
Allan H. Spear
University of Chicago Press. Cloth, $8.75; Pap. $3.45.

BLACK COMMUNITY CONTROL: A STUDY OF TRANSITION IN A TEXAS GHETTO
Joyce E. Williams
292 pp. Praeger Pubs., 1973. $17.50.

THE BLACK GHETTO: PROMISED LAND OR COLONY?
Richard Meister
235 pp. D. C. Heath and Co., 1972. Pap. $2.95.

THE BLACK GHETTO: A SPATIAL BE-HAVIORAL PERSPECTIVE
Harold M. Rose
McGraw-Hill Book Co., 1971. Cloth, $5.50; Pap. $3.50.

BLACK GHETTOS, WHITE GHETTOS AND SLUMS
Robert E. Forman
The causes and problems of black ghettos and the history of other ghettos. Prentice-Hall, Inc., 1971.

BLACK NEIGHBORHODDS: AN ASSESS-MENT OF COMMUNITY POWER
Donald I. Warren
Based on a study of nearly 2,000 respondents in Detroit, this analysis shows how and why the power structure of the black ghetto is unique in terms of the functioning of local neighborhoods, community groups, and status processes. 240 pp. University of Michigan Press, 1975. $9.00.

THE BLACK NORTH IN 1901: A SOCIAL STUDY
W. E. B. DuBois
An in-depth look at the black ghettos of Boston, Philadelphia, and New York at the turn of the Century. Arno Press. Reprint of the 1901 edition. $4.00.

BEYOND THE BURNING: LIFE AND DEATH OF THE GHETTO
Sterling Tucker
Association Press, 1968. Pap. $2.50.

COMING UP BLACK: PATTERNS OF GHETTO SOCIALIZATION
David A. Schultz
The author gives particular attention to ten families, five complete and five broken, all of whom lived in a housing project. Prentice-Hall, Inc., 1969. Pap. $2.45.

*DARK GHETTO: DILEMMAS OF SO-CIAL POWER
Kenneth B. Clark
Harper and Row Pubs., 1965. Cloth, $7.95; Pap. $1.75. Below college level.

THE ENDURING GHETTO
David R. Goldfield, and James B. Lane, Editors
Compares and contrasts white ethnic ghettos with their black counterparts, and examines the pathology of past and present ghettos and their disparate moods. 264 pp. J. B. Lippincott Co., 1973. Pap. $3.95.

GEOGRAPHY OF THE GHETTO: PER-CEPTIONS, PROBLEMS, AND ALTER-NATIVES

Harold Rose and Harold McConnell
Northern Illinois University Press, 1972.
$15.00.

GHETTO FEVER
Thomas V. Millea
Bruce Books, 1968. $3.95.

GHETTO REVOLTS: THE POLITICS OF VIOLENCE IN AMERICAN CITIES
Joe Feagin and Harlan Hahn
Macmillan Publishing Co., Inc., 1973. Cloth,
$8.95; Pap. $3.95.

GHETTO SOCIAL STRUCTURE: A SURVEY OF BLACK BOSTONIANS
Joe R. Feagin
R & E Research Associates, 1975. Pap. $9.00.

HARLEM: THE MAKING OF A GHETTO, 1890 TO 1830
Gilbert Osofsky
Harper and Row Pubs., 1966. Cloth, $8.95;
Pap. $2.95.

HARLEM NEGRO METROPOLIS
Claude McKay
An account of the world's largest black community during the 1920s and 1930s. 262 pp.
Harcourt Brace Jovanovich, Inc. Pap. $2.95.

HARLEM ON MY MIND, 1900 TO 1968
Allen Schoener, Editor
Random house, Inc., 1969. $12.95.

HARLEM, U. S. A.
John H. Clarke
Macmillan Publishing Co., Inc., 1971. Pap.
$2.45.

HUNTER'S POINT: A BLACK GHETTO IN AMERICA
Arthur E. Hippler
Basic Books, 1974. $11.95.

LIFE STYLES IN THE BLACK GHETTO
William McCord, et al
W. W. Norton and Co., 1969. Cloth, $6.95;
Pap. $2.95.

THE NEGRO GHETTO
Robert Weaver
Russell and Russell. Reprint of the 1948 edition.
$16.00.

*A PECK OF SALT: A YEAR IN THE GHETTO

John Hough, Jr.
Little, Brown, and Co., 1970. Pap. $5.95.
Below college level.

THE POLITICAL ECONOMY OF THE BLACK GHETTO
William K. Tabb
W. W. Norton and Co., 1971. Cloth, $5.95;
Pap. $2.45.

THE RISE OF THE GHETTO
John H. Bracey, Jr., Editor
27 readings and writings on the history and conditions of the black ghetto. 222 pp. Wadsworth Publishing Co., 1974. Pap. $4.50.

SOULSIDE: INQUIRIES IN GHETTO CULTURE AND COMMUNITY
Ulf Hannerz
Columbia University Press, 1969. Cloth,
$10.00; Pap. $2.95.

SPOUT SPRING: BLACK COMMUNITY IN THE OZARKS
P. H. Kunkel and S. S. Kennard
Holt, Rinehart, and Winston, 1971. Pap. $2.75.

HIGHER EDUCATION

AMERICAN CASTE AND NEGRO COLLEGE
Buell G. Gallagher
478 pp. Gordian Press. Reprint of the 1938 edition. $10.00.

A BACKGROUND STUDY OF NEGRO COLLEGE STUDENTS
Ambrose Caliver
132 pp. Negro Universities Press. Reprint of the 1933 edition. Illus. $8.75.

BETWEEN THE TWO WORLDS: A PROFILE OF NEGRO HIGHER EDUCATION
Bowles and Decosta, Editors
Problems confronting over 100 Negro colleges.
340 pp. McGraw-Hill Book Co., 1971. $7.95.

BLACK EDUCATORS IN WHTIE COLLEGES: PROGRESS AND PROSPECT
William Moore, Jr. and Lonnie Wagstaff
Jossey-Bass, Inc., 1974. $9.50.

BLACK ELITE: DISCRIMINATION AND EDUCATION

Richard Freeman
The author proposes that the decade of the 1960's may well have marked the beginning of the end of labor market discrimination against black college graduates, and, possibly, all black workers. 300 pp. McGraw-Hill book Co., 1975. $12.50.

BLACK STUDENTS AT WHITE COLLEGES
Charles Willie and Arline McCord
136 pp. Praeger Pubs., 1972. $10.00.

BLACKER THAN THOU: THE STRUGGLE FOR CAMPUS UNITY
George Napper
Depicts the tension of the black student, who is caught between the two poles of white middle-class values and emerging black identity. William B. Eerdmans Publishing Co., 1973. Cloth, $4.95; Pap. $2.45.

BLACK STUDENTS IN PREDOMINANTLY WHITE NORTH CAROLINA COLLEGES AND UNIVERSITIES: RESEARCH REPORT NO. 2
Junius Davis and Anne Borders-Patterson
28 pp. College Entrance Examination Board, 1973. Pap. $1.50.

BLACKS IN WHITE COLLEGES: OKLAHOMA'S LANDMARK CASES
George Lynn Cross
A college President's story of the events leading to the desegregation of the University of Oklahoma in 1948. 130 pp. University of Oklahoma Press, 1974. Illus. Cloth, $7.95; Pap. $3.95.

THE CAMPUS AND THE RACIAL CRISIS
David C. Nichols and Olive Mills, Editors
44 papers on admissions criteria, black studies, and supplementary education to compensate for inadequate preparation. 309 pp. American Council on Education, 1970. $8.75.

THE COLLEGE-BRED NEGRO AMERICAN
W. E. B. DuBois
Kraus Reprint Co. Reprint of the 1910 edition. Pap. $2.00.

COLLEGE LEVEL EXAMINATION SERIES AFRO-AMERICAN HISTORY
Jack Rudman
National Learning. Cloth, $11.50; Pap. $7.50.

THE EVOLUTION OF THE NEGRO COLLEGE

Dwight Oliver Wendell Holmes
A study of black education and the status of Negro colleges and their graduates. Arno Press. Reprint of the 1934 edition. $7.50. AMS Press, $5.50.

FROM SERVITUDE TO SERVICE
American Unitarian Association
An early twentieth century symposium on the aspirations of American Negroes to higher education. Arno Press. Reprint of the 1905 edition. $8.50. Negro Universities Press, $10.00.

GENERAL EDUCATION IN THE NEGRO COLLEGE
Irving Derbigny
255 pp. Negro Universities Press. Reprint of the 1947 edition. $11.50.

THE NEGRO COLLEGE GRADUATE
Charles Spurgion Johnson
399 pp. Negro Universities Press. Reprint of the 1938 edition. Illus. $16.50. McGrath Publishing Co., $18.00.

THE NEW NEGRO IN CAMPUS: BLACK COLLEGE REBELLIONS OF THE 1920'S
Raymond Wolters
Princeton University Press, 1974. $15.00.

A PERSONNEL STUDY OF NEGRO COLLEGE STUDENTS: A STUDY OF THE RELATIONS BETWEEN CERTAIN BACKGROUND FACTORS OF NEGRO COLLEGE STUDENTS AND THEIR SUBSEQUENT CAREERS IN COLLEGE
Ambrose Caliver
146 pp. Negro Universities Press; AMS Press, Inc. Reprint of the 1931 edition. Illus. $8.75.

PRIVATE BLACK COLLEGES AT THE CROSSROADS
Daniel C. Thompson
308 pp. Greenwood Press, Inc., 1973. $12.50.

QUARTERLY REVIEW OF HIGHER EDUCATION AMONG NEGROES VOL. 1 TO 28
Negro Universities Press. Reprint of the 1933 to 1960 edition. $395.00.

THE READING INTERESTS AND NEED OF NEGRO COLEGE FRESHMEN REGARDING SOCIAL SCIENCE MATERIALS
Walter Green Daniel
AMS Press, Inc. Reprint of the 1942 edition. $10.00.

SURVEY OF NEGRO COLLEGES AND UNIVERSITIES
United States Office of Education
964 pp. Negro Universities Press. Reprint of the 1929 edition. $40.00.

THIRD PRESS GUIDE TO BLACK COLLEGES AND UNIVERSITIES
George M. Daniels
A look at each institution's history, scholarship and tuition assistance programs available, as well as total enrollment. 120 pp. Third Press, 1974. Cloth, $8.95; Pap. $3.95.

HISTORY

*ABC'S OF BLACK HISTORY
Deloris H. Holt
Ritchie, Ward Press, 1971. $4.50. Ages 6 to 12.

THE AFRICAN ABROAD: OR, HIS EVOLUTION WESTERN CIVILIZATION
William H. Ferris
1004 pp. Two vols. Johnson Reprint Corporation. Reprint of the 1913 edition. $42.00 set.

THE AFRO-AMERICAN EXPERIENCE: A CULTURAL HISTORY THROUGH EMANCIPATION
James H. Dormon and Robert R. Jones
Synthesizes the new scholarship in the field of Afro-American history and culture from African beginnings through emancipation and to the present synthesis. 274 pp. John Wiley & Sons, 1974. Cloth, $8.95; Pap. $4.50.

AFRO-AMERICAN HISTORY
Charles W. Simmons and Harry W. Morris.
Charles E. Merrill Publishing Co., 1972. Pap. $5.95.

AFRO-AMERICAN HISTORY: THE MODERN ERA
Herbert Aptheker
Citadel Press, 1971. Cloth, $7.95; Pap. $2.95.

AFRO-AMERICAN HISTORY: *Primary Sources*
Thomas R. Frazier
An introduction to the history of Afro-Americans through the use of historical documents that originated in the black community. 514 pp. Harcourt Brace Jovanovich, Inc., 1971. Pap. $5.50.

AFRO-AMERICAN HISTORY PROGRAM, INCLUDING:
A People Uprooted [1500-1800]
Chains of Slavery [1800-1865]
Separate and Unequal [1865-1910]
Quest for Equality [1910 to Present]
160 pp. ea. Encyclopedia Brittanica Educational Corporation, 1972. $1.45 each. Set of ten, $13.25.

AFRO-AMERICAN HISTORY: SEPARATE OR INTER-RACIAL?
Meyer Weinberg
An address made to a black sorority which suggests a new approach to U. S. history, black and white. 20 pp. Integrateducation Associates. Pap. $.50.

AFRO-AMERICAN HISTORY SERIES, 10 VOLS.
Mazwell Whiteman, Editor
Scholarly Resources, Inc. $160.00 set.

AFTER SLAVERY: THE NEGRO IN SOUTH CAROLINA DURING RECONSTUUCTION, 1861 TO 1877
Joel Williamson
442 pp. University of North Carolina Press, 1969. Cloth, $8.50; Pap. $3.45.

AMERICA'S BLACK PAST: *A Reader in Afro-American History*
Eric Foner, Editor
Readings trace the development of the black community in America, its institutions and its leadership, and highlight contributions made by black people throughout American history. 684 pp. Harper & Row Publishers, 1971. Cloth, $12.50; Pap. $6.95.

AN AMERICAN DILEMMA: THE NEGRO PROBLEM & MODERN DEMOCRACY
Gunnar Myrdal
An analysis of the facts as they were at the end of the 1930s and the beginning of the 1940s. Two volumes. Each; Pap. $5.95.

THE AMERICAN NEGRO ACADEMY, OCCASIONAL PAPERS: NUMBERS 1-22
American Negro Academy
Scholarly papers on various aspects of American Negro life: sociology, history, and education. Arno Press. Reprint of the 1897-1924 edition. $21.50.

*THE AMERICAN NEGRO: OLD WORLD BACKGROUND AND NEW WORLD EX-

PERIENCE
Rayford W. Logan and Irving S. Cohen
The history of America's black minority from
the achievements of civilization in Africa to
developments during the Nixon years.
Houghton-Mifflin, 1970. Cloth, $4.35; Pap.
$2.97, Ages 12-18.

**BEFORE THE MAYFLOWER: A HISTORY
OF BLACK AMERICA**
Lerone Bennett, Jr.
Johnson Publishing Co. 1969. $6.95.

**BEFORE THE MAYFLOWER: A HISTORY
OF THE NEGRO IN AMERICA 1619-1964**
Lerone Bennett, Jr.
A history of the American Negro, from his
origins in Africa through the Negro revolt of the
1960s. Penguin Books, 1962. $2.45.

**THE BETRAYAL OF THE NEGRO: FROM
RUTHERFORD B. HAYES TO WOODROW
WILSON**
R. W. Logan
Macmillan Publishing Co., Inc., 1965. Pap.
$1.50.

**THE BLACK ALMANAC FROM INVOLUN-
TARY SERVITUDE TO THE AGE OF DIS-
ILLUSIONMENT [1619-1973]**
Alton Hornsby, Jr.
All of the important biographical details, in-
stitutions, significant events, laws, court
decisions, programs and manifestos affecting
the black-American. 212 pp. Barron's
Educational Series, 1974. Cloth, $7.25; Pap.
$2.95.

**THE BLACK AMERICAN: A BRIEF DOCU-
MENTARY HISTORY**
Leslie H. Fishel and Benjamin Quarles
Covers the ghetto crisis, the rural crisis, the
race-oriented national crisis, and the
development of black power. sources include
official documents, personal accounts,
newspaper articles, travel tales, memoirs and
speeches. 418 pp. Scott Foresman & Co., 1970.
Illus. Pap. $4.35.

**THE BLACK AMERICAN: A PERSPEC-
TIVE LOOK**
M. H. Manoni
Afro-American history dwelling on the question
of "Why?" more than on "What?" and
"When?" 177 pp. Michie Company, 1970.
Illus. Pap. $2.95.

**BLACK AMERICANS: A STUDY GUIDE
AND SOURCE BOOK**
Lynn P. Dunn
R & E Research Associates, 1975. Pap. $6.00.

**BLACK CAROLINIANS: A HISTORY OF
BLACKS IN SOUTH CAROLINA FROM
1895 TO 1968**
I. A. Newby
University of South Carolina Press, 1973.
$14.95.

*BLACK CHRONICLE
Blackslide, Inc.
Holt, Rinehart, and Winston, 1972. $110.00 per
kit. Below college level.
THE BLACK CODES OF THE SOUTH
T. B. Wilson
192 pp. University of Alabama Press, 1966.
$7.50.

**BLACK DIALOGUES: TOPICS IN AFRO-
AMERICAN HISTORY**
This text studies speeches, diaries, editorials,
court decisions, short stories, poems, songs,
magazine articles, and books. 512 pp. Encyclopedia Britannica Educational Corporation. Illus. $6.95.

THE BLACK EXPERIENCE IN AMERICA
Norman Coombs
Begins with the history of Africa at the
beginning of European civilization and continues to the present. Twayne Pulishers, 1972.
$7.95.

**THE BLACK EXPERIENCE: AMERICAN
BLACKS, 1865 TO 1972**
Mary Ellison
Barnes and Noble, 1974. $14.50.

THE BLACK FRONTIERSMEN: *Adventures of Negroes among American Indians, 1528
to 1918*
J. Norman Heard
John Day Publishing Co., 1969. Illus. $3.95.

**BLACK HEROES IN OUR NATION'S
HISTORY**
Philip Drotning
Henry Regnery Co., 1969. Cloth, $6.95.
Washington Square Press, Pap. $.95.

*BLACK HISTORY BOOKLETS
Ida Meltzer
A series of 32 page illustrated booklets which
provides reading and language activities for

students grades 4-12. Features stories about the lives of famous black men and women and events in black history. Titles included are: *Blacks in Early American History, Montgomery Bus Story, A School at Midnight, Events in Gebruary, Robert Smalls, Great Seaman, Phillis Wheatley, Young Poet, Frederick Douglass, Great Abolitionist, Harriet Tubman, Moses of Her People.* Book-Lab Inc., 1972. Set of 30; each, $16.50.

BLACK HISTORY: LOST, STOLEN OR STRAYED
Otto Lindenmeyer
The social contribution of the American Negro. Avon Books. Illus. Pap. $1.25.

*BLACK HISTORY: PAST AND PRESENT
James Egert Allen
A collection of vignettes revealing the black man's role in the great events of history. Exposition Press, 1971. $7.50.

BLACK HISTORY: A REAPPRAISAL
Melvin Drimmer, Editor
A history of Negro participation in American events from Colonial times to the present. Doubleday & Co., 1969. Illus. Cloth, $7.95; Pap. $3.95.

BLACK HISTORY VIEWPOINTS
African Bibliographic Center
Negro Universities Press, 1969. Pap. $5.00.

BLACK HISTORY VIEWPOINTS: A SELECTED BIBLIOGRAPHICAL GUIDE TO RESOURCES FOR AFRO-AMERICAN AND AFRICAN HISTORY
389 pp. Greenwood Press, 1970. Pap. $12.50.

BLACK LEADERSHIP IN AMERICAN HISTORY
T. T. Lyons
Addison-Wesley Publishing Co., 1971. Pap. $2.60.

*THE BLACK MAN IN AMERICA, 1619-1970
Florence and J. B. Jackson
The story of black Americans from their arrival at Jamestown to the formation of the United States government. 83 pp. Franklin Watts, Inc., 1971. Ages 10-15. $3.90.

*THE BLACK MAN IN AMERICA, 1791-1861
Florence Jackson

The "Cotton Kingdom," expansion of slavery, the abolitionist movement, the Underground Railroad, and more. 89 pp. Franklin Watts, Inc., 1971. Illus. Ages 10-15. $3.90.

*THE BLACK MAN IN AMERICA, 1861-1877
Florence Jackson
The Civil War, Reconstruction, black servicemen and black codes, and more. 96 pp. Franklin Watts, Inc., 1972. Illus. Ages 10-15. $3.90.

*THE BLACK MAN IN AMERICA, 1877-1905
Florence Jackson
Du Bois and Booker T. Washington led the black race from Reconstruction to the Niagara Movement. 90 pp. Franklin Watts, Inc., 1973. Illus. Ages 10-15. $3.90.

*THE BLACK MAN IN AMERICA, 1905-1932
Florence Jackson
The development of the NAACP and its effect on black Americans. 96 pp. Franklin Watts, Inc., 1974. Illus. Ages 10-15. $3.90.

*THE BLACK MAN IN AMERICA
Florence Jackson
The history of blacks in the United States from Roosevelt's New Deal to the Supreme Court's ruling on *Brown vs. Board of Education of Topeka.* 96 pp. Franklin Watts, Inc., 1975. Illus. Ages 10-15. $3.90.

BLACK MAN OF THE SOUTH, AND THE REBELS
Charles Stearns
562 pp. Negro Universities Press. Reprint of the 1872 edition. Illus. $17.50.

THE BLACK PEOPLE OF AMERICA: ILLUSTRATED HISTORY
R. Ethel Dennis
Reviews African history from the rise of the earliest black civilizations to the outbreak of the slave trade in the fifteenth century. It then explores the roles played by black people in the social, economic, and political development of the United States. 400 pp. McGraw-Hill Book Co., 1970. Illus. Cloth, $10.28; Pap. $7.80.

THE BLACK PIONEER IN MICHIGAN: FLINT AND GENESEE COUNTY
Melvin E. Banner
A hostile Indian environment provided a haven

for the fugitive Negro. 88 pp. Pendell Publishing Co., 1973. Pap. $3.95.

BLACK RECONSTRUCTION IN AMERICA, 1860 TO 1880
William Edward Burghardt Du Bois
Russell and Russell. Reprint of the 1935 edition. Cloth, $16.50. Atheneum Publications, Pap. $4.95.

BLACK RECONSTRUCTIONISTS
Emma Lou Thornbrough, Editor
Prentice-Hall, 1972. $5.95.

THE BLACK SIDE
Edward R. Carter
A partial history of the business, religious and educational side of the Negro in Atlanta, Georgia. Books for Libraries, 1894. $27.75.

BLACK TEXANS: A HISTORY OF NEGROES IN TEXAS, 1528-1971
Alwyn Barr
A discussion of the political, economic, educational, and social developments of the black people of Texas, who number over a million and constitute the largest black community of any state except New York. 259 pp. Jenkins Publishing Co., 1973. Illus. $8.50.

*BLACKS IN AMERICA, 1492 TO 1970, A CHRONOLOGY AND FACT BOOK
Irving Sloan
Oceana Pubns., 1971. $5.00. Below college level.

BOOKER T. WASHINGTON AND HIS CRITICS: THE PROBLEM OF NEGRO LEADERSHIP
Hugh Hawkins, Editor
113 pp. D. C. Heath and co., 1962. Pap. $2.50.

BOOKER T. WASHINGTON AND THE NEGRO'S PLACE IN AMERICAN LIFE
Samuel R. Spencer, Jr.
212 pp. Little, Brown, and Co., 1965. Cloth, $5.00; Pap. $2.95.

BROWN AMERICANS
Edwin R. Embree
The history of the Afro-American: his origin, development, culture, and struggle for liberty and self-respect. 248 pp. August M. Kelley Publishers. Reprint of the 1945 edition. Illus. $11.50.

CALIFORNIA'S BLACK PIONEERS: A

BRIEF HISTORICAL SURVEY
Kenneth G. Goode
McNally and Lofton, Pubns. Cloth, $6.95; Pap. $3.50.

CHRONOLOGICAL HISTORY OF THE NEGRO IN AMERICA
Peter and Mort Bergman
Harper and Row Pubs., 1969. Cloth, $13.50. New American Library, Pap. $1.50.

THE CONQUEST: THE STORY OF A NEGRO PIONEER
Oscar Micheaux
Books for Libraries, Inc. Reprint of the 1913 edition. $11.75.

COOPERATIVES AND RURAL POVERTY IN THE SOUTH
Ray Marshall and Lamond Godwin
Johns Hopkins Press, 1971. Cloth, $6.00; Pap. $1.95.

A DOCUMENTARY HISTORY OF THE NEGRO PEOPLE IN THE UNITED STATES: FROM COLONIAL TIMES THROUGH THE CIVIL WAR, VOL. 1
Herbert Aptheker
Citadel Press, 1962. Pap. $4.95.

A DOCUMENTARY HISTORY OF THE NEGRO PEOPLE IN THE UNITED STATES: FROM THE RECONSTRUCTION YEARS TO THE FOUNDING OF THE NAACP, 1910, VOL. 2
Herbert Aptheker
Citadel Press, 1964. Pap. $4.95.

A DOCUMENTARY HISTORY OF THE NEGRO PEOPLE IN THE UNITED STATES, 1910-1932
Herbert Aptheker
Lyle Stuart, Inc. $17.50.

A DOCUMENTARY HISTORY OF THE NEGRO PEOPLE IN THE UNITED STATES, VOL. 3: 1932 TO 1945
Herbert Aptheker
Citadel Press, 1974. $17.50.

AN ENCYCLOPEDIA OF THE NEGRO IN AFRICA AND AMERICA, 18 VOLS.
Scholarly Press. $540.00 per set.

ESSAYS IN THE HISTORY OF THE AMERICAN NEGRO
Herbert Aptheker

Covers Negro slave revolts, the struggle for emancipation during the War of Independence, and Negroes in the Abolitionist movement and the Civil War. 216 pp. International Publishers, 1964. Pap. $2.25.

EVIDENCES OF PROGRESS AMONG COLORED PEOPLE
G. F. Richings

An illustrated record of achievement in education, religion, business and the professions by Afro-Americans from 1865 to 1900. 544 pp. Metro Books, Inc. Reprint of the 1900 edition. $18.00.

THE EVOLUTION OF THE NEGRO, TWO VOLS. IN ONE
Norman Eustace Cameron

Negro Universities Press. Reprint of the 1934 edition. 1975. $22.50.

*EXPLORING BLACK AMERICA: *A History and Guide*
Marcella Thum

Guide to the museums, monuments and historic sites that commemorate the achievements of Black-Americans, plus discussions about slavery, the underground railroad, abolitionists, pioneers and cowboys, military heroes, artists and craftsmen, authors and historians, musicians, scholars, and scientists. Atheneum Publishers, 1975. $10.95. Ages 10 up.

*EYEWITNESS: THE NEGRO IN AMERICAN HISTORY
William Loren Katz

The contributions of blacks in every period of U. S. history, from the early explorers of the New World to today's black leaders. 603 pp. Pitman Publishing Corp., 1974. Illus. Cloth, $9.28; Pap. $7.00. Age 15 up.

*THE FIRST BOOK OF AMERICAN NEGROES
Margaret B. Young

The Negro's contributions to literature, music, art, the theatre, and sports. 86 pp. Franklin Watts, Inc., 1966. Illus. Cloth, $3.90; Pap. $1.25. Ages 9-12.

THE FREE NEGRO IN VIRGINIA 1619-1865
John H. Russell

A study of Negroes who were free men prior to the Emancipation Proclamation; The Free Negro's legal and social status in Virginia; blacks who owned white servants; Negroes who bought other blacks; free men who married

slave women; 194 pp. Dover Publications. Pap. $2.00.

IN FREEDOM'S BIRTHPLACE: A STUDY OF BOSTON NEGROES
John Daniels

Details the part Negroes played in Boston's growth and development from the early days of colonial slave trade through the first part of the 20th century. Arno Press. Reprint of the 1914 edition. $12.50.

FROM AFRICA TO THE UNITED STATES AND THEN . . . A CONCISE AFRO-AMERICAN HISTORY
Kenneth G. Goode

Traces the path of the black-American from earliest African civilization to the present time. 177 pp. Scott, Foresman & Co., 1969. Pap. $2.95.

FROM DARKNESS TO LIGHT: THE STORY OF NEGRO PROGRESS
Mary Helms

218 pp. Negro Universities Press. Reprint of the 1909 edition. Illus. $11.50.

FROM SLAVERY TO FREEDOM: A HISTORY OF AMERICAN NEGROES
John Franklin

Alfred A. Knopf, Inc., 1967. Cloth, $13.95. Random House, Inc., Pap. $3.95.

THE GEORGIA NEGRO, A HISTORY
Asa H. Gordon

448 pp. Reprint Co. Reprint of the 1937 edition. Illus. $15.00.

GEORGIA NIGGER
John L. Spivak

241 pp. Patterson Smith Publishing Corp. Reprint of the 1932 edition. Illus. $10.00.

GREAT DOCUMENTS IN BLACK AMERICAN HISTORY
George Ducas and Charles Van Doren, Editor

354 pp. Praeger Pubs., 1970. Illus. Cloth, $12.50; Pap. $4.95.

A GUIDE TO NEGRO HISTORY IN AMERICA
Phillip Drotning

Doubleday and Co., 1968. $5.95.

A HALF CENTURY OF FREEDOM OF THE NEGRO IN OHIO

William A. Joiner, Compiler and Arranger
Book for Libraries. Reprint of the 1915 edition.
$18.25.

HISTORICAL RESEARCH RESPECTING THE OPINION OF FOUNDERS OF THE REPUBLIC ON NEGROES AS SLAVES, CITIZENS, AND AS SOLDIERS

George Livermore
184 pp. Burt Franklin Pubs. Reprint of the 1863
edition. $12.50.

HISTORICAL ROMANCE OF THE AMERICAN NEGRO

Charles Henry Fowler
269 pp. Johnson Reprint. Reprint of the 1902
edition. $21.00.

HISTORY OF THE COLORED RACE IN AMERICA, CONTAINING ALSO THEIR ANCIENT AND MODERN LIFE IN AFRICA, THE ORIGIN AND DEVELOPMENT OF SLAVERY, THE CIVIL WAR, 2ND EDITION

William T. Alexander
600 pp. Negro Universities Press. Reprint of the
1887 edition. Illus. $22.50.

HISTORY OF THE NEGRO RACE IN AMERICA FROM 1619 TO 1880

George W. Williams
A massive reference of primary sources by a
significant Negro historian. Arno Press. Reprint
of the 1833 edition. $34.50.

A HISTORY OF THE NEGROES OF MISSISSIPPI FROM 1865 TO 1890

Jesse Thomas Wallace
190 pp. Johnson Reprint. Reprint of the 1927
edition. $7.75.

ILLUSTRATED HISTORY OF BLACK AMERICANS

John Franklin
Time-Life Books, 1970. $7.95.

*IMPORTANT DATES IN AFRO-AMERICAN HISTORY

Lee Bennett Hopkins
Birthdays, special events, and holidays relating
to Afro-Americans. 188 pp. Franklin Watts,
Inc., 1969. Illus. Ages 8-12. $4.90.

IN FREEDOM'S BIRTHPLACE: A STUDY OF THE BOSTON NEGROES

John Daniels

496 pp. Johnson Reprint. Reprint of the 1914
edition. $17.50.

INTERNATIONAL LIBRARY OF NEGRO LIFE AND HISTORY, 10 VOLS.

Association for the Study of Negro Life
and History
United Publishing Corp., 1970. $138.00.

JIM CROW

Jesse Walters Dees, and James S. Hadley
529 pp. Negro Universities Press. Reprint of the
1951 edition. Illus. $22.50.

*A JUNIOR HISTORY OF THE AMERICAN NEGRO

Morris C. Goodman
A factual chronicle of the contributions black
people have made to the history and culture of
America. Vol. I: Discovery to the Civil War;
Vol. II: The Civil War to the Civil Rights War.
Illus. Fleet Press, 1970. $5.00 per volume.
Teacher's manual, $.50.

JUSTICE DENIED: *The Black Man in White America*

William M. Chace and Peter Collier
A collection of 53 essays and primary sources
surveying Afro-American history from the start
of the slave trade to the present. 548 pp.
Harcourt Brace Jovanovich, Inc., 1970. Pap.
$4.95.

KEY ISSUES IN THE AFRO-AMERICAN EXPERIENCE

Nathan I. Huggins, Martin Kilson, Daniel
M. Fox
A two-volume work in which specialists in Afro-
American History present their views on the
crucial issues of the black-American experience.
Vol. I: To 1877; Vol. II: Since 1865. Harcourt
Brace Jovanovich, Inc., 1971. Each volume,
Pap. $4.50; Combined one-volume hardbound,
$10.50.

LONESOME ROAD: THE STORY OF THE NEGRO IN AMERICA

Saunders Redding
Doubleday and Co., 1958. $6.95.

THE MALIGNANT HERITAGE: YANKEE PROGRESSIVES AND THE NEGRO QUESTION 1901-1914

David W. Southern
Discusses recial tension in relation to the politics
of the Progressive era. 116 pp. Loyola
University Press, 1968. $3.50.

*MARCH TOWARD FREEDOM: A HISTORY OF BLACK AMERICANS
James Banks
Fearon Pubs., 1970. $5.20. Ages 16 and up.

MONARCH COLLEGE OUTLINE ON BLACK HISTORY
Norman Hodges
Monarch Press. Pap. $2.95.

THE MYTH OF THE NEGRO PAST
Melville J. Herskovitz
Peter Smith Publishers. $5.00.

NATIONAL CYCLOPEDIA OF THE COLORED RACE
Clement Richardson
Gordon Press. $30.00.

NEGRO AMERICANS THE EARLY YEARS
Pendulum Press, 1974. $.60.

NEGRO BUILDERS AND HEROES
Benjamin Brawley
The history of the Negro in the United States from the Revolution until the late 1930s. 330 pp. University of North Carolina Press, 1937. $5.50.

NEGRO CIVILIZATION IN THE SOUTH
Charles Edwin Roberts
Books for Libraries, Inc. Reprint of the 1880 edition. $12.00.

THE NEGRO FREEDMAN: LIFE CONDITIONS OF THE AMERICAN NEGRO IN THE EARLY YEARS AFTER EMANCIPATION
Donald H. Henderson
Cooper Square Publishers, 1952. $9.00.

THE NEGRO FROM AFRICA TO AMERICA
Willis Duke Weatherford
487 pp. Greenwood Press. Reprint of the 1924 edition. $15.00.

THE NEGRO IMMIGRANT: HIS BACKGROUND, CHARACTERISTICS AND SOCIAL ADJUSTMENT, 1899-1937
Ira De A. Reid
A study of the 100,000 foreign-born Negroes in the United States. Arno Press. Reprint of the 1939 edition. $7.50.

THE NEGRO IMPACT ON WESTERN CIVILIZATION
Joseph Roucek, Editor

International Pubns. Service, 1970. $15.00.

*THE NEGRO IN AMERICA
Earl Spangler
The experiences of American blacks from 1619 through the integration, civil rights, and black power struggles of recent years. 112 pp. Lerner Publications, 1971. Illus. Ages 11-17. $3.95.

THE NEGRO IN AMERICAN HISTORY
Louis R. Harlan
American Historical Association, 1974. Pap. $1.00.

*THE NEGRO IN AMERICAN HISTORY, VOL. 1, WHICH WAY TO CITIZENSHIP?
Stanley Seaberg
Scholastic Book Service, 1974. Pap. $1.25. Ages 16 and up.

*THE NEGRO IN AMERICAN HISTORY, VOL. 2, WHICH WAY TO EQUALITY?
Stanley Seaberg
Scholastic Book Service, 1974. Pap. $1.25. Ages 16 and up.

THE NEGRO IN AMERICAN HISTORY: MEN AND WOMEN EMINENT IN THE EVOLUTION OF THE AMERICAN OF AFRICAN DESCENT
John W. Cromwell
284 pp. Johnson Reprint. Reprint of the 1914 edition. $12.00.

THE NEGRO IN THE AMERICAN REVOLUTION
Benjamin Quarles
252 pp. University of North Carolina Press, 1961. Cloth, $7.50; Pap. $1.95.

THE NEGRO IN CALIFORNIA BEFORE 1890
Odell A. Thurman
Historical coverage of early California. Thesis. R & E Research Associates. Reprint of the 1945 edition. Pap. $7.00.

THE NEGRO IN THE DISTRICT OF COLUMBIA
Edward Norman Ingle
110 pp. Johnson Reprint. Reprint of the 1893 edition. Pap. $8.50. Books for Libraries, Inc., $10.00.

THE NEGRO IN LOUISIANA
Charles Barthelemy Rousseve
212 pp. Johnson Reprint. Reprint of the 1937 edition. Illus. $9.75.

*THE NEGRO IN MARYLAND
Vera F. Rollo
The story of the Negro in Maryland from the 17th century to the present day. 75 pp. Maryland Historical Press, 1972. Illus. Pap. $2.75.

THE NEGRO IN MISSISSIPPI, 1865 TO 1890
Vernon L. Wharton
Harper and Row Pubs. Cloth, $4.25; Pap. $1.95.

THE NEGRO IN NEW JERSEY
New Jersey Conference of Social Work
116 pp. Negro Universities Press. Reprint of the 1932 edition. Illus. $14.50.

THE NEGRO IN THE NEW WORLD
Harry H. Johnson
449 pp. Johnson Reprint. Reprint of the 1910 edition. Illus. $24.50.

THE NEGRO IN OHIO, 1802 TO 1870
Charles Thomas Hickok
AMS Press, Inc. Reprint of the 1896 edition. $14.50.

THE NEGRO IN PENNSYLVANIA HISTORY
Ira V. Brown
65 pp. Pennsylvania Historical Association, 1970. Pap. $1.25.

THE NEGRO IN PENNSYLVANIA: SLAVERY-SERVITUDE-FREEDOM, 1639-1861
Edward Raymond Turner
314 pp. Greenwood Press. Reprint of the 1921 edition. $11.75.

THE NEGRO IN RECONSTRUCTION
Robert Crunden
Prentice-Hall, 1969. Cloth, $5.95; Pap. $2.45.

THE NEGRO IN THE RECONSTRUCTION OF VIRGINIA
Alrutheus Ambush Taylor
Russell and Russell. Reprint of the 1926 edition. $9.50.

THE NEGRO IN THE SOUTH
Booker T. Washington and W. E. B. DuBois
Citadel Press, 1970. Cloth, $6.50; Pap. $2.45.

THE NEGRO IN THE SOUTH SINCE 1865
C. E. Wynes, Editor

253 pp. University of Alabama Press, 1965. $6.95.

THE NEGRO IN SOUTH CAROLINA DURING THE RECONSTRUCTION
Alrutheus Ambush Taylor
AMS Press, Inc. Reprint of the 1924 edition. $8.75.

THE NEGRO IN TENNESSEE, 1790-1865
Caleb Perry Patterson
213 pp. Greenwood Press. Reprint of the 1922 edition. $9.25.

THE NEGRO IN TENNESSEE, 1865 TO 1880
Alrutheus A. Taylor
316 pp. Reprint Co. Reprint of the 1941 edition. $15.00.

THE NEGRO IN THE UNITED STATES
E. Franklin Frazier
Macmillan Publishing Co., Inc., 1957. $10.95.

THE NEGRO IN THE UNITED STATES, VOL. 1: A HISTORY TO 1945: FROM SLAVERY TO SECOND-CLASS CITIZENSHIP
Rayford W. Logan
Peter Smith Publishers. Cloth, $4.50. Van Nostrand Reinhold Co., Pap. $3.50.

THE NEGRO IN THE UNITED STATES, VOL. 2: THE ORDEAL OF DEMOCRACY
Rayford W. Logan and Michael R. Winston
Peter Smith Publisher. $5.50. Van Nostrand Reinhold Co., Pap. $3.50.

THE NEGRO IN THE UNITED STATES OF AMERICA: A BRIEF HISTORY
R. W. Logan
Peter Smith Publishers. $4.00.

NEGRO LIFE IN THE SOUTH
Willis Duke Weatherford
Books for Libraries, Inc. Reprint of the 1911 edition. $11.25.

THE NEGRO ON THE AMERICAN FRONTIER
Kenneth Wiggins Porter
Negro frontier history in early America. Arno Press, 1971. $15.00.

THE NEGRO PEOPLE IN AMERICAN HISTORY
William Z. Foster

The history of Afro-Americans in the United States. 608 pp. International Publishers, 1970. Cloth, $8.50; Pap. $3.45.

THE NEGRO SINCE EMANCIPATION
Harvey Wish, Editor
Peter Smith Publishers. $4.95.

THE NEGRO SINGS A NEW HEAVEN
Mary Allen Grisson
AMS Press, Inc. Reprint of the 1930 edition. $5.00.

NEGRO TRAIL BLAZERS OF CALIFORNIA
Delilah Leontium Beasley
317 pp. Negro Universities Press. Reprint of the 1919 edition. $17.25. D and E Research Associates, Pubs., $15.00.

THE NEGRO VANGUARD
Richard Bardolph
388 pp. Negro Universities Press. Reprint of the 1959 edition. $19.25.

NEGRO'S PROGRESS IN FIFTY YEARS
American Academy of Political and Social Science
266 pp. Negro Universities Press. Reprint of the 1913 edition. $12.00.

*NEGROES IN AMERICAN LIFE
Richard C. Wade
History of the black race in America from 1619 to the present. Houghton-Mifflin, 1970. Illus. Ages 12-18. $3.99; Pap. $2.97.

*NEGROES IN THE EARLY WEST
Olive W. Burt
Messner, 1969. $4.29. Below college level.

NEGROES IN THE UNITED STATES, 1920-32
United States Bureau of the Census
344 pp. Greenwood Press. Reprint of the 1935 edition. Illus. $40.00. Kraus Reprint Co., $37.50.

NEGROES AND THEIR TREATMENT IN VIRGINIA FROM 1865 TO 1867
John Preston McConnell
126 pp. Negro Universities Press. Reprint of the 1910 edition. $7.50.

A NEW NEGRO FOR A NEW CENTURY
Booker T. Washington
Reviews development of the black race, and changes that have taken place in American.

Mnemosyen Publishing Co. Reprint of the 1900 edition. Illus. $3.95.

NO MORE LIES: THE MYTH AND THE REALITY OF AMERICAN HISTORY
Dick Gregory
Harper and Row Pubs. Pap. $1.95.

NORTH STAR SHINING: A PICTORIAL HISTORY OF THE AMERICAN NEGRO
Hildegard Swift
William Morrow and Co., 1947. $6.50.

NOTES ON THE PROGRESS OF THE COLORED PEOPLE OF MARYLAND SINCE THE WAR: A SUPPLEMENT TO *The Negro in Maryland: A Study of the Institution of Slavery*
Jeffrey Richardson Brackett
96 pp. Johnson Reprint Corporation. Reprint of the 1890 edition. Pap. $7.75.

*ONE HUNDRED YEARS OF NEGRO FREEDOM
Arna Bontemps
The struggle of the American Negro through the past century. 276 pp. Dodd, Mead & Co., 1961. Age 16 up. $6.00.

ORIGINS OF AFRO-AMERICANS
J. H. Clark and V. Harding
Holt, Rinehart, and Winston, 1975. $2.25.

OUR BROTHER IN BLACK: HIS FREEDOM AND HIS FUTURE
Atticus G. Haygood
Books for Libraries, Inc. Reprint of the 1848 edition. $12.25.

THE PAST AND PRESENT CONDITION, AND THE DESTINY OF THE COLORED RACE
Henry Garnet
Books for Libraries, Inc., reprint of the 1848 edition. $5.75.

PICTORIAL HISTORY OF BLACK AMERICA, 4 VOLS.
Ebony Editors
Johnson Publishing Co., Chicago, 1971. $38.90 set.

A PICTORIAL HISTORY OF BLACK AMERICANS
Langston Hughes and Milton Meltzer
380 pp. Crown Publishers, 1973. Over 1,000 illustrations. Cloth, $7.95; Pap. $4.95.

PIONEERS OF NEGRO ORIGIN IN CALIFORNIA
Sue Thruman
R and E Research Associates, Pubs. Reprint of the 1949 edition. $6.00.

THE PLANTATION NEGRO AS A FREE MAN: OBSERVATIONS ON HIS CHARACTER, CONDITIONS AND PROSPECTS IN VIRGINIA
Philip Alexander Bruce
262 pp. Metro Books, Inc. Reprint of the 1889 edition. $13.50.

PROGRESS OF A RACE: OR THE REMARKABLE ADVANCEMENT OF THE AFRO-AMERICAN FROM THE BONDAGE OF SLAVERY, IGNORANCE, AND POVERTY TO THE FREEDOM OF CITIZENSHIP, INTELLIGENCE, AFFLUENCE, HONOR, AND TRUST
Henry F. Kletzing and William Henry Crogman
663 pp. Negro Universities Press. Reprint of the 1897 edition. Illus. $24.75.

PROLOGUE TO LIBERATION: A HISTORY OF BLACK PEOPLE IN AMERICA
Rodney P. Carlisle
Prentice-Hall, 1972. Pap. $4.25.

THE PROPHETIC FAMILIES, OR THE NEGRO: HIS ORIGIN, DESTINY, AND STATUS
J. Troup Taylor
Books for Libraries, Inc. Reprint of the 1895 edition. $6.75.

IN RED AND BLACK: *Marxian Explorations in Southern and Afro-American History*
Eugene Genovese
Pantheon Books, 1971. Cloth, $10.00; Pap. $2.95.

THE RURAL NEGRO
Carter Godwin Woodson
Russell and Russell. Reprint of the 1930 edition. Illus. $12.50.

SEVEN ON BLACK: REFLECTIONS OF THE NEGRO EXPERIENCE IN AMERICA
William G. Shade and Roy C. Herrenkohl
Covers slavery, reconstruction, Booker T. Washington, migration from farm to city, contemporary urban politics, and "black power." 177 pp. J. B. Lippincott Co., 1969. $2.95.

A SHORT HISTORY OF THE AMERICAN NEGRO
Benjamin Brawley
288 pp. Greenwood Press, Inc. Reprint of the 1939 edition. $12.50.

SKETCHES OF NEGRO LIFE AND HISTORY IN SOUTH CAROLINA
Asa H. Gordon
University of South Carolina Press, 1971. Cloth, $14.95; Pap. $2.25.

SOCIAL HISTORY OF THE AMERICAN NEGRO: *A History of the Negro Problem in the United States*
Benjamin G. Brawley
Johnson Reprint. Reprint of the 1921 edition. Cloth, $17.50. Macmillan Publishing Co., Inc., Pap. $2.95.

SOUTH CAROLINA NEGROES, 1877 TO 1900
George B. Tindall
University of South Carolina Press. Reprint of the 1952 edition. Cloth, $9.95. Louisiana State University Press, Pap. $1.95.

THE STORY OF KING COTTON
Harris Dickson
309 pp. Negro Universities Press. Reprint of the 1937 edition. Illus. $14.50.

*STORY OF THE NEGRO
Arna Bontemps
Alfred A. Knopf, Inc., 1958. $3.95. Below college level.

THE STORY OF THE NEGRO: THE RISE OF THE RACE FROM SLAVERY, 2 VOLS.
Booker T. Washington
Peter Smith Publishers. $12.00.

THE STORY OF A RISING RACE: THE NEGRO IN REVELATION, IN HISTORY AND CITIZENSHIP
J. J. Pipkin
Books for Libraries. Reprint of the 1902 edition. $31.50.

*STRUGGLE FOR FREEDOM: *The History of Black Americans*
Daniel S. Davis
A study of the black experience in America from the early slave trade through the civil rights movement of the 1960s. 256 pp. Harcourt Brace Jovanovich, Inc., 1972. Ages 14 up. $6.50.

A SUGGESTED OUTLINE FOR THE STUDY OF THE NEGRO HISTORY
Lloyd King
R and E Research Associates, Pubs. Reprint of the 1941 edition. $5.00.

TEN YEARS ON A GEORGIA PLANTATION SINCE THE WAR
Frances Butler Leigh
347 pp. Negro Universities Press. Reprint of the 1883 edition. $12.25.

TEXTBOOK OF THE ORIGIN AND HISTORY OF THE COLORED PEOPLE
James Pennington
Scholarly Press. Reprint of the 1841 edition. $8.00.

THEY CAME IN CHAINS: AMERICNS FROM AFRICA
Saunders Redding
Three centuries of American Negro history. 336 pp. J. B. Lippincott Co., 1973. Reprint of the. 1950 edition. $3.25.

THE THIN DISGUISE: TURNING POINT IN NEGRO HISTORY
A full study of the Supreme Court decision which "legalized segregation." American Institute for Marxist Studies. $4.00.

TIME OF TRIAL, TIME OF HOPE: THE NEGRO IN AMERICA, 1919 TO 1941
Milton Meltzer and August Meier
Doubleday and Co., 1966. Cloth, $3.75; Pap. $1.45.

TO BE FREE: STUDIES IN AMERICAN NEGRO HISTORY
Herbert Aptheker
Covers slave guerilla warfare, black soldiers and sailors in the Civil War, freedom organization under slavery, Reconstruction in Mississippi. 256 pp. International Publishers, 1968. Pap. $2.25.

*TOWARD FREEDOM: THE HISTORY AND HERITAGE OF BLACK AMERICANS
These five books portray the black people's struggle through centuries for freedom and equality, and highlight their social, political and cultural contributions to America. 128 pp. *Human Cargo: The Story of the Atlantic Slave Trade,* Anne Terry White; *North to Liberty: The Story of the Underground Railroad,* Anne Terry White; *Their Eyes on the Stars: Four Black Writers,* Margaret Goff Clark; *The Long*

Bondage: 1441-1815, James McCague; *The Road to Freedom: 1815-1900,* James McCague. Age 10-15. $17.90 per set.

THE TRAGEDY OF THE NEGRO IN AMERICA: A CONDENSED HISTORY OF THE ENSLAVEMENT, SUFFERINGS, EMANCIPATION, PRESENT CONDITION AND PROGRESS OF THE NEGRO RACE IN THE UNITED STATES OF AMERICA
P. Thomas Stanford
Books for Libraries. Reprint of the 1897 edition. $17.25.

THE TRUMPET SOUNDS: A MEMOIR OF NEGRO LEADERSHIP
Anna A. Hedgeman
Holt, Rinehart, and Winston, 1964. $4.95.

TUSKEGEE AND THE BLACK BELT
Anne K. Walker
Dietz Press, 1945. $3.00.

UNCLE TOM OF THE OLD SOUTH
M. F. Surghnor
A story of the South in reconstruction days. Books for Libraries. Reprint of the 1896 edition. $18.25.

*UNDERSTANDING NEGRO HISTORY
Dwight W. Hoover
The problems involved in both reading and writing the history of the Negro in America. 43½ pp. Franklin Watts, Inc., 1968. Age 16 up. Cloth, $12.50; Pap. $2.95.

*THE UNFINISHED MARCH: THE HISTORY OF THE NEGRO IN THE UNITED STATES; RECONSTRUCTION TO WORLD WAR I
Carol Drisko
Doubleday and Co., 1967. Illus. Cloth, $3.75; Pap. $1.45. Below college level.

THE WHITE SIDE OF A BLACK SUBJECT: A VINDICATION OF THE AFRO-AMERICAN RACE, FROM THE LANDING OF SLAVES AT ST. AUGUSTINE, FLORIDA, IN 1565, TO THE PRESENT TIME
Norman Barton Wood
390 pp. Greenwood Press. Reprint of the 1896 edition. Illus. $16.00.

WORTH FIGHTING FOR: THE HISTORY OF THE NEGRO IN THE UNITED STATES DURING THE CIVIL WAR AND RECON-

STRUCTION
Agnes McCarthy and Lawrence Reddick
Doubleday and Co., 1965. Cloth, $3.75; Pap.
$1.45.

INTELLECTUALS

BLACK AMERICAN SCHOLARS-A STUDY OF THEIR BEGINNINGS
Horace Mann Bond
A presentation of the beginnings of Negro intellectualism in America. 210 pp. Balamp Publishing, 1972. Cloth $8.95; Pap. $3.95.

BLACK INTELLIGENCE VS. WHITE GENES
Moyibi Amoda and Benjamin Jah
Emerson Hall Pubs., 1973. Cloth, $10.00; Pap. $6.95.

THE CRISIS OF THE NEGRO INTELLECTUAL
Harold Cruse
Examination of the Negro intellectual from the 1920's to the present. William Morrow & Co., 1967. Cloth, $10.00; Pap. $3.50.

AN INQUIRY CONCERNING THE INTELLECTUAL AND MORAL FACULTIES AND LITERATURE OF NEGROES
Henri Gregoire
McGrath Publishing Co. Reprint of the 1810 edition. $12.00.

HOLDERS OF DOCTORATES AMONG AMERICAN NEGROES
Harry Washington Greene
A veritable "Who's Who" of Black intellectualism in America from 1876 to 1943. 275 pp. Crofton Publishing Corp., 1946. $15.00.

THE IDEOLOGY OF BLACKNESS
Raymond F. Betts
An anthology which demonstrates the common themes of cultural protest voiced by black intellectuals in the United States, the Caribbean, and Africa. 192 pp. D. C. Heath and Co., 1971.

THE MIND OF THE NEGRO: AN INTELLECTUAL HISTORY OF AFRO-AMERICANS
Earl Thorpe
562 pp. Negro Universities Press. Reprint of the 1961 edition. $22.50.

NEGRO GENIUS
Benjamin G. Brawley
Biblo Tanner Booksellers Pubs. Reprint of the 1937 edition. $8.50.

NEGROES IN SCIENCE: NATURAL SCIENCE DOCTORATES, 1876-1969
James M. Jay
This book presents a profile study of 587 of the then estimated total of 650 American-born Negroes to earn doctorates in the natural sciences. 99 pp. Balamp Publishing., 1971. Paper only, $2.50.

A TRIBUTE FOR THE NEGRO: BEING A VINDICATION OF THE MORAL, INTELLECTUAL, AND RELIGIOUS CAPABILITIES OF THE COLORED PORTION OF MANKIND; WITH PARTICULAR REFERENCE TO THE AFRICAN RACE. ILLUSTRATED BY NUMEROUS BIOGRAPHICAL SKETCHES, FACTS, ANECDOTES, ETC.
Wilson Armistead
564 pp. Greenwood Press. Reprint of the 1848 edition. Illus. $21.00.

JEWISH-BLACK RELATIONS

BITTERSWEET ENCOUNTER: THE AFRO-AMERICAN AND THE AMERICAN JEW
Robert G. Weisbord and Arthur Stein
The authors have composed and analyzed the earlier contributions of both groups and placed them within an historical context. Schocken Books. Pap. $2.95.

BLACK ANTI-SEMITISM AND JEWISH RACISM
Nat Hentoff
Articles by James Baldwin, "Negroes Are Anti-Semitic Because They're Anti-White;" Julius Lester, "A Response;" and Rabbi Jay Kaufman, "Thou Shalt Surely Rebuke Thy Neighbor" are among the eight authors who comprise this book. Schocken Books, 1975. Pap. $2.45.

BLACK-JEWISH RELATIONS IN NEW YORK CITY
Louis Harris and Bert E. Swanson
260 pp. Fraeger Publishers, 1970. $15.00.

THE BLACK JEWS OF HARLEM: *Negro Nationalism and the Dilemmas of Negro Leadership*
Howard M. Brotz

The sustaining myth of an Ethopian-Hebrew origin, however inaccurate and set against a white Christianity, has put this small sect on the path toward "remoralization," shared dignity, and a sense of self-reclamation. Schocken Books, 1975. Cloth, $5.00; Pap. $1.75.

JEWS AND BLACKS: A COURSE ON THE JEWISH PERSPECTIVE AND THE RACIAL CRISIS
Jerald l. Rosenthal
Provides required reading, points of emphasis, questions for discussion, research topics, related films and filmstrips, resources for research and additional reading, and a selected bibliography. 60 pp. Union of American Hebrew Congregations, 1971. Pap. $1.45.

JUSTICE, JUSTICE: A JEWISH VIEW OF THE BLACK REVOLUTION.
Rabbi Henry Cohen
A high school text that summarizes 15 years of dramatic events in race relations. 205 pp. Union of American Hebrew Congregations, 1968. $3.15; teacher's guide, $1.15.

NEGRO AND JEW: AN ENCOUNTER IN AMERICA
Shlomo Katz
Macmillan Publishing Co., Inc., 1967. Cloth, $4.95; Pap. $1.45.

NEGRO-JEWISH RELATIONS IN THE UNITED STATES
Conference on Jewish Social Studies
Citadel Press, 1966. Pap. $1.50.

THE NEGROES AND THE JEWS
Lenora Berson
Random House, Inc., 1971. $8.95.

JOURNALISM

THE AFRO-AMERICAN PRESS AND ITS EDITORS
I. Garland Penn
The earliest survey of the black press in the United States from its beginnings in the pre-Civil War era. Arno Press. Reprint of the 1891 edition. $18.00.

AMERICAN NEGRO REFERENCE GUIDE
Contains a listing of American Negro newspapers and publications. World Mutual

Exchange, 79 Wall St., New York, N.Y. 10005. $4.00.

THE BLACK AMERICAN AND THE PRESS
Jack Lyle, Editor
Ritchie, Ward Press, 1968. Cloth, $4.95; Pap. $1.95.

BLACKS IN COMMUNICATIONS: JOURNALISM, PUBLIC RELATIONS AND ADVERTISING
M. L. Stein
Julian Messner Publications, 1972. $4.79.

THE BLACK PRESS, 1827 TO 1890: THE QUEST FOR NATIONAL IDENTITY
Martin Dann
G. P. Putnam's Sons, 1971. Cloth, $7.95; Pap. $2.95.

THE BLACK PRESS, U.S.A.
Roland E. Wolseley
A discussion of the historical development and current situation of the black press. 352 pp. Iowa State University Press, 1971. Cloth, $10.50; Pap. $4.95.

THE BLACK PRESS VIEWS AMERICAN IMPERIALISM, 1898-1900
George P. Marks III Editor
Gives insight into the enduring black tradition of criticizing American wars against weaker nations. Arno Press, 1971. $11.00.
THE NEGRO NEWSPAPER
Vishnu Vitthal Oak
170 pp. Greenwood Press. Reprint of the 1948 edition. Illus. $8.50.

THE NEGRO PRESS IN THE UNITED STATES
Frederick G. Detweiler
McGrath Publishing Co. Reprint of the 1922 edition. $15.00.

NEW WORLD A-COMING: INSIDE BLACK AMERICA
Roi Ottley
A black reporter's story of Negroes in and out of the government during the New Deal. Arno Press. Reprint of the 1943 edition. $11.50.

PACIFIC APPEAL
Philip A. Bell, Editor
The first Negro newspaper published in California, San Francisco. R & E Research Associates. Reprint of the 1862 edition. Pap. $10.00.

ROBERT VANN OF THE PITTSBURG COURIER: POLITICS AND BLACK JOURNALISM
   Andrew Buni
University of Pittsburgh Press, 1974. $12.95.

THE SELECTED WRITINGS OF JOHN EDWARD BRUCE: MILITANT BLACK JOURNALIST
   Peter Gilbert, EDitor
The man espoused both black political power and economic independence, flayed white hypocrisy, and repeatedly exhorted his readers to rejoice in their blackness and study their history. Arno Press, 1971. $9.00.

THE TROUBLE I'VE SEEN: WHITE JOURNALIST-BLACK MOVEMENT, 1964 TO 1974
   Paul Good
Howard University Press, 1974. $7.95.

THE VOICE OF THE NEGRO, 1919
   Robert T. Kerlin
A compilation of comment and opinion published in the Negro press during the Washington riot of 1919. Arno Press. Reprint of the 1920 edition. $7.50.

VOICES OF A BLACK NATION: POLITICAL JOURNALISM IN THE HARLEM RENAISSANCE
   Theodore G. Vincent, Editor
A collection of over 100 selections from the first black nationalist, socialist, and communist newspapers, which present divergent positions on black identity, the significance of Africa, black capitalism, trade unions, alliances with whites and the importance of the cultural Renaissance in the struggle for black liberation. 396 pp. Ramparts Press, 1972. Cloth, $10.00; Pap. $3.45.

LABOR

THE AMERICAN REVOLUTION: PAGES FROM A NEGRO WORKER'S NOTEBOOK
   James Boggs
Monthly Review Press, 1963. Pap. $1.65.

BLACK BELONGING: A STUDY OF THE SOCIAL CORRELATES OF WORK RELATIONS AMONG NEGROES
   Jack Ross and Raymond Wheeler
292 pp. Greenwood Press, Inc., 1971. Illus. $11.50.

BLACK COAL MINERS IN THE UNITED STATES
   Paul Nyden
Provides a history and analysis of present conditions, with special emphasis on trade-union activities, of black coal miners. American Institute for Marxist Studies. $2.00.

BLACK EMPLOYMENT AND THE LAW
   Alfred Blumrosen
Rutgers University Press, 1971. $15.00.

BLACK LABOR IN AMERICA
   Milton Cantor, Editor
Probing the corners of black labor history. 170 pp. Greenwood Press, 1969. $11.00.

BLACK LABORERS AND BLACK PROFESSIONALS IN EARLY AMERICA, 1750 TO 1830
   Dr. Robert E. Perdue
Vantage Press, Inc., 1974. $6.95.

BLACK WORKER IN THE DEEP SOUTH
   Hosea Hudson
The life story of the son of a sharecropping family who escaped to the city to become a metal worker, and participated in the union and civil rights movements in the South in the 1930's and 1940's. 130 pp. International Publishers, 1972. Cloth, $6.95; Pap. $1.95.

BLACK WORKERS AND THE CLASS STRUGGLE
   Roscoe Proctor
Discusses the rise of black caucuses within trade unions, the reasons, and the need for class-unity approach in order to challenge the power of the big corporations. New Outlook Pubs. $.45.

BLACK WORKERS AND THE NEW UNIONS
   Horace R. Cayton and George S. Mitchell
473 pp. Greenwood Press. Reprint of the 1939 edition. $16.50.

BLACK WORKERS AND ORGANIZED LABOR
   John H. Bracey, et al, Editors
A collection of 12 essays concerning the Negro and the American Labor Movement. 227 pp. Wadsworth Publishing Co., 1971. Pap. $4.50.

BLACKS IN THE THE INDUSTRIAL WORLD: ISSUES FOR THE MANAGER
   Theodore Purcell and Gerald Cavanagh
Free Press, 1973. Cloth, $10.95; Pap. $3.95.

BLACKS, UNIONS, AND THE EEOC: A STUDY OF ADMINISTRATIVE TUTILITY
Benjamin W. Wolkinson
The economic and political bases of union discrimination. 224 pp. Lexington Books, 1973. $12.50.

BROWN AMERICAN:: NATIONAL ASSOCIATION OF NEGROES IN AMERICAN INDUSTRIES VOLS. 1 TO 5
Negro Universities Press. Reprint of the 1936 to 1945 editions. $225.00.

EMPLOYMENT OF BLACKS IN THE SOUTH
Ray Marshall and Virgil Christian, Editors
Examines employment status and trends among the black population of the South. Olympus Publishing Co., 1975. Two volumes. $29.95.

FARM TENANCY: BLACK AND WHITE: TWO REPORTS
New Deal Reports
The Report of the Special Committee on Farm Tenancy, and the Federal Emergency Relief Association on Rural Negroes shows an awareness of the problems of tenant farmers, black and white, during the Depression. Arno Press. Reprint of the 1935, 1937 editions. $10.00.

FREE NEGRO LABOR AND PROPERTY HOLDING IN VIRGINIA, 1830 TO 1860
Luther Porter Jackson
Atheneum Publications, 1969. Pap. $3.45.

THE INDUSTRIAL HISTORY OF THE NEGRO RACE OF THE UNITED STATES
Giles B. Jackson and D. Webster Davis
Books for Libraries, Inc. Reprint of the 1908 edition. $29.95.

*JOBS AND THE COLOR BARRIER
Kenneth Wegner
Pendulum Press, Inc., 1969. Pap. $.60. Below College Level.

THE LIFE AND STRUGGLES OF NEGRO TOILERS
George Padmore
Sun Dance Press, 1971. $7.50.

THE MOBILITY OF THE NEGRO: A STUDY IN THE AMERICAN LABOR SUPPLY
Edward Lewis
AMS Press, Inc. Reprint of the 1931. $12.50.

THE NEGRO AND THE AMERICAN LABOR MOVEMENT
Julius Jacobson, Editor
Doubleday and Co., 1968. $1.95.

NEGRO AND APPRENTICESHIP
F. Ray Marshall and Vernon Briggs
Johns Hopkins Press, 1967. $9.00.

THE NEGRO IN THE AIR TRANSPORT INDUSTRY
Herbert R. Northrup, et al
University of Pennsylvania Press, 1971. $5.95.

NEGRO EMPLOYMENT IN BASIC INDUSTRY: A STUDY OF RACIAL EMPLOYMENT POLICIES IN SIX INDUSTRIES
Herbert Northrup and Richard Rowan
University of Pennsylvania Press, 1970. $15.00.

THE NEGRO IN THE BITUMINOUS COAL-MINING INDUSTRY
Darold BArnum
University of Pennsylvania Press, 1970. Pap. $4.50.

THE NEGRO IN THE DEPARTMENT STORE INDUSTRY
Charles Perry
University of Pennsylvania Press, 1971. $5.95.

THE NEGRO IN THE DRUG MANUFACTURING INDUSTRY
F. Marion Fletcher
University of Pennsylvania Press, 1970. $5.95.

THE NEGRO IN THE DRUGSTORE INDUSTRY
F. Marion Fletcher
University of Pennsylvania Press, 1972. $5.95.

THE NEGRO IN THE ELECTRICAL MANUFACTURING INDUSTRY
Theodore Purcell and Daniel Mulvey
University of Pennsylvania Press, 1971. $5.95.

THE NEGRO IN THE FARM EQUIPMENT AND CONSTRUCTION MACHINERY INDUSTRY
Robert Ozanne
University of Pennsylvania Press, 1972. $5.95.

THE NEGRO IN FEDERAL EMPLOYMENT: THE QUEST FOR EQUAL OPPORTUNITY
Samuel Krislov

Provides a basic analysis of the role and requirements of the public service which will serve as a standard for the future investigation and assessment of progress in the opening of the federal service to Negroes. University of Minnesota Press, 1967. $5.00.

NEGRO EMPLOYMENT IN FINANCE: A STUDY OF RACIAL POLICIES IN BANKING AND INSURANCE
Armand Thieblot
University of Pennsylvania Press, 1970. $9.50.

THE NEGRO IN THE FURNITURE INDUSTRY
William Fulmer
University of Pennsylvania Press, 1972. $5.95.

THE NEGRO IN THE INSURANCE INDUSTRY
Linda Fletcher
University of Pennsylvania Press, 1970. $5.95.

NEGRO EMPLOYMENT IN LAND AND AIR TRANSPORT: A STUDY OF RACIAL POLICIES IN THE RAILROAD, AIRLINES, TRUCKING, AND URBAN TRANSIT INDUSTRIES
Herbert Northrup, et al
University of Pennsylvania Press, 1971. $13.50.

THE NEGRO IN THE LONGSHORE INDUSTRY
Lester Rubin
University of Pennsylvania Press, 1972. $5.95.

NEGRO EMPLOYMENT IN THE MARITIME INDUSTIRES: A STUDY OF RACIAL POLICIES IN SHIPBUILDING, LONGSHORE, AND OFFSHORE MARITIME INDUSTRIES
Lester Rubin
University of Pennsylvania Press, 1974. $12.00.

NEGRO EMPLOYMENT IN PUBLIC UTILITIES: A STUDY OF THE RACIAL POLICIES IN THE ELECTRIC POWER, GAS, AND TELEPHONE INDUSTRIES
Bernard Anderson
University of Pennsylvania Press, 1970. $8.50.

THE NEGRO IN THE RAILROAD INDUSTRY
Howard Risher
University of Pennsylvania Press, 1970. $5.95.

THE NEGRO IN THE RUBBER TIRE INDUSTRY
Herbert Northrup and Alan Batchelder
University of Pennsylvania Press, 1969. $3.50.

THE NEGRO IN THE SHIPBUILDING INDUSTRY
Lester Rubin
University of Pennsylvania Press, 1970. $5.95.

THE NEGRO IN THE SLAUGHTERING AND MEAT-PACKING INDUSTRY IN CHICAGO
Alma Hebst
The focus of this book is on the Negro in the succession of ethnic and racial groups entering the plants in the stockyards. Arno Press. Reprint of the 1932 edition. $10.00.

NEGRO EMPLOYMENT IN SOUTHERN INDUSTRY: A STUDY OF THE RACIAL POLOCIES OF PAPER, LUMBER, TOBACCO, COAL, AND TEXTILE INDUSTRIES
Herbert Northrup and Richard Rowan
University of Pennsylvania Press, 1971. $13.50.

THE NEGRO IN THE SUPERMARKET INDUSTRY
Marion Fletcher
University of Pennsylvania Press, 1972. $5.95.

THE NEGRO IN THE TEXTILE INDUSTRY
Richard Rowan
University of Pennsylvania Press, 1970. $5.95.

THE NEGRO IN THE TRUCKING INDUSTRY
Richard Leone
University of Pennsylvania Press, 1970. $4.50.

THE NEGRO IN THE URBAN TRANSIT INDUSTRY
Philip Jeffress
University of Pennsylvania Press, 1970. $4.50.

NEGRO IRONWORKERS OF LOUISIANNA
Marcu B. Christian
Pelican Publishing House, 1972. Pap. $2.50.

NEGRO LABOR: A NATIONAL PROBLEM
Robert C. Weaver
Kennikat Press. Reprint of the 1946 edition. $11.00.

NEGRO LABOR IN THE UNITED STATES, 1850 TO 1925: A STUDY IN AMERICAN

ECONOMIC HISTORY
Charles Wesley
Russell and Russell. Reprint of the 1927 edition.
$11.00.

THE NEGRO LABOR UNIONIST OF NEW YORK
Charles Franklin
AMS Press, Inc. Reprint of the 1936 edition.
$15.00.

NEGRO MEMBERSHIP, AMERICAN LABOR UNIONS
National Urban League
175 pp. Greenwood Press. Reprint of the 1930 edition. $8.50.

19 NEGRO MEN: PERSONALITY AND MANPOWER RETRAINING
Aaron Rutledge and Gertrude Gass
Jossey-Bass, Inc., 1967. $7.75.

THE NEGRO WAGE EARNER
Lorenzo Greene and Carter Woodson
AMS Press, Inc. Reprint of the 1930 edition.
$10.25.

THE NEGRO AT WORK DURING THE WORLD WAR AND DURING RECONSTRUCTION: STATISTICS, PROBLEMS AND POLICIES RELATING TO THE GREATER INCLUSION OF NEGRO WAGE EARNERS IN AMERICAN INDUSTRY AND AGRICULTURE
United States Department of Labor-Division of Negro Economics
144 pp. Greenwood Press. Reprint of the 1921 edition. Illus. $9.00.

THE NEGRO AT WORK IN NEW YORK CITY: A STUDY OF ECONOMIC PROGRESS
George Edmund Haynes
An early study of Negro economic conditions written by one of the founders of the Urban League. Arno Press. Reprint of the 1912 edition. $4.50. AMS Press, Inc. $5.50.

NEGRO WORKER
Ray Marshall
Random House, Inc., 1967. Pap. $2.00.

NEGROES AND JOBS: A BOOK OF READINGS
Louis A. Ferman, et al. Editors
608 pp. University of Michigan Press, 1968.
$12.50; Pap. $6.25.

OFFICIAL HISTORY OF FREE-MASONRY AMONG THE COLORED PEOPLE IN NORTH AMERICA
William Henry Grimshaw
Tracing the growth of Masonry from 1717 down to the present day. Books for Libraries. Reprint of the 1903 edition. $18.25.

OPENING UP THE SKILLED CONSTRUCTION TRADES TO BLACKS: A STUDY OF THE WASHINGTON AND INDIANAPOLIS PLANS FOR A MINORITY EMPLOYMENT
Richard Rowan and Lester Rubin
University of Pennsylvania Press, 1972. $5.95.

ORGANIZED LABOR AND THE NEGRO
H. R. Northrup
Kraus Reprint Co. Reprint of the 1944 edition.
$15.00.

RACISM AND THE CLASS STRUGGLE: FURTHER PAGES FROM A BLACK WORKER'S NOTEBOOK
James Boggs
Monthly Review Press, 1970. Cloth, $6.00; Pap.
$2.45.

ROBESON: LABOR'S FORGOTTEN CHAMPION
Charles H. Wright
A narrative of Paul Robeson's outstanding achievements to America by Charles Wright, founder of the Afro-American Museum of Detroit. 170 pp. Balamp Publishing. 1975.
$7.95.

UNTAPPED HUMAN RESOURCE: THE URBAN NEGRO AND EMPLOYMENT EQUALITY
Marvin J. Levine
237 pp. General Learning Corp., 1972. $8.50.

THE URBAN NEGRO WORKER IN THE UNITED STATES, 1925-1936; AN ANALYSIS OF THE TRAINING, TYPES, AND CONDITIONS OF EMPLOYMENT AND THE EARNINGS OF 200,000 SKILLED AND WHITE-COLLAR NEGRO WORKERS
United States Office of Adviser on Negro Affairs
127 pp. Greenwood Press. Reprint of the 1938-39 edition. Illus. $20.00.

WHITE CAPITAL AND COLOURED LABOR
Sydney Haldan Olivier

175 pp. Negro Universities Press. Reprint of the 1910 edition. $8.75.

THE WORKING POOR: MINORITY WORKERS IN LOW-WAGE, LOW-SKILL JOBS
Dennis Sobin
Kennikat Press, 1974. $8.50.

LANGUAGE

BEFO' DE WAR: ECHOES IN NEGRO DIALECT
A.C. Gordon and Thomas Nelson Page
Books for Libraries, Inc. Reprint of the 1888 edition. $11.00

BLACK DIALECTS AND READING
Bernice Cullinan, Editor
Examines the interrelationship among black dialect, oral language, and reading. 208 pp. National Council of Teachers of English, 1974. $3.95.

BLACK ENGLISH
J.L. Dillard
Traces the development of Black English from its African roots through the period of slavery to the present. Vintage Press. $2.45.

BLACK ENGLISH: ITS HISTORY AND USES IN THE UNITED STATES
J.L. Dillard
Random House, Inc., 1972. Cloth, $10.00; Pap. $2.45.

BLACK LANGUAGE READER
Robert H. Bentley and Samuel D. Crawford
Readings which explore the origins of black English, its characteristics and relation to the total black experience today, and the problems of education and social progress for speakers of the black dialect. 245 pp. Scott, Foresman & Co., 1973. Illus. Pap. $2.95.

BLACK TALK
Ben Sidran
Holt, Rinehart, and Winston, 1971. Cloth, $5.95; Pap. $2.95.

BLACK—WHITE SPEECH RELATIONSHIPS
Walt Wolfram and Nona H. Clarke, Editors

Eight papers dealing with dialect research from differing perspectives. 176 pp. Center for Applied Linguistics, 1971. $6.50.

BLACK WORDS
Arthur Boze
Broadside Press, Pubns., 1972. Pap. $1.00.

A COMPREHENSIVE ANNOTATED BIBLIOGRAPHY OF AMERICAN BLACK ENGLISH
Ila Wales Brasch and Walter Milton Brasch
290 pp. Louisiana State University Press, 1974. $15.00.

LANGUAGE, COMMUNICATIONS, AND RHETORIC IN BLACK AMERICA
Arthur L. Smith
Harper and Row Pubs., 1972. Pap. $6.50.

THE PSYCHOLOGY OF BLACK LANGUAGE
James Haskins and Hugh F. Butts
95 pp. Harper & Row Publishers, 1973. Pap. $1.50.

TEACHING BLACK CHILDREN TO READ
Joan C. Baratz and Roger W. Shuy, Editors
Eight papers concerned with the relationship of language to reading and the role of the childs's own language behavior in the process of learning to read. 219 pp. Center for Applied Linguistics, 1969. $7.00.

TENSE MARKING IN BLACK ENGLISH: A LINGUISTIC AND SOCIAL ANALYSIS
Ralph W. Fasold
A sociolinguistic study of Washington, D.C. black English. 254 pp. Center for Applied Linguistics, 1972. $8.00.

LITERATURE

AN ABC OF COLOR
W.E.B. DuBois
Selections from over a half century of his writings, edited by the author himself. 216 pp. International Publishers, 1970. Pap. $1.35.

AFRO—AMERICAN LITERATURE: *An Introduction*

Robert Hayden, David J. Burrows,
Frederick R. Lapides
A collection of 52 readings: short stories,
peoms, autobiographical pieces, critical essays
and one complete play. 309 pp. Harcourt Brace
Jovanovich, Inc., 1971. Pap. $4.50.

**AFRO—AMERICAN LITERATURE:
DRAMA**
William Adams, et al, Editors
Houghton Mifflein Co., 1969. Pap. $2.64.

**AFRO—AMERICAN LITERATURE:
FICTION**
William Adams, Editor
Houghton Mifflin Co., 1969. Pap. $2.64.

**AFRO—AMERICAN LITERATURE:
NONFICTION**
William Adams, et al, Editors
Houghton Mifflin Co., 1970. Pap. $2.64.

AFRO—AMERICAN READINGS
Ross K. Baker
Van Nostrand Reinhold Co., 1970. Pap. $6.50.

AFTER—YUH MAMMA
Howard E. Seals, 1972. Pap. $1.00.

AMERICAN NEGRO SHORT STORIES
John Henrick Clarke, Editor
31 stories by Richard Wright, Langston
Hughes, Arna Bontemps, James Baldwin,
LeRoi Jones, and others. Hill & Wang, 1966.
Pap. $2.45.

ANOTHER VIEW: *To Be Black In America*
Gerald Messner
An anthology of expository prose that describes
the present condition fo the black man in
America. 400 pp. Harcourt Brace Jovanovich,
Inc., 1970. Pap. $4.80.

**ANTHOLOGY OF AMERICAN NEGRO
LITERATURE**
V.F. Calverton, Editor
Kraus Reprint Co. Reprint of the 1929 edition.
$20.00.

**BACKGROUNDS TO BLACK AMERICAN
LITERATURE**
R. Miller
Chandler Publishing Co., 1971. Pap. $6.00.

**BALTIMORE AFRO—AMERICAN: BEST
SHORT STORIES BY AFRO—AMERICAN
WRITERS**

H.L. Faggett and Nick Aaron Ford,
Editors
Kraus Reprint Co. Reprint of the 1950 edition.
$12.50.

**THE BEST SHORT STORIES BY NEGRO
WRITERS**
Langston Hughes
Little, Brown, and Co., 1967. Cloth, $10.00;
Pap. $2.95.

**BLACK AMERICAN FICTION SINCE
1952: A PRELIMINARY CHECKLIST**
Frank Deodene and William French
Chatham Bookseller, 1970. Pap. $2.50.

**THE BLACK AMERICAN IN BOOKS FOR
CHILDREN: READINGS IN RACISM**
Donnarae MacCann and Gloria Woodard,
Editors
230 pp. Scarecrow Press, 1972. $7.50.

BLACK AMERICAN LITERATURE
Ruth Miller
An anthology of black American literature form
1760 to the present. Macmillan Publishing Co.
$3.95.

**BLACK AMERICAN LITERATURE: A
CRITICAL HISTORY, NO. 278**
Roger Whitlow
Littlefield, Adams, and Co., 1974. Pap. $3.95.

**BLACK AMERICAN LITERATURE: A
CRITICAL HISTORY**
Roger Whitlow
Includes the traditions, works, movements, and
influences of forty-five black writers from 1746,
form Lucy Terry to Nikki Biovanni. 303 pp. -
Nelson-Hall Publishers, 1973. $8.95.

**BLACK AMERICAN LITERATURE:
ESSAYS**
D.T. Turner
Charles E. Merrill Publishing Co., 1969. Pap.
$2.95.

**BLACK AMERICAN LITERATURE:
ESSAYS, POETRY, FICTION, DRAMA**
Darwin T. Turner
Charles E. Merrill Publishing Co., 1970. Cloth,
$8.95; Pap. $5.95.

*BLACK B C'S
Lucille Clifton
E.P. Dutton and Co., 1970. Illus. $3.95. Below
college level.

THE BLACK BOOK
Harris A. Middleton, et al,
Random House, Inc., 1973. Cloth, $15.00; Pap.
$5.95.

BLACK DEFIANCE
Jay David, Editor
In autobiography, dramatic account, and
poetry, 23 blacks tell of their struggles to combat racism. William Morrow & Co., Cloth,
$6.95; Pap. $2.45.

**THE BLACK EXPERIEINCE IN CHILD-
REN'S BOOKS**
Augusta Baker
109 pp. New York Public Library, 1971. Illus.
$.50.

BLACK FICTION
Roger Rosenblatt
Harvard University Press, 1974. $9.50.

**BLACK FIRE: AN ANTHOLOGY OF
AFRO—AMERICAN WRITING**
Le Roi Jones and Larry Neal, Editors
Essays, poems, short stories and plays of over
70 black writers. William Morrow & Co., 1968.
Cloth, $10.00; Pap. $3.50.

***BLACK HANDS ON A WHITE FACE, A
TIMEPIECE OF EXPERIENCES IN BLACK
AND WHITE AMERICA**
Whit Burnett, Editor
A collection of fiction and non-fiction
mirroring the Negro experience in America
through 25 writers. 416 pp. Dodd, Mead & Co.,
1971. Age 16 up. $7.95.

**BLACKS IN AMERICA: BIBLIO-
GRAPHICAL ESSAYS**
James McPherson, et al.
Doubleday and Co., 1972. Cloth $10.00; Pap.
$3.95.

**BLACK INSIGHTS: SIGNIFICANT LIT-
ERATURE BY AFRO—AMERICANS, 1970
TO THE PRESENT**
Nick A. Ford
Xerox College Publishing, 1971. Pap. $6.95.

BLACK IS . . . .
Committee of Children's Librarians
Enoch-Pratt Free Library, 1972. Pap. $0.75.

**BLACK LIKE IT IS/WAS: ERSKINE
CALDWELL'S TREATMENT OF RACIAL
THEMES**

William A. Sutton
Provides an examination of the racial and
racial/sexual factors in Cladwell's Depression
era works. 164 pp. Scarecrow Press, 1974.
$6.00.

*BLACK LIKE ME
John H. Griffin
New American Library, 1961. Pap. $1.25.

BLACK LITERATURE IN AMERICA
H.A. Baker
Included are bibliographies of reference works,
historical and literary introductions, and
selections that reflect dominant literary conventions as well as prevalent historical concerns.
443 pp. McGraw-Hill Book Co., 1971. $6.95.

**BLACK LITERATURE IN AMERICA: A
CASEBOOK**
R.K. Singh and P. Fellowes, Editors
Thomas Y. Crowell Co., 1970. Pap. $4.75.

**BLACK LITERATURE IN HIGH SCHOOLS
IN ILLINOIS**
A survey of over 600 English teachers explores
attitudes toward teaching black lierature, when
and why courses in black literature and culture
were inaugurated, and purposes and techniques
in teaching such courses. 41 pp. National
Council of Teachers of English, 1971. Pap.
$.75.

**THE BLACK MAN AND THE PROMISE OF
AMERICA**
Lettie J. Austin, et al
Essays, speeches, letters, documents, historical
and biographical narratives, fictional selections
and poems. 523 pp. Scott, Foresman & Co.,
1970. Pap. $4.95.

BLACK MAN'S BURDEN
John Oliver Killens
Trident Press. $4.95.

**BLACK MASKS: NEGRO CHARACTERS
IN MODERN SOUTHERN FICTION**
Nancy M. Tischler
Pennsylvania State University Press, 1969.
$8.50.

***BLACK ON BLACK: COMMENTARIES
BY AMERICAN NEGROES**
Arnold Adoff, Editor
Macmillan Publishing Co., Inc., 1968. $5.95.
Below college level.

BLACK ON WHITE: A CRITICAL SURVEY OF WRITINGS BY AMERICAN NEGROES
David Littlejohn
192 pp. Viking Press, 1969. Pap. $1.45.

BLACK PORTRAITURE IN AMERICAN FICTION: STOCK CHARACTERS, ARCHETYPES, AND INDIVIDUALS
Catherine J. Starke
Basic Books, 1971. $7.95.

THE BLACK ROOM
John M. Akili
Carlton Press. $3.75.

THE BLACK SEVENTIES
Floyd B. Barbour, Editor
Essays by sixteen contemporary black authors.
352 pp. Porter Sargent Publisher, Inc. Cloth, $5.95; Pap. $2.95.

BLACK TALES
Imamu Amiri Baraka (LeRoi Jones)
16 tales. Vintage Press. $1.25.

BLACK TITAN: W.E.B. DuBOIS
The editors of *Freedomways*
An anthology; Langston Hughes, Paul Robeson, Martin Luther King and others recall the intellectual forerunner of contemporary black militancy. Beacon Press. Pap. $2.95.

BLACK THUNDER
Arna Bontemps
A novel of slavery and rebellion. Beacon Press. Pap. $2.95.

THE BLACK TRADITION IN AMERICAN FICTION SERIES, 24 VOLS.
McGrath Publishing Co. $275.00 set.

BLACK VIEWPOINTS
Arthur Littleton and Mary Burger, Editors
New American Library, 1971. Pap. $1.50.

BLACK VOICES: AN ANTHOLOGY OF AFRO—AMERICAN LITERATURE
Abraham Chapman, Editor
New American Library, 1968. $1.75.

BLACK VOICES FORM PRISON
Ethridge Knight and fellow inmates of Indiana State Prison
192 pp. Pathfinder Press. Cloth, $5.95; Pap. $2.45.

*BORN BLACK: AN ANTHOLOGY
Jay David and Catherine Green, Editors
Lothrop, Lee, and Shepard Co., 1971. $4.95.
Ages 16 and up.

BROTHERS BLACK
James R. Adair
Baker Book House, 1973. Pap. $0.95.

CALVACADE OF THE AMERICAN NEGRO
Writers Program, Illinois
AMS Press, Inc., 1973. Reprint of the 1940 edition. $5.00.

CALVACADE: NEGRO AMERICAN WRITING FROM 1760 TO THE PRESENT
A.P. Davis and S. Reading, Editors
Houghton Mifflin Co., 1970. Cloth, $12.50; Pap. $2.00.

A CENTURY OF FICTION BY AMERICAN NEGROES: 1853 TO 1952.
Maxwell Whiteman
Albert Saifer Pub., 1969. $10.00.

COLLECTED PAPERS AND DOCUMENTS
Marcus Garvey
Humanities Press, 1974.

CYRILL
Ernest C. Oliver
A collection of essays that analyze the past, present and future of the black race in America. Vintage Press. $4.95.

DARK SYMPHONY: NEGRO LITERATURE IN AMERICA
J.A. Emanuel and T.L. Gross, Editors
Free Press, 1968. Cloth, $8.95; Pap. $4.95.

THE DEVIL, THE GARGOYLE AND THE BUFFOON: THE NEGRO AS METAPHOR IN WESTERN LITERATURE
Lemuel A. Johnson
An examination of the mythology and theological concepts of the Black Muslims. Kennikat Press, 1971. Cloth, $10.95; Pap. $3.95.

THE DIMENSIONS OF BLACK
Jehanne Teilhet
Laurence McGilvery, 1970. Pap. $7.50.

DIRECTORY OF BLACK LITERARY MAGAZINES
Minority Research Center, Inc. 117 R St., N.E., Washington, D.C. 20002, $5.00.

EARLY NEGRO WRITING, 1760-1837
Dorothy Porter, Editor
Beacon Press, 1971. $20.00.

ELY: TOO BLACK, TOO WHITE
Ely Green and E. Chittly, Editors
New American Library, 1971. Pap. $1.95.

THE EMERGING THOUGHT OF W.E.B. DuBOIS: ESSAYS AND EDITORIALS FROM THE CRISES WITH AN INTRODUCTION, COMMENTARIES, AND A PERSONAL MEMOIR
Henry Lee Moon
Simon and Schuster, 1972. $12.95.

FROM APOLOGY TO PROTEST: THE BLACK AMERICAN NOVEL
Noel Schraufnagel
The black movement in black-American literature. 240 pp. Everett-Edwards, Inc., 1973. $12.00.

FROM THE DARK TOWER
Arthur P. Davis
An overview of significant black writers and their works from 1900 to 1960. 332 pp. 28 photos. Howard University Press, 1974. $10.95.

*FROM THE ROOTS: SHORT STORIES BY BLACK AMERICANS
Charles L. James, Editor
The development of black American literature is reflected in 27 short stories by 23 authors, ranging from Charles Chestnutt's "The Goophered Grapevine" to James Alan McPherson's "A Matter of Vocabulary." 370 pp. Dodd, Mead & Co., 1970. Age 16 up. Pap. $4.95.

THE FUTURE OF THE AMERICAN NEGRO
Booker T. Washington
244 pp. Greenwood Press, 1969. Reprint of the 1907 edition. $10.25.

THE FUTURE OF THE AMERICAN NEGRO
Booker T. Washington
244 pp. Metro Books, Inc. Reprint of the 1899 edition. $10.00.

THE GIFT OF BLACK FOLK
W.E. Burghart Du Bois
349 pp. Johnson Reprint, 1969. Reprint of the 1924 edition. $14.00.

HARLEM GALLERY
Melvin Tolson
Macmillan Publishing Co., Inc., 1969. $1.50.

*THE HARLEM RENAISSANCE REMEMBERED
Arna Bontemps, Editor
An array of black writers of prose, poetry, and drama. 310 pp. Dodd, Mead & Co., 1972. Illus. Age 16 up. $6.95.

I, TOO, SING AMERICA: BLACK VOICES IN AMERICAN LITERATURE
Barbara Dodds
320 pp. Hayden Book Co., 1971. Cloth, $6.85; Pap. $4.95.

IMAGE OF THE BLACK IN CHILDREN'S FICTION
Dorothy M. Broderick
Study of how blacks are treated in traditional children's literature. 219 pp. R.R. Bowker Co., 1973. $12.75.

IMAGES OF THE NEGRO IN AMERICAN LITERATURE
Seymour Gross, Editor
University of Chicago Press, 1966. Cloth, $8.75; Pap. $2.95.

IN WHITE AND BLACK: A STORY
W.W. Pinson
Books for Libraries, Inc. Reprint of the 1900 edition. $16.00.

INTRICATE KNOT: THE NEGRO IN AMERICAN LITERATURE
J.F. Yellin
New York University Press, 1971. Cloth, $10.00; Pap. $3.25.

INTRODUCTION TO BLACK LITERATURE IN AMERICA
Patterson
United Publishing Corp. $13.88.

THE INVENTION OF THE NEGRO
Earl Conrad
Paul Erikson, Inc., 1969. Cloth, $5.95; Pap. $1.95.

JAMES BALDWIN: A CRITICAL EVALUATION
Therman B. O'Daniel, Editor
An assesment of James Baldwin the novelist, short story writer, playwright, scenarist, and conversationalist. 192 pp. Howard University Press, 1976. $8.95.

JUST BETWEEN US BLACKS
Carl Rowan
Random House, Inc., 1974. $5.95.

A KEY TO UNCLE TOM'S CABIN: PRE-SENTING THE ORIGINAL FACTS AND DOCUMENTS UPON WHICH THE STORY IS FOUNDED, TOGETHER WITH CORRO-BORATIVE STATEMENTS VERIFYING THE TRUTH OF THE WORK
Harriet Beecher Stowe
The object of the author is to bring the subject of slavery, as a moral and religious question, before the minds of all those who profess to be followers of Christ. Kennikat Press. Reprint of the 1853 edition. $12.50.

LONG BLACK SONG: ESSAYS IN BLACK AMERICAN LITERATURE AND CULTURE
Houston A. Baker, Jr.
156 pp. University Press of Virginia, 1972. $7.95.

*LONG JOURNEY HOME: STORIES FROM BLACK HISTORY
Julius Lester
Six pieces of black historical fiction. 160 pp. Dell Publishing Co., 1972. Age 12 up. $4.95.

THE MAKING OF BLACK AMERICA
August Meier and Elliott Rudwick, Editors
A collection of essays depicting attitudes and institutions of American Negro Life. Atheneum Publishers, 1969. Cloth, $12.50; Pap. $4.25.

THE MIND OF THE NEGRO AS REFLECT-ED IN LETTERS WRITTEN DURING THE CRISIS, 1800 TO 1860
Carter Woodson
672 pp. Greenwood Press, Inc. Reprint of the 1926 edition. $17.00.

MINGO AND OTHER SKETCHES IN BLACK AND WHITE
Joel Chandler Harris
Books for Libraries, Inc. Reprint of the 1884 edition. $12.25.

MODERN BLACK STORIES
Martin Mirer, Editor
Stories for a realistic view of black culture and personality. 256 pp. Barron's Educational Series. Pap. $1.95.

NARRATIVES OF COLORED AMERICANS
Lindley Murray
Books for Libraries, Inc. Reprint of the 1877 edition. $14.50.

A NARRATIVE OF THE NEGRO
Mrs. Leila Amos Pendleton

Books for Libraries, Inc. Reprint of the 1912 edition. $16.00.

THE NEGRO
W. Burghardt DuBois
184 pp. Oxford University Press, 1970. Pap. $2.50.

NEGRO ANTHOLOGY
Nancy Cunard
854 pp. Greenwood Press. Reprint of the 1934 edition. Illus. $85.00.

NEGRO: AN ANTHOLOGY
Nancy Cunard and Hugh Ford, Editors
460 pp. Frederick Ungar Publishing Co., 1970. Illus. $32.50.

THE NEGRO A BEAST
Charles Carroll
Books for Libraries, Inc. Reprint of the 1900 edition. $16.50.

THE NEGRO CHARACTER IN AMERICAN LITERATURE
John H. Nelson
McGrath Publishing Co. Reprint of the 1926 edition. AMS Press, Inc. Cloth, $12.00. Pap. $5.00.

THE NEGRO CARAVAN
Sterling Brown, et al, Editors
An extensive collection of pre-World War II Negro writing including poetry, speeches, short stories, folk literature, music, essays, selections from novels, plays, biographies, and autobiographies. Arno Press, 1969. Reprint of the 1941 edition. $35.00.

NEGRO IN AMERICA: CONDENSED VERSION OF GUNNAR MYRDAL'S *American Dilemma*
Arnold Rose
Peter Smith Publishers. $4.50.

THE NEGRO IN AMRICAN FICTION AND NEGRO POETRY AND DRAMA
Sterling Brown
Arno Press, 1969. Reprint of the 1937 edition. $10.50.

THE NEGRO IN CONTEMPORARY AMERICAN LITERATURE: AN OUTLET FOR INDIVIDUAL AND GROUP STUDY
Elizabeth L. Green
McGrath Publishing Co., 1928. $9.50.

***THE NEGRO IN DEPRESSION AND WAR: PRELUDE TO REVOLUTION, 1930-1945**
Bernard Sternsher
A collection of historical literature on black America. 348 pp. Franklin Watts, Inc., 1969. Age 16 up. Pap. $2.95.

THE NEGRO IN LITERATURE AND ART IN THE UNITED STATES
Benjamin Griffith Brawley
AMS Press, Inc. Reprint of the 1930 edition. 1971. $6.50.

THE NEGRO IN LITERATURE AND ART IN THE UNITED STATES
Benjamin Brawley
Scholarly Press. Reprint of the 1929 edition. $14.50.

THE NEGRO IS A MAN
W.S. Armistead
A reply to Professor Charles Carroll's book, "The Negro is a Beast, or, In the Image of God." Books for Libraries, 1903. $16.00.

THE NEGRO NOVEL IN AMERICA
Robert A. Bone
Yale University Press, 1965. Cloth, $13,50; Pap. $3.25.

NEGRO VOICES IN AMERICAN FICTION
Hugh Morris Gloster
Russell and Russell, 1965. Reprint of the 1948 edition. $13.00.

THE NEW NEGRO: AN INTERPRETATION
Alain Locke, Editor
A collection of poems, stories and essays by Negroes, edited by the first Negro Rhodes Scholar. Arno Press, 1968. Reprint of the 1925 edition. $9.00.

THE NEW NEGRO RENAISSANCE: AN ANTHOLOGY
Arthur P. Davis and Michael Peplow, Editors
One-act plays, poems, short stories and essays by DuBois, Garvey, Hughes, and scores more. 544 pp. Holt, Rinehart & Winston, 1974. $12.95.

NIGGER
Dick Gregory
McGraw Hill Book Co., 1970. $1.80.

NOMMO: AN ANTHOLOGY OF MODERN BLACK AFRICA AND BLACK AMERICAN LITERATURE
W.H. Robinson
Macmillan Publishing Co., Inc., 1972. $5.95.

***THE OLD SOUTH: "A SUMMER TRAGEDY" AND OTHER STORIES OF THE THIRTIES**
Arna Bontemps
A collection of 14 short stories of black Southern life in the 1930's. 200 pp. Dodd, Mead & Co., 1973. Age 16 up. $6.95.

ON BEING BLACK
Charles T. Davis and Daniel Walden, Editors
An anthology of writings by Afro-Americans, from Frederick Douglass to the present. Fawcett World Library. Pap. $1.25.

OUT OF OUR LIVES
Quandra Prettyman Stadler, Editor
A collection of contemporary black fiction. The life-cycle approach of this anthology shows the myriad life styles of a people and the unique spiritual continuity of that people. 324 pp. Howard University Press, 1975. $9.95.

PHILOSOPHY AND OPINIONS OF MARCUS GARVEY
Marcus Garvey
Collected writings of the leader of the "Back to Africa" movement. Atheneum Publishers, 1969. Illus. Pap. $4.95.

POSITIVELY BLACK
Roger Abrahams
Irvington Books Press, 1970. Pap. $3.95.

THE POSSIBILITIES OF THE NEGRO IN SYMPOSIUM
165 pp. Negro Universities Press. Reprint of the 1904 edition. $8.50.

SEVENTH SON: THE THOUGHTS AND WRITINGS OF W.E. DuBOIS, 2 VOLS
Julius Lester, Editor
Random House, Inc., 1971. Boxed, $25.00. Vols. I and II, Pap. $3.95 ea.

SINGERS OF DAYBREAK: STUDIES IN BLACK AMERICAN LITERATURE
Houston A. Baker, Jr.
Examines black writers and surveys a multiplicity of themes tied to an introductory discussion of an age-old polemic-didacticism and

black literature. 128 pp. Howard University Press, 1975. $6.95.

SOON ONE MORNING: NEW WRITING BY AMERICAN NEGROES
H. Hill
Alfred A. Knopf, Inc., 1963. $7.95.

THE SOUL OF JOHN BROWN
Stephen Graham
AMS Press, Inc., 1970. Reprint of the 1920 edition. $12.50.

SOULS OF BLACK FOLK
W.E.B. DuBois
New American Library, 1969. Pap. $1.25.

*THE SOULS OF BLACK FOLK
W.E. Burghardt DuBois
A collection of essays of the co-founder of the NAACP. 204 pp. Dodd, Mead & Co., 1970. Illus. Age 16 up. $5.50.

*SPEAK OUT IN THUNDER TONES: LETTERS AND OTHER WRITINGS BY BLACK NORTHERNERS, 1787 TO 1865
Dorothy Sterling
Doubleday and Co., 1973. Illus. $5.95. Below college level.

100 STORIES IN BLACK
Bridges Smith
A collection of bright, breezy, humourous stories of the colored race as seen in the sunny south. Books for Libraries. Reprint of the 1910 edition. $15.25.

TALES AND STORIES FOR BLACK FOLKS: WRITTEN BY BLACK AUTHORS
Toni Cade Bambara, Editor
Doubleday and Co. Cloth, $3.95; Pap. $1.75.

THREE NEGRO CLASSICS
John Hope Franklin, Editor
Up From Slavery, the autobiography of Booker T. Washington; *The Souls of Black Folk*, W.E.B. DuBois' essay on the social history of blacks in America; and *The Autobiography of an Ex-Colored Man*, the phenomenon of "passing", by James Weldon Johnson. Avon Books, 1965. Pap. $1.65.

TEN TIMES BLACK: STORIES FROM THE BLACK EXPERIENCE
Julian Mayfield, Editor
Bantam Books, 1972. Pap. $.95.

A TRIBUTE FOR THE NEGRO: BEING A VINDICATION OF THE MORAL, IN-TELLECTUAL, AND RELIGIOUS CAPA-BILITIES OF THE COLOURED PORTION OF MANKIND; WITH PARTICULAR RE-FERENCE TO THE AFRICAN RACE
Wilson Armistead
Books for Libraries, 1848. $21.50.

TWENTIETH CENTURY NEGRO LITERA-TURE
Daniel Wallace Culp, Editor
A cyclopedia of thought on the vital topics relating to the American Negro by one hundred of America's greatest Negroes. Books for Libraries. Reprint of the 1902 edition. $21.50. Arno Press, $20.00.

UNCLE TOM'S CABIN, OR LIFE AMONG THE LOWLY
Harriet Beecher Stowe
442 pp. Dodd, Mead & Co., 1952. Illus. Age 16 up. $5.50.

THE VENGEANCE OF THE GODS, AND THREE OTHER STORIES OF REAL AMERICAN COLOR LINE LIFE
William Pickens
AMS Press. Reprint of the 1922 edition. $7.50. Books for Libraries, Inc., $10.00.

VIOLENCE IN THE BLACK IMAGINA-TION: ESSAYS AND DOCUMENTS
Ronald Takaki
G.P.Putnam's Sons, 1972. Cloth, $6.95; Pap. $3.25.

W.E.B. DuBOIS: THE CRISIS WRITINGS
Daniel Walden, Editor
An anthology of W.E.B. DuBois' writings, taken from the *Crisis*, the magazine he founded and edited. Fawcett World Library, 1972. Pap. $1.25.

A W.E.B. DuBOIS READER
Meyer Weinberg, Editor
Harper and Row Pubs., 1970. Cloth, $10.00; Pap. $2.95.

THE WAY OF THE NEW WORLD, *The Black Novel in America*
Addison Gayle, Jr.
A critical study of the black novel in America from mid-nineteenth century to the present. Doubleday, 1976. $3.95.

WHAT WE MUST SEE: YOUNG BLACK STORYTELLERS
Orde M. Coombs, Editor
An anthology of 16 short stories by relatively unknown and unpublished black writers. 210 pp. Dodd, Mead & Co., 1971. Age 16 up. $5.95.

WHETHER WHITE OR BLACK, A MAN
Edith Smith Davis
Books for Libraries. Illus. Reprint of the 1898 edition. $13.00.

YOU AIN'T THUH MAN YUH MAMMA WUZ
Howard E. Seals
Howard E. Seals, 1969. Pap. $.45.

MAGAZINES AND JOURNALS

THE ANGLO-AFRICAN MAGAZINE, VOLUME 1, 1859
The first years issues of a New York-based Negro magazine containing the work of leading Negro poets, spokesmen and authors, including the original "Confessions of Nat Turner." Arno, Press. Reprint of the 1859 edition. $12.50.

BLACK REVIEW: NUMBER 1
Mel Watkins, Editor
Peter Smith Publishers. Cloth, $4.50. William Morrow and Co., pap. $1.95.

BLACK REVIEW NO. 2
Mel Watkins, Editor
William Morrow and Co., 1972. Pap. $2.95.

COLOR LINE: A MONTHLY ROUNDUP OF THE FACTS OF NEGRO AMERICAN PROGRESS AND OF THE GROWTH OF AMERICAN DEMOCRACY VOL. 1 AND 2
Negro Universities Press. Reprint of the 1946 to 1947 editions. $14.50.

COLORED AMERICAN MAGAZINE
Volume 1-17. Reprint of the 1900-1909 editions. Greenwood Press, 1975. $765.00.

COMPETITOR, VOLS. 1 TO 3
Negro Universities Press. Reprint of the 1920 to 1921 editions. $145.00.

THE CRISIS: A RECORD OF THE DARKER RACES, 1910-1960

National Association for the Advancement of Colored People
Volumes from the first fifty years of the journal of the N.A.A.C.P. Arno Press, 1975. Vols. 1-16, $25.00 ea.; 17-30, $40.00 ea.; 31-50, $45.00 ea. Complete set: $1450.00.

HARLEM QUARTERLY Nos. 1 TO 4
Negro Universities Press. Reprint of the 1949 To 1950 edition. $14.00.

JOURNAL OF NEGRO HISTORY, 56 VOLS.
Association for the Study of Negro Life and History
United Publishing Corp., 1969. $775.00.

MESSENGER: WORLD'S GREATEST NEGRO MONTHLY Vol. 1 TO 10, No. 5
Negro Universities Press. Reprint of the 1917 to 1928 edition. $495.00.

NATIONAL NEGRO HEALTH NEWS: VOL. 1 TO 18
Negro Universities Press. Reprint of the 1933 to 1950 edition. $245.00.

NEGRO QUARTERLY: A REVIEW OF NEGRO LIFE AND CULTURE, VOL. 1 TO 4
Negro Universities Press. Reprint of the 1942 to 1943 edition. $19.50.

NEGRO STORY, A MAGAZINE FOR ALL AMERICANS, VOLS. 1 AND 2
Negro Universities Press. Reprint of the 1944 to 1946 editions. $49.00.

OPPORTUNITY, JOURNAL OF NEGRO LIFE: CUMULATIVE INDEX, VOLS. 1 TO 27, 1923 TO 1949
E.M. Ellis
Kraus Reprint Co., 1971. $15.00.

RACE: DEVOTED TO SOCIAL, POLITICAL, AND ECONOMIC EQUALITY VOL. 1 TO 2
Negro Universities Press. Reprint of the 1935 to 1936 edition. $15.00.

MALCOLM X

THE ASSASSINATION OF MALCOLM X
George Breitman and Herman Porter
32 pp. Pathfinder Press. $.60.

THE AUTOBIOGRAPHY OF MALCOLM X
Malcolm X and Alex Haley
Grove Press, Inc., 1965. Pap. $1.95. Below college level.

BY ANY MEANS NECESSARY
Malcolm X
Speeches and statements from Malcolm X's last year, including three speeches to his Organization of Afro-American Unity. 192 pp. Pathfinder Press, 1974. Cloth, $5.95; Pap. $1.95.

FROM THE DEAD LEVEL: MALCOLM X AND ME
H.A. Jamal
Warner Paperback Library, 1973. Pap. $1.50.

THE LAST YEAR OF MALCOLM X: THE EVOLUTION OF A REVOLUTIONARY
George Breitman
169 pp. Pathfinder Press, Inc., 1970. Cloth, $5.95; Pap. $1.95.

MALCOLM X ON AFRO-AMERICAN HISTORY
Malcolm X
80 pp. Pathfinder Press, Inc., 1972. Pap. $1.25.

MALCOLM X, THE MAN AND HIS IDEAS
George Breitman
24 pp. Pathfinder Press, Inc., Pap. $0.50.

MALCOM X SPEAKS: SELECTED SPEECHES AND STATEMENTS
George Breitman, Editor
242 pp. Photos. Pathfinder Press. Cloth, 6.95. Grove Press, Inc., pap. $1.65.

MALCOLM X TALKS TO YOUNG PEOPLE
Malcolm X
32 pp. Pathfinder Press. $.35.

MYTHS ABOUT MALCOLM X: TWO VIEWS
Rev. Albert Cleage and George Breitman
32 pp. Pathfinder Press. Pap. $.50.

MIGRATION

A BIBLIOGRAPHY OF NEGRO MIGRATION
Frank Alexander Ross
251 pp. Burt Franklin Pubs., 1969. Reprint of the 1934 edition. $17.50.

BLACK AMERICA, *Geographic Perspectives*
Robert T. Ernst and Lawrence Hugg, Editors
A collection and assessment of works on the geographical and demographic patterns of Black America. Illus. Doubleday, 1975. $5.95.

BLACK MIGRATION, MOVEMENT NORTH, 1900-1920
Florette Henri
A study which charts the demographic, economic, political, social, and psychological changes wrought by black migration between the years 1900-1920. Doubleday, 1975. $3.95.

CENTURY OF NEGRO MIGRATION
Carter Godwin Woodson
AMS Press, Inc. Reprint of the 1918 edition. $8.00.

THE NEGRO IMMIGRANT: HIS BACKGROUND, CHARACTERISTICS AND SOCIAL ADJUSTMENT, 1899-1937
Ira De A. Reid
An analysis of the Carribean Negro, this book deals with the characteristics and social adjustment of the 100,000 foreign-born Negroes in the United States in the late 1930's. Arno Press. Reprint of the 1939 edition. $7.50.

THE NEGRO MIGRANT IN PITTSBURGH: A STUDY IN SOCIAL ECONOMICS
Abraham Epstein
The Negro migration during the World War I industrial boom. Arno Press. Reprint of the 1918 edition. $4.50.

NEGRO MIGRATION: CHANGES IN RURAL ORGANIZATION AND POPULATION OF THE COTTON BELT
Thomas Jackson Woofter
195 pp. Greenwood Press; AMS Press, Inc. Reprint of the 1920 edition. Illus. $7.50.

NEGRO MIGRATION DURING THE WAR
Emmett J. Scott
A study of the Negro migrations of World War I that led to today's ghettos in the Northern urban centers. Arno Press. Reprint of the 1920 edition. $6.00.

NEGRO MIGRATION IN 1916 TO 1917
United States Department of Labor-Division of Negro Economics
158 pp. Negro Universities Press. Reprint of the 1919 edition. $9.75.

NEGRO MIGRATION TO LOS ANGELES, 1930-1950
Lawrence B. de Graaf
Dissertation. R & E Research Associates, 1974. Reprint of the 1962 paper. $10.00.

THE NEGRO PEASANT TURNS CITY-WARD
Louise Venable Kennedy
AMS Press, Inc. Reprint of the 1930 edition. $9.00.

NEGRO POPULATION, 1790 TO 1915
United States Bureau of the Census
Kraus Reprint Co. Reprint of the 1918 edition. $37.50.

NEGRO POPULATION IN THE UNITED STATES, 1790-1915
John Cummings
An important statistical study of the growth and mobility of the Negro population over 125 years. Arno Press, 1968. Reprint of the 1918 edition. $23.50.

NEGROES IN THE UNITED STATES, 1920-32
Charles Hall
Population movements in the U.S. during the Prohibition era. Arno Press. Reprint of the 1935 edition. $25.00.

NEGROES IN THE UNITED STATES
United States Bureau of the Census
333 pp. Negro Universities Press. Reprint of the 1904 edition. $22.00.

SOME ASPECTS OF THE MIGRATION OF THE NEGRO TO THE SAN FRANCISCO BAY AREA SINCE 1940
Edward E. France
Dissertation. R & E Research Associates. Reprint of the 1962 paper. Pap. $9.00.

MILITARY

ARMY LIFE IN A BLACK REGIMENT
Thomas W. Higginson
A first-hand account of Negro soldiering during the Civil War by the white commanding officer of the first all-black, all ex-slave regiment in the Union Army. 296 pp. Corner House Publishers, 1974. $9.00.

BLACK AMERICANS AND THE WHITE MAN'S BURDEN, 1898-1903
William B. Gatewood, Jr.
Includes letters of black soldiers, articles in black newspapers, and other materials of the period to show how blacks dealt with the dilemmas posed by the Spanish-American War. 350 pp. University of Illinois Press. $12.95.

BLACK ARMED FORCES OFFICERS
Jesse J. Johnson
Male and female black officers in the U.S., with biographical notes on many. 170 pp. Jesse J. Johnson. $8.95.

THE BLACK BRIGADE OF CINCINNATI
Peter Clark
Blacks who aided the Union war effort. Arno Press. Reprint of the 1864 edition. $4.50.

BLACK DEFENDERS OF AMERICA: 1775-1973: A REFERENCE AND PICTORIAL HISTORY
Robert E. Greene
A history of black participation in America's military--the army, navy, marines and air force--contributions spanning two centuries. 416 pp. Johnson Publishing Co., Chicago, 1974. Illus. $17.95.

THE BLACK INFANTRY IN THE WEST, 1869-1891
Arlen L. Fowler
A study of the 24th and 25th U.S. Infantry Regiments. 167 pp. Greenwood Press, 1971. Illus. $10.75.

BLACK MILITARY EXPERIENCE IN THE AMERICAN WEST
John M. Carroll, Editor
Liveright Publishing Corp., 1974. Cloth, $17.50; Pap. $3.95.

THE BLACK MUTINY: THE REVOLT ON THE SCHOONER AMISTAD
William A. Owens
Peter Smith Publishers. $5.50.

THE BLACK PHALANX: A HISTORY OF THE NEGRO SOLDIERS OF THE UNITED STATES IN THE WARS OF 1775-1812, 1861-1865
Joseph T. Wilson
Arno Press. Reprint of the 1890 edition. $15.50.

THE BLACK PRESENCE IN THE ERA OF THE REVOLUTION

Sidney Kaplan
New York Graphic Society, 1973. $17.50.

*BLACK SOLDIER
John Clarke
Novel about a Northern Negro who is drafted and the discrimination he encounters. Doubleday & Co., 1968. Illus. Ages 12-14. $3.95.

THE BLACK SOLDIER
Jay David and Elaine Crane
The saga of America's black soldiers from the Revolution to Vietnam. William Morrow & Co., 1971. Cloth, $6.95; Pap. $2.95.

THE BLACK SOLDIER
Jesse J. Johnson
Describes American utilization of the Negro from 1619-1815 for military defense. 100 pp. Jesse J. Johnson. Cloth, $3.95; Pap. $1.50; Pocketbook $1.10.

THE BLACK SOLDIER AND OFFICER IN THE UNITED STATES ARMY, 1891-1917
Marvin E. Fletcher
The author examines years in which blacks found themselves affected by growing institutionalization of prejudice and separation of the races in society at large, and the mirroring of that division in the military. 224 pp. University of Missouri Press, 1974. $11.00.

BLACKS AND THE MILITARY IN AMERICAN HISTORY: A NEW PERSPECTIVE
Jack Foner
160 pp. Praeger Publishers, 1973. Cloth, $7.50; Pap. $2.95.

BLACKS IN AMERICA'S WARS: *The Shift In Attitudes From The Revolutionary War To Vietnam*
Robert W. Mullen
The history of blacks in the U.S. military service. 96 pp. Pathfinder Press, 1974. Illus. Cloth, $5.00; Pap. $1.45.

THE BROWNSVILLE AFFAIR: NATIONAL CRISIS AND BLACK REACTION
Ann J. Lane
The U.S. Army finally clears the records of 167 soldiers who were dishonorably discharged for a frontier shooting incident in Brownsville, Texas, 1906, after 66 years. This is the history of that event. Kennikat Press, 1971. $10.95; Pap. $3.95.

THE BUFFALO SOLDIERS: A NARRATIVE OF THE NEGRO CAVALRY IN THE WEST
William H. Leckie
Negro soldiers who remained in the U.S. Army became the Ninth and Tenth Cavalry Regiments, controlling Indians on the Great Plains. 304 pp. University of Oklahoma Press, 1975. Illus. Pap. $2.95.

CAMP-FIRES OF THE AFRO-AMERICAN: OR, THE COLORED MAN AS A PATRIOT, SOLDIER, SAILOR AND HERO, IN THE CAUSE OF FREE AMERICA
James M. Guthrie
710 pp. Johnson Reprint. Reprint of the 1899 edition. Illus. $38.50.

CAPTAIN BLACKMAN
John A. Williams
Novel about a black soldier in the American Army through each war, from revolutionary times to Vietnam. Doubleday & Co., 1975. $6.95.

THE COLORED CADET AT WEST POINT
Henry Ossian Flipper
The first black man to graduate from the U.S. Military Academy tells of his training during the 1870's. Arno Press. Reprint of the 1878 edition. $8.00.

THE COLORED PATRIOTS OF THE AMERICAN REVOLUTION, WITH SKETCHES OF SEVERAL DISTINGUISHED COLORED PERSONS: TO WHICH IS ADDED A BRIEF SURVEY OF THE CONDITION AND PROSPECTS OF COLORED AMERICANS
William C. Nell
The story of the forgotten black heroes who helped the colonies secure their independence from Britain. Arno Press. Reprint of the 1855 edition. $12.00.

THE COLORED REGULARS IN THE UNITED STATES ARMY
T.G. Steward
Negro military accomplishments on the frontier and during the Spanish-American War. Arno Press. Reprint of the 1904 edition. $10.50.

THE CONDITIONS, ELEVATION, EMIGRATION, AND DESTINY OF THE COLORED PEOPLE OF THE UNITED STATES: POLITICALLY CONSIDERED
Martin Robinson Delany

The author was the first Negro to hold the rank of field officer in the Civil War. Arno Press. Reprint of the 1852 edition. $6.50.

THE CONFEDERATE NEGRO: VIRGINIA'S CRAFTSMEN AND MILITARY LABORERS, 1861 TO 1865
James Brewer
212 pp. Duke University Press, 1969. $7.50.

CONNECTICUT'S BLACK SOLDIERS 1775-1783
David O. White
The role of the black in the military and the colonies' revolutionary ideology about freedom for all. Pequot Press, 1973. 71 pp. Illus. Pap. $2.50.

EBONY BRASS
Jesse J. Johnson
A group portrait of the daily working relations between white and Negro officers and men in the Armed Forces. 160 pp. Jesse J. Johnson. Cloth, $6.95; Pap. $1.95; Pocketbook $1.00.

*GIVE ME LIBERTY: BLACK VALOR IN THE AMERICAN REVOLUTION
Thomas Fleming
Scholastic Book Service, 1974. Pap. $1.65. Ages 12 to 15.

HISTORY OF THE AMERICAN NEGRO IN THE GREAT WORLD WAR: HIS SPLENDID RECORD IN THE BATTLE ZONES OF EUROPE INCLUDING A RESUME OF HIS PAST SERVICES TO HIS COUNTRY
William Allison Sweeney
307 pp. Negro Universities Press. Reprint of the 1919 edition. Illus. $19.00. Johnson Reprint, $16.75.

HISTORY OF NEGRO SOLDIERS IN THE SPANISH-AMERICAN WAR
Edward Augustus Johnson
147 pp. Johnson Reprint Corporation. Reprint of the 1899 edition. $9.75.

A HISTORY OF THE NEGRO TROOPS IN THE WAR OF REBELLION, 1861-1865, PRECEDED BY A REVIEW OF THE MILITARY SERVICES OF NEGROES IN ANCIENT AND MODERN TIMES
G.W. Williams
Kraus Reprint Co. Reprint if the 1888 edition. $24.00.

MISSING PAGES IN AMERICAN HISTORY: REVEALING THE SERVICES OF NEGROES IN THE EARLY WARS IN THE UNITED STATES OF AMERICA, 1641 TO 1815
Laura Eliza Wilkes
AMS Press, 1972. Reprint of the 1919 edition. $7.50.

THE NEGRO AND THE WAR
Earl Brown and George Leighton
AMS Press, Inc. Reprint of the 1942 edition. $8.50.

THE NEGRO, DEMOCRACY, AND THE WAR
Walter W. Delsarte
135 pp. Negro Universities Press. Reprint of the 1919 edition. $8.25.

THE NEGRO IN THE AMERICAN REBELLION: HIS HEROISM AND HIS FIDELITY
William Wells Brown
380 pp. Johnson Reprint Corp. Reprint of the 1867 edition. $16.75. Kraus Reprint Co., $16.00.

THE NEGRO IN THE AMERICAN REBELLION: HIS HEROISM AND HIS FIDELITY
William Wells Brown
Books for Libraries. Reprint of the 1880 edition. $12.75.

THE NEGRO IN WORLD WAR II
John D. Silvera
A picture history of the part black men played in World War II. Arno Press. Reprint of the 1947 edition. $14.00.

NEGRO MEDAL OF HONOR MEN, REVISED EDITION
Irvin H. Lee
The personal lives and heroic actions under fire of all the Negro medal of honor winners in the American wars: Civil War, Indian battles, Spanish-American War, both World Wars, Korea, and Viet Nam. 152 pp. Dodd, Mead & Co., 1968. Illus. Age 16 up. $4.50.

THE NEGRO MILITIA AND RECONSTRUCTION
Otis Singletary
University of Texas Press, 1971. $8.50.

THE NEGRO SOLDIER: A SELECT COM-PILATION
Contents: *The Loyalty and Devotion of Colored Americans in the Revolution and War of 1812,* by William Lloyd Garrison; *Historical Notes on the Employment of Negroes in the American Army of the Revolution,* by George Henry Moore; and *Missing Pages in American History, Revealing the Service of Negroes in the Early Wars in the United States of America, 1641-1815,* by Laura Eliza Wilkes. 24, 24, 91 pp. Greenwood Press. $8.25.

NEGRO SOLDIERS IN WORLD WAR I: THE HUMAN SIDE
Charles Halston Williams
AMS Press. Reprint of the 1923 edition. $12.50.

NEGRO SOLDIERS AND OTHER POEMS
Roscoe C. Jamison
AMS Press, Inc. Reprint of the 1918 edition. $7.50.

THE NEGRO VANGUARD
Richard Bardolph
388 pp. Greenwood Press, 1974. Reprint of the 1959 edition. $16.75.

NEGRO AT WORK DURING THE WORLD WAR AND DURING RECONSTRUCTION
United States Department of Labor-Division of Negro Economics
144 pp. Negro Universities Press. Reprint of the 1921 edition. Illus. $10.50.

A PICTORIAL HISTORY OF BLACK SERVICEMEN
Jesse J. Johnson
Afro-Americans in the Air Force, Army, Navy, and Marines, as well as the WAFS, WACs, WAVEs, and SPARs. 300 photos. Jesse J. Johnson. $8.95.

A PICTORIAL HISTORY OF THE BLACK SOLDIERS IN THE UNITED STATES IN PEACE AND WAR
Jesse J. Johnson
Black service from the colonial era to Vietnam. 130 pp. Jesse J. Johnson. $8.95. Pap. $3.00.

SABLE ARM: NEGRO TROOPS IN THE UNION ARMY, 1861 TO 1865
Dudley T. Cornish
W.W.Norton and Co., 1966. Pap. $1.95.

SERVICES OF COLORED AMERICANS IN THE WARS OF 1776 AND 1812

William Cooper Nell
AMS Press, Inc. Reprint of the 1851 edition. $10.00.

"SMOKED YANKEES" AND THE STRUGGLE FOR EMPIRE: LETTERS FROM NEGRO SOLDIERS, 1898 TO 1902
Willard B. Gatewood, Jr.
329 pp. University of Illinois Press, 1971. Illus. $9.50.

*THE STORMING OF FORT WAGNER: BLACK VALOR IN THE CIVIL WAR
Irving Werstein
Scholastic Book Service, 1974. Pap. $1.65. Ages 12 to 15.

THE UNKNOWN SOLDIERS
Arthur E. Barbeau and Florette Henri
Black-American troops in World War I. It discloses racism and the black soldier's lot in segregated U.S. training camps in France and at home. 297 pp. Illus. Temple University Press, 1974. $12.50.

MUSIC

AFRO-AMERICAN FOLKSONGS: A STUDY IN RACIAL AND NATIONAL MUSIC
Henry Edward Krehbiel
Includes an analysis of the idioms of music; an examination of the songs; and discussion of the language, customs, dances, and background relative to music. 176 pp. Frederick Ungar Publishing Co., 1962. $2.95.

AMERICAN NEGRO FOLKSONGS
Newman I. White
Gale Research. Reprint of the 1928 edition. $10.00.

AMERICAN NEGRO SONGS AND SPIRITUALS
J.W. Work, Editor
Spirituals, blues, and hollers. Words and music to over 200 songs. 259 pp. Crown Publishers, 1940. $5.00.

BEALE STREET: WHERE THE BLUES BEGAN
George W. Lee
McGrath Publishing Co., 1969. Reprint of the 1934 edition. $12.00.

*BIG STAR FALLIN' MAMA: FIVE WOMEN IN BLACK MUSIC
Hettie Jones
152 pp. Viking Press, 1974. Illus. $6.95. Ages 12 up.

BLACK AMERICAN MUSIC: PAST AND PRESENT
Hildred Roach
A survey of Afro-American composers and their music from colonial times to the present day. Crescendo Publishing Co. Cloth, $9.50; Pap. $5.00.

BLACK MAMMY: SONG OF THE SUNNY SOUTH, IN THREE CANTOS AND "MY VILLAGE HOME"
William Lightfoot Visscher
Books for Libraries, Inc. Reprint of the 1885 edition. $8.75.

BLACK MUSIC
Le Roi Jones
Today's young jazz musicians: Ornette Coleman, John Coltrane, Sonny Rollins, and more. William Morrow & Co., 1967. Cloth, $7.95; Pap. $1.95.

BLACK MUSIC, *Four Lives*
A.B. Spellman
A portrait of four jazz musicians--Cecil Taylor, Ornette Coleman, Herbie Nichols, and Jackie McLean--tells what it means to be a black artist in America today. Told in the musicians' own words, the reader is taken into the jazz culture: the drug scene, the fight for work and recognition, and the effects of racism. Originally titled *Four Lives in the Bebop Business.* Schocken Books, 1975. Pap. $1.95.

BLACK MUSIC IN AMERICA
John Rublowsky
Basic Books, 1971. $7.95. Below college level.

BLACK MUSIC IN OUR CULTURE: CURRICULAR IDEAS ON THE SUBJECTS, MATERIALS, AND PROBLEMS
Dominique-Rene De Lerma
Kent State University Press.

BLACK MUSIC OF TWO WORLDS
John Storm Roberts
296 pp. Praeger Pubs., 1972. Illus. $10.00.

BLACK NATIONALISM AND THE REVOLUTION IN MUSIC
Frank Kofsky

Selected discography of John Coltrane's works. 280 pp. Pathfinder Press, 1970. Cloth, $7.95; Pap. $2.95.

BLUES AND GOSPEL RECORDS, 1902 TO 1942
John Godrich
International Pubns. Service, 1969. $22.50.

BLUES PEOPLE: NEGRO MUSIC IN WHITE AMERICA
Le Roi Jones
The social and musical history of the American Negro. William Morrow & Co., 1963. Cloth, $7.95; Pap. $1.95.

ECHOES OF AFRICA IN FOLK SONGS OF THE AMERICAS
Beatrice Landeck
David McKay, 1969. $7.95. Ages 16 and up.

FAMOUS NEGRO MUSIC MAKERS
Langston Hughes
Leadbelly, Ethel Waters, Louis Armstrong, and Mahalia Jackson, among others. 179 pp. Dodd, Mead & Co., 1955. Illus. Age 16 up. $3.95.

FOLK SONG OF THE AMERICAN NEGRO
John Wesley Work
131 pp. Negro Universities Press. Reprint of the 1915 edition. Illus. $8.50. Music.

JAZZMEN
Frederic Ramsey and Charles Smith, Editors
Scholarly Press. Reprint if the 1939 edition. $19.50.

LIVING COUNTRY BLUES
Harry Oster
A book on Negro blues gives the setting, history, definition, themes and functions, and poetry of this unique American art form. 230 songs. 464 pp. Gale Research Co., 1969. Illus. $15.00.

THE MUSIC OF BLACK AMERICANS
Eileen Southern
Biographical sketches, bibliographical guide, from colonial times to the present. 552 pp. W.W. Norton & Co., 1975. Illus. Cloth, $10.00; Pap. $4.45.

MUSIC: BLACK, WHITE AND BLUE
Ortiz Walton
The author claims that had there been no black music, there would be no popular American

music. William Morrow & Co., 1972. Illus. Cloth, $6.95; Pap. $2.45.

NEGRO AUTHORS AND COMPOSERS OF THE UNITED STATES
William Christopher Handy
AMS Press. Reprint of the 1938 edition. $15.00.

NEGRO FOLK MUSIC, UNITED STATES OF AMERICA
Harold Courlander
Columbia University Press, 1963. Cloth, $12.50; Pap. $3.95.

THE NEGRO AND HIS MUSIC AND NEGRO ART, PAST AND PRESENT
Alain Locke
Black contributions to music and art. Arno Press. Reprint of the 1936 edition. $8.00.

NEGRO AND HIS SONGS: A STUDY OF TYPICAL NEGRO SONGS IN THE SOUTH
Howard Odum and Guy Johnson
306 pp. Negro Universities Press. Reprint of the 1925 edition. $13.00.

THE NEGRO IN MUSIC AND ART
Patterson
United Publishing Corp. $13.88.

NEGRO MUSIC JOURNAL: DEVOTED TO THE EDUCATIONAL INTEREST OF THE NEGRO IN MUSIC, VOL. 1 AND 2
Negro Music Journal
Negro Universities Press. Reprint of the 1902 to 1903 editions. $30.00.

NEGRO MUSICIANS AND THEIR MUSIC
Maud Cuney-Hare
Da Capo Press, 1974. $22.50.

THE NEGRO SINGS A NEW HEAVEN
Mary Allen Grissom
A collection of 45 authentic Negro spirituals, transcribed exactly as they were found and sung at church meetings in Kentucky. 101 pp. Dover Publications, 1969. Pap. $2.00.

NEGRO SLAVE SONGS IN THE UNITED STATES
Miles Mark Fisher
Russell and Russell. Reprint of the 1953 edition. $13.00. Citadel Press, pap. $2.45.

NEGRO SONGS FROM ALABAMA
Harold Courlander
75 transcriptions of authentic field recordings.

Music Sales Corporation, 1975. $3.95.

NEGRO SPIRITUALS
Harry T. Burliegh
Two volumes in one. AMS Press. Reprint of the 1917-1922 edition. $45.00.

NEGRO WORKADAY SONGS
Howard Odum and Guy Johnson
278 pp. Negro Universities Press. Reprint of the 1926 edition. Illus. Music. $12.50.

OLD PLANTATION HYMNS: A COLLECTION OF HITHERTO UNPUBLISHED MELODIES OF THE SLAVE AND THE FREED MAN
William Eleazar Barton
AMS Press. Reprint of the 1899 edition. $7.50.

ON THE TRAIL OF NEGRO FOLKSONGS
Dorothy Scarborough
Gale Research. Reprint of the 1925 edition. $8.50.

POETRY OF THE BLUES
Samuel Charters
Explores the poetry of black Americans through the music and lyrics of the blues. Avon Books. Pap. $1.25.

READINGS IN BLACK AMERICAN MUSIC
Eileen Southern, Editor
Selection of authentic, contemporary documents illustrating the history of black American music from the seventeenth century to the present. 302 pp. W.W. Norton & Co., 1975. Cloth, $12.00; Pap. $3.95.

RELIGIOUS FOLK-SONGS OF THE NEGRO
Robert Dett, Editor
AMS Press, Inc. Reprint of the 1927 edition. $12.50.

SEVENTY NEGRO SPIRITUALS
William Arms Fisher, Editor
AMS Press, Inc. Reprint of the 1926 edition. $18.50.

*SINGERS OF THE BLUES
Frank Surge
The life-stories of 17 great blues artists, including Ma Rainey, Bessie Smith, Leadbelly, Billie Holiday, Sonny Terry and Brownie McGhee. 64 pp. Lerner Publications. Ages 11-16. $3.95.

SINGING BLACK
  Homer Rodeheaver
AMS Press, Inc. Reprint of the 1936 edition.
$5.00.

SLAVE SONGS OF THE UNITED STATES
  William F. Allen, et al, Editors
Books for Libraries, Inc. Reprint of the 1867
edition. Cloth, $8.75. Peter Smith Publishers,
pap. $3.50.

**THE SOCIAL IMPLICATIONS OF EARLY
NEGRO MUSIC IN THE UNITED STATES**
  Bernard Katz, Editor
A collection of articles, largely from the 19th
century, evaluating music. 150 songs and spirit-
uals. Arno Press, 1968. Cloth, $7.50; Pap.
$2.45.

**SOME CURRENT FOLKSONGS OF THE
NEGRO**
  Will H. Thomas
16 pp. Southern Methodist University Press.
Reprint of the 1912 edition. Pap. $1.00.

**SOUL MUSIC, BLACK AND WHITE: THE
INFLUENCE OF BLACK MUSIC ON THE
CHURCHES**
  Johannes Riedel
Augsburg Publishing House, 1974. Pap. $3.50.

SOUND OF SOUL
  Phyl Garland
Henry Regnery Co., 1969. Pap. $2.95.

**SOURCEBOOK OF AFRICAN AND AFRO-
AMERICAN MATERIALS FOR MUSIC
EDUCATORS**
  James A. Standifer and Barbara Reeder
Provides lists of books, articles, recordings, and
other materials dealing with African and Afro-
American music traditions. 147 pp. Music Edu-
cators National Conference, 1972. $3.50.

THE STORY OF THE BLUES
  Paul Oliver
From slavery to the modern city ghetto. 176 pp.
Chilton Book Co., 1969. Illus. Cloth, $12.50;
Pap. $4.95.

THE TREASURY OF NEGRO SPIRITUALS
  Henry A. Chambers, Editor
30 of the best-known spirituals and six modern
compositions. Emerson Books, 1963. $7.50.

***UNCLE REMUS: HIS SONGS AND HIS
SAYINGS**
  Joel C. Harris
Hawthorn Books, 1921. $4.95. Ages 6 to 12.

**WAKE UP DEAD MAN: AFRO-AMERICAN
WORKSONGS FROM TEXAS PRISONS**
  Bruce Jackson
326 pp. Harvard University Press, 1972. Illus.
65 songs. Cloth, $14.95; Pap. $4.95.

NATIONALISM

**AMERICAN NEGRO: WHAT HE WAS,
WHAT HE IS, AND WHAT HE MAY BE-
COME**
  William Hannibal Thomas
440 pp. Negro Universities Press. Reprint of the
1901 edition. $14.75.

**BLACK AMERICAN AND THE WORLD
REVOLUTION**
  Claude M. Lightfoot
Five speeches, 1966-1970, showing the growing
revolutionary character of the black liberation
struggle and its relationship to the worldwide
revolutionary process. New Outlook Pubs.
$.90.

THE BLACK DILEMMA
  John Herbers
John Day Publishing Co., 1972. Cloth, $5.95;
Pap. $1.95.

BLACK FORTUNE
  Eldred Kurtz Means
Books for Libraries, Inc., 1972. Reprint of the
1931 edition. $13.50.

BLACK HOMELAND/BLACK DIASPORA:
Cross-Currents of the African Relationship
  Jacob Drachler, Editor
Explores the question of black Zionism.
Kennikat Press, 1975. $12.00.

BLACK IS
  T. Brown, Jr.
Grove Press, Inc., 1969. Pap. $1.25.

**BLACK LIBERATION AND SOCIAL-
ISM: AN ANTHOLOGY**
  Tony Thomas, Editor
Written by young black militants, these essays
probe the relationship between Marxism and
black nationalism, the need for an independent
black political party, and the importance of the

black liberation movement to a socialist re-volution in the U.S. Also included are a socialist program and strategy for ending racial op-pression, and a discussion of Black women's liberation. 256 pp. Pathfinder Press, 1974. Cloth, $10.00; Pap. $2.95.

BLACK MAJORITY
    Peter H. Wood
Alfred A. Knopf, Inc., 1974. $10.00.

THE BLACK MAN, HIS ANTECEDENTS, HIS GENIUS, AND HIS ACHIEVEMENTS
    William Wells Brown
Books for Libraries, Inc. Reprint of the 1865 edition. $10.00.

BLACK NATIONALISM IN AMERICA
    John H. Bracey, et al, Editors
634 pp. Bobbs-Merrill Co., 1970. Cloth, $8.50; Pap. $3.60.

BLACK NATIONALISM: THE SEARCH FOR AN IDENTITY
    E.U. Essien-Udom
University of Chicago Press, 1962. Cloth, $10.00; Pap. $3.45.

THE BLACK POSITION
    Gwendolyn Brooks, Editor
Broadside Press Pubns. Vol. 1. 1971. $1.00; Vol.2. 1972. $1.50; Vol.3. 1973. $3.00.

*BLACK PRIDE: A PEOPLE'S STRUGGLE
    J.Harris and J.W.Hobson
Bantam Books, 1974. Pap. $.75. Below college level.

BLACK PROTEST THOUGHT IN THE TWENTIETH CENTURY
    August Meier, et al
An updated second edition, this book focuses on the ideologies of black power, people's power, and revolutionary nationalism, along with 23 new documents. 712 pp. Bobbs-Merrill Co., 1971. Cloth, $8.50; Pap. $3.95.

THE CASE FOR BLACK REPARATIONS
    Boris Bittker
Random House, Inc., 1973. Cloth, $7.95; Pap. $1.95.

IN DEFENSE OF BLACK NATION-ALISM: AN ANSWER TO THE COM-MUNIST PARTY AND TME YOUNG WORKERS LIBERATION LEAGUE
    Tony Thomas

32 pp. Pathfinder Press, 1971. Pap. $.60.

THE DIVISIBLE REPUBLIC
    Matthew Holden, Jr.
Abelard, 1973. $12.00.

FOR BLACK PEOPLE
    D.L.Lee
Third World Press, 1968. Pap. $.50.

THE FUTURE OF THE AMERICAN NEGRO
    Booker T. Washington
244 pp. Metro Books, Inc., 1969. Reprint of the 1899 edition. $10.00.

THE FUTURE OF THE NEGRO: SOME CHAPTERS IN THE DEVELOPMENT OF A RACE
    Frederick Guggisberg and A.G. Fraser
152 pp. Negro Universities Press. Reprint of the 1919 edition. $8.50.

GOODBYE TO UNCLE TOM
    J.C. Furnas
The past, present and possible future of the American Negro. William Morrow & Co., 1964. $2.95.

THE IDEOLOGICAL ORIGINS OF BLACK NATIONALISM
    Sterling Stuckey
Explores the 19th-century black-American dream of an independent nation. Beacon Press, 1974. Cloth, $8.95; Pap. $3.95.

LEON TROTSKY ON BLACK NATIONAL-ISM AND SELF-DETERMINATION
    Leon Trotsky
68 pp. Pathfinder Press, Inc. Pap. $1.05.

LIGHT AHEAD FOR THE NEGRO
    Edward Augustus Johnson
AMS Press, Inc. Reprint of the 1904 edition. $6.00.

THE MOST CONTROVERSIAL AMERICAN AND WHY THE NEGRO LACKS UNITY
    Don Ben Owens, Jr.
Commonsense Pubns., 1963. Pap. $5.95.

THE NEGRO POTENTIAL
    Eli Ginzberg
Columbia University Press, 1956. Pap. $1.65.

THE NEGRO'S STRUGGLE FOR SUR-VIVAL
    Samuel J. Holmes

The biological trend of the American Negro. Kennikat Press, 1966. Reprint of the 1937 edition. $11.00.

A NEW DEAL FOR BLACKS: SUGGESTION FOR SALVATION
Ensen X. Douglas (pseud.)
The author suggests that white America support blacks in setting up a new nation outside America in which blacks can preserve their dignity, values, and culture. Exposition Press, 1974. $4.50.

THE NEW NEGRO
Mathew Ahmann
Biblo and Tanner Booksellers and Pubs., 1969. Reprint of the 1961 edition. $7.50.

NEW NEGRO: AN INTERPRETATION
Alan LeRoy Locke, Editor
446 pp. Johnson Reprint, 1968. Reprint of the 1925 edition. $12.50.

THE NEW NEGRO, HIS POLITICAL, CIVIL, AND MENTAL STATUS, AND RELATED ESSAYS
William Pickens
AMS Press, Inc. Reprint of the 1916 edition. $10.00.

THE NEW WORLD OF NEGRO AMERICANS
Harold R. Issacs
Based on interviews with Negroes. 384 pp. Viking Press, 1963. Pap. $1.65.

THE OMNI-AMERICANS
Albert Murray
The author argues against separatism or cultural nationalism. Avon Books. Pap. $1.50.

ON BLACK SEPARATISM
Robert S. Browne and Robert Vernon
32 pp. Pathfinder Press. Pap. $.60.

ONE CONTINUAL CRY: WALKER'S APPEAL TO THE COLORED CITIZENS OF THE WORLD, 1829 AMERICAN INSTITUTE FOR MARXIST STUDIES
The full text of the earliest published expression of militancy by an American Negro, with a long essay on Walker's life and time by H. Aptheker. Cloth, $4.00 Pap. $2.95. American Institute for Marxist Studies.

PROGRESS OF A RACE, OR, THE REMARKABLE ADVANCEMENT OF THE

AMERICAN NEGRO
Henry F. Kletzing and William Henry Crogman
663 pp. Johnson Reprint. Reprint of the 1897 edition. Illus. $34.75.

PROGRESS OF A RACE: OR, THE REMARKABLE ADVANCEMENT OF THE AMERICAN NEGRO FROM THE BONDAGE OF SLAVERY, IGNORANCE, AND POVERTY TO THE FREEDOM OF CITIZENSHIP, INTELLIGENCE, AFFLUENCE, HONOR, AND TRUST
J.L. Nichols and William H. Crogman
A history of black-Americans, with particular stress on the efforts of black men and women to better their lives economically and culturally. Arno Press, 1969. Reprint of the 1920 edition. $16.50.

THE REDISCOVERY OF BLACK NATIONALISM
Theodore Draper
Traces black nationalism throughout American history. 224 pp. Viking Press, 1970. Cloth, $5.95; Pap. $2.45.

THE RISING SON: THE ANTECEDENTS AND ADVANCEMENT OF THE COLORED RACE
William Wells Brown
Books for Libraries, Inc. Reprint of the 1874. edition. $18.25.

THE ROOTS OF BLACK NATIONALISM
Rodney Carlisle
Examines black nationalism as a body of political views with a continuous history. Kennikat Press, 1975. $11.50.

STRATEGY FOR A BLACK AGENDA: A CRITIQUE OF NEW THEORIES OF LIBERATION IN THE UNITED STATES AND AFRICA
Henry Winston
The chairman of the Communist Party, U.S.A. analyzes current ideological variants such as neo-Pan-Africanism, black nationalism and Maoism. 324 pp. International Publishers, 1973. Cloth, $7.50; Pap. $2.50.

A TRANSITIONAL PROGRAM FOR BLACK LIBERATION 1972
Socialist Workers Party
24 pp. Pathfinder Press, Inc., 1972. Pap. $.35.

THE UNITED NEGRO: HIS PROBLEMS AND HIS PROGRESS
Negro Young People's Christian and Educational Congress Atlanta 1902
600 pp. Negro Universities Press. Reprint of the 1902 edition. $27.75.

POETRY

AFRO-AMERICAN LITERATURE: POETRY
William Adams, et al, Editors
Houghton Mifflin Co., 1970. Pap. $2.64.

AMERICA'S FIRST NEGRO POET: THE COMPLETE WORKS OF JUPITER HAMMON OF LONG ISLAND
Jupiter Hammon
Kennikat Press, 1969. $10.00.

AMERICAN NEGRO POETRY
Arna Bontemps, Editor
56 black American poets, from Paul Laurence Dunbar to Nikki Giovanni. Hill & Wang, 1963. $2.65.

AN ANTHOLOGY OF VERSE BY AMERICAN NEGROES
Newman White and Walter Jackson
Folcroft Library Editions, 1924. $6.75.

BID THE VASSAL SOAR
M.A. Richmond
Interpretive essays on the life and poetry of Phyllis Wheatley and George Moses Horton, two black American poets. 234 pp. Howard University Press, 1974. $8.95.

BLACK AMERICAN LITERATURE: POETRY
D.T.Turner
Charles E. Merrill Publishing Co., 1969. Pap. $2.95.

BLACK AMERICAN POETRY SINCE 1944: A PRELIMINARY CHECK LIST
Frank Deodene and William French
Chatham Bookseller, 1971. Pap. $3.50.

BLACK POETRY IN AMERICA: TWO ESSAYS IN HISTORICAL INTERPRETATION
Blyden Jackson and Louis D. Rubin, Jr.
A look at black-American writing from its beginning to the present. Louisiana State University Press, 1974. $5.95.

BLACK POETS OF THE UNITED STATES: FROM PAUL LAWRENCE DUNBAR TO LANGSTON HUGHTS
Jean Wagner
584 pp. University of Illinois Press, 1973. Cloth, $15.00; Pap. $5.50.

BLACKSPIRITS: A FESTIVAL OF NEW BLACK POETS IN AMERICA
Woodie King, Editor
A collection of contemporary black-American poetry by 30 authors. Vintage Press. $1.95.

BONDAGE, FREEDOM AND BEYOND: - THE PROSE OF BLACK AMERICANS
Addison Gayle, Jr., Editor
Doubleday and Co., 1971. Cloth, $3.95; Pap. $1.75.

THE BOOK OF AMERICAN NEGRO POETRY: *An Anthology*
James Weldon Johnson
300 pp. Harcourt Brace Jovanovich, Inc. Cloth, $6.95; Pap. $1.45.

THE BROWN THRUSH: ANTHOLOGY OF VERSE BY NEGRO STUDENTS
Lillian W. Voorhees, and Robert W. O'Brien, Editors
Books for Libraries, Inc., 1973. Reprint of the 1932 edition. $10.50.

COLOR
Countee Cullen
The poetry of Afro-American culture in the 1920's. Arno Press, 1970. Reprint of the 1925 edition. $4.50.

THE COMPLETE POEMS OF PAUL LAURENCE DUNBAR
Paul Laurence Dunbar
The verse of an outstanding American Negro poet. 479 pp. Dodd, Mead & Co., 1913. Age 16 up. $5.95.

THE CONCEPT OF NEGRITUDE IN THE POETRY OF LEOPOLD SEDAR SENGHOR
Sylvia W. Ba
Princeton University Press, 1973. $11.00.

CONTEMPORARY POETRY OF THE NEGRO
Robert T. Kerlin
Books for Libraries. Reprint of the 1921 edition. $9.50.

DYNAMITE VOICES: BLACK POETS OF THE 1960'S
Don L. Lee
Broadside Press, Pubns., 1971. Pap. $2.75.

*FAMOUS AMERICAN NEGRO POETS
Charlemae Rollins
Backgrounds and appraisals given on Paul Laurence Dunbar, William Stanley Braithwaite, Frances Ellen Harper, Countee Cullen, and Arna Bontemps. 95 pp. Dodd, Mead & Co., 1965. Illus. Age 11-15. $3.95.

OLK ROOTS OF AFRO-AMERICAN POETRY
Bernard Bell
Broadside Press, 1974. Cloth, $5.00; Pap. $2.75.

THE FORERUNNERS, *Black Poets in America*
Woodie King, Jr., Editor
An anthology of sixteen poets who bridged the gap between poets of the twenties and those of the sixties and seventies. 134 pp. Howard University Press, 1975. $8.95.

FROM THE DEPTHS OF MY SOUL
Arnold J. Kelly
A poetic journey into the world of the modern, young, educated Southern black. Exposition Press. $3.50.

GET YOUR ASS IN THE WATER AND SWIM LIKE ME: NARRATIVE POETRY FROM BLACK ORAL TRADITION
Bruce Jackson and Snell
Harvard University Press, 1974. $12.50.

THE HARLEM GALLERY: BOOK ONE, THE CURATOR
Melvin B. Tolson
The Negro poet's vision of Harlem with all its diversities, potentialities, and tragicomedies. Twayne Publishers, 1971. $6.00.

I AM CURIOUS (BLACK)
Jack Chancellor
Poetry about hedonistic Americans, bigotry, and racial identities. Exposition Press. $3.00.

*I AM THE DARKER BROTHER: AN ANTHOLOGY OF MODERN POEMS BY NEGRO AMERICANS
Arnold Adoff, Editor
Macmillan Publishing Co., Inc., 1968. Cloth, $4.95; Pap. $1.25. Below college level.

I KNOW WHY THE CAGED BIRD SINGS
Maya Angelou
Bantam Books, 1971. Pap. $1.25.

IF WORDS COULD SET US FREE
Gertrude Blackwell Bailey
A collection of poems reflecting the Black Renaissance in America. Exposition Press. $4.00.

INVISIBLE POETS: AFRO-AMERICANS OF THE NINETEENTH CENTURY
Joan R. Sherman
300 pp. University of Illinois Press, 1974. Illus. $10.00.

JUPITER HAMMIN, AMERICAN NEGRO POET
Oscar Wegelin
Books for Libraries, Inc. Reprint of the 1915 edition. $5.75.

KALEIDOSCOPE: *Poems By American Negro Poets*
Robert Hayden, ed.
Included among others are Paul Laurence Dunbar, Gwendolyn Brooks, Arna Bontemps, and Langston Hughes. 231 pp. Harcourt Brace Jovanovich, Inc., 1968. Ages 14 up. $4.95.

NEGRITO
John Mason Brewer
Negro dialect poems of the Southwest. Illus. Books for Libraries, 1933. $10.00.

PHILLIS WHEATLEY IN THE BLACK AMERICAN BEGINNINGS
William H. Robinson
The racial, social, religious and literary realities of colonial times are assessed in Phillis Wheatley's poetry. 95 pp. Broadside Press, 1975. Cloth, $6.00; Pap. $3.50.

*THE POETRY OF BLACK AMERICA: ANTHOLOGY OF THE 20th CENTURY
Arnold Adoff, Editor
Harper and Row Pubs., 1973. $12.50. Below college level.

REFLECTIONS OF A BLACK MAN
Efton F. Geary
Book of black poetry. The Naylor Co. $4.95.

A ROCK AGAINST THE WIND: BLACK LOVE POEMS
Lindsay Patterson, Editor
85 poets and over 140 poems, including Gwendolyn Brooks, Nikki Giovanni, Sonia

Sanchez, and Langston Hughes, among others. 200 pp. Dodd, Mead & Co., 1973. Age 16 up. $5.95

WE SPEAK AS LIBERATORS: YOUNG BLACK POETS
Orde M. Coombs, Editor
An assemblage of poems of blacks who came of age during the American sixties. 252 pp. Dodd, Mead & Co., 1970. Age 16 up. $5.95.

POLITICS

*ADAM CLAYTON POWELL: PORTRAIT OF A MARCHING BLACK
James Haskins
A biography bqsed on interviews with associates of the late Congressman. 160 pp. Photos. Dell Publishing Co., 1974. Ages 12 up. $5.95.

AMERICA'S BLACK CONGRESSMEN
Maurine, Christopher
Thomas Y. Crowell, Co., 1971. $8.95.

THE BENCH AND THE BALLOT: SOUTHERN FEDERAL JUDGES AND BLACK VOTERS
Charles Hamilton
270 pp. Oxford University Press, 1974. Cloth, $7.95; Pap. $2.95.

BLACK AMERICANS AND THE MIDDLE EAST CONFLICT
Henry Winston
Exposure of the Nixon Administration's attempts to win black support for Israeli aggression. New Outlook Pubs. $.25.

BLACK EXPERIENCE IN AMERICAN POLITICS
Charles V. Hamilton
G.P.Putnam's Sons, 1973. Cloth, $7.95; Pap. $3.25.

BLACK LIBERATION AND POLITICAL POWER: *The Meaning of the Gary Convention*
Derrick Morrison and Tony Thomas
24 pp. Pathfinder Press, Inc., 1972. Pap. $.35.

BLACK PANTHERS
J.L.Sutton
William Frederick Press, 1973. $5.50.

BLACK POLITICAL DEVELOPMENT: AN ADVOCACY ANALYSIS
Reginald E. Gilliam, Jr.
The author focuses on practical programs for political development: Using electoral politics, the courts, tenant organizations, Community Development Corporations, black control of media, alignment with African economic interests, eliminating organized crime from the ghettos, and focusing the issue of ecology on ghetto conditions. Kennikat Press, 1975. $18.50.

THE BLACK POLITICAL EXPERIENCE IN AMERICA
Milton D. Morris
A comprehensive survey of the political experience attitudes, and behavior of black Americans from the earliest political activities through the 1970's. Harper & Row Publishers, 1975. Paper.

BLACK POLITICAL PARTIES: AN HISTORICAL AND POLITICAL ANALYSIS
Hanes Walton, Jr.
Free Press, 1972. $7.95.

*BLACK POLITICANS
Richard W. Bruner
David McKay Co., 1971. $4.25. Ages 6 to 12.

THE BLACK POLITICIAN: HIS STRUGGLE FOR POWER
Mervyn Dymally
Wadsworth Publishing Co., 1971. $4.50.

BLACK POLITICS AND BLACK VISION
Moyibi Amoda
Aspects of the black movement and racism in America. 208 pp. Westminster Press, 1972. $6.50.

BLACK POLITICS AND PUBLIC POLICY
Norman J. Powell and Robert A. Holmes
Emerson Hall Pubs., 1973. Cloth, $8.95; Pap. $.95.

BLACK POLITICS IN NEW YORK CITY
Edwin R. Lewinson
Traces the involvement of blacks in the political life of New York City. Twayne Publishers, 1974. $10.95.

BLACK POLITICS IN PHILADELPHIA
Miriam Ershowitz and Joseph Zikmund, Editors
Basic Books, 1973. $10.00.

BLACK POLITICS, *A Theoretical and Structural Analysis*
   Hanes Walton, Jr.
An historical and analytical approach to the black political experience in America. 246 pp. Illus. Bib. J.B. Lippincott Co., 1972. Pap. `$4.95.

BLACK PROTEST: ISSUES AND TACTICS
   Robert C. Dick
From 1827 to the Civil War. Examines the role of blacks in the governmental system, black functions in political parties, civil obedience versus disobedience, violence versus non-violence, separation versus integration, and black abolitionism. 338 pp. Greenwood Press, 1974. Illus. $12.95.

BLACK REPUBLICANS: THE POLITICS OF THE BLACK AND TANS
   Hanes Walton, Jr.
An analysis of those blacks who joined and worked in the Republican Party from 1856 to 1972. 217 pp. Scarecrow Press, 1975. $8.00.

CAN A NEGRO HOLD OFFICE IN GEORGIA?
   Richard W. White
179 pp. Negro Universities Press. Reprint of the 1869 edition. $9.75.

THE CASE FOR AN INDEPENDENT BLACK PARTY
   Socialist Workers Party
24 pp. Pathfinder Press, Inc. Pap. $0.50.

*CHANGING OF THE GUARD: THE NEW BREED OF BLACK POLITICIANS
   Alfred Duckett
Coward, McCann, and Geohegan, 1972. Illus. $3.60. Below college level.

CLIMBING JACOB'S LADDER: *The Arrival of Negroes in Southern Politics*
   Pat Watters and Reese Cleghorn
A history of Negroes' struggles to gain the ballot in the 1960s. 389 pp. Harcourt Brace Jovanovich, Inc., 1972. Cloth, $8.95; Pap. $2.95.

THE DEVELOPMENT OF STATE LEGIS-LATION CONCERNING THE FREE NEGRO
   Franklin Johnson
207 pp. Greenwood Press, 1974. Reprint of the 1919 edition. $10.25.

*FIGHTING SHIRLEY CHISHOLM

James Haskins
A biography of Congresswoman Shirley Chisholm, whose 1972 campaign slogan was "Unbought and Unbossed." 244 pp. Dell Publishing Co., 1975. Photos. Ages 12 up. $5.95.

FROM CONTRABAND TO FREEDMAN: FEDERAL POLICY TOWARD SOUTHERN BLACKS, 1861-1865
   Louis S. Gerteis
255 pp. Greenwood Press, 1973. $12.50.

FROM THE VIRGINIA PLANTATION TO THE NATIONAL CAPITOL; OR THE FIRST AND ONLY NEGRO REPRESEN-TATIVE IN CONGRESS FROM THE OLD DOMINION
   J.M. Langston
Kraus Reprint Co. Reprint of the 1894 edition. $20.00.

MARXISM AND THE NEGRO STRUGGLE
   Harold Cruse, George Breitman and Clifton DeBarry
48 pp. Pathfinder Press, 1968. Pap. $.75.

THE MORNING BREAKS: *The Trial of Angela Davis*
   Bettina Aptheker
A personal account of the author's experiences. Provides an informative historical picture of the development of the political movement around the case. 300 pp. International Publishers, 1975. Cloth, $9.50; pap. $3.75.

THE NEGRO AND THE COMMUNIST PARTY
   Wilson Record
The relationship between the American Negro and the party from 1919 to 1950. Atheneum Publishers, 1971. Pap. $3.45.

THE NEGRO AND FUSION POLITICS IN NORTH CAROLINA 1894 TO 1901
   Helen G. Edmonds
Russell and Russell, 1973. Reprint of the 1951 edition. $18.00.

NEGRO IN AMERICAN NATIONAL POLITICS
   William Felbert Nowlin
Russell and Russell, 1970. Reprint of the 1931 edition. $7.50.

THE NEGRO IN MARYLAND POLITICS, 1870-1912
   Margaret Law Callcott

In this book, the desire of blacks to stay free prevented a racist Democratic party from rigging elections or depriving blacks of their rights. 214 pp. Johns Hopkins University Press, 1975. Cloth, $9.00; Pap. $2.95.

THE NEGRO IN NORTH CAROLINA POLITICS SINCE RECONSTRUCTION
William Alexander Mabry
AMS Press, Inc., 1970. Reprint of the 1940 edition. $7.50.

THE NEGRO IN THIRD PARTY POLITICS
Hanes Walton, Jr.
Dorrance and Co., 1969. $3.95.

THE NEGRO IN VIRGINIA POLITICS, 1865 TO 1902
Richard L. Morton
199 pp. Reprint Co.. Reprint of the 1918 edition. $12.00.

THE NEGRO IN VIRGINIA POLITICS, 1902 TO 1965
Andrew Buni
296 pp. University Press of Virginia, 1967. $7.50.

NEGRO LAWMAKERS IN THE SOUTH CAROLINA LEGISLATURE, 1868 TO 1902
Lawrence C. Bryant
Lawrence C. Bryant, 1968. Cloth, $10.00; Pap. $8.00.

NEGRO LEGISLATORS OF TEXAS
J. Mason Brewer
The role Negroes have played in Texan legislative history. 250 pp. Jenkins Publishing Co. Reprint of the 1932 edition. Updated. $12.50.

NEGRO LEGISLATORS OF TEXAS AND THEIR DESCENDANTS
J. Mason Brewer
R and E Research Associates, Pubs., 1970. Reprint of the 1935 edition. $7.00.

NEGRO POLITICAL LEADERSHIP IN THE SOUTH
Everett C. Ladd, Jr.
Cornell University Press, 1966. Cloth, $12.50; Pap. $3.95.

NEGRO POLITICAL LEADERSHIP IN THE SOUTH
Everett Carll Ladd, Jr.
Negro leadership in two North Carolina communities in the 20th century. Atheneum

Publishers, 1969. Pap. $3.95.

THE NEGRO POLITICIAN
Edward T. Clayton
Johnson Publishing Co., Chicago, 1964. $4.95.

NEGRO POLITICIANS: THE RISE OF NEGRO POLITIC IN CHICAGO
Harold F. Gosnell
University of Chicago Press, 1935. Cloth, $10.00; Pap. $2.95.

NEGRO POLITICS
J.Q. Wilson
Free Press, 1960. Cloth, $7.95; Pap. $2.95.

THE NEGRO PROBLEM: ABRAHAM LINCOLN'S SOLUTION
William Passmore Pickett
580 pp. Greenwood Press, 1974. Reprint of the 1909 edition. $17.50.

NEGRO SOCIAL AND POLITICAL THOUGHT, 1850-1920: *A Reader*
Howard Brotz, Editor
The place of the Negro in American society between 1850 and 1920, grouped under four main themes: Emigration, assimilation, cultural nationalism, and political nationalism. 593 pp. Harper & Row Publishers, 1966. Pap. $4.95.

THE NEGRO AND SOUTHERN POLITICS: A CHAPTER OF FLORIDA HISTORY
Hugh Douglas Price
133 pp. Greenwood Press, 1974. Reprint of the 1957 edition. $8.50.

NEGROES AND THE NEW SOUTHERN POLITICS
Donald R. Matthews and James W. Prothro
A description and analysis of the part Negroes have played in the political life of the South. 551 pp. Harcourt Brace Jovanovich, Inc. $12.50.

THE NEW NEGRO: HIS POLITICAL, CIVIL, AND MENTAL STATUS, AND RELATED ESSAYS
William Pickens
239 pp. Negro Universities Press. Reprint of the 1916 edition. $10.00.

*A PIECE OF THE POWER: FOUR BLACK MAYORS
James Haskins
Brief biographies of Carl Stokes, Richard Hatcher, Charles Evers, and Kenneth Gibson.

192 pp. Dell Publishing Co., 1972. Photos. Ages 12 up. $5.95.

THE POLITICAL STATUS OF THE NEGRO IN THE AGE OF F.D.R.: A CARNEGIE-MYRDAL REPORT EMPHASIZING THE AMERICAN SOUTH
Ralph J. Bunche
University of Chicago Press, 1973. $17.50.

THE POLITICS OF THE BLACK "NATION"
Matthew Holden, Jr.
Chandler Publishing Co., 1973. Pap. $5.95.

THE POLITICS OF THE SOUTHERN NEGRO: FROM EXCLUSION TO BIG CITY ORGANIZATION
Harry Holloway
Random House, Inc., 1969. $8.95.

RACE AND RADICALISM: THE NAACP AND THE COMMUNIST PARTY IN CONFLICT
Wilson Record
Cornell University Press, 1963. Cloth, $8.50; Pap. $1.95.

THE REPUBLICAN PARTY AND BLACK AMERICA: FROM MCKINLEY TO HOOVER, 1896 TO 1933
Richard B. Sherman
274 pp. University of Virginia Press, 1973. $9.50.

REVOLUTIONARY TRACINGS IN WORLD POLITICS AND BLACK LIBERATION
James E. Jackson
Points the way to correct struggle and to eventual but sure socialist liberation. Includes the author's speech in a debate with Senator Edmund Muskie, his essay "Lenin and National Liberation" and his speech on Engels, Marcuse and Angela Davis. 263 pp. International Publishers, 1975. Cloth, $9.50; pap. $3.50.

ROOTS OF REBELLION: *The Evolution of Black Politics and Protest Since World War II*
Richard P. Young, Editor
Traces the development of black protest from the 1940's to the present. 482 pp. Harper & Row Publishers, 1970. Pap. $6.50.

A SKETCH OF THE NEGRO IN POLITICS, ESPECIALLY IN SOUTH CAROLINA AND MISSISSIPPI
Frederic Bancroft

AMS Press, Inc. Reprint of the 1885 edition. $7.50.

THE STUDY AND ANALYSIS OF BLACK POLITICS: A BIBLIOGRAPHY
Hanes Walton, Jr.
179 pp. Scarecrow Press, 1973. $7.00.

THINKING BLACK: AN INTRODUCTION TO BLACK POLITICAL POWER
Frank McQuilkin
Bruce Books, 1970. Pap. $2.95.

TOGETHER: A REPORTER'S JOURNEY INTO THE NEW BLACK POLITICS
L.H. Whittemore
A documentation of those black Americans still committed to America. William Morrow & Co., 1971. $7.95.

VOICES OF A BLACK NATION: POLITICAL JOURNALISM IN THE HARLEM RENAISSANCE
Theodore G. Vincent
Monthly Review Press, 1972. Cloth, $10.00; Pap. $3.45.

WHAT BLACK POLITICIANS ARE SAYING
Nathan Wright, Jr.
Hawthorn Books, 1972. Cloth, $7.95; Pap. $2.95.

WHAT COUNTRY HAVE I?: POLITICAL WRITINGS OF BLACK AMERICANS
J.J.Storing
St. Martin's Press, 1970. Cloth, $6.95; Pap. $4.25.

PROFESSIONALS

*THE ADVENTURES OF THE NEGRO COWBOYS
Philip Durham and Everett L. Jones
The heroes and villains of the Negro race whose sagas as cowboys are an integral part of the story of the building of the American West. 160 pp. Dodd, Mead & Co., 1966. Illus. Age 11-15. $3.95.

BLACK ENGINEERS IN THE UNITED STATES: A DIRECTORY
Kames K. Ho, Editor
Howard University Press, 1974. $18.00.

BLACK IN BLUE: A STUDY OF THE NEGRO POLICEMAN
Nicholas Alex
How the black policeman feels about himself, his occupation, the community, and his white colleagues. 210 pp. Prentice-Hall, Inc., 1969. Pap. $4.50.

BLACK INVENTORS OF AMERICA
Burt McKinley
ERA Press. $5.25.

THE BLACK LIBRARIAN IN AMERICA
E.J. Josey, Editor
336 pp. Scarecrow Press, 1970. $8.50.

*BLACK PIONEERS OF SCIENCE AND INVENTION
Louis Haber
A study of the life and work of 14 outstanding black scientists. 192 pp. Harcourt Brace Jovanovich, Inc., 1970. Ages 10 up. $5.50.

BLACKS, MEDICAL SCHOOLS, AND SOCIETY
James L. Curtis
188 pp. University of Michigan Press, 1971. $7.95.

THE COLORED INVENTOR: A RECORD OF FIFTY YEARS
Henry E. Baker
A list of black inventors and their inventions. Arno Press, 1971. Reprint of the 1913 edition. Pap. $1.00.

THE FIRST BLACK CAPTAIN
Edward D. Williams
The story of the first black police captain in the city of Newark. Vantage Press. $4.95.

*THE HIDDEN CONTRIBUTORS: BLACK SCIENTISTS AND INVENTORS IN AMERICA
Aaron E. Klein
Doubleday and Co., 1971. $4.95. Up to 14.

HISTORY OF THE NEGRO IN MEDICINE
Morias
United Publishing Corp., 1970. $13.88.

THE NEGRO COWBOYS
Philip Durham and Everett L. Jones
Cowboys of the Negro race in America. 278 pp. Dodd, Mead & Co., 1965. Illus. Age 16 up. $5.00.

THE NEGRO PROFESSIONAL MAN AND THE COMMUNITY, WITH SPECIAL EMPHASIS ON THE PHYSICIAN AND LAWYER
Carter Godwin Woodson
365 pp. Negro Universities Press. Reprint of the 1934 edition. $16.00. Johnson Reprint, $16.75.

NEGROES FOR MEDICINE
Lee Cogan
Johns Hopkins Press, 1969. $4.95.

A PORTRAIT OF THE BLACK ATTORNEY IN CHICAGO
Marion S. Goldman
Field study of members of the black bar in Chicago, focusing on demographic characteristics and the black bar's response to the criminal justice system's treatment of black persons during and following the Chicago riots of April 1968. 62 pp. American Bar Foundation, 1972. Pap. $1.00.

PORTRAITS OF TWENTIETH CENTURY AMERICANS OF NEGRO LINEAGE
Louise E. Jefferson, Compiler
Portfolio of photographs of 24 outstanding contemporary blacks representing a variety of vocations. Friendship Press. $1.75.

PROFILE OF THE NEGRO IN AMERICAN DENTISTRY
Foster Kidd, D.D.S., Editor
Examines and profiles the cultural, educational, social, civic, and professional advancements of the Negro in dentistry in the United States. 168 pp. Howard University Press, 1976. $9.95.

WHAT BLACK LIBRARIANS ARE SAYING
E.J. Josey, Editor
324 pp. Scarecrow Press, 1972. $8.50.

PSYCHOLOGY

BEING BLACK: *Psychological-Sociological Dilemmas*
Robert V. Guthrie, Editor
Articles present information pertinent to the mental health of black-Americans. Explores how black people perceive themselves and white people in socio-psychological relationships. 223 pp. Canfield Press, 1970. Pap. $3.95.

BEYOND BLACK AND WHITE
James P. Comer, M.D.
An account by a black psychiatrist of the effects of racism on the "black mind" and the "white mind." 272 pp. Quadrangle Books, 1972. $7.95.

BLACK AMERICANS: A PSYCHOLOGICAL ANALYSIS
E. Earl Baughman
Academic Press, 1971. Pap. $2.95.

BLACK PSYCHE: MODAL PERSONALITY PATTERNS OF BLACK AMERICANS
S.S.Guterman, Editor
Glendessary Press, 1972. Cloth, $9.95; Pap. $4.95.

BLACK PSYCHOLOGY
Reginald L. Jones, Editor
Writings by black psychologists and social scientists provide reinterpretations of the psychological literature on blacks. 432 pp. Harper & Row Publishers, 1972. Pap. $6.95.

THE BLACK SELF
Marvin D. Wyne, et al
114 pp. Prentice-Hall, 1974. Cloth, $6.95; Pap. $2.95.

BLACK SELF-CONCEPT
James A. Banks/Jean D. Grambs, Editors
A collection of essays that examines the relationship between education, social science, and the development of the self-concepts of black youth. 185 pp. McGraw-Hill Book Co., 1972. Cloth, $5.95; Pap. $2.95.

BLACK SKIN, WHITE MASKS
Franz Fanon
Grove Press, Inc., 1967. Cloth, $5.00; Pap. $1.65.

BLACK SUICIDE
Herbert Hendin
Basic Books, 1969. $5.95.

BOY'S NO MORE: A BLACK PSYCHOLOGIST'S VIEW OF COMMUNITY
Charles W. Thomas
Glencoe Press, 1971. Pap. $2.95.

COLOR, CLASS, AND PERSONALITY
Robert Lee Sutherland
135 pp. Negro Universities Press. Reprint of the 1942 edition. Illus. $9.00.

COUNSELING NEGROES
Clemmont Von Tress

Houghton Mifflin, Co., 1971. Pap. $1.60.

INTERRACIAL HOUSING: A PSYCHOLOGICAL EVALUATION OF A SOCIAL EXPERIMENT
Morton Deutsch and Mary Collins
Russell and Russell, 1968. Reprint of the 1951 edition. $7.00.

THE MARK OF OPPRESSION: EXPLORATIONS IN THE PERSONALITY OF THE AMERICAN NEGRO
Abram Kardiner and L. Ovesey
New American Library; Peter Smith Publishers. Cloth, $5.00; Pap. $3.95.

MENTAL HEALTH AND SEGREGATION
Martin M. Grossack, Editor
Springer Publishing Co., 1963. $4.50.

THE POSSIBILITIES OF THE NEGRO IN SYMPOSIUM: A SOLUTION OF THE NEGRO PROBLEM PSYCHOLOGICALLY CONSIDERED
Books for Libraries. Reprint of the 1904 edition. $11.75.

PSYCHOLOGY AND THE BLACK EXPERIENCE
Roderick W. Pugh
Wadsworth Publishing Co., 1972. Pap. $3.95.

THE PSYCHOLOGY OF THE NEGRO: AN EXPERIMENTAL STUDY
George Oscar Ferguson
138 pp. Greenwood Press, 1974. Reprint of the 1916 edition. Illus. $8.50.

RACIAL ATTITUDES IN AMERICA:
Analysis and Findings of Social Psychology
John C. Brigham and Theodore A. Weissbach
Psychological research and theorizing in the area of black-white attitudes. Presents empirical findings within the context of broad social issues. 401 pp. Harper & Row Publishers, 1972. Pap. $7.95.

WHY BLACKS KILL BLACKS
Alvin F. Poussaint
Emerson Hall Pubs., 1973. $7.95.

RACE RELATIONS

AFRO-AMERICANS AND THE RACE PROBLEM: A BRIEF HISTORICAL SKETCH OF

THE COLORED PEOPLE OF THE UNITED STATES, AND A METHOD OF HARMONIUS SOLUTION OF THE RACE PROBLEM IN THE SOUTH, BENEFICIAL TO THE FREED MEN AND THEIR FORMER OWNERS IN ACCORD WITH OUR REPUBLICAN FORM OF GOVERNMENT
William H. Payne
120 pp. Greenwood Press. Reprint of the 1920 edition. $8.00.

THE AFTERMATH OF SLAVERY: A STUDY OF THE CONDITION AND ENVIRONMENT OF THE AMERICAN NEGRO
William Albert Sinclair
An evaluation of race relations in the South from 1865 to 1900. 358 pp. Metro Books, Inc. Reprint of the 1905 edition. $11.00.

AMERICAN CIVILIZATION AND THE NEGRO: THE AFRO-AMERICAN IN RELATION TO NATIONAL PROGRESS
Charles Victor Roman
434 pp. Negro Universities Press. Reprint of the 1916 edition. $18.75.

ANOTHER NATION: THE NEGRO AND YOU
Philip Hurley
Paulist-Newman Press. $.25.

BECAUSE THEY'RE BLACK
John Gus and Derek Humphry
Peter Smith Publishers. $3.50.

BEFORE AND AFTER: OR THE RELATIONS OF THE RACES IN THE SOUTH
Issac DuBose Seabrook
158 pp. Louisiana State University Press, 1967. $5.50.

THE BLACK ANGLO-SAXONS
N. Hare
Macmillan Publishing Co., 1970 Pap. $1.50.

BLACK CONFLICT WITH WHITE AMERICA
Jack Van Der Slik
Charles E. Merrill Publishing Co., 1970. Pap. $5.95.

THE BLACK EXPERIENCE IN AMERICA
Norman Coombs
Hippocrene Books, Inc., 1972. Pap. $2.95.

THE BLACK IMAGE IN THE WHITE MIND: THE DEBATE ON AFRO-

AMERICAN CHARACTER AND DESTINY, 1817 TO 1914
George Frederickson
Harper and Row Pubs., 1971. Cloth, $10.00; Pap. $3.95.

THE BLACK MAN IN AMERICA: INTEGRATION AND SEPARATION
James A. Moss
An overview of the black revolution that marked the 1960s. 320 pp. Dell Publishing Co. $2.45.

BLACK RACIAL ATTITUDES: TRENDS AND COMPLEXITIES
Howard Schuman and Shirley Hatchett
Gives descriptive and analytic attention to the attitudes, beliefs, and actions of blacks. 160 pp. Institute for Social Research, 1974. Cloth, $10.00; Pap. $5.50.

BLACK REFLECTIONS ON WHITE POWER
Sterling Tucker
A picture of white power in action. William B. Eerdmans Publishing Co., 1969. Pap. $1.95.

BLACK AND WHITE
J.C. Byars, Compiler and Editor
Books for Libraries. Reprint of the 1927 edition. $9.25.

BLACK AND WHITE
William Brink and Louis Harris
Simon and Schuster, 1967. Cloth, $5.95; Pap. $1.95.

BLACK AND WHITE IN AMERICAN CULTURE: AN ANTHOLOGY FROM THE MASSACHUSETTS REVIEW
Jules Chametsky and Sidney Kaplan, Editors
University of Massachusetts Press, 1969. $15.00.

BLACK AND WHITE: LAND, LABOR, AND POLITICS IN THE SOUTH
Timothy Thomas Fortune
A leading 19th century Negro intellectual assesses the causes and cures of the economic, political, and social problems of the Southern Negro. Arno Press, Reprint of the 1884 edition. $9.00.

BLACK AND WHITE POWER SUBREPTION
Joseph R. Washington, Jr.
Examines the history of deception underlying

racial relations in America. Beacon Press, 1971. Cloth, $6.00; Pap. $2.95.

BLACK AND WHITE STORIES OF AMERICAN LIFE
Donald Gibson and Carol Anselment, Editors
Washington Square Press. $.95.

THE BURDEN OF RACE: A DOCUMENTARY HISTORY OF NEGRO-WHITE RELATIONS IN AMERICA
Gilbert Osofsky
Harper and Row Pubs., 1967. Cloth, $8.95; Pap. $3.75.

CITIZEN'S GUIDE TO DESEGREGATION: A STUDY OF SOCIAL AND LEGAL CHANGE IN AMERICAN LIFE
Herbert Hill
185 pp. Negro Universities Press. Reprint of the 1955 edition. $9.50.

COLOR AT HOME AND ABROAD
George Mallison
AMS Press, Inc. Reprint of the 1929 edition. $17.50.

THE COLOR LINE: A BRIEF IN BEHALF OF THE UNBORN
William Benjamin Smith
261 pp. Negro Universities Press. Reprint of the 1905 edition. $10.75. Books for Libraries, Inc. $11.00.

COMPARATIVE STUDIES OF BLACKS AND WHITES IN THE UNITED STATES
Kent S. Miller and Ralph M. Dreger, Editors
Academic Press, 1973. $18.50.

CRISIS IN BLACK AND WHITE
Charles Silberman
Random House, Inc., 1964. Cloth, $7.95; Pap. $1.95.

DEEP SOUTH SAYS, "NEVER"
John Bartlow Martin
181 pp. Negro Universities Press. Reprint of the 1957 edition. $9.75.

FOLLOWING THE COLOR LINE: *An Account of Negro Citizenship in the American Democracy*
Ray Stannard Baker
Observations and interpretations of race relations in the U.S. at the turn of the 20th cen-

tury. 314 pp. Corner House Publishers, 1974. Reprint of the 1908 edition. $4.98.

FOR BLACKS ONLY: BLACK STRATEGIES FOR CHANGE IN AMERICA
Sterling Tucker
It is the author's contention that in spite of white oppression and black rage, there are at hand, within the system, effective tools for change. William B. Eerdmans Publishing Co., 1971. Pap. $2.95.

HOW TO GET ALONG WITH BLACK PEOPLE: A HANDBOOK FOR WHITE FOLKS, AND SOME BLACK FOLKS TOO
Chris Clark and Shiela Rush
Race relations, private and public, social, and business. 156 pp. Third Press, 1971. Cloth, $5.95; Pap. $2.95.

HOW TO SOLVE THE RACE PROBLEM: THE PROCEEDINGS OF THE WASHINGTON CONFERENCE ON THE RACE PROBLEM IN THE UNITED STATES
Jesse Lawson
286 pp. Metro Books, Inc., 1969. Reprint of the 1904 edition. $11.50.

IMAGES OF THE NEGRO IN AMERICA
Darwin Turner and Joan Bright, Editors
113 pp. D.C.Heath and Co., 1965. Pap. $2.50.

INQUIRY INTO THE CONDITION AND PROSPECTS OF THE AFRICAN RACE IN THE UNITED STATES
Books for Libraries, Inc. Reprint of the 1839 edition. $12.75.

LINCOLN ON BLACK AND WHITE
Arthur Zilversmit, Editor
A collection of Abraham Lincoln's writings from 1837 to 1865 that reflect his thought on black-white relationships in the United States. 187 pp. Wadsworth Publishing Co.

THE MULATTO IN THE UNITED STATES, INCLUDING A STUDY OF THE ROLE OF MIXED-BLOOD RACES THROUGHOUT THE WORLD
Edward Byron Reuter
417 pp. Greenwood Press. Reprint of the 1918 edition. $13.75.

NATURE KNOWS NO COLOR LINE
J.A. Rogers
The Negro ancestry in the white race. Illus. H.M. Rogers Publishing Co., 1952. $5.95.

THE NEGRO AND THE WHITE MAN
Wesley John Gaines
218 pp. Greenwood Press. Reprint of the 1897 edition. $9.50.

NEGRO AND WHITE IN A CONNECTICUT TOWN: A STUDY IN RACE RELATIONS
Frank F. Lee
College and University Press. $7.50.

THE NEGRO IN AMERICAN CIVILIZATION: A STUDY OF NEGRO LIFE AND RACE RELATIONS IN THE LIGHT OF SOCIAL RESEARCH.
Charles Spurgeon Johnson
538 pp. Johnson Reprint, 1970. Reprint of the 1930 edition. $23.00.

NEGRO: NATIONAL ASSET OR LIABILITY? THE BATTLE OF BLOODS
John Louis Hill
233 pp. Johnson Reprint Corporation. Reprint of the 1930 edition. $10.50.

THE NEGRO PROBLEM
Booker T. Washington, Editor
AMS Press, Inc. Reprint of the 1903 edition. $7.00.

THE NEGRO PROBLEM IN THE UNITED STATES: RISE, DEVELOPMENT AND SOLUTION
Frank Gage
116 pp. Negro Universities Press. Reprint of the 1892 edition. $8.25.

THE NEGRO: THE SOUTHERNER'S PROBLEM
Thomas Nelson Page
316 pp. Johnson Reprint. Reprint of the 1904 edition. $14.00.

NEGRO THOUGHT IN AMERICA, 1880 TO 1915: RACIAL IDEOLOGIES IN THE AGE OF BOOKER T. WASHINGTON
August Meier
348 pp. University of Michigan Press, 1963. Cloth, $8.95; Pap. $2.25.

THE NEGRO'S IMAGE IN THE SOUTH: THE ANATOMY OF WHITE SUPREMACY
Claude H. Nolen
232 pp. University of Kentucky Press, 1967. Cloth, $6.50; Pap. $2.50.

PROFILE IN BLACK AND WHITE: A FRANK PORTRAIT OF SOUTH CAROLINA

Howard H. Quint
214 pp. Greenwood Press. Reprint of the 1958 edition. $11.00.

RACE ADJUSTMENT: ESSAYS ON THE NEGRO IN AMERICA
Kelly Miller
A collection of essays reviewing education, the Negro problem, social equality, etc. Mnemosyne Publishing Co. Reprint of the 1908 edition. Pap. $2.95. Books for Libraries, Inc., Cloth, $11.50.

RACE ADJUSTMENT: ESSAYS ON THE NEGRO IN AMERICA: AND THE EVERLASTING STAIN
Kelly Miller
Two collections of the best lectures and letters by a dean of Howard University. Arno Press, 1968. Reprint of the 1924 edition. $20.50.

RACE AND REGION: A DESCRIPTIVE BIBLIOGRAPHY WITH SPECIAL REFERENCE TO THE RELATIONS BETWEEN WHITES AND NEGROES IN THE UNITED STATES
E.T. and Alma M. Thompson
Kraus Reprint Co. Reprint of the 1949 edition. $12.00.

RACE AND THE SOUTH: TWO STUDIES, 1914/1922
Lily Hardy Hammond
In Black and White: An Interpretation of Southern Life, and *In The Vanguard of a Race.* Arno Press, 1972. $23.00.

RACE ORTHODOXY IN THE SOUTH, AND OTHER ASPECTS OF THE NEGRO QUESTION
Thomas Pearce Bailey
386 pp. Greenwood Press. Reprint of the 1914 edition.

RACE RELATIONS: ADJUSTMENT OF WHITES AND NEGROES IN THE UNITED STATES
Willis D. Weatherford
590 pp. Negro Universities Press. Reprint of the 1934 edition. $20.00.

RACE TRAITS AND TENDENCIES OF THE AMERICAN NEGRO
Frederick Ludwig Hoffman
AMS Press, Inc., Reprint of the 1896 edition. $13.50.

RACIAL INTEGRITY AND OTHER FEATURES OF THE NEGRO PROBLEM
Alexander Harvey Shannon
Books for Libraries, Inc. Reprint of the 1907 edition. $15.00.

RISING ABOVE COLOR
Philip Henry Lotz, Editor
Books for Libraries, Inc. Reprint of the 1943 edition. $8.75.

SURVIVAL--BLACK/WHITE
Florence Halpern
Seeks to explain how the black people's struggle for survival has determined their particular way of perceiving and responding to their world. 248 pp. Pergamon Press, 1973. Cloth, $11.50; Pap. $5.00.

THROUGH AFRO-AMERICA, AN ENGLISH READING OF THE RACE PROBLEM
William Archer
295 pp. Greenwood Press. Reprint of the 1910 edition. $12.00.

WHAT THE NEGRO WANTS
Rayford W. Logan
Agathon Press. Reprint of the 1944 edition. $12.00.

THE WHITE MAN'S BURDEN: A DISCUSSION OF THE INTERRACIAL QUESTION WITH SPECIAL REFERENCE TO THE RESPONSIBILITY OF THE WHITE RACE TO THE NEGRO PROBLEM
Benjamin Franklin Riley
239 pp. Greenwood Press. Reprint of the 1910 edition. $11.50.

WHITE OVER BLACK: AMERICAN ATTITUDES TOWARD THE NEGRO, 1550-1812
Winthrop D. Jordan
672 pp. University of North Carolina Press, 1969. $13.95.

RACE RIOTS

ANATOMY OF FOUR RACE RIOT RACIAL CONFLICT IN KNOXVILLE, ELAINE [ARK.], TULSA AND CHICAGO, 1919-1921
Lee E. Williams and Lee E. Williams II
University Press of Mississippi. $5.95.

ANTI-NEGRO RIOTS IN THE NORTH, 1863
The year of the Emancipation Proclamation was also the year of fierce anti-Negro rioting in the North. Arno Press, 1969. $3.50.

BLACK GHETTO RIOTS AND CAMPUS DISORDERS
Roger B. Canfield
A subcultural and philosophical study of democratic legitimacy and American political violence, 1964-1970. R & E Research Associates, 1973. $12.00.

BLACK RIOT IN LOS ANGELES: THE STORY OF THE WATTS TRAGEDY
Spencer Crump
Trans-Anglo Books. $9.95.

BLACK RIOTERS: A STUDY OF SOCIAL FACTORS AND COMMUNICATION IN THE DETROIT AREA
Benjamin D. Singer, et al
126 pp. Lexington Books, 1970. $10.00.

THE BLACK UPRISINGS
Paul Boutelle, et al
30 pp. Pathfinder Press. $.35.

THE COMPLETE REPORT OF MAYOR LA GUARDIA'S COMMISSION ON THE HARLEM RIOT OF MARCH 19, 1935
Mayor's Commission on Conditions in Harlem
The Report reveals that memories of injustice and lynching in the South, poverty, discrimination, the lack of confidence in the integrity of the police, and other ghetto characteristics of alienation were among the conditions leading to the Harlem riots. Arno Press. Reprint of the 1936 edition. $4.50.

THE LOS ANGELES RIOTS
Robert Fogelson, Editor
A report of the Watts riots of 1965. Arno Press. Reprint of the 1969 edition. $7.50.

THE NEGRO IN CHICAGO: A STUDY OF RACE RELATIONS AND A RACE RIOT
The Chicago Commission on Race Relations
A documentary on the bloody 1919 Chicago race riot. Arno Press. Reprint of the 1922 edition. $15.00.

RACE RIOT AT EAST ST. LOUIS, JULY 2, 1917
Eilliott M. Rudwick
Southern Illinois University Press, 1964. $6.00.

RACE RIOT: CHICAGO IN THE RED SUMMER OF 1919
    William M. Tuttle, Jr.
A study of the clash between the black and white blue-collar workers in Chicago. Atheneum Publishers, 1970. Cloth, $8.95; Pap. $3.25.

RACE RIOT: A FIRST HAND OBSERVATION OF THE 1943 DETROIT RIOTS
    Alfred McClung Lee and Norman D. Humphrey
143 pp. Octagon Books. Reprint of the 1943 edition. $9.00.

RACE RIOTS IN BLACK AND WHITE
    J. Paul Mitchess, Editor
Prentice-Hall, 1970. Cloth, $5.95; Pap. $1.95.

RAPE OF DETROIT
    Argie White Post
The Detroit riots of July, 1967, and the devastation that resulted. Exposition Press. $4.00.

RIVERS OF BLOOD, YEARS OF DARKNESS: THE UNFORGETTABLE CLASSIC ACCOUNT OF THE WATTS RIOT
    Robert Conot
William Morrow and Co., 1968. $7.50.

STORY OF THE RIOT, PERSECUTION OF NEGROES BY ROUGHS AND POLICEMEN IN THE CITY OF NEW YORK, AUGUST 1900
    Frank Moss
The black riot in New York, of August 12, 1900. Arno Press. Reprint of the 1900 edition. $4.50.

THE TULSA RACE WAR OF 1921
    R. Halliburton, Jr.
A documented study with photographs of the burning and violence. R & E Research Associates, 1975. Pap. $9.00.

VIOLENCE AND RIOTS IN URBAN AMERICA
    R.F.Allen and C.H.Adair
Charles A. Jones Publishing Co., 1969. Pap. $5.25.

WATTS: THE AFTERMATH BY THE PEOPLE OF WATTS
    P. Bullock, Editor
Grove Press, Inc., 1970. Pap. $1.50.

WHY RACE RIOTS?
    Earl Louis Brown

Lessons from Detroit. AMS Press. Reprint of the 1944 edition. $5.00.

RACISM

AFRO-AMERICANS IN PITTSBURGH: THE RESIDENTIAL SEGREGATION OF A PEOPLE
    Joe T. Darden
96 pp. Lexington Books, Inc., 1973. $9.50.

AM I A RACIST?
    Robert Heyer and Fortune Monte
Paulist-Newman Press, 1969. Pap. $2.25. Ages 16 and up.

THE AMERICAN NEGRO AS DEPENDENT, DEFECTIVE, AND DELINQUENT
    Charles H. McCord
Gordon Press. $25.00.

THE AMERICAN RACE PROBLEM
    Edward Byron Reuter
432 pp. Apollo Editions. Reprint of the 1927 edition. $4.95.

AN APPEAL TO CONSCIENCE: AMERICA'S CODE OF CASTE, A DISGRACE TO DEMOCRACY
    Kelly Miller
A polemic against lawlessness and segregation. Arno Press. Reprint of the 1918 edition. $3.50.

BACKGROUNDS TO PATTERNS OF NEGRO SEGREGATION
    Charles S. Johnson
The state of black segregation and discrimination since 1940. 352 pp. Apollo Editions, 1970. Pap. $2.95.

BASIC ECONOMICS OF THE URBAN RACIAL CRISIS
    D. Fusefeld
Holt, Rinehart, and Winston, 1973. Pap. $3.50.

THE BASIS OF RACIAL ADJUSTMENT
    Thomas Jackson Woofter, Jr.
Books for Libraries, Inc. Reprint of the 1925 edition. $15.25.

BEYOND RACISM
    Whitney M. Young, Jr.
This book describes the sickness of racism and the crisis to be faced by black and white

America. 255 pp. McGraw-Hill Book Co., 1971. Pap. $2.95.

BI-RACIAL POLITICS: CONFLICT AND TO EMANCIPATION AND RECONSTRUCTION
Chandler Davidson
324 pp. Louisiana State University Press, 1972. $11.95.

BLACK LEADERSHIP FENCED IN BY RACISM
Spurgeon Q. Bryant
A study of the handicaps placed on black leadership, this book traces the effects of the white color caste system on blacks from the time of the Civil War to the present. 224 pp. Dorrance & Co., 1974. $7.95.

BLACK PROFESSIONALS' PERCEPTIONS OF INSTITUTIONAL RACISM IN HEALTH AND WELFARE
C.L.Sanders
International Publications Service, 1973. $9.50.

BLACK RESISTANCE/WHITE LAW: A HISTORY OF CONSTITUTIONAL RACISM IN AMERICA
Mary Frances Berry
Attempts to describe and analyze constitutionally sanctioned violence against blacks and violent suppression of black resistance throughout the American experience. 268 pp. Prentice-Hall, Inc., 1971. Pap. $4.25.

BLACK SCARE: THE RACIST RESPONSE TO EMANCIPATION AND RE-CONSTRUCTION
Forrest G. Wood
University of California Press, 1968. Cloth, $8.50; Pap. $2.45.

BLACK AND WHITE-ONE CLASS, ONE FIGHT: THE ROLE OF WHITE WORKERS IN THE STRUGGLE AGAINST RACISM
Henry Winston
New Outlook Pubs., 1972. Pap. $.50.

CASTE AND CLASS IN A SOUTHERN TOWN
John Dollard
Peter Smith Publishers. Cloth, $4.25. Doubleday, Pap. $1.95.

CHALLENGE TO THE COURT: SOCIAL SCIENTISTS AND THE DEFENSE OF SEGREGATION 1954 TO 1966

I.A.Newby
382 pp. Louisiana State University Press. 1969. $8.50.

CHILDREN OF THE STORM: BLACK CHILDREN AND AMERICAN CHILD WELFARE
Billingsley and Giovannoni
The historical effects of racism on child welfare, recent efforts to improve conditions, and recommendations for definitive changes. 263 pp. Harcourt Brace Jovanovich, 1972. $3.95.

THE COLOR LINE IN OHIO: A HISTORY OF RACE PREJUDICE IN A TYPICAL NORTHERN STATE
Frank Uriah Quillin
178 pp. Greenwood Press. Reprint of the 1913 edition. $9.00.

COLOUR PREJUDICE, WITH PARTICULAR REFERENCE TO THE RELATIONSHIP BETWEEN WHITES AND NEGROES
Sir Alan C. Burns
164 pp. Negro Universities Press, 1972. Reprint of the 1948 edition. $10.50.

DESEGRATION LAW: AN INTRODUCTION
Integrated Education Associates
Editorial Staff, Editors
56 pp. Integrated Education Associates. Pap. $1.00.

DESEGREGATION RESEARCH: AN APPRAISAL
Meyer Weinberg
460 pp. Integrated Education Associates, 1970. Pap. $5.00.

DESEGREGATION: RESISTANCE AND READINESS
Melvin M. Tumin
Princeton University Press, 1958. $10.00.

DESEGREGATION AND THE SUPREME COURT
Benjamin Munn Ziegler
116 pp. D.C.Heath and Co., 1958. Pap. $2.25.

DEVELOPMENT AND ADMINISTRATION OF THE NEW YORK STATES LAW AGAINST DISCRIMINATION
J.A.Higbee
420 pp. University of Alabama Press, 1967. $10.00.

DIRTY WORK, RACE, AND SELF-ESTEEM
Edward J. Walsh
Insights into the concept of the black subculture. 95 pp. Institute of Labor and Industrial Relations, 1975. Cloth, $6.50; Pap. $2.50.

DISCRIMINATION, PERSONALITY, AND ACHIEVEMENT: A SURVEY OF NORTHERN NEGROES
Robert L. Crain and Carlos S. Weisman
Academic Press, 1972. $11.00.

DISCRIMINATION, POVERTY, AND THE NEGRO: ARIZONA IN THE NATIONAL CONTEXT
John E. Crow
Discusses the interrelation of discrimination and poverty among the Negro citizens of Arizona. 53 pp. University of Arizona Press, 1968. Pap. $1.50.

DISCRIMINATION: WHAT DOES IT MEAN?
Richard E. Biddle
An interpretation of the various court cases which help define the relationship of selection procedures to employment. 27 pp. International Personnel Management Association, 1973. $4.50.

THE DYNAMICS OF RACE RELATIONS
Graham C. Kinloch
305 pp. McGraw-Hill Book Co., 1974. Pap. $5.95.

DYNAMICS OF RACISM IN SOCIAL WORK PRACTICE
James A. Goodman, Editor
The many issues the practitioner must face in seeking to understand racism and its effect on the client, our society, and his own inner consciousness. 388 pp. National Association of Social Workers, 1973. $6.50.

E. FRANKLIN FRAZIER ON RACE RELATIONS
G. Franklin Edwards, Editor
University of Chicago Press, 1968. Cloth, $12.50; Pap. $3.95.

THE ECONOMICS OF RACISM U.S.A.: ROOTS OF BLACK INEQUALITY
Victor Perlo
Focusing on income, types of employment, and unemployment, this study examines conditions in housing, health services and education. International Publishers, 1975. Cloth, $10.50; Pap. $4.25.

EMPLOYMENT, RACE AND POVERTY
Arthur M. Ross and Herbert Hill, Eds.
An examination of racial bias in American employment practices. 598 pp. Harcourt Brace Jovanovich, Inc., 1967. Pap. $4.45.

ESSAYS ON SEGREGATION
T. Robert Ingram, et al
St. Thomas. Pap. $1.50.

THE ETIQUETTE OF RACE RELATIONS IN THE SOUTH: A STUDY IN SOCIAL CONTROL
Bertram W. Doyle
A differentiation between natural, moral and civil law. Kennikat Press, 1968. Reprint of the 1937 edition. $8.50.

EXPERIMENT IN MODIFYING ATTITUDES TOWARD THE NEGRO
Fred Tredwell Smith
AMS Press, Inc., Reprint of the 1943 edition. $10.00.

FEW COMFORTS OR SURPRISES: THE ARKANSAS DELTA
Eugene Richards
M.I.T. Press, 1973. Cloth, $15.00; Pap. $7.95.

FIGHT RACISM — FOR UNITY AND PROGRESS
Henry Winston
A call to the people's movements, the working-class movement in particular, and the Communist Party, for a fight against racism as a basic condition for victories and the development of working-class consciousness. New Outlook Pubs., 1971. $.25.

FORBIDDEN NEIGHBORS: A STUDY OF PREJUDICE IN HOUSING
Charles Abrams
Kennikat Press. Reprint of the 1955 edition. $13.50.

THE GREAT FEAR: RACE IN THE MIND OF AMERICA
Gary B. Nash and Richard Weiss, Editor
Holt, Rinehart, and Winston, 1970. $5.95.

THE HIGH COST OF PREJUDICE
Bucklin Moon
168 pp. Negro Universities Press. Reprint of the 1947 edition. $9.50.

HOW TO SOLVE THE RACE PROBLEM
Jesse Lawson

The proceedings of the Washington Conference on the race problem in the United States. 286 pp. Metro Books, Inc. Reprint of the 1904 edition. $11.50.

INSTITUTIONAL RACISM IN AMERICA
Louis Knowles and Kenneth Prewitt, Editors
Explains the conclusions of the black militants and the Kerner Commission showing how the United States is indeed a racist country. Prentice-Hall, Inc., 1969. Cloth, $5.95; Pap. $1.95.

JIM CROW'S DEFENSE: ANTI-NEGRO THOUGHT IN AMERICA, 1900 TO 1930
I.A.Newby
230 pp. Louisiana State University Press, 1968. Pap. $2.45.

JIM CROW GUIDE TO THE U.S.A.: THE LAWS, CUSTOMS, AND ETIQUETTE GOVERNING THE CONDUCT OF NON-WHITES, AND OTHER MINORITIES AS SECOND-CLASS CITIZENS
Stetson Kennedy
230 pp. Greenwood Press, 1974. Reprint of the 1959 edition. $9.25.

LAW ADMINISTRATION AND NEGRO-WHITE RELATIONS IN PHILADEL-PHIA: A STUDY OF RACE RELATIONS
Bureau of Municipal Research, Philadelphia
183 pp. Greenwood Press. Reprint of the 1947 edition. $9.00.

THE LEOPARD'S SPOTS: SCIENTIFIC ATTITUDES TOWARD RACE IN AMER-ICA, 1815 TO 1859
William Stanton
University of Chicago Press, 1960. Cloth, $7.50; Pap. $2.75.

THE METROPOLITAN AREA AS A RACIAL PROBLEM
Morton Grodzins
University of Pittsburgh Press. Reprint of the 1958 edition. Pap. $1.95.

THE MIND AND MOOD OF BLACK AMERICA: 20TH CENTURY THOUGHT
S.P. Fullinwider
Shows how myths, based on psychological needs, were developed to become the core of a racist ideology spanning two centuries. 266 pp. Dorsey Press, 1969. Cloth, $10.00; Pap. $5.50.

MINORITIES IN AMERICAN HIS-TORY: RECONSTRUCTION AND NATIONAL GROWTH, 1865-1900
William Loren Katz
The plight of the newly-freed black man in the post-Civil War Soth. 96 pp. Franklin Watts, Inc., 1974. Age 12 up. $4.33.

THE MORALITY OF THE COLOR LINE: AN EXAMINATION OF THE RIGHT AND THE WRONG OF THE DIS-CRIMINATIONS AGAINST THE NEGRO IN THE UNITED STATES
Francis James Gilligan
222 pp. Greenwood Press. Reprint of the 1928 edition. $9.50.

THE NEGRO: HIS RIGHTS AND WRONGS
Francis J. Grimke
Gordon Press. $29.95.

NEGRO-MANIA: EXAMINATION OF THE FALSELY ASSUMED EQUALITY OF THE VARIOUS RACES OF MEN
John Campbell
Books for Libraries, Inc. Reprint of the 1851 edition. $16.00.

NEGRO-WHITE UNITY
Henry Winston
Discusses the fight against racism, Black Power, and the black liberation struggle. New Outlook Pubs. $.25.

THE NEGROES OF COLUMBIA, MIS-SOURI: A CONCRETE STUDY OF RACE PROBLEM
William Wilson Elwang
A look at racial prejudice as it existed in one university at the turn of the century. 84 pp. Metro Books, Inc. Reprint of the 1904 edition. $9.00.

THE NEW RACISM: REVERSE DIS-CRIMINATION IN AMERICA
Lionel Lokos
Arlington House Pubs., 1971. $9.95.

OREO: A PERSPECTIVE ON RACE AND MARGINAL MEN AND WOMEN
Charles V. Willie
A book about living in, between, and beyond the races. 95 pp. Parameter Press, 1975. Pap. $3.95.

ORIGINS OF SEGREGATION
Joel R. Williamson, Editor

113 pp. D.C.Heath & Co., 1968. Pap. $2.50.

OUR RACE PROBLEMS
Henry Ferdinand Suksdorf
Books for Libraries. Reprint of the 1911 edition. $12.25.

PATTERNS OF RACIAL DISCRIMINATION, VOLUME 1: HOUSING
George von Furstenberg, Editor
Contains hitherto unpublished studies on racial discrimination in housing. 240 pp. Lexington Books, 1974. $16.00.

PATTERNS OF RACIAL DISCRIMINATION, VOLUME 2: EMPLOYMENT AND INCOME
George von Furstenberg, Editor
Stresses the interplay between the demand for and the supply of educational services and discrimination, unemployment and income equality. 272 pp. Lexington Books, 1974. $16.00.

PATTERNS OF RESIDENTIAL SEGREGATION
Linton C. Freeman and Morris H. Sunshine
160 pp. General Learning Corp., 1970. $9.50.

PLANTATION SOCIETIES, RACE RELATIONS, AND THE SOUTH
Edgar T. Thompson
A study of the general social order which formed around the plantation, and the areas which it dominated. 420 pp. Duke University Press, 1975. Cloth, $12.75; Pap. $6.75.

POLICE, POLITICS AND RACE: THE NEW YORK CITY REFERENDUM ON CIVILIAN REVIEW
David W. Abbott et al
American Jewish Committee, 1969.

POLITICAL STRATEGIES IN NORTHERN DESEGREGATION
Robert Crain and David Kirby
288 pp. Lexington Books, 1973. $10.00.

POLITICS OF EQUALITY
Thomas R. Dye
252 pp. Bobbs-Merrill Co., 1971. Cloth, $8.00; Pap. $3.95.

POVERTY AND DISCRIMINATION
Lester C. Thruow
214 pp. Brookings Institution, 1969. $7.95.

POWER AND THE BLACK COMMUNITY: A READER ON RADICAL SUBORDINATION IN THE UNITED STATES
Sethard Fisher
Alfred A. Knopf, Inc., 1970. Pap. $5.95.

PREJUDICE AND RACE RELATIONS
Raymond W. Mack
Contributors include Nathan Glazer, Bayard Rustin, and Julian Bond. 272 pp. Franklin Watts, Inc., 1970. Age 16 up. Cloth, $6.95; Pap. $2.45.

PREJUDICE AND YOUR CHILD
Kenneth B. Clark
A guide to understanding and preventing the damage which racial prejudice can cause to young minds and personalities, whether aggressors or victims. Beacon Press, 1963. Pap. $1.95.

*PREJUDICE IN THE UNITED STATES OF AMERICA
Charles I. Glock and Ellen Siegleman, Editors
220 pp. Praeger Pubs., 1969. Cloth, $6.95; Pap. $2.50. Below college level.

PREJUDICE: 21 TALES OF OPPRESSION AND LIBERATION
C.R.Lawson, Editor
New American Library, 1975. $1.50.

PRUDENCE CRANDALL: AN INCIDENT OF RACISM IN 19TH CENTURY CONNECTICUT
Edmond Fuller
133 pp. Wesleyan University Press, 1971. Illus. $7.50.

RACE ATTITUDES IN CHILDREN
Bruno Lasker
394 pp. Greenwood Press, Inc. Reprint of the 1929 edition. $15.75.

RACE AWARENESS: THE NIGHTMARE AND THE VISION
Ruth Miller and Paul J. Dolan, Editors
488 pp. Oxford University Press, 1971. Pap. $4.95.

RACE, CLASS AND POLITICAL CONSCIOUSNESS
John C. Leggett
243 pp. General Learning Press, 1972. Cloth, $6.50; Pap. $5.25.

RACE AND CULTURE
Robert E. Park
Free Press, 1950. Cloth, $7.95; Pap. $3.45.

RACE DISTINCTIONS IN AMERICAN LAW
Gilbert Thomas Stephenson
388 pp. Negro Universities Press. Reprint of the 1910 edition. $16.00.

RACE: THE HISTORY OF AN IDEA IN AMERICA
Thomas F. Gossett
A history of racial theories, beliefs, and practices, and of their consequences in the United States from colonial days until the present. 522 pp. Southern Methodist University Press. Reprint of the 1963 edition. $12.50.

RACE IN THE CITY: POLITICAL TRUST AND PUBLIC POLICY IN THE NEW URBAN SYSTEM
Joel D. Aberbach and Jack L. Walker
293 pp. Little, Brown, and Co., 1973. Pap. $5.95.

RACE, JOBS AND POLITICS: THE STORY OF THE FEPC
Louis Ruchames
255 pp. Negro Universities Press. Reprint of the 1953 edition. $13.75.

RACE AND THE NEWS MEDIA
Paul Fisher and Ralph Lowenstein, Editors
168 pp. Praeger Pubs., 1967. $6.00.

RACE ORTHODOXY IN THE SOUTH: AND OTHER ASPECTS OF THE NEGRO QUESTION
Thomas Pearce Bailey
AMS Press, Inc. Reprint of the 1914 edition. $15.00.

RACE AND POLITICS: "BLEEDING KANSAS" AND THE COMING OF THE CIVIL WAR
James A. Rawley
The controversies that followed the repeal of the Missouri Compromise, and the theory that the real issue was not slavery as such, but race. 304 pp. J.B. Lippincott Co., 1970. $2.45.

RACE AND POVERTY: THE ECONOMICS OF DISCRIMINATION
John F. Kahn, Editor
Prentice-Hall, 1969. Pap. $1.95.

RACE PREJUDICE: *How It Began, When It Will End*
George Breitman
16 pp. Pathfinder Press. $.35.

RACE PREJUDICE
Jean Finot
Books for Libraries, Inc. Reprint of the 1906 edition. $11.75.

THE RACE PROBLEM IN THE SOUTH
Joseph LeConte
Books for Libraries. Reprint of the 1892 edition. $5.75.

RACE, RACISM, AND AMERICAN LAW
Derrick A. Bell, Jr.
1087 pp. Little, Brown, and Co., 1973. $19.00.

RACE RELATIONS: ADJUSTMENT OF WHITES AND NEGROES IN THE UNITED STATES
Willis Duke Weatherford and Charles S. Johnson
590 pp. Greenwood Press. Reprint of the 1934 edition. $17.50.

RACE RELATIONS AND AMERICAN LAW
Jack Greenberg, Editor
Columbia University Press, 1959. $14.00.

RACE RELATIONS: ELEMENTS AND SOCIAL DYNAMICS
Oliver C. Cox
Traces the effects of the political, economic, and cultural forces on race relations in American society. 576 pp. Wayne State University Press, 1975. $19.95.

RACE RELATIONS: A MONTHLY SUMMARY OF EVENTS AND TRENDS Vols. 1 TO 5
Negro Universities Press. Reprint of the 1943 to 1948 edition. $115.00.

RACE RELATIONS AND THE RACE PROBLEM: A DEFINITION AND AN ANALYSIS
Edgar Tristan Thompson, Editor
338 pp. Greenwood Press, Inc. Reprint of the 1939 edition. $14.50.

RACE RELATIONS IN THE UNITED STATES
Keesing
Traces relations between whites and blacks since

the Supreme Court decision on public school desegregation. Charles Scribner's Sons. $2.95.

RACE, RESEARCH, AND REASON: SOCIAL WORK PERSPECTIVES
Roger R. Miller, Editor
Report of the Institute on Research Toward Improving Race Relations, 1967. Ten papers. 190 pp. National Association of Social Workers, 1969. $3.75.

RACE AND RESIDENCE: AN ANALYSIS OF PROPERTY VALUES IN TRANSITIONAL AREAS: ATLANTA, GEORGIA, 1960 TO 1971
Howard Openshaw
Georgia State University, School of Business Administration. Pap. $3.00.

RACE AND RUMORS OF RACE: CHALLENGE TO AMERICAN CRISIS
Howard Washington Odum
245 pp. Negro Universities Press. Reprint of the 1943 edition. $11.50.

RACE AND THE SOCIAL SCIENCES
Irwin Katz and Patricia Gurin, Editors
Basic Books, 1969. $8.95.

RACIAL CONFLICT AND THE AMERICAN MAYOR: POWER, POLARIZATION AND PERFORMANCE
Charles H. Levine
Case studies of mayoral leadership in New York, Chicago, Los Angeles, Gary, Cleveland, and Birmingham demonstrates how racial polarization minimizes the prospects of the "civic entrepreneur" style of leadership. 176 pp. Lexington Books, 1974. $13.50.

RACIAL CONFLICT AND NEGOTIATIONS: PERSPECTIVES AND FIRST CASE STUDIES
W. Ellison Chalmers and Gerald W. Cormick, Editors
Examines the use of the negotiations process in racial conflict. 252 pp. Institute of Labor and Industrial Relations, 1971. Cloth, $12.00; Pap. $5.95.

RACIAL AND CULTURAL MINORITIES: AN ANALYSIS OF PREJUDICE AND DISCRIMINATION
George E. Simpson and Milton Yinger, Jr. Harper and Row Pubs., 1972. $14.95.

RACIAL DESEGREGATION AND IN-

TEGRATION: 1956
The American Academy of Political and Social Service, 1975. Cloth, $5.00; Pap. $4.00.

RACIAL DISCRIMINATION AND ECONOMIC DEVELOPMENT: A CASE STUDY OF SOUTH CAROLINA
Joan Hoffman
Analyzes the relationship between racial cocupational discrimination and economic growth. Lexington Books, 1975.

RACIAL DISCRIMINATION AND PUBLIC POLICY IN THE UNITED STATES
Richard M. Burkey
144 pp. Lexington Books, Inc., 1971. $10.00.

RACIAL DISCRIMINATION IN THE UNITED STATES
Thomas F. Pettigrew, Editor
A selection of recent studies on discrimination against blacks in the United States. Harper & Row Publishers, 1975. Paper.

RACIAL FACTORS IN AMERICAN HISTORY
Herman Feldman
Jerome S. Ozer Pubs. Reprint of the 1931 edition. $13.50.

RACIAL NEGOTIATIONS: POTENTIALS AND LIMITATIONS
W. Ellison Chalmers
New institutional and racial relationships. 281 pp. Institute of Labor and Industrial Relations, 1974. $15.00.

RACIAL OPPRESSION IN AMERICA
Robert Blauner
Harper and Row Pubs., 1972. Pap. $5.50.

RACIAL POLICIES AND PRACTICES OF REAL ESTATE BROKERS
Rose Helper
The author attempts to find out how real estate personnel regard their racial practices and analyzes the ideology on which their practice is based. University of Minnesota Press, 1969. $9.50.

RACIAL PRIDE AND PREJUDICE
Eric John Dingwall
246 pp. Negro Universities Press. Reprint of the 1946 edition. $11.00.

RACIALLY SEPARATE OR TOGETHER?
Thomas F. Pettigrew

A presentation of specific and concrete elements of American race relations. 288 pp. McGraw-Hill Book Co., 1971. Cloth, $6.50; Pap. $4.95.

RACIAL THOUGHT IN AMERICA: FROM THE PURITANS TO ABRAHAM LINCOLN
Louis Ruchames
University of Massachusetts Press, 1969. $15.00.

RACISM: A CASEBOOK
Frederick Lapides and David Burrows
Thomas Y. Crowell Co., 1971. Pap. $4.50.

RACISM: THE NATION'S MOST DANGEROUS POLLUTANT
Gus Hall
A call to white workers, the Left, radical movements, and the Communist Party for a struggle against racism and white chauvinism within people's movements. New Outlook Pubs. $.50.

RACISM IN THE UNITED STATES
D. Reimers
Holt, Rinehart, and Winston, 1972. Pap. $3.00.

RELUCTANT REFORMERS: THE IMPACT OF RACISM ON AMERICAN SOCIAL REFORM MOVEMENTS
Robert Allen
Howard University Press, 1974. $8.95.

RESISTANCE TO RACIAL CHANGE IN THE URBAN NORTH
John Michael Ross
Examines the sources of opposition and challenges current theories of anti-racial change. 240 pp. Ballinger Publishing Co., 1975. $13.50.

THE RHETORIC OF RACIAL REVOLT
Roy Hill, Editor
Golden Bell Press, 1964. $5.50.

THE RISE OF MASSIVE RESISTANCE: RACE-POLITICS IN THE SOUTH DURING THE 1950's
Numan V. Bartley
384 pp. Louisiana State University Press, 1969. Illus. $10.00.

RUMORS, RACE AND RIOTS
Terry Ann Knopf
An examination and critique of three major models of rumor formation: the psychological, functional, and conspiratorial approaches. 390 pp. Transaction Books, 1975. $12.95.

SECRET CITY: A HISTORY OF RACE RELATIONS IN THE NATION'S CAPITOL
Constance M. Green
Princeton University Press, 1967. Cloth, $10.00; Pap. $3.95.

SELECT DISCUSSIONS OF RACE PROBLEMS
J.A. Bigham, Editor
Kraus Reprint Co. Reprint of the 1916 edition. Pap. $2.00.

*THE SEGREGATION ERA, EIGHTEEN SIXTY THREE TO NINETEEN FIFTY FOUR
Allen Weinstein and Frank O. Catell
320 pp. Oxford University Press, 1970. $9.95; Pap. $3.50. Below college level.

THE SEGREGATION FACTOR IN THE FLORIDA DEMOCRATIC GUBERNATORIAL PRIMARY OF 1956
Helen Jacobstein
84 pp University of Florida Press, 1972. Pap. $2.00.

SEGREGATION: THE INNER CONFLICT OF THE SOUTH
Robert Penn Warren
Random House, Inc., 1956. $4.50.

THE SEGREGATION STRUGGLE IN LOUISIANA, 1862 TO 1877
Roger A. Fischer
180 pp. University of Illinois Press, 1974. $6.95.

THE SISTERS OF ORLEANS: A TALE OF RACE AND SOCIAL CONFLICT
Books for Libraries, Inc. Reprint of the 1871 edition. $15.50.

TO STEM THIS TIDE: A SURVEY OF RACIAL TENSION AREAS IN THE UNITED STATES
Charles Spurgeon Johnson
AMS Press. Reprint of the 1943 edition. $6.00.

THE STRUGGLE WITHIN: RACE RELATIONS IN THE UNITED STATES
David Bowen
Grosset and Dunlap, Inc., 1972. $4.95.

STUDIES IN THE AMERICAN RACE PROBLEM
Wlfred Holt Stone
555 pp. Greenwood Press. Reprint of the 1908 edition. $17.00.

THE SUBJECT IS RACE: TRADITIONAL IDEOLOGIES AND THE TEACHING OF RACE RELATIONS
Peter I. Rose
Gives a brief history of the teaching of race relations in the United States from the late nineteenth century on. Also offers a critique on the content and methodology of present courses, and suggestions for their improvement. 192 pp. Oxford University Press, 1968. Cloth, $5.95; Pap. $2.50.

*THE SUPREME COURT ON RACIAL DISCRIMINATION
Joseph Tussman, Editor
412 pp. Oxford University Press, 1963. Pap. $3.50. Below college level.

THROUGH DIFFERENT EYES: BLACK AND WHITE PERSPECTIVES ON AMERICAN RACE RELATIONS
Peter I. Rose, et al, Editors
The views of 20 sociologists and journalists, both black and white, on race relations in the United States today. 472 pp. Oxford University Press, 1973. Cloth, $12.50; Pap. $3.95.

TOWARD INTERRACIAL COOPERATION
National Interracial Conference
192 pp. Negro Universities Press. Reprint of the 1926 edition. $9.50.

THE TREND OF THE RACES
George Edmund Haynes
Books for Libraries, Inc. Reprint of the 1922 edition. $10.00.

TWO, FOUR, SIX, EIGHT, WHEN YOU GONNA INTEGRATE?
Ernest Hirsch, et al
Liveright Publishing Corp., 1971. Pap. $2.75.

UNDERSTANDING RACE RELATIONS
Ina C. Brown
A study of the various historical, economic, and cultural factors necessary for an understanding of black and white relations in the United States. 288 pp. Prentice-Hall, Inc., 1973. Cloth, $7.95; Pap. $4.25.

WHITE ATTITUDES TOWARD BLACK PEOPLE
Angus Campbell
The future of race relations in the United States. 177 pp. Institute for Social Research, 1972. Cloth, $9.00; Pap. $5.00.

THE WHITE MAN'S BURDEN: HISTORICAL ORIGINS OF RACISM IN THE UNITED STATES
Winthrop Jordan
246 pp. Oxford University Press, 1974. Cloth, $8.95; Pap. $2.50.

WHITE RACISM AND BLACK AMERICANS
David G. Bromley and Charles F. Longino
662 pp. General Learning Press, 1972. Cloth, $12.50; Pap. $7.95.

WHITE RACISM AND THE LAW
Lois B. Moreland
Charles E. Merrill Publishing Co., 1970. Pap. $4.95.

WHITE SAVAGE: RACIAL FANTASIES IN THE POSTBELLUM SOUTH
Lawrence J. Friedman
192 pp. Prentice-Hall, 1970. Pap. $2.45.

THE WHITE USE OF BLACKS IN AMERICA
Dan Lacy
Recounts the policies of whites toward blacks in America for the period of 1619 to the present, and views and interprets the aggregate of laws, judicial decisions, racial etiquette, extra-legal violence, and personal attitudes that have marked the past 350 years. 288 pp. McGraw-Hill Book Co., 1973. Pap. $2.95.

WHY RACISM IS USED AGAINST WELFARE PROGRAMS: WHY WORKERS SHOULD JOIN WELFARE RECIPIENTS' STRUGGLES
Julia Barnes
The racist and bureaucratic practices of welfare officials. New Outlook Pubs. $.10.

YAZOO: INTEGRATION IN A DEEP-SOUTHERN TOWN
Willie Morris
Harper's Magazine Press, 1971. $6.95.

RELIGION

AFRO-AMERICAN RELIGIOUS STUDIES: A COMPREHENSIVE BIBLIOGRAPHY WITH LOCATIONS IN AMERICAN LIBRARIES

Ethel E. Williams and Clifton F. Brown, Editors
454 pp. Scarecrow Press, 1972. $13.50.

THE AMERICAN CHURCHES: THE BULWARKS OF AMERICAN SLAVERY
James Gillespie Birney
The author presents this indictment of the church's indifference to the slavery issue. Arno Press. Reprint of the 1842 edition. $4.50.

AMERICAN CHURCHES AND THE NEGRO
W.D. Weatherford
Pre-Civil War to the present. 310 pp. Christopher Publishing House. $5.95.

BLACK AWARENESS: A THEOLOGY OF HOPE
Major J. Jones
An examination of the black experience and the nature of the church, from pre-Civil War days until the present Black Awareness movement. 144 pp. Abingdon Books, 1971. Pap. $2.45.

BLACK BELIEF
Henry H. Mitchell
An interpretation of the black religious experience in this country from slavery to the contemporary storefront church. 192 pp. Harper & Row Publishers, 1974. Pap. $6.95.

THE BLACK CHRISTIAN EXPERIENCE
Emmanuel McCall
Broadman Press, 1972. $3.95.

BLACK CHRISTIAN NATIONALISM: NEW DIRECTIONS FOR THE BLACK CHURCH
Albert B. Cleage, Jr.
The Black Christian Nationalists seek to radicalize the Black church and ultimately create a national cultural revolution. This book is the manifesto of this movement. William Morrow & Co., 1972. Cloth, $7.95; Pap. $3.45.

THE BLACK CHURCH IN AMERICA
Hart M. Nelsen, et al, Editors
Basic Books, 1971. $10.75.

BLACK CHURCH IN THE SIXTIES
Hart M. Nelsen and Anne Kusener Nelsen
Attacks the view that the black church tends to inhibit civil rights militancy and discredit the stereotype of religion that it is oblivious to black problems or hesitant to fight against them. University Press of Kentucky, 1975. $11.50.

THE BLACK CHURCH IN THE UNITED STATES, ITS ORIGIN, GROWTH, CONTRIBUTIONS, AND OUTLOOKS
William L. Banks
Moody Press, 1972. Pap. $2.25.

THE BLACK CHURCHMEN
Andrew W. Tilly
Crescent Pubns., 1973. Pap. $5.95.

THE BLACK EXPERIENCE IN RELIGION: A COLLECTION OF READINGS
C. Eric Lincoln, Editor
Doubleday and Co., 1974. $3.95.

BLACK GODS OF THE METROPOLIS: NEGRO RELIGIOUS CULTS OF THE URBAN NORTH
Arthur H. Fauset
University of Pennsylvania Press, 1971. Pap. $1.95.

THE BLACK MAN IN THE OLD TESTAMENT AND ITS WORLD
Alfred G. Dunston, Jr.
Dorrance and Co., 1974. $6.95.

THE BLACK MUSLIMS IN AMERICA
C. Eric Lincoln
A sociological analysis of the history, workings, and ideology of the Muslim movement. Beacon Press, 1973. Cloth, $12.50; Pap. $3.95.

A BLACK POLITICAL THEOLOGY
J. Deotis Roberts
Presents the place of the black church as the main institution poised to implement the liberation of whole persons and a whole people. 240 pp. Westminster Press, 1974. Pap. $3.95.

BLACK POWER AND CHRISTIAN RESPONSIBILITY
C. Freeman Sleeper
The author gives a new interpretation to the Bible through the ethical problem of Black Power. 224 pp. Abingdon Books, 1969. $4.50.

BLACK POWER AND WHITE PROTESTANTS: A CHRISTIAN RESPONSE TO THE NEW NEGRO PLURALISM
Joseph C. Hough, Jr.
240 pp. Oxford University Press, 1968. $6.95.

THE BLACK PREACHER IN AMERICA
Charles V. Hamilton
William Morrow and Co., 1972. Cloth, $7.95; Pap. $2.95.

BLACK RELIGION AND AMERICAN EVANGELICALISM: WHITE PROTESTANTS, PLANTATION MISSIONS, AND THE FLOWING OF NEGRO CHRISTIANITY, 1787-1865
Milton C. Sernett
Examines the life and work, the faith and order of Black Christians. 320 pp. Scarecrow Press, 1975. $12.50

BLACK RELIGION AND BLACK RADICALISM
Gayraud S. Wilmore
Historical documentation that black radicalism in the U.S. is related directly to black Christianity. Doubleday & Co., 1975. Cloth, $7.95; Pap. $3.50.

BLACK RELIGION: ThE NEGRO AND CHRISTIANITY IN THE UNITED STATES
Joseph R. Washington, Jr.
How segregation has forced black religion to become a freedom substitute, divorced from the mainstream of the Christian heritage. Beacon Press, 1964. Cloth, $5.00; Pap. $2.95.

BLACK SECTS AND CULTS
Joseph R. Washington, Jr.
A study of the religious cults and sects in the black community. Doubleday & Co., 1972. Cloth, $5.95; Pap. $2.95.

BLACK THEOLOGY AND BLACK POWER
James H. Cone
Seabury Press, 1969. Pap. $2.95.

THE CATHOLIC CHURCH AND THE NEGRO
John T. Gillard
324 pp. Johnson Reprint. Reprint of the 1929 edition. Illus. $14.00.

CHILDREN OF FREEDOM, BLACK LIBERATION IN CHRISTIAN PERSPECTIVE
Peter C. Hodgeson
Fortress Press, 1975. Pap. $2.95.

CHRISTIAN FAITH IN BLACK AND WHITE: A PRIMER IN THEOLOGY FROM THE BLACK PERSPECTIVE
Warner R. Traynham
Religious and social ideas as seen by the black community. 121 pp. Parameter Press, 1973. Cloth, $7.00; Pap. $4.60.

COLD BLACK PREACH
Robert H. De Coy

Holloway House Publishing Co., 1971. Pap. $1.50.

COMMUNITY IN A BLACK PENTECOSTAL CHURCH: AN ANTHPOLOGICAL STUDY
Melvin D. Williams
A look at the black Southern peasant transplanted to the urban North, the role of the black church in this transition, the concept of community in modern society, and the cultural content of poverty. 202 pp. University of Pittsburgh Press, 1974. $9.95.

A COMPASSIONATE ADDRESS TO THE CHRISTIAN NEGROES IN VIRGINIA
Benjamin Fawcett
AMS Press, Inc. Reprint of the 1755 edition. $5.00.

THE DARK CENTER: A PROCESS THEOLOGY OF BLACKNESS
Eulqlio Baltazar
Paulist-Newman Press, 1974. Pap. $4.95.

THE EDUCATION OF NEGRO MINISTERS
William Daniel
187 pp. Negro Universities Press. Reprint of the 1925 edition. $9.50.

GOD STRUCK ME DEAD
Charles H. Johnson, Editor
United Church Press, 1969. $3.45.

GOD'S MEN OF COLOR: THE COLORED CATHOLIC PRIESTS OF THE UNITED STATES, 1854-1954
Albert S. Foley
The story of the black Catholic clergy of the United States. Arno Press, 1969. Reprint of the 1955 edition. $10.00.

THE GOSPEL AMONG THE SLAVES: A SHORT ACCOUNT OF MISSIONARY OPERATIONS AMONG THE AFRICAN SLAVES OF THE SOUTHERN STATES
William Pope Harrison
AMS Press. Reprint of the 1893 edition. $15.50.

THE HISTORY OF THE COLORED METHODIST EPISCOPAL CHURCH IN AMERICA: COMPRISING ITS ORGANIZATION, SUBSEQUENT DEVELOPMENT, AND PRESENT STATUS
Charles H. Phillips
From the farm to the bishopric. Arno Press. Reprint of the 1898 edition. $12.00.

IDEOLOGY OF BLACKNESS
Raymond F. Betts
192 pp. D.C.Heath & Co., 1971. Pap. $4.50.

IS GOD A WHITE RACIST? A PREAMBLE TO BLACK THEOLOGY
William R. Jones
Doubleday and Co. Cloth, $7.95; Pap. $2.95.

LIBERATION AND RECONCILIATION: A BLACK THEOLOGY
J. Deotis Roberts
Examine the essential categories of theology as they relate to the prospects for blacks in this country. 208 pp. Westminster Press, 1971. Pap. $3.50.

MAJOR THEMES IN NORTHERN BLACK RELIGIOUS THOUGHT, 1800-1860
Monroe Fordham
Afro-American religious thought during the antebellum period, the formative years of the independent black church in the United States; an analysis of the principal ideas and their social significance. Exposition Press, 1975. $8.50.

METHODISM AND THE NEGRO
Issac Lemuel Thomas
328 pp. Negro Universities Press. Reprint of the 1910 edition. Illus. $14.50.

THE NEGRO CHURCH IN AMERICA, THE BLACK CHURCH SINCE FRAZIER
E. Franklin Frazier; C. Eric Lincoln
Two volumes in one. A religious study with an historical perspective combined with Lincoln's view of black institutional religion. Schocken Books, 1975. Cloth, $10.00; Pap. $2.95.

NEGRO IN THE CHRISTIAN PULPIT; OR THE TWO CHARACTERS AND TWO DESTINIES, AS DELINEATES IN 21 PRACTICAL SERMONS
James Walker Hood
363 pp. Negro Universities Press. Reprint of the 1884 edition. $14.75.

THE NEGRO'S CHURCH
Benjamin J. Mays and Joseph W. Nicholson
A first-hand investigation of 609 urban and 185 rural Negro churches in twelve major cities and four non-urban areas. Arno Press. Reprint of the 1933 edition. $11.00.

THE NEGRO'S GOD AS REFLECTED IN HIS LITERATURE
Benjamin Elijah Mays
Russell and Russell. Reprint of the 1938 edition. Illus. Cloth, $8.00. Athenum Publishers, pap. $2.75.

THE POLITICS OF GOD: THE FUTURE OF THE BLACK CHURCHES
Joseph R. Washington, Jr.
A theological basis for the black revolution, arguing that blacks have a sacred mission to free white souls from the sins of racism. Beacon Press, 1969. Pap. $2.95.

THE PROTESTANT CHURCH AND THE NEGRO: A PATTERN OF SEGREGATION
Frank Samuel Loescher
159 pp. Negro Universities Press. Reprint of the 1948 edition. $10.50.

THE QUEST FOR A BLACK THEOLOGY
James J. Gardiner and J. Deotis Roberts, Editors
United Church Press, 1971. $5.95.

RELIGION IN HIGHER EDUCATION AMONG NEGROES
Richard I. McKinney
The scene in leading colleges and universities: status of religious workers, attitudes of administrators, students and teachers towards religion's educational role, and an extensive bibliography. Arno Press. Reprint of the 1945 edition. $9.00.

THE RELIGIOUS INSTRUCTION OF THE NEGROES IN THE UNITED STATES
Charles C. Jones
Books for Libraries. 277 pp. Reprint of the 1842 edition. $12.25. Kraus Reprint Co., $11.50. Negro University Press, $11.00.

SAY AMEN BROTHER! OLD-TIME NEGRO PREACHING: A STUDY IN AMERICAN FRUSTRATION
William H. Pipes
210 pp. Negro Universities Press. Reprint of the 1951 edition. $11.00.

A SCRIPTURAL EXAMINATION OF THE INSTITUTION OF SLAVERY IN THE UNITED STATES
Howell Cobb
Books for Libraries, 1856. $11.75.

SLAVERY AND THE CHURCHES IN EARLY AMERICA
Lester B. Scherer

Traces the record of American Christianity with respect to slavery. 208 pp. William B. Eerdmans Publishing Co., 1975. $7.95.

SOUL-FORCE: AFRICAN HERITAGE IN AFRO-AMERICAN RELIGION
Leonard E. Barrett
A study which describes the means of survival for the African in "diaspora." Doubleday & Co., 1974. Cloth, $7.95; Pap. $3.50.

THE SOUTHERN NEGRO NUN
Sister Mary Gabriella Guidry
Autobiography of a black member of the Congregation of Sisters of the Holy Family, and her work as a teacher in the South. Exposition Press, 1974. Illus. $6.50.

WHITE PROTESTANTISM AND THE NEGRO
David M. Reimers
248 pp. Oxford University Press, 1965. $7.50.

SLAVERY

AFTER SLAVERY: THE NEGRO IN SOUTH CAROLINA DURING RECONSTRUCTION, 1861-1877
Joel Williamson
456 pp. University of North Carolina Press, 1965. Cloth, $9.25; Pap. $3.45.

THE AFTERMATH OF SLAVERY: A STUDY OF THE CONDITION AND ENVIRONMENT OF THE AMERICAN NEGRO
William A. Sinclair
An analysis of the conditions facing black men in the Southern states during Reconstruction. Arno Press. Reprint of the 1905 edition. Cloth, $11.00; Pap. $3.45.

AMERICAN LIBERTIES AND AMERICAN SLAVERY: MORALLY AND POLITICALLY ILLUSTRATED
S.B. Treadwell
Books for Libraries. Reprint of the 1838 edition. $15.75.

AMERICAN NEGRO SLAVE REVOLTS
Herbert Aptheker
A documented study of slave revolts and other forms of resistance to slavery in the United States. 416 pp. International Publishers, 1969. $3.75.

AMERICAN NEGRO SLAVERY: A SURVEY OF THE SUPPLY, EMPLOYMENT, AND CONTROL OF NEGRO LABOR AS DETERMINED BY THE PLANTATION REGIME
Ulrich Bonnell Phillips
530 pp. Louisiana State University Press, 1966. Pap. $2.95.

THE AMERICAN PREJUDICE AGAINST COLOR: AN AUTHENTIC NARRATIVE, SHOWING HOW EASILY THE NATION GOT INTO AN UPROAR, BY WILLIAM G. ALLEN, A REFUGEE FROM AMERICAN DESPOTISM
William G. Allen
A black abolitionist who married one of his white students, and was subsequently driven out. Arno Press. Reprint of the 1853 edition. $4.50.

THE AMERICAN SLAVE: A COMPOSITE AUTOBIOGRAPHY
George P. Rawick
This nineteenth volume work provides a comprehensive view of the culture and life of the American slave. Volume 1 appraises the history of the blacks in America. Volumes 2-19 comprise the entire collection of 2,000 personal accounts of ex-slaves recorded by the WPA and Fisk University project of the 1920s and 1930s. 19 volumes. Greenwood Press, 1972. $450.00.

THE AMERICAN SLAVE CODE IN THEORY AND PRACTICE
William Goodell
A collection of documents, statutes, and court decisions on slavery. Arno Press. Reprint of the 1853 edition. $15.00.

THE AMERICAN SLAVE TRADE
John R. Spears
The development, peak and decline of the slave trade between the United States and Africa. 232 pp. Corner House Publishers. Reprint of the 1900 edition. $7.50.

AMERICAN SLAVERY AS IT IS: TESTIMONY OF A THOUSAND WITNESSES
Theodore Dwight Weld
A pre-Emancipation Proclamation anti-slavery pamphlet. Arno Press. Reprint of the 1839 edition. $7.00.

AMERICAN SLAVERY AND COLOUR
William Chambers

216 pp. Metro Books, Inc. Reprint of 1857 edition. $9.50.

AMERICAN SLAVERY: THE QUESTION OF BLACK RESISTANCE
John H. Bracey, Jr., Editor
Eleven essays on the history of black resistance in America. 200 pp. Wadsworth Publishing Co., 1974. $4.50.

ANTI-SLAVERY ADDRESSES OF 1844 AND 1845
Salmon Portland Chase and Charles Dexter Cleveland
167 pp. Greenwood Press. Reprint of the 1867 edition. $8.00.

THE ANTI-SLAVERY HISTORY OF THE JOHN BROWN YEAR: THE TWENTY SEVENTH ANNUAL REPORT OF THE AMERICAN ANTI-SLAVERY SOCIETY
American Anti-Slavery Society
The views of prominent abolitionists toward John Brown's raid on Harper's Ferry. Arno Press. Reprint of the 1861 edition. $12.00.

THE ANTI-SLAVERY IMPULSE:1830-1844
Gilbert Hobbs Barnes
An account of the religious zeal and organizing genius of Theodore Weld in the struggle for Negro rights. 336 pp. Harcourt Brace Jovanovich, Inc., 1974. Pap. $2.65.

AN ANTI-SLAVERY MANUAL
John Gregg Fee
A Southern abolitionist who was disowned by his slaveholding father. Arno Press. Reprint of the 1848 edition. $8.50.

ANTISLAVERY ORIGINS OF THE CIVIL WAR IN THE UNITED STATES
Dwight Lowell Dumond
142 pp. University of Michigan Press. Pap. $1.95.

AUNT DICE: THE STORY OF A FAITHFUL SLAVE
Nina HIll Robinson
Books for Libraries, Inc. Reprint of the 1897 edition. $11.00.

AUTOBIOGRAPHY OF A FEMALE SLAVE
Mattie Griffiths
Books for Libraries. Reprint of the 1856 edition. $13.25.

THE BIBLE DEFENCE OF SLAVERY
Josiah Priest and W.S.Brown
Scholarly Press. Reprint of the 1851 edition. $27.50.

BLACK AMERICA: A STUDY OF THE EX-SLAVE AND HIS LATE MASTER
Sir William Laird Clowes
240 pp. Negro Universities Press. Reprint of the 1891 edition. $12.25.

BLACK BONDAGE: THE LIFE OF SLAVES IN THE SOUTH
Walter Goodman
Life in the South using the slaves' own narratives. 160 pp. Farrar, Straus and Giroux, 1969. Photos. Age 12 up. $3.95.

THE BLACK MAN OF THE SOUTH AND THE REBELS; OR, THE CHARACTERISTICS OF THE FORMER, AND THE RECENT OUTRAGES FOR THE LATTER
C. Stearns
Kraus Reprint Co. Reprint of the 1872 edition. $20.00.

BLACK REBELLION
Thomas Wentworth Higginson
The principal slave insurrections are told by a militant white abolitionist minister. Arno Press. Reprint of the 1889 edition. $7.00.

BLACK SLAVE NARRATIVES
J. Bayliss, Editor
Macmillan Publishing Co., 1970. Cloth, $5.95; Pap. $1.50.

BLACKS IN THE ABOLITIONIST MOVEMENT
John H. Bracey, et al, Editors
Thirteen readings and writings about the abolition of slavery, written by black abolitionists. 168 pp. Wadsworth Publishing Co., 1974. Pap. $4.50.

BLACKS IN BONDAGE: LETTERS OF AMERICAN SLAVES
Robert S. Starobin
Daily existence, flights to freedom in the North, attempts at rebellion, and new life in Liberia. 196 pp. Franklin Watts, Inc., 1974. Cloth, $8.95; Pap. $3.95. Age 16 up.

BOND AND FREE: A TRUE TALE OF SLAVE TIMES
James H.W. Howard
Books for Libraries, Inc. Reprint of the 1886 edition. $12.75.

BOSTON SLAVE RIOT AND TRIAL OF ANTHONY BURNS
Anonymous

An eyewitness account by an anonymous observer of the apprehension, trial and extradition of a slave under the Fugitive Slave Law of 1850 that so enraged Bostonians that they rioted in the streets of Boston until Federal troops were called to restore order to the city. 86 pp. Metro Books, Inc. Reprint of the 1854 edition. $9.00.

THE CHILD'S ANTI-SLAVERY BOOK
Contains a few words about American slave children, and stories of slave life. Books for Libraries. Reprint of the 1859 edition. $9.00.

CHILDREN OF THE SLAVES
Stephen Graham

315 pp. Johnson Reprint. Reprint of the 1920 edition. $18.25.

THE DOMESTIC SLAVE TRADE OF THE SOUTHERN STATES
Winfield H. Collins

Slavery in the United States, particularly the Southern states. Kennikat Press. Reprint of the 1904 edition. $6.50.

*THE DRED SCOTT DECISION, MARCH 6, 1857: SLAVERY AND THE SUPREME COURT'S "SELF-INFLICTED WOUND"
Frank B. Latham

The case that drew America closer to the Civil War. 54 pp. Franklin Watts, Inc., 1968. Cloth, $3.90; Pap. $1.25. Age 12 up.

EARLY AMERICAN VIEWS ON NEGRO SLAVERY
M. Mellon

New American Library, 1975. $1.25.

EARLY STUDIES OF SLAVERY BY STATES
464 pp. This book consists of five titles: HISTORY OF SLAVERY IN CONNECTICUT, Bernard Christian Steiner, 1893; SLAVERY IN THE STATE OF NORTH CAROLINA, James Spencer Bassett, 1899; A STUDY OF SLAVERY IN NEW JERSEY, Henry Scofield Cooley, 1896; SLAVERY AND SERVITUDE IN NEW JERSEY, Alfred Miller Heston, 1903; HISTORY OF SLAVERY IN VIRGINIA, James Curtis Ballagh, 1902. Metro Books Inc., 1972. $20.00.

EMANCIPATION
William Ellery Channing

An abolitionist argues that since emancipation of the slaves had worked well in the West Indies, it could work in the United States. Arno Press. Reprint of the 1840 edition. $4.50.

THE ENORMITY OF THE SLAVE TRADE; AND THE DUTY OF SEEKING THE MORAL AND SPIRITUAL ELEVATION OF THE COLORED RACE.
American Tract Society

Speeches of Wilberforce, and other documents and records. Books for Libraries, 18-? $8.75.

ESSAYS AND PAMPHLETS ON ANTI-SLAVERY
Negro Universities Press. Reprint of the 1833 to 1898 editions. $12.75.

THE ETIQUETTE OF RACE RELATIONS IN THE SOUTH: *A Study in Social Control*
Bertram Wilbur Doyle

This black historian describes the content of interracial relations between slaves, masters, and freedmen in the various spheres of their lives--on the plantation, in the church, in family life--and gives insight into the foundation on which the structure of racism rested. Schocken Books. Pap. $2.75.

AN EXPOSITION OF THE AFRICAN SLAVE TRADE
From the year 1840 to 1850, inclusive. Prepared from official documents, and published by direction of the representatives of the Religious Society of Friends in Pennsylvania, New Jersey and Delaware. Books for Libraries. Reprint of the 1851 edition. $10.00.

THE FAITHFUL SLAVE
Robert Morris

Books for Libraries, Inc. Reprint of the 1852 edition. $11.25.

FIVE SLAVE NARRATIVES: A COMPENDIUM
William Loren Katz, Editor

Arno Press, 1968. $15.00.

THE FREEDMAN'S BUREAU IN SOUTH CAROLINA, 1865-1872
Martin Abbott

172 pp. University of North Carolina Press, 1967. $6.95.

THE FREEDMEN OF THE SOUTH
Linda W. Slaughter

Kraus Reprint Co. Reprint of the 1869 edition. $10.00.

THE FREEDMEN'S BOOK
Lydia Maria Child

Originally used as a textbook in schools attended by ex-slaves, this book contains essays on slavery, black heroes, and the abolition movement. Arno Press. Reprint of the 1865 edition. $8.50.

FROM SUNDOWN TO SUNUP: THE MAKING OF THE BLACK COMMUNITY
George P. Rawick

208 pp. Greenwood Press, 1972. Volume 1 of *The American Slave, A Composite Autobiography.* $10.00.

THE FRONTIER AGAINST SLAVERY: WESTERN ANTI-NEGRO PREJUDICE AND THE SLAVERY EXTENSION CONTROVERSY
Eugene H. Berwanger

176 pp. University of Illinois Press, 1971. Cloth, $5.95; Pap. $1.95.

THE FUGITIVE SLAVE LAW AND ANTHONY BURNS: A PROBLEM IN LAW ENFORCEMENT
Jane H. and William H. Pease

The story of one of the most dramatic fugitive slave incidents which reinforced both Northern fears, that slavery eroded the rights of free men, and white Southern fears that abolitionism increasingly threatened their property rights and personal security. 103 pp. J.V. Lippincott Co., 1975. $2.75.

GOD AGAINST SLAVERY: AND THE FREEDOM AND DUTY OF THE PULPIT TO REBUKE IT, AS A SIN AGAINST GOD
George Barrell Cheever

A founder of the Church Anti-Slavery Society who called on all Christians to denounce bondage. Arno Press. Reprint of the 1857 edition. $9.50.

THE HIGHER LAW, IN ITS RELATION TO CIVIL GOVERNMENT: WITH PARTICULAR REFERENCE TO SLAVERY AND THE FUGITIVE SLAVE LAW
William Hosmer

Books for Libraries, Inc. Reprint of the 1852 edition. $10.00.

THE HISTORY OF THE ANTI-SLAVERY CAUSE IN STATE AND NATION
Austin Willey

Books for Libraries. Reprint of the 1866 edition. $16.00.

AN HISTORICAL RESEARCH RESPECTING THE OPINION OF THE FOUNDERS OF THE REPUBLIC ON NEGROES AS SLAVES, AS CITIZENS, AND AS SOLDIERS
George Livermore

A documentary historical study of the opinions of famous Americans on the Negro during our nation's early years. Arno Press. Reprint of the 1862 edition. $6.50.

THE HISTORY OF NEGRO SERVITUDE IN ILLINOIS AND OF THE SLAVERY AGITATION IN THAT STATE 1719 TO 1864
Norman Dwight Harris

276 pp. Negro Universities Press. Reprint of the 1904 edition. $11.50. Haskell House Publishers, $10.95.

A HISTORY OF NEGRO SLAVERY IN NEW YORK
Edgar J. McManus

Syracuse University Press, 1966. $5.95.

A HISTORY OF THE STRUGGLE FOR SLAVERY EXTENSION OR RESTRICTION IN THE U.S.
Horace Greeley

From the Declaration of Independence to the present day. Mainly compiled and condensed from the journals of Congress and other official records. Books for Libraries. Reprint of the 1856 edition. $11.00.

THE HOUSE OF BONDAGE; OR, CHARLOTTE BROOKS AND OTHER SLAVES, ORIGINAL AND LIFE-LIKE, AS THEY APPEARED IN THEIR OLD PLANTATION AND CITY SLAVE LIFE
Mrs. Octavia V. Rogers Albert

Books for Libraries, 1890. $12.25.

INQUIRY INTO THE CHARACTER AND TENDENCY OF THE AMERICAN COLONIZATION AND AMERICAN ANTI-SLAVERY SOCIETIES
William Jay

Books for Libraries, Inc. Reprint of the 1835 edition. $10.50.

JUDICIAL CASES CONCERNING AMERICAN SLAVERY AND THE NEGRO, 5 VOLS.
Helen T. Catterall, Editor

Octagon Books. Reprint of the 1926 to 1937 editions. $115.00 per set. negro University Press, $123.00 per set.

LECTURES ON THE PHILOSOPHY AND PRACTICE OF SLAVERY, AS EXHIBITED IN THE INSTITUTION OF DOMESTIC SLAVERY IN THE U.S.; WITH THE DUTIES OF MASTERS TO SLAVES
William A. Smith
Books for Libraries. Reprint of the 1856 edition. $12.75.

LECTURES ON SLAVERY
Benjamin Godwin
258 pp. Greenwood Press. Reprint of the 1836 edition. $10.25.

LIBERIA: OR, EARLY HISTORY AND SIGNAL PRESERVATION OF THE AMERICAN COLONY OF FREE NEGROES ON THE COAST OF AFRICA
William Innes, Editor
Books for Libraris, Inc. Reprint of the 1831 edition. $11.75.

MANY THOUSAND GONE: THE EX-SLAVES' ACCOUNT OF THEIR BONDAGE AND FREEDOM
Charles H. Nichols
Indiana University Press, 1969. Pap. $2.95.

MULES AND MEN
Zora Neale Hurston
Harper and Row Pubs., 1970. Cloth, $12.00; Pap. $1.50.

NAT TURNER'S SLAVE REVOLT, 1831
H. Aptheker
A full-length examination of the major slave rebellion in U.S. history. American Institute for Marxist Studies. Cloth, $4.00;Pap. $1.00.

THE NEGRO AND THE NATION: A HISTORY OF AMERICAN SLAVERY AND ENFRANCHISEMENT
George Spring Merriam
436 pp. Greenwood Press. Reprint of the 1906 edition. $14.00.

THE NEGRO IN PENNSYLVANIA: SLAVERY, SERVITUDE, FREEDOM, 1639-1861
Edward Raymond Turner
Details the economic, social, political, and cultural problems slaves and free Negroes faced in a liberal Northern state. Arno Press. Reprint of the 1911 edition. $10.00.

THE NEGRO IN MARYLAND: A STUDY OF THE INSTITUTION OF SLAVERY
Jeffrey Richardson Brackett
268 pp. Negro Universities Press. Reprint of the 1889 edition. $10.50. Books for Libraries, $12.25.

THE NEGRO IN PENNSYLVANIA: SLAVERY, SERVITUDE, FREEDOM, 1639 TO 1861
Edmund Raymond Turner
314 pp. Negro Universities Press. Reprint of the 1911 edition. $11.75.

THE NEGRO QUESTION: FROM SLAVERY TO CASTE, 1863-1910
Otto H. Olsen, Editor
A wide range of arguments of many different views dealing with the debate over the status of the Negro in the United States from the Civil War up to the founding of the NAACP. Pitman Publishing Corp. Cloth, $8.75; Pap. $4.20.

NEGRO SLAVERY IN LOUISIANA
Joe Gray Taylor
260 pp. Greenwood Press, 1960. $10.50.

NEGROES AND NEGRO SLAVERY: THE FIRST AN INFERIOR RACE, THE LATTER ITS NORMAL CONDITION
John H. Van Evrie
Books for Libraries, Inc. Reprint of the 1863 edition. $12.50.

NOTES ON THE PROGRESS OF THE COLORED PEOPLE OF MARYLAND SINCE THE WAR: A SUPPLEMENT TO THE NEGRO IN MARYLAND
Jeffrey R. Brackett
A study of the institution of slavery. Books for Libraries, 1890. $10.00.

OUT OF THE HOUSE OF BONDAGE
Kelly Miller
Arno Press. Reprint of the 1914 edition. Cloth, $7.50 Schocken Books. Cloth, $7.50; Pap. $2.45.

PICTURES OF SLAVERY AND ANTI-SLAVERY
John Bell Robinson
The advantages of Negro slavery and the benefits of Negro freedom are morally, socially, and politically considered. Books for Libraries. Reprint of the 1863 edition. $13.75.

PICTURE OF SLAVERY IN THE UNITED STATES OF AMERICA
George Bourne

The author shows relentless, moral indignation towards the hypocrisy of slaveholders who call themselves Christian, as well as the clergy who condones or ignores slavery. 227 pp. Scholarly Press. Reprint of the 1834 edition. Illus. $14.50.

PLANTATION LIFE: THE NARRATIVES OF MRS. HENRY ROWE SCHOOLCRAFT
Mary Howard Schoolcraft
569 pp. Negro Universities Press. Reprint of the 1852 to 1860 edition. $21.50.

THE PLANTATION NEGRO AS A FREE-MAN: OBSERVATIONS ON HIS CHARAC-TER, CONDITION, AND PROSPECTS IN VIRGINIA
Philip Alexander Bruce
262 pp. Metro Books, Inc. Reprint of the 1889 edition. $13.50. Humanities Press, $18.95.

THE PROGRESS OF SLAVERY IN THE UNITED STATES
George M. Weston
Books for Libraries. Reprint of the 1857 edition. $12.25.

PUTTIN' ON OLE MASSA: THE SLAVE NARRATIVES OF HENRY BIBB, WILLIAM W. BROWN AND SOLOMON NORTHRUP
Gilbert Osofsky, Editor
Harper and Row Pubs., 1969. Illus. Cloth, $10.00; Pap. $3.25.

REMINISCENCES OF FUGITIVE SLAVE DAYS IN BOSTON
Austin Bearse
The author was an active member of the Boston Vigilance committee that rescued fugitive slaves from slavery. Arno Press. Reprint of the 1880 edition. $4.50.

THE RESULTS OF SLAVERY
Augustin Cochin
413 pp. Greenwood Press. Reprint of the 1863 edition. $13.75.

THE RISE AND FALL OF BLACK SLAVERY
C. Duncan Rice
The history of black slavery in the Atlantic world from the beginning of the fifteenth to the end of the nineteenth century. 448 pp. Harper and Row, 1975. $12.50.

RUM, SLAVES AND MOLASSES: THE STORY OF NEW ENGLAND'S TRI-ANGULAR TRADE
Clifford Lindsey Alderman
A focus on the Northern role in the slave trade. Macmillan Publishing Co. $4.95.

SHADOW OF THE PLANTATION
Charles S. Johnson
University of Chicago Press, 1934. Cloth, $7.50; Pap. $2.25.

SLAVE GIRL REBA AND HER DES-CENDANTS IN AMERICA
Nora Louis Hicks
A history of her family's achievements by a fifth-generation descendant of a half-black, half-French girl, sold as a slave to a South Carolina plantation. owner. Exposition Press, 1974. Illus. $5.00.

SLAVE INSURRECTIONS SELECTED DOC-UMENTS
114 pp. Greenwood Press. Reprint of the 1822-1860 editions. $8.25.

SLAVE LIFE IN GEORGIA
John Brown
A narrative of the life, sufferings, and escape of John Brown, a fugitive slave, now in England. Books for Libraries, 1855. $14.50.

THE SLAVE POWER
Theodore Parker
Speeches of a Boston abolitionist minister in the early 20th century. Arno Press. Reprint of the 1907 edition. $14.50.

THE SLAVE TRADE: SLAVERY AND COLOR
Theodore Dehon Jervey
Written by a southerner who believes in the in-feriority of Afro-Americans, this study records their early importation into South Carolina, traces their development under the state's slavery system, and cites their progress in South Carolina politics from 1865 to the 1890's. 344 pp. Metro Books, Inc. Reprint of 1925 edition. $13.00. Negro University Press, $12.75.

SLAVERY
William Ellery Channing
The author points out that the most essential property right of the individual is the right to the fruits of his own abilities, and slavery de-prived its victims of this right. Arno Press. Reprint of the 1835 edition. $6.50.

SLAVERY AND THE DOMESTIC SLAVE-TRADE IN THE UNITED STATES

Ethan Allen Andrews
A series of letters. Books for Libraries, 1836. $10.00.

SLAVERY IN AMERICA: THEODORE WELD'S AMERICAN SLAVERY AS IT IS
Richard O. Curry and Joanna Dunlap Cowden, Editors
An edited and abridged version of Theodore Weld's classic. 248 pp. F.E. Peacock Publishers, 1972. Cloth, $7.00; Pap. $3.95.

SLAVERY IN AMERICA: WITH NOTICES OF THE PRESENT STATE OF SLAVERY AND THE SLAVE TRADE THROUGHOUT THE WORLD
Numbers 1-14. Greenwood Press. Reprint of the 1836-37 editions. $16.50.

SLAVERY IN AMERICAN SOCIETY
Richard D. Brown
The history of slavery in America. 108 pp. D.C. Heath and Co., 1969.

SLAVERY AND THE INTERNAL SLAVE TRADE IN THE UNITED STATES OF NORTH AMERICA
Theodore Dwight Weld
The author presents a vivid picture of the United States abolitionists to his British counterparts. Arno Press. Reprint of the 1841 edition. $10.00.

SLAVERY AND PLANTATION GROWTH IN FLORIDA, 1821-1860
Julia Floyd Smith
249 pp. University Presses of Florida, 1972. Illus. $8.50.

SLAVERY IN SOUTH CAROLINA, AND THE EX-SLAVES; OR, THE PORT ROYAL MISSION
A.M. French
312 pp. Greenwood Press. Reprint of the 1862 edition. Illus. $11.50.

SLAVERY IN THE STATES: SELECTED ESSAYS
Slavery in North Carolina, New Jersey, Rhode Island, New York, Connecticut, and Missouri. 500 pp. Greenwood Press, 1968. Reprint of the 1893-1914 editions. $32.00.

SLAVERY IN THE STRUCTURE OF AMERICAN POLITICS, 1765-1820
Donald L. Robinson
A study of the role of slavery in the American

experience that places the prime responsibility on the founding fathers. 560 pp. Harcourt Brace Jovanovich, Inc. $13.95.

SLAVERY IN THE UNITED STATES
Charles Ball
A narrative of the life and adventures of Charles Ball, a black man, who lived forty years in Maryland, South Carolina and Georgia, as a slave. Kraus Reprint Co. Reprint of the 1836 edition. $15.00.

*SLAVERY IN THE UNITED STATES
Leonard W. Ingraham
From the 20 indentured Africans shipped to Virginia in 1619, to the legal end of slavery in 1863. 89 pp. Franklin Watts, Inc., 1968. Illus. Ages 9-12. Cloth, $3.90; Pap. $1.25.

SLAVERY: A PROBLEM IN AMERICAN INSTITUTIONAL AND INTELLECTUAL LIFE
Stanley M. Elkins
University of Chicago Press, 1968, 2nd edition. Cloth, $7.50; Pap. $2.45.

THE SLAVERY QUESTION
John Lawrence
Books for Libraries, 1854. $14.50.

A SOUTH-SIDE VIEW OF SLAVERY: THREE MONTHS AT THE SOUTH IN 1854
Nehemiah Adams
A New England minister describes the institution of slavery in the United States. Kennikat Press. Reprint of the 1885 edition. $8.50.

SOUTHERN INSTITUTES: OR, AN INQUIRY INTO THE ORIGIN AND EARLY PREVALENCE OF SLAVERY AND THE SLAVE TRADE
George S. Sawyer
Books for Libraries. Reprint of the 1858 edition. $13.75.

THE STRUGGLE BETWEEN THE CIVILIZATION OF SLAVERY AND THAT OF FREEDOM
Edward C. Billings
Books for Libraries, Inc. Reprint of the 1873 edition. $7.50.

THE SUPPRESSED BOOK ABOUT SLAERY!
Herschel V. Cashin, et al
An abolitionist indictment of slavery based on newspaper interviews, court testimony and

letters. Arno Press. Reprint of the 1864 edition. $13.50.

THE SUPPRESSION OF THE AFRICAN SLAVE TRADE TO THE UNITED STATES OF AMERICA
W.E.B. DuBois

A history of the efforts made to control, limit or suppress the profitable slave trade between the U.S. and Africa from colonial times to 1870. 325 pp. Corner House Publishers. Reprint of the 1896 edition. $7.50. Dover Publications, Pap. $2.50. Schocken Books: Cloth, $7.50; Pap. $2.45.

THEY CAME IN CHAINS, *Americans from Africa*
Saunders Redding

An account of the tragedies, struggles, and attainments of blacks in America. 336 pp. J.B. Lippincott Co., 1973. Pap. $3.25.

*TO BE A SLAVE
Julius Lester

160 pp. Dell Publishing Co., 1968. Age 12 up. $5.95.

A TREATISE ON THE UNCONSTITU-TIONALITY OF AMERICAN SLAVERY: TOGETHER WITH THE POWERS AND DUTIES OF THE FEDERAL GOVERN-MENT, IN RELATION TO THAT SUBJECT
Joel Tiffany, Esq.

Books for Libraries. Reprint of the 1849 edition. $8.00.

THE UNWRITTEN HISTORY OF SLAVERY
Social Science Institute: Fish University IHS Microcard Editions. $5.95.

VIEWS OF AMERICAN SLAVERY, TAKEN A CENTURY AGO
Anthony Benezet

A Quaker who was the leading Anti-Slavery propagandist of pre-Revolutionary War America. Arno Press. Reprint of the 1858 edition. $5.50.

WHERE I'M BOUND: PATTERNS OF SLAVERY AND FREEDOM IN BLACK AMERICAN AUTOBIOGRAPHY
Sidonie Smith

The earliest black American autobiographies, the slave narratives. 194 pp. Greenwood Press, 1974. $9.95.

WHITE SUPREMACY AND NEGRO SUB-ORDINATION; OR, NEGROES, A SUB-ORDINATE RACE, AND SO-CALLED SLAVERY ITS NORMAL CONDITION
John H. Van Evrie

399 pp. Negro Universities Press. Reprint of the 1868 edition. Illus. $16.75.

WILLIAM JOHNSON'S NATCHEZ: THE ANTE-BELLUM DIARY OF A FREE NEGRO
William Ransom Hogan and Edwin Adams Davis, Editors

Chronicles of a former slave. Two vols. Kennikat Press. Reprint of the 1951 edition. $34.50.

THE WRONG OF SLAVERY, THE RIGHT OF EMANCIPATION AND THE FUTURE OF THE AFRICAN RACE IN THE UNITED STATES
R.D.Owen

Kraus Reprint Co. Reprint of the 1864 edition. $10.00.

SPEECHES

AN ADDRESS TO THE NEGROES OF THE STATE OF NEW YORK
Jupiter Hammon

Gordon Press. $25.00.

BLACK-BELT DIAMONDS: GEMS FROM THE SPEECHES, ADDRESSES, AND TALKS TO STUDENTS OF BOOKER T. WASHINGTON
Booker Taliaferro Washington

115 pp. Greenwood Press. Reprint of the 1898 edition. $7.50.

BLACK SPOKESMAN: SELECTED PUB-LISHED WRITINGS OF EDWARD WILMOT BLYDEN
Hollis R. Lynch

Humanities Press, 1971. $11.00.

THE BOOKER T. WASHINGTON PAPERS
Louis R. Harlan, Editor

Covers Washington's career from 1895 to 1898, including all of his speeches and correspondence. 740 pp. University of Illinois Press. Volume 4, Illus. $20.00.

NEGRO ORATORS AND THEIR ORATIONS

Carter Godwin Woodson, Editor
Russell and Russell. Reprint of the 1925 edition. $20.00.

THE NEGRO SPEAKS: THE RHETORIC OF CONTEMPORARY BLACK LEADERS

Jamye and McDonald Williams, Editors
A collection of speeches by Roy Wilkins, Ralph Bunche, Thurgood Marshall, Martin Luther King, Malcolm X, and other prominent black Americans. Noble & Noble Pubs., 1970. Pap. $3.20; teacher's guide, $1.72.

ThE ORATORY OF NEGRO LEADERS, 1900-1968

Marcus H. Boulware
The black speechmaking of politicians, preachers, labor leaders, lecturers, cultists, civil rights advocates, and militants. 312 pp. Greenwood Press, 1969. $13.50.

PROCEEDINGS OF THE NATIONAL NEGRO CONFERENCE, 1909

National Negro Conference
The speeches delivered at the conference that launched the NAACP. Arno Press. Reprint of the 1909 edition. $7.00.

THE RHETORIC OF BLACK AMERICANS

James L. Golden and Richard Rieke
Charles E. Merrill Publishing Co., 1971. Pap. $7.95.

SPEECHES BY BLACK AMERICANS

D.O'Neill
Dickenson Publishing Co., 1971. Pap. $6.95.

THE VOICE OF BLACK AMERICA

Philip Foner, Editor
Simon and Schuster, 1972. $19.95.

THE VOICES OF BLACK AMERICA: MAJOR SPEECHES BY NEGROES IN THE UNITED STATES, 1791 TO 1971, 2 VOLS.

Philip S. Foner, Editor
G.P.Putnam's Sons, 1974. Each volume, pap. $3.25.

W.E.B. DuBOIS SPEAKS: SPEECHES AND ADDRESSES

Philip S. Foner, Editor
Vol. 1: 1890-1919, 289 pp. Vol 2: 1920-1963, 346 pp. Set $15.90; Pap. $5.90. Pathfinder Press.

URBAN EXPERIENCE

BLACK HOME OWNERSHIP: A SOCIOLOGICAL CASE STUDY OF METROPOLITAN JACKSONVILLE

William A. Stacey
152 pp. Praeger Publishers, 1972. $12.50.

THE BLACK MAN COMES TO THE CITY: A DOCUMENTARY ACCOUNT FROM THE GREAT MIGRATION TO THE GREAT DEPRESSION, 1915-1930

Robert B. Grant
Personal letters, official testimony, contemporary magazine pieces, items from newspapers, and reports from investigative agencies authenticate the black migrant's disillusionment with the unfulfilled promise of life in the North after World War I. 287 pp. Nelson-Hall Publishers, 1972. $12.00.

BLACK MANHATTAN

James Weldon Johnson
An account of the black man's role in New York from the time of the earliest Dutch settlements. Arno Press. Reprint of the 1930 edition, $13.00.

BLACK METROPOLIS: *A Study of Negro Life in a Northern City*

St. Clair Drake and Horace R. Cayton
A study of an urban Negro community. Vol. I, Introductions by Richard Wright and E.C. Hughes, 377 pp. Vol. II, 390 pp. Harcourt Brace Jovanovich, Inc., 1970. Pap. each volume, $2.85.

BLACK NEW ORLEANS 1860 to 1880

John W. Blassingame
University of Chicago Press, 1973. $9.95.

THE BLACK NEW YORKERS

Regina M. Andrews
Robert Speller and Sons, 1974. $17.50.

THE BLACK SIDE: A PARTIAL HISTORY OF THE BUSINESS, RELIGIOUS AND EDUCATIONAL SIDE OF THE NEGRO IN ATLANTA, GEORGIA

Edward Randolph Carter
323 pp. Negro Universities Press. Reprint of the 1894 edition. Illus. $13.75.

THE BLACK URBAN CONDITION

Hollis Lynch
The impact of cities on Negroes. 480 pp. Thomas Y. Crowell Co., 1973. Age 16 up. $12.50.

BLACKS IN THE CITY
Guichard Parris and Lester Brooks
Little, Brown, and Co., 1971. $12.50.

BEFORE THE GHETTO: BLACK DETROIT IN THE NINETEENTH CENTURY
David M. Katzman
261 pp. University of Illinois Press, 1973. Illus. $10.00.

BLACKS AND METROPOLITAN GOVERNANCE: THE STAKES OF REFORM
Willis D. Hawley
34 pp. Institute of Government Studies at Berkeley, 1972. Pap. $1.50.

THE BUS STOPS HERE: A STUDY OF SCHOOL DESEGREGATION IN THREE CITIES
Anna Holden
Agathon Press, 1974. $15.00.

*CHICAGO'S BLACKS: A TRUE STORY
Rose J. Hayes
Chicago Historical Society, 1974. $5.00. Ages 15 and up.

CINCINNATI'S COLORED CITIZENS: HISTORICAL, SOCIOLOGICAL, AND BIOGRAPHICAL
Wendell Phillips Dabney
440 pp. Negro Universities Press. Reprint of the 1926 edition. Illus. $19.00

CIRCLE OF DISCRIMINATION: AN ECONOMIC AND SOCIAL STUDY OF THE BLACK MAN IN NEW YORK CITY
Herman D. Bloch
New York University Press, 1969. $9.95.

COLOR AND HUMAN NATURE: NEGRO PERSONALITY DEVELOPMENT IN A NORTHERN CITY
William Warner
301 pp. Negro Universities Press. Reprint of the 1941 edition. $12.25.

COMMUNITY CONTROL: THE BLACK DEMAND FOR PARTICIPATION IN LARGE AMERICAN CITIES
Alan Altshuler
Pegasus Press, 1970. Cloth, $6.95; Pap. $2.75.

DARK METROPOLIS
Arthur Joseph
AMS Press, Inc. Reprint of the 1936 edition. $11.50.

A GHETTO TAKES SHAPE: BLACK CLEVELAND, 1870-1930
Kenneth L. Kusmer
University of Illinois Press, 1975.

HALF A MAN: THE STATUS OF THE NEGRO IN NEW YORK
Mary White Ovington
236 pp. Negro Universities Press. Reprint of the 1911 edition. $10.00.

HISTORY OF THE CHICAGO URBAN LEAGUE
Arvarh E. Strickland
286 pp. University of Illinois Press, 1966. $7.50.

IN FREEDOM'S BIRTHPLACE: A STUDY OF THE BOSTON NEGROES
John Daniels
496 pp. Negro Universities Press. Reprint of the 1914 edition. Illus. $15.50.

NATIONALITY, COLOR, AND ECONOMIC OPPORTUNITY IN THE CITY OF BUFFALO
Niles Carpenter
194 pp. Negro Universities Press. Reprint of the 1927 edition. Illus. $17.00.

NEGRO AND THE CITY
Richard B. Sherman, Editor
Prentice-Hall, 1970. $5.95.

NEGRO HISTORY TOUR OF MANHATTAN
M.A.Harris
113 pp. Greenwood Press, Inc., 1968. Illus. $3.95.

NEGRO ILLEGITIMACY IN NEW YORK CITY
Ruth Reed
AMS Press, Inc. Reprint of the 1926 edition. $10.00.

THE NEGRO IN THE CITY
Gerald Leinwand
Pocket Books, Inc. Pap. $.95.

THE NEGRO IN EIGHTEENTH-CENTURY WILLIAMSBURG
Thad W. Tate, Jr.
136 pp. University Press of Virginia, 1965. Cloth, $5.00; Pap. $3.00.

THE NEGRO IN LOS ANGELES: DISSERTATION
J. Max Bond

R and E Research Associates, Pubs., 1972. Reprint of the 1936 edition. $9.00.

THE NEGRO IN NEW YORK
James Egert Allen
The black New Yorker's relationship to the entire nation. Exposition Press, 1964. Age 16 up. $5.00.

THE NEGRO IN SAVANNAH 1865-1900
Robert E. Perdue
A study of black urbanization in the years following the Civil War. Exposition Press, 1973. $7.50.

NEGRO MECCA: A HISTORY OF THE NEGRO IN NEW YORK CITY, 1865 TO 1920.
Seth M. Scheiner
New York University Press, 1965. Cloth, $8.50; Pap. $2.75.

THE NEGRO NEWCOMERS IN DETROIT AND THE NEGRO IN WASHINGTON
George Edmund Haynes and Sterling Brown
The change in black America from fundamentally rural to largely urban people is the subject of these two works. Arno Press. Reprint of the 1918 edition. $4.50.

THE NEGRO PEASANT TURNS CITY-WARD
Louise V. Kennedy
McGrath Publishing Co. Reprint of the 1930 edition. $12.00.

THE NEGRO POPULATION OF CHICAGO: A STUDY OF RESIDENTIAL SUCCESSION
Otis Dudley Duncan and Beverly Duncan
University of Chicago Press, 1957. $12.50.

NEGRO PROBLEMS IN CITIES
Thomas Jackson Woofter, Editor
284 pp. Greenwood Press. Reprint of the 1928 edition. Pap., $11.00.

NEGROES IN CITIES: RESIDENTIAL SEGREGATION AND NEIGHBORHOOD CHANGE
Karl and Alma Taeuber
Atheneum Publications, 1969. Pap. $3.95.

NEGROES IN NEW YORK: AN INFORMAL HISTORY
Roi Ottley and William J. Weatherby, Editors

New York Public Library, 1967. Cloth, $7.50; Pap. $2.95. Ages 16 and up.

NEW HAVEN NEGROES: A SOCIAL HISTORY
Robert Austin Warner
The plight of the Northern Negro before and after the Civil War. Arno Press. Reprint of the 1940 edition. $14.00.

OUR NEGRO POPULATION: A SOCIOLOGICAL STUDY OF THE NEGROES OF KANSAS CITY, MISSOURI
Asa Earl Martin
189 pp. Negro Universities Press. Reprint of the 1913 edition. Illus. $11.00.

THE PARTICIPATION OF THE NEGRO IN THE COMMUNITY LIFE OF LOS ANGELES: THESIS
James M. Ervin
R and E Research Associates, Pubs., 1973. Reprint of the 1932 edition. Pap. $8.00.

THE PHILADELPHIA NEGRO, *A Social Study*
W.E.B. DuBois
An inquiry into the social and economic problems, as well as the daily lives, of Negroes in Philadelphia's Seventh Ward in 1896-98. Schocken Books. Cloth, $8.50; Pap. $3.45.

POLITICS OF VIOLENCE: THE NEW URBAN BLACKS AND THE WATTS RIOT
David O. Sears and John B. McConahay
Houghton Mifflin Co., 1973. Pap. $5.50.

RECREATION AND AMUSEMENT AMONG NEGROES IN WASHINGTON, D.C.: A SOCIOLOGICAL ANALYSIS OF THE NEGRO IN AN URBAN ENVIRONMENT
William Henry Jones
216 pp. Greenwood Press. Reprint of the 1927 edition. Illus. $12.00.

SAN FRANCISCO BLACK COMMUNITY 1870 TO 1890
Francis M. Lortie
R and E Associates, Pubs. Reprint of the 1970 edition. Pap. $7.00.

SEA ISLAND TO CITY: A STUDY OF ST. HELENA ISLANDERS IN HARLEM AND OTHER URBAN CITIES
Clyde Vernon Kiser
AMS Press, Inc. Reprint of the 1932 edition. $10.00.

SKETCHES OF THE HIGHER CLASSES OF COLORED SOCIETY IN PHILADELPHIA, BY A SOUTHERNER
Joseph Willson
Books for Libraries, Inc. Reprint of the 1841 edition. $10.50.

SOCIAL AND PHYSICAL CONDITIONS OF NEGROES IN CITIES
Conference for the Study of Problems Concerning Negro City Life
Kraus Reprint Co. Reprint of the 1897 edition. $12.00.

THE STORY OF THE NEGRO IN LOS ANGELES COUNTY
WPA-Federal Writers' Project
R and E Research Associates, Pubs. Reprint of the 1936 edition. Pap. $3.00.

THE SYRACUSE BLACK COMMUNITY, 1970: A COMPARATIVE STUDY
Seymour Sacks and Ralph Andrew
Syracuse University Press, 1973. $3.00.

URBAN BLUES
Charles Keil
University of Chicago Press, 1966. Cloth, $7.50; Pap. $2.45.

THE URBAN NEGRO IN THE SOUTH
Wilmoth Annette Carter
Russell and Russell. Reprint of the 1962 edition. $17.00.

WOMEN

ALL ABOUT HEALTH AND BEAUTY FOR THE BLACK WOMAN
Naomi Sims
A compendium of a top black model's beauty and health secrets. Illus. Doubleday, 1976. $8.95.

BLACK-EYED SUSANS
Mary Helen Washington, Editor
Classic stories by and about black women. Doubleday, 1975. $2.95.

BLACK GIRL: FROM GENESIS TO RE-VELATIONS
J.E. Franklin
The experiences of a young writer's first confrontation with New York. 124 pp. Illus. Howard University Press, 1976. $7.95.

THE BLACK WOMAN IN AMERICA: SEX, MARRIAGE AND THE FAMILY
Robert Staples
287 pp. Nelson-Hall Publishers, 1973. $8.95.

A BLACK WOMAN'S EXPERIENCE: FROM SCHOOLHOUSE TO WHITE HOUSE
Alice Allison Dunnigan
The autobiography of the first Negro woman journalist to receive White House accreditations. 673 pp. Dorrance & Co., 1974. $15.00.

BLACK WOMEN'S LIBERATION
Maxine Williams and Pamela Newman
16 pp. Pathfinder Press. $.35.

BLACK WOMEN IN WHITE AMERICA: A DOCUMENTARY HISTORY
Gerda Lerner
Black women relate the struggles against racist and sexist stereotypes that have oppressed them from the colonial period to the present day. Vintage Press. $3.95.

A CRY FROM A CHILD OF THE GHETTO
Janet Dubose
A nonfiction novel by a black woman who bases the story on her own life and her ambivalent feelings toward whites and blacks. Vantage Press. $4.95.

GOALS AND PLANS OF BLACK WOMEN: A SOCIOLOGICAL STUDY
Kelly Hamilton
This study compares the goals and aspirations of two groups of black women; a sample group from a predominantly black college and another group from an ethnically mixed college. Exposition Press, 1975. $5.00.

*I, CHARLOTTE FORTEN, BLACK AND FREE
Charlotte Forten
A first-person account of 1854-64 in America, based on the actual journal of a young, educated, free-born black woman. 247 pp. Thomas Y. Crowell Co., 1970. Ages 11-15. $4.95.

KEEPING THE FAITH: BLACK WOMEN ON WRITING
Pat Crutchfield Exum, Editor
Selections of poetry, fiction and literary criticism give insights into the experience of black women in the United States. Fawcett World Library. $.95.

NOTED NEGRO WOMEN: THEIR TRI-UMPHS AND ACTIVITIES
Monroe A. Majors
Books for Libraries. Reprint of the 1893 edition. $18.25.

A POETIC EQUATION
Nikki Giovanni and Margaret Walker
Two black women writers express their views on a number of topics: Vietnam; the racial struggle; sex roles; literature and art; violence. 160 pp. 55 photos. Howard University Press, 1974. $6.95.

THE THIRD DOOR: THE AUTOBIOGRA-PHY OF AN AMERICAN NEGRO WOMAN
Ellen Tarry
304 pp. Greenwood Press. Reprint of the 1955 edition. $13.50.

TO BE A BLACK WOMAN: PORTRAITS IN FACT AND FICTION
Jay David and Mel Watkins, Editors
Portrait of the black woman throughout American history. William Morrow & Co., 1970. $6.95.

TRAILBLAZER: *Negro Nurse in the American Red Cross*
Jean Maddern Pitrone
A biography of the first Negro nurse officially enrolled in the American Red Cross. 191 pp. Harcourt Brace Jovanovich, Inc., 1969. $5.50. Ages 12 up.

WOMEN, SEX AND RACE
Bernard Braxton
Petticoats, prejudice and persecution. 228 pp. Verta Press, 1973. Cloth, $6.95; Pap. $2.95.

THE WORK OF THE AFRO-AMERICAN WOMAN
Mrs. N.F. Mossell
Books for Libraries. Reprint of the 1894 edition. $11.75.

YOUTH

THE BLACK CHILD: A PARENT'S GUIDE
Phyllis Harrison-Ross and Barbara Wyden
Berkley Publishing Corp., 1974. Pap. $1.50.

BLACK CHILD, WHITE CHILD: THE DEVELOPMENT OF RACIAL ATTITUDES
Judith D. Porter

278 pp. Harvard University Press, 1971. Illus. $8.95.

BLACK CHILDREN, WHITE DREAMS
Thomas J. Cottle
Conversations between a sociologist/psychotherapist and two black 11-year-olds. 187 pp. Dell Publishing Co., 1975. Pap., $2.25. Houghton Mifflin Co. Cloth, $5.95.

CAREER GUIDANCE FOR BLACK ADOLESCENTS: A GUIDE TO SELECTED PROFESSIONAL OCCUPATIONS
John G. Cull and Richard E. Hardy
Medicine, economics, the ministry, elementary and secondary education, general business enterprises, the physical sciences, and professional counseling and guidance. 124 pp. Charles C. Thomas Publishers, 1974.

CHILDREN OF BONDAGE
Allison Davis and John Dollard
The personality development of Negro youth in the urban South is represented in eight composite cases. 299 pp. American Council on Education. Reprint of the 1940 edition. Pap. $4.00.

COUNSELLING THE CULTURALLY DIFFERENT BLACK YOUTH
Elsie Smith
Charles E. Merrill Publishing Co., 1973. Pap. $4.50.

I'M SOMEBODY IMPORTANT: YOUNG BLACK VOICES FROM RURAL GEORGIA
George Mitchell
254 pp. University of Illinois Press, 1973. Illus. $7.95.

IN A MINOR KEY: NEGRO YOUTH IN STORY AND FACT
Ira Reid
134 pp. Greenwood Press, Inc. Reprint of the 1940 edition. $13.00.

INNER-CITY NEGRO YOUTH IN A JOB TRAINING PROJECT: A STUDY OF FACTORS RELATED TO ATTRITION AND JOB SUCCESS
Gerald Gurin
University of Michigan Institute for Social Research, 1968. Pap. $5.00.

JOB OPPORTUNITIES FOR YOUNG NEGROES
Adrian Paradis

David McKay Co., 1969. $4.95. Ages 16 and up.

NEGRO YOUTH AT THE CROSSWAYS, *Their Personality Development in the Middle States*

E. Franklin Frazier

The author analyzes what he heard in listening to black teenagers in Louisville and Washington describe how they came to terms with their blackness. Schocken Books. Cloth, $6.50; Pap. $2.45.

PROBLEMS AND EMOTIONAL DIFFICULTIES OF NEGRO CHILDREN AS STUDIED IN SELECTED COMMUNITIES AND ATTRIBUTED BY PARENTS AND CHILDREN TO THE FACT THAT THEY ARE NEGRO

Regina Mary Goff

AMS Press, Inc. Reprint of the 1949 edition. $10.00.

A PSYCHOLOGICAL STUDY OF DELINQUENT AND NON-DELINQUENT NEGRO BOYS

Robert Prentiss Daniel

AMS Press, Inc. Reprint of the 1932 edition. $10.00.

*SWEET PEA: *A Black Girl Growing up in the Rural South*

Jill Krementz

A ten-year-old girl living at the poverty level in a small town in Alabama talks about her life. 95 pp. Photos. Harcourt Brace Jovanovich, Inc., 1969. $5.75. Ages 8 up.

TASK FORCE ON EMPLOYMENT PROBLEM OF BLACK YOUTH

Twentieth Century Fund

Kraus Reprint Co. Reprint of the 1971 edition. Pap. $3.95.

THUS BE THEIR DESTINY: THE PERSONALITY DEVELOPMENT OF NEGRO YOUTH IN THREE COMMUNITIES

Jesse Howell Atwood, et al, Editors

AMS Press, Inc., Reprint of the 1941 edition. $9.00.

YOUNG BLACK ADULTS: LIBERATION AND FAMILY ATTITUDES

George B. Thomas

An analysis of the liberation consciousness and its effects on the attitudes of blacks regarding marriage and family life. Friendship Press, 1974. Pap. $1.95.

*YOUNG AND BLACK IN AMERICA

Rae Pace Alexander and Julius Lester, Editors

Malcolm X, Jimmy Brown, Anne Moody, Richard Wright and others recall youthful experiences that shaped their outlooks and destinies. Vintage Press. $1.50. Teacher's guide, $1.00. Random House, Inc., $1.50. Ages 11 and up.

OTHER MINORITIES

This section contains books on ethnic minorities other than American Indians and Black-Americans. Ethnic groups are arranged alphabetically with some groups sub-categorized for easy subject reference.

ARAB-AMERICANS

ARAB MOSLEMS IN THE UNITED STATES
Abdo A. Elkholy
College and University Press, 1966. Cloth, $5.00; Pap. $1.95.

ARABIC SPEAKING COMMUNITIES IN AMERICAN CITIES
Barbara C. Aswad
Center for Migration Studies, 1974. Pap. $5.95.

A STUDY OF THE SYRIAN POPULATION OF GREATER NEW YORK
Lucius Hopkins Miller
R & E Research Associates. Reprint of the 1902 edition. Pap. $5.00.

THE SYRIAN-LEBANESE IN AMERICA
Philip M. and Joseph M. Kayal
Twayne Publishers. $12.50.

ARMENIAN-AMERICANS

AN ABSTRACT OF THE HISTORICAL AND SOCIOLOGICAL ASPECTS OF ARMENIAN IMMIGRATION TO THE UNITED STATES, 1890-1930
Gary A. Kulhanjian
R & E Research Associates, 1975. Pap. $8.00.

THE ARMENIANS IN AMERICA
Malcolm M. Vartan
R and E Research Associates. Reprint of the 1919 edition. $8.00.

THE ARMENIANS OF THE UNITED STATES AND CANADA
James H. Tashjian
R and E Research Associates. Reprint of the 1947 edition. Illus. $5.00.

A HISTORY OF ARMENIAN IMMIGRATION TO AMERICA WITH SPECIAL REFERENCE TO LOS ANGELES: THESIS
Aram S. Yeretzian
R and E Research Associates. Reprint of 1923 edition. Pap. $8.00.

HISTORY OF ARMENIANS IN CALIFORNIA
Charles Mahakian
Covers immigration, history, missionaries in Armenia, economic life, agriculture, business, urban centers, religion, the family-marriage-divorce social customs, organizations, crime, and American attitudes toward Amenians. Thesis. R & E Research Associates. Reprint of the 1935 edition. Pap. $8.00.

CHINESE-AMERICANS

Assimilation

BIBLIOGRAPHY OF THE CHINESE QUESTION IN THE UNITED STATES
Robert E. Cowan
R and E Research Associates. Reprint of the 1909 edition. 5.00.

CHINATOWN, SAN FRANCISCO
Phil Palmer and Jim Walls
Howell-North Books, 1960. Illus. Pap. $1.00.

CHINESE AMERICANS: SCHOOL AND COMMUNITY PROBLEMS
Integrated Education Associates
Editorial Staff, Editors
76 pp. Integrated Education Associates. Pap. $2.25.

THE CHINESE AND THE CHINESE QUESTION
James A. Whitney
R and E Research Associates. Reprint of the 1888 edition. $9.00.

A CHINESE COMMUNITY IN AMERICA
Melford Stephen Weiss
Schenkman Publishing Co., 1974. Cloth, $8.95; Pap. $5.95.

THE CHINESE COMMUNITY IN NEW YORK, 1920-1940
I. Hsuan Julia Chen
Thesis. R & E Research Associates. Reprint of the 1942 paper. Pap. $9.00.

CHINESE PROBLEM
    L.T.Townsend
R and E Research Associates, 1970. Reprint of the 1876 edition. $5.00.

CHINESE RESIDENTS IN CHICAGO
    Ting C. Fan
Covers history, population, business, schools, wages, crime. Thesis. R & E Research Associates. Reprint of the 1926 edition. Illus. Pap. $8.00.

CHINESE TEMPLES IN CALIFORNIA: THESIS
    Mariann Kaye Wells
R and E Research Associates, 1962. $7.00.

THE COMING STRUGGLE: OR WHAT THE PEOPLE ON THE PACIFIC COAST THINK OF THE COOLIE INVASION
    M. Starr
Anti-Chinese feeling and hysteria. R & E Research Associates. Reprint of the 1873 edition. $6.00.

THE DAYS OF THE TONG WARS
    C.Y.Lee
Ballantine Books, 1974. Pap. $1.25.

THE HISTORY OF SAN FRANCISCO'S CHINATOWN
    Helen V. Cather
Thesis. R & E Research Associates. Reprint of the 1932 paper. Pap. $7.00.

THE I HING OR "PATRIOTIC RISING"
    Steward Culin
Chinese Secret Societies in the U.S.; customs of the Chinese in America. R & E REsearch Associates. Reprint of the 1890 edition. $3.00.

LONGTIME CALIFORN: A DOCUMENTARY STUDY OF AN AMERICAN CHINATOWN
    Victor G. and Brett De Bary Nee
Houghton Mifflin Co., 1974. Pap. $4.75.

THE MISSISSIPPI CHINESE: BETWEEN BLACK AND WHITE
    James W. Loewen
237 pp. Harvard University Press, 1971. $10.00.

MUST THE CHINESE GO?
    Mrs. S.L.Balwin
R and E Research Associates. Reprint of the 1890. $5.00.

THE OTHER SIDE OF THE CHINESE QUESTION
    Testimony of California's Leading Citizens
R & E Research Associates. Reprint of the 1886 edition. $5.00.

PARTICIPATION OF CHINESE IN THE COMMUNITY LIFE OF LOS ANGELES
    Kim Fong Tom
Thesis. R & E Research Associates. Reprint of the 1944 paper. Pap. $8.00.

PRESSURES ON CONGRESS: A STUDY OF THE REPEAL OF CHINESE EXCLUSION
    Fred Warren Riggs
260 pp. Greenwood Press, Inc. Reprint of the 1950 edition. $11.50.

VALLEY CITY: A CHINESE COMMUNITY IN AMERICA
    Melford S. Weiss
269 pp. General Learning Corp., 1974. Pap. $4.20.

Discrimination

THE ANTI-CHINESE MOVEMENT IN CALIFORNIA
    Elmer C. Sandmeyer
136 pp. University of Illinois Press, 1973. Cloth, $5.95; Pap. $2.25.

CHINK: EVIDENCE OF THE ANTI-CHINESE PREJUDICE PERVADING OUR COUNTRY
    Cheng-Tsu Wu
New American Library, 1972. Pap. $3.95.

THE INDISPENSABLE ENEMY: LABOR AND THE ANTI-CHINESE MOVEMENT IN CALIFORNIA
    Alexander Saxton
University of California Press, 1971. $10.00

SAN FRANCISCO ANTI-CHINESE ORDINANCES, 1850-1900
    William J. Courtney
Thesis. R & E Research Associates. Reprint of the 1956 paper. Pap. $7.00.

History

BITTER STRENGTH: A HISTORY OF THE CHINESE IN THE UNITED STATES, 1850 TO 1870
Gunther P. Barth
305 pp. Harvard University Press, 1964. $12.50.

CALIFORNIA AND CHINESE: THE FIRST DECADE
Ellen R. Wood
Dissertation. R & E Research Associates. Reprint of the 1961 paper. Pap. $8.00.

CALIFORNIA AND THE ORIENTAL
William D. Stephens
R and E Research Associates. Reprint of the 1922 edition. $12.00.

THE CHALLENGE OF THE AMERICAN DREAM: THE CHINESE IN THE UNITED STATES
Francis L.K. Hsu
Contact and conflict between two different ways of life: the Chinese assimilation into America. 155 pp. Wadsworth Publishing Co., 1971. Pap. $3.95.

CHINESE AMERICAN INTERACTIONS: A HISTORICAL SUMMARY
John K. Fairbank
Rutgers University Press, 1975. Cloth, $6.50; Pap. $2.95.

CHINESE AMERICANS
Stanford Lyman
Random House, Inc., 1974. Pap. $2.95.

CHINESE AMERICANS, A BRIEF HISTORY
Larry Stevens
32 pp. Relevant Instructional Materials, 1970. $.75.

CHINESE-BORN: AN AMERICAN EXPERIENCE
Nick Dybman
Vantage Press. $3.95.

CHINESE AT HOME AND ABROAD
Willard B. Farwell
R and E Research Associates. Reprint of the 1885 edition. $11.00.

*THE CHINESE IN AMERICA
Claire Jones

A look at the Chinatowns across the United States and their inhabitants. 96 pp. Lerner Publications, 1973. Ages 11-17. $3.95.

THE CHINESE IN AMERICA: A CHRONOLOGY AND FACTBOOK, 1820 TO 1973
William Tung
Oceana Publications, 1974. $5.00.

CHINESE IN AMERICAN LIFE: SOME ASPECTS OF THEIR HISTORY, STATUS, PROBLEMS, AND CONTRIBUTIONS
Shien-woo Kung
352 pp. Greenwood Press, 1962. $15.00.

THE CHINESE IN CALIFORNIA: A BRIEF BIBLIOGRAPHIC HISTORY
G.C.Hansen, Editor
International Scholarly Book Service, 1970. $15.00.

THE CHINESE IN THE CALIFORNIA MINES, 1848 TO 1860: THESIS
Stephen Williams
R and E Research Associates. Reprint of the 1930 edition. $7.00.

THE CHINESE HELPED BUILD AMERICA
Dorothy and Joseph Dowdell
Messner, 1972. $4.79.

THE CHINESE IN EASTERN OREGON, 1860-1890
Christopher H. Edson
R & E Research Associates, 1974. Illus. Pap. $8.00.

CHINESE AND JAPANESE IN AMERICA
American Academy of Political and Social Science
R & E Research Associates, 1970. Reprint of the 1909 edition. $12.00.

CHINESE IN THE MOTHER LODE, 1850-1870
Pauline Minke
R & E Research Associates. Reprint of the 1960 edition. Pap. $7.00.

ETHNIC ENTERPRISE IN AMERICA: BUSINESS AND WELFARE AMONG CHINESE, JAPANESE, AND BLACKS
Ivan H. Light
University of California Press, 1973. Pap. $2.85.

A HISTORY OF THE CHINESE IN NEVADA, 1855-1904
Gary P. BeDunnah
The Chinese contribution to mining and railroading in Nevada. Thesis. R & E Research Associates. Reprint of the 1966 edition. Pap. $7.00.

THE IMAGES OF CHINA AND THE CHINESE IN THE OVERLAND MONTHLY, 1868-1875, 1883-1935
Limin Chu
A survey of an historical publication. Dissertation. R & E Research Associates. Reprint of the 1965 paper. Pap. $11.00.

MEMORIAL OF THE SIX CHINESE COMPANIES
California Legislature
R and E Research Associates. Reprint of the 1877 edition. $5.00.

PASSAGE TO THE GOLDEN GATE: A HISTORY OF THE CHINESE IN AMERICA TO 1910
Daniel and Samuel Chu
Doubleday and Co., 1967. Illus. Cloth, $3.95; Pap. $1.45.

THE REAL CHINESE IN AMERICA
J.S.Tow
R and E Research Associates. Reprint of the 1923 edition. $8.00.

THE STORY OF THE CHINESE IN AMERICA
Betty L. Sung
Macmillan Publishing Co., Inc., 1971. Pap. $2.95.

WRITINGS ON THE CHINESE IN CALIFORNIA
Pearl Ng
Chapters on attitudes, agitation, exclusion, legislation, California's development, religion, education and newspapers. Thesis. R & E Research Associates. Reprint of the 1939 edition. Pap. $7.00.

Immigration

THE ASSIMILATION OF CHINESE IN AMERICA: THESIS
Stanly L. Fong
R and E Research Associates. Reprint of 1967 edition. Pap. $7.00.

CHINESE IMMIGRATION
Mary Roberts Coolidge
A documentary of every aspect of the Chinese immigrant: his home, his politics, and the laws that attempted to exclude his migration to America. Arno Press. Reprint of the 1909 edition. $15.00.

CHINESE IMMIGRATION
Frank Shay
R and E Research Associates. Reprint of the 1876 edition. $8.00.

CHINESE IMMIGRATION IN THE PACIFIC AREA
Ching-Chao Wu
Covers the Pacific area, islands and continents. R & E Research Associates. Reprint of the 1926 dissertation. Pap. $8.00.

CHINESE IMMIGRATION IN ITS SOCIAL AND ECONOMICAL ASPECTS
George F. Seward
A discussion of the Chinese immigration issue at the very moment the nation was considering exclusion legislation. Arno Press. Reprint of the 1881 edition. $17.50.

CHINESE IMMIGRATION: ITS SOCIAL, MORAL, AND POLITICAL EFFECT
California State Senate, Special Committee on Chinese Immigration
Jerome S. Ozer Pubs. Reprint of the 1878 edition. $12.50.

GAMBLING GAMES OF THE CHINESE IN AMERICA
Steward Culin
University of Pennsylvania study on the two games brought to America by Chinese immigrants. One is played today in the casinos of Nevada under the name of Keno. 18 pp. Gambler's Book Club. Reprint of the 1891 edition. Pap. $1.25.

In Hawaii

THE CHINESE IN HAWAII: AN ANNOTATED BIBLIOGRAPHY
Nancy Foon Young
144 pp. University Press of Hawaii, 1973. Pap. $4.00.

HAWAII'S PEOPLE FROM CHINA
Margaret Young
The cultural contribution of the Chinese to Hawaii's way of life. 64 pp. Hogarth Press, 1973. Illus. $1.95. Age 8-18.

THE SANDAL WOOD MOUNTAINS: READINGS AND STORIES OF THE EARLY CHINESE IN HAWAII
Tin Yuke Char, Editor
368 pp. University Press of Hawaii, 1975. Illus. $12.00.

CROATIAN-AMERICANS

AMERICANIZATION OF THE CROATS IN ST. LOUIS, MISSOURI DURING THE PAST THIRTY YEARS: THESIS
C.S.Mihanovich
R and E Research Associates. Reprint of the 1936 edition. $7.00.

BIOGRAPHICAL DIRECTORY OF AMERICANS AND CANADIANS OF CROATIAN DESCENT
Vladimir Markotic
Also contains organizational directory, church and priest directory, as well as current newspapers and periodicals. R & E Research Associates, 1973. Pap. $10.00.

BIOGRAPHICAL DIRECTORY OF SCHOLARS, ARTISTS AND PROFESSIONALS OF CROATIAN DESCENT IN THE UNITED STATES AND CANADA
Francis H. Eterovich
R & E Research Associates, 1970 Pap. $10.00.

CONTEMPORARY IOWA OPINIONS REGARDING THE INFLUENCE OF CROATIANS IN WATERLOO AND VICINITY, 1907 TO 1949; DISSERTATION
Mary A. Bresson
R and E Research Associates, 1951. $7.00.

THE CROATIAN IMMIGRANTS IN AMERICA
George J. Prpic
503 pp. R and E Research Associates, 1971. $12.00.

CROATIAN NEWSPAPER AND CALENDARS IN THE UNITED STATES: THESIS
Nada Kestercanek

R and E Research Associates, 1952. $7.00.

DALMATIANS FROM CROATIA AND MONTENEGRIN SERBS IN THE WEST AND SOUTH 1800 TO 1900
Adam S. Eterovich
R and E Research Associates, 1971. $7.00.

THE SOCIAL AND ECONOMIC ADJUSTMENT OF THE CROATIAN DISPLACED PERSONS IN CLEVELAND COMPARED WITH THAT OF THE EARLIER CROATIAN IMMIGRANTS: THESIS
Joseph C. Brentar
R and E Research Associates, 1951. $7.00.

CZECH-AMERICANS

THE CZECHOSLOVAKS
Thomas Capek
The Czech and Slovak community of New York. R & E Research Associates. Reprint of the 1921 edition. $5.00.

THE CZECHS [BOHEMIANS] IN AMERICA: A STUDY OF THEIR NATIONAL, CULTURAL, POLITICAL, SOCIAL, ECONOMIC, AND RELIGIOUS LIFE
Thomas Capek
AMS Press, Inc. Reprint of the 1920 edition. Pap. $8.25. Greenwood Press, $16.50; Arno Press, $13.00.

*THE CZECHS AND SLOVAKS IN AMERICA
Joseph S. Roucek
Lerner Pubns., 1967. Illus. $3.95. Ages 10 and up.

THE STORY OF A BOHEMIAN-AMERICAN VILLAGE: A STUDY OF THE SOCIAL PERSISTANCE AND CHANGE
Robert I. Kutak
The permutation of the Czech community of Milligan, Nebraska. Arno Press. Reprint of the 1933 edition. $7.00.

DUTCH-AMERICANS

*AN AMISH BOY REMEMBERS
Jesse W. Hofer

The life-style of a boy in an Amish community during the first decades of the twentieth century. 248 pp. The Naylor Co. Ages 12 up. $8.95.

ANTHOLOGY OF NEW NETHERLAND OR TRANSITIONS FROM EARLY DUTCH POETRY OF NEW YORK
Henry Cruse Murphy, Editor
MSS Information Corp. Reprint of the 1865 edition. $14.25.

DUTCH EMIGRATION TO NORTH AMERICA, 1624 TO 1860
Bertus Harry Wabeke
Books for Libraries, Inc. Reprint of the 1944 edition. $12.25.

DUTCH EXPLORERS, TRADE, SETTLERS IN THE DELAWARE VALLEY
Clinton A. Weslager
University of Pennsylvania Press, 1964. $10.00.

THE DUTCH IN AMERICA
Gerald F. DeJong
Describes why the Hollanders left their homeland and the problems they encountered on arrival in the United States. Twayne Publishers, 1975. $9.95.

THE DUTCH IN AMERICA
Gerritt Tenzythoff
Lerner Publications, 1969. $3.95.

THE DUTCH IN AMERICA: A CHRONOLOGY AND FACT BOOK, 1609 TO 1970
J.W.Smit and Pamela Smit
Oceana Publications, 1973. $5.00.

DUTCH IN NEW NETHERLAND, 1609 TO 1900, AND THE UNITED STATES
Netherland Chamber of Commerce
R and E Research Associates. Reprint of the 1909 edition. $5.00.

THE GANESVOORTS OF ALBANY: DUTCH PATRICIANS IN THE UPPER HUDSON VALLEY
Alice P. Kenney
Syracuse University, 1969.

THE HOLLANDERS IN AMERICA
Martinus Nijhoff
A collection of books, maps and pamphlets relating to the early colonization, voyages, exploration, etc. by the Hollanders in different parts of North and South America. 94 pp. R &

E Research Associates. Reprint of the 1925 edition. $6.00.

THE PENNSYLVANIA DUTCH
Frederick Klees
Their religions, history, folk arts, and contributions to the American culture. Macmillan Publishing Co. $8.95.

"PENNSYLVANIA DUTCH" AND OTHER ESSAYS
Phebe H. Gibbons
AMS Press, Inc. Reprint of the 1882 edition. $17.00.

PENNSYLVANIA DUTCH AMERICAN FOLK ART
H.J.Kauffman
Peter Smith Publishers. Cloth, $12.95; Pap. $5.50.

PRE-REVOLUTIONARY DUTCH HOUSES AND FAMILIES IN NORTHERN NEW JERSEY AND SOUTHERN NEW YORK
Rosalie Fellows Bailey
Study of early Dutch houses and families of Brooklyn, Queens, Staten Island, nearby New York and New Jersey and western New Jersey. 612 pp. Dover Publications, 1968. Illus. Pap. $5.00.

RED HILLS: A RECORD OF GOOD DAYS OUTDOORS AND IN, WITH THINGS PENNSYLVANIA DUTCH
Cornelius Weygandt
Kennikat Press. Reprint of the 1929 edition. Illus. $9.50.

REVOLUTIONARY WAR IN THE HACKENSACK VALLEY: THE JERSEY DUTCH AND THE NEUTRAL GROUND, 1775 TO 1783
Adrian C. Leiby
Rutgers University Press, 1963. $10.00.

STUBBORN FOR LIBERTY, THE DUTCH IN NEW YORK
Alice P. Kenney
Explorers and settlers, traders, soldiers, merchants, statesmen and patriots. 304 pp. Syracuse University Press, 1975. $10.00.

WILLIAM PENN AND THE DUTCH QUAKER MIGRATION TO PENNSYLVANIA
William I. Hull

445 pp. Genealogical Publishing Co. Reprint of the 1935 edition. Illus. $14.00.

EAST INDIAN-AMERICANS

EAST INDIAN IMMIGRATION ON THE PACIFIC COAST
Jogesh Chandler Misrow
R and E Research Associates. Reprint of the 1915 edition. $7.00.

*THE EAST INDIANS AND THE PAKISTANIS IN AMERICA
Leona B. Bagai
One of the smallest U.S. minorities. 64 pp. Lerner Publications, 1967. Illus. Aves 11-17. $3.95.

ENGLISH-AMERICANS

BRITISH CHARTISTS IN AMERICA, 1839 TO 1900
Ray Boston
110 pp. Rowman and Littlefield, 1971. Illus. $9.00.

BRITISH EMIGRATION TO NORTH AMERICA: PROJECTS AND OPINIONS IN THE EARLY VICTORIAN PERIOD
Wilbur S. Shepperson
302 pp. University of Minnesota Press, 1957. Illus. $7.50.

BRITISH IMMIGRANTS IN INDUSTRIAL AMERICA, 1790 TO 1950
Rowland Tappan Berthoff
Russell and Russell. Reprint of the 1953 edition. $10.00.

THE BRITISH IN AMERICA FROM 1578 TO 1970: A CHRONOLOGY AND FACTBOOK
Howard B. Furer
Oceana Publications, 1973. $5.00.

BRITISH PIONEERS IN CALIFORNIA: THESIS
Douglas H. Maynard
R and E Research Associates. Reprint of 1948 edition. Pap. $9.00.

THE ELIZABETHANS' AMERICA: A

COLLECTION OF EARLY REPORTS BY ENGLISHMEN ON THE NEW WORLD
Louis B. Wright, Editor
295 pp. Harvard University Press, 1965. $8.00.

*THE ENGLISH IN AMERICA
Edwin H. Cates
Lerner Publications, 1966. Illus. $3.95. Ages 10 and up.

ENGLISH ON THE DELAWARE: 1610 TO 1682
C.A. Weslager
Rutgers University Press, 1967. $7.50.

INVISIBLE IMMIGRANTS: THE ADAPTATION OF ENGLISH AND SCOTTISH IMMIGRANTS IN NINETEENTH CENTURY AMERICA
Charlotte Erickson
Contains the hundreds of letters of twenty-five families of English and Scottish immigrants who settled in the United States in the nineteenth century. 531 pp. University of Miami Press, 1972. Illus. $17.50.

LIST OF EMIGRANTS TO AMERICA FROM LIVERPOOL, 1697-1707
Elizabeth French
55 pp. Genealogical Publishing Co. Reprint of the 1913 edition. $5.00.

PRARIE ALBION: AN ENGLISH SETTLEMENT IN PIONEER ILLINOIS
Charles Boewe
Southern Illinois University Press, 1962. $10.00.

SELF-CONCEPT: A COMPARISON OF NEGRO, ANGLO AND SPANISH-AMERICAN STUDENTS ACROSS ETHNIC SEX AND SOCIO-ECONOMIC VARIABLES
Gary W. Healy
Dissertation. R & E Research Associates. Reprint of the 1969 paper. Pap. $8.00.

SOME EARLY EMIGRANTS TO AMERICA FROM LIVERPOOL
Cregoe D.P. Nicholson
110 pp. Genealogical Publishing Co. Reprint of the 1955 edition. $7.50.

TOPOGRAPHICAL DICTIONARY OF 2,885 ENGLISH EMIGRANTS TO NEW ENGLAND, 1620 TO 1650
Charles Edward Banks
295 pp. Genealogical Publishing Co. Reprint of the 1937 edition. $12.00.

ESKIMO-AMERICANS

*ALASKA AND THE ESKIMOS
Allyn and Bacon, 1974. Pap. $3.24; teacher's guide, $3.00. Below college level.

ALASKA INDIAN BASKETRY
L.W.MacDowell
Shorey Publications. Reprint of the 1904 edition. Pap. $1.00. Ages 16 and up.

ALASKA IN TRANSITION: THE SOUTH-EAST REGION
G.W. Rogers
Johns Hopkins Press, 1960. $12.00.

ALASKA NATIVES IN HIGHER EDU-CATION
Karen Kohout and Judith Kleinfeld
University of Alaska Press, 1974. $3.00.

ALASKA NATIVES: A SURVEY OF THEIR SOCIOLOGICAL AND EDUCATIONAL STATUS
H.D. Anderson and W.C. Eells
Kraus Reprint Co. Reprint of the 1935 edition. $40.00.

ALASKAN ESKIMO CEREMONIALISM
Margaret Lantis
143 pp. University of Washington Press, 1947. $5.95.

ALASKAN ESKIMO LIFE IN THE 1890's AS SKETCHED BY NATIVE ARTISTS
George E. Phebus, Jr.
Smithsonian Institution Press, 1972. $15.00.

ALASKAN ESKIMOS
Wendell Oswalt
Chandler Publishing Co., 1967. Cloth, $8.50; Pap. $6.50.

ALASKAN IGLOO TALES
Edward L. Keithahn
35 original Eskimo stories combine with illustrations of a well-known Eskimo artist. Alaska Northwest Publishing Co., 1975. Pap. $4.95.

AMONG THE ESKIMOS OF WALES, ALASKA, 1890 TO 1893
Harrison Robertson Thornton
AMS Press, Inc., 1931. $27.50.

AND THE LAND PROVIDES: ALASKAN NATIVES IN A YEAR OF TRANSITION

Lael Morgan
Doubleday and Co., 1974. Illus. $10.00.

*BLIND BOY AND THE LOON, *And Other Eskimo Myths*
R. Maher
John Day Publishing Co., 1969. Illus. $4.29. Below college level.

ESKIMO BOY TODAY
Photography and reporting on the day-to-day life of a modern Eskimo youngster. Alaska Northwest Publishing Co., 1975. Cloth, $6.95; Pap. $3.95.

ESKIMO CHILDHOOD AND INTER-PERSONAL RELATIONSHIPS: NUNIVAK BIOGRAPHIES AND GENEALOGIES
Margaret Lantis
236 pp. University of Washington Press, 1960. Illus. $5.95.

*ESKIMO CRAFTS AND THEIR CULT-URAL BACKGROUNDS
Jeremy Comins
The sculpture, stencil prints, masks, and leather applique of Eskimo artists, complete with photo and readable instructions. 128 pp. William Morrow & Co., 1975. Illus. $5.95. Ages 10 up.

ESKIMO MASKS: ART AND CEREMONY
Dorothy Jean Ray
Discusses the forms, meanings, and uses of masks in the context of 19th century aboriginal Alaskan Eskimo culture. 272 pp. University of Washington Press, 1967. Illus.

THE ESKIMO OF NORTH ALASKA: CASE STUDIES IN CULTURAL ANTHROPO-LOGY
Norman A. Chance
Holt, Rinehart, and Winston, 1966. Pap. $2.75.

THE SOCIAL ECONOMY OF THE TLINGIT INDIANS
Kalvervo Oberg
New light is thrown on such matters as class and rank, marriage patterns, the economic and ritual use of slaves, and the significance of the potlatch. 144 pp. University of Washington Press, 1973. Illus. $8.50.

THE STORY OF COMOCK THE ES-KIMO: AS TOLD TO ROBERT FLAHERTY
Edmund Carpenter, Editor
A collection of Eskimo sketches describes ten

years on a frozen island in Hudson's Bay. Fawcett World Library. Pap. $.95.

A STUDY OF THE TLINGETS OF ALASKA
Livingston French Jones
261 pp. Johnson Reprint. Reprint of the 1914 edition. $17.50.

TANAINA TALES FROM ALASKA
Bill Vaudrin
132 pp. University of Oklahoma Press, 1969. Illus. $4.95.

THE TLINGIT INDIANS: RESULTS OF A TRIP TO THE NORTHWEST COAST OF AMERICA AND THE BERING STRAITS
Aurel Krause
320 pp. University of Washington Press, 1970. Illus. Cloth, $5.95; Pap. $2.95.

TLINGIT MYTHS AND TEXTS
J.R.Swanton
451 pp. Scholarly Press. Reprint of the 1909 edition. $24.50.

FILIPINO-AMERICANS

AN ANALYSIS OF THE RACIAL ADJUSTMENT ACTIVITIES AND PROBLEMS OF THE FILIPINO-AMERICAN CHRISTIAN FELLOWSHIP IN LOS ANGELES
Severino F. Corpus
Thesis. R & E Research Associates. Reprint of the 1938 edition. Pap. $8.00.

CHARACTERISTICS OF FILIPINO ORGANIZATIONS IN LOS ANGELES
Marion P. Ave
Covers fraternal organizations, associations, relationships of organizations, religious beliefs, democracy, duty and obligations, service to humanity. Thesis. R & E Research Associates. Reprint of the 1952 edition. Pap. $7.00.

FACTS ABOUT FILIIPINO IMMIGRATION INTO CALIFORNIA
California Department of Industrial Relations.
R and E Research Associates. Reprint of the 1930 edition. $6.00.

THE FILIPINO COMMUNITY IN LOS ANGELES

Valentin R. Aquino
Thesis. R & E Research Associates. Reprint of the 1952 paper. Pap. $7.00.

THE FILIPINO IMMIGRANTS IN THE UNITED STATES: THESIS
Honorante Mariano
R and E Research Associates. Reprint of the 1934 edition. Pap. $7.00.

FILIPINO IMMIGRATION: TO THE CONTINENTAL UNITED STATES AND TO HAWAII
Bruno Lasker
In 1920 there were about 5,600 Filipinos in the United States; in 1929 the estimated figures were over 56,000. Anti-Filipino agitation passed into a movement for their exclusion and on May 19, 1928 Rep. R.J. Welch of California introduced in Congress a bill for the exclusion of Filipinos from U.S. territories. The author investigates this situation. Arno Press. Reprint of the 1931 edition. $14.50.

THE FILIPINO SOCIAL ADJUSTMENT IN THE UNITED STATES: DISSERTATION
B.T.Catapusan
R and E Research Associates. Reprint of the 1940 edition. Pap. $7.00.

FILIPINOS IN CALIFORNIA: THESIS
Sonia Wallovits
R and E Research Associates. Reprint of the 1966 edition. Pap. $7.00.

THE FILIPINOS IN HAWAII: THESIS
Roman R. Cariaga
R and E Research Associates. Reprint of the 1936 edition. Pap. $9.00.

ORIENTAL IMMIGRATION FROM AN AMERICAN DEPENDENCE [PHILLIPINES]: THESIS
Generoso P. Provido
R and E Research Associates. Reprint of 1931 edition. Pap. $7.00.

A STUDY OF THE FILIPINO REPATRIATION MOVEMENT: THESIS
Casiano Coloma
R and E Research Associates. Reprint of the 1939 edition. Pap. $8.00.

A STUDY OF THE PROBLEMS OF FILIPINO STUDENTS IN THE UNITED STATES
Aquino B. Obando
Student movement, early legislative induce-

ments, Legislative Act of 1924, pensionado students, self-supporting students, geographical distribution in America, East, Midwest and West, educational interest, cultural and social status, attitudes, contributions, race, success, occupational outlook in United States and Phillipines. Thesis. R & E Research Associates. Reprint of the 1936 edition. Pap. $8.00.

FINNISH-AMERICANS

THE AMERICANIZATION OF THE FINNS
John Wargelin
185 pp. R and E Research Associates. Reprint of the 1924 edition. $9.00.

THE FAITH OF THE FINNS: HISTORICAL PERSPECTIVES OF THE FINNISH-LUTHERAN CHURCH IN AMERICA
Ralph J. Jalkanen, Editor
360 pp. Michigan State University Press, 1972. $12.50.

FINNISH IMMIGRANTS IN AMERICA, 1880 TO 1920
William A. Hogland
University of Wisconsin Press, 1960. $10.00.

FINNS IN AMERICA
John I. Kolehmainen
Teachers College Press, 1968. Pap. $1.50.

THE FINNS IN NORTH AMERICA: A SOCIAL SYMPOSIUM
Ralph J. Jalkanen, Editor
230 pp. Michigan State University Press, 1969. $7.50.

THE FINNS ON THE DELAWARE, 1638 TO 1655
John Henry Wuorinen
AMS Press, Inc. Reprint of the 1938 edition. $7.00.

HAVEN IN THE WOODS: THE STORY OF THE FINNS IN WISCONSIN
John I. Kolehmainen and George Hill
State Historical Society of Wisconsin. Reprint of the 1951 edition. $4.00.

FRENCH-AMERICANS

FRANCE IN AMERICA

W.J. Eccles
Harper and Row Pubs., 1972. $10.00.

THE FRANCO-AMERICANS
Maurice Violette
Vantage Press. $6.95.

THE FRANCO-TEXAN LAND COMPANY
Virginia H. Taylor
University of Texas Press, 1969. $8.75.

THE FRENCH BLOOD IN AMERICA
Lucian J. Fosdick
448 pp. Genealogical Publishing Co. Reprint of the 1906 edition. Illus. $14.00.

FRENCH EMIGRE PRIESTS IN THE UNITED STATES (1791-1815)
Leo Francis Ruskowski
AMS Press. Reprint of the 1940 edition. $7.00.

*THE FRENCH IN AMERICA
Virginia Brainard Kunz
Lerner Publications, 1966. Illus. $3.95. Ages 10 and up.

FRENCH IN NORTH AMERICA: A BIBLIOGRAPHICAL GUIDE TO FRENCH ARCHIVES, REPRODUCTIONS, AND RE-SEARCH MISSIONS
Henry P. Beers
414 pp. Louisiana States University Press, 1957. $12.50.

FRENCHMEN AND FRENCH WAYS IN THE MISSISSIPPI VALLEY
John Francis McDermott, Editor
320 pp. University of Illinois Press, 1969. Illus. $10.95.

THE INFLUENCE OF FRENCH IMMI-GRATION ON THE POLITICAL HISTORY OF THE U.S.
Elizabeth Huntington Avery
Includes chapters on the revolutionary period, state constitutions, the French Catholics and the old Northwest. 75 pp. R & E Research Associates. Reprint of the 1890 edition. $6.00.

SOCIAL AND ECONOMIC ASPECTS OF FRENCH ACTIVITIES IN EARLY CALI-FORNIA
Geraldine Wimmer
Thesis. R & E Research Associates. Reprint of the 1940 paper. Pap. $7.00.

TALES FROM THE FRENCH FOLKLORE OF MISSOURI
Joseph Medard Carriere
AMS Press, Inc. Reprint of the 1937 edition. $17.50.

GERMAN-AMERICANS

History

AMERICANS FROM GERMANY: A STUDY IN CULTURAL DIVERSITY
Robert H. Billgmeier
The author concerns himself with the strong ethnic identification of German Americans: their culturally heterogeneous backgrounds, national and regional social character, and the different types of German immigrants. He discusses their various responses to the American frontier, the ways they preserved their heritage, and the general importance of cultural diversity. 160 pp. Wadsworth Publishing Co., 1974. Pap. $4.95.

ANGLO-GERMAN AND AMERICAN-GERMAN CROSSCURRENTS
Philip Allison Shelley, et al, Editors
303 pp. Johnson Reprint Corporation Reprint of the 1957 edition. $21.00.

BIBLIOGRAPHY ON GERMAN SETTLEMENTS IN COLONIAL NORTH AMERICA
Emil Meynen
Gale Research. Reprint of the 1937 edition. $20.00.

CONSERVATIVE REFORMERS: GERMAN-AMERICAN CATHOLICS AND THE SOCIAL ORDER
Philip Gleason
University of Notre Dame Press, 1968. $10.95.

THE EARLY GERMAN THEATRE IN NEW YORK, 1840 TO 1872.
Frederick Adolph Leuchs
AMS Press, Inc. Reprint of the 1928 edition. $12.00.

THE EARLY GERMANS OF NEW JERSEY: THEIR HISTORY, CHURCHES, AND GENEALOGIES
Theodore Frelinghuysen Chambers
Genealogical Publishing Co. Reprint of the 1895 edition. Illus. $18.50.

THE EFFECT OF PROHIBITION ON THE GERMAN-AMERICANS
H.W.Ronnenberg
Carlton Press. $4.50.

FIELDS OF PEACE: A PENNSYLVANIA GERMAN ALBUM (PHOTOGRAPHIC STUDY)
Millen Brand
Doubleday and Co., 1970. Cloth, $8.95. E.P. Dutton and Co., pap. $3.95.

GERMAN ACHIEVEMENTS IN AMERICA
Rudolf Cronau
Gordon Press. $27.00.

GERMAN-AMERICANA: *A Bibliography*
Don H. Tolzmann, Editor
Lists 5,300 books, pamphlets, articles, records, and other materials covering all aspects of German-Americana. 396 pp. Scarecrow, 1975. $15.00.

THE GERMAN-AMERICANS
Richard O'Connor
Little, Brown, and Co., 1968. $10.00.

THE GERMAN ELEMENT IN THE UNITED STATES: WITH SPECIAL REFERENCE TO ITS POLITICAL, MORAL, SOCIAL, AND EDUCATIONAL INFLUENCE
Albert Bernhardt Faust
This study of German immigration first covers the German settlers before the American Revolution and then continues through the nineteenth century. Volume 2 discusses the German influences on industrial development, politics and agriculture with specific reference to German settlements in various parts of America. Arno Press. Reprint of the 1927 edition. Two volumes. $37.50. Scholarly Press, $34.50.

GERMAN INTEREST IN CALIFORNIA BEFORE 1850: THESIS
George Peter Hammon
R and E Research Associates. Reprint of the 1921 edition. $7.00.

THE GERMAN PIETISTS OF PROVINCIAL PENNSYLVANIA, 1694 TO 1708
Julius Friedrich Sachse
AMS Press, Inc. Reprint of the 1895 edition. $25.00.

GERMAN PIONEERS IN EARLY CALIFORNIA

Erwin G. Gudde
R and E Research Associates. Reprint of the
1927 edition. $3.00.

GERMAN SECTARIANS OF PENNSYL-VANIA, 1708 TO 1800, TWO VOLS.
Julius Friedrich Sachse
AMS Press, Inc. Reprint of the 1899 to 1900
edition. $45.00 per set; $24.00 each.

THE GERMAN SETTLEMENT AT ANA-HEIM
Dorothea Paule
Study of the first German colonization of
California. Thesis. R & E Research Associates.
Reprint of the 1952 paper. Pap. $7.00.

GERMANIA, U.S.A.: SOCIAL CHANGE IN NEW ULM, MINNESOTA
Noel Iverson
A historical and sociological study of a rural
ethnic community. 188 pp. University of
Minnesota Press, 1966. $5.50.

THE GERMANS HELPED BUILD AMER-ICA
Kathlyn Gay
Messner, 1971. $4.50.

GERMANS IN AMERICA
Carl Wittke
Teachers College Press, 1967. Pap. $1.50.

*THE GERMANS IN AMERICA
Virginia Brainard Kunz
Lerner Publications, 1966. Illus. $3.95. Ages 10
and up.

THE GERMANS IN AMERICA, 1607 TO 1970, A CHRONOLOGY AND FACTBOOK
Howard B. Furer
Oceana Publications, 1973. $5.00.

THE GERMANS IN AMERICAN LIFE
Rachel Davis-DuBois, and Emma
Schweppe, Editors
Books for Libraries, Inc. Reprint of the 1936
edition. $11.50.

THE GERMANS IN COLONIAL TIMES
Lucy F. Bittinger
Russell and Russell. Reprint of the 1901 edition.
$8.50.

GERMANS IN COLORADO: THESIS
Mildred S. MacArthur

R and E Research Associates. Reprint of the
1917 edition. $5.00.

GERMANS IN LOS ANGELES COUNTY, 1850 TO 1909
Lamberta Vogeth
R and E Research Associates. Reprint of the
1933 edition. Pap. $5.00.

THE GERMANS IN THE MAKING OF AMERICA
Frederick Franklin Schrader
Haskell House Pubs., Inc. Reprint of the 1924
edition. $11.95.

HISTORIC BACKGROUND AND ANNALS OF THE SWISS AND GERMAN PIONEERS OF SOUTHEASTERN PENNSYLVANIA AND OF THEIR REMOTE ANCESTORS
Frank Eshleman
386 pp. Genealogical Publishing Co. Reprint of
the 1917 edition. $12.50.

JOHN O. MEUSEBACH: GERMAN COLONIZER IN TEXAS
Irene M. King
University of Texas Press, 1966. $6.50.

MARYLAND GERMANS: A HISTORY
Dieter Cunz
Kennikat Press. Reprint of the 1948 edition.
Illus. $17.50.

PENNSYLVANIA GENEALOGIES: CHIEF-LY SCOTCH-IRISH AND GERMAN
William Henry Egle
798 pp. Genealogical Publishing Co. Reprint of
the 1896 edition. $22.50.

THE SETTLEMENT OF THE GERMAN COAST OF LOUISIANNA AND THE CREOLES OF GERMAN DESCENT
J. Hanno Dieler
154 pp. Genealogical Publishing Co. Reprint of
the 1909 edition. Cloth $10.00. R and E
Research Associates. Pap. $5.00.

THE SETTLEMENT OF GERMANTOWN, PENNSYLVANIA AND THE BEGINNING OF GERMAN EMIGRATION TO NORTH AMERICA
Samuel W. Pennypacker
Benjamin Blom Pubs. Reprint of the 1899
edition. $12.50.

THE SO-CALLED WENDS OF GERMANY AND THEIR COLONIES IN TEXAS AND IN AUSTRALIA

George C. Engerrand

Slavic colonies in Texas from Germany from 1850-1900. R & E Research Associates. Reprint of the 1934 edition. $9.00.

THE STORY OF THE PENNSYLVANIA GERMANS: EMBRACING AN ACCOUNT OF THEIR ORIGIN, THEIR HISTORY, THEIR DIALECY

William Biedelman

Gale Research. Reprint of the 1898 edition. $10.00.

SUNBONNETS AND SHOOFLY PIES: PENNSYLVANIA DUTCH CULTURAL HISTORY

John Joseph Stoudt
A S Barnes, 1973. $25.00.

THREE CENTURIES OF GERMAN LIFE IN AMERICA

Rudolf Cronau
Gordon Press. $27.00.

THE TRAGEDY OF GERMAN-AMERICA: THE GERMANS IN THE UNITED STATES OF AMERICA DURING THE NINETEENTH CENTURY AND AFTER

John Arkas Hawgood

After a brief overview of German-American settlement, the author designates nativism in the 1850's especially Know-Nothingism as the force shaping German-America. Arno Press. Reprint of the 1940 edition. $13.50.

*A YANKEE IN GERMAN-AMERICA: TEXAS HILL COUNTRY

Vera Flach
188 pp. Naylor Co., 1973. $5.95. Ages 12 and up.

Immigration

DETAILED REPORTS ON THE SALZBURGER EMIGRANTS WHO SETTLED IN AMERICA, 1736

Samuel Urlsperger
368 pp. University of Georgia Press, 1972. $10.00.

GERMAN SEED IN TEXAS SOIL: IMMI-

GRANT FARMERS IN 19TH CENTURY TEXAS

Terry G. Jordan
University of Texas Press, 1966. $7.50.

THE GERMANS IN TEXAS: A STUDY IN IMMIGRATION

Gilbert G. Benjamin

The history of Germans in Texas between 1821 and 1909. 155 pp. Illus. Jenkins Publishing Co., 1974. Cloth, $12.95. R and E Research Associates, pap. $8.00.

PENNSYLVANIA GERMAN PIONEERS: A PUBLICATION OF THE ORIGINAL LISTS OF ARRIVALS IN THE PORT OF PHILADELPHIA, 1727 TO 1808, TWO VOLS

Ralph Beaver Strassburger

Genealogical Publishing Co. Reprint o the 1934 edition. $32.50.

TRUE AND AUTHENTIC REGISTER OF PERSONS WHO IN THE YEAR 1709 JOURNEYED FROM GERMANY TO AMERICA

Ulrich Simmendinger

20 pp. Genealogical Publishing Co. Reprint of the 1934 edition. Pap. $3.00.

Literature

BIBLIOGRAPHY OF GERMAN CULTURE IN AMERICA TO 1940

Henry A. Pochmann and Arthur R. Schultz, Editors

University of Wisconsin Press, 1953. $15.00.

THE FIRST CENTURY OF GERMAN PRINTING IN AMERICA, 1728 TO 1830

O. Seidensticker

Kraus Reprint Co. Reprint of the 1893 edition. $14.00.

GERMAN EXILE LITERATURE IN AMERICA, 1933 TO 1950: A HISTORY OF THE FREE GERMAN PRESS AND BOOK TRADE

Robert E. Cazden
American Library Assn., 1970. $10.00.

THE GERMAN LANGUAGE PRESS IN AMERICA

Carl F. Wittke

Haskell House Pubs., Inc. Reprint of the 1957 edition. $11.95.

GERMAN LANGUAGE IN AMERICA: A SYMPOSIUM
Glenn G. Gilbert, Editor
University of Texas Press, 1971. $8.50.

THE GERMAN LANGUAGE PRESS OF THE AMERICAS, 1732 TO 1968: HISTORY AND BIBLIOGRAPHY, VOL. II
Karl J. Arndt aNd May E. Olson
708 pp. Rowman and Littlefield, 1973. Illus. $50.00.

LOCAL LIVES: POEMS ABOUT THE PENNSYLVANIA GERMANS
Millen Brand
Poems about the people living in the Allentown-Reading area. 464 pp. Crown Publishers, 1975. $12.50.

Politics

GEORGE SYLVESTER VIERECK: GERMAN-AMERICAN PROPAGANDIST
Niel M. Johnson
282 pp. University of Illinois Press, 1972. Illus. $9.95.

THE GERMAN-AMERICANS IN POLITICS, 1914-1917
Clifton James Child
This book focuses on the growth of the National German-American Alliance whose aim was to maintain friendly German-American relations, protect German-American culture, and propagandize their cause to the American public. Arno Press. Reprint of the 1939 edition. $8.50.

GERMAN POLITICAL REFUGEES IN THE UNITED STATES, 1815 TO 1860
Ernest Bruncken
R and E Research Associates. Reprint of the 1904 edition. $5.00.

IMMIGRANTS AND POLITICS: THE GERMANS OF NEBRASKA, 1880 TO 1900
Frederick C. Luebke
220 pp. University of Nebraska Press, 1969. $9.95.

Wars

BONDS OF LOYALTY: GERMAN AMERICAN DURING WORLD WAR I
Frederick C. Luebke
University of Illinois Press, 1974. Cloth, $10.00; Pap. $3.00.

THE GERMAN ALLIED TROOPS IN THE NORTH AMERICAN WAR OF INDEPENDENCE, 1776-1783
Max von Eelking
360 pp. Genealogical Publishing Co. Reprint of the 1893 edition. $12.00.

THE GERMAN SOLDIER IN THE WARS OF THE U.S.
Joseph S. Rosengarten
Coverage of the Revolutionary and Civil War periods. R & E Research Associates. Reprint of the 1886 edition. $9.00.

GREEK-AMERICANS

THE ASSIMILATION OF GREEKS IN THE UNITED STATES
Evangelos C. Vlachos
International Publications Service, 1969. $9.50.

A BIBLIOGRAPHIC GUIDE TO MATERIALS ON GREEKS IN THE UNITED STATES 1890 TO 1968
Michael N. Cutsumbis
Center for Migration Studies, 1970. Pap. $4.50.

FIRST AND SECOND GENERATION GREEKS IN CHICAGO: AN INQUIRY INTO THEIR STRATIFICATION AND MOBILITY PATTERNS
George A. Kourvetaris
International Publications Service, 1971. $10.00.

GREEK SETTLEMENT OF THE SAN FRANCISCO BAY AREA: THESIS
Demitra Georgas
R and E Research Associates, Pubs., 1974. Written: 1951. Pap. $7.00.

GREEKS IN AMERICA
Thomas Burgess
R and E Research Associates. Reprint of the 1913 edition. $11.00.

*THE GREEKS IN AMERICA
Jayne Clark Jones
Lerner Pubns., 1969. Illus. $3.95. Ages 10 and up.

GREEKS IN AMERICA
Theodore Saloutos
Teachers College Press, 1967. Pap. $1.50.

THE GREEKS IN AMERICA
J.P. Xenides
R and E Research Associates. Reprint of the 1922 edition. $8.00.

GREEKS IN AMERICA: AN ACCOUNT OF THEIR COMING, PROGRESS, CUSTOMS, LIVING, AND ASPIRATIONS, WITH AN HISTORICAL INTRODUCTION AND THE STORIES OF SOME FAMOUS AMERICAN-GREEKS
Thomas Burgess
Covers every feature of the Greek experience in America, from conditions in Greece to industrial employment here, community institutions, their New World colonies, and their religious and cultural life in general. Arno Press Reprint of the 1913 edition. $12.00.

THE GREEKS IN THE UNITED STATES
Theodore Saloutos
445 pp. Harvard University Press, 1964. Illus. $12.00.

WELFARE ACTIVITIES AMONG THE GREEK PEOPLE IN LOS ANGELES
Mary Antoniou
Thesis. R & E Research Associates. Reprint of the 1939 paper. Pap. $8.00.

HAWAIIAN-AMERICANS

ANCIENT HAWAIIAN MUSIC
H.H. Roberts
Kraus Reprint Co. Reprint of the 1926 edition. Pap. $25.00.

THE ANCIENT HAWAIIANS: HOW THEY CLOTHED THEMSELVES
Margaret Titcomb
The story of *tapa* (cloth) making, the art involved and its uses. 64 pp. Hogarth Press Hawaii, 1974. Illus. Age 8-18. $1.95.

*THE ANCIENT HAWAIIANS: WHO

WERE THEY? HOW DID THEY LIVE?
Dorothy Hazama
An account of Hawaiian family and class systems, the types of homes they had and what they used in them. 80 pp. Hogarth Press Hawaii, 1974. Illus. Age 8-18. $1.95.

AN ANTHROPOMETRIC STUDY OF HAWAIIANS OF PURE AND MIXED BLOOD
L.C.Dunn
Kraus Reprint Co. Reprint of the 1928 edition. Pap. $3.00.

CULTURE AND BEHAVIOR IN HAWAII: AN ANNOTATED BIBLIOGRAPHY
Judith Rubano
147 pp. University Press of Hawaii, 1971. Pap. $4.00.

FOLK SONGS HAWAII SINGS
John M. Kelly, Jr., Editor
80 pp. 60 pages of music. Charles E. Tuttle Co. Illus. $5.45.

FOLKTALES FROM HAWAII
L.Green
Krishna Press. $25.95.

HAWAIIAN AMERICANS
Edwin J. Burrows
An account of the mingling of the cultures in Hawaii. Hogarth Press Hawaii, 1975. $8.00.

HAWAIIAN LEGENDS OF GHOSTS AND GHOST-GODS
W.D. Westervelt, Editor
The fantastic world of the Shark God of Molokai, the Ghost of Wahuala Temple, and the King of Ghosts. 280 pp. Charles E. Tuttle Co., 1963. Photos. $3.25.

HAWAIIAN LEGENDS OF OLD HONO-LULU
W.D. Westervelt, Editor
Centuries-old folk tales. 300 pp. Charles E. Tuttle Co. $3.75.

HAWAIIAN LEGENDS OF VOLCANOES
W.D. Westervelt, Editor
Stories of volcanoes and the gods who live in them. 291 pp. Charles E. Tuttle Co. Photos. $3.75.

HAWAIIAN MYTHOLOGY
Martha Warren Beckwith
608 pp. University Press of Hawaii, 1970. $12.00.

HAWAIIAN PROVERBS AND RIDDLES
H.P.Judd
Kraus Reprint Co. Reprint of the 1930 edition.
Pap. $6.00.

*KAMEHAMEHA, FIRST KING OF HAWAII
A. Grove Day
64 pp. Hogarth Press Hawaii, 1974. Illus. Age 8-18. $1.95.

LANGUAGE AND DIALECT IN HAWAII: A SOCIOLINGUISTIC HISTORY TO 1935
John E. Reinecke
272 pp. University Press of Hawaii, 1970. $9.00.

LEGENDS OF HAWAII
P.Colum
Ballantine Books, 1973. Pap. $1.50.

THE LEGENDS AND MYTHS OF HAWAII: THE FABLES AND FOLK-LORE OF A STRANGE PEOPLE
His Hawaiian Majesty Kalakaua
568 pp. Charles E. Tuttle Co. Illus. Pap. $3.50.

SELECTIONS FROM FORNANDER'S HAWAIIAN ANTIQUITIES AND FOLKLORE
Samuel H. Elbert, Editor
306 pp. University Press of Hawaii, 1959. Illus. Pap. $6.50.

THOSE KINGS AND QUEENS OF OLD HAWAII
Paul Bailey
The Hawaiin Monarchy before American statehood, a 200 year history. 300 pp. Westernlore Press, 1975. Illus. $11.95.

THE UNWRITTEN LITERATURE OF HAWAII: THE SACRED SONGS OF THE HULA
Nathaniel B. Emerson
A study of the Hawaiian hula in song and dance form. 340 pp. Charles E. Tuttle Co., 1965. Pap. $3.25.

HISPANIC-AMERICANS

*THE ART OF THE SPANISH IN THE UNITED STATES AND PUERTO RICO
S.Glubok
Macmillan Publishing Co., Inc., 1972. $6.95. Below college level.

EDUCATION AND ECONOMIC SUCCESS OF URBAN SPANISH-SPEAKING IMMIGRANTS
Paul M. Zisman
R & E Research Associates, 1975. Pap. $11.00.

THE HISPANIC SOCIETY OF AMERICA. CATALOGUE OF THE LIBRARY OF THE HISPANIC SOCIETY OF AMERICA, 10 VOLS.
G.K. Hall and Co., 1962. $745.00.

*HISPANO-AMERICAN CONTRIBUTORS TO AMERICAN LIFE
John M. Franco
The purpose of this book is to develop and build an appreciation of the contributions of Hispano-Americans to life in the United States. 21 biographies of successful Hispano-Americans of primarily Mexican, Cuban or Puerto Rican origin. Benefic Press. Age 7-12. $4.45.

LATIN AMERICAN CULTURE: *An Anthropological Synthesis*
Emilio Willems
Examines such institutions of Latin American society as family, religion, economy, and political organization within the context of a common culture. Illus. Harper & Row Publishers, 1975.

LATIN AMERICAN NEWSPAPERS IN THE UNITED STATES LIBRARIES: A UNION LIST
Steven M. Charno, Editor
University of Texas Press, 1969. $20.00.

LOS PRIMEROS: HISPANIC AMERICANS OF THE UTE FRONTIER
F.L.Swadesh
University of Notre Dame Press, 1974. Cloth, $9.95; Pap. $3.45.

MY HOUSE IS YOUR HOUSE
Rafael V. Martinez
The accomplishments and problems of Spanish-Americans living among Anglo-Americans. Friendship Press. Pap. $2.50.

NORTH FROM MEXICO: THE SPANISH SPEAKING PEOPLE OF THE UNITED STATES
Carey McWilliams
324 pp. Greenwood Press, Inc. Reprint of the 1949 edition. $12.50.

OUR CITIZENS FROM THE CARRIBEAN
Clarence Senior
McGraw Hill Book Co. 1965. $1.96.

PROBLEMS IN LATIN AMERICAN HISTORY: *The Modern Period*
Joseph S. Tulchin, Editor
An in-depth study of major issues in contemporary Latin American history which draws on the hypothesis of various social sciences to broaden understanding of Latin American problems. 529 pp. Harper & Row Publishers, 1973. Pap. $6.95.

PROSPECTS FOR THE SPANISH AMERICAN CULTURE OF NEW MEXICO
Thomas R. Lopez, Jr.
R & E Research Associates, 1974. $12.00.

RELATIONS BETWEEN THE SPANISH-AMERICANS AND ANGLO-AMERICANS IN NEW MEXICO: A STUDY OF CONFLICT AND ACCOMODATION IN A DUAL-ETHNIC SITUATION
Carolyn Zeleny
Includes such topics as the land conflict, religious separatism, the problem of education, and economic, social, and political relations. Arno Press, 1974. Illus. $21.00.

SPANISH-AMERICANS OF NEW MEXICO: A HERITAGE OF PRIDE
Nancie L. Gonzales
University of New Mexico Press, 1969. Cloth, $7.95; Pap. $3.95.

SPANISH COLONIAL LIFE IN NEW MEXICO
12 photos with text and background information. Museum of New Mexico Press; 1974. $1.00.

SPANISH HARLEM: ANATOMY OF POVERTY
Patricia Cayo Sexton
Harper and Row Pubs., Pap. $1.60.

SPANISH-SPEAKING GROUPS IN THE UNITED STATES
John H. Burma
The author brings together the facts and problems of Spanish-speaking groups in the U.S., particularly Mexicans. Stresses the value of accepting cultural plurality as a means of improving intergroup relations. 214 pp. Blain Ethridge Publications. Reprint of the 1954 Durham-Duke University Press edition. $12.00.

SPANISH SPEAKING HEROES
Roger W. Axford
Sketches, over two dozen, include Puerto Ricans, Mexicans, Cubans, Dominicans, and Spanish people claiming American citizenship. 88 pp. Pendell Publishing Co., 1973. Pap. $3.95.

THE SPANISH SPEAKING IN THE UNITED STATES: A GUIDE TO MATERIALS
U.S. Cabinet Committee On Opportunities for Spanish Speaking People
More then 1,700 books, articles, dissertations, audiovisual units, and other materials are covered, and several hundred broadcast and print outlets devoted wholly or in part to Spanish language content are listed, with addresses. Annotated. Blaine Ethridge Publications. 175 pp. Reprint of the 1971 edition. $16.50.

SPANISH-SPEAKING PEOPLE IN THE UNITED STATES
June Helm, Editor
Thirteen studies by anthropologists and sociologists that demonstrate the tenacity of the cultural heritage of the people as well as the dimensions of their responses to the total society. 224 pp. University of Washington Press, 1968. Pap. $4.00.

VOICES OF CHANGE IN THE SPANISH-AMERICAN THEATER: AN ANTHOLOGY
William I. Oliver
University of Texas Press, 1971. $8.00.

HUNGARIAN-AMERICANS

A HISTORY OF AMERICAN HUNGARIAN LITERATURE
Leslie Konnyu
American Hungarian Review. $3.00.

HUNGARIAN LANGUAGE MAINTENANCE IN THE UNITED STATES
Joshua A. Fishman
Indiana University Research Center for the Language Sciences, 1966. Pap. $4.00.

*HUNGARIANS IN AMERICA
Rezsoe and Margaret Gracza
Lerner Publications, 1969. Illus. $3.95. Ages 10 and up.

HUNGARIANS IN THE UNITED STATES OF AMERICA, AN IMMIGRATION STUDY
    Leslie Konnyu
American Hungarian Review, 1967. Cloth, $5.50; Pap. $4.25.

ITALIAN, SLAVIC, AND HUNGARIAN UNSKILLED LABORERS IN THE UNITED STATES
    Frank J. Sheridan
Jerome S. Ozer Pubs. Reprint of the 1907 edition. $5.95.

IRISH-AMERICANS

*AN ALBUM OF THE IRISH AMERICANS
    Eugene Murphy and Timothy Driscoll
Topics include the Irish heritage, the Church, the Western Irish, the Fighting Irish, and 20th-century Irish leaders. 96 pp. Franklin Watts, Inc., 1974. Age 12 up. $4.90.

*AMERICA IS ALSO IRISH
    Robert N. Webb
G.P.Putnam's Sons, 1973. Illus. $3.89. Below college level.

THE AMERICAN-IRISH AND THEIR INFLUENCE ON IRISH POLITICS
    Philip H. Bagenal
Jerome S. Ozer Pubs. Reprint of the 1882 edition. $10.50.

THE AMERICAN-IRISH: A POLITICAL AND SOCIAL PORTRAIT
    William V. Shannon
Macmillan Publishing Co., Inc., 1974. Cloth, $9.95.; Pap. $4.95.

FENIAN MOVEMENT IN THE UNITED STATES, 1858 TO 1886
    William D'Arcy
Russell and Russell. Reprint of the 1947 edition. $18.00.

FORGOTTEN PIONEERS: IRISH LEADERS IN EARLY CALIFORNIA
    Thomas F. Prendergast
Books for Libraries, Inc. Reprint of the 1942 edition. $14.50.

A HIDDEN PHASE OF AMERICAN HISTORY: IRELAND'S PART IN AMERICA'S STRUGGLE FOR LIBERTY

    Michael J. O'Brien
533 pp. Genealogical Publishing Co. Reprint of the 1919 edition. Illus. $15.00.

A HISTORY OF THE IRISH SETTLERS OF NORTH AMERICA FROM THE EARLIEST PERIOD TO THE CENSUS OF 1850
    Thomas D'Arcy McGee
R and E Research Associates, Pubs. Reprint of the 1852 edition. $12.00 Genealogical Publishing Co., $10.00. Jerome S. Ozer Publications, $9.95.

HOW THE IRISH BECAME AMERICANS
    Joseph P. O'Grady
A history of the Irish in America, with an emphasis on political leverage. Twayne Publishers. $7.95.

I AM OF IRELAND
    Richard Howard Brown
One Irish-American's growing involvement with Ireland and the IRA. Harper & Row Pubs., 1972. $6.95.

IMMIGRATION OF THE IRISH QUAKERS INTO PENNSYLVANIA, 1682-1750
    Albert Cook Myers
With their early history in Ireland. 477 pp. Genealogical Publishing Co. Reprint of the 1902 edition. Illus. $16.00.

IRELAND AND THE AMERICAN EMIGRATION, 1850 TO 1900.
    Arnold Schrier
Russell and Russell. Reprint of the 1958 edition. Illus. $9.50.

IRELAND AND IRISH EMIGRATION TO THE NEW WORLD FROM 1815 TO THE FAMINE
    William Forbes Adams
Russell and Russell. Reprint of the 1932 edition. $10.00.

IRISH EMIGRATION TO THE UNITED STATES: WHAT IT HAS BEEN, AND WHAT IT IS
    Stephen Byrne
Written in an effort to forewarn Irish immigrants of making the fatal mistake of crowding into large cities when they reached America. Arno Press. Reprint of the 1873 edition. $5.00.

THE IRISH HELPED BUILD AMERICA
    Virginia B. McDonnell
Messner, 1969. $3.95.

IRISH IMMIGRATION IN THE UNITED STATES: IMMIGRANT INTERVIEWS

Jeremiah O'Donovan

A collection of eyewitness accounts of Irish immigrants and their lives in the U.S. during the first half of the nineteenth century. Arno Press. Reprint of the 1864 edition. $11.50.

*THE IRISH IN AMERICA

James E. Johnson

Lerner Publications, 1966. Illus. $3.95. Ages 10 and up.

THE IRISH IN AMERICA

John Francis Maguire

Personal observations made soon after the height of the Irish immigration to America, written in the form of a novel. Arno Press. Reprint of the 1868 edition. $18.50.

THE IRISH IN AMERICA

Carl Wittke

Russell and Russell. Reprint of the 1956 edition. Cloth, $13.50. Teachers College Press, pap. $1.50.

THE IRISH IN AMERICA: CHRONOLOGY AND FACTBOOK, 1550 TO 1972

William D. Griffin

Oceana Publications, 1973. $5.00.

THE IRISH IN AMERICA: EXCERPTED FROM THE JOURNAL OF THE AMERICAN IRISH HISTORICAL SOCIETY, VOL 13

Michael J. O'Brien

63 pp. Genealogical Publishing Co. Reprint of the 1914 edition. $5.00.

THE IRISH IN PHILADELPHIA

Dennis Clark

Ten generations of urban experience. Insights into Irish immigrant history in America. 264 pp. Temple University Press, 1974. $12.50.

THE IRISH IN THE UNITED STATES

John B. Duff

The author examines the Irish in America: their hatred of the English, the early American settlements, the potato famine, employment struggles, political skill and reliance on the democratic process to change their lives, their continuous loyalty to their homeland, and the strength and influence of the Roman Catholic Church. 87 pp. Wadsworth Publishing Co., 1974. Pap. $3.50.

IRISH AND IRISH POLITICIANS: A STUDY OF SOCIAL AND CULTURAL ALIENATION

Edward M. Levine

University of Notre Dame Press, 1966. $7.95.

REAL LACE: AMERICA'S IRISH RICH

Stephen Birmingham

Harper and Row Pubs., 1973. Illus. $10.00.

WHAT BRINGS SO MANY IRISH TO AMERICA!

Hibericus

78 pp. R and E Research Associates, Pubs. Reprint of the 1845 edition. $6.00.

ITALIAN-AMERICANS

Assimilation

DAYS PLEASANT AND UNPLEASANT IN THE ORDER: SONS OF ITALY IN AMERICA

Robert Ferrari

The problem of races and racial societies in the United States: assimilation or isolation? The author helps explain the alienation of Italian-Americans. 147 pp. August M. Kelley, Publishers. Reprint of the 1926 edition. $10.00.

FACING THE CHAIR: SACCO AND VANZETTI

John Dos Passos

The story of the Americanization of two foreign-born workmen. Oriole Editions, 1971. First published 1927. $2.00.

THE ITALIAN COMMUNITY AND ITS LANGUAGE IN THE UNITED STATES

Francesco Cordasco, Editor

472 pp. Rowman & Littlefield, 1975. $25.00.

ITALIAN OR AMERICAN? THE 2ND GENERATION IN CONFLICT

Irvin L. Child

Russell and Russell. Reprint of the 1943 edition. $11.00.

ITALIAN WOMEN IN INDUSTRY

Louise C. Odencrantz

Describes their home life, their incomes, the standards they are able to maintain, the effect of American industrial and living conditions upon their standards, and conversely, the effect of their Italian standards of life and work on the industries they engage in. 345 pp. August M. Kelley. Reprint of the 1919 edition. $15.00.

THE ITALIANS: SOCIAL BACKGROUNDS OF AN AMERICAN GROUP

Fancesco Cordasco and Eugene Bucchioni
Provides a sourcebook of documents and other materials which re-creates the period of the great migrations to America. 598 pp., 1974. Illus. August M. Kelley, Publishers $19.95.

THE SOCIAL BACKGROUND OF THE ITALO-AMERICAN SCHOOL CHILD: A STUDY OF THE SOUTHERN ITALIAN FAMILY MORES AND THEIR EFFECT ON THE SCHOOL SITUATION IN ITALY AND AMERICA

Leonard Covello
488 pp. Rowman and Littlefield. Reprint of the 1967 edition. $25.00.

SOCIAL AND RELIGIOUS LIFE OF ITALIANS IN AMERICA

Enrico C. Sartorio
The author deals with the twin dynamics of conflict and acculturation in a discussion of "Americanization" as well as with the role of the churches. 152 pp. August M. Kelley. Reprint of the 1918 edition. $10.00.

STUDIES IN ITALIAN AMERICAN SOCIAL HISTORY:

Francesco Cordasco, Editor
A collection of essays on diverse facets of the Italian experience in the United States. 300 pp. Rowman and Littlefield, 1975. $25.00.

History

*AN ALBUM OF THE ITALIAN-AMERICAN

Salvatore John LaGumina
The roles of Italian-Americans throughout history, their problems, accomplishments, and relationships with other ethnic groups. 96 pp. Franklin Watts, Inc., 1972. Ages 9-12. $4.90.

ALCOHOL IN ITALIAN CULTURE: FOOD AND WINE IN RELATION TO SOBRIETY AMONG ITALIANS AND ITALIAN AMERICANS

G. Lolli et al
Rutgers Center of Alcohol Studies. $6.00.

THE AMERICAN ITALIANS: THEIR HISTORY AND CULTURE

Andrew F. Rolle
Wadsworth Publishing Co., 1972. Pap. $3.95.

BLOOD OF MY BLOOD: THE DILEMA OF ITALIAN AMERICANS

Richard Gambino
Doubleday and Co., 1973. $7.95.

THE CHILDREN OF COLUMBUS: AN INFORMAL HISTORY OF THE ITALIANS IN THE NEW WORLD

Erik Amfitheatrof
Little, Brown, and Co., 1973. $8.95.

ETHNIC ALIENTATION: THE ITALIAN-AMERICANS

Patrick J. Gallo
Fairleigh Dickinson University Press, 1974. $10.00.

THE ITALIAN IN AMERICA

Eliot Lord, et al, Editors
Books for Libraries, Inc. Reprint of the 1905 edition. $11.25. R and E Research Associates, $12.00.

THE ITALIAN IN AMERICA: THE PROGRESSIVE VIEW, 1891 TO 1914

Lyido F. Tomasi
Center for Migration Studies, 1972. Pap. $4.95.

THE ITALIAN-AMERICANS

Luciano J. Torizzo and Salvatore Mondello
Evaluates their contributions to agriculture, viniculture, the arts, politics, and organized crime. Twayne Publishers. $7.50.

ITALIAN-AMERICANS

Joseph Lopreato
Peter Smith Publishers. Cloth, $5.00. Random House, Inc., pap. $3.25

THE ITALIAN-AMERICANS: THEIR HISTORY AND CULTURE

Andrew F. Rolle
This book takes an historical approach to the immigrant experience as well as describing why immigrants left Italy, how they were changed by American culture, and where they settled. Also discusses current attitudes, problems of the second generation, and recent immigration. 122 pp. Wadsworth Publishing Co. Pap. $3.50.

THE ITALIAN EXPERIENCE IN THE UNITED STATES

S.M.Tomasi and M.H.Engel
Center for Migration Studies, 1970. Cloth,
$8.00; Pap. $4.95.

ITALIAN, SLAVIC, AND HUNGARIAN UNSKILLED LABORERS IN THE UNITED STATES

Frank J. Sheridan
Jerome S. Ozer Pubs. Reprint of the 1907
edition. $5.95.

*THE ITALIANS IN AMERICA

Ronald Grossman
Lerner Publications, 1966. Illus. $3.95. Ages 10
and up.

THE ITALIANS IN AMERICA

Pietro Militello
Franklin Publishing Co., 1973. $4.95.

THE ITALIANS IN AMERICA: A CHRONO-LOGY AND FACTBOOK, 1492 TO 1972

Anthony F. LoGatto
Oceana Pubns., 1972. $5.00.

ITALIANS IN THE UNITED STATES

Francesco Cordasco and Salvatore J.
LaGumina
A bibliography of reports, texts, critical studies
and related materials. Oriole Editions, 1972.
$20.00.

SOME ASPECTS OF THE EFFECT OF THE DOMINANT AMERICAN CULTURE UPON CHILDREN OF ITALIAN-BORN PARENTS

Joseph Wilfrid Tait
AMS Press, Inc. Reprint of the 1942 edition.
$10.00.

SONS OF ITALY: A SOCIAL AND RE-LIGIOUS STUDY OF THE ITALIANS IN AMERICA

Antonio Mangano
Jerome S. Ozer. Rerpint of the 1917 edition.
Illus. $11.50. Russell and Russell, $14.00.

SOUTH ITALIAN FOLKWAYS IN EUROPE AND AMERICA: A HANDBOOK FOR SOCIAL WORKERS, VISITING NURSES, SCHOOL TEACHERS, AND PHYSICIANS

Phyllis H. Williams
Russell and Russell. Reprint of the 1938 edition.
$8.50.

Immigration

THE IMMIGRANT UPRAISED: ITALIAN ADVENTURES AND COLONISTS IN AN EXPANDING AMERICA

Andrew F. Rolle
391 pp. University of Oklahoma Press. Reprint
of the 1968 edition. Illus. Cloth, $8.95; Pap.
$3.95.

THE ITALIAN EMIGRATION OF OUR TIMES

Robert Franz Foerster
A study of the Italian migratory movement
which analyzes the causes of emigration by considering conditions in Italy, follows the emigrants into the countries of settlement in
Europe, Africa, South America and the United
States, and attempts to discover their economic
and cultural contributions as well as the nature
of their personal fortunes. Arno Press. Reprint
of the 1919 edition. $16.50. Russell and Russell,
$15.00.

ITALIAN REPATRIATION FROM THE UNITED STATES, 1900 TO 1914

Betty B. Caroli
Center for Migration Studies, 1973. Pap. $4.50.

ROSA: THE LIFE OF AN ITALIAN IMMI-GRANT

Marie Hall Ets
The life story of an Italian woman who came to
America in 1884, told in her own words. 254 pp.
University of Minnesota Press, 1970. $7.50.

SOME ASPECTS OF THE EFFECT OF THE DOMINANT AMERICAN CULTURE UPON CHILDREN OF ITALIAN-BORN PARENTS

Joseph W. Tait
The author explores the relationships between
character traits of Italian-American children
and the influence of "background" traits. 74
pp. August M. Kelley. Reprint of the 1942
edition. $7.50.

SOME ASPECTS OF ITALIAN IMMI-GRATION TO THE UNITED STATES

Antonio Stella
R and E Research Associates, Pubs. Reprint of
the 1924 edition. $7.00.

Literature

AN ETHNIC CONNECTION AND GOALS BEYOND: REFLECTIONS OF AN ITALIAN-AMERICAN POET
Ron Iannone
The poet blends and reveals his Italian-American heritage and nature. McClain Printing Co., 1975. $3.50.

THE ITALIAN—AMERICAN NOVEL
Rose B. Green
Fairleigh Dickenson University Press, 1974. $18.00.

THE ITALIAN INFLUENCE ON AMERICAN LITERATURE
C. Waller Barrett
Grolier Club, 1962. $10.50.

ITALO-AMERICAN BALLADS, POEMS, LYRICS AND MELODIES
Regina and Roy D'Ariano
Melodies and songs with words for Italian-American song lover. McClain Printing Co., 1975.

Urban Experience

THE ITALIAN SETTLEMENT OF SAN FRANCISCO
Raymond S. Dondero
Thesis. R & E Research Associates, 1974. Reprint of the 1950 paper. Pap. $8.00.

THE ITALIANS IN CHICAGO, 1880 TO 1930; A STUDY IN ETHNIC MOBILITY
Humbert S. Nell
320 pp. Oxford University Press, 1973. Cloth, $9.95; Pap. $2.95.

THE ITALIANS IN CHICAGO: A SOCIAL ECONOMIC STUDY
Carroll D. Wright
This work is based on a census of 7000 Italians in Chicago, covering by statistical tables their educational level, occupation, health, and other features. Arno Press. Reprint of the 1897 edition. $16.50.

THE ITALIANS IN MILWAUKEE, WISCONSIN
G. La Piana

R and E Research Associates, Pubs. Reprint of the 1915 edition. $4.00.

THE ITALIANS OF NEW YORK CITY
Somerset Publications, 1938. $14.50.

THE ITALIANS OF NEW YORK: A SURVEY
W.P.A. Federal Writers Project
Covers every aspect of local Italian life in New York City in the 1930's. Arno Press. Reprint of the 1938 edition. $5.00.

ITALIANS IN SAN FRANCISCO
Paul Radin
R and E Research Associates, Pubs. Reprint of the 1935 edition. Pap. $10.00.

STREET CORNER SOCIETY: THE SOCIAL STRUCTURE OF AN ITALIAN SLUM
William Whyte
University of Chicago Press, 1955. Cloth, $10.00; Pap. $3.45.

JAPANESE-AMERICANS

Assimilation

*THE BIRTHDAY VISITOR
Yoshiko Uchida
Picture book of family life in a Japanese-American household. Charles Scribner's Sons, 1974. Ages 6-8. $5.95.

CALIFORNIA AND THE JAPANESE
Kiichi Kanzaki
R and E Research Associates, Pubs. Reprint of the 1921 edition. $6.00.

CHANGING CULTURES, CHANGING LIVES: AN ETHNOGRAPHIC STUDY OF THREE GENERATIONS OF JAPANESE AMERICANS
Christie W. Kiefer
Jossey-Bass, Inc., 1974. $12.50.

CHINESE AND JAPANESE IN AMERICA
American Academy of Polictical and Social Science
R & E Research Associates. Reprint of the 1909 edition. $12.00.

ETHNIC ENTERPRISE IN AMERICA:

BUSINESS AND WELFARE AMONG CHINESE, JAPANESE, AND BLACKS
Ivan H. Light
University of Claifornia Press, 1973. Pap. $2.85.

JAPAN AND THE CALIFORNIA PROBLEM
Toyokichi Iyenaga and Kenosake Sato
Scholarly Resources Inc. R and E Research Associates Publishers, $12.00. Reprint of the 1921 edition. $13.50.

JAPANESE-AMERICANS IN THE PACIFIC NORTHWEST
Tacoma Public Library Staff
A bibliography of materials in the collections of the Tacoma Public Library. 15 pp. Tacoma Public Library, 1971, c/o Gary F. Reese, 1102 Tacoma Ave. South, Tacoma, Wash. 98402.

THE JAPANESE-AMERICAN STORY
Budd Fukei
A look at life in America for people of Japanese descent, from internment during World War II to current admiration of Japanese culture. 200 pp. Dillon Press. $6.95.

JAPANESE-AMERICANS: THE EVOLUTION OF A SUBCULTURE
Harry H.L. Kitano
Analyzes adaption of the Japanese immigrant and his family to the United States. 186 pp. Prentice-Hall, Inc., 1969. Cloth, $6.40; Pap. $2.95.

THE JAPANESE HELPED BUILD AMERICA
Dorothy and Joseph Dowdell
Messner, 1970. $4.79.

JAPANESE IN AMERICA
E. Manchester Boddy
R and E Research Associates, Pubs. Reprint of the 1921 edition. $8.00.

THE JAPANESE IN AMERICA
Masako Herman
Oceana Pubns., 1974. $5.00.

*THE JAPANESE IN AMERICA
Noel Leathers
Topics covered include the background of Japanese immigrants, the problems of prejudice, wartime treatment and wartime contributions of the people, the Japanese in Hawaii, and the present-day Japanese-Americans. 72 pp. Lerner Publications, 1967. Illus. Ages 11-17. $3.95.

THE JAPANESE IN THE CITY OF SAN FRANCISCO
President Roosevelt
R and E Research Associates, Pubs. Reprint of the 1901 edition. $5.00.

THE JAPANESE PROBLEM IN CALIFORNIA
Tasuka Harada
R and E Research Associates, Pubs. Reprint of the 1922 edition. $6.00.

THE MENTAL CAPACITY OF AMERICAN-BORN JAPANESE CHILDREN
M.L. Darsie
Kraus Reprint Co. Reprint of the 1926 edition. Pap. $4.00.

THE REAL JAPANESE IN CALIFORNIA
Jean Pajus
R and E Research Associates, Pubs. Reprint of the 1937 edition. $12.00.

THE SECOND-GENERATION JAPANESE PROBLEM
Edward K. Strong, Jr.
Reviews the history of the Japanese immigration, tthe anti-Japanese prejudice which occured, the group's vital statistics, and the educational and occupational potential for second-generation Japanese-Americans. Arno Press. Reprint of the 1934 edition. $12.00.

SOCIAL AND ECONOMIC CONDITIONS AMONG JAPANESE FARMERS IN CALIFORNIA
Kaizo Naka
Thesis. R & E Research Associates. Reprint of the 1913 paper. Pap. $7.00.

THE STORY OF JAPANESE FARMING IN CALIFORNIA
Emil Bunje
A WPA project. R & E Research Associates. Reprint of the 1937 edition. $11.00.

THEODORE ROOSEVELT AND THE JAPANESE-AMERICAN CRISIS
Thomas A. Baily
Peter Smith Publishers. $5.50.

Discrimination

CALIFORNIA NATIVISM: ORGANIZED

OPPOSITION TO THE JAPANESE, 1890 TO 1913
Eldon R. Penrose
R and E Research Associates, Pubs., 1973. $10.00.

DISCRIMINATION AGAINST THE JAPANESE IN CALIFORNIA: A REVIEW OF THE REAL SITUATION
Herbert Johnson
R and E Research Associates, Pubs. Reprint of the 1907 edition. $7.00.

JAPANESE-AMERICANS: OPPRESSION AND SUCCESS
William Peterson
Peter Smith Publishers. $5.00.

THE POLITICS OF PREJUDICE: THE ANTI-JAPANESE MOVEMENT IN CLAIFORNIA AND THE STRUGGLE FOR JAPANESE EXCLUSION
Roger Daniels
Peter Smith Publishers. $4.00. Atheneum Publications. $2.65.

PREJUDICE: JAPANESE-AMERICANS; SYMBOL OF RACIAL INTOLERANCE
Carey McWilliams
337 pp. Shoe String Press. Reprint of the 1944. $10.00.

History

THE AMERICAN JAPANESE PROBLEM: A STUDY OF THE RACIAL RELATIONS OF THE EAST AND WEST
Sidney L. Gulick
Jerome S. Ozer Pubs. Reprint of the 1914 edition. $15.50.

THE DECISION TO RELOCATE THE JAPANESE-AMERICANS
Roger Daniels
Based on research of new available sources, the author ananlyzes the decision to relocate Japanese-Americans after Pearl Harbor. 135 pp. J.B. Lippincott Co., 1975. Pap. $3.25.

A HISTORY OF THE JAPANESE COMMUNITY IN SACRAMENTO, 1833-1972: ORGANIZATIONS, BUSINESSES, AND GENERATIONAL RESPONSE TO

MAJORITY DOMINATION AND STEREOTYPES
Cheryl L. Cole
R & E Research Associates, 1975. Pap. $10.00.

THE HISTORY OF THE JAPANESE PEOPLE IN OREGON: THESIS
Marjorie R. Stearns
R and E Research Associates, Pubs. Reprint of the 1938 edition. Pap. $8.00.

JUSTICE DENIED: A HISTORY OF THE JAPANESE IN THE UNITED STATES
Jennifer Cross
Scholastic Book Service, 1974. Pap. $1.65.

NISEI: THE QUIET AMERICANS
Bill Hosokawa
The 100 year history of the Japanese in the U.S. Photos. William Morrow & Co., 1969. Cloth, $10.95; Pap. $3.95.

Immigration

JAPANESE IMMIGRATION
Yamato Ichihashi
R and E Research Associates, Pubs. Reprint of the 1915 edition. $5.00.

JAPANESE IMMIGRATION AND COLONIZATION
V.S. McClatchy
R and E Research Associates, Pubs. Reprint of the 1921 edition. $7.00.

JAPANESE IMMIGRATION: AN EXPOSITION OF ITS REAL STATUS
Japanese Association of the Pacific Northwest, Seattle
48 pp. R and E Research Associates, Pubs. Reprint of the 1907 edition. $5.00.

JAPANESE IMMIGRATION: ITS STATUS IN CALIFORNIA
Yamato Ichihashi
Jerome S. Ozer Pubs. Reprint of the 1915 edition. $5.95.

JAPANESE IN THE UNITED STATES: A CRITICAL STUDY OF THE PROBLEMS OF THE JAPANESE IMMIGRANTS AND THEIR CHILDREN
Yamato Ichihashi
After introductory chapters on Japanese inter-

national migration in general and on the immigration to the Hawaiian Islands, the book has
four subdivisions: the coming of the Japanese,
an analysis of the salient fact relating to alien
Japanese residents, an historical examination of
anti-Japanese agitations, and a survey of the
second-generation problems. Arno Press.
Reprint of the 1932 edition. $13.00.

**PRESENT-DAY IMMIGRATION WITH
SPECIAL REFERENCE TO JAPANESE**
American Academy of Political and Social
Science
R & E Research Associates. Reprint of the 1921
edition. $11.00.

In Hawaii

**THE JAPANESE EXPANSION INTO
HAWAII, 1868-1898**
Francis H. Conroy
A study of the diplomatic, economic and social
movement of Japanese into Hawaii. Dissertation. R & E Research Associates. Reprint of
the 1949 edition. $12.00.

**THE JAPANESE AND THE HAOLES OF
HONOLULU: DURABLE GROUP INTER-
ACTION**
Frederick Samuels
College and University Press, 1970. Cloth,
$6.00; Pap. $2.95.

**JAPANESE IN HAWAII: AN ANNO-
TATED BIBLIOGRAPHY**
Mitsuga Matsuda
300 pp. University Press of Hawaii, 1975. Pap.
$6.00.

THINGS JAPANESE IN HAWAII
John De Francis
224 pp. University Press of Hawaii, 1973. Illus.
Pap. $8.50.

World War II

**AMERICANS BETRAYED: POLITICS AND
THE JAPANESE EVACUATION**
Morton Grodzins
University of Chicago Press, 1969. Pap. $16.50.

**CITY ON THE SUN: THE JAPANESE
CONCENTRATION CAMP AT POSTON,
ARIZONA**
Paul Bailey
What life was like in America's largest Japa-
nese-American concentration camps during the
Second World War. Westernlore Press, 1972.
Illus. $7.95.

**CONCENTRATION CAMPS, UNITED
STATES OF AMERICA: JAPANESE
AMERICANS AND WORLD WAR II**
Roger Daniels
Holt, Rinehart, and Winston, 1972. Cloth,
$5.95; Pap. $3.50.

EXECUTIVE ORDER 9066
Maisie and Richard Conrat
A photographic study of the internment of
110,000 Japanese-Americans during World War
II. 64 photos. California Historical Society,
1975. Pap. $3.95.

**THE GREAT BETRAYAL: THE EVAC-
UATION OF THE JAPANESE-AMERICANS
DURING WORLD WAR II**
Audrie Girdner and Anne Loftis
Macmillan Publishing Co., Inc., 1969. $12.95.

**IMPOUNDED PEOPLE: JAPANESE-
AMERICANS IN THE RELOCATION
CENTERS**
Edward H. Spicer, et al
Describes the growth and changes in community
life; how attitudes of Japanese-American relo-
catees and WRA administrators evolved, ad-
justed and affected one another on political,
social and psychological levels. 342 pp.
University of Arizona Press, 1969. $8.50.

**THE MANAGED CASUALTY: THE
JAPANESE-AMERICAN FAMILY IN
WORLD WAR II**
John I. Kitsuse and Leonard Broom
University of California Press, 1974. $12.75.

**REMOVAL AND RETURN: THE SOCIO-
ECONOMIC EFFECTS OF THE WAR ON
JAPANESE-AMERICANS**
Leonard Broom and Ruth Riemer
University of California Press, 1974. $14.75.

**THE SPOILAGE: JAPANESE-AMERICAN
EVACUATION AND RESETTLEMENT**
Dorothy S. Thomas and Richard S.
Nishimoto
University of California Press, 1969. Pap.
$2.45.

UPROOTED AMERICANS: THE JAPA-NESE-AMERICANS AND THE WAR RELO-CATION AUTHORITY
Dillon S. Myer
The author reflects on the crucial decision to establish the centers, policy information when there were no precedents or guidelines, pressures and rumors of the times, the reloca-tion program, and legal aspects of the events of 1942. 360 pp. University of Arizona Press, 1971. Pap. $5.95.

JEWISH-AMERICANS

Assimilation

AMERICANS OF JEWISH DESCENT: A COMPENDIUM OF GENEALOGY
Malcom H. Stern
Basic biographical data on 372 families and their descendants, more than 25,000 individuals, who sttled in America between 1654 and 1840. 307 pp. Ktav Publishing House, 1960. $40.00.

FUTURE OF THE AMERICAN JEW
Mordecai M. Kaplan
A survey of American Jewish life and its problems. Reconstructionist Press. Pap. $3.50.

THE FUTURE OF THE JEWISH COM-MUNITY IN AMERICA
David Sidorsky
Basic Books, 1974. $11.95.

THE HASIDIC COMMUNITY OF WIL-LIAMSBURG, A STUDY IN THE SOCI-OLOGY OF RELIGION
Solomon Poll
Schocken Books. Cloth, $7.50; Pap. $3.45.

AN HOUR WITH THE AMERICAN JEW
Herbert N. Eaton
R and E Research Associates, Pubs. Reprint of the 1879 edition. $6.00.

THE JEW IN AMERICAN SOCIETY
M. Sklare, Editor
Behrmen House, 1974. $12.50.

JEW IN CHRISTIAN AMERICA
A. Gilbert
Sheed and Ward, 1966. $4.95.

THE JEW WITHIN AMERICAN SOCI-

ETY: A STUDY IN ETHNIC INDIVID-UALITY
C. Bezalel Sherman
280 pp. Wayne State University Press, 1965. Pap. $2.00.

JEWISH COMMUNITY ORGANIZATION IN THE UNITED STATES
M.J. Karpf
Arno Press. Reprint of the 1938 edition. $11.00.

JEWISH PHILANTHROPY: AN EXPOSI-TION OF PRINCIPLES AND METHODS OF JEWISH SOCIAL SERVICE IN THE UNITED STATES
Boris D. Bogen
391 pp. Patterson Smith Publishing Corp. Reprint of the 1917 edition. $12.50.

JEWS IN SUBURBIA
Albert Issac Gordon
Greenwood Press, Inc. Reprint of the 1959 edition. $12.00.

THE OTHER JEWS: PORTRAITS IN POVERTY
D. Rabinowitz
American Jewish Committee, 1972. $1.25.

POOR JEWS: AN AMERICAN AWAKEN-ING
Naomi Levine and Martin Hochbaum, Editors
The special characteristics of Jewish poverty: age groups, locations, special needs and problems, are all considered in this book. 275 pp. Transaction Books, 1974. Cloth, $12.95; Pap. $3.45.

STATISTICS OF JEWS AND JEWISH ORGANIZATIONS
H.S. Linfield
R and E Research Associates, Pubs. Reprint of the 1939 edition. $5.00.

THEORIES OF AMERICANIZATION: A CRITICAL STUDY, WITH SPECIAL RE-FERENCE TO THE JEWISH GROUP
Issac Baer Berkson
AMS Press, Inc. Reprint of the 1920 edition. $8.00.

Black-Jewish Relations

BITTERSWEET ENCOUNTER: THE AFRO-

AMERICAN AND THE AMERICAN JEW
Robert G. Weisbord and Arthur Stein
The authors have compiled and analyzed the earlier contributions of both groups and placed them within an historical context. Schocken Books. Pap. $2.95.

BLACK ANTI-SEMITISM AND JEWISH RACISM
Nat Hentoff, Editor
Articles by James Baldwin, "Negroes Are Anti-Semitic Because They're Anti-White;" Julius Lester, "A Response;" and Rabbi Jay Kaufman, "Thou Shalt Surely Rebuke Thy Neighbor" are among the eight authors who comprise this book. Schocken Books, 1975. Pap. $2.45.

BLACK-JEWISH RELATIONS IN NEW YORK CITY
Louis Harris and Bert E. Swanson
260 pp. Praeger Publishers, 1970. $15.00.

JEWS AND BLACKS: A COURSE ON THE JEWISH PERSPECTIVE AND THE RACIAL CRISIS
Jerald L. Rosenthal
Provides required reading, points of emphasis, questions for discussion, research topics, related films and filmstrips, resources for research and additional reading, and a selected bibliography. 60 pp. Union of American Hebrew Congregations, 1971. Pap. $1.45.

JUSTICE, JUSTICE: A JEWISH VIEW OF THE BLACK REVOLUTION
Rabbi Henry Cohen
A high school text that summarizes 15 years of dramatic events in race relations. 205 pp. Union of American Hebrew Congregations, 1968. $3.15; teacher's guide, $1.15.

NEGRO AND JEW: AN ENCOUNTER IN AMERICA
Shlomo Katz
Macmillan Publishing Co., Inc., 1967. Cloth, $4.95; Pap. $1.45.

NEGRO-JEWISH RELATIONS IN THE UNITED STATES
Conference on Jewish Social Studies
Citadel Press, 1966. Pap. $1.50.

THE NEGROES AND THE JEWS
Lenora Berson
Random House, Inc., 1971. $8.95.

Civil Rights

JEWISH RADICALISM: A SELECTED ANTHOLOGY
J.N. Porter and P. Drier, Editors
Grove Press, Inc., 1973. $7.95.

THE JEWS AND MINORITY RIGHTS, (1898 TO 1919)
Oscar I. Janowsky
AMS PRess, Inc. Reprint of the 1933 edition. $12.50.

THE JEWS STRUGGLE FOR RELIGIOUS AND CIVIL LIBERTY IN MARYLAND
E.M. Altfeld
Da Capo Press. Reprint of the 1924 edition. $12.50.

NOT FREE TO DESISTS: THE AMERICAN JEWISH COMMITTEE 1906 TO 1966
N.W. Cohen
Jewish Publications Society of America, 1972. $9.00.

THE STORY OF THE JEWISH DEFENSE LEAGUE
Rabbi Meir Kahane
The real reasons for the demonstrations, riots, Jewish militant bombings, harrassment of Soviet officials, cooperation with alleged Mafia kingpins, denunciations of establishment Jews, and confrontations with the Black Panthers, told by the founder of the JDL. 288 pp. Chilton Book Co., 1975. $7.95.

Discrimination

ANTI-SEMITISM IN THE UNITED STATES: ITS HISTORY AND CAUSES
Lee Joseph Levinger
120 pp. Greenwood Press. Reprint of the 1925 edition. $7.00.

THE CHOSEN FEW: A STUDY OF DISCRIMINATION IN EXECUTIVE SELECTION
Robert P. Quinn, et al
Discusses those aspects of executive selection which deal particularly with discrimation against Jews. 49 pp. Institute for Social Research. Reprint of the 1968 edition. Pap. $4.00.

THE JEW IN THE OLD AMERICAN FOLK-LORE
Rudolf Glanz
A study not only of the migration of ideas, stereotypes, and prejudices, but of the acclimatization of the Jews in the New World. 240 pp. Ktav Publishing House, 1961. $10.00.

"KIKE," AN ANTHOLOGY OF ANTI-SEMITISM
M. Selzer, Editor
New American Library, 1972. Pap. $3.95.

165 TEMPLES DESECRATED: THE INSIDE STORY OF ANTI-SEMITISM IN AMERICA
Saul Carson
Popular Library, 1971. Pap. $.95.

THE TENACITY OF PREJUDICE: ANTI-SEMITISM IN CONTEMPORARY AMERICA
Gertrude J. Selznick and Stephen Steinberg
Harper and Row Pubs., 1969. Cloth, 10.00; Pap. $1.95.

Education

JEWISH EDUCATION IN NEW YORK CITY
Alexander N. Dushkin
Covers the whole field of educational activities undertaken by Jews expressly for the continuance of Jewish ideas and traditions in America through transmission of a distinct cultural heritage. 596 pp. August M. Kelley. Reprint of the 1915 edition. $17.50.

JEWISH EDUCATION IN A PLURALIST SOCIETY: SAMSON BENEDERLY'S ROLE IN JEWISH EDUCATION IN THE UNITED STATES
N.S. Winter
New York University Press, 1966. 8.95.

JEWISH EDUCATION IN THE UNITED STATES
Lloyd P. Gartner, ed.
This book deals with the types of Jewish schools, their curricula and their teachers since the 1750's, paying special attention to the place of Jewish education within the philosophies which have shaped and guided education. 240 pp. Teachers College Press, 1970. Cloth, $6.95; Pap. $2.75.

SELECTED WRITINGS OF LEO L. HONOR
Abraham P. Gannes, Editor
A history of Jewish education in the United States and the programs, methods and principles of one of America's leading Jewish educators. Reconstructionist Press. 3.00.

History

*AN ALBUM OF THE JEWS IN AMERICA
Yuri Suhl
Jewish-Americans in the United States. 96 pp. Franklin Watts, Inc., 1972. Age 12 up. $4.90.

THE AMBIVALENT AMERICAN JEW
C.S.F. Liebman
Jewish Publication Society of America, 1973. $5.95.

*AMERICA IS ALSO JEWISH
Richard Goldhurst
G.P. Putnam's Sons, 1972. Illus. $3.89. Below college level.

AMERICA'S JEWS
M. Sklare
Random House, Inc., 1971. Pap. $3.25.

AMERICAN JEW
Oscar Isaiah Janowsky
Books for Libraries, Inc. Reprint of the 1942 edition. $13.25.

THE AMERICAN JEW AS PATRIOT, SOLDIER, AND CITIZEN
S. Wolf
Gregg Press, 1972. Reprint of the 1895 edition. $20.00.

THE AMERICAN JEW: A REAPPRAISAL
O.I. Janowsky
Jewish Publications Society of America, 1964. $6.00.

THE AMERICAN JEWISH YEAR BOOK, 1973
M. Himmelfarb, et al
Jewish Publications Society of America, 1973. $13.95.

AMERICAN JEWISH YEAR BOOK INDEX
Emily Solis-Cohen
A reference guide to source material for fifty

years of Jewish history. 384 pp. Ktav Publishing House, 1968. $15.00.

AMERICAN JEWRY; DOCUMENTS; EIGHTEENTH CENTURY
Jacob Rader Marcus
A picture of the life of the 18th-century Jew in North America. 492 pp. Ktav Publishing House, 1958. $10.00.

THE AMERICAN JEWS
James Yaffe
Random House, Inc., 1968. $10.95.

AMERICAN JEWS: THEIR HISTORY
Oscar Handlin
A brief history of Jewish life in America from 1654 to the present. Anti-Defamation League of B'nai B'rith. Illus. 48 pp. Pap. $.75.

A CALIFORNIA JEWISH HISTORY: A DESCRIPTIVE BIBLIOGRAPHY
N.B. Stern
Arthur H. Clark Co., 1967. $17.50.

CHILDREN OF THE GILDED GHETTO: CONFLICT RESOLUTIONS OF THREE GENERATIONS OF AMERICAN JEWS
Judith T. Kramer and Seymour Leventman
Shoe string press. Reprint of the 1961 edition. $8.50.

THE COLONIAL AMERICAN JEW, 1492 TO 1776. 3 VOLS.
Jacob R. Marcus
1650 pp. Wayne State University Press, 1970. Illus. $36.00.

CONFERENCE OF HISTORIANS CONVENED BY THE AMERICAN JEWISH HISTORICAL SOCIETY ON THE OCCASION OF THE 300th ANNIVERSARY OF THE SETTLEMENT OF JEWS IN THE UNITED STATES
Kraus Reprint Co. Reprint of the 1957 edition. $7.00.

CRITICAL STUDIES IN AMERICAN JEWISH HISTORY
Jacob Rader Marcus
Selected studies from the publications of the American Jewish Archives. 1000 pp. Three volumes. Ktav Publiching House, 1971. $29.50.

DECADES OF DECISION: AN APPRAISAL OF AMERICAN JEWISH LIFE

M.J. Routtenberg
Bloch Publishing Co., 1973. $8.95.

A DOCUMENTARY HISTORY OF THE JEWS IN THE UNITED STATES *1654-1875*
Morris U. Schappes, Editor
In the 159 documents that comprise the study, the editor illustrates many aspects of Jewish life--social, economic, politcal, religious, legal, cultural, and philanthropic--from colonial times to the era of reconstruction. A number of these sources are printed here for the first time. Schocken Books. Third Edition. $12.50.

EARLY AMERICAN JEWRY
Jacob Rader Marcus
The history of the American Jews in the 17th and 18th centuries. Three volumes in two, 1350 pp. Ktav Publishing House. Reprint of the 1953 edition. $35.00.

ETHNIC GROUPS OF AMERICA: THEIR MORBIDITY, MORTALITY AND BEHAVIOR DISORDERS. VOLUME 1: THE JEWS
Ailon Shiloh and Ida Cohen Selavan, Editors
Reveals that specific gene-linked diseases have an affinity for certain ethnic groups. 446 pp. Charles C. Thomas Publishers, 1973. Illus. Cloth $17.50; Pap. $12.95.

THE FUTURE OF THE JEWISH COMMUNITY IN AMERICA
American Jewish Committee, 1972.

THE GHETTO AND BEYOND: ESSAYS ON JEWISH LIFE IN AMERICA
Peter I. Rose, Editor
Random House, 1969. Cloth, $8.95; Pap. $4.95.

HISTORY OF THE JEWS IN AMERICA
D. Pessin
United Synagogue Book Service, 1957. $3.75.

*A HISTORY OF THE JEWS IN THE UNITED STATES
Lee J. Levinger
616 pp. Union of American Hebrew Congregations, 1961. Reprint of the 1930 edition. Illus. Cloth, $4.90; Pap. $1.75. Ages 16 and up.

HISTORY OF THE JEWS OF LOS ANGELES
Max Vorspan and Lloyd P. Gartner
362 pp. Henry E. Huntington Library and Art Gallery, 1970. Illus. $10.00.

THE HISTORY OF THE JEWS IN UTAH AND IDAHO
Juanita Brooks
The chronicle of the growth of the Jewish community in Utah from 1853, when the first Jewish couple opened a bakery in Salt Lake City, to the present. Western Epics Publishing Co., 1973. $7.95.

A HISTORY OF PIONEER JEWS IN CALIFORNIA: THESIS
Jack B. Goldman
R and E Research Associates, Pubs. Reprint of the 1939 edition. $7.00.

AN INDEX TO SCIENTIFIC ARTICLES ON AMERICAN JEWISH HISTORY
Jacob R. Marcus
Articles in Jewish periodicals dealing with the life, culture and history of the American Jew. Ktav Publishing House, 1971. $17.50.

THE JEW IN AMERICA: A HISTORY
Rufus Learsi
The Jews in America from 1654 to the middle of the twentieth century. 422 pp. Ktav Publishing House, 1972. $5.95.

A JEW IS . . .
Howard H. Hirschhorn
Case history on ethnic identity. 90 pp. Christopher Publishing House. $3.95.

JEWISH AMERICANS: THREE GENERATIONS IN A JEWISH COMMUNITY
S. Goldstein and C. Goldscheide
Prentice-Hall, Inc., 1968. Pap. $3.95.

JEWISH COMMUNITY IN AMERICA
M. Sklare
Behrman House, 1974. $12.50.

THE JEWISH EXPERIENCE IN AMERICA
Abraham J. Karp
Selected studies from the publications of the American Jewish Historical Society. Five volumes, 2300 pp. Ktav Publishing House, 1969. $49.50. American Jewish Historical Society, $49.50.

*THE JEWS IN AMERICA
Frances Butwin
Lerner Publications, 1969. Illus. $3.95. Ages 10 and up.

*JEWS IN AMERICA, 1621 TO 1970
Irving J. Sloan

Oceana Publications, 1971. $5.00. Below college level.

*THE JEWS OF AMERICA: HISTORY AND SOURCES
F. Butwin
Behrman House, 1973. Pap. $3.25. Ages 16 and up.

THE JEWS OF CALIFORNIA: FROM THE DISCOVERY OF GOLD UNTIL 1880
Rudolf Glanz
The settling of the Jews in early California. 196 pp. Ktav Publishing House, 1960. $7.50.

*THE JEWS HELPED BUILD AMERICA
Arlene Harris Kurtis
Messner, 1970. $3.64. Below college level.

THE JEWS: SOCIAL PATTERNS OF AN AMERICAN GROUP
M. Sklare, Editor
Free Press, 1958. $10.95.

JEWS IN THE SOUTH
Leonard Dinnerstein and Mary Dale Palsson, Editors
392 pp. Louisiana State University Press, 1973. $12.50.

THE JEWS OF SOUTH CAROLINA, FROM THE EARLIEST TIMES TO THE PRESENT DAY
Barnett A. Elzas
376 pp. Reprint Co. Reprint of the 1905 edition. Illus. $15.00.

JEWS OF THE UNITED STATES, 1790 TO 1840: A DOCUMENTARY HISTORY
J.L. Blau and S.W. Baron, Editors
Columbia University Press, 1964. $45.00. Set.

MAKING OF AN AMERICAN JEWISH COMMUNITY
I.M. Fein
Jewish Publications Society of America, 1971. $6.50.

MEMORIES OF AN AMERICAN JEW
Philip Cowen
The history of the Jews in the United States in the past fifty years. Arno Press. Reprint of the 1932 edition. $28.00.

MINIATURES AND SILHOUETTES OF EARLY AMERICAN JEWS
Hannah R. London

Great artists and noted American Jews are the subjects of this book dealing with the pictorial representation of Jews in early American life. 382 pp. Charles E. Tuttle Co. 124 plates. $16.50.

MY BROTHER'S KEEPER: A HISTORY OF THE AMERICAN JEWISH JOINT DISTRIBUTION, 1929 TO 1938
Bauer Yehuda
Jewish Publications Society of America, 1974. $7.95.

NEW YORK JEWS' QUEST OF COMMUNITY: THE KEHILLA EXPERIMENT, 1908 TO 1922
A.A. Goren
Columbia University Press, 1970. $12.50.

THE PROVINCIALS: JEWS IN THE SOUTH
Eli N. Evans
Atheneum Publications, 1973. $10.95.

THE SETTLEMENT OF THE JEWS IN NORTH AMERICA
C.P. Daly
Gordon Press. $25.00.

STUDIES IN AMERICAN JEWISH HISTORY
Jacob Rader Marcus
A history of the American Jew from the earliest days to the present. 278 pp. Ktav Publishing House, 1968. $7.50.

STUDIES IN JUDAICA AMERICANA
Rudolf Glanz
The 19th century experience of American Jews of German descent who settled in the urban centers of the Atlantic and Pacific Coasts, the Great Lakes, and the Mississippi Basin. 425 pp. Ktav Publishing House, 1970. $14.95.

THREE CENTURIES OF ANGLO-JEWISH HISTORY
V.D. Lipman
Albert Saifer Pub., 1971. $5.00.

TRAVELS THROUGH JEWISH AMERICA
Harry Golden and Richard Goldhurst
A documentation of the changes in ten Jewish communities throughout the country. Doubleday & CO., 1973. $7.95.

THE TWO HUNDRED AND FIFTIETH ANNIVERSARY OF THE SETTLEMENT OF

THE JEWS IN THE UNITED STATES
American Jewish Historical Society
Kraus Reprint Co. Reprint of the 1904 edition. Pap. $10.00.

THE WRITING OF AMERICAN JEWISH HISTORY
American Jewish Historical Society-Moshe Davis and Isidore S. Meyer, Editors
Proceedings of the conference of historians convened by the American Jewish Historical Society on the occasion of the 300th anniversary of the settlement of the Jews in the United States. Kraus Reprint Co. Reprint of the 1957 edition. $7.00.

ZION IN AMERICA
Henry L. Feingold
How the reciprocity of America and its Jews originated, developed, and prospered. 376 pp. Twayne Publishers, 1975. Cloth, $12.95. Hippocrene Books. Pap. $5.95.

Immigration

DOWNTOWN JEWS: PORTRAITS OF AN IMMIGRANT GENERATION
R. Sanders
Harper and Row Pubs., 1969. Illus. $10.00.

HISTORY OF THE BARON DE HIRSCH: THE AMERICANIZATION OF THE JEWISH IMMIGRANT
Samuel Joseph
A record and evaluation of the Baron de Hirsch Fund, created to deal with the needs of Jewish immigrants in a period which witnessed the transplantation of nearly one-third of the Jews of Eastern Europe to the United States. 305 pp. August M. Kelley. Reprint of the 1935 edition. $12.50.

IMMIGRANTS TO FREEDOM: JEWISH COMMUNITIES IN RURAL NEW JERSEY SINCE 1882
J. Brandes and M. Douglas
University of Pennsylvania Press, 1971. $12.50.

JEW AND IRISH: HISTORIC GROUP RELATIONS AND IMMIGRATION
Rudolf Glanz
Two transplanted cultures brought together, one fleeing from hunger and famine, the other

from persecution and pogroms. 160 pp. Ktav Publishing House, 1966. $7.50.

JEW AND ITALIAN: HISTORIC GROUP RELATIONS AND THE NEW IMMIGRATION (1881-1924)
Rudolf Glanz
Reviews the history of the development of Italian-Jewish cooperation in the American Labor movement, and in the neighborhoods in which they lived, often side by side. 220 pp. Ktav Publishing House, 1971. $10.00.

JEWISH IMMIGRATION TO THE UNITED STATES FROM 1881 TO 1910
Samuel Joseph
A history of Jewish immigration, this book first presents an "analysis of the economic, social and political conditions in Russia, Roumania and Austria-Hungary which bear upon the Jewish question . . . then comes a discussion of the movement and characteristics of the Jewish immigration to the United States followed by a carefully prepared set of statistical tables. Arno Press. Reprint of the 1914 edition. Pap. $6.00. AMS Press, Inc. Cloth, $10.00.

NO HAVEN FOR THE OPPRESSED: UNITED STATES POLICY TOWARD JEWISH REFUGEES, 1938 TO 1945
Saul S. Friedman
315 pp. Wayne State University Press, 1973. $15.95.

SEND THESE TO ME: JEWS AND OTHER IMMIGRANTS IN URBAN AMERICA
John Higham
288 pp. Atheneum Publishers, 1975. Cloth, $10.00; Pap. $4.95.

Language

SCHLEMIEL AS METAPHOR: STUDIES IN THE YIDDISH AND AMERICAN JEWISH NOVEL
S. Pinkser
Southern Illinois University Press, 1971. $5.95.

YIDDISH IN AMERICA: SOCIAL AND CULTURAL FOUNDATIONS
M. Doroshkin
Fairleigh Dickinson University Press, 1970. $12.00.

YIDDISH IN AMERICA: SOCIO-LINGUISTIC DESCRIPTION AND ANALYSIS
J.A. Fishman
Indiana University Research Center for the Language Sciences, 1965. Pap. $3.00.

Leaders

AUTOBIOGRAPHIES OF AMERICAN JEWS
H.U. Riblow, Editor
Jewish Publications Society of America, 1965. $6.00.

DISTINGUISHED AMERICAN JEWS
Philip Henry Lotz, Editor
Books for Libraries, Inc. Reprint of the 1945 edition. $9.00.

*EMINENT AMERICAN JEWS: 1776 TO THE PRESENT
C.A. Madison
400 pp. Frederick Ungar Publishing Co., 1971. Illus. $10.00. Below college level.

*HEROES OF AMERICAN JEWISH HISTORY
Deborah Karp
American Jews who helped build our nation. 155 pp. Anti-Defamation League of B'nai B'rith. Illus. Ages 12-18. $4.75.

MEMOIRS OF AMERICAN JEWS: 1775-1865
Jacob Rader Marcus
Autobiographical writings of American Jews from the beginning of the Republic to the days just prior to the Civil War. 3 volumes in 2, 1230 pp. Ktav Publishing House. Reprint of the 1955 edition. $35.00.

"OUR CROWD": THE GREAT JEWISH FAMILIES OF NEW YORK
Stephen Birmingham
Harper and Row Pubs., 1967. Illus. $12.50.

PORTRAITS OF JEWS
Hannah R London
A reprint of a series of sketches and biographies on the most famous Jews in Colonial America. 210 pp. Charles E. Tuttle Co. Reprint of the 1927 edition. $13.75.

Literature

AN AMERICAN JEWISH BIBLIOGRAPHY, BEING A LIST OF BOOKS AND PAMPHLETS BY JEWS OR RELATING TO THEM, IN THE UNITED STATES . . . UNTIL 1850
A.S. Rosenbach
Kraus Reprint Co. Reprint of the 1926 edition. $14.00.

CONTEMPORARY AMERICAN-JEWISH LITERATURE: CRITICAL ESSAYS
Irving Malin, Editor
Indiana University Press, 1973. $8.95.

DIRECTORY OF JEWISH ARCHIVAL INSTITUTIONS
Phillip P. Mason Editor
Published for the National Foundation for Jewish Culture, this directory of Jewish Archival Insttutions describes the collections of the American Jewish Archives, the American Jewish Historical Society, the Leo Baeck Institute, the Bund Archives of the Jewish Labor Movement, Dropsie University, Jewish Theoological Seminary of America, and the YIVO Institute for Jewish Research, among other institutions. 72 pp. Wayne State University, 1975. Pap. $3.00.

THE GERMAN JEW IN AMERICA: AN ANNOTATED BIBLIOGRAPHY INCLUDING BOOKS, PAMPHLETS AND ARTICLES OF SPECIAL INTEREST
Rudolf Glanz
Covers the main period of German Jewish immigration to the United States, 1820-1880. 192 pp. Ktav Publishing House, 1969. $15.00.

THE JEW IN AMERICAN LITERATURE
S. Liptzin
Bloch Publishing Co. $5.50.

JEWISH-AMERICAN LITERATURE: AN ANTHOLOGY
A. Chapman, Editor
New American Library, 1975. $2.25.

JEWISH AMERICANA
American Jewish Archives
A supplement to A.S.W. Rosenbach's, *An American Jewish Bibliography*. 126 pp. Ktav Publishing House, 1954. $5.95.

JEWISH REFERENCE BOOKS: A SELECT LIST
A bibliography of Jewish reference books. 16 pp. Jewish Book Council, 15 E. 26th St., New York, N.Y. 10010. $25.00.

JEWISH WRITER IN AMERICA: ASSIMILATION AND THE CRISIS OF IDENTITY
Allen Guttmann
266 pp. Oxford University Press, 1971. $7.95.

LEESER OCCIDENT
Nathan·M. Kaganoff, Editor
The story of the editor of the first American Jewish periodical in the United States, the *Occident*. 400 pp. Ktav Publishing House, 1973. $20.00.

THE LITERATURE OF THE AMERICAN JEWS
Theodore L. Gross, Editor
Songs, short stories, poems, and criticism. Macmillan Publishing Co. $12.95. Free Press, $12.95.

A MANUSCRIPT CATALOG OF THE AMERICAN JEWISH ARCHIVES FIRST SUPPLEMENT
G.K. Hall and Co., 1973.

PLAYS OF JEWISH INTEREST ON THE AMERICAN STAGE
E.D. Coleman
Gordon Press. $29.00.

THE RISE OF AMERICAN JEWISH LITERATURE
Angoff and Levin, Editors
Simon and Schuster, 1970. $15.00.

THE SOCIO-CULTURAL CHANGES IN AMERICAN JEWISH LIFE AS REFLECTED IN SELECTED JEWISH LITERATURE
B. Cohen
Fairleigh Dickinson University Press, 1972. $12.00.

STEELED BY ADVERSITY: ESSAYS AND ADDRESSES ON AMERICAN JEWISH LIFE
S.W. Baron
Jewish Publication Society of America, 1971. $9.00.

*A TIME TO SEEK: AN ANTHOLOGY OF CONTEMPORARY JEWISH AMERICAN POETS
Samuel Hart Joseloff, Editor

65 poems by twenty-one poets. Union of American Hebrew Congregations, 1974. Age 16 up. $5.00.

YIDDISH PRESS: AN AMERICANIZING AGENCY
Mordechai Soltes
Arno Press. Reprint of the 1925 edition. $8.50.

Military Experience

THE AMERICAN JEW IN THE CIVIL WAR
Isidore S. Meyer, Editor
American Jewish Historical Society, 1961. $5.00. Kraus Reprint Co., $7.00.

AMERICAN JEWRY AND THE CIVIL WAR
Bertram W. Korn
Atheneum Publications, 1970. Pap. $4.50.

JEWS, WARS, AND COMMUNISM, VOL. I: THE ATTITUDE OF AMERICAN JEWS TO WORLD WAR I, THE RUSSIAN REVOLUTIONS OF 1917, AND COMMUNISM (1914-1945)
Zosa Szajkowski
742 pp. Ktav Publishing House, 1972. Illus. $20.00.

JEWS, WARS AND COMMUNISM VOL. II: THE IMPACT OF THE 1919-20 RED SCARE ON AMERICAN JEWISH LIFE
Zosa Szajkowski
Lays to rest once and for all the accusation of a "Jewish Communist Conspiracy." 400 pp. Ktav Publishing House. $20.00.

UNRECOGNIZED PATRIOTS: THE JEWS IN THE AMERICAN REVOLUTION
Samuel Rezneck
Greenwood Press, 1975. $13.95.

Politics

AMERICAN JEWISH VOTING BEHAVIOR: A HISTORY AND ANALYSIS
Wm. Ray Heitzmann
R & E Research Associates, 1975. Pap. $8.00.

THE JEW IN AMERICAN POLITICS
N. Weyl
Arlington House Pubs., 1968. $6.95.

JEWISH LABOR IN THE U.S.A.: AN INDUSTRIAL, POLITICAL AND CULTURAL HISTORY OF THE JEWISH LABOR MOVEMENT 1882-1952
Melech Epstein
942 pp. Two volumes in one. Ktav Publishing House, 1950, 1953. $25.00.

THE NEW LEFT AND THE JEWS
M.S. Chertoff, Editor
Pitman Publishing Corp., 1971. $6.50.

Religion

AGENDA FOR AMERICAN JEWS
Eli Ginzberg
Identifies strategic problem areas with which American Jews should be concerned and seeks to make explicit the boundaries within which solutions should be found. Reconstructionist Press, 1964. Pap. $1.95.

*AMERICAN JUDIASM
John A. Hardon
A study of the history, beliefs and practices of the Jewish people in America. 372 pp. Loyola University Press, 1971. $5.95.

AMERICAN JUDAISM
Nathan Glazer
University of Chicago Press, 1972. Cloth, $5.95; Pap. $1.95.

ASPECTS OF THE RELIGIOUS BELIEF OF AMERICAN JEWS
Charles Liebman
Essays on Orthodoxy, rabinical training, and Reconstructionism. 296 pp. Ktav Publishing House. $12.50.

CONSERVATIVE JUDAISM: AN AMERICAN RELIGIOUS MOVEMENT
Marshall Sklare
One of the leading sociologists of American Jewry analyzes the changing needs of the Jewish Community, the influence of Orthodox Judaism upon the Conservative movement, the rise of Conservative synagogues, and the evolving patterns of Conservative religious worship, social activities, Jewish education, and lay-Rabbinic relationships. Schocken Books. New, Augmented Edition. Cloth, $10.00; Pap. $3.95.

FAITH OF AMERICA
Mordecai M. Kaplan
A book of readings, songs, and prayers for the celebration of American holidays. Reconstructionist Press. Pap. $2.50.

GRANDEES: AMERICA'S SEPHARDIC ELITE
Stephen Birmingham
Harper and Row Pubs., 1971. $10.00.

INDIANS OR JEWS? AN INTRODUCTION . . TO A REPRINT OF MANASSEH BEN ISRAEL'S "THE HOPE OF ISRAEL"
Lynn Glaser, Editor
The question of the Jewish ancestry, through the lost ten tribes of Israel, of the American Indians is entertained by the author. 160 pp. Burt Franklin Publishers. Reprint of the 1650 edition. Illus. $18.50.

JEW AND MORMON: HISTORIC GROUP RELATIONS AND RELIGIOUS OUTLOOK
Rudolf Glanz
Two groups who were discriminated against because of their religious beliefs. 388 pp. Ktav Publishing House, 1963. $12.50.

THE JEWISH WAY
Rabbi David H. Weisenberg
The practice and belief of American Judaism. 185 pp. Christopher Publishing House. Illus. $4.95.

JUDAISM AS A CIVILIZATION: TOWARD A RECONSTRUCTION OF AMERICAN-JEWISH LIFE
Mordecai M. Kaplan
In this classic of modern Jewish thought, the author proposes a program for a reconstruction of Judaism that would include a living language and literature, social organization, religious folkways, mores, laws, and art. Schocken Books. Pap. $3.95.

JUDAISM AND THE COMMUNITY
Jacob Freid, Editor
A S Barnes, 1967. $6.00.

MY LIFE AMONG THE GENTILES
Miriam Biskin
A S Barnes, 1968. $1.98.

Urban Experience

BROWNSVILLE: THE BIRTH, DEVELOP-
MENT, AND PASSING OF A JEWISH COMMUNITY
A.E. Landesman
Bloch Publishing Co., 1969. $7.95.

BY MYSELF, I'M A BOOK!: AN ORAL HISTORY OF THE IMMIGRANT JEWISH EXPERIENCE IN PITTSBURGH
Ailon Shiloh, Editor
A record of the East European Jews who settled in the Pittsburgh area between 1890 and 1924. 188 pp. Ktav Publishing House. $8.50.

A CENTURY OF JEWISH LIFE IN DIXIE: THE BIRMINGHAM EXPERIENCE
Mark H. Elovitz
A social history of the Jewish community in Birmingham, Alabama. 256 pp. University of Alabama Press, 1974. $10.00.

CONSIDER THE YEARS: THE STORY OF THE JEWISH COMMUNITY OF EASTON, 1752 TO 1942
J. Trachtenberg
Hive Publishing Co. Reprint of the 1944 edition. $17.50.

THE EARLY JEWS OF NEW ORLEANS
Bertram Wallace Korn
Jewish life under French, Spanish, and American rule during the period of 1757 to 1850. 382 pp. Ktav Publishing House, 1970. $15.00.

THE FACE OF FAITH: AN AMERICAN HASSIDIC COMMUNITY
George Kranzler
A sociological photo essay portraying the cultural and religious life of the Hassidic community of Williamsburg, Brooklyn, New York. 118 pp. Ktav Publishing House, 1966. $12.50.

FROM MINYAN TO A COMMUNITY: HISTORY OF THE JEWS OF SYRACUSE
B.G. Rudolph
Syracuse University Press, 1970. $7.50.

THE GREATEST JEWISH CITY IN THE WORLD
Harry Golden
A nostalgic look at New York City as a Jewish city. Doubleday & Co., 1972. Illus. $12.95.

JEWISH LIFE ON NEW YORK'S LOWER EAST SIDE, 1912 TO 1962
Rogers Book Service, 1972. $15.00.

THE JEWS OF JACKSON, CALIFORNIA
I.H. Sharfman
Arthur H. Clark Co., 1969. $10.00.

PORTAL TO AMERICA: THE LOWER EAST SIDE, 1870 TO 1925
A. Schoener
Holt, Rinehart, and Winston, 1967. Illus. Cloth, $12.95; Pap. $5.95.

THE PROMISED CITY: NEW YORK'S JEWS, 1870 TO 1914
Moses Rischin
Harper and Row Pubs., 1970. Pap. $3.25.

THE RUSSIAN JEW IN THE UNITED STATES
Charles S. Bernheimer, Editor
Studies of social conditions in New York, Philadelphia and Chicago, focusing on: General aspects of population; philanthropy; economic and industrial condtitions; religious activity; educational influences; amusements and social life; politics; health and sanitation; law and litigation; and distribution. 426 pp. August M. Kelley. Reprint of the 1905 edition. $13.50.

THE RUSSIAN JEW IN THE UNITED STATES: STUDIES OF SOCIAL CONDI-TIONS IN NEW YORK, PHILADELPHIA, AND CHICAGO, WITH A DESCRIPTION OF RURAL SETTLEMENTS
Charles S. Bernheimer
Jerome S. Ozer Pubs. Reprint of the 1905 edition. $11.95.

THE SPIRIT OF THE GHETTO: STUDIES OF THE JEWISH QUARTER OF NEW YORK
Hutchins Hapgood
The Jewish community on New York's Lower East Side in the early part of this century is the subject of this book. 1966. 315 pp. Schocken Books. Illus. Pap. $2.95. Harvard University Press. Cloth, $8.50; Pap. $2.95.

SYNAGOGUE IN THE CENTRAL CITY: TEMPLE ISRAEL OF GREATER MIAMI, 1922 TO 1972
Charlton W. Tebeau
170 pp. University of Miami Press, 1972. $7.95.

WILLS OF EARLY NEW YORK JEWS (1704-1799)
Leo Hershkowitz
A view of the 18th century social, economic and religious world. 229 pp. Ktav Publishing House, 1967. $10.00.

KOREAN-AMERICANS

THE KOREAN COMMUNITY IN LOS ANGELES
Helen L. Givens
Thesis. R & E Research Associates. Reprint of the 1939 paper. Pap. $7.00.

THE KOREANS IN AMERICA
Hyung-Chan Kim
Oceana Pubns., 1974. $5.00.

MEXICAN-AMERICANS

Assimilation

ACCROSS THE TRACKS: MEXICAN-AMERICANS IN A TEXAS CITY
Arthur J. Rubel
University of Texas Press, 1966. Cloth, $7.50; Pap. $2.95.

ANDO SANGRANDO: A STUDY OF MEXICAN-AMERICAN POLICE CON-FLICT
Armando Morales
International Scholarly Book Service, 1973. $7.95.

ANGLO-AMERICANS AND MEXICAN AMERICANS IN SOUTH TEXAS: A STUDY IN DOMINANT-SUBORDINATE GROUP RELATIONS
Ozzie G. Simmons
An analysis of the social function of stereo-typing and discrimination in order to maintain Anglo hegemony. Arno Press, 1974. $37.00.

CHICANOS AND RURAL POVERTY
Vernon M. Briggs
John Hopkins Press, 1973. Cloth, $6.00; Pap. $1.95.

CHICANOS: SOCIAL AND PSYCHOLOGICAL PERSPECTIVES

Nathaniel N. Wagner and Marsha J. Haug
An anthology of readings into the social and emotional aspects of minority group membership in the United States. 303 pp. C.V. Mosby Co., 1971. Pap. $6.75.

CLASS CONSCIOUSNESS AND SOCIAL MOBILITY IN A MEXICAN-AMERICAN COMMUNITY: THESIS

Fernando Penalosa
R and E Research Associates, Pubs. Reprint of the 1963 edition. pap. $7.00.

A COMPARISON OF CHICANO AND AGLO WOMEN

Carmen Carillo-Beron
Covers family structure, authoritarianism, conventionalism, discipline, moralistic rejection, learning theory, anthropology, achievement, alienation, socio-economic. With figures and tables. Thesis. R & E Research Associates. Reprint of the 1971 edition. Pap. $8.00.

CONDITIONS SURROUNDING MEXICANS IN CHICAGO: THESIS

Anita Edgar Jones
R and E Research Associates, Pubs. Reprint of the 1928 edition. Pap. $7.00.

THE DISTRIBUTION OF MEXICAN POPULATIONS IN THE UNITED STATES: THESIS

Elizabeth Broadbent
R and E Research Associates, Pubs. Reprint of the 1944 edition. Pap. $7.00.

ECONOMIC ASPECTS OF THE MEXICAN RURAL POPULATION IN CALIFORNIA: THESIS

Lloyd W. Fellows
R and E Research Associates, Pub. Reprint of the 1929 edition. $7.00.

EQUALITY OF OPPORTUNITY FOR LATIN-AMERICANS IN TEXAS: A STUDY OF THE ECONOMIC, SOCIAL AND EDUCATIONAL DISCRIMINATION AGAINST LATIN-AMERICANS IN TEXAS, AND OF THE EFFORTS OF THE STATE GOVERNMENT ON THEIR BEHALF

Everett Ross Clinchy, Jr.
A history of discrimination against Mexican Americans in Texas. Arno Press, 1974. $14.00.

FACTORS INFLUENCING THE ASSIMILA-

TION OF THE MEXICAN IN TEXAS

Gladys Wells
Thesis. R & E Research Associates. Reprint of the 1941 edition. Pap. $7.00.

THE FORGOTTEN ONES: A SOCIOLOGICAL STUDY OF ANGLO AND CHICANO RETARDATES

Anne-Marie Henshel
University of Texas Press, 1973. $8.50.

LA VIDA CHICANA: HEALTH CARE ATTITUDES AND BEHAVIORS OF HOUSTON CHICANOS

Emil J. Farge
R & E Research Associates, 1975. Pap. $11.00.

HEALTH IN THE MEXICAN-AMERICAN CULTURE: A COMMUNITY STUDY

Margaret Clark
University of California Press, 1970. Cloth, $10.00; Pap. $2.85.

LATIN-AMERICANS IN TEXAS

Pauline R. Kibbe
A picture of legal, economic, residential, and governmental discrimination against Mexicans in Texas. Arno Press. Reprint of the 1946 edition. $18.00.

MEXICAN-AMERICAN SOCIO-CULTURAL PATTERNS: IMPLICATIONS FOR SOCIAL CASEWORK

Consuelo Salcedo
Thesis. R & E Research Associates. Reprint of the 1955 paper. Pap. $7.00.

MEXICAN-AMERICAN YOUTH: FORGOTTEN YOUTH AT THE CROSSROADS

Celia S. Heller
Peter Smith Publishers, 1966. Cloth, $4.50. Random House, Inc., Pap. $2.95.

MEXICAN-AMERICANS

A bibliography of books, films, fimstrips, records, periodicals and other media in English. Libraries Unlimited, P.O. Box 263, Littleton, Colo. 80120. $8.50.

MEXICAN-AMERICANS IN CALIFORNIA, A HISTORY

Larry Stevens
29 pp. Relevant Instructional Materials, 1970. $.75.

MEXICAN-AMERICANS: SONS OF THE SOUTHWEST

Ruth S. Lamb

Tells the story of the Mexican Americans in the Southwest, describes the traditional behavior patterns, and developing trends in community associations and radical organizations. Ocelot Press, 1970. $5.95.

MEXICAN-AMERICANS OF SOUTH TEXAS
 W. Madsen
Holt, Rinehart, and Winston, 1973. Pap. $3.00.

MEXICAN-AMERICANS IN THE SOUTH-WEST
 Ernesto Galarza
McNally and Lofton, Pubns., 1970. Pap. $2.50.

THE MEXICAN FAMILY IN SAN AN-TONIO, TEXAS: THESIS
 Kathleen M. Gonzales
R and E Research Associates, Pubs., 1972. Written in 1928. Pap. $7.00.

MEXICANS IN CALIFORNIA
 C.C. Young
R and E Research Associates, Pubs. Reprint of the 1930 edition. $10.00.

THE MEXICAN IN MINNESOTA
 Minnesota-Governor's Interracial Commission
R & E Research Associates, 1972. Reprint of the 1953 edition. $5.00.

THE MEXICAN POPULATION OF AUSTIN, TEXAS: THESIS
 Earl M. Connell
R and E Research Associates, Pubs. Reprint of the 1925 edition. Pap. $7.00.

MEXICANS IN LOS ANGELES
 G. Oxnam
R and E. Research Associates, Pubs. Reprint of the 1920 edition. $3.00.

MONOGRAPH IN CULTURAL ANTHRO-POLOGY: THE MEXICAN-AMERICAN POPULATION OF HOUSTON: A SURVEY IN THE FIELD, 1965 TO 1970
 Mary E. Goodman
Rice University Press, 1971. Pap. $3.25.

NEW CONVERTS TO THE AMERICAN DREAM? MOBILITY ASPIRATIONS OF YOUNG MEXICAN-AMERICANS
 Celia S. Heller
College and University Press, 1972. Cloth, $7.50; Pap. $2.95.

NOT WITH THE FIST: MEXICAN-AMERI-CANS IN A SOUTHWEST CITY
 Ruth D. Tuck
A portrait of Mexican-Americans in San Bernadino, California. Arno Press. Reprint of the 1946 edition. $16.00.

PAIN AND PROMISE: THE CHICANO TODAY
 Edward Simmen, Editor
New American Library, 1972. Pap. $1.25.

SOCIAL LIFE IN A MEXICAN-AMERICAN COMMUNITY: SOCIAL CLASS OR ETH-NIC GROUPING?
 T. Allen Caine
R & E Research Associates, 1974. Illus. $12.00.

THE SOCIO-ECONOMIC STATUS TRENDS OF THE MEXICAN PEOPLE RESIDING IN ARIZONA: THESIS
 Raymond J. Flores
R and E Research Associates, Pubs. Reprint of the 1951 edition. Pap. $8.00.

URBANIZATION AND SOCIOCULTURAL CHANGE IN A MEXICAN-AMERICAN EN-CLAVE
 Thomas G. Thurston
Thesis. R & E Research Associates. Reprint of the 1957 paper. Pap. $9.00.

Civil Rights

AN AWAKENED MINORITY: THE MEXI-CAN-AMERICANS
 Manuel P. Servin
Glencoe Press, 1974. Pap. $3.95.

AWAKENING MINORITIES: AMERICAN INDIANS, MEXICAN AMERICANS, PUERTO RICANS
 John R. Howard, Editor
Partial minority groups submerged below the threshhold of national awareness. 191 pp. Transaction Books, 1972. Cloth, $7.95; Pap. $3.45.

CHICANO REVOLT IN A TEXAS TOWN
 John S. Shockley
University of Notre Dame Press, 1974. Cloth, $9.95; Pap. $3.95.

THE CHICANOS: LIFE AND STRUGGLES OF THE MEXICAN MINORITY IN THE UNITED STATES
Gilberto Lopez Y Rivas
Monthly Review Press, 1974. Cloth, $7.95; Pap. $3.25.

CHICANOS: MEXICAN AMERICAN VOICES
Ludwig and Santobanez, Editors
Penguin Books, Inc.

CHICANOS AND NATIVE AMERICANS: THE TERRITORIAL MINORITIES
Rudolphe de la Garza, et al, Editors
An anthology contributing to the rise in cultural nationalism of the Mexican-American and American Indian communities in the United States. Prentice-Hall, Inc., 1973. $6.95.

LA CAUSA CHICANA: THE MOVEMENT FOR JUSTICE
Margaret M. Mangold, Editor
Seventeen articles reflect the perspectives of Chicanos working in various settings, geographical regions, and disciplines. Family Service Association of America, 1972. $7.50.

LULAC: LEAGUE OF UNITED LATIN-AMERICAN CITIZENS: THESIS
Edward D, Garza
R and E Research Associates, Pubs. Reprint of the 1951 edition. Pap. $7.00.

THE MEXICAN-AMERICAN AND THE LAW
Carlos E. Cortes, Editor
An anthology of eight selections examine the various aspects of the relationship of the Mexican-American with the U.S. legal system. Arno Press, 1974. Illus. $20.00.

MEXICAN-AMERICANS IN THE U.S.: *A Reader*
John H. Burma, Editor
A collection of essays portraying the problems of the Mexican-American as the forgotten minority int the United States. The plight of the militant Mexican-American striving for social and economic justice. 487 pp. Canfield Press, 1970. Pap. $6.95.

SOMOS CHICANOS: STRANGERS IN OUR OWN LAND
David F. Gomez
A personal history of the Chicano movement told by a Chicano activist, Catholic priest, and writer. Beacon Press, 1873. $8.95.

VIVA LA RAZA! THE STRUGGLE OF THE MEXICAN AMERICAN POPLE
Elizabeth Sutherland Martinez and Enriqueta Vasquez
Doubleday and Co., 1974. $4.95.

Education

ACCESS TO COLLEGE FOR MEXICAN AMERICANS IN THE SOUTHWEST
Richard I. Ferrin, et al
42 pp. College Board Publications, 1972. Free.

A COMPARITIVE STUDY OF MEXICAN AND AMERICAN CHILDREN IN THE SCHOOLS OF SAN ANTONIO, TEXAS: THESIS
Eunice Parr
R and E Research Associates, Pubs. Written in 1926. Pap. $7.00.

A COMPARITIVE STUDY OF THE MEXICAN-AMERICAN GRADUATE AND DROP-OUT: THESIS
Sarkis A. Takesian
R and E Research Associates, Pubs. Written in 1967. Pap. $7.00.

EDUCATING THE MEXICAN AMERICAN
Henry S. Johnson and William J. Hernandez-Martinez
This anthology of readings reflects concerns of educating a significant minority group. Judson Press, 1971. Pap. $6.95.

EDUCATING THE MEXICAN CHILD IN THE ELEMENTARY SCHOOL: THESIS
K.H. Meguire
R and E Research Assocaites, Pubs. Reprint of the 1938 edition. Pap. $8.00.

EDUCATION AND THE MEXICAN-AMERICAN
Carlos E. Cortes, Editor
Five selections provide perspectives on the educational system's relationship to the Mexican American. Arno Press, 1974. Illus. $30.00.

A GUIDE OF UNDERSTANDING AND TEACHING OF MECICAN-AMERICAN ADOLESCENTS: THESIS
Dorothy K. Chang

R and E Research Associates, Pubs. Reprint of the 1957 edition. Pap. $8.00.

INTRODUCTION TO CHICANO STUDIES: A READER
I. Livie Duran and R.H. Bernard
Macmillan Publishing Co., Inc., 1973. Pap. $5.95.

METHODS OF ORIENTATION OF SPANISH-SPEAKING CHILDREN TO AN AMERICAN SCHOOL: THESIS
Manuel V. Ceja
R and E Research Associates, Pubs. Reprint of the 1957 edition. Pap. $8.00.

METHODS OF TEACHING MEXICANS: THESIS
Betty Gould
R and E Research Associates, Pubs. Reprint of the 1932 edition. Pap. $8.00.

MEXICAN-AMERICAN CHILDREN IN AN INTEGRATED ELEMENTARY SCHOOL
Alexander Ynigo
Covers the community, integration, social adjustment, and academic adjustment. Thesis. R & E Research Associates. Reprint of the 1957 edition. Pap. $7.00.

MEXICAN-AMERICANS AND EDUCATIONAL CHANGE
Alfredo Castaneda, et al, Editors
Focuses on four major areas: educational change in historical perspective, the politics of educational change, bicultural education, and bilingual education. Arno Press, 1974. $24.00.

MEXICAN-AMERICANS IN SCHOOL: A HISTORY OF EDUCATIONAL NEGLECT
Thomas P. Carter
Mexican-American Children in five Southwestern States. 248 pp. College Entrance Examination Board, 1970. $4.75.

OCCUPATIONAL AND EDUCATIONAL LEVELS OF ASPIRATION OF MEXICAN-AMERICAN YOUTH: THESIS
Arturo De Hoyos
R and E Research Assocaites, Pubs. Written in 1961. Pap. $7.00.

POLITICAL SOCIALIZATION OF CHICANO CHILDREN: A COMPARATIVE STUDY WITH ANGLO IN CALIFORNIA SCHOOLS
F. Chris Garcia

250 pp. Praeger Pubs., 1973. $15.00.

SOME DIFFERENCES IN FACTORS RELATED TO EDUCATIONAL ACHIEVEMENT OF TWO MEXICAN-AMERICAN GROUPS
Phillip Montez
Thesis. R & E Research Associates. Reprint of the 1960 paper. Pap. $7.00.

SOME FACTORS AFFECTING LEADERSHIP OF MEXICAN-AMERICANS IN A HIGH SCHOOL
Marguertie De La Vega
Thesis. R & E Research Associates. Reprint of the 1951 paper. Pap. $7.00.

A STUDY OF AMERICAN AND MEXICAN-AMERICAN CULTURE VALUES AND THEIR SIGNIFICANCE IN EDUCATION: THESIS
Ysidro A. Cabrera
R and E Research Associates, Pubs., 1972. Written in 1963. Pap. $7.00.

History

BARRIO BOY
Ernesto Galarza
University of Notre Dame Press, 1971. Cloth, $7.95; Pap. $3.95.

BARRIO EXPRESSIONS
Luis Javier Rodriguez
A self-history about ganga and urban barrio life in the barrios of Southern California. Quinto Sol Pubs., 1974. Price not set.

A BIBLIOGRAPHY FOR CHICANO HISTORY
Matt S, Meier and Feliciano Rivera
R and E Research Associates, Pubs., 1972. Pap. $5.00.

CHICANO: EVOLUTION OF A PEOPLE
R. Rosaldo
Holt, Rinehart, and Winston, 1973. Pap. $6.95.

THE CHICANO: FROM CARICATURE TO SELF-PORTRAIT
E.R. Simmen, ed.
New American Library, 1975. $1.25.

THE CHICANOS: A HISTORY OF MEXI-CAN-AMERICANS

Matt S. Meier and Feliciano Rivera
The Mexican-American experience in the Southwest. Hill & Wang, 1972. Cloth, $8.95; Pap. $2.65.

*CHICANOS: MEXICANS IN THE UNITED STATES

Patricia Miles Martin
Parents Magazine Press, 1971. $4.59. Ages 7 to 9.

CHICANOS: THE STORY OF MEXICAN-AMERICANS

Patricia De Garza
Messner, 1973. $5.29.

CHICANOS: A STUDY GUIDE AND SOURCE BOOK

Lynn P. Dunn
R 9 E Research Associates, 1975. Pap. $6.00.

DOCUMENTARY HISTORY OF MEXICAN-AMERICANS

Wayne Moquin, Editor
430 pp. Praeger Pubs., 1972. Illus. Cloth, $13.50; Pap. $4.95.

A DOCUMENTARY HISTORY OF THE MEXICAN-AMERICANS

Wayne Moquin and Charles Van Doren
Bantam Books, 1972. Pap. $1.50.

EMERGING FACES: THE MEXICAN-AMERICANS

Y. Arturo Cabera
The social problems of education, religion, housing, and politics that Mexcican-Americans face today. 99 pp. William C. Brown Pubs., 1971. Pap. $2.50.

THE FOLKLORE, MANNERS, AND CUSTOMS OF THE MEXICANS IN SAN ANTONIO, TEXAS: THESIS

Charles A. Arnold
R and E Research Associates, Pubs., 1970. Written in 1928. Pap. $7.00.

FOREIGNERS IN THEIR NATIVE LAND: HISTORICAL ROOTS OF THE MEXICAN AMERICANS

David J. Weber
University of New Mexico Press, 1973. Cloth, $12.00; Pap. $4.95.

FORGOTTEN AMERICAN

Luis F. Hernandez
Surveys the historical-sociological background of the Mexican-American community; offers special guidelines for teaching the mexican-americans; and lists a bibliography of recommended readings. 56 pp. Anti-Defamation League of B'nai B'rith. Pap. $.75.

FOUNDLINGS ON THE FRONTIER

A. Blake Brophy
Race, religion, and intolerance in the turbulant Arizona Territory of the early 1900's. An explosive incident at Clifton-Morenci involving placement in Mexican foster homes of forty Anglo foundlings from New York City. 129 pp. University of Arizona Press, 1972. Pap. $3.95.

FROM OVER THE BORDER: A STUDY OF THE MEXICANS IN THE UNITED STATES

Vernon M. McCombs
R and E Research Associates, Pubs. Reprint of the 1925 edition. $9.00.

LA RAZA: THE MEXICAN-AMERICANS

Stan Steiner
Harper and Row Pubs., 1970. Illus. Cloth, $10.00; Pap. $2.75.

THE MEXICAN ADAPTATION IN AMERICAN CALIFORNIA, 1846 TO 1875: THESIS

Richard H. Morefield
R and E Research Associates, Pubs. Written in 1955. $8.00.

A MEXICAN-AMERICAN COLORING BOOK

Ed Ludwig and James Santibanez
Polaris Press, 1973. Pap. $1.95.

THE MEXICAN-AMERICAN HERITAGE

Ernest F. Garcia and George Shaftel
Fearson Pubs., 1972. $5.60.

*THE MEXICAN-AMERICAN: HIS LIFE ACROSS FOUR CENTURIES

Gilbert T. Martinez and Jane Edwards
Discusses contributions Mexican-Americans have made, problems they face, and the equal rights programs they ahve evolved. Houghton-Mifflin, 1973. Pap. $3.20. Ages 12-18.

THE MEXICAN-AMERICAN PEOPLE: THE NATION'S SECOND LARGEST MINORITY

Leo Grebler, et al
Free Press, 1970. $14.95.

MEXICAN-AMERICAN SOURCE BOOK

Feliciano Rivera

Eduational Consortium of America, 1970. Pap.
$6.00.$

MEXICAN-AMERICANS
Joan Moore and Alfredo Cuellar
A combination of history and socio-economic
insight into the nation's second largest minority
group. 172 pp. Prentice-Hall, Inc., 1970. Cloth,
$6.40; Pap. $3.50.

MEXICAN-AMERICANS
Ellwyn R. Stoddard
Random House, Inc., 1973. Pap. $3.95.

**MEXICAN-AMERICANS: A BRIEF LOOK
AT THEIR HISTORY**
Julian Nava
Examines the distortions and stereotyping that
still surronds Mexican-Americans. 55 pp. Anti-
Defamation League of B'nai B'rith. Pap. $.75.

**MEXICAN-AMERICANS IN THE UNITED
STATES: A READER**
John H. Burma, Editor
Schenkman Publishing Co., 1970. Cloth, $8.95;
Pap. $5.95.

THE MEXICAN IN THE UNITED STATES
Emory S. Bogardus
The Mexican-American community in the
1930's, covering health, labor, crime,
amusements, and cultural life. Arno Press.
Reprint of the 1934 edition. $6.00. R an E
Research Associates Pubs. $6.00. Jerome S.
Bogardus. $5.50.

MEXICANS IN AMERICA
Carey McWilliams
Teachers College Press, 1968. Pap. $1.50.

*THE MEXICANS IN AMERICA
Jane Pinchot
The story of the second-largest minority group
in the United States. 100 pp. Lerner Publications, 1973. Illus. Ages 11-17. $3.95.

**MEXICO AND THE OLD SOUTH-
WEST: PEOPLE, PALAVER AND
PLACES**
Haldeen Braddy
Kennikat Press, 1971. Cloth, $12.50; Pap.
$3.95.

MISFORTUNES OF A CHICANO
Roy L Carpenter
William Frederick Press. $6.25.

***THE NEW LIFE--LA VIDA NUEVA: THE
MEXICAN-AMERICAN TODAY**
Arnold Dobrin
How many Mexican-Americans feel about
prejudice, education, and political action. 112
pp. Dodd, Mead & Co., 1971. Illus. Age 11-15.
$4.50.

OCCUPIED AMERICA: *The Chicano's
Struggle Toward Liberation*
Rodolfo Acuna
A social and political history of the Mexican
Americans in what is now the United States.
Describes the colonization of the people of the
Southwest and their struggle to attain equality
in society. 282 pp. Canfield Press, 1972. Cloth,
$5.95; Pap. $4.95.

**PERSPECTIVES ON MEXICAN-AMERI-
CAN LIFE**
Carlos E. Cortes, Editor
An anthology of Mexican-American life in the
1920's and the 1930's. Arno Press, 1974.
$15.00.

**A SOCIAL AND POLITICAL HISTORY OF
THE MEXICAN-AMERICAN POPULA-
TION OF TEXAS, 1929 TO 1963: THESIS**
Robert A. Cuellar
R and E Research Associates, Pubs. Written in
1969. Pap. $8.00.

**SOUTH BY SOUTHWEST: THE MEXICAN-
AMERICAN AND HIS HERITAGE**
John Tebbel and Ramon E. Ruiz
Doubleday and Co., 1969. Illus. $3.75; Pap.
$1.45.

**THAT MEXICAN! AS HE REALLY IS,
NORTH AND SOUTH OF THE RIO
GRANDE**
Robert N McLean
R and E Research Associates, Pubs., 1971.
Reprint of the 1928 edition. $9.00.

**TIJERINA AND THE LANDS GRANTS:
MEXICAN-AMERICANS IN STRUGGLE
FOR THEIR HERITAGE**
Patricia Bell Blawis
The story of the leader of the Alianza and the
struggle of the Mexican-Americans for return of
their traditional lands. 192 pp. International
Publishers, 1971. Illus. Cloth, $6.95; Pap.
$2.95.

Immigration

AMERICAN ATTITUDES TOWARD MEXICAN IMMIGRATION, 1924 TO 1952; THESIS
Robert J. Lipschultz
R and E Research Associates, Pubs. Written in 1962. Pap. $7.00.

THE APPERCEPTIVE MASS OF FOREIGNERS AS APPLIED TO AMERICANIZATION, THE MEXICAN GROUP: THESIS
Alfred E. White
R and E Research Associates, Pubs. Written in 1923. $8.00.

THE ECONOMIC STATUS OF THE MEXICAN IMMIGRANT IN SAN ANTONIO THESIS
William J. Knox
R and E Research Associates, Pubs. Written in 1927. Pap. $7.00.

THE LIFE STORY OF THE MEXICAN IMMIGRANT
Manuel Gamio
A collection of more than 75 life-stories told by the immigrants themselves. Accounts describe reasons for immigrating, economic insecurity in the U.S., ingratitude of the gringo and racial prejudice. 288 pp. Dover Publications, 1972. Pap. $3.00. Peter Smith Publishers. $5.00.

MEXICAN ILLEGAL IMMIGRATION INTO CALIFORNIA, PRINCIPALLY SINCE 1945: THESIS
Horace E. Newton
R and E Research Associates, Pubs. Reprint of the 1954 edition. Pap. $8.00.

THE MEXICAN IMMIGRANT: HIS LIFE STORY
Manuel Gamio
More than 75 interviews with Mexican immigrants. Arno Press, 1969. Reprint of the 1931 edition. $8.50.

MEXICAN IMMIGRATION TO THE UNITED STATES: A STUDY OF HUMAN IMMIGRATION AND ADJUSTMENT
Manuel Gamio
Studies the cultural backgrounds of Mexican immigrants, the effect which their sojourn to the United States had upon them, their mental development, their religion, and their reaction to the new conditions under which they lived while in the U.S. 262 pp. Arno Press. Reprint of the 1930 edition. $11.00. Dover Publications. Pap. $3.00.

MEXICAN IMMIGRATION TO THE UNITED STATES: THESIS
John R. Martinez
R and E Research Associates, Pubs., 1957. $9.00.

THE MEXICAN-UNITED STATES BORDER: PUBLIC POLICY AND CHICANO ECONOMIC WELFARE
Vernon M. Briggs, Jr.
University of Texas Bureau of Business Research, 1974. Pap. $1.50.

POLITICAL AND ECONOMIC ASPECTS OF MEXICAN IMMIGRATION IN CALIFORNIA AND THE UNITED STATES SINCE 1941: THESIS
Dean L. Williams
R and E Research Associates, Pubs. Reprint of the 1950 edition. Pap. $7.00.

THE SOCIAL AND ECONOMIC EFFECTS OF THE MEXICAN MIGRATION INTO TEXAS: THESIS
Charles H. Hufford
R and E Research Associates, Pubs. 1972. Written in 1929. Pap. $7.00.

A STUDY OF THE SOCIAL ATTITUDES OF ADULT MEXICAN IMMIGRANTS IN LOS ANGELES AND VICINITY
Evangeline Hymer
Thesis. R & E Research Associates. Reprint of the 1923 edition. $7.00.

A SURVEY OF THE PROBLEMS INVOLVED IN THE AMERICANIZATION OF THE MEXICAN-AMERICAN: THESIS
Ignacio Reyes
R and E Research Associates, Pubs. Reprint of the 1957 edition. Pap. $7.00.

THE UNUSUAL MEXICAN: A STUDY IN ACCULTURATION: THESIS
Ruth L. Martinez
R and E Research Associates, Pubs. Reprint of the 1942 edition. Pap. $7.00.

Labor

CHRONICLE OF AZTLAN

Arturo Alvarado
A self-history about Chicano migrant Texas agricultural life, written by one who experienced it. Quinto Sol Pubs., 1974. Price not set.

THE EMPLOYMENT OF MEXICAN WORKERS IN UNITED STATES AGRICULTURE, 1900 TO 1960: DISSERTATION
John C. Elac
R and E Research Associates, Pubs. Reprint of the 1961 edition. Pap. $7.00.

LOS MOJADOS: THE WETBACK STORY
Julian Samora, Editor
University of Notre Dame Press, 1971. Cloth, $6.95; Pap. $2.95.

MEXICAN-AMERICAN LABOR PROBLEMS IN TEXAS: THESIS
Lamar B. Jones
R and E Research Associates, Pubs., 1972. Written in 1965. Pap. $7.00.

MEXICAN LABOR IN ARIZONA DURING THE TERRITORIAL PERIOD
Joseph F. Park
Conflicts between Anglos and Mexican-Americans. University of Arizona Press, 1975.

MEXICAN LABOR IN THE UNITED STATES
Carlos E. Cortes, Editor
An anthology of five works examining various aspects of the Mexican labor experience. Arno Press, 1974. Illus. $26.00.

MEXICAN LABOR IN THE UNITED STATES
Paul S. Taylor
A description of the Mexican Workingman's existence, employment, fraternal life, and church. Arno Press. Reprint of the 1930-32 edition. Two volumes. $30.00.

MEXICAN LABOR IN THE UNITED STATES
Paul Schuster Taylor
816 pp. Johnson Reprint, reprint of the 1928 to 1934 editions. Set. Pap. $55.25.

MINORITY MIGRANTS IN THE URBAN COMMUNITY: MEXICAN-AMERICAN AND NEGRO ADJUSTMENT TO INDUSTRIAL SOCIETY
Lyle Shannon
Sage Publications, 1972. $15.00.

RIO GRANDE WETBACKS: MEXICAN MIGRANT WORKERS
Carrol norguest
University of New Mexico Press, 1972. $4.95.

SMALL HANDS, BIG HANDS: SEVEN STORIES OF MEXICAN-AMERICAN MIGRANT WORKERS AND THEIR FAMILIES
Sandra Wiener
Pantheon Books, 1970. $3.95.

WETBACK LABOR IN THE LOWER RIO GRANDE VALLEY
Bruce S. Meador
A study of the Chicano as a labor factor in the southwest. Thesis. R & E Research Associates. Reprint of the 1951 edition. Pap. $9.00.

WETBACKS AND BRACEROS: MEXICAN MIGRANT LABORERS AND AMERICAN IMMIGRATION POLICY
Nelson G. Copp
Thesis. R & E Research Associates. Reprint of the 1963 edition. Pap. $7.00.

Language

EL LENGUAJE DE LOS CHICANOS: REGIONAL AND SOCIAL CHARACTERISTICS OF LANGUAGE USED BY MEXICAN-AMERICANS
Eduardo Hernandez-Chavez, et al, Editors
Twenty essays on bilingualism, dialectal and non-standard forms of language, speech mixture, code switching, language maintenance, an Chicano Spanish and education. 250 pp. Center for Applied Linguistics, 1974. $7.00.

SOCIAL FUNCTIONS OF LANGUAGE IN A MEXICAN-AMERICAN COMMUNITY
Goerge Carpenter Barker
Examines the relationship of language usage to the total cultural pattern; interpersonal relationships, family structure, the neighborhood, and general cultural orientation. 56 pp. Univerity of Arizona Press, 1972. Pap. $3.95.

A SOCIOLINGUISTIC APPROACH TO BILINGUAL EDUCATION
Andrew D. Cohen
A report on the findings of the Redwood City Study. The assessment of bilingual education of Mexican-Americans in a Spanish-speaking community in California. Newbury House Publishers, Inc. Pap. $9.95.

A STUDY OF SEVERAL LINGUISTIC FUNCTIONS OF MEXICAN-AMERICAN CHILDREN IN A TWO LANGUAGE ENVIRONMENT

George B. Linn
R and E Research Associates, Pubs. Written in 1965. Pap. $7.00.

Leaders

BETWEEN TWO CULTURES: THE LIFE OF AN AMERICAN-MEXICAN

John J. Poggie, Jr.
The life story and thought patterns of Ramon Gonzales, Mexican by nationality but American by culture and pleasures. 94 pp. University of Arizona Press, 1973. Pap. $2.50.

*FAMOUS MEXICAN-AMERICNS

Clarke Newlon
Biographies of Mexican-Americans include Lee Trevino, Cesar Chavez, Joseph Montoya, Henry Ramirez, and others. 187 pp. Dodd, Mead & Co., 1972. Illus. Age 11-16. $3.95.

A PORTFOLIO OF OUTSTANDING AMERICANS OF MEXICAN DESCENT

David Rodriguez and Benjamin Lelevier
Educational Consortium of America. $10.00.

*STRANGERS IN THEIR OWN LAND: A HISTORY OF MEXICAN-AMERICANS

Albert Prago
Discusses the efforts of Cesar Chavez, Zapata, Pancho Villa, Benito Juarez and others. 192 pp. Four Winds Press, 1973. Illus. Ages 12-16. $5.95.

Literature

AZTLAN: AN ANTHOLOGY OF MEXICAN-AMERICAN LITERATURE

Stan Steiner and Luis Valdez
Alfred A. Knopf, Inc., 1972. $8.95.

AZTLAN: AN ANTHOLOGY OF MEXICAN-AMERICAN LITERATURE

Luis Valdez and Stan Steiner, Editors
Collection of Mexican-American documents, essays and fictional writings span the centuries from Cortez to Chavez. Vintage Press. $2.45.

CHICANAS EN LA LITERATURA Y EL ARTE

Drama, short stories. poetry and art by 12 Chicana authors. Entire book devoted to women in literature. 88 pp. Spanish and English. Quinto Sol Pubs. Pap. $1.50.

THE CHICANOS: MEXICAN-AMERICAN VOICES

Edward W. Ludwig and James Santibanez, Editors
An anthology of writings by an about Mexican-Americans, including fiction, poetry, and articles. Penguin Books, 1971. Pap. $1.50.

DOORS AND MIRRORS: FICTION, AND POETRY FROM SPANISH AMERICA, 1920 TO 1970

Hortense Carpentier and Janet Brof, Editors
Grossman Publishers, 1972. $15.00.

DRAMA CHICANO: CHICANO DRAMA

Six works. Spanish and English. 88 pp. Quinto Sol Pubs. Pap. $1.50.

EL ESPEJO: THE MIRROR

Octavio I. Romano-V and Herminio Rios, Editors
An anthology of Chicano literature by Chicano authors who reflect Chicano experiences from a Chicano perspective. Quinto Sol Pubs. Reprint of the 1969 edition. Cloth, $6.75; Pap. $3.75.

FROM THE BARRIO: A CHICANO ANTHOLOGY

Luis O. Salinas and Lillian Faderman
Canfield Press, 1973. Pap. $2.95.

LA VOZ POETICA DEL CHICANO

Lyric, concrete, baiku, and poetic axiom poetry by 12 Chicano poets, in a surrealistic, satirical historical vein. English and Spanish. 80 pp. Quinto Sol Pubs. Pap. $1.50.

THE MEXICAN-AMERICAN

A collection of 21 books, including autobiographies and biographies, scholarly studies and critical exposes, government reports and church tracts, anti-Chicano diatribes and pleas for social justice, ethnocentric treatises and nostalgic reminiscences. Arno Press, 1974. $495.00.

MEXICAN-AMERICAN BIBLIOGRAPHIES

Carlos E. Cortes, Editor
A collection of five of the earliest bibliographies

of materials concerning the Mexican-American people. Arno Press, 1974. $22.00.

MEXICAN-AMERICANS? RESOURCES TO BUILD CULTURAL UNDERSTANDING
Lois B. Jordan
A selection of books, films, filmstrips, records, periodicals, and other media that provide information about distinguished Mexican-American personalities, Mexican-American organizations, periodicals and newspapers. 265 pp. Libraries Unlimited, 1973. $8.50.

THE NEW MEXICAN HISPANO
Carlos E. Cortes, Editor
An anthology of four works spotlighting the Hispanos, or Spanish-American people in Northern New Mexico. Arno Press, 1974. Illus. $30.00.

READINGS ON LA RAZA: THE TWENTIETH CENTURY
Matt S. Meier and Feliciano Rivera, Editors
Describes the social, political, and economic history of the Chicano people in modern America. Hill & Wang, 1974. Cloth, $8.95; Pap. $3.50.

TOWARD A CHICANO/RAZA BIBLIOGRAPHY: DRAMA, PROSE, POETRY
Guillermo Rojas
Comprehensive bibliography for 1965-1972. Over 800 authors listed. 89 pp. Quinto Sol Pubs. Pap. $1.50.

VIVA LA RAZA: READINGS ON MEXICAN-AMERICANS
Julian Nava
D. Van Nostrand Co., 1973. Pap. $3.25.

VOICES OF AZTLAN: CHICANO LITERATURE OF TODAY
Dorothy Harth and Lewis M. Baldwin
New American Library, 1974. Pap. $1.95.

VOICES: SELECTED READINGS FROM *El Grito,* **1967-1973**
Octavio I. Romano-V, Editor
Chicano perspectives in history, anthropology, psycholoby, sociology, social welfare, penology, etc. 542 pp. Quinto Sol Pubs., 1970. Pap. $3.95.

WE ARE CHICANOS: AN ANTHOLOGY OF CHICANO LITERATURE
Philip Ortego, Editor
Washington Square Press, 1973. Pap. $1.25.

Politics

THE CHANGING MEXICAN-AMERICAN: A READER
Rudolph Gomez, Editor
Deals with the background problems and growth of Mexican-Americans toward political strength. 312 pp. Pruett Publishing Co., 1972. Pap. $6.50.

CHICANO POLITICS: READINGS
F. Chriss Garcia, Editor
MSS Information Corp., 1873. $13.00.

CHICANO POWER: THE EMERGENCE OF MEXICAN AMERICA
Tony Castro
Saturday Review Press, 1974. Cloth, $8.95; Pap. $3.95.

LA CAUSA POLITICA: A READER
F. Chris Garcia
University of Notre Dame Press, 1974. Cloth, $13.95; Pap. $4.50.

THE LIBERATION OF A CHICANO MIND
Ricardo Sanchez
Peter Smith Publishers. $5.00.

OCCUPIED AMERICA: THE CHICANO'S STRUGGLE TOWARD LIBERATION
Rudy Acuna
Canfield Press, 1972. Cloth, $6.95; Pap. $4.50.

THE PENITENTES OF NEW MEXICO
Carlos E. Cortes, Editor
An anthology of selections about the Penitentes, leaders of Chicano cultural resistance. Arno Press, 1974. Illus. $30.00.

POLICTICAL CONDITIONS AMONG TEXAS MEXICANS ALONG THE RIO GRANDE: THESIS
Edgar E. Chelton, Jr.
R and E Research Assocaites, Pubs. Written in 1946. Pap. $8.00.

SPANISH-AMERICANS AS A POLITICAL FACTOR IN NEW MEXICO, 1912-1950
E.B. Fincher
Analyzes the roots of, and obstacles to Chicano political power in New Mexico. Arno Press, 1974. $19.00.

TOWARD CHICANO LIBERATION: THE COMMUNIST PARTY POSITION

Communist Party 20th National Convention
New Outlook Pubs., 1972. Pap. $.40.

Religion

CHURCH VIEWS OF THE MEXICAN AMERICAN
Carlos E. Cortes, Editor
An anthology of seven works on the Mexican American and his religious beliefs. Arno Press, 1974. Illus. $38.00.

THE RELIGIOUS STATUS OF THE MEXICAN POPULATION OF LOS ANGELES: THESIS
Samuel Ortegon
R and E Research associates, Pubs. Reprint of the 1932 edition. pap. $7.00.

NORWEGIAN-AMERICANS

AMERICANS FROM NORWAY
Leola Marjorie Bergmann
324 pp. Greenwood Press, Inc. Reprint of the 1950 edition. $13.00.

A FOLK EPIC: THE BYGDELAG IN AMERICA
Odd Sverre Lovoll
A history of the growth of the Norwegian social organizations known as the *bygdelag,* which first appeared in America at the turn of the century. Twayne Publishers. $8.50.

THE HISTORY OF THE NORWEGIAN CLUB OF SAN FRANCISCO
Ralph Enger
R and E Research Associates, Pubs. Reprint of the 1947 edition. Pap. $7.00.

HISTORY OF THE NORWEGIAN PEOPLE IN AMERICA
Olaf Morgan Norlie
Haskell House Pubs., Inc. Reprint of the 1925 edition. $19.95.

THE LUTHERAN CHURCH AMONG NORWEGIAN AMERICANS, TWO VOLS.
Clifford Nelson and Eugene L. Fevold
Augsburg Publishing House, 1960. $12.50 per set.

NORWEGIAN-AMERICAN STUDIES
Kenneth O. Bjork, Editor
A collection of articles on Norwegian immigration to the United States, published in conjunction with the Norwegian-American Historical Association. Twayne Publichers. $7.50.

THE NORWEGIAN-AMERICANS
Arlow W. Anderson Twayne Publishers. $8.95.

NORWEGIAN IMMIGRANT CONTRIBUTIONS TO AMERICA'S MAKING
Harry Sunby-Hansen
R and E Research Associates, Pubs. Reprint of the 1921 edition. $8.00.

NORWEGIANS IN AMERICA
Einar Haugen
Teachers College Press, 1967. Pap. $1.50.

*THE NORWEGIANS IN AMERICA
Percie V. Hillbrand
Lerner Publications, 1967. Illus. $3.95. Ages 10 and up.

NORWEGIAN LANGUAGE IN AMERICA: A STUDY IN BILINGUAL BEHAVIOR
Einar Haugen
Indiana University Press, 1969. $17.50.

NORWEGIAN MIGRATION TO AMERICA: 1825-1860
Theodore C. Blegen
Details the history of economic pressure and religious intolerance that forced Norwegians to migrate, as well as their successful settlements in America. Arno Press. Reprint of the 1931 edition. $12.50.

NORWEGIAN MIGRATION TO AMERICA, TWO VOLS.
Theodore C. Blegen
Haskell House Pubs., Inc. Reprint of the 1931 edition. $32.95.

NORWEGIAN SETTLEMENT IN THE UNITED STATES
Carlton C. Qualey
Traces the course of movement from Norway successively through the American west. Arno Press. Reprint of the 1938 edition. $12.00.

100 YEARS WITH THE NORWEGIANS IN THE EAST BAY
Soren C. Roinstad
R and E Research Associates, Pubs. Reprint of the 1963 edition. Pap. $5.00.

ORIENTAL-AMERICANS

AIIIEEEEE!
  Frank Chin, Jeffery Chan, Lawson Inada, and Shawn Wong
An anthology of Asian-American writers. 256 pp. Howard University Press, 1974. $7.95.

AMERICANS IN PROCESS: A STUDY OF OUR CITIZENS OF ORIENTAL ANCESTRY
  William Carlson Smith
The authors interest is in tracing the effects of racial discrimination and rejection by whites on Oriental-Americans. Arno Press. Reprint of the 1937 edition. $15.00.

ASIAN-AMERICANS: A STUDY GUIDE AND SOURCE BOOK
  Lynn P. Dunn
R & E Research Associates, 1975. Pap. $6.00.

CHINESE AND JAPANESE IN AMERICA
  American Academy of Politcal and Social Science
R and E Research Associates, Pubs. Reprint of the 1909 edition. $12.00.

*EAST MEETS WEST: THE STORY OF THE CHINESE AND JAPANESE IN CALIFORNIA
  George Goldberg
144 pp. Harcourt Brace Jovanovich, Inc., 1970. Ages 12 up. $5.50.

THE ORIENTAL-AMERICANS
  H. Brett melendy
The history of the Chinese and Japanese in America. Twayne Publishers. Cloth $7.95. Hippocrene Books, Inc. Pap. $2.95.

ORIENTAL EXCLUSION: THE EFFECT OF AMERICAN IMMIGRATION LAWS, REGULATIONS, AND JUDICIAL DECISIONS UPON THE CHINESE AND JAPANESE ON THE AMERICAN PACIFIC COAST
  Roderick Mckenzie
Jerome Ozer Pubs. Reprint of the 1927 edition. $7.95.

ORIENTALS IN AMERICAN LIFE
  Albert W. Palmer
The Chinese, Japanese and Filipino in America. R & E Research Associates. Reprint of the 1934 edition. $10.00.

OUT OF THE FAR EAST
  Allan A. Hunter
The Filipino, Japanese and Chinese in America. R & E Research Associates. Reprint of the 1934 edition. $9.00.

POLISH-AMERICANS

AMERICA'S POLISH HERITAGE: A SOCIAL HISTORY OF THE POLES IN AMERICA
  Joseph A. Wytrwal
380 pp. Endurance Press, 1961. $6.75.

AMERYKA: A HYNDRED YEARS AGE: A GLOBETROTTER'S VIEW
  Sygurd Wisniowski
A portrait of the Polish settlements in the U.S. in the early 1870's. 140 pp. Cherry Hill Books, 1972. Pap. $5.00.

THE FIRST POLISH COLONIES OF AMERICANS IN TEXAS
  Edward J. Dworaczyk
R & E Research Associates. Reprint of the 1936 edition. $10.00.

HAMTRACK: A SOCIOLOGICAL STUDY OF A POLISH-AMERICAN COMMUNITY
  Arthur E. Wood
College and University Press, 1955. Pap. $2.45.

*THE POLES IN AMERICA
  Joseph Wytrwal
Lerner Pubns., 1969. $3.95. Illus. Ages 10 and up.

THE POLES IN AMERICA
  Paul Fox
Studies the European background and the American experience of the Polish people in the United States. Arno Press. Reprint of the 1922 edition. $6.00.

THE POLES IN AMERICA, 1608 TO 1972
  Frank Renkiewicz
Oceana Publications, 1973. $5.00.

POLES IN AMERICAN HISTORY AND TRADITION
  Joseph A. Wytrwal
From their beginnings in Jamestown to the present. 498 pp. Endurance Press, 1969. $6.75.

POLES IN NEW YORK IN THE 17th AND 18th CENTURIES
Haiman Mieczyslaw
R & E Research Associates. Reprint of the 1938 edition. $5.00.

POLISH-AMERICAN COMMUNITY LIFE: A SURVEY OF RESEARCH
Irwin T. Sanders and Ewa T. Morawska
Bibliography of ethnic community studies of Polish life. Polish Institute of Arts and Sciences In America, 1975. $6.50.

POLISH-AMERICAN POLITICS IN CHICAGO 1888-1940
Edward R. Kantowicz
Focuses on the goals which the Polish-American community pursued in politics, the issues they deemed important, and the functions which politics served for them. 288 pp. University of Chicago Press, 1975. $12.95.

THE POLISH-AMERICAN STORY
Rev. Joseph Swastek
Endurance Press. $.60.

A POLISH CHAPTER IN JACKSONIAN AMERICA
Jerzy Jan Lerski
Endurance Press. $5.00.

THE POLISH COLONY OF CALIFORNIA, 1876-1914
Milton Kosberg
Thesis. R & E Research Associates. Reprint of the 1952 paper. $7.00.

THE POLISH PEASANT IN EUROPE AND AMERICA
William I. Thomas and Florian Znaniecki
Octagon Books, 1975. Reprint of the 1927 edition. $67.50.

POLISH PIONEERS OF CALIFORNIA
Haiman Mieczyslaw
R & E Research Associates. Reprint of the 1940 edition. $5.00.

POLISH PIONEERS OF PENNSYLVANIA
Haiman Mieczyslaw
R & E Research Associates. Reprint of the 1941 edition. $5.00.

POLISH PIONEERS OF VIRGINIA AND KENTUCKY
Haiman Mieczyslaw
R & E Research Associates. Reprint of the 1937 edition. $5.00.

THE POLISH PRESS IN AMERICA
Edmund Olszyk
The development and character of Polish American journalism. Endurance Press. $3.25.

REGISTER OF POLISH-AMERICAN SCHOLARS, SCIENTISTS, WRITERS, AND ARTISTS
Damian Wandycz
80 pp. Polish Institute of Arts and Sciences in America, 1969. Pap. $2.00.

*THEY CAME FROM POLAND: THE STORIES OF FAMOS POLISH-AMERICANS
Laura Pilarski
Dodd, Mead, and Co., 1969. $4.50. Ages 13 and up.

WE, THE MILWAUKEE POLES, 1846-1946
Thaddeus Borun, Compiler
The history of Milwaukeeans of Polish descent and a record of their contributions. Endurance Press. $3.75.

WHO'S WHO IN POLISH-AMERICA: A BIOGRAPHICAL DIRECTORY OF POLISH-AMERICAN LEADERS AND DISTINGUISHED POLES RESIDENT IN THE AMERICAS
Francis Bolek, Editor
Contains a listing of some 5000 brief biographies of outstanding Poles. Arno Press. Reprint of the 1943 edition. $23.50.

WOODROW WILSON AND THE REBIRTH OF POLAND, 1914 TO 1920: A STUDY IN THE INFLUENCE ON AMERICAN POLICY OF MINOITY GROUPS OF FOREIGN ORIGIN
Louis L. Gerson
166 pp. Shoe String Press. Reprint of the 1953 edition. $7.00.

PORTUGUESE-AMERICANS

CALIFORNIA AND THE PORTUGUESE
Celestino Soares
R and E Research Associates, Pubs. Reprint of the 1939 edition. $5.00.

A HISTORICAL STUDY OF THE PORTU-GUESE IN CALIFORNIA: THESIS
W.S. Brown
R and E Research Associates, Pubs. Reprint of the 1944 edition. Pap. $7.00.

PORTUGUESE IMMIGRATION TO THE UNITED STATES: THESIS
Christian John Bannik
R and E Research Associates, Pubs., 1971. $7.00.

SOCIAL PLACEMENT OF THE PORTU-GUESE IN HAWAII AS INDICATED BY FACTORS IN ASSIMILATION
Gerald A. Estep
Thesis. R & E Research Associates. Reprint of the 1941 paper. Pap. $7.00.

TWO PORTUGUESE COMMUNITIES IN NEW ENGLAND
Donald R. Taft
A study of the assimilation of Portuguese immigrants in America. Arno Press. Reprint of the 1923 edition. $10.50. AMS Press, Inc. $9.50.

PUERTO RICAN-AMERICANS

Assimilation

AWAKENING MINORITIES: AMERICAN INDIANS, MEXICAN AMERICANS, PUERTO RICANS
John R. Howard, Editor
Partial minority groups submerged below the thrreshhold of national awareness. 191 pp. Transaction Books, 1972. $7.95; Pap. $3.45.

THE PUERTO RICAN IN AMERICAN SOCIETY
Anthony L. LaRuffa and J. Vazquez
Gordon Press, 1973. Price not set.

THE PUERTO RICANS: CULTURE AND LANGUAGE DEVIANCE
Ruby Rohrlich Leavitt
A study of Puerto Ricans in New York and San Juan; and integration of Anthropology and speech pathology investigates the theory that stuttering is a deviant linguistic response to sociocultural stress. 268 pp. University of Arizona Press, 1974. Pap. $4.95.

PUERTO RICANS ON THE U.S. MAINLAND
A bibliography of reports, texts, critical studies and related materials. 146 pp. Rowan and Littlefield, 87 Adams Dr., Totowa, N.J. 07512. $12.50.

THE PUERTO RICANS: A SOCIOLOGI-CAL SOURCEBOOK
Francesco Cordasco and Eugene Bucchioni
370 pp. Rowan and Littlefield, 1972. $10.00.

*THE PUERTO RICANS: STRANGERS--THEN NEIGBORS
Clarence Senior
Problems of adjustment, interchange of ideas with other Americans, and neighborhood communication. 128 pp. Franklin Watts, Inc., 1965. Age 16 up. Pap. $2.95.

SOCIOLINGUISTIC ASPECTS OF ASSIM-ILATION: PUERTO RICAN ENGLISH IN NEW YORK CITY
Walt Wolfram
A study of language varieties in contact. 241 pp. Center for Applied Linguistics, 1973. $8.00.

THE VOICE OF THE CHILDREN: WRITINGS BY BLACK AND PUERTO RICAN YOUNG PEOPLE
June Jordan and Terri Bush, Editors
Washington Square Press, 1974. Pap. $.95.

Education

THE PUERTO RICAN COMMUNITY AND ITS CHILDREN ON THE MAINLAND: A SOURCE BOOK FOR TEACHERS, SOCIAL WORKERS, AND OTHER PROFESSION-ALS
Francesco Cordasco and Eugene Bucchioni
465 pp. Scarecrow Press, 1972. $11.00.

THE PUERTO RICAN COMMUNITY DE-VELOPMENT PROJECT: A PROPOSAL FOR A SELF-HELP PROJECT TO DE-VELOP THE COMMUNITY BY STRENGTHENING THE FAMILY, OPENING OPPORTUNITIES FOR YOUTH AND MAKING FULL USE OF EDUCATION
Puerto Rican Forum
This proposal includes a rationale for a culturally-based project; a research proposal; programs; organization of programs with a

project framework; and a history of the Puerto Rican migration and its trends. Arno Press. Reprint of the 1964 edition. $9.00.

THE PUERTO RICAN STUDY 1953-1957
New York City Board of Education
A report of the education and adjustment of Puerto Rican pupils in the public schools of New York City. Oriole Editions, 1972. $12.50.

PUERTO RICANS AND EDUCATIONAL OPPORTUNITY
An anthology of five studies of the Puerto Rican in American education. Arno Press, 1975. $12.00.

History

*AN ALBUM OF PUERTO RICANS IN THE UNITED STATES
Stuart Brahs
Their history and culture, migration, aspirations, and achievements. 84 pp. Franklin Watts, Inc., 1973. Age 11 up. $4.90.

CONTRA VIENTOY MAREA (AGAINST THE STORMY SEAS)
Information about Puerto Ricans in the United States: their uniqueness, cultural heritage, values, and achievements. Family Service Association of America. $1.75.

THE ETHNIC QUEUE IN THE U.S.: THE CASE OF PUERTO RICANS
Clara Rodriguez
R & E Research Associates, 1973. $12.00.

THE NEWCOMERS
Oscar Handlin
Problems of the Negro and Puerto Rican in New York. Doubleday & Co., 1959. Pap. $1.95.

PUERTO RICAN-AMERICANS: THE MEANING OF MIGRATION TO THE MAINLAND
Joseph P. Fitzpatrick
An examination of the experience of Puerto Ricans who have migrated to the U.S. mainland. 192 pp. Prentice-Hall, Inc., 1971. Cloth, $6.95; Pap. $3.50.

THE PUERTO RICANS: AN ANNOTATED BIBLIOGRAPHY
Paquita Vivo, Editor

Over 2600 entries cover history, education, economics, juvenile literature, migration, arts, music, and the Puerto Rican experience on the U.S. mainland. 299 pp. R.R. Bowker Co., 1973. $14.95.

THE PUERTO RICANS: A CHRONOLGY AND FACT BOOK, 1493 TO 1973
Francisco Cordasco
Oceana Pubns. 1973. $5.00.

THE PUERTO RICANS: A DOCUMEN-TARY HISTORY
Kal Wagenheim and Olga Jimenez de Wagenheim, Editors
352 pp. Praeger Pubs., 1973. Illus. $12.50.

*PUERTO RICANS: FROM ISLAND TO MAINLAND
Arlene Harris Kurtis
Messner, 1969. $3.95. Below college level.

*THE PUERTO RICANS IN AMERICA
Ronald J. Larsen
The Spanish, Indian and Africans from Puerto Rico who have settled in the United States. 88 pp. Lerner Publications, 1973. Illus. Ages 11-17. $3.95.

PUERTO RICAN PERSPECTIVES
Edward Mapp, Editor
18 essays about the Puerto Rican experience on the mainland; education, the arts, the community and the individual. 179 pp. Scarecrow Press, 1974. $6.00.

PUERTO RICANS ON THE UNITED STATES MAINLAND: A BIBLIOGRAPHY OF REPORTS, TEXTS, CRITICAL STUDIES AND RELATED MATERIALS
Francisco Cordasco
146 pp. Rowan and Littlefield, 1972. $12.50.

PUERTO RICO AND THE PUERTO RICANS
Clifford A. Hauberg
Puerto Rican history and migration to the United States. Hippocrene Books, 1975. Pap. $3.95.

UP FROM PUERTO RICO
Elena Padilla
Columbia University Press, 1958. $12.00.

Urban Experience

*CARLITO'S WORLD: A BLOCK IN

SPANISH HARLEM
Veronica Nash
McGraw Hill Book Co., 1969. $3.83. Below college level.

EIGHTY PUERTO RICAN FAMILIES IN NEW YORK CITY: HEALTH AND DISEASE STUDIED IN CONTEXT
Beatrice Bishop Berle
Includes recommendations for realistic, long-range resolutions of the health-related problems of the Puerto Rican community, such as family service centers. Arno Press. Reprint of the 1958 edition. $20.00.

ISLAND IN THE CITY: THE WORLD OF SPANISH HARLEM
Dan Wakefield
Daily life in the *barrio* of East Harlem, looking at migration, education, housing, employment, and religious practices. Arno Press. Reprint of the 1959 edition. $16.00.

LA VIDA: A PUERTO RICAN FAMILY IN THE CULTURE OF POVERTY: SAN JUAN AND NEW YORK
Oscar Lewis
Random House, Inc., 1966. Cloth, $12.50; Pap. $2.95.

THE NEWCOMERS: NEGROES AND PUERTO RICANS IN A CHANGING METROPOLIS
Oscar Handlin
171 pp. Harvard University Press, 1959. $5.00.

A PUERTO RICAN IN NEW YORK AND OTHER SKETCHES
Jesus Colon
Recollections of the author's life in New York City in the early 1920's, and his experiences as a writer for a socialist newspaper. Arno Press. Reprint of the 1961 edition. $11.00.

PUERTO RICAN JOURNEY: NEW YORK'S NEWEST MIGRANTS
Charles Wright Mills, et al
Russell and Russell. Reprint of the 1950 edition. $13.50.

PUERTO RICAN MIGRANT IN NEW YORK CITY
Lawrence R. Chenault
Russell and Russell. Reprint of the 1938 edition. $13.50.

PUERTO RICAN POPULATION OF NEW YORK CITY
Abraham J. Jaffe, Editor
The demography of the New York City Puerto Rican Community. Arno Press. Reprint of the 1954 edition. $7.00.

THE PUERTO RICAN IN NEW YORK
Christopher Rand
188 pp. Oxford University Press, 1958. $5.75.·

PUERTO RICANS IN NEW YORK CITY: THE REPORT OF THE COMMITTEE ON PUERTO RICANS IN NEW YORK CITY OF THE WELFARE COUNCIL OF NEW YORK CITY
New York City Welfare Council
Deals with the size and location of the Puerto Rican population; problems of neighborhood groups of Puerto Ricans; education, employment and health; Spanish-speaking personnel in social agencies; migration and resettlement. Arno Press. Reprint of the 1948 edition. $7.00.

PUERTO RICANS IN PHILADELPHIA: A STUDY OF THEIR DEMOGRAPHIC CHARACTERISTICS, PROBLEMS AND ATTITUDES
Arthur Siegel, Harold Orlans and Loyal Greer
Includes an examination of the migration of Puerto Ricans to Philadelphia; the history of its Puerto Rican community; educational programs for Puerto Rican children, and relations between police and the Puerto Rican community. Arno Press. Reprint of the 1954 edition. $8.00.

RESIDENCE, EMPLOYMENT AND MOBILITY OF PUERTO RICANS IN NEW YORK CITY
Terry J. Rosenberg
University of Chicago Press, Department of Geography, 1974. $5.00; Subscription $4.00.

A STUDY IN SLUM CULTURE: BACKGROUND FOR *La Vida*
Oscar Lewis
Random House, Inc., 1968. $7.00.

RUSSIAN-AMERICANS

ALASKA HERALD AND FREE PRESS

(SLOBODA) NEWSPAPER

Agapu Honcharenko

First Russian-English paper published in AMerica (San Francisco). Six volumes from 1868-1874. An anti-czarist Russian-Ukranian revolutionar. R & E Research Associates, 1968-70. Reprint of the 1868 edition. Pap. $10.00 per volume.

LIEUTENANT ZAGOSKIN'S TRAVELS IN RUSSIAN-AMERICA, 1848 TO 1844; THE FIRST ETHNOGRAPHIC AND GEOGRAPHIC INVESTIGATIONS IN THE YUKON AND KUSKOKIM VALLEYS OF ALASKA

Henry N. Michael, Editor

358 pp. Univeristy of Toronto Press, 1967. $15.00.

RUSSIAN CALIFORNIA: 1805 TO 1841

Emil Theodore Bunje

R and E Research Associates, Pubs. Reprint of the 1937 edition. Pap. $7.00.

THE RUSSIAN IMMIGRANT

Jerome Davis

A scientific study of the Russian immigrant in this country and also of his environment in Russia before he came to America. Arno Press. Reprint of the 1922 edition. $7.00.

THE RUSSIAN SETTLEMENT IN CALIFORNIA

R.A. Thompson

R and E Research Associates, Pubs. Reprint of the 1896 edition. $3.00.

*THE RUSSIANS IN AMERICA

Nancy Eubank

Lerner Publications, 1973. Illus. $3.95. Ages 10 and up.

SCANDINAVIAN-AMERICANS

*AMERICA IS ALSO SCANDINAVIAN

Carl Malmberg

G.P. Putnam's Sons, 1970. Illus. $3.86. Below college level.

THE AMERICAN-SCANDINAVIAN FOUNDATION

Friis

The 50 year history of the ASF; philosophy, goals, personalities, charter, fellows and publications. 135 pp. American-Scandinavian Foundation. $2.00.

AMERICAN-SCANDINAVIAN STUDIES

Benson, Editor

32 studies of Scandinavian-American culture and immigration, drama, withcraft, literature and more. 381 pp. American-Scandinavian Foundation. $5.00.

THE DIVIDED HEART: SCANDINAVIAN IMMIGRANT EXPERIENCE THROUGH LITERARY SOURCES

Dorothy Burton Skardal

394 pp. University of Nebraska Press, 1974. $20.00.

THE HISTORY AND REVIEW OF THE SCADINAVIAN SOCIETY OF SAN FRANCISCO

August Wetterman

R and E Research Associates, Pubs. Reprint of the 1912 edition. Pap. $7.00.

HISTORY OF THE SCANDINAVIANS AND SUCCESSFUL SCANDINAVIANS IN THE UNITED STATES, TWO VOLS. IN ONE

O.N. Nelson

Haskell House Pubs., Inc. Reprint of the 1904 edition. $37.50.

HOMEWARD TO ZION: THE MORMON MIGRATION FROM SCANDINAVIA

William Mulder

375 pp. University of Minnesota Press, 1957. $10.00.

THE SCANDINAVIAN-AMERICAN

Alfred O. Fonkalsrud

R and E Research Associates, Pubs. Reprint of the 1915 edition. $8.00.

THE SCANDINAVIAN ELEMENT IN THE UNITED STATES

Kendric Charles Babcock

Details the life of American Scandinavians located in the Northern Mississippi Valley from the 1850's to the early 1900's. Arno Press, Hohnso Reprint. Reprint of the 1914 edition. $6.50.

SCANDINAVIAN IMMIGRANTS IN NEW YORK, 1630 TO 1674

John O. Evjen

438 pp. Genealogical Publishing Co. Reprint of the 1916 edition. Illus. $15.00.

THE SCANDINAVIANS IN AMERICA
FROM 986 TO 1970
Howard B. Furer
Oceana Pubs., 1973. $5.00.

SCANDINAVIANS ON THE PACIFIC
Thomas Ostensen Stine
R and E Research Associates, Pubs. Reprint of
the 1900 edition. $10.00

SCOTCH-IRISH-AMERICANS

CHRONICLES OF THE SCOTCH-IRISH
SETTLEMENT IN VIRGINIA: EXTRAC-
TED FROM THE ORIGINAL COURT
RECORDS OF AUGUSTA COUNTY, 1745-
1800
Lyman Chalkley
Three volumes. Genealogical Publishing Co.
Reprint of the 1912 edition. $60.00.

PENNSYLVANIA GENEALOGIES: CHIEF-
LY SCOTCH-IRISH AND GERMAN
William Henry Egle
798 pp. Genealogical Publishing Co. Reprint of
the 1896 edition. $22.50.

THE SCOTCH-IRISH IN AMERICA
Henry Jones Ford
Includes a study of the causes that led to the
emigration from Ulster to America, and descriptions of the Scotch-Irish settlements in this
country. Arno Press; Shoe String Press. Reprint
of the 1915 edition. $15.00. Gordon Press,
$27.00.

THE SCOTCH-IRISH IN AMERICA
Sameul Swett Green
R and E Research Associates, Pubs. Reprint of
the 1895 edition. $5.00.

THE SCOTCH-IRISH OR THE SCOT IN
NORTH BRITAIN, NORTH IRELAND, AND
NORTH AMERICA, 2 VOLS
Charles A. Hanna
Genealogical Publishing Co. Reprint of the
1902 edition. $27.50 per set.

SCOTCH-IRISH PIONEERS IN ULSTER
AND AMERICA
Charles Bolton
398 pp. Genealogical Publishing Co. Reprint of
the 1910 edition. Illus. $12.00.

*THE SCOTS AND THE SCOTCH-IRISH IN
AMERICA
James E. Johnson
Lerner Publications, 1966. Illus. $3.95. Ages 10
and up.

SCOTTISH-AMERICANS

A DICTIONARY OF SCOTTISH EMI-
GRANTS TO THE UNITED STATES OF
AMERICA
Donald Whyte
Magna Carta Book Co., $16.90.

THE HIGHLAND SCOTS OF NORTH
CAROLINA, 1732 TO 1776
Duane Meyer
218 pp. University of North Carolina, 1961.
Cloth, $7.50. North Carolina Office of Archives
and History. Pap. $.50.

AN HISTORICAL ACCOUNT OF THE SET-
TLEMENTS OF SCOTCH HIGHLANDERS
IN AMERICA PRIO TO THE PEACE OF
1783, WITH NOTICES OF HIGHLAND RE-
GIMENTS AND BIOGRAPHICAL SKET-
CHES
John Patterson MacLean
455 pp. Genealogical Publishing Co. Reprint of
the 1900 edition. $13.50.

INVISIBLE IMMIGRANTS: THE ADAP-
TATION OF ENGLISH AND SCOTTISH
EMMIGRANTS IN NINETEENTH CEN-
TURY AMERICA
Charlotte Erickson
Contains the hundreds of letters of twenty-five
families of English and Scottish immigrants
who settled in the United States in the
nineteenth century. 531 pp. University of Miami
Press, 1972. Illus. $17.50.

THE SCOT IN AMERICA AND THE
ULSTER SCOT
Whitelaw Reid
R and E Research Associates, Pubs. 1970.
Reprint of the 1912 edition. $5.00.

SCOTLAND'S MARK ON AMERICA
George Fraser Black
126 pp. R and E Research Assocaites, Pubs.
Reprint of the 1921 edition. $7.00.

*THE SCOTS AND THE SCOTCH-IRISH IN AMERICA
James E. Johnson
Lerner Publications, 1966. Illus. $3.95. Ages 10 and up.

*THE SCOTS HELPED BUILD AMERICA
Nancy Wallace Henderson
Messner, 1969. $3.95. Below college level.

SCOTTISH POETS IN AMERICA
John D. Ross, Editor
Benjamin Blom Pubs. Reprint of the 1889 edition. $13.50.

SLAVIC-AMERICANS

AMERICAN ASSOCIATION FOR THE AD-VANCEMENT OF SLAVIC STUDIES — DIRECTORY OF MEMBERS
Lists about 2,500 members with information as to their positions, fields of interest, and home addresses. 80 pp. Published every two years by the Association, c/o Ohio State University, 190 W. Nineteenth Ave., Room 254, Columbus, Ohio 43210. $5.00.

THE COMING OF THE SLAV
Charles Eugene Edwards
The movement into the United States of the Poles, Czechs, Slovaks, Croatians, Slovencs. Russians, Ukranians, and the Serbians; and a historical background on their heritage. 148 pp. R & E Research Associates. Reprint of the 1921 edition. $8.00.

HIGH ADVENTURE
The story of Slavic pioneers in America.
R & E Research Associates. Reprint of the 1923 edition. $8.00.

HISTORY OF SLAVS IN ARIZONA (1864-1912)
Joan Werling
R & E Research Associates, 1968. Pap. $5.00.

ITALIAN, SLAVIC, AND HUNGARIAN UNSKILLED LABORERS IN THE UNITED STATES
Frank J. Sheridan
Jerome S. Ozer Pubs. Reprint of the 1907 edition. $5.95.

OUR SLAVIC FELLOW CITIZENS
Emily Greene Balch
Details the living conditions and cultural development of Slavs in Europe and presents an overview of Slavic immigrant life in the United States. Arno Press. Reprint of the 1910 edition. $20.00.

PEASANT PIONEERS
Kenneth D. Miller
An interpretation of the Slavic peoples in the U.S. R & E Research Associates. Reprint of the 1925 edition. $10.00.

THE SLAV INVASION AND THE MINE WORKERS: A STUDY IN IMMIGRATION
Frank J. Warne
Jerome S. Ozer Pubs. Reprint of the 1904 edition. $8.95.

THE SLAVIC IMMIGRANT WOMAN
Bessie Olga Pehotsky
R & E Research Associates. Reprint of the 1925 edition. $7.00.

SLAVS IN CALIFORNIA
Stephen N. Sestanovich
R & E Research Assocaites. Reprint of the 1937 edition. $7.00.

SOUTH SLAV SETTLEMENT IN WESTERN WASHINGTON: PERCEPTION AND CHOICE
Roger H. Green
R & E Research Associates, 1974. Illus. $9.00.

THE SOUTH SLAVS IN UTAH: A SOCIAL HISTORY
Joseph Stipanovich
R & E Research Associates, 1975. Pap. $9.00.

SWEDISH-AMERICANS

BACKGROUND OF SWEDISH EMIGRA-TION TO THE UNITED STATES: AN ECONOMIC AND SOCIOLOGICAL STUDY IN THE DYNAMICS OF MIGRATION
John S. Lindberg
Jerome S. Ozer Pub. Reprint of the 1930 edition. $10.95.

THE BACKGROUND OF SWEDISH IMMI-GRATION, 1840-1930
Florence Edith Janson

The standard account of the material and social conditions in Sweden which influenced group members to leave home and go to the United States. Arno Press. Reprint of the 1931 edition. $21.50.

LETTERS FROM THE PROMISED LAND: SWEDES IN AMERICA, 1840-1914
    H. Arnold Benton, Editor
Letters Swedish immigrants sent home to Sweden, plus diaries, memoirs, and travel accounts, during the Swedish migration to the United States. 368 pp. University of Minnesota Press, 1975. Illus. $16.50.

PIONEER SWEDISH-AMERICAN CULTURE IN CENTRAL KANSAS
    Ruth Bildt
William A. Linder Company, 1965. $5.00.

THE RELATION OF THE SWEDISH-AMERICAN NEWSPAPER TO THE ASSIMILATION OF SWEDISH IMMIGRANTS
    Albert Ferdinand Schersten
Augustana Library Publications of Augustana College, 1935. 102 pp. $1.00.

THE RELIGIOUS ASPECTS OF SWEDISH IMMIGRATION: A STUDY OF IMMIGRANT CHURCHES
    George Malcolm Stephenson
"This is an historical description of the development of radical religious sects in Sweden about the middle of the 19th century as a reaction against the rigidity and intolerance of the state church, of the migration of these religious groups to the United States, and the development of their religious organizations in America. Arno Press. Reprint of the 1932 edition. $16.50.

*THE SWEDES IN AMERICA
    Percie V. Hillbrand
Lerner Publications, 1966. Illus. $3.95. Ages 10 and up.

SWEDES IN AMERICA, 1638 TO 1938
    Adolph Benson and Naboth Hedin
Haskell House Pubs., Inc. Reprint of the 1938 edition. $25.00.

THE SWEDES IN CHICAGO: A DEMOGRAPHIC AND SOCIAL STUDY OF THE 1846 TO 1880 IMMIGRATION
    Ulf Beijbom
Chicago Historical Society, 1971. $12.50.

THE SWEDISH IMMIGRANT COMMUNITY IN TRANSITION: ESSAYS IN HONOR OF DR. CONRAD BERGENDOFF
    J.I. Dowie and E.M. Espelie, eds.
Augustana Library Publications of Augustana College, 1963. 246 pp. $5.95.

SWISS-AMERICANS

LISTS OF SWISS EMIGRANTS IN THE 18th CENTURY TO THE AMERICAN COLONIES, TWO VOLS. IN ONE
    Albert B. Faust and Gaius M. Brumbaugh
Genealogical Publishing Co. Reprint of the 1920 edition. $17.50.

THE OLD LAND AND THE NEW: THE JOURNALS OF TWO SWISS FAMILIES IN AMERICA IN THE 1820's
    Robert Billigmeier and Fred Picard, Editors
281 pp. University of Minnesota Press, 1965. Illus. $5.75.

THE SWISS IN THE UNITED STATES
    John Paul Von Grueningen
R and E Research Associates, Pubs. Reprint of the 1940 edition. $8.00.

UKRANIAN-AMERICANS

AHAPIUS HONCHARENKO AND THE ALASKAN HERALD
    Wesyl and Theodore Luciw
A Ukranian pioneer of the 1860's in San Francisco and Alaska: Priest, newspaper editor and revolutionary. R & E Research Associates, 1963. $7.00.

UKRANIANS IN THE UNITED STATES
    Wasyl Halich
An overview of Ukranian-American life, why they left and how they went about building communities in the U.S., with an emphasis upon the cultural contributions of the Ukranians to America. Arno Press. Reprint of the 1937 edition. $7.50. R and E Research Associates, $7.00.

*THE UKRANIANS IN AMERICA
    Myron Kuropas

Lerner Publications, 1972. Illus. $3.95. Ages 10
and up.

WELSH-AMERICANS

AMERICANS FROM WALES
Edward G. Hartmann
Information on Welsh settlements, religion,
societies, and migration. 294 pp. Christopher
Publishing House. $6.50.

WELSH FOUNDERS OF PENNSYLVANIA
Thomas Allen Glenn
Two volumes in one. Genealogical Publishing
Co. Reprint of the 1911 and 1913 edition. Illus.
$16.50.

WELSH IN AMERICA: LETTERS FROM THE IMMIGRANTS
Alan Conway, Editor
341 pp. University of Minnesota Press, 1961.
$7.50.

WELSH PEOPLE OF CALIFORNIA, 1849-1906
David Hughes
R & E Research Associates. Reprint of the 1906
edition. $7.00.

YUGOSLAV-AMERICANS

AMERICANS FROM YUGOSLAVIA
Gerald Gilbert Govorchin
352 pp. University of Florida Press, 1961. Illus.
$8.50. R and E Research Associates, $10.00.

ASSIMILATION OF YUOGOSLAVS IN FRANKLIN COUNTY, OHIO: DISSERTATION
Walter Vladimir Babics
R and E Research Associates, Pubs. Reprint of
the 1964 edition. $7.00.

LAUGHING IN THE JUNGLE: THE AUTOBIOGRAPHY OF AN IMMIGRANT IN AMERICA
Louis Adamic
Story of a Yugoslavian boy coming to America
in 1913. Arno Press. Reprint of the 1932
edition. $9.50.

THE SLAVONIC PIONEERS OF CALIFORNIA
Vjekoslav Meler
A study on Yugoslavs (Dalmatians/Croations)
in the United States. R & E Research Associates.
Reprint of the 1932 edition. Pap. $7.00.

THE SOCIAL SYSTEM OF A RURAL YUGOSLAV-AMERICAN COMMUNITY: OYSTERVILLE, LOUISIANA
Frank M. Lorvich
R and E Research Associates, Pubs. 1963.
$7.00.

YUGOSLAV CALIFORNIA MARRIAGES: 1880 TO 1948
Adam S. Eterovich
R and E Research Associates, Pubs. 1968. Pap.
$3.00.

YUGOSLAV CEMETERY RECORDS IN SAN FRANCISCO 1849 TO 1930
Adam S. Eterovich
R and E Research Associates, 1968. Pap. $3.00.

YUGOSLAV CENSUS OF POPULATION IN CALIFORNIA, 1850 TO 1880
Adam S. Eterovich
R and E Research Associates, Pubs., 1968. Pap.
$3.00.

YUGOSLAV IMMIGRANT BIBLIOGRAPHY
Adam S. Eterovich
R and E Research Associates, Pubs., 1968. Pap.
$3.00.

YUGOSLAV MIGRATIONS TO AMERICA
Branko Mita Colakovic
This study illustrates the coming, distribution
and dispersion of Croatians, Serbians, Slovenes
and other South Slavs to the U.S. R & E
Research Associates, 1973. Illus. $9.00.

YUGOSLAV SURVEY OF CALIFORNIA, NEVADA, ARIZONA, AND THE SOUTH, 1830 TO 1900
Adam S. Eterovich
R and E Research Associates, Pubs., 1971.
$7.00.

YUGOSLAVS IN LOS ANGELES: 1733 TO 1900
Adam S. Eterovich
R and E Research Associates, Pubs., 1968. Pap.
$5.00.

YUGOSLAVS IN LOUISIANA
Milos M. Vujnovich
Covers Dalmatians and Serbs from the Boka area, from 1770-1870. 246 pp. R & E Research Associates; Pelican Publishing House, 1974. Illus. $12.50.

YUGOSLAVS IN NEVADA, 1859-1900
Adam S Eterovich
A small group with a large representation in Nevada during the Silver Boom: Dalmatian and Montenegrin gunfighters, killers saloonkeepers, and silvermine owners. R & E Research Associates, 1972. $7.00.

YUGOSLAVS IN SAN FRANCISCO: 1870 TO 1875
Adam S. Eterovich
R and E Research Associates, 1968. Pap. $3.00.

YUGOSLAVS IN THE WILD WEST: 1840 TO 1900
Adam S. Eterovich
R and E Research Associates, Pubs., 1968. Pap. $5.00.

MISCELLANEOUS ETHNIC GROUPS

BASQUE AMERICANS
Grant E. McCall
Theories of migration and adaptation. Covers Nevada, California and other areas of the west. Thesis. R & E Research Associates. Reprint of the 1968 edition. Pap. $7.00.

CHANGES AND SOCIO-RELIGIOUS CONFLICT IN AN EHTNIC MINORITY GROUP: THE SERBIAN ORTHODOX CHURCH IN AMERICA
Djuro J. Vrga and Frank J. Fahey
R & E Research Associates, 1975. Pap. $8.00.

THE CHILENOS IN THE CALIFORNIA GOLD RUSH: THESIS
George E. Faugsted, Jr.
R and E Research Associates, Pubs. Reprint of the 1963 edition. Pap. $7.00.

CHILENOS IN CALIFORNIA: A STUDY OF THE 1850, 1852 and 1860 CENSUSES
Carlos U. Lopez
Contains the names and other pertinent data of all individuals. Graphs, charts and statistics with historical analysis. R & E Research Associates, 1973. Illus. $10.00.

CUBANS IN EXILE: DISAFFECTION AND THE REVOLUTION
Richard R. Fagen, et al
A study on the demographic characteristics of the Cuban migrants; on their economic-occupational status before leaving; and on their atitudes toward the Batista regime and the rebels who ultimately overthrew it. 161 pp. Stanford University Press, 1968. $5.95.

THE DOMINICAN DIASPORA: FROM THE DOMINICAN REPUBLIC TO NEW YORK CITY--VILLAGERS IN TRANSITION
Glenn Hendricks
The ethnographic account of the people of one Dominican village who settled in New York City. 171 pp. Teachers College Press, 1974. Photos. Cloth, $9.00; Pap. $5.95.

GOLD FLEET FOR CALIFORNIA: 49ERS FROM AUSTRALIA AND NEW ZEALAND
Charles Bateson
167 pp. Michigan State University Press, 1964. Illus. $7.50.

A HISTORY OF THE DANES IN AMERICA
John H. Bille
R and E Research Associates, Pubs. Reprint of the 1896 edition. $5.00.

THE LATVIANS IN AMERICA: A CHRONOLOGY SERIES
Maruta Karklis, et al, Editors
Oceana Pubns., 1974. $5.00.

THE MORAVIANS IN GEORGIA, 1735-1740
Adelaide L. Fries
252 pp. Genealogical Publishing Co. Reprint of the 1905 edition. Illus. $11.50.

THE NORMAN PEOPLE: AND THEIR EXISTING DESCENDANTS IN THE BRITISH DOMINIONS AND THE UNITED STATES OF AMERICA
Norman names and ancestry in the United States and England. 484 pp. Genealogical Publishing Co. Reprint of the 1874 edition. $17.50.

SPOKEN AND WRITTEN ALBANIAN: A PRACTICAL HANDBOOK
Nelo Drizari
188 pp. Frederick Ungar Publishing Co., 1959. $7.50.

A STUDY OF ASSIMILATION AMONG THE ROUMANIANS IN THE UNITED STATES
Christine Avghi Galitzi
AMS Press. Reprint of the 1929 edition. $15.00.

RECEIVED TOO LATE FOR CLASSIFICATION

GENERAL ETHNOLOGY

AMERICAN ANTHROPOLOGICAL ASSO-CIATION: *Memoirs*
Kraus Reprint Co.

AMERICAN FOLKLORE SOCIETY: *Memoirs*
Kraus Reprint Co.

A BIBLICAL PERSPECTIVE OF THE RACE PROBLEM
Thomas O. Figart
Deals with the race problem from a basic Biblical starting point. 185 pp. Baker Book House. $3.95.

BILINGUAL, BICULTURAL
Twelve articles dealing with the ethnic identity of Hispanic-Americans. Council on Interracial Books for Children. $1.75.

*COLORS AROUND ME
Designed to develop positive self-images by relating portraits representing various complexions to child-appeal objects of similar colors. 32 pp. Afro-Am Publishing Co., Inc. $5.95. Pre-school thru first grade.

THE CULTURAL DIMENSION IN LEARN-ING AND CHILD DEVELOPMENT: NEW POLICY IMPLICATIONS
Jerome M. Seelig
Recommendations for creating child development programs that are sensitive to and supportive of a child's own cultural heritage. Institute on Pluralism & Group Identity. $1.00.

DEFINITIONS OF RACISM
Differentiates between prejudice and racism and defines individual, institutional, cultural and paternal racism. For classroom students and workshop participants. Council on Interracial Books for Children. Bib. $.10.

EDUCATION AND RACISM: AN ACTION MANUAL
National Education Association
A guide for people who plan to conduct racism awareness training sessions or workhops. Includes an essay on racism in education, exercises, etc. Council on Interracial Books for Children. Bib. $2.50.

ELIMINATING ETHNIC BIAS IN IN-STRUCTIONAL MATERIALS: COMMENTS AND BIBLIOGRAPHY
Noted educators list and comment upon basic resources that will aid school people in deepen-ing and broadening their appreciation for the richness and diversity of the various American cultural groups. 64 pp. Association for Supervision and Curriculum Development, 1974. $3.25.

ETHNIC CULTURE SERIES
Gordon Press Publishers

ETHNIC MODIFICATION OF THE CUR-RICULUM
Points out the need for immediate curriculum evaluation and revision in terms of a pluralistic society. 52 pp. Association for Supervision and Curriculum Development, 1970. $1.00.

ETHNICITY AND AMERICAN EDUCA-TION
Irving M. Levine
An edited compendium of writings dealing with the ethnic factor in public education. Institute on Pluralism & Group Identity. $1.25.

FACT SHEETS ON INSTITUTIONAL RACISM
Current statistics documenting institutional racism in business, unions, health care, housing, publishing, media, education and government. Details both the white control and the minority oppression still commonplace in most American institutions. Council on Interracial Books for Children. $.50.

HARVARD UNIVERSITY, PEABODY MU-SEUM OF ARCHAEOLOGY AND ETHNOL-OGY: *Memoirs and Papers*
Kraus Reprint Co.

THE LANGUAGE EDUCATION OF MINORITY CHILDREN
Bernard Spolsky, Editor
Brings together some of the writings on the problem of minority groups in the United States. Provides the basis for courses in language education. Newbury House Publishers. Cloth, $10.95; Pap. $5.95.

MAJORITY AND MINORITY: THE DY-NAMICS OF RACIAL AND EHTNIC RELA-TIONS
Norman R. Yetman and C. Hoy Steele
Studies the dynamics of differential power and inter-group conflicts in racial and ethnic relations. 670 pp. Allyn and Bacon, Inc., 1975. Pap. $8.50.

*MINORITIES VERSUS COURTS: JUSTICE STANDS TRIAL FOR RACISM
Student-oriented leaflets presenting minority viewpoints on current affairs including: *Minorities and the News Media; Minorities and Police; Minorities and Jobs; Minorities and Prisons; Minorities and Courts; Minorities and Education; Minorities and Housing.* Also, the *Proud Series* of five titles including: *Indian and Proud; Puerto Rican and Proud; Chicano and Proud; Black Woman and Proud;* and *Black-American Freedom Fighters.* Four pages each. Council on Interracial Books for Children. $.10 each.

MODIFYING THE SMALL GROUP EXPERIENCE FOR MULTI-CULTURAL AMERICA
Nicholas V. Montalto
A critique of multi-cultural education of the past, with an emphasis on the educational benefits to be derived from emphasizing cultural differences. Institute on Pluralism & Group Identity. $.75.

MULTIETHNIC MEDIA: SELECTED BIBLIOGRAPHIES IN PRINT
David Cohen, Editor
American Library Association. $2.00. prepaid.

THE MULTINATIONAL SOCIETY: *Papers of the Ljubljana Seminar*
William F. Mackey and Albert Verdoodt, Editors
81 persons representing 27 countries exchange views on such problems as minority rights, anti-discrimination laws, ethnic diversity and cultural identity. Newbury House Publishers. Pap. $9.95.

THE NEW JERSEY CONSULTATION ON ETHNIC FACTORS IN EDUCATION
Nancy Seifer
A guide for programming around ethnic factors in education; recommendations for school-community relations; etc. Institute on Pluralism & Group Identity. $.50.

PEOPLE ON THE MOVE: A UNITED STATES HISTORY
Ray Ginger
Among other themes, this text describes the important sub-themes of ethnicity and culture-conflict. Two volumes. 800 pp. Allyn and Bacon, Inc., 1975. Pap. $13.95.

PURSUING THE AMERICAN DREAM: WHITE ETHNICS AND THE NEW POPULISM

Richard J. Krickus
Considers what role ethnic politics will take in the future and whether increasing ethnic awareness can support a 'new politics' in an era of needed reform. Doubleday and Co. 1976. $3.50.

RACE, COLOR, AND THE YOUNG CHILD
John E. Williams and J. Kenneth Morland
Represents the collaborative efforts of a social-developmental psychologist and a social anthropologist to describe what is known -and what needs to be investigated-concerning the development of race and color concepts in young children. 400 pp. University of North Carolina Press. 1976. $12.95.

RACE DECADENCE
William Sadler
Gordon Press Publishers. $39.95.

RACE AND SOCIAL DIFFERENCE
Baxter and Sansom, Editors
Penguin Books, Inc. $3.95.

RACIAL HISTORY OF MAN
Roland B. Dixon
Two volumes. Gordon Press Publishers. $100.00.

RACISM IN CAREER EDUCATION MATERIALS: HOW TO DETECT IT AND HOW TO COUNTERACT IT
Presents the findings of a major study of 100 Career Education materials from all grade levels—print and AV. Council on Interracial Books for Children. $2.50.

THE REDUCTION OF INTERGROUP TENSION: A SURVEY OF RESEARCH ON PROBLEMS OF EHTNIC, RACIAL, AND RELIGIOUS GROUP RELATIONS
Robin M. Williams
Kraus Reprint Co., 1947. Pap. $3.25.

RELIGION AND OUR RACIAL TENSIONS
Williard Sperry
Consortium Books. $14.00.

THE ROLE OF WHITE ETHNIC COMMUNITIES IN THE URBAN ADJUSTMENT OF NEWCOMERS
Joseph P. Fitzpatrick
A stable well-organized ethnic community can assist newcomers by creating links to the mainstream of urban life. Institute on Pluralism & Group Identity. $.50.

SOCIAL POLICY AND MULTI-ETHNICITY IN THE 1970's

Irving M. Levine

A coalitionist's analysis of major domestic public policy problems in our multi-ethnic society. Institute on Pluralism & Group Identity. $1.00.

SPEAKING IN MANY TONGUES: ESSAYS IN FOREIGN LANGUAGE TEACHING

Wilga M. Rivers

Eleven articles addressed to teachers of foreign languages, and to those involved in bilingual education or language problems of minority groups. Newbury House Publishers. Pap. $5.50.

TRANSRACIAL ADOPTION TODAY: VIEWS OF ADOPTIVE PARENTS AND SOCIAL WORKERS

Grow and Shapiro

A study of current practices as seen by both. 91 pp. Child Welfare League of America, Inc. 1975. $3.95.

UNITED STATES BUREAU OF AMERICAN ETHNOLOGY: *Bulletins*

Kraus Reprint Co.

URBAN ETHNIC ORGANIZING

Daniel F. Reidy

Summary of a research project describing elements of effective organizing in urban ethnic communities; includes policy recommendations for community organizers. Institute on Pluralism & Group Identity. $1.00.

THE WORKING POOR: MINORITY WORKERS IN LOW-WAGE, LOW-SKILL JOBS

Dennis P. Sobin

Suggests plans for government and industry for shifting the focus of planning from curtailing unemployment to finding meaningful jobs for the unskilled. Kennikat Press. 1974. $8.50.

AMERICAN INDIANS

THE AMERICAN HERITAGE BOOK OF INDIANS

A.M. Josephy, Jr.

An illustrated history of the American Indians from prehistoric times to the present. Superior Publishing Co. $12.98.

THE AMERICAN INDIAN

Gordon Press Publishers

THE AMERICAN INDIAN TODAY

Levine and Lurie, Editors

Penguin Books, Inc. $3.25.

AMERIND FOUNDATION: *Publications*

Kraus Reprint Co.

*ANCIENT INDIANS OF THE SOUTHWEST

96 pp. Doubleday and Co. 1976. Photos. $4.95. Grades 5 thru 7.

THE BUFFALO WAR: THE HISTORY OF THE RED RIVER INDIAN UPRISING OF 1874

James L. Haley

Doubleday and Co. 1976. Photos. $7.95.

THE CAMP GRANT MASSACRE

Elliott Arnold

The conflict between a tribe of Apache Indians led by chief Eskiminzin and the settlers of Arizona. Simon and Schuster. $9.95.

CRAZY HORSE AND CUSTER: THE PARALLEL LIVES OF TWO AMERICAN WARRIORS

Stephen E. Ambrose

Doubleday and Co. Photos, illus. $12.50.

CURTIS' WESTERN INDIANS

Ralph W. Andrews

Over 200 of Curtis' best works on Indian life are portrayed. Covered are the Apache, Navajo and other plains people as well as Northwest Coast tribes. Superior Publishing Co. $8.95.

FAR FROM THE RESERVATION: THE TRANSRACIAL ADOPTION OF AMERICAN INDIAN CHILDREN

David Fanshel

Research on American Indian children adopted by white families. 388 pp. Child Welfare League of America, Inc., 1972. $13.50.

A GUIDE TO AMERICA'S INDIANS: CEREMONIALS, RESERVATIONS, AND MUSEUMS

Arnold Marquis

Tells where to find Indian reservations and what to expect when you get there. 267 pp. The University of Oklahoma Press. Cloth, $9.95; pap. $4.95.

GUIDE TO INDIAN ROCK CARVINGS OF THE PACIFIC NORTHWEST COAST

Beth Hill

49 pp. Superior Publishing Co. Pap. $2.50.

INDIAN HERITAGE, INDIAN PRIDE: STORIES THAT TOUCHED MY LIFE
Jimalee Burton

Paintings, poetry, and stories of Indian legends. 176 pp. The University of Oklahoma Press. $12.50.

INDIAN RAWHIDE: AN AMERICAN FOLK ART
Mable Morrow

Shows patterns and designs representative of tribes from Apache to Yakima which indicate flourishing folk art prior to the annihilation of the buffalo. 140 illustrations. 200 pp. The University of Oklahoma Press. $20.00.

THE INDIAN TIPI: ITS HISTORY, CONSTRUCTION, AND USE
Reginald and Gladys Laubin

208 pp. The University of Oklahoma Press. $6.95.

INDIANS AS THE WESTERNERS SAW THEM
Ralph W. Andrews

Old manuscripts and photographs reveal experiences of pioneers, settlers, traders, teamsters and Army wives with the Indians of the great plains. Superior Publishing Co. $7.95.

INDIANS OF THE AMERICAN SOUTHWEST
Bertha Dutton

An overview of past and present Indian life in the Southwest. Information is given for each major tribe, including: Historical background, current facts on social and religious customs and ceremonies, educational and employment opportunities, etc. 298 pp. Prentice-Hall, 1975. $14.95.

INDIANS OF NORTH AMERICA
Books and monographs. Kraus Reprint Co.

THE INVASION OF AMERICA: INDIANS COLONIALISM, AND THE CANT OF CONQUEST
Francis Jennings

The crime of the white man's seizure of North America from the Indians. 369 pp. University of North Carolina Press. 1975. Illus. $14.95.

THE LIFE AND ART OF THE NORTH AMERICAN INDIAN
A survey of the art and culture of the Indian nations. 100 full color photos; 50 in black and white. Superior Publishing Co. $11.98.

THE MEXICAN KICKAPOO INDIANS
Felipe A. Latorre and Dolores L. Latorre

A study by two anthropologists who lived for ten years with the Kickapoos of Muzquiz, of northern Mexico. The Latorres explore everyday life, social structure, language, sex, etc. University of Texas Press. $15.95.

THE PLAINS APACHE
John Upton Terrell

A study of why the Plains Apache became an instant symbol of terror among the first Americans who settled the high plains. Thomas Y. Crowell. $7.95.

RECONSTRUCTION IN INDIAN TERRITORY
M. Thomas Bailey

A story of avarice, discrimination and opportunism. Kennikat Press. 1972. $11.50.

THE REFORMERS AND THE AMERICAN INDIAN
Robert W. Mardock

Surveys reform activities from the 1830's trhough the Dawes Act. Discusses Grant's Peace Policy, and the conflict of eastern and western views. University of Missouri Press, 1971. $9.00.

THE SIOUX OF THE ROSEBUD: A HISTORY IN PICTURES
Henry W. and Jean Tyree Hamilton

From 1891 until 1948, John A. Anderson phographed the painful adjustment of the Brule Sioux to reservation life. 200 photos. 300 pp. The University of Oklahoma Press. $12.50.

SOUTHERN INDIANS IN THE AMERICAN REVOLUTION
O'Donnell

The University of Tennessee Press. $8.50.

THE TEN GRANDMOTHERS
Alice Marriott

Kiowa history through the sacred "medicine" bundles, surrounded by legends and power. 306 pp. The University of Oklahoma Press. $5.95.

THE TRAIL OF TEARS
Gloria Jahoda

The story of the forced removal of the so-called Five Civilized Tribes from 1830 to 1850. Chronicles the forced migration of more than 50 tribes. Holt, Rinehart and Winston. Illus. $12.95.

VOICES OF THE RAINBOW: CONTEMPORARY POETRY

Kenneth Rosen, Editor

The works of 21 poets from 20 different tribes are represented. 232 pp. Illus. Viking Press, Inc., 1975. $10.00.

WHY GONE THOSE TIMES?

James Willard Schultz; Illustrated by Charles M. Russell

The University of Oklahoma Press. $7.95.

BLACK-AMERICANS

*ACCOMPLISHMENTS OF FAMOUS BLACK AMERICANS

Stories written to acquaint children with the African-American contributions to our culture. Afro-Am Publishing Co., Inc. $3.85. Primary thru intermediate grades.

AFRICAN STUDIES

Gordon Press Publishers

*AFRO-AMERICAN READER

Includes puzzles, games, songs, practice pages, eye-hand coordination work. Emphasis of African heritage. Afro-Am Publishing Co., Inc. $3.85. Primary grades.

*BLACK ABC's

A set of picture-stories of the alphabet. The pictures and words are those with which black children readily identify. Afro-Am Publishing Co., Inc. $28.50. Pre-school thru third grade.

BLACK CONSCIOUSNESS: IDENTITY AND ACHIEVEMENT

Patricia Gurin and Edgar G. Epps

A study of students in historically black colleges. Provides data on black students' educational and occupational goals and achievement motivation. 560 pp. John Wiley & Sons, Inc. (Center for Professional Development Programs.) 1975. $13.95.

THE BLACK FAMILY IN MODERN SOCIETY

John H. Scanzoni

Focuses on the "middle-class" black family in urban America. 353 pp. Allyn and Bacon, Inc., 1971. Pap. $4.95.

BLACK PERIODICALS AND NEWSPAPERS

Susan Bryl and Erwin K. Welsch, Editors

Wisconsin State Historical Society. $3.00.

*BLACK STUDIES BIBLIOGRAPHY

Lists paperbacks in the areas of black studies. Afro-Am Publishing Co., Inc. Pap. $1.00. Grade nine up.

BLACK TRADITION IN AMERICAN FICTION

A 22 volume collection. See publisher for titles. Consortium Books. $275.00.

BOOKER T. WASHINGTON

Basil J. Mathews

A bibliography. Consortium Books. $21.00.

CIVIL RIGHTS: A CURRENT GUIDE TO THE PEOPLE, ORGANIZATIONS AND EVENTS

Joan Martin Burke, Editor

Provides details on 250 people and organizations active as of late 1973. Listings of civil rights laws in various states; black elected officials; and major sources and collections of works on minority rights are also included. 266 pp. Bib. R.R. Bowker and Co., 1974. $12.50.

AN ECONOMIC DETOUR

Merah S. Stuart

Shows the acievements of Afro-Americans in the insurance business while pointing out the destructiveness of "race business." Consortium Books. $21.00.

EDUCATION FOR LIFE

Francis G. Peabody

The story of Samuel Armstrong and his fight for the education of an oppressed people. In 1868 he opened Hampton Institute, the first Negro educational institution. Consortium Books. $21.00.

AN ENQUIRY . . . . CONCERNING NEGROES

Henri Gregoire

On Negro American history and literature. Concortium Books. $15.00.

EVOLUTION OF THE NEGRO COLLEGE

Dwight O.W. Holmes

A study of the challenge of Afro-Americans - to construct a seperate education system in the face of White hostility and indifference. Consortium Books. $17.00.

*HAYES AFRO-AMERICAN ABC

A workbook which uses African subjects for illustrating alphabet letter. Afro-Am Publishing Co., Inc. $3.85. Pre-school thru sixth grade.

*HAYES STORY READER OF YOUNG BLACK AMERICANS

Twenty-eight biographies dealing mostly with childhood incidents with which black children can readily identify. Afro-Am Publishing Co., Inc. $3.85. Primary thru intermediate grades.

HISTORY OF MOREHOUSE COLLEGE
Benjamin Brawley

Portrays the struggles and achievements of a group of early Afro-American leaders who showed their people the way to higher education. Consortium Books. $14.00.

JULIUS ROSENWALD: BENEFACTOR OF MANKIND
Dr. Alfred Q. Jarrette

A documented biography of Julius Rosenwald, a man who gave over fifty million to aid black-Americans. His gifts helped build over five thousand schools for black children. Southeastern University Press. $5.00.

LIVING BLACK AMERICAN AUTHORS: A BIOGRAPHICAL DIRECTORY
Ann Allen Shockley, Editor

More than 425 black authors are profiled. Entries provide: name, occupation, educational background, organizations, publications, etc. 220 pp. R.R. Bowker and Co. 1973. $13.95.

NIGHT RIDERS IN BLACK FOLK HISTORY
Gladys-Marie Fry

Describes black's own feelings about the various supernatural and bogey figures used to terrorize them down through the years. 252 pp. The University of Tennessee Press. 1976. Illus. $9.50.

PHILLIS WHEATLEY IN THE BLACK AMERICAN BEGINNINGS
Robinson

Broadside Press. Cloth, $6.00; pap.. $3.50.

SIMPLE JUSTICE: THE HISTORY OF BROWN VS. BOARD OF EDUCATION AND BLACK AMERICA'S STRUGGLE FOR EQUALITY
Richard Kluger

Examines the systematic exploitation of blacks from the time of Reconstruction to the end of World War II. Describes small court battles engaged in by the NAACP and other groups in the struggle for equality. Also includes interviews with Supreme Court Justices on the Brown vs. Board of Education case. 768 pp. Alfred A. Knopf, Inc. $15.95.

SOUTHERN URBAN NEGRO AS A CONSUMER
Paul K. Edwards

A study in the participation of Afro-Americans in our conspicuous consumption society. Consortium Books. $17.00.

TEACHERS' GUIDE TO AMERICAN NEGRO HISTORY
William Loren Katz

A plan for integrating American history curriculums and initiating black history courses. Provides bibliographic, text and audio-visual information, etc. 192 pp. Afro-Am Publishing Co., Inc. Pap. $3.50.

A TREASURY OF AFRO-AMERICAN FOLKLORE
Harold Courlander

A collection of stories, tales, poetry, and songs of Afro-American culture - a culture made up of many related strains. 640 pp. Crown Publishers, Inc. Cloth, $14.95; pap. $5.95.

WHO IS CHAUNCEY SPENCER?
Chauncey E. Spencer

An autobiography telling of Spencer's efforts to obtain pilot training for Negroes in World War II. Spencer stresses Americanism over Blackness, and defends human dignity, regardless of race. 150 pp. Broadside Press. 1975. $7.95.

OTHER MINORITIES

ALASKAN-AMERICANS

LOST HERITAGE OF ALASKA: THE ADVENTURES AND ART OF THE ALASKA COASTAL INDIANS
P. & L. Miller

A study of the arts and history of the Tlingit and Haida Indians. 230 illustrations. Superior Publishing Co. $6.95.

ESKIMO ADVENTURE
E.L. Keithahn

An account of primitive life in the igloo villages at Shishmaref, Kake, Hydaburg, and Wrangell - the way of life of the Eskimos, etc. 53 photos. Superior Publishing Co. $3.95.

THE ESKIMO STORYTELLER
Edwin S. Hall, Jr.

Includes folktales from Noatak, Alaska. Professor Hall includes an analysis of the tales and provides brief autobiographies of the informants. 492 pp. The University of Tennessee Press. $18.50.

FRENCH-AMERICANS

AMERICAN AND FRENCH CUTLURE, 1800-1900
Henry Blumenthal
An encyclopedic study of the social and cultural interchanges between France and America in the nineteenth century. 576 pp. Louisiana State Univerity Press. 1975. $17.50.

GERMAN-AMERICANS

ENCYCLOPEDIA OF GERMAN-AMERICAN GENEALOGICAL RESEARCH
Clifford Neal Smith
Offers insight to the social, religious, political, and economic conditions in Germany that led to the migration from that country to America over the past three centuries. 400 pp. R.R. Bowker and Co. 1976. $26.50.

JEWISH-AMERICANS

THE AMERICAN JEW IN THE CIVIL WAR
Isadore S. Meyer, Editor
This catalog of the exhibit of the Civil War Centennial Jewish Historical Commission tells of the role played by American Jews, both in the North and South. 28 illustrations. Kraus Reprint Co. Reprint of the 1962 edition. Cloth, $8.50; pap. $3.50.

BEGINNINGS: EARLY AMERICAN JUDAICA
A collection of ten publications, in facsimile, illustrative of the religious, communal, cultural and political life of American Jewry, 1761-1845. The Jewish Publication Society of America. $20.00.

THE HISTORY OF THE JEWS OF PHILADELPHIA: FROM COLONIAL TIMES TO THE AGE OF JACKSON
Edwin Wolf 2nd, and Maxwell Whiteman 552 pp. The Jewish Publication Society of America. Illus. $8.50.

JEWISH BOOK ANNUAL
A. Alan Steinbach, Editor
Contains seven bibliographies and ten articles dealing with aspects of Jewish literature throughout the world. Includes eight special articles and bibliographies commemorating the Bicentennial. 278 pp. Jewish Book Council. $7.00.

THE JEWISH WOMAN IN AMERICA
Charlotte Baum, Paula Hyman and Sonya Michel
Dial Press.

REBELS AND REFORMERS: THE LIVES OF FOUR JEWISH AMERICANS
Alberta Eiseman; Illus. by Herb Steinberg Biographies of Uriah P. Levy, Ernestine L. Rose, Louis D. Brandeis, and Lillian D. Wald. Doubleday and Co. 1976. Illus. Cloth, $4.95; pap. $2.50.

REMEMBER THE DAYS: A SHORT HISTORY OF THE JEWISH-AMERICANS
Doubleday and Co.

STUDIES IN JEWISH LITERATURE
Gordon Press Publishers

MEXICAN-AMERICANS

CHICANO BIBLIOGRAPHY
Charles J. Boorkman
Gordon Press Publishers. $25.00.

POLISH-AMERICANS

AN APPRAISAL OF THOMAS AND ZNANIECKI'S *The Polish Peasant In Europe And America*
Herbert Blumer
Statements, discussion; summary and analysis of the work. Kraus Reprint Co., 1939. Pap. $4.50.

UKRANIAN-AMERICANS

UKRANIANS IN AMERICA: A Biographical Directory
Dmytro M. Shtohryn, Editor
Includes about 2,000 of selected boigraphical and bio-bibliographical notes of persons of Ukranian origin living in the United States and Canada. 424pp. Association for the Advancement of Ukranian Studies, Inc., $27.50.

Publisher Index

The following is a list of publishers whose books appear in the bibliography. Entries are arranged alphabetically, with complete, zip-coded addresses.

A

A.S. Barnes & Co., Inc., P.O. Box 421, Cranbury, N.J. 08512

Abelard-Schuman Ltd., 257 Park Ave. S., Nashville, Tenn. 37202

Abingdon Press, 201 Eighth Ave. S., Nashville, Tenn. 37202

Academic Press, Inc., 111 Fifth Ave., New York, N.Y. 10003

Academic Press of Arkansas, 300 Spring Bldg., Little Rock, Ark. 72201

Addison-Wesley Pub. Co.,Jacob Way, Reading, Mass. 01867

Afro-Am Publishing Co., 1727 S. Indiana Ave., Chicago, Ill. 60616

Agathon Press, Inc., 150 Fifth Ave., New York, N.Y. 10011

AHM Publishing Corp., 1500 Skokie Blvd., Northbrook, Ill. 60062

Alaska Northwest Pub. Co., P.O. Box 4EEE, Anchorage, Alaska 99509

Alaska Travel Publications Inc., P.O. Box 4-2031, Anchorage, Alaska 99509

Albert Safer, Publisher, Town Center, Box 56, West Orange, N.J. 07052

Albert Whitman & Co., 560 W. Lake St., Chicago, Ill. 60605

Aldine Publishing Co., 529 S. Wabash Ave., Chicago, Ill. 60605

Alfred A. Knopf, Inc., c/o Random House, Inc., 400 Hahn Rd., Westminster, Md.

Allyn & Bacon, Inc., 470 Atlantic Ave., Boston, Mass. 02210

American Academy of Political and Social Science, 3937 Chestnut St., Philadelphia, Pa. 19104

American Anthropological Assn., Publications Dept., 1703 New Hampshire Ave., NW, Washington, D.C. 20009

American Association of School Administration, 1801 N. Moore St., Arlington, Va. 22209

American Association for State & Local History, 1315 Eighth Ave., S., Nashville, Tenn. 37203

American Bar Foundation, 1155 E. 60th St., Chicago, Ill. 60637

American Bibliographic Center-Clio Press, Riviera Campus, 2040 Alameda Padre Serra, Santa Barbara, Calif. 93103

American Book Co., Division of Litton Educational Publishers, Inc., 450 W. 33rd St., New York, N.Y. 10001

American-Canadian Publishers, Inc., Drawer 2078, Portales, N.M. 88130

American Council on Education, 1 Dupont Circle, Suite 800, Washington, D.C. 20036

American Federation of Arts, 41 E. 65th St., New York, N.Y. 10021

American Heritage Publishing Co., 1221 Ave. of the Americas, New York, N.Y. 10036

American Historical Association, 400 "A" St., S.E., Washington, D.C. 20003

American History Research Associates, P.O. Box 140, Brookeville, Md. 20729

American Hungarian Review, 5410 Kerth Rd., St. Louis, Mo. 63128

American Institute for Marxist Studies, 20 E. 30th St., New York, N.Y. 10016

American Jewish Committee, 165 E. 56th St., New York, N.Y. 10022

American Jewish Historical Society, 2 Thornton Rd., Waltham, Mass. 02154

American Library Association, 50 E. Huron St., Chicago, Ill. 60611

American Management Association, c/o Macmillan Co., 866 Third Ave., New York, N.Y. 10022

American Museum of Social Anthropology Books, Natural History Press, c/o Doubleday & Co., Inc., 501 Franklin Ave., Garden City, N.Y. 11530

American Philosophical Society, 104 S. Fifth St., Philadelphia, Pa. 19106

American-Scandinavian Foundation, 127 E. 73rd St., New York, N.Y. 10021

American Society Press, P.O. Box 145, Naperville, Ill. 60540

AMS Press, Inc., 56 E. 13th St., New York, N.Y. 10003

Ann Arbor Publishers, 2057 Charlton, Ann Arbor, Mich, 48103

Apollo Editions, 201 Park Ave. S., New York, N.Y. 10003

Appalachian Books, P.O. Box 248, Oakton, Va. 22124

Appalachian Press, P.O. Box 8074, Huntington, W. Va. 25705

Arbor House Publishing Co., 641 Lexington Ave., New York, N.Y. 10022

Arco Publishing Co., Inc., 219 Park Ave., S., New York, N.Y. 10003

Argosy-Antiquarian, Ltd., 116 E. 59th St., New York, N.Y. 10022

Arlington House Publishers, 81 Centre Ave., New Rochell, N.Y. 10801

Arno Press, 330 Madison Ave., New York, N.Y. 10017

Arthur H. Clark Co., 1264 S. Central Ave., Glendale, Calif. 91204

Asia Publishing House, 420 Lexington Ave., New York, N.Y. 10017

Associated Press, 50 Rockefeller Plaza, New York, N.Y. 10020

Association for the Advancement of Ukranian Studies, Inc., P.O. Box 3295, County Fair Station, Champaign, Ill. 61820

Association for Supervision & Curriculum Development, 1701 "K" St., N.W., Washington, D.C. 20006

Association Press, 291 Broadway, New York, N.Y. 10007

Atheneum Publishers, c/o Book Warehouse, Inc., Vreeland Ave., Boro of Totowa, Patterson, N.J. 07512

Augsburg Publishing House, 426 S. Fifth St., Minneapolis, Minn. 55415

Augusta M. Kelley, Publishers, 305 Allwood Dr., Clifton, N.J. 07012

Augustana Historical Society, Augustana Harvard Sq., Cambridge, Mass. 02138

Avon Books, 959 Eighth Ave., New York, N.Y. 10019

B

Baker Book House, 1019 Wealthy St., S.E., Grand Rapids, Mich. 49506

Balamp Publishing, 7430 Second Ave., Suite 442, Detroit, Mich. 48202

Ballantine Books, Inc., c/o Random House, Inc., Westminster, Md. 21157

Ballena Press, P.O. Box 711, Ramona, Calif. 92065

Ballinger Publishing Co., 17 Dunster St., Harvard Sq. Cambridge, Mass. 02138

Bantam Books, Inc., 666 Fifth Ave., New York, N.Y. 10019

Barnes & Noble, Inc., c/o Harper & Row Publishers, Inc., Keystone Industrial Park, Scranton, Pa. 18512

Barre-Westover, 419 Park Ave. S., New York, N.Y. 10016

Barron's Educational Series, 113 Crossways Park Dr., Woodbury, N.Y. 11797

Bascom Books, P.O. Box 78, St. Albans, N.Y. 11412

Basic Books, Inc., 10 E. 53rd St., New York, N.Y. 10022

Beacon Press, 25 Beacon St., Boston, Mass. 02108

Beekman Publishing Inc., 53 Park Place, New York, N.Y. 10007

Behavioral Publications Inc., 72 Fifth Ave., New York, N.Y. 10011

Behrman House, Inc., 1261 Broadway, New York, N.Y. 10001

Benefic Press, Div. of Beckley-Cardy Co. , 10300 W. Roosevelt Rd., Westchester, Ill. 60153

Benjamin Blom, Inc., Publishers, 2521 Broadway, New York, N.Y. 10025

Benjamin D. Smallwood, 2112 New Hampshire Ave., N.W., Washington, D.C. 20009

Berkley Publishing Corp., Affiliate of G.P. Putnam's Sons, 200 Madison Ave., New York, N.Y. 10016

Berkshire Traveller Press, Stockbridge, Mass. 01262

Biblo & Tannen Booksellers & Publishers, P.O. Box 14174, University Station, Minneapolis, Minn. 55414

Binfords & Mort, Publishers, 2505 S.E. 11th Ave., Portland, Oregon 97202

Black Letter Press, 663 Bridge St., N.W., Grand Rapids, Mich. 49504

Blaine-Ethridge Books, 13977 Penrod St., Detroit, Mich. 48223

Bloch Publishing Co., 915 Broadway, New York, N.Y. 10010

Blue & Gray Press, Inc., 605 Merrit St., Nashville, Tenn. 37203

B'nai Brith Career Counseling Services, 1640 Rhode Island Ave., N.W., Washington, D.C. 20036

Bobbs-Merrill Co., Inc., Subs. of Howard Sams & Co., 4300 W. 62nd St., Indianapolis, Ind. 46268

Book-Lab, Inc., 1449 37th St., Brooklyn, N.Y. 11218

Books for Libraries, Inc., 1 Dupont St., Plainview, N.Y. 11803

Bowling Green University, c/o Popular Press, 101 University Hall, Bowling Green, Ohio 43403

Branden Press, Inc., 221 Columbus Ave., Boston, Mass. 02116

Brigham Young University Press, 205 University Press Bldg., Provo, Utah 84601

British American Books, P.O. Box 302, Willits, Calif. 05490

Broadman Press, 127 Ninth Ave. N., Nashville, Tenn. 37203

Broadside Press Publications, 12651 Old Mill Place, Detroit, Mich. 48238

Bro-Dart Publishing Co., 1609 Memorial Ave., Williamsport, Pa. 17701

Brookings Institution, 1775 Massachusetts Ave., N.W., Washington, D.C. 20036

Brooks-Cole Publishing Co., 10 Davis Dr., Belmont, Calif. 94002

Brown Book Co., 519 Acorn St., Deer Park, N.Y. 11729

Bruce Books, Macmillan Publishing Co., Riverside, N.J. 08075

Bucknell University Press, P.O. Box 421, Cranbury, N.J. 08512

Burgess Publishing Co., c/o Eliot Books, 35-53 24th St., Long Island City, N.Y. 11106

Burt Franklin Publishing, c/o Lenox Hill Publishing & Distributing Corp., 235 E. 44th St., New York, N.Y. 10017

C

C.E. Tuttle Co., Inc., 28 S. Main St., Rutland, Vermont 05701

C.V. Mosby Co., 11836 Westline Industrial Drive., St. Louis, Mo. 63141

California Book Co., Ltd., 2310 Telegraph Ave., Berkeley, Calif. 94704

California Historical Society, 2090 Jackson St., San Francisco, Calif. 94109

Cambridge University Press, 32 E. 57th St., New York, N.Y. 10022

Canfield Press, 850 Montgomery St., San Francisco, Calif. 94133

Carlton Press, 84 Fifth Ave., New York, N.Y. 10011

Caxton Printers, Ltd., 312 Main St., Caldwell, Idaho 83605

Center for Applied Linguistics, 1611 N. Kent St., Arlington, VA. 22209

Center for Migration Studies, c/o Jerome Ozer Publishing Inc., 475 Fifth Ave., New York, N.Y. 10017

Chandler Publishing Co., Div. of Intext Education Publishers, Oak St. & Pawnee Ave., Scranton, Pa. 18512

Charles A. Jones Publishing Co., Div. of Wadsworth Publishing Co., 10 Davis Drive, Belmont, Calif. 94002

Charles E. Merrill Publishing Co., Div. of Bell & Howell Co., 1300 Alum Creek Dr., Columbus, Ohio 43216

Charles Scribner's Sons, Shipping & Service Ctr., Vreeland Ave., Totowa, N.J. 07512

Charles C. Thomas Publishers, 301-327 E. Lawrence Ave., Springfield, Ill. 62703

Chatham Bookseller, 38 Maple St., Chatham, N.J. 07928

Chatham Press, c/o E.P. Dutton & Co., 201 Park Ave. S., New York, N.Y. 10003

David McKay Co., 750 Third Ave., New York, N.Y. 10017

Delacorte Press, c/o Dial Press, 750 Third Ave., New York, N.Y. 10017

Dell Publishing Co., Inc., 1 Dag Hammerksjold Plaza, 245 E. 47th St., New York, N.Y. 10017

Devin-Adair Co., Inc., 1 Park Ave., Old Greenwich, Conn. 06870

Dexter & Westbrook, Ltd., 958 Church St., Baldwin, N.Y. 11510

Dial Press, 1 Dag Hammerksjold Plaza, 245 E. 47th St., New York, N.Y. 10017

Dickenson Publishing Co., 16561 Ventura Blvd., Encino, Calif. 91316

Dietz Press, 109 E. Carey, Richmond, Va. 23219

Dillon Press, Inc., 500 S. Third St., Minneapolis, Minn. 55415

Dodd, Mead & Co., 79 Madison Ave., New York, N.Y. 10016

Dorrance & Co., 1617 J.F. Kennedy Blvd., Philadelphia, Pa. 19103

Dorsey Press, Inc., Div. of Richard Irwin, Inc., 1818 Ridge Rd., Homewood, Ill. 60430

Doubleday & Co., Inc., 501 Franklin Ave., Garden City, N.Y. 11530

Dover Publications Inc., 180 Varick St., New York, N.Y. 10014

Drama Book Specialists, 150 W. 52nd St., New York, N.Y. 10019

Drum & Spear Press, 1371 Fairmont St., N.W., Washington, D.C. 20009

Duke University Press, 6697 College Station, Durham, N.C. 27708

Dunellen Publishing Co., c/o Kennikat Press, 90 W. Bayles Ave., Port Wash-Washington, N.Y. 10050

E

E.P. Dutton & Co., 201 Park Ave. S., New York, N.Y. 10003

Educational Consortium of America, P.O. Box 1057, Menlo Park, Calif. 94025

Educational Service, Inc., P.O. Box 219, Stevensville, Mich. 49127

Emerson Books, Reynolds Lane, Buchanan, N.Y. 10511

Emerson Hall Publishers, 62 W. 85th St., New York, N.Y. 10025

Encyclopedia Brittanica Education Corp., c/o Encyclopedia Brittanica, 425 N. Michigan Ave., Chicago, Ill. 60611

Endurance Press, 5695 Lumley St., Detroit, Mich. 48210

Enoch Pratt Free Library, 400 Cathedral St., Baltimore, Md. 21201

ERA Press, P.O. Box 767, Amherst, Mass. 01002

Everett/Edwards, Inc., P.O. Box 1060, Deland, Fla. 32720

Exposition Press, 50 Jericho Tpke., Jericho, N.Y. 11753

F

F.T. Peacock Publishers, 401 W. Irving Park Rd., Itasca, Ill. 60143

Fairleigh Dickenson University Press, P.O. Box 421, Cranbury, N.J. 08512

Family Service Association of America, 44 E. 23rd St., New York, N.Y. 10010

Farrar, Straus & Giroux, Inc., 19 Union Sq. W., New York, N.Y. 10003

Fawcett World Library, 1515 Broadway, New York, N.Y. 10036

Fearon Publications, Division of Lear Siegler, Inc., 6 Davis Drive, Belmont, Calif. 94002

Finch Press, 220 E. Huron St., Ann Arbor, Mich. 48108

Fleet Press Corp., 160 Fifth Ave. New York, N.Y. 10010

Folcroft Library Editions, P.O. Box 182, Folcroft, Pa. 19032

Fontana Paperbacks, 750 Fifth Ave., New York, N.Y. 10019

Fortress Press, 2900 Queen Lane, Philadelphia, Pa. 19129

Foundation for Research in the Afro-American Creative Arts, Inc., P.O. Box 11049, Cambria Heights, N.Y. 11411

Franklin Publishing Co., 2047 Locust St., Philadelphia, Pa. 19103

Franklin Watts, Inc., c/o Grolier, Inc., 845 Third Ave., New York, N.Y. 10022

Frederick Ungar Publishing, 250 Park Ave. S., New York, N.Y. 10003

Free Press, c/o Macmillan Co., 886 Third Ave., New York, N.Y. 10022

Friendship Press, 475 Riverside Dr., New York, N.Y. 10027

Funk & Wagnalls Co., c/o Thomas Crowell Co., 666 Fifth Ave., New York, N.Y. 10019

G

G.K. Hall & Co., 70 Lincoln St., Boston, Mass. 02111

G.P. Putnam's Sons, 200 Madison Ave., New York, N.Y. 10016

Gale Research Co., Book Tower, Detroit, Mich. 48226

Gambler's Book Club, P.O. Box 4115, Las Vegas, Nev. 89106

Garland Publishing Co., 10 E. 44th St., New York, N.Y. 10017

Garrard Publishing Co., 1607 N. Market St., Champaign, Ill. 61820

Garrett Park Press, Garrett Park, Md. 20766

Gasper Kici, P.O. Box 5801, Presidio, Monterey, Calif. 93940

Genealogical Publishing Co., 521-523 St. Paul Pl., Baltimore, Md. 21202

General Learning Corp., 250 James St., Morristown, N.J. 07960

George Braziller, Inc., 1 Park Ave., New York, N.Y. 10016

George Wahr Publishing Co., 304 1/2 S. State St., Ann Arbor, Mich. 48108

Georgetown University School of Language & Linguistics, Publications Department, Washington, D.C. 20007

Georgia State University, School of Business Administration, Publishing Services Division, 33 Gilmer St., S.E., Atlanta, Georgia 30303

Glencoe Press, c/o Macmillan Co., Riverside, N.J. 08075

Glendessary Press, 2512 Grove St., Berkeley, Calif. 94704

Golden Bell Press, 2403 Champa St., Denver, Colo. 80205

Gordian Press, 85 Hompkins St., Staten Island, N.Y. 10304

Gordon Press, P.O. Box 459, Bowling Green Station, New York, N.Y. 10004

Great Outdoors Publishing Co., 4747 28th St. N., St. Petersburg, Fla. 33714

Greenwood Press, Inc., 51 Riverside Ave., Westport, Conn. 06880

Gregg Press, 70 Lincoln St., Boston, Mass. 02111

Grolier Club, c/o University Press of Virginia, University Station, P.O. Box 3608, Charlottesville, Va. 22903

Grosset & Dunlap, 51 Madison Ave., New York, N.Y. 10010

Grossman Publishers, c/o Viking Press, 625 Madison Ave., New York, N.Y. 10022

Grove Press, 53 E. 11th St., New York, N.Y. 10003

Group for the Advancement of Psychiatry, 419 Park Ave. S., New York, N.Y. 10016

H

H.S. Stuttman Co., Inc., 404 Park Ave. S., New York, N.Y. 10016

Hacher Art Books, 54 W. 57th St., New York, N.Y. 10019

Hafner Press, c/o Collier-Macmillan Distributing Center, Riverside, N.J. 08075

Harcourt Brace Jovonovich, 757 Third Ave., New York, N.Y. 10017

Harmony, c/o Crown Publishers, 419 Park Ave. S., New York, N.Y. 10016

Harper Magazine Press, 2 Park Ave., New York, N.Y. 10016

Harper & Row, Publishers, College Department, 10 East 53rd St., New York, N.Y. 10022

Harry Abrams, Inc., Subsidiary of Times Mirror Co., 110 E. 59th St., New York, N.Y. 10022

Harvard University Press, 79 Garden St., Cambridge, Mass. 02138

Haskell House Publishers, 280 Lafayette St., New York, N.Y. 10012

Hawthorn Books, 260 Madison Ave., New York, N.Y. 10016

Hayden Book Co., Inc., 50 Essex St., Rochelle Park, N.J. 07662

Helga M. Rogers, 1270 Fifth Ave., New York, N.Y. 10029

Hennessey & Ingalls, 8321 Campion Dr., Los Angeles, Calif. 90045

Henry E. Huntington, Library & Art Gallery, 1151 Oxford Rd., San Marino, Calif. 91108

Henry Regnery Co., 114 W. Illinois St., Chicago, Ill. 60610

Herald Press, 616 Walnut Ave., Scottdale, Pa. 15683

Heritage Press, Avon, Conn. 06001

Highlights for Children, 2300 W. Fifth St., Columbus, Ohio 43216

Hill & Wang, Division of Farrar, Straus & Giroux, Inc., 19 Union Sq., New York, N.Y. 10003

Hippocrene Books, Inc., 171 Madison Ave., New York, N.Y. 10016

Historic Pensacola Preservation Board, c/o John C. Pace Library, University of W. Florida, Pensacola, Fla. 32504

Hive Publishing Co., P.O. Box 1004, Easton, Pa. 18042

Hogarth Press, P.O. Box 6012, Honolulu, Hawaii 96818

Holbrook Press, Rockleigh, N.J. 07647

Holloway House Publishing Co., 8060 Melrose Ave., Los Angeles, Calif. 90046

Holt, Rinehart & Winston, Inc., 383 Madison Ave., New York, N.Y. 10017

Houghton Mifflin Co., 551 Fifth Ave., New York, N.Y. 10017

House of Collectibles, Inc., 17 Park Ave., New York, N.Y. 10016

House of Gemini, P.O. Box 7803, Philadelphia, Pa. 19101

Howard E. Seals, 3831 S. Michigan Ave., Rear Bldg., Chicago, Ill. 60653

Howard University Press, 2935 Upton St., N.W., Washington, D.C. 20001

Howell-North Books, 1050 Parker St., Berkeley, Calif. 94710

Hubbard Press, 2855 Shermer Rd. Box 442, Norhtbrook, Ill. 60052

Human Relations Area File Press, P:O. Box 2015, Yale Station, New Haven, Conn. 06520

Humanities Press, Atlantic Highlands, N.J. 07716

I

I H S-Microcard Editions, 5500 S. Valentine Way, Englewood, Colo. 80110

Indian Historian Press, 1451 Masonic Ave., San Francisco, Calif. 94117

Indiana University Press, Tenth & Morton Sts., Bloomington, Ind. 47401

Indiana University Research Center for the Language Sciences, c/o Humanities Press, Inc., Atlantic Highlands, N.J. 07716

Initial Teaching Alphabet Publications, 6 E. 43rd St., New York, N.Y. 10017

Institute of Labor and Industrial Relations, The University of Michigan, Wayne State University, Publications Office, P.O. Box B-1, Ann Arbor, Mich. 48106

Institute of Pluralism and Group Identity, 165 East 56th St., New York, N.Y. 10022

Institute of Race Relations, c/o Oxford University Press, 16-00 Pollitt Dr., Fair Lawn, N.J. 10022

Integrated Education Association, Northwestern University, School of Education, 2003 Sheridan Rd., Evanston, Ill. 60201

Inter-American University Press of Puerto Rico, P.O. Box 1298, Hate Rey, Puerto Rico 00919

Interbook, Inc., 545 Eighth Ave., New York, N.Y. 10018

Interculture Associates, Quaddick Rd. P.O. Box 277, Thompson, Conn. 06277

Interland Publishing Inc., 799 Broadway, New York, N.Y. 10003

International Personnel Management Association, 1313 E. 60th St., Chicago, Ill. 60637

International Publishers, 381 Park Ave. S., New York, N.Y. 10016

International Publications Service, 114 E. 32nd St., New York, N.Y.10016

International Scholarly Book Service, Inc., P.O. Box 4347, Portland, Oreg. 97208

International Universities Press, Inc., 239 Park Ave. S., New York, N.Y. 10003

Interstate, 19-27 N. Jackson St., Danville, Ill. 61832

Intext Educational Publications, 257 Park Ave. S., New York, N.Y. 10010

Iowa State University Press, Press Bldg. Ames, Iowa 50010

Ira J. Friedman, c/o Kennikat Press, 90 S. Bayles Ave., Port Washington, N.Y. 11050

Irish University Press, 485 Madison Ave., New York, N.Y. 10022

Irvington Books, 27 W. 44th St., Box 19, New York, N.Y. 10036

J

J.B. Lippincott Co., Division of Higher Education, E. Washington Square, Philadelphia, Pa. 19105

Jack Delaney, 1136 Fort View Place, Cincinnati, Ohio 45202

James T. White Co., 1700 State Hwy 3, Clifton, N.J. 07013

Jenkins Publishing Co., P.O. Box 2085, Austin, Texas 78767

Jerome S. Ozer Publishing, 475 Fifth Ave., New York, N.Y. 10017

Jesse J. Johnson, Hapton Institute, Hampton, Va. 23668

Jewish Book Council, Jewish Welfare Board, 15 East 26th St., New York, N.Y. 10010

Jewish Publication Society of America, 222 N. 15th St., Philadelphia, Pa. 19102

Jewish Reconstructionist Foundation, 15 W. 86th St., New York, N.Y. 10024

John F. Blair, Publishing, 1406 Plaza Dr., S.W., Winston-Salem, N.C. 27103

John Day Co., c/o Intext Educational Publishers, Galerie St. Etienne, 24 W. 57th St., New York, N.Y. 10019

John M. Fontana, Publisher, 829 E. 45th St., Brooklyn, N.Y. 11203

John Muir Publications, c/o Book People, 2940 Seventh St., Berkeley, Calif. 94710

John Wiley & Sons, 605 Third Ave., New York, N.Y. 10016

Johns Hopkins Press, Baltimore, Md. 21218

Johnson Publishing Co., P.O. Box 317, Murfreesboro, N.C. 27855

Johnson Publishing Co., 820 S. Michigan Ave., Chicago, Ill. 60605

Johnson Reprint Corp., c/o Harcourt, Brace, Jovanovice, Inc., 111 Fifth Ave., New York, N.Y. 10003

Jonathan David Publications, 68-22 Eliot Ave., Middle Village, N.Y. 11379

Jossey-Bass, Inc., 615 Montgomery St., San Francisco, Calif. 94111

Judson Press, Valley Forge, Pa. 19481

Julian Messner, Inc., c/o Simon & Schuster, Inc., 1 W. 39th St., New York, N.Y. 10018

K

K C Publications, P.O. Box 14883, Las Vegas, Nev. 89114

Kennikat Press Corp., c/o Taylor Publishing Co., 90 S. Bayles Ave., Port Washington, N.Y. 11050

Kent State University Press, Kent, Ohio 44240

Kraus Reprint Co., c/o Kraus-Thompson Organization Ltd., Millwood, N.Y. 10546

Krause Publications Inc., Iola, Wisc. 54945

Krishna Press, P.O. Box 459, Bowling Green Station, New York, N.Y. 10004

Ktav Publishing House, Inc., 120 E. Broadway, New York, N.Y. 10022

L

Landfall Press, Inc., 4077 E. Town & Country Rd., Dayton, Ohio 45429

Lawrence C. Bryant, Rte 1, P.O. Box 1069-C, Orangeburg, S.c. 29115

Lawrence Verry, Inc., 16 Holmes St., Mystic, Conn. 06355

Learning Systems Co., 1818 Ridge Rd., Homewood, Ill. 60430

Lerner Publications, 241 First Ave., N., Minneapolis, Minn. 55401

Lexington Books, Division of D.C. Heath & Co., 125 Spring St., Lexington, Mass. 02173

Libraries Unlimited, Inc., c/o Colorado Bibliographic Institute, P.O. Box 263, Littleton, Colo. 80120

Library of Armenian Studies, Publishers, 129 Robbins Rd., Watertown, Mass. 02172

Lion Press, c/o Sayre Publishing Co., 52 Park Ave., New York, N.Y. 10016

Little, Brown & Co., 200 West St., Waltham, Mass. 02154

Littlefield, Adams & Co., 81 Adams Dr., Totowa, N.J. 07512

Little Glass Shack, 3161 56th St., Sacramento, Calif. 95820

Liveright Publishing Corp., c/o E.P. Dutton & Co., 201 Park Ave. S., New York, N.Y. 10003

Llewellyn Publications, P.O. Box 3383, St. Paul, Minn. 55165

Logos International, 185 North Ave., Plainfield, N.J. 07060

Lone Star Publishers, Inc., 1912 W. Anderson Lane, Austin, Tex. 78757

Long Island University Press, 385 Flatbush Ave. Ext., Brooklyn, N.Y. 11201

Lothrop, Lee & Shepard Co., 105 Madison Ave., New York, N.Y. 10016

Louisiana State University Press, Baton Rouge, La. 70803

Loyola University Press, 3441 N. Ashland Ave., Chicago, Ill. 60657

Lunan-Fergeson Library, 2219 Clement St., San Francisco, Calif. 94121

Lyle Stuart, Inc., 120 Enterprise Ave., Secausus, N.J. 07094

M

Museum of New Mexico Press, P.O. Box 2087, Santa Fe, N.M. 87501

Museum Restoration Service, Bridge Authority Bldg., Ogdensburg, N.Y. 13669

Music Educators National Conference, 1201 16th St. N.W., Washington, D.C. 20036

Music Treasure Publications, 620 Fort Washington Ave., Apt. 1-F, New York, N.Y. 10040

Myrin Institute, Inc., 521 Park Ave., New York, N.Y. 10021

N

Nash Publishing Corporation, Order Service Center, 50 Liberty Ave., Freeport, N.Y. 11520

National Art Education Association, 1201 16th St., N.W., Washington, D.C. 20036

National Association of Social Workers, P.O. Box 504, Murray Hill Station, New York, N.Y. 10016

National Council of Teachers of English, 1111 Kenyon Rd. Urbana, Ill. 61801

National Council for the Social Studies, National Education Association, 1201 16th St., N.W., Washington, D.C. 20036

National Education Association, The Academic Bldg., Saw Mill Rd., West Haven, Conn. 06516

National Geographic Society, 17th & "M" Sts., N.W., Washington, D.C. 20036

National Learning Corp., 20 DuPont St., Plainview, N.Y. 11803

Natural History Press, c/o Doubleday & Co., 501 Franklin Ave., Garden City, N.Y. 11530

Naturegraph Publishers, 8339 W. Dry Creek Rd., Healdsburg, Calif. 95448

Naylor Co., P.O. Box 1838, San Antonio, Texas 78206

Negro Universities Press, c/o Greenwood Press, 51 Riverside Ave., Westport, Conn. 06880

Nelson-Hall Co., 325 W. Jackson Blvd., Chicago, Ill. 60606

New Age Press, 4636 Vineta Ave., La Canada, Calif. 91011

Newbury House Publishers, 68 Middle Rd., Rowley, Mass. 01969

New American Library, 1301 Ave. of the Americas, New York, N.Y. 10019

New Outlook Publishers & Distributors, 205 W. 19th St., New York, N.Y. 10011

New York Graphic Society, 140 Greenwich Ave., Greenwich, Conn. 06830

New York Public Library, Rm. 50 A, Fifth Ave. & 42nd St., New York, N.Y. 10018

New York State School of Industrial & Labor Relations, Publications Division, 214 Research Bldg., Cornell University, Ithaca, N.Y. 14850

New York University Press, Washington Sq., New York, N.Y. 10003

Noble & Noble Publishers, 1 Dag Hammersikjold Plaza, New York, N.Y. 10017

North Carolina Office of Archives & History, 109 E. Jones St., Raleigh, N.C. 27611

Northland Press, P.O. Box N, Flagstaff, Ariz. 86001

North Star Press, P.O. Box 451, St. Cloud, Minn. 56301

Norwood Editions, P.O. Box 38, Norwood, Pa. 19074

O

Oceana Publications, Dobbs Ferry, N.Y. 10522

Ocelot Press, P.O. Box 504, Claremont, Calif. 91711

Octagon Books, 19 Union Sq. W., New York, N.Y. 10003

Olympus Publishing Co., c/o Olympus Research Corp., 955 E. Ninth St., Salt Lake City, Utah 84102

Organization of American States, Dept. of Publications & Conferences, Washington, D.C. 20006

Oriole Editions, 19 W. 44th St., New York, N.Y. 10036

P

Pantheon Books, Division of Random House, 457 Hahn Rd., Westminster, Md. 21157

Panther House Ltd., P.O. Box 3552, New York, N.Y. 10017

Paragon Book Reprint Corp., 14 E. 38th St., New York, N.Y. 10016

Parameter Press, 705 Main St., Wakefield, Mass. 01880

Parents Magazine Press, 52 Vanderbilt Ave., New York, N.Y. 10017

Parnassus Press, 4080 Halleck St., Emeryville, Calif. 94608

Pathfinder Press, Inc., 410 West St., New York, N.Y. 10003

Patterson Smith Publishing Corp., 23 Prospect Terrace, Montclair, N.J. 07042

Paul S. Eriksson, Inc., c/o David White, Inc., 60 E. 55th St., New York, N.Y. 10022

Paulist/Newman Press, 400 Sette Dr., Paramus, N.J. 07652

Pegasus, c/o Bobbs-Merrill Co., 4300 W. 62nd St., Indianapolis, Ind. 46268

Pelican Publishing House, 630 Burmaster St., Gretna, La. 70053

Pendell Publishing Co., P.O. Box 1666 PT, Midland, Mich. 48640

Pendle Hill Publications, Quaker Study, 338 Plush Mill Rd., Wallingford, Pa. 19086

Pendulum Press, Inc., Academic Bldg., Saw Mill Rd., West Haven, Conn. 06516

Penguin Books, 7110 Ambassador Rd., Baltimore, Md. 21207

Pennsylvania Historical & Museum Commission, Wm. Penn Museum & Archives Bldg., Box 1026, Harrisburg, Pa. 17120

Pequot Press, Old Chester Rd., Chester, Conn. 06412

Pergamon Press, Maxwell House, Fairview Park, Elmsford, N.Y. 10523

Peter Smith Publisher, 6 Lexington Ave., Gloucester, Mass. 01930

Peter H. Wyden, Inc., c/o David McKay Co., 750 Third Ave., New York, N.Y. 10017

Philadelphia Book Co., Inc., Philadelphia, Pa. 19127

Philosophical Library, Inc., 15 E. 40th St., New York, N.Y. 10016

Pilot Books, 347 Fifth Ave., New York, N.Y. 10016

Pitman Publishing Corp., 6 E. 43rd St., New York, N.Y. 10017

Pocket Books, Inc., 1 W. 39th St., New York, N.Y. 10018

Polaris Press, 16540 Camellia Terrace, Los Gatos, Calif. 95030

Polish Institute of Arts & Sciences in America, 59 E. 66th St., New York, N.Y. 10021

Polish Publishing Co., 1455 W. Division St., Chicago, Ill. 60622

Popular Library, Inc., Unit of CBS Publications, 600 Third Ave., New York, N.Y. 10011

Porter Sargent Publisher, Inc., 11 Beacon St., Boston, Mass. 02108

Potomac Books, Inc., 4832 MacArthur Blvd., N.W., Washington, D.C. 20005

Prakken Publications, Inc., 416 Longshore Dr., Ann Arbor, Mich. 48107

Preager Publishers, 111 Fourth Ave., New York, N.Y. 10003o

Prentice-Hall, Inc., Englewood Cliffs, N.J. 07632

Prescott College Press, Prescott, Ariz. 86301

Princeton University Press, Princeton, N.J. 08540

101 Productions, 834 Mission St., San Francisco, Calif. 94110

Pruett Publishing Co., P.O. Box 1560J, Boulder, Colo. 80302

Q

Quadrangle Press, c/o The New York Times Co., 10 E. 53rd St., New York, N.Y. 10022

Quick Fox, 33 W. 60th St., New York, N.Y. 10023

Quinto Sol Publications, Inc., P.O. Box 9275, Berkeley, Calif. 94709

R

R & E Research Associates, 4843 Mission St., San Francisco, Calif. 94112

R.R. Bowker, A Xerox Education Co., P.O. Box 1807, Ann Arbor, Mich. 48106

Ramparts Press, P.O. Box 10128, Palo Alto, Calif. 94303

Random House, Inc., Order Dept., 457 Hahn Rd., Westminster, Md. 21157

Rand McNally & Co., P.O. Box 7600, Chicago, Ill. 60680

Reilly & Lee Co., c/o Henry Regnery Co., 114 W. Illinois St., Chicago, Ill. 60610

Relevant Instructional Materials, c/o Hammer Press, P.O. Box 794, Stockton, Calif. 95201

Reprint Co., P.O. Box 5401, Spartenburg, S.C. 29301

Rice University Press, Houston, Texas 77001

Richard W. Baron Publishing Co., c/o E.P. Dutton & Co., 210 Park Ave. S., New York, N.Y. 10003

Rio Grande Press, Glorieta, N.M. 87535

Robert Speller & Sons, Publishing, P.O. Box 461, Times Square Station, New York, N.Y. 10036

Rogers Book Service, 217 W. 18th St., Box V, New York, N.Y. 10011

Ronald Press Co., 79 Madison Ave., New York, N.Y. 10016

Ross & Haines, Inc., 3021 Nicollet Ave., Minneapolis, Minn. 55408

Rowman & Littlefield, Inc., Division of Littlefield, Adams, 81 Adams Dr., Totowa, N.J. 07512

Russell & Russell, Division of Atheneum Publishers, 122 E. 42nd St., New York, N.Y. 10017

Rutgers Center of Alcohol Studies Publications, Rutgers University, New Brunswick, N.J. 08903

Rutgers University Press, 30 College Ave., New Brunswick, N.J. 08903

S

Sage Publications, 2755 Beverly Dr., Beverly Hills, Calif. 90212

Saphrograph Co., 194 Elizabeth St., New York, N.Y. 10012

Saturday Review Press, c/o E.P. Dutton & Co., 201 Park Ave. S., New York, N.Y. 10003

Scarecrow Press, Inc., c/o Grolier Educational Corp., Box 656, 52 Liberty St., Metuchen, N.J. 08840

Schenkman Publishing Co., 3 Revere St., Cambridge, Mass. 02107

Scholastic Book Services, 50 W. 44th St., New York, N.Y. 10036

Schocken Books, Inc., 200 Madison Ave., New York, N.Y. 10016

Scholarly Press, 22929 Industrial Dr. E., St. Clair Shores, Mich. 48080

Scholarly Resources, Inc., 1508 Pennsylvania Ave., Wilmington, Del. 19806

Science Research Associates, c/o IBM, 259 E. Erie St., Chicago, Ill. 60611

Scott Foresman & Co., 1900 E. Lake Ave., Glenview, Ill. 60025

Seabury Press, Inc., 815 Second Ave., New York, N.Y. 10017

Serina Press, 70 Kennedy St., Alexandria, Va. 22305

Sheed & Ward, Inc., 475 Fifth Ave., New York, N.Y. 10017

Sherbourne Press, 1640 S. La Cienega Blvd., Los Angeles, Calif. 90035

Shields Publishing Co., 155 N. College Ave., Ft. Collins, Colo. 80521

Shoe String Press, Inc., 995 Sherman Ave., Hamden, Conn. 06514

Shorey Publications, 815 Third Ave., Seattle, Wash. 98104

Singing Tree Press, c/o Gale Research Co., Book Tower, Detroit, Mich. 48226

Silver Burdett Co., c/o General Learning Corp., 250 James St., Morristown, N.J. 07960

Simon & Schuster, Inc., 630 Fifth Ave., New York, N.Y. 10020

Smithsonian Institution Press, c/o George Braziller, Inc., 1 Park Ave., New York, N.Y. 10016

Social Science & Sociological Resources, P.O. Box 241, Aurora, Ill. 60542

Somerset Publishers, 200 Park Ave., Suite 303 E., New York, N.Y. 10017

Southeastern University Press, P.O. Box 2351, Greenville, S.C. 29602

Southern Methodist University Press, Dallas, Texas 75222

Spectrum Productions, 979 Casiano Rd., Los Angeles, Calif. 90049

Springer Publishing Co., 200 Park Ave. S., New York, N.Y. 10003

St. Heironymous Press, Inc., P.O. Box 9431, Berkeley, Calif. 94709

St. Martin's Press, 175 Fifth Ave., New York, N.Y. 10010

St. Thomas Press, P.O. Box 35096, Houston, Texas 77035

Stackpole Books, Cameron & Keller Sts., Harrisburg, Pa. 17105

Stanford University Press, Stanford, Calif. 94305

State Historical Society of Wisconsin, 816 State St., Madison, Wis. 53706

State Printing Co., 1305 Sumter St., Columbia, S.C. 29201

Structures Publishing Co., P.O. Box 423, Farmington, Mich. 48024

Summer Institute of Linguistics, P.O. Box 1028, Fairbanks, Alaska 99701

Sun Dance Press, 1520 N. Crescent Heights, Hollywood, Calif. 90046

Superintendent of Documents, U.S. Government Printing Office, Washington, D.C. 20402

Superior Publishing Co., 708 Sixth Ave. Box 170, Seattle, Wash. 98111

Swallow Press, 1139 S. Wabash Ave., Chicago, Ill. 60605

Swanson Publishing Co., P.O. Box 334, Moline, Ill. 61265

Syracuse University Press, P.O. Box 8, University Station, Syracuse, N.Y. 13210

Syracuse University Publications in Continuing Education, 105 Roney Lane, Syracuse, N.Y. 13210

T

Tandem Press, Inc., P.O. Box 237, Tannersville, Pa. 18372

Teachers College Press, Columbia University, 1234 Amsterdam Ave., New York, N.Y. 10027

Temple University Press, Philadelphia, Pa. 19122

Texian Press, 1301 Jefferson, Waco, Texas 76703

Third Press-Joseph Okpaku Publishing Co., Inc., 444 Central Park W., New York, N.Y. 10025

Third World Press, 7850 S. Ellis Ave., Chicago, Ill. 60019

Thomas Y. Crowell Co., 666 Fifth Ave., New York, N.Y. 10003

Thomas-Newell, 1201 Monroe St., Endicott, N.Y. 13760

Thoreau Foundation, Inc., Thoreau Lyceum, 156 Belknap St., Concord, Mass. 01742

Time-Life Books, c/o Morgan & Morgan Co., 400 Warburton Ave., Hastings-on-Hudson, N.Y. 10706

Todd Publications, 11 Third St., Rye, N.Y. 10580

Tower Publications, c/o Belmont-Tower Books, 185 Madison Ave., New York, N.Y. 10016

Transaction Books, c/o E.P. Dutton Co., 201 Park Ave S., New York, N.Y. 10003

Trans-Anglo Books, P.O. Box 38, Corona Del Mar, Calif. 92625

Transatlantic Arts, Inc., N. Village Green, Levittown, N.Y. 11756

Trend House Publishers, 13-06 W. Kennedy Blvd., Box 2350, Tampa, Fla. 33601

Trident Press, 630 Fifth Ave., New York, N.Y. 10020

Twayne Publishers, c/o G.K. Hall & Co., 70 Lincoln St., Boston, Mass. 02111

U

Union of American Hebrew Congregations, 838 Fifth Ave., New York, N.Y. 10021

United Church Press, 1505 Race St., Philadelphia, Pa. 19102

United Publishing Corp., 1316 Arch St., Philadelphia, Pa. 19107

United Synagogue Book Service, 155 Fifth Ave., New York, N.Y. 10010

University Associates, P.O. Box 80637, San Diego, Calif. 92138

University Microfilm, 300 N. Zeeb Rd., Ann Arbor, Mich. 48106

University of Alabama Press, Drawer 2877, University, Alaska 35486

University of Alaska Press, c/o University Washington Press, Seattle, Wash. 98105

University of Alaska, Institute of Social, Economic & Government Research, College, Alaska 99701

University of Arizona Press, P.O. Box 3398, Tucson, Ariz. 85722

University of California Press, 2229 Fulton St., Berkeley, Calif. 94720

University of California, Center for Chinese Studies, Berkeley, Calif. 94720

University of California Institute of Governmental Studies, Berkeley, Calif. 94720

University of Chicago Press, 5801 Ellis Ave., Chicago, Ill. 60637

University of Florida Press, 15 N.W. 15th St., Gainesville, Fla. 32601

University of Georgia Press, Waddell Hall, Athens, Ga. 30601

University of Illinois Press, Urbana, Ill. 61801

University of Massachusetts Press, Amherst, Mass. 01002

University of Miami Press, Drawer 9088, Coral Gables, Fla. 33124

University of Michigan Press, 615 E. University, Ann Arbor, Mich. 48106

University of Michigan, Graduate School of Business Administration, c/o Bureau of Business Research, Ann Arbor, Mich. 48104

University of Michigan, Wayne State Institute of Labor & Industrial Relations, P.O. Box B-1, Ann Arbor, Mich. 48106

University of Michigan, Institute for Social Research, Dept. 74, Ann Arbor, Mich. 48106

University of Minnesota Press, 2037 University Ave. S.E., Minneapolis, Minn. 55455

University of Missouri Press, 107 Swallow Hall, Columbia, Mo. 65201

University of Nebraska Press, 901 N. 17th St., Lincoln, Neb. 68508

University of New Mexico Press, Albuquerque, N.M. 87106

University of North Carolina Press, Chapel Hill, N.C. 27514

University of Notre Dame Press, c/o Harper & Row Publishers, Keystone Industrial Park, Scranton, Pa. 18512

University of Oklahoma Press, 1005 Asp Ave., Norman, Okla. 73069

University of the Pacific Press, Stockton, Calif. 95205

University of Pennsylvania Press, 3933 Walnut St., Philadelphia, Pa. 19104

University of Pittsburg Press, 127 N. Bellefield Ave., Pittsburg, Pa. 15213

University Place Book Shop, 821 Broadway, New York, N.Y. 10003

University Press of Hawaii, 535 Ward Ave., Honolulu, Hawaii 96814

University Press of Kansas, 366 Watson Library, Lawrence, Kansas 66044

University Press of Kentucky, Lexington, Ky. 40506

University Press of Mississippi, 3825 Ridgewood Rd., Jackson, Miss. 39211

University Press of New England, P.O. Box 979, Hanover, N.H. 03755

University Press of Virginia, P.O. Box 3608, University Station, Charlottesville, Va. 22903

University of South Carolina Press, Columbia, S.C. 29208

University of South Dakota Press, Vermillion, S.D. 57069

University of Tennessee Press, Communications Bldg., Knoxville, Tenn. 37916

University of Texas Press, P.O. Box 7819, University Station, Austin, Texas

University of Texas, Bureau of Business Research, Austin, Texas 78712

University of Toronto Press, 33 E. Tupper St., Buffalo, N.Y. 14208

University of Utah Press, Bldg. 513, Salt Lake City, Utah 84112

University of Washington Press, Seattle, Wash. 98105

University of West Florida, c/o Historic Pensacola Preservation Board, 200 E. Zaragoza St., Pensacola, Fla. 32501

University of Wisconsin Press, P.O. Box 1379, Madison, Wisc. 53701

V

Vanderbilt University Press, Nashville, Tenn. 37203

Vanguard Press, Inc., 424 Madison Ave., New York, N.Y. 10017

Van Nostrand Reinhold Co., c/o Litton Educational Publishing, 300 Pike St., Cincinnati, Ohio 45202

Vantage Press, Inc., 516 W. 34th St., New York, N.Y. 10001

Verta Press, 15 Randolph Place, N.W., Washington, D.C. 20001

Vic Press, P.O. Box 883, Cheyenne, Wyom. 82001

Vigo Press, P.O. Box 959, El Paso, Tex. 79946

Viking Press, Inc., 625 Madison Ave., New York, N.Y. 10022